The Handbook of
SOCIAL WORK RESEARCH METHODS

Respectfully dedicated to the memory of
Walter W. Hudson, teacher, scholar,
and beloved friend to many

The Handbook of
SOCIAL WORK RESEARCH METHODS

Edited by
Bruce A. Thyer

Sage Publications, Inc.
International Educational and Professional Publisher
Thousand Oaks ■ London ■ New Delhi

For information:

Sage Publications, Inc.
2455 Teller Road
Thousand Oaks, California 91320
E-mail: order@sagepub.com

Sage Publications Ltd.
6 Bonhill Street
London EC2A 4PU
United Kingdom

Sage Publications India Pvt. Ltd.
M-32 Market
Greater Kailash I
New Delhi 110 048 India

Printed in the United States of America

Library of Congress Cataloging-in-Publication Data

The handbook of social work research methods / edited by Bruce A. Thyer.
    p. cm.
  Includes bibliographical references and index.
  ISBN 0-7619-1905-8 (cloth: alk. paper)
  ISBN 0-7619-1906-6 (pbk.: alk. paper)
  1. Social service—Research. I. Thyer, Bruce A. II. Title.
  HV11 .H342 2000
  361'.007'2—dc21   00-010587

01 02 03 04 05 06 07 7 6 5 4 3 2 1

Acquisition Editor:	Nancy S. Hale
Production Editor:	Diane S. Foster
Editorial Assistant:	Cindy Bear
Typesetter/Designer:	Marion Warren
Indexer:	Cristina Haley
Cover Designer:	Michelle Lee

Contents

Acknowledgments

The editing of a book is a massive exercise in group cooperation, and many individuals are responsible for helping to produce the present volume. Jim Nageotte, then a senior editor at Sage Publications, was responsible for conceiving the idea of a handbook of social work research methods and of approaching the editor of this volume with the opportunity to prepare it. For this and other collaborative projects, I gratefully acknowledge Jim's capable assistance and friendship over the years. His successors at Sage have been Nancy Hale, Heather Gotlieb, and Diane Foster, three talented publishing professionals whose expertise has been exceeded only by their patience. The authors of the individual chapters deserve the lion's share of the credit for creating what merits reside within this handbook. All of them experts in their respective fields of research, it has been a real pleasure collaborating with such a superb group of academics and practitioners. To them, I extend my heartfelt thanks. My students—B.S.W., M.S.W., and Ph.D.—always serve as a source of inspiration, enlightenment, and challenge, and they have been valued stimuli in helping to prepare this handbook. I hope that future generations of social workers derive benefits from this text proportionate to those that I have obtained from my work with students. Lastly, and most important, I express my appreciation to my wife, Laura Myers, for her many kindnesses expressed throughout the course of our marriage—kindness, love, and support that has made undertaking a project like this possible. Our children—John, William, Joseph, and Cynthia—will get to see more of Daddy now that this handbook is completed.

—Bruce A. Thyer

Preface

Welcome to this new *Handbook of Social Work Research Methods,* a volume specifically written by social workers for a social work audience interested in learning more about research related to social work practice. Every chapter has been authored by one or more social workers, most of whom are senior academics with extensive histories in the worlds of both practice and research. This social work focus is important given the applied nature of most of the work and research that we undertake as a separate discipline. Some other social work research books are simply texts originally written by sociologists for sociology students and then given a facelift for a social work audience. Others are generalist research texts written by one or more social workers, but which lack the depth possible in an edited handbook such as the present volume, wherein it is possible to recruit a leading scholar or scholars to write each individual chapter. No one (or even several) social work researcher can legitimately claim extensive expertise in all areas of social work research, whereas an edited handbook can overcome this all-too-human limitation.

This handbook is organized in a relatively straightforward manner. After an introductory chapter by the editor, placing the importance of scientific research into its historic and contemporary context, the remainder of the volume is divided into four major parts. Part I is devoted to quantitative approaches, the type of inquiry that most readers think of when the term *research* comes to mind. Introductory chapters present an overview of these methods of study and introduce topics that are central to most scientific studies—probability theory and sampling, determining the reliability and validity of measurement methods, how to find suitable instruments for use in research, and an overview of some statistical methods that are most useful in quantitative investigations. These introductory chapters are followed by individual chapters authored by expert researchers presenting information about the various types of quantitative studies—descriptive studies, surveys, needs assessments, single-systems designs, randomized controlled trials, program evaluations, and cost → procedure → process → outcome analysis.

Part II deals with qualitative approaches to scientific research. In contrast to quantitative studies in which many data are presented in the form of numbers, in qualitative inquiry data and evidence are justified using words alone and often lack the numerical focus of quantitative methods. As is noted, qualitative studies always have been an important part of mainstream science, from the beginnings of social work until the present. In fact, there currently is a resurgence of interest is qualitative methods as applied to social work research. Both quantitative and qualitative methods share an interest in obtaining reliable and valid information, and the first chapter in this part is followed by one dealing with a description of the qualitative approach to justifying research evidence. These two introductory chapters are followed by five others that present specific methods of qualitative research—narrative case studies, in-depth interviews, ethnographic research methods, participant observation, and grounded theory. Each of these is an important tool that social work researchers may use for specific purposes. Each has its strengths and limitations, as outlined by some of the foremost qualitative researchers to be found within contemporary social work.

Part III presents four chapters on different forms of conceptual research, approaches to inquiry that might not fit into either the quantitative or qualitative category—studies on theory development, historical research, literature reviews, and critical analyses. Depending on its slant, an individual study using these methods may be more closely aligned with either quantitative or qualitative research methods. For example, a historical study may be very quantitative in nature (e.g., Almgren, Kemp, & Eisinger, 2000) and aimed at presenting historical "facts" as accurately as possible, perhaps using archival statistical data, or it may be more oriented to an examination of the perceptions of people who experienced a particular historic event and have diaries, newspaper articles, and journal editorials as the primary data source (e.g., Knupfer, 1999). Similarly, reviews of the literature may involve a focus on aggregating statistical findings across studies (e.g., Gorey, Thyer, & Pawluck, 1998) or present a narrative summary of the authors' impressions of an array of research studies (e.g., Stubbs & Bozarth, 1994). Each approach has its merits and limitations. The type of research labeled *theory development* may be purely conceptual in nature or involve a presentation of empirical research studies supportive or disconfirming of a particular theoretical model.

Part IV presents chapters that deal with more general issues—ethical factors in social work research; the significance of gender, ethnicity, and race variables; comparative international research; the value of integrating qualitative and quantitative approaches to research; applying for research grants; and disseminating research findings. Each of these is important to the research process. Increasingly, social work research is being funded through competitively awarded, externally funded grants. The most sophisticated researcher in the world who cannot obtain needed funding to undertake important studies will be seriously disadvantaged. Social work must be grounded in a thorough knowledge of ethical principles and governed accordingly. During recent years, the research programs of entire universities have been temporarily halted by the federal government, pending the correction of internal review mechanisms established for the protection of human subjects. Pity the poor academic social work researcher whose eagerness to collect data prior to obtaining approval from his or her university's human subjects institutional review board results in a shutdown of all university-conducted research by the federal government. Obviously, research findings must be disseminated to the social work community and to others for such findings to be of value to society. The unpublished research study might as well not even have been conducted. Although dissemination usually is construed to mean published in a peer-reviewed hard-copy journal, other useful vehicles to share research information include conference presentations, electronic journals, articles in popular media, and teaching. Too often, our research programs teach social workers how to design and conduct research but fail to teach the intricacies of how to get published. Fortunately, there are some excellent resources available to remedy this deficit (e.g., Thyer, 1994).

Together, these four parts provide the reader with a comprehensive overview to major research methods used in contemporary social work. This handbook joins related volumes published by Sage Publications including the *Handbook of Social Work Direct Practice* (edited by Allen-Meares & Garvin, 2000), the *Handbook of Social Policy* (edited by Midgley, Tracy, & Livermore, 2000), and the *Handbook of Social Welfare Management* (edited by Patti, 2000). This comprehensive series promises to be an exceedingly valuable, if not definitive, compilation of scholarly resources for social work students, academics, and practitioners alike.

Keep in mind the applied nature of social work research. Our field is not primarily interested in the development of theoretical knowledge for knowledge's sake alone; we can leave that to the academic disciplines. As noted by Thyer (1759), "The end of all knowledge is to understand what is fit to be done, for to know what has been, and what is, and what may be, does but tend to that" (pp. 487-488). As a practicing profession, our mandate is to provide credible evidence regarding what can be done to help solve societal and interpersonal problems. To the extent that we adhere to this task, we are carrying out the mission given to us by society at large and expected of us by our clients.

—*Bruce A. Thyer*

REFERENCES

Allen-Meares, P., & Garvin, C. (Eds.). (2000). *The handbook of social work direct practice*. Thousand Oaks, CA: Sage.

Almgren, G., Kemp, S. P., & Eisinger, A. (2000). The legacy of Hull House and the Children's Bureau in the American mortality transition. *Social Service Review, 74*, 1-27.

Gorey, K. M., Thyer, B. A., & Pawluck, D. E. (1998). Differential effectiveness of prevalent social work practice models: A meta-analysis. *Social Work, 43*, 269-278.

Knupfer, A. M. (1999). Professionalizing probation work in Chicago, 1900-1935. *Social Service Review, 73*, 478-495.

Midgley, J., Tracy, M. B., & Livermore, M. (Eds.). (2000). *The handbook of social policy*. Thousand Oaks, CA: Sage.

Patti, R. J. (Ed.). (2000). *The handbook of social welfare management*. Thousand Oaks, CA: Sage.

Stubbs, J. P., & Bozarth, J. D. (1994). The dodo bird revisited: A qualitative study of psychotherapy efficacy research. *Applied and Preventive Psychology, 3*, 109-120.

Thyer, B. A. (1994). *Successful publishing in scholarly journals*. Thousand Oaks, CA: Sage.

Thyer, R. (Ed.). (1759). *Samuel Butler*. London: J. & R. Tonson.

CHAPTER ONE

Introductory Principles of Social Work Research

BRUCE A. THYER

The scientific approach to unsolved problems is the
only one which contains any hope of learning to deal
with the unknown.
—*Bertha Capen Reynolds (1942, p. 20)*

An emphasis on the value of scientific research *always* has characterized professional social work education and practice. Indeed, this emphasis is one of the
hallmarks that distinguishes genuinely "professional" services from other forms of
private/public philanthropy and charity and the provision of social care motivated by
religious, familial, altruistic, or philosophical reasons. Of course, a focus of science
can be, and often is, legitimately compatible with these latter motivations, and this
may represent the ideal circumstance. In the history of social work in North America
and Great Britain, as well as in other European nations, the system of poor laws and
other relatively unsystematic attempts to care for the destitute gave rise during
the latter part of the 19th century to an orientation labeled *scientific philanthropy.*
Coincident with the emergence of "friendly visiting," formalized academic training,
and other precursors to the professionalization of social work, the development of
charitable services guided by science, and practiced by humans who were motivated
by their personal religious beliefs or secular humanistic values, has evolved to the
present day.

Social work historian John Graham provides a good case study on the transition of a Toronto charity home for women called The Haven, established in 1878 by religious elites, that gradually made the transition to a more secularly oriented and professional service. Graham (1992) describes the completion of this transition in 1927 as follows:

> Professional social work, therefore, had been firmly installed at *The Haven,* and the last vestiges of the benevolent philanthropy of the nineteenth century were abandoned. A growing sense of professional identity moreover demanded a strict delineation between the social worker and the social agency volunteer. Differentiating the former from the latter was a *scientific knowledge base and specialized skills* which were the social worker's alone. (p. 304, italics added)

Such a transition can be said to characterize the majority of social work programs across North America during the early part of the 20th century.

Where do we social workers come from organizationally? We have many roots, but a central one was the establishment in 1865 of the American Social Science Association (ASSA), a generalist organization influenced by French sociologist Auguste Comte's then novel philosophy of science labeled *positivism,* which called for the objective study of human society and behavior using the same tools of scientific inquiry that were proving so successful in the biological and physical sciences. From the ASSA sprouted numerous offshoots, some of which thrive to this day, although the parent group crumbled in 1909. From the ASSA, in 1879, emerged the Conference of Charities, which in 1884 evolved into the National Conference of Charities and Correction (NCCC), described as "a forum for the communication of the ideas and values connected with scientific charity" (Germain, 1970, p. 9). In turn, the NCCC was renamed the National Conference on Social Work in 1917. This label lasted until 1957, when it was altered to the National Conference on Social Welfare, which gradually expired during the 1980s.

The role of scientific research in social welfare can be seen through many early writings including an article titled "Scientific Charity" presented at the 1889 meeting of the NCCC (cited in Germain, 1970, p. 8) and one titled "A Scientific Basis for Charity" (Wayland, 1894), which appeared in the influential journal *The Charities Review.* Such perspectives culminated in 1917 with the publication of Richmond's (1917) *Social Diagnosis,* an influential text that wholeheartedly extolled the virtues of positivist science. Indeed, in 1921, Richmond received an honorary M.A. degree from Smith College for "establishing the scientific basis of a new profession" (cited in Germain, 1970, p. 12).

The possible examples of conference talks, journal articles, chapters, and books illustrating the central reliance on scientific research as a guiding force within early social work are too numerous to mention here. Germain (1970) remains one of the very best reviews of this "ancient" history of our profession. More recent is the history of the Social Work Research Group (SWRG), a short-lived professional membership organization established in 1949 that became one of the original seven constituents of the National Association of Social Workers (NASW) in 1955, transmogrifying itself into the NASW's Research Section. In 1963, this became the NASW's Council on Social Work Research, where it gradually faded from view by the mid-1960s. Graham, Al-Krenawi, and Bradshaw (2000) have prepared an excellent historical study of the rise and demise of the SWRG.

More recently, in 1994, a small ground of social workers led by Janet B. W. Williams established a new scientifically oriented social work membership organization known as the Society for Social Work and Research (SSWR). All social workers with an interest in scientific research in social work are eligible to join. The SSWR quickly grew from 271 members in 1995 to more than 900 in 2000, and the organization has an active newsletter and program of annual international conferences. The first professional conference was held in 1995 in Washington, D.C., and was followed by conferences in Miami, Florida (1998); Austin, Texas (1999); and Charleston, South Carolina (2000). The next conferences are scheduled for Atlanta, Georgia (2001) and San Diego, California (2002). The SSWR conferences offer a host of competitively reviewed symposia, papers, and posters; plenary addresses by prominent social work researchers; and an awards program that recognizes outstanding examples of recently published social work research. Because of its superb organization and the top quality of its presentations, the SSWR conference has rapidly become the preferred venue for social work researchers to present their research findings. Moreover, it has become the conference of choice for schools of social work to seek interviews with potential new faculty and for potential new faculty to seek academic positions. In 1999, the SSWR began providing its members a subscription to the bimonthly peer-reviewed journal *Research on Social Work Practice,* an independent periodical established in 1991. This growth of the SSWR augurs well for the continuing voice of science within mainstream social work.

A related but independent development during the 1990s was the establishment of the Institute for the Advancement of Social Work Research (IASWR) in 1993. The mission of the IASWR is

to advance the scientific knowledge base of social work practice by building the research capacity of the profession. Ensuring that social work is represented within the national scientific community, [the] IASWR strengthens the voice of the profession in public policy determinations. (IASWR, 2000)

Five national professional social work organizations contributed to the development of the IASWR and are represented on its governing board. Among its initiatives have been co-sponsorship of the SSWR conferences, information dissemination, the commissioning of a major appraisal of the state of research resources within social work (Austin, 1998), and effective advocacy for the establishment of a federal Center for Social Work Research under the auspices of the National Institutes of Health. A bill proposing such a center presently is before Congress.

SCIENTIFIC PERSPECTIVES ON PRACTICE

Coincident with these organizational and policy developments related to the integration of science and social work during the past quarter century have been three related perspectives on practice. The first is known as *empirical clinical practice* (ECP), the second is called *empirically validated treatments* (EVT), and the third is labeled *evidence-based practice* (EBP). These are reviewed briefly in turn.

Empirical Clinical Practice

Empirical clinical practice was the name of a book authored by social workers Jayaratne and Levy (1979), who describe the characteristics of the ECP model they espouse: "Empirical practice is conducted by clinicians who strive to measure and demonstrate the effect of their clinical practice by adapting traditional experimental research techniques to clinical practice" (p. xiii). The authors focus on teaching social workers the use of relatively simple research methods called single-system research designs to empirically evaluate the outcomes of their work. They believe that "clinical practice that can empirically demonstrate its effect provides the basis for the best service to the client" (p. xiv). They contend that ECP can be adopted by practitioners using virtually any theoretical model of practice so long as it is possible to measure changes in the client, relate these changes (provisionally) to social work intervention, and then base future services on these observations. The authors do advocate that social workers should rely on previous research to help guide their choices of interventions that they offer clients. In their words, "The clinician would first be interested in using an intervention strategy that has been successful in the past. . . . When established techniques are available, they should be used, but they should be based on objective evaluation rather than subjective feeling" (p. 7). ECP involves the careful and repeated measure of client functioning, using reliable and valid measures repeated over time, combined with selected treatments based on the best available scientific evidence. Their entire book is devoted to describing how to do these activities. A similar social work text by Wodarski (1981), titled *The Role of Research in Clinical Practice*, advocates for much the same thing—a preference to make use of psychosocial treatments that scientific research had really demonstrated to be of benefit to clients, measuring client functioning in reliable and valid ways, and empirically evaluating outcomes with individual clients and larger groups.

The banner of ECP was picked up by a number of subsequent social workers, and a rather large (and not uncontroversial) literature has grown around these notions (e.g., Corcoran, 1985; Ivanoff, Blythe, & Briar, 1987; Ivanoff, Robinson, & Blythe, 1987; MacDonald, 1994; Thyer, 1996). The influence of ECP has not been inconsiderable. For example, in 1982, just 3 years following the publication of *Empirical Clinical Practice* (Jayaratne & Levy, 1979), the curriculum policy statement of the Council on Social Work Education (CSWE, 1982) included a new mandate that research courses must now teach "designs for the systematic evaluation of the student's own practice . . . [and should] prepare them systematically to evaluate their own practice and contribute to the generation of knowledge for practice" (pp. 10-11). Similar standards still can be found in the current CSWE guidelines. Insisting that individual practitioners conduct systematic outcome evaluations of their own services was a remarkable professional standard, one that has not yet been emulated by educational and practice guidelines within clinical psychology or psychiatry in the present day.

Empirically Validated Treatments

Subsequent to the ECP movement within social work, a related initiative developed within clinical psychology called *empirically validated treatments*. During the mid-1990s, the president of Section III (Society for a Science of Clinical Psychology) of Division 12 (Clinical Psychology) of the American Psychological Association convened a Task Force on Promotion and Dissemination of Psychological Procedures, a group charged with two functions: (a) develop a scientifically defensible set of criteria that can be used to determine whether or not a given psychological technique can be called *empirically validated* and (b) conduct comprehensive reviews of the research literature, apply these criteria, and come up with, in effect, lists of psychological procedures that fulfill these criteria and, therefore, can be considered, in a scientific sense, empirically validated.

The evidentiary standards ultimately decided on by the task force actually were rather modest, consisting of the following criteria:

I.   At least two good between-group design experiments demonstrating efficacy in one or more of the following ways:
     A.   Superior to pill or psychological placebo or to another treatment
     B.   Equivalent to an already established treatment in experiments with adequate statistical power

or

II. A large series of single-case design experiments ($N > 9$) demonstrating efficacy
     that must have done the following:
     A. Used good experimental designs
     B. Compared the intervention to another treatment (as in I.A.)

Among the further criteria are that the psychological techniques must be based on
well-proceduralized treatment manuals, that the characteristics of the client samples
are clearly defined, and that the positive effects must have been demonstrated by at
least two different investigators or investigatory teams. A psychological treatment
meeting the preceding criteria could be said to be *well established*. A somewhat less
stringent set of criteria could be followed to potentially label a treatment as *probably
efficacious* (Chambless et al., 1996).

     With the criteria in place, the task force busily got to work in seeing which psycho-
logical treatments could be labeled *empirically validated* and *probably efficacious*,
and reports soon began appearing indicating EVT for a wide array of psychological
disorders such as depression, panic disorder, pain, and schizophrenia. As with the
ECP movement within social work, the EVT task force within psychology did not es-
cape controversy. For one thing, the task force recognized that labeling a treatment as
empirically validated seemed to close the discussion off, implying perhaps a stronger
level of research evidence than was justified. Subsequent reports of the task force
used the more tempered language of *empirically supported treatments* or *empirically
based*. Entire issues of leading professional journals (i.e., a 1996 issue of *Clinical Psychology: Science and Practice*, a 1998 issue of the *Journal of Consulting and Clinical
Psychology*, a 1998 issue of *Psychotherapy Research*) were devoted to the topic, as
were considerable independent literatures (e.g., Nathan & Gorman, 1998; Sanderson & Woody, 1995; Task Force on Promotion and Dissemination of Psychological
Procedures, 1995). The influence of the EVT movement also has been strong, and the
work of the Division 12 task force was commented on extremely favorably in the recent *Mental Health: A Report of the Surgeon General* (Hatcher, 2000).

Evidence-Based Practice

     Coincident with the EVT initiatives in clinical psychology have been related activi-
ties in medicine labeled *evidence-based practice*, defined as "the conscientious, explicit, and judicious use of the current best evidence in making decisions about the
care of individual patients" (Sackett, Richardson, Rosenberg, & Haynes, 1997, p. 2).
On its face, EBP would not seem to be a radical notion, and indeed, most readers
would be assumed to infer that such a standard already was in place in most of the
health professions. Sadly, to a great extent, this is not the case, although a small but
influential group of health care providers is attempting to make it so. EBP and EVT

actually are variations of the earlier ECP model of social work, which mandates not only the *selection* of treatments based on their level of scientific research support but also the ongoing empirical *evaluation of outcomes* using single-system and other research designs. But the spirit and intent of all three movements—ECP (developed within social work), EVT (developed within psychology), and EBP (developed within medicine)—are the same. And it seems as though the EBP language will gradually supplant that of ECP and EVT. Already, one can find social workers and psychologists adopting the EBP terminology. The current president of the Society for the Science of Clinical Psychology (a section of Division 12 of the American Psychological Association) recently published an editorial titled "Evidence-Based Psychotherapy: A Graduate Course Proposal" (Persons, 1999), and some social workers have begun using the EBP language, most notably Gambrill (1999) with her thoughtful article titled "Evidence-Based Practice: An Alternative to Authority-Based Practice" and Corcoran (2000) with her recent book titled *Evidence-Based Social Work Practice With Families* (see also Lloyd, 1998; Thyer, in press a). The melding of these *disciplinary* perspectives into an *interdisciplinary* human services movement generically called *evidence-based practice* seems likely. Consider Persons's (1999) description of EBP:

> The evidence-based practitioner:
> - Provides informed consent for treatment
> - Relies on the efficacy data (especially from RCTs [randomized clinical trials]) when recommending and selecting and carrying out treatments
> - Uses the empirical literature to guide decision-making
> - Uses a systematic, hypothesis-testing approach to the treatment of each case:
>   - Begins with careful assessment
>   - Sets clear and measurable goals
>   - Develops an individualized formulation and a treatment plan based on the formulation
>   - Monitors progress toward the goals frequently and modifies or ends treatment as needed (p. 2)

Well, perhaps Jayaratne and Levy were simply two decades ahead of their time. A recent issue of *NASW News* contained an article on the Surgeon General's Report on Mental Health and noted, "A challenge in the near term is to speed transfer of new *evidence-based treatments* and prevention interventions into diverse service delivery settings and systems" (O'Neill, 2000, p. 6, italics added). The surgeon general's report itself states clearly,

> Responding to the calls of managed mental health and behavioral health care systems for evidence-based interventions will have a much needed and discernable impact on practice.

. . . It is essential to expand the supply of effective, evidence-based services throughout the nation. (Hatcher, 2000, Chap. 8)

EBP requires knowing what helps social work clients and what does not help them. It requires being able to distinguish between unverified *opinions* about psychosocial interventions and *facts* about their effectiveness. And separating facts from fictions is what science is pretty good at doing. Not perfectly, and not without false starts, but the publicly verifiable and potentially testable conclusions of scientific research render this form of knowledge building an inherently self-correcting one (in the long run), a considerable advantage over other "ways of knowing."

ON TERMS

The preceding brief overview helps to bring us to the present, wherein social work is attempting to really implement our original aspirations pertaining to being based on a foundation of scientific research. As in most intellectual undertakings, it always is helpful to begin by defining one's terms. Accordingly, the following language is being used to help set the stage for subsequent chapters in this handbook.

Research refers to "systematic procedures used in seeking facts or principles" (Barker, 1999, p. 410), and the phrase *scientific method* means

a set of rigorous procedures used in social and physical research to obtain and interpret facts. The procedures include defining the problem, operationally stating in advance the method for measuring the problem, defining in advance the criteria to be used to reject hypotheses, using measuring instruments that have validity and reliability, observing and measuring all the cases or a representative sample of those cases, presenting for public scrutiny the findings and the methods used in accumulating them in such detail as to permit replication, and limiting any conclusions to those elements that are supported by the findings. (p. 427)

The term *empirical* often is bandied about in the social work literature, and in some interpretations it seems synonymous with the assertion, "If I can see it, then it is real." Well, evidence obtained via the senses certainly is a part (and a very important one) of the meaning of the term, but simply having a single person sense (e.g., see, hear, smell) something does not really suffice for something to be considered a piece of scientific data. For research purposes, data "should also be obtained through *systematic* observations capable of being *replicated* (i.e., verified) by other individuals and subject to some evidentiary standards (Thyer & Wodarski, 1998, p. 2, italics in original). Perhaps it is true that a neighbor was removed from his bed by aliens one night and subjected to invasive medical procedures prior to being returned home. But unless others see the abduction occur, or unless other evidence is available (e.g., the aliens left objects inside his body), to label this experience of his as *empirical* is true only in the loosest sense of the term. Certainly, one-time private events leaving no detectable evidence behind, or purely subjective experiences, are difficult phenomena on which to conduct scientific research. This is not to say that such experiences are false or otherwise unimportant, only that they rarely are the subject matter of science.

SOME PHILOSOPHICAL ASSUMPTIONS

Professional social work's dual origins in the worlds of religion and of science require contemporary practice and research to rest a bit uneasily on a Procrustean bed of philosophical assumptions. The philosophical positions described in what follows, while for the most part being simply seen as common sense, cannot in any way be said to be *proved* or demonstrated to be valid. Each is vulnerable to attack and, indeed, to apparent refutation, but these views nevertheless have stood the test of both time and practice sufficiently well for us to have some degree of confidence in them. First, I describe principles that most contemporary researchers accept as philosophically axiomatic (i.e., self-evident truths), followed by some selected philosophical positions that are rejected by most scientists today.

Accepted Principles:

Realism: the point of view that the world has an independent or objective existence apart from the perceptions of the observer

Determinism: the assumption that all phenomena, including psychosocial ones, have physical (as opposed to metaphysical) causes that are potentially amenable to scientific investigation and discovery

Positivism: the belief that valid knowledge about the objective world *can* be arrived at through scientific research

Rationalism: the belief that reason and logic are useful tools for scientific inquiry and that, ultimately, truthful or valid accounts of human behavior will be rational or logically understandable

Empiricism: a preference to rely on evidence gathered systematically through observation or experiment and capable of being replicated (i.e., reproduced and verified) by others using satisfactory standards of evidence

Operationism: the assertion that it is important to develop dependent (e.g., outcome measures) and independent (e.g., social work treatments) variables that can be reliably replicated by others

Parsimony: a preference to seriously consider the simpler of the available and adequate explanations of a phenomenon prior to accepting a more complex account

Scientific skepticism: the point of view that all scientific claims (e.g., Treatment X helps clients) should be considered to be of doubtful validity until substantiated by credible empirical data

Rejected Principles:

Metaphysics: explanations involving supernatural, incorporeal, or immaterial entities or factors

Nihilism: the doctrine that all values are baseless and that nothing is known or can be learned

Dualism: the view that the world consists of the two fundamental entities of mind and matter

Reification: attributing reality to an abstract or hypothetical construct (e.g., the superego) in the absence of adequate evidence supporting the existence of that construct

Circular reasoning: an explanation for human behavior in which causes and effects cannot be distinguished from each other

Scientism: the theory that the investigational methods used in the natural sciences should be applied in all fields of inquiry

Now, certainly, some words of clarification might be needed here because a few of the preceding positions could be seen as challenging or confusing to the reader. Let us begin with *realism*. Most of us accept the idea that the world continues merrily along, even though we might not be aware of it, for example, when we are asleep or under anesthesia. But to accept realism is not to reject the potentially important role of individual perceptions in the construction of an individual's world. To be a realist means to accept that at least *some* part of our world has an objective existence, and for many areas of social work practice it is these objective realities that are the focus of intervention. Actually, most social workers are hard-core realists, and it is only a small (but vocal) minority who challenge this notion, mostly philosophically oriented sherry-sippers located within the academy. The wisdom of Reynolds (1942) remains the mainstream view: "A second characteristic of scientifically oriented social work is that it accepts the objective reality of forces outside itself with which it must cooperate" (p. 24).

We accept *determinism* whenever we attempt intervention by the tacit assumption that treatment can have effects. If we did not believe that clients' problems or social ills had causes, then what would be the point of having an entire profession devoted to discovering those causes and remedying them?

Although the term *positivism* usually is not uttered kindly, in reality most of the criticisms against it have portrayed a straw man. Most of us believe that scientific inquiry about the world of our clients and the amelioration of their difficulties can be a useful undertaking. *That* simple idea is positivism in a nutshell. It always is a good idea to turn to original sources when discussing controversial topics, so let us see how one of the founders of the logical positivist movement describes this perspective:

Our position is related to that of *Positivism* which, like ourselves, rejects Metaphysics and requires that every scientific statement should be based on and reducible to statements of empirical observations. On this account many (and we ourselves at times) have given our position the name of Positivism (or New Positivism or Logical Positivism). The term may be employed, provided it is understood that we agree with Positivism only in its logical components, but make no assertions as to whether the Given is real and the Physical World appearance, or *vice versa*, for Logical Analysis shows that such assertions belong to the class of unverifiable pseudo-statements. (Carnap, 1934/1995, p. 27)

For the logical positivists, many philosophical problems are essentially unresolvable by the methods of science and are, therefore, seen as pseudo-problems and serve only to distract us from more serious issues. Whether this handbook that you are reading is "real" or whether you are simply dreaming about it (a nightmare!) cannot be ascertained with certainty by scientific methods. Thus, positivism dismisses such issues from the purview of science (calling them *unverifiable pseudo-statements,* as in the Carnap [1934/1995] quote) and moves on to the more practical matters that concern most social workers. Asking provocative philosophical questions, posing tautologies, and pointing out professional paradoxes can be both interesting and fun at times. But if we become preoccupied with such issues to the extent that we become professionally immobilized, then what was a harmless distraction has become a destructive influence.

Positivism does *not* mean that scientific research is the *only* way in which to discover useful knowledge. Positivism does *not* mean that all knowledge obtained from nonscientific sources is incorrect or useless. And positivism does *not* mean that any supposed finding obtained from a "scientific study" is free from error or that science does not make mistakes. Remember the excitement of the discovery of "cold" fusion a decade ago, with its unfulfilled promise of unlimited, pollution-free energy for humankind? How about the early astronomer who discovered "canals" on Mars? Canals then also were claimed to be seen by other "scientific" astronomers. (Sorry, there are no canals on Mars.) And if mistakes occur in the relatively "cleaner" disciplines such as physics and astronomy, then think how much more difficult it can be to design and conduct sound scientific studies in the field of social work, studies taking place not in a germ-free laboratory using purified reagents but rather in the hurly-burly of clients' *lives,* in the real world contexts in which social problems exist. Social workers can envy bench scientists' degree of experimental control over their subject matters and the reliability of the findings that they can obtain. Envy, perhaps, but with the appreciation that our field is more intrinsically difficult and challenging. Research into the causes of social problems and into the development and evaluation of interventions designed to ameliorate or prevent them can be seen as more difficult and as requiring greater intelligence and perseverance than rocket science.

Certainty in science is relative, provisional, and fallible, with any given finding always susceptible to being overturned by new and better data. "Science does not claim to have complete knowledge of the truth or to have established perfect order out of chaos in this world. It is less an accomplished fact than an attitude" (Todd, 1920, p. 71). Through scientific research, we may perhaps come closer to nature's truth, even if we are unable to completely understand it.

Few would argue that *rationalism* and *empiricism* are not noble attributes, and most accept that it is necessary for both practice and research purposes to *operationalize* our measures so as to elevate what we do beyond the level of art to that of a teachable skill and a communicable method. We make use of *parsimony* wherever we check out the simplest and most obvious explanations of a problem first. And *scientific skepticism* is our protection against being overwhelmed by an ever growing number of claims. Skepticism originally arose during the Enlightenment as a reaction to traditional theological explanations for things. Scientific skepticism deals with claims made with respect to areas that are the purview of scientific research. Scientific skepticism is not applicable to nonscientific claims (but other forms of skepticism might be, e.g., religious skepticism), although there is some overlap (e.g., testing the claims of fraudulent faith healers, designing and conducting randomized controlled trials of the purported healing powers of prayer).

Social workers do not usually invoke spiritual explanations for domestic violence, rape, or child abuse and neglect. Nor are demons usually seen as the cause of unemployment, poverty, or sudden infant death syndrome. A social worker might subscribe to *metaphysics* or supernatural beliefs in his or her personal life, but in professional social work metaphysical accounts typically are eschewed in favor of material ones. *Nihilism* is, in a sense, the reverse of positivism (although social work researchers with a sense of humor have noted that the opposite of positivism is negativism), basically denying that advances in scientifically supported knowledge are possible. This view is, of course, refuted each time a new issue of a social work research journal is published. Few of us are *dualists* today. We might use the language of the "mind," but we really know that we are talking about the physical processes of the brain as opposed to some immaterial entity called the mind that exists independent of the brain and body. Rejecting the concept of mind is an example of avoiding *reification, and we also avoid reification every time we reject characterological explanations of why people act the way they do in favor of social, economic, or person-in-environment explanations. Circular* reasoning remains rampant in social work, and it requires careful attention to avoid falling into this trap. Following are a couple of examples:

Q: Why don't inner-city residents vote?
A: They are apathetic.
Q: How do you know they are apathetic?

A: They do not vote.

Q: Why does Allen drink so much?
A: He is an alcoholic.
Q: How do you know he is an alcoholic?
A: He drinks too much.

In these simple examples, the only evidence in support of the existence of the presumed "cause" (apathy or alcoholism, actual things said to reside within the person [i.e., characterological traits]) is the very behavior one is attempting to explain. If the only evidence for the existence of alcoholism is the very drinking that the alcoholism is said to cause, then despite the appearance of closure in explanation, in reality nothing has been explained. Pseudo-explanations involving circular reasoning often involve reification as well. Contrast the preceding examples with the following:

Q: Why is Allen crying so much?
A: His wife left him.

Q: Why does Allen scream and run away at
   the sight of dogs?
A: When he was 4 years old, he was
   attacked by a Rottweiler.

In these latter examples, the possible causes are potentially verifiable and *not* inferred from the behavior that they are trying to explain. Thus, in a scientific sense, they are much more satisfactory explanations than the former ones.

The sin of *scientism* occurs when one ignores the fact that *many* very important issues of social work policy and practice are *not* matters capable (at least not at present) of being resolved by scientific inquiry. Whether or not same-sex partners should be permitted to be legally married is not a public policy issue on which science can shed much light. Whether or not pregnant minors should be legally required to obtain parental consent to undergo abortions, or whether or not the Georgia state flag should be altered to delete the Confederate stars and bars, is similarly a matter of values, morality, religion, philosophy, and social justice, not an issue particularly capable of being resolved by scientific research. "The goals of social work are determined in large part by values, or philosophic rather than scientific considerations, and the means of social work are also affected not only by considerations of efficiency but also by moral and philosophical convictions" (Macdonald, 1960, p. 4). And this is as it should be. Science is modest and knows its limits. It also knows its purview, and although a great deal of social work is the legitimate subject matter of scientific research, much is not.

Another point is worth stressing. To advocate for one position (e.g., that social work practice needs to rely more on scientific research findings) does not imply acceptance of a more extreme position (e.g., that we must eliminate all "art" from clinical practice). For example, Myers and Thyer (1997) argue that as EBPs emerge, clients should have a right to be offered those interventions by their social workers as treatment options of first choice. This has been misconstrued by some to imply that evidence-based or scientific considerations should be the *only* voice in practice decisions. Such is not the case. Urging that science be invited to the dinner party does not mean that other guests cannot attend or should be cast out hungry into the darkness of the stormy night. Empirical research at present continues to play a relatively minor role in practice. Augmenting practice wisdom, insight, and art *with* the findings of science would merely seem to be the hallmark of professional practice, not a threat to these traditional sources of guidance. But, one might ask, what if the findings of scientific research *conflict* with the dictates of these other sources of knowledge? At present, that is a matter of personal choice and conviction. But certainly, forces external to, as well as within, the profession are urging that greater consideration be given to research findings.

THE PROGRESSIVE NATURE OF SCIENTIFIC RESEARCH

Another feature of science is its generally progressive nature. During the 18th, 19th, and early 20th centuries, large-scale systematic surveys of the plight of the poor were undertaken by individuals, private groups, and governments in Great Britain, Europe, and the United States documenting the incidence of social problems as well as their correlates and consequences. John Howard investigated the conditions of prisoners, prisons, and jailers in Britain, Europe, and Russia. Sir Frederic Morton Eden examined the state of the poor in Britain and published a large-scale study of his findings in 1797. Charles Booth studied the living and working conditions of the people of London, and Beatrice Webb conducted social investigations in Britain. These are only a few of the pioneers in scientific social work. In the United States, Dorothea Dix conducted systematic investigations of conditions in mental hospitals. These and the Pittsburgh Survey of 1907 (the American equivalent to Booth's work) are just two of many similar examples. In turn, the results of these early scientific surveys, having elevated the plight of the poor beyond that of real or fictitious anecdotes (as in Charles Dickens's *Oliver Twist*), helped to set the stage for progressive welfare legislation aimed at ameliorating human misery. Indeed, by the early part of the 20th century, progressive social reform movements had become almost *synonymous* with a reliance on scientific research. As noted by Larson (1995),

> Progressive reforms characteristically reflected a "belief in interventionism" and "relied upon organization, the application of scientific (or social-scientific) expertise, and the value of efficiency and rationality" to solve the pressing social, political, and economic problems of the day. Thus, individual progressive reform movements typically began with the formulation of a rational or scientific solution to a pressing social problem, proceeded to the organization of a public education campaign to promote voluntary acceptance of the solution, and concluded with the passage of laws to compel conformity with it. . . . Progressives relied heavily on the scientific and social-scientific expertise provided by leading universities. (pp. 15, 17)

In short, a reliance on the findings of scientific research has long been associated with the fields of social work and social welfare, and the tools of science have been harnessed to promote progressive social welfare legislation to such an extent that the very term *progressive* implied a reliance on science. This can be contrasted with the widespread contemporary association of the term *progressive* with left-wing politics or of the views of some who see scientific research as inherently conservative, if indeed not anti-progressive. These latter voices are heard commonly enough with social work to cause Allen Rubin, then president of the Society for Social Work and Research, to devote an editorial rebutting such erroneous views, claiming,

> We need to test out our noble intentions with research. We need to do this for three reasons. The first reason is to be sure we are supporting something that is really helpful (and not harmful). The second reason is that scientific evidence strengthens our ability to persuade others to support our proposals and, thus, helps us build stronger coalitions and ultimately have more influence as a profession. The third reason is that to eschew such research is to belie our claim to be a profession. (Rubin, 1999, p. 281)

The more things change, the more they stay the same. Contrast Rubin's (1999) recent editorial with the following statement made more than 60 years ago:

> Employment of scientifically approved and tested techniques will [e]nsure the profession the confidence and respect of clients and the public, for increasingly the social casework process will operate more certainly for known and desired ends in the area of social adjustment. (Strode, 1940, p. 142)

Or, how about 80 years ago:

Social science and its applications must share the spirit, if not the strict technique, of the exact sciences. The elements of scientific approach and scientific precision must be back of all social reform which hopes to weather the storms. (Todd, 1920, p. iv)

Or, how about nearly 90 years ago: "To make benevolence scientific is the great problem of the present age" (Toynbee, 1912, p. 74).

By now, the point made initially in this chapter should be adequately reinforced. Both philosophically and practically, professional social work has espoused a reliance on the findings of scientific research and has encouraged social workers to actually undertake such research studies themselves. This means that social workers need to be trained in scientific research methods. This commitment is pervasive throughout the profession. For example, the *Code of Ethics* of the National Association of Social Workers (1996) states,

Social workers should base practice on recognized knowledge, including empirically based knowledge, relevant to social work and social work ethics. . . . Social workers should contribute to the knowledge base of social work. . . . Social workers should promote and facilitate evaluation and research to contribute to the development of knowledge. . . . Social workers should educate themselves, their students, and their colleagues about responsible research practices. (pp. 22, 24-26)

Research training is deemed an essential component of the B.S.W. and M.S.W. curricula by the organization that accredits social work educational programs, the Council on Social Work Education. So, it is fair to claim that research training, research use in practice, and the conduct of research can be considered part-and-parcel of the activities of a professionally trained social worker.

SOME PURPOSES OF RESEARCH

There are many ways in which to try to conceptualize research activities within social work, and a commonly used framework classifies research efforts as those aimed at generating *descriptive* knowledge, those aimed at producing *explanatory* knowledge, and those focused on *interventive* knowledge (some call this *control* knowledge). Most research in various fields of science begins, by necessity, with descriptive work. We could not have a genuine science of chemistry until we had established a periodic table of the elements that corresponded reasonably well with the way in which elements actually occur in nature. Similarly, developing a way of classifying species of plants and animals that accurately reflected the way in which they are divided in the natural world was a great impetus to the development of biology. Although social work lacks such comprehensive descriptive systems, devising ways in which to reliably and validly measure psychosocial phenomena that we are interested in (i.e., to *describe* them accurately) is an essential feature of legitimate scientific inquiry. Measurement, of course, means the assignment of a number or quantity to some phenomenon, and just about everything that social workers are concerned about has the potential to be measured. In fact, this can be considered *axiomatic:*

Axiom 1: If something exists, then it has the potential to be measured.

If the reader does not believe this, then he or she should try to come up with an example of some *social work* issue, client concern, or problem that *cannot* be measured. The reader will be hard-pressed to do so. Alcohol abuse? Child abuse? Domestic violence? Schizophrenia? Depression? Poverty? Each and every one has been the focus of decades of increasingly rigorous efforts to measure these things. Occasionally, one might hear someone claim, "Well, you just can't measure X." An interesting question to pose at this point is, "Well, do you mean that no one, ever, anywhere, has ever been successful at measuring X? Or, do you really mean that *you* do not know how to measure X?" Lacking omniscience, most such nay-sayers will quickly back down, for in truth there is such a vast array of scientific literature out there on how to measure things of concern to social workers that one will very likely be able to locate relevant studies describing reasonably justifiable ways in which to measure X. Why this emphasis on measurement? Because of the following:

Axiom 2: If something is measured, then the social worker is in a better position to do research on it.

Imagine trying to study temperature prior to the development of measuring heat in terms of degrees (as in the Centigrade scale) or before having thermometers as measuring instruments. Closer to home, imagine trying to study poverty prior to defining it along some reasonable dimensions such as income, assets, and/or debt. In fact, the federal government has a number of definitions of poverty that it uses in its various entitlement programs. Early studies on schizophrenia and other so-called mental disorders were hampered by the use of vague, loose, and poorly operationalized terms, and over the past three decades immense advances have been made in trying to more accurately capture the realities of human psychopathology via the development of a more reliable system of classifying psychiatric disorders. *Child abuse* is defined legally in most states, and even though it sometimes is extremely detailed, often there still are loopholes. Nevertheless, these legal definitions do go far to help protect children from certain harsh experiences (even if they are not perfect operational definitions). More than 80 years ago, Richmond (1917) prudently noted, "To state that we think our client is mentally deranged is futile; to state the observations that have created this impression is a possible help" (p. 335). Clearly, Richmond was arguing for greater precision in observing and measuring client function. To be sure, the process of measuring aspects of clients' lives can be immensely challenging. For one thing, "In social work, there is this significant difference that the observer cannot avoid being a part of the social situation he is studying. Special methods must be worked out to take this factor into effect" (Reynolds, 1942, p. 23). Note that Reynolds (1942) does not suggest that we abandon as hopeless efforts to measure psychosocial phenomena, only that we be aware of the problems posed and cope with them with suitable research methods.

This leads us to the following:

> *Axiom 3:* If a client problem can be validly measured, then the social worker is in a better position to effectively help the client and to see whether the efforts are followed by improvement in the client's life.

Again turning to Richmond (1917), "Special efforts should be made to ascertain whether abnormal manifestations are *increasing* or *decreasing* in number and intensity, as this often has a practical bearing on the management of the case" (p. 435, italics in original). If the social worker does this with clients as individuals, or with larger groups of consumers, then he or she has undertaken intervention research. But more on that later.

Explanatory research efforts essentially aim at developing and testing theory, and a very large amount of valuable scholarly effort goes into such endeavors. Theory has been defined as "a group of related hypotheses, concepts, and constructs, based on facts and observations, that attempts to explain a particular phenomen[on]" (Barker, 1999, p. 485). Some theories are relatively small scale and attempt to develop accounts of very limited phenomena. The theory of the "insular mother" as a precipitant for child abuse is one example and leads logically to interventions intended to prevent or ameliorate child abuse by getting the mother more involved with a social network of adults or by instituting a program of frequent home visits. The "tension reduction theory" of alcohol abuse hypothesizes that individuals drink too much so as to cope with internally imposed or external stressors. This theory leads to interventions designed to teach stress-coping skills or to reduce aversive experiences undergone by the individual. Other theories are more comprehensive. Freud's psychodynamic theory made a valiant effort to account for a very wide array of human psychopathology, and social learning theory similarly encompasses explanations for both psychopathology and everyday actions. Usually, it is the social and behavioral sciences (e.g., psychology, sociology, economics, political science) that focus on the development and testing of theory. There has been little indigenous *theory* developed exclusively within and by social workers, who traditionally have been involved more in the application of theory through direct and community practice. Indeed, given the interdisciplinary wellsprings from which social work draws sustenance, it is not very likely that social work itself will be able to develop a large body of knowledge that is discipline specific (Thyer, 2000). And indeed, given the focus of social work as an *applied* field made up primarily of practitioners, and given the very limited number of doctorates in social work earned each year, efforts to emulate the academic social and behavioral sciences by focusing on explanatory research seem misguided. Surveys, correlational studies, needs assessments, predictor investigations (e.g., who among a group of people is more liable to develop a particular problem), comparisons, and the like are some of the types of research methods often used in conducting explanatory studies.

A far more useful undertaking for social work researchers to engage in is the third form of scientific inquiry, interventive research or studies aimed at empirically evaluating the outcomes of social work services. Here, the pragmatic research methods involve conducting single-system evaluations of clinical outcomes, quasi-experimental group outcome studies, randomized controlled clinical trials, cost-benefit analyses, and policy evaluations. The design and conduct of interventive studies may produce findings that bear on the corroboration or refutation of selected hypotheses derived from a given theory, but often they do not. Some authorities even go so far as to distinguish *evaluation* studies as different from *research* studies because of the applied focus of the former. This probably is a mistake. Interventive studies are part-and-parcel of the research enterprise and make use of many of the same principles of science as do descriptive and explanatory studies. Shaw and Lishman (1999) state this well: "Evaluation and research can often be distinguished only by general tendency and not by watertight categories. For example, *some* evaluation will involve theorizing and knowledge development . . . , while probably *all* research will involve theorizing" (p. 17, italics in original).

Many social work interventions are designed and carried out in the absence of any formal theory, and evaluation studies of the effectiveness of such interventions should not be retrospectively construed as tests of a particular theory. Genuine tests of theory should be limited to interventive programs explicitly derived from a particular theory, not retrofitted. Because theories are *explanations* of phenomena, they should not be confused with related concepts such as philosophical assumptions undergirding the science used to conduct research and models of practice that describe what to do but in themselves are not explanations for the rise of problems and do not account for why an intervention might work (e.g., the task-centered model of social work practice). Thyer (in press b) elaborates on the relationship between theory and research more extensively, arguing that not all interventive research studies need to be based on some theoretical framework or seek to test theoretical propositions. An interventive study that attempts to empirically find out whether a given social work program has been followed by improvements in client well-being is an exceedingly useful research endeavor and need not be disparaged if it fails to address theory.

A very large proportion of contemporary social work research may be classified as descriptive, perhaps around 36%, according to one survey by Rosen, Proctor, and Staudt (1999), with about 49% being explanatory in nature and only 15% being aimed at evaluating social work interventions. These figures need to be placed in the context that less than half (47%) of the articles actually appearing in mainstream social work journals from 1993 to 1997 presented empirical research findings at all, with the balance (the majority) being devoted to conceptual, theoretical, or methodological articles or to literature reviews. So, in actuality, only about 1 in 14 (7%) of social work articles reported research on intervention. The reader can check these proportions out for himself or herself by picking up a recent issue of any social work journal and classifying each article as descriptive, explanatory, or interventive in focus.

The failure of the social work profession to focus more on interventive studies has been commented on extensively by many leading authorities. Numerous individuals have explicitly urged the field to conduct more studies on the outcomes of social work practice, claiming that such investigations have a far more practical and valuable impact on the field and client services than do descriptive or explanatory research. For example, in Austin's (1998) report titled *A Report on Progress in the Development of Research Resources in Social Work,* he states,

> Of highest priority are strategies . . . for the development of research-based, practice-relevant knowledge for using in services dealing with children and their families. . . . Research on actual service interventions is the critical element in connecting research to the knowledge base used by professional practitioners. . . . Research on the effectiveness of service interventions is a major form of representation of the profession to the larger society. *The most important issue for the immediate future is to bring the practice effectiveness concerns of social work practitioners together with the resources represented by social work researchers.* . . . The issue is now one of developing investigations of social work intervention initiatives, studies that go beyond descriptive and explanatory research. (pp. 6, 17, 27, 43, italics in original)

Ell (1996), former executive director of the IASWR, expresses similar sentiments:

> Studies are needed on the effectiveness of psychosocial intervention, including interventions previously tested under ideal controlled circumstances, in real-world health-care systems. This growing area of research affords social work opportunities to conduct research

on actual programs and services. . . . Intervention research is costly and time-consuming. Social work is also disadvantaged in that it has yet to fully develop natural practice-research partnerships between researchers and service providers. . . . The collective commitment of the profession is needed to successfully address the current gaps in research on social work interventions. (pp. 587, 589)

Whether or not one agrees that interventive research should be seen as a more valuable form of inquiry for social workers than descriptive or explanatory studies, it does seem clear that there is a grave—indeed harmful—shortage of the former and that greater efforts aimed at promoting research on social work practice are needed (Harrison & Thyer, 1988).

THE METHODS OF SCIENCE

Scientific research always has been characterized by methodological pluralism. No one approach to inquiry is suitable for answering all questions or for all purposes. There *is* a sort of hierarchy of methods arranged in loose order in which we can have confidence in the strength of the conclusions. For example, observational and correlational studies are seen as generally less persuasive than experimental studies. This is a pecking order that has been around since Aristotle, if not before his time. But some disciplines lend themselves more readily to experimentation than do others. For example, take legitimate scientific fields such as meteorology, geology, astronomy, and paleontology. Here, scientists primarily rely on observations and correlations among these observations. There are few, if any, genuine experiments intended to influence the weather, the movement of tectonic plates, the rotation of the planets, or the placement of fossils in the Earth's strata, yet these disciplines certainly are recognized as "hard" sciences. True experimentation is exceedingly difficult in the world of social work, and this makes those few examples that have been undertaken all the more precious and admirable. So, we too rely, to a great extent, on naturalistic observations, correlational methods, and quasi-experiments of less than ideal design so as to advance knowledge in our field.

Charles Darwin did not conduct any true "experiments," but by soaking seeds in salt water and retrieving them from bird feces, he was able to create some very plausible hypotheses on how plant species could become widely distributed. And his naturalistic observations of many plant and animal species conducted around the world during his voyage as a naturalist on the British naval vessel *Beagle* gave him the raw data that, after germinating for years, culminated in his theory of the evolution of species via natural selection, perhaps the greatest idea in history to affect biology. It took anthropologist Jane Goodall only one naturalistic observation of chimpanzees in the wild eating another animal to disprove the hypothesis that chimps were natural vegetarians. David Rosenhan's clever pseudo-patient study conducted during the early 1970s involved no "experiments." He simply sent graduate students out to seek admission to mental hospitals and, after their admissions, had them record their experiences. This marvelous qualitative investigation was published in *Science,* perhaps the most prestigious research periodical in the world (Rosenhan, 1973). The field of science always has embraced a variety of research methods, both quantitative and qualitative, and both always have been fruitfully employed by social work investigators.

The balance of this handbook presents a number of the major methods used in social work research. We start off with some fundamentals such as probability, reliability, validity, and statistics—not that these are easy, but they set the stage for understanding much of the subsequent material. Next comes a presentation of some of the various types of quantitative studies—descriptive studies, surveys, needs assessments, and various forms of outcome studies. This is followed by a substantial section of the book reviewing various qualitative research methods—how we can use narrative case studies, in-depth interviews, ethnographic research, and participant observation. A smaller section then deals with conceptual forms of inquiry—the development of theory, historical research, literature reviews, and critical analyses. The final section covers more general topics—ethical issues in the design and conduct of social work research; the roles of gender, ethnicity, and race in research; comparative international research; integrating qualitative and quantitative methods; applying for research grants; and suggestions for publishing research findings.

Working with clients and communities can be fun. Knowing what one is doing by relying on EBP makes social work not only fun but also effective and ethical. Today's practice environment is increasingly expecting human service providers to deliver evidence-based psychosocial treatments where such knowledge has been developed. Scientific research is what enables us to figure out valid descriptive, explanatory, and interventive knowledge. A handbook such as this hopes to teach for the purposes of enhancing reader comprehension. The reader is urged to attempt the further step of *application.* Perhaps by collaborating with others, the reader should try to undertake some of the research methods described herein—a small-scale survey, a needs assessment, a single-system study, or a pretest-posttest group outcome study. The reader should write up a narrative case study of his or her work with an interesting client or should author a historical study of a local social service agency. The truly ambitious reader can attempt to publish his or her work in a professional journal or apply for a research grant. All of these actions are intrinsic parts of social work *practice.* The reader should try them out.

REFERENCES

Austin, D. (1998). *A report on progress in the development of research resources in social work*. Austin: University of Texas, School of Social Work.

Barker, R. L. (Ed.). (1999). *The social work dictionary* (4th ed.). Washington, DC: NASW Press.

Carnap, R. (1995). *The unity of science*. Bristol, UK: Thoemmes Press. (Originally published in 1934)

Chambless, D. L., Sanderson, W. C., Shoham, V., Bennet-Johnson, S., Pope, K. S., Crits-Christoph, P., Baker, M., Johnson, B., Woody, S. R., Sue, S., Beutler, L., Williams, D. A., & McCurry, S. (1996). An update on empirically validated therapies. *The Clinical Psychologist, 49*(2), 5-18.

Corcoran, J. (2000). *Evidence-based social work practice with families*. New York: Springer.

Corcoran, K. J. (1985). Clinical practice with nonbehavioral methods: Strategies for evaluation. *Clinical Social Work Journal, 13*, 78-86.

Council on Social Work Education. (1982). Curriculum policy for the master's degree and baccalaureate degree program in social work education. *Social Work Education Reporter, 30*(3), 5-12.

Ell, K. (1996). Social work research and health care policy and practice: A psychosocial research agenda. *Social Work, 41*, 583-592.

Gambrill, E. (1999). Evidence-based practice: An alternative to authority-based practice. *Families in Society, 80*, 341-350.

Germain, C. (1970). Casework and science: A historical encounter. In R. Roberts & R. Nee (Eds.), *Theories of social casework* (pp. 3-32). Chicago: University of Chicago Press.

Graham, J. R. (1992). The Haven, 1878-1930: A Toronto charity's transition from a religious to a professional ethos. *Histoire Sociale* [Social History], *25*, 283-306.

Graham, J. R., Al-Krenawi, A., & Bradshaw, C. (2000). The Social Work Research Group/NASW Research Section/Council on Social Work Research: 1949-1865—An emerging research identity in the American profession. *Research on Social Work Practice.*

Harrison, D. F., & Thyer, B. A. (1988). Doctoral research on social work practice. *Journal of Social Work Education, 24*, 107-114.

Hatcher, D. (2000). *Mental health: A report of the surgeon general*. Washington, DC: Government Printing Office.

Institute for the Advancement of Social Work Research. (2000). Available: http://www.sc.edu/swan/iaswr

Ivanoff, A., Blythe B. J., & Briar, S. (1987). The empirical clinical practice debate. *Social Casework, 68*, 290-298.

Ivanoff, A., Robinson, E. A., & Blythe, B. J. (1987). Empirical clinical practice from a feminist perspective. *Social Work, 32*, 417-423.

Jayaratne, S., & Levy, R. (1979). *Empirical clinical practice*. New York: Columbia University Press.

Larson, E. J. (1995). *Sex, race, and science*. Baltimore, MD: Johns Hopkins University Press.

Lloyd, E. (1998). Introducing evidence-based social welfare practice in a national child care agency. In A. Buchanan & B. L. Hudson (Eds.), *Parenting, schooling, and children's behaviour* (pp. 161-177). Aldershot, UK: Ashgate.

MacDonald, G. (1994). Developing empirically based practice in probation. *British Journal of Social Work, 24*, 405-427.

Macdonald, M. W. (1960). Social work research: A perspective. In N. A. Polansky (Ed.), *Social work research* (pp. 1-23). Chicago: University of Chicago Press.

Myers, L. L., & Thyer, B. A. (1997). Should social work clients have the right to effective treatment? *Social Work, 42*, 288-298.

Nathan, P., & Gorman, J. (Eds.). (1998). *A guide to treatments that work*. New York: Oxford University Press.

National Association of Social Workers. (1996). *Code of ethics*. Washington, DC: NASW Press.

O'Neill, J. V. (2000, February). Surgeon general's report lauded. *NASW News*, pp. 1, 6.

Persons, J. B. (1999, Fall). Evidence-based psychotherapy: A graduate course proposal. *Clinical Science*, pp. 2, 12.

Reynolds, B. C. (1942). *Learning and teaching in the practice of social work*. New York: Farrar & Rinehart.

Richmond, M. (1917). *Social diagnosis*. New York: Russell Sage.

Rosen, A., Proctor, E., & Staudt, M. (1999). Social work research and the quest for effective practice. *Social Work Research, 23*, 4-14.

Rosenhan, D. L. (1973). On being sane in insane places. *Science, 179*, 250-258.

Rubin, A. (1999). Do National Association of Social Workers leaders value research? A summit follow-up [editorial]. *Research on Social Work Practice, 9*, 277-282.

Sackett, D. L., Richardson, W. S., Rosenberg, W., & Haynes, R. B. (1997). *Evidence-based medicine: How to practice and teach EBM*. New York: Churchill Livingston.

Sanderson, W. C., & Woody, S. (1995). Manuals for empirically validated treatments. *The Clinical Psychologist, 48*(4), 7-11.

Shaw, I., & Lishman, J. (Eds.). (1999). *Evaluation and social work practice*. London: Sage.

Strode, J. (1940). *Introduction to social case work*. New York: Harper & Brothers.

Task Force on Promotion and Dissemination of Psychological Procedures. (1995). Training in and dissemination of empirically validated psychological treatments: Report and recommendations. *The Clinical Psychologist, 48*(1), 3-23.

Thyer, B. A. (1996). Guidelines for applying the empirical clinical practice model to social work. *Journal of Applied Social Sciences, 20*, 121-127.

Thyer, B. A. (2000). *Developing disciplinary-specific knowledge for social work: Is it possible?* Unpublished manuscript, University of Georgia.

Thyer, B. A. (in press a). Evidence-based approaches to community practice. In K. Corcoran & H. Briggs (Eds.), *Structuring change: Effective practice for common client problems* (2nd ed.). Chicago: Lyceum.

Thyer, B. A. (in press b). The role of theory in research on social work practice. *Journal of Social Work Education*.

Thyer, B. A., & Wodarski, J. S. (1998). First principles of empirical social work practice. In B. A. Thyer & J. S. Wodarski (Eds.), *Handbook of empirical social work practice* (Vol. 1, pp. 1-31). New York: John Wiley.

Todd, A. J. (1920). *The scientific spirit and social work*. New York: Macmillan.

Toynbee, A. (1912). *Lectures on the industrial revolution of the eighteenth century in England*. London: Longmans, Green.

Wayland, H. L. (1894). A scientific basis for charity. *The Charities Review: A Journal of Practical Sociology, 3*, 263-275.

Wodarski, J. S. (1981). *The role of research in clinical practice: A practical approach for the human services*. Baltimore, MD: University Park Press.

PART I

Quantitative Approaches

Quantitative approaches are what usually come to mind when the subject of research is raised. Although it certainly is true that these are a major form of scientific inquiry, they are by no means the sole legitimate method of studying social work clients and their problems. Barker (1999) gives a simple definition of quantitative research as "systematic investigations that include descriptive or inferential statistical analysis. Examples are experiments, survey research, and investigations that make use of numerical comparisons" (p. 394).

This sounds simple enough. If data are presented, even partially, in the form of numbers, then one is dealing with a quantitative research method. This part of the handbook contains overviews of six major categories of quantitative research, prefaced by five chapters that introduce fundamental principles common to all quantitative methods.

Phyllis Solomon and Jeffrey Draine (Chapter 2) begin Part I with an overview of quantitative research methods, grounding these approaches as a part of the field's larger quest for obtaining valid knowledge about social work clients and interventions. They are clear in describing the assumptions underlying these quantitative approaches to study, and they illustrate these through their own research on social work practice.

Bill Nugent (Chapter 3) describes the numerical theory underlying the subsequent chapters related to reliability and validity and to measuring client problems. Probability and sampling concepts also are central to a later chapter on statistics. Before he became a social worker, Nugent was an acrobat in a circus and an engineer. He continues to demonstrate the virtues of agility and clear thinking associated with his past training in his present treatment of probability and sampling.

Catheleen Jordan and Richard Hoefer (Chapter 4) have written a gripping overview of the importance of reliability and validity in quantitative measurement. They show how to look for and interpret evidence that a particular indicator is both reliable and valid. They describe the different forms of reliability, validity, and errors in measurement associated with quantitative studies as well as how the latter can be minimized.

Practitioners in particular will appreciate Kevin Corcoran's (Chapter 5) chapter on locating instruments. A common misconception among research students is that developing one's own measure is a necessary part of conducting a scientific study. This most certainly is not true if someone already has undertaken this important step. Corcoran's chapter will teach the reader how to find out whether outcome measures related to his or her topic of interest already exist (they usually do) and how they can be tracked down for use in one's own study. There is no need to reinvent the wheel.

Do not be dismayed by the length of Tim Stocks's chapter (Chapter 6) on statistics for social workers. Stocks possesses a remarkable gift for rendering difficult material intelligible to the average reader. There are lots of formulas and tables in this chapter, but if the reader takes his or her time and walks through it carefully, the reader will be rewarded with a much better understanding of this important topic.

Barbara Thomlison (Chapter 7) describes the design and conduct of purely descriptive research studies. Such studies attempt to answer *what* without trying to provide an answer to *why*. They can be used to describe the characteristics and features of clients, of crimes, of disorders, of resources—virtually any area of concern to social work practice. Agencies undertake descriptive studies of their clientele, community organizers of disparities in resources across neighborhoods, and policymakers of the prevalence of particular psychosocial problems. Very often, theory gets its genesis through well-crafted descriptive studies.

An overlapping approach is the survey, and this chapter was prepared by Carol Mowbray and Mieko Yoshihama (Chapter 8). Survey-type studies are among the most prevalent forms of empirical research to be found in social work journals, and many social workers almost seem to equate the idea of "doing research" with conducting surveys.

Canadian social workers Leslie Tutty and Michael Rothery (Chapter 9) authored the chapter on needs assessments, a specialized form of survey study (usually) that produces a particular type of descriptive information. Needs assessments can be vital in documenting the need for new social welfare programs or, conversely, in helping social workers avoid needless efforts in developing a program for whom there are few constituents.

Ram Cnaan and Guy Enosh (Chapter 10) present one of the most sophisticated types of quantitative research studies, the randomized controlled trial (RCT). Such studies can be exceedingly difficult to undertake and are intensive of both time and resources. But the payoffs in terms of valid knowledge are among the strongest of all research activities. RCTs are widely seen as the type of study most likely to produce findings in which we can have confidence.

Using group research designs can be helpful in the design and conduct of program evaluations, and T. K. Logan and David Royse (Chapter 11) discuss this specialized form of study.

A specialized form of a cost-benefit study, cost → procedure → process → outcome analysis, is presented by Brian Yates, Peter Delany, and Dorothy Dillard (Chapter 12). Determining the costs of demonstrably effective social work programs is receiving increasing attention in these fiscally conservative times. It no longer is enough to show that clients receiving services from Program X are getting better. It also is becoming important to show that Program X is not prohibitively expensive or far more costly than Program Y.

Part I finishes with a chapter I prepared (Chapter 13) on using single-system designs (SSDs) to evaluate the outcomes of practice. SSDs are a practitioner-friendly approach to evaluative research and have been employed by social workers for over 30 years.

The ability to understand quantitative research is an essential skill expected of all social workers. Such an ability is necessary to comprehend research studies in our field and to successfully undertake such studies in one's own right. Part I of the handbook will get the reader off to a good start in acquiring these skills.

REFERENCE

Barker, R. L. (Ed.). (1999). *The social work dictionary* (4th ed.). Washington, DC: NASW Press.

C H A P T E R   T W O

Overview of Quantitative Research Methods

PHYLLIS SOLOMON

JEFFREY DRAINE

Social work practitioners have multiple ways of gaining knowledge and understanding about their clients and the intervention strategies to help their clients. Frequently, they learn through their own experiences in the field and from the practice wisdom of their supervisors and coworkers who have been doing this work for years. Although these approaches are based on personal observations and logical reasoning, the validity of these assumed truisms might be questionable. We know that the logic of an idea does not make it true. Similarly, our experiences in observing phenomena can easily be distorted. For example, when we have a group of clients who have particularly difficult problems, such as homeless individuals with severe and persistent mental illness, we project our difficulties with a small group of clients into overgeneralizations about an entire population, such as believing that all homeless individuals are mentally ill. Other distortions that we often encounter in practice include when we generalize from clients who use services to those who do not seek services and when we generalize about mentally ill individuals in crises as to how they will behave when stable. Distortions such as these have been referred to as the clinician's illusion (Cohen & Cohen, 1984).

Another means to gain knowledge about the practice of social work is through empirically based research. This approach incorporates the strengths of rational reasoning while controlling for these potential misperceptions. Research methods offer strategies to control the influence of these distortions on our conclusions, whether they are on the types of clients served or on the effectiveness of social work practice. In quantitative research, these strategies include sampling, measurement, design, and inferential statistics, all of which are discussed in the subsequent chapters of this handbook. This chapter focuses on the basic assumptions of the scientific method (specifically, quantitative research methods), functions served by research methodology, and the need for conceptual frameworks and clear conceptualization of the phenomena being studied.

ASSUMPTIONS OF QUANTITATIVE RESEARCH METHODS

One of the first assumptions underlying the scientific method is that "scientific knowledge is not self-evident" (Nachmias & Nachmias, 1987, p. 8). The rational basis for knowing, common sense, and practice wisdom cannot be relied on for verifying a social work knowledge base. There are too many sources of error in these ways of knowing. Consequently, sound knowledge about social work practice requires objective procedures for verification.

Another fundamental assumption of the scientific method is that there is orderliness and regularity to all phenomena in the world that can be discerned (Nachmias & Nachmias, 1987). Social events, human behaviors, attitudes, and other social phenomena related to the practice of social work do not occur randomly; rather, there is a pattern that social work researchers can detect. Although there may be exceptions to these regularities, these exceptions do not diminish the fact that an overarching pattern exists. There is not an expectation that these observations will occur 100% of the time or even 80% to 90% of the time, but it is expected that they will occur more often than not.

For example, there have been a number of studies demonstrating quite consistently that when a family continues with psychoeducation interventions for at least 9 months, there is a reduction in psychiatric rehospitalizations of the person with a severe psychiatric disorder (Lam, 1991). Although this does not occur every time a family participates in such an intervention, it occurs with a high probability. Similarly, when psychiatric clients stop taking their prescribed medication, they frequently have exacerbations of their symptomatic behavior. Relapse does not occur every time a client stops taking the prescribed medication or for every client who ceases taking prescribed medication, but one event seems to precede the other with a good deal of regularity. Consequently, these relationships can be demonstrated through scientific investigation.

Another fundamental assumption of quantitative research is that there is a shared reality among relevant individuals that can be discerned and described. Quantitative researchers today are more sophisticated than the early logical positivists who believed that they could "study society rationally and objectively" (Babbie, 1998). Or, as the concept of "logical positivism" implies, research is dependent on logic and rational reasoning as well as objective empirical observation. Thus, this approach is a combination of both rationalist and positivist philosophies. Currently, social and behavioral researchers recognize that there is no way of knowing a "true" objective reality. All individuals view the world through their own subjective experiences. Consequently, a true objective reality cannot be known.

However, through communication with other relevant individuals (i.e., individuals working in the same substantive area, whether they are researchers or direct service providers), a "shared agreement" of what constitutes the meaning of a concept can emerge (Reynolds, 1971). Therefore, "objectivity" or "objective reality" develops through what Reynolds (1971) calls the process of "intersubjectivity." Although individual social workers have their own particular meanings for a given concept, through communicating with others who also have their own meanings of a similar phenomenon, we can come to a common understanding of the concept. This common agreement requires all relevant individuals to describe the phenomenon in explicit detail so that commonalities can be found (Reynolds, 1971). Without this common understanding, we are not able to communicate with one another about a given phenomenon. This is true not only in our professional lives but also in our personal lives. For example, we need to agree on what food, clothing, and shelter are; otherwise, we cannot survive in society because we would not know what to eat, what to wear, and where to live.

Quantitative researchers recognize that individuals have their own subjective views and understandings about any given phenomenon that is based on their own experiences. Through the process of conceptualizing the phenomenon, an objective (or, more precisely, an intersubjective) reality can be created. Without accepting this assumption, we would be studying an individual phenomenon that would have little or no meaning to anyone other than the individual person or the situation being studied. As Babbie (1998) indicates, subjectivity is individualist, but objectivity is socially derived.

Another assumption is that this objective reality is empirical and, therefore, can be known through perceptions, experiences, and observations (Nachmias & Nachmias, 1987). In other words, social work phenomena that include, but are not limited to, clients served, their social problems, and intervention strategies employed to ameliorate these problems can be known through direct observation. If they are internal to individuals, then the phenomena can be known through the direct reports of individuals' perceptions and experiences. We can observe certain characteristics about our clients, and clients can express their views about their problems.

A further assumption of the scientific method is that all social phenomena relevant to social work investigations have "natural causes or antecedents" and that, with time and the proper methods, these causes can be identified. This assumption directs us to focus our research efforts on cause-and-effect relationships (Nachmias & Nachmias, 1987, p. 8). Social work investigators recognize that some of the phenomena addressed by social workers may have causes in the biological or psychological domain. Therefore, to investigate these phenomena thoroughly, interdisciplinary investigators are essential. This does not diminish the fact that causes for social work phenomena are naturally occurring ones.

FUNCTIONS OF RESEARCH METHODOLOGY

Social work research employs the same rules and procedures of social and behavioral science. Thus, much of social work research can be integrated within this broader arena and can influence other disciplines. By following the established rules and procedures of social and behavioral science, a body of knowledge is developed against which information obtained from other ways of knowing about social work practice can be evaluated. This system of rules is changing constantly as new and innovative methodologies, measurement techniques, and statistical procedures are developed. For example, multivariate analysis of variance (MANOVA) and ordinary least squares regression techniques once were the mainstay statistical tools for social work researchers. Now, more sophisticated techniques, such as hierarchical linear models, more effectively model change over time and also handle missing data. Such innovations in statistical techniques challenge methodologists to update established research strategies.

Scientific methodology serves three functions for the researcher. It provides the researcher with the rules for communication with other investigators, with the rules for reasoning, and with the rules for determining objectivity or, more appropriately, intersubjectivity (Nachmias & Nachmias, 1987).

The explicit rules for the conduct of research enable investigators to communicate with other researchers regarding the methods and procedures they employed in their investigations. This information provides the details necessary for other researchers to either replicate or constructively criticize the study methods. Replication of research studies serves to guard against possible scientific errors, whether they are intentional or unintentional, and increased generalizability of the results. Criticism provides an impetus for improvements in methodological rigor. Public presentation of results is extremely important to the entire process of building knowledge in the field of social work. When a study is well presented, it allows for replication and appropriate methodological improvements.

Scientific methodology requires logical reasoning in a diversity of functional areas. First, a study is based on a conceptually sound and well-reasoned argument that justifies the relationship of the explanatory or predictive factors to the concept being explained or predicted. Each of the concepts in the argument is conceptually defined. Consequently, the study hypothesis flows logically from a well-reasoned argument. The means to testing the study hypothesis are then logically derived from conceptualization, design, and measurement procedures. Similarly, each aspect of the research process, including design, sampling, measurement, and analysis, has a set of logical rules that provide direction for the investigator.

Intersubjectivity is the process whereby independent observers of the same phenomenon or activity arrive at the same conclusion, although they have different subjective experiences. This outcome is considered "objective truth" in that it is independent of the observer but is derived from the research process of verification (Babbie, 1998). The prerequisite for intersubjectivity is that empirical observations are unaffected by any factors other than those that are common to all observers. The rules for intersubjectivity establish criteria for what is considered empirically objective and employ the techniques for verification of objectivity. These two aspects of determining objective truth are interrelated because researchers cannot make claims for objectivity until the measurement of the concept has been verified (Nachmias & Nachmias, 1987). Therefore, objectivity is inexplicably intertwined within the process of verification. It is through the process of replication that empirical observations are further confirmed and eventually considered objective.

Strong social work research builds on common terms of social work practice to conceptualize meaningful research questions and hypotheses. Hypotheses can then be empirically tested when the terms are operationalized in quantitative terms. Research methods provide procedures that enhance confidence in the degree of correspondence between quantitative terms (variables) and abstract concepts. Well-delineated conceptualization is the basis for the benefit that research provides to the social work profession and its clients. In operationalizing concepts, research often refines perspectives on social work practice.

CONCEPTUALIZATION IN SOCIAL WORK RESEARCH

In social work, conceptualization is the process of defining and operationalizing all aspects of intervention. These aspects include problem definitions, assumptions, client characteristics, provider characteristics, program implementation, system outputs, and client outcomes (among others). Conceptualization applies to practice as well as to research about practice. The conceptualization of intervention and outcome often is left unstated in social work practice. However, making these conceptualizations explicit so that they can be critically analyzed creates numerous opportunities to add to our understanding of how services work and how to improve services for clients. To this end, the most useful conceptualizations incorporate logical linkages of concepts (e.g., client characteristics, program components, outcomes) and are validated in practice settings.

A recurring weakness of social work research has been the failure, if specifying a theoretical framework taken from previous literature, to adequately operationalize and test the framework in the practice setting. Therefore, the usefulness of the research is undercut on two fronts. First, the study does not succeed in producing adequate information to test the framework. Second, and most important, the study does not provide enough information to answer important research questions for practice.

This is easily overcome by capitalizing on one of the social work profession's strengths—engagement in the community with persons in need and the organizations that attempt to help them. Using engagement in community settings as the primary source of information for conceptualization is a win-win situation for both research and practice. This is consistent with the rules of empirical social research. It enriches research with field-tested relevance of the concepts under study. Furthermore, it enriches practice with new knowledge that can be more easily applied to various practice, program, and policy problems.

Given a choice between testing an a priori theory and conceptualizing a problem based in the experience of providing services, practicing social workers likely would choose the latter. Does this mean that these social workers are atheoretical? (Thyer, 1999). No, it does not. These social workers are constructing meaningful theory through their engagement in their service environment. Without this "small theory" (Lipsey & Pollard, 1989) or conceptual framework, no sense can be made of data collected or results obtained from analysis. A strong conceptual framework ensures that a quantitative research project is about ideas rather than about numbers.

Conceptualization in social work research generates a framework for understanding the process and outcome of service. Furthermore, its application to service settings requires the operationalization of the key concepts in measurable terms. This is the key intellectual task of the quantitative researcher in planning empirical research. Typically, constructing a conceptual framework is an iterative process. The researcher begins with an initial understanding of the service setting, clients, providers, service processes, and expected outcomes. The researcher then reviews and revises this understanding based on information continuously gathered about the setting.

The researcher assumes that there is order in the process and outcome of intervention. This order might not be readily apparent to providers immersed in a service environment. Providers usually have views of their clientele or their outcomes that are shaped by their more memorable or difficult cases. Research adds a dimension of objectivity to understanding these settings. By "objective," we do not imply "value free." Individuals conducting research use the terms and processes of the service setting that often are laden with priorities and value judgments. The choices made by researchers in conceptualization, beginning with a topic, are value driven. Objectivity refers to a strategic and systematic process of observation. Systematic observation provides a unique perspective of process over time and the overall scope of services, recipients, and providers. New perspectives offered by research often lead program leaders and policymakers in different directions than if they relied on the accounts of service providers and administrators immersed in the day-to-day functions of an intervention or a service.

ITERATIVE PROCESS OF CONCEPTUALIZATION

The iterative process of conceptualization does not end with fielding a research design. As researchers encounter constraints on implementing research studies, these often are opportunities to further understand the client population served by the setting. Examples from a recent study help to illustrate this.

In a randomized field trial of post-release case management services for persons with serious mental illness who also were homeless and leaving a large city jail system, recruitment of new participants in the study was taking longer than expected. The service providers in the recruitment setting believed that because so many of their clients were homeless, it should not take so long to recruit study participants. Researchers instituted a simple checklist as part of the intake process to operationalize whether or not new clients were homeless. In a systematic review of charts for clients over a 1-year period, researchers found that the incidence of homelessness was far less than estimates based on the reports of providers (Draine, Solomon, & Meyerson, 1994; Solomon, Draine, Marcenko, & Meyerson, 1992). Furthermore, they found that the recruitment rate for the study was keeping pace with the incidence of homelessness and serious mental illness in the jail mental health service. Thus, by operationalizing homelessness and measuring it systematically in the setting, both researchers and service providers learned something new about the research population. Responding to homelessness was indeed an important part of the work of jail mental health workers. However, this level of effort was explained more by a few people returning to jail more frequently and for longer periods of time than by a large homeless population in their clientele.

In this study, it was found that there was a relationship between more intensive mental health services and jail recidivism. Because this was counter to the hypotheses for the study, a closer examination of recidivism seemed in order. Many case managers were using probation and parole violations to access treatment for acute psychiatric illness for their clients in an environment where mental health treatment in the jail was assured and involuntary psychiatric treatment was perceived as inaccessible. These clients were returning to jail on technical violations of probation and parole. Technical violations consisted of nonadherence to the rules of probation and parole including standard stipulations such as not leaving the state without notifying a probation officer, not using alcohol or drugs, and not living in one's residence of record. For persons with psychiatric illness, judges also were adding stipulations to take medication, to attend certain day programs, and to participate in case management. With these stipulations, many case managers had additional leverage with which to coerce clients to adhere to psychiatric treatment and to access acute psychiatric treatment in the criminal justice system (Draine & Solomon, 1994; Solomon & Draine, 1995a, 1995b, 1995c).

Therefore, a new study reconceptualized jail incarceration to be broken down into types of reincarceration (Solomon & Draine, 1995b; Solomon, Rogers, Draine, & Meyerson, 1995). These types of incarceration were new charges (i.e., new criminal behaviors for which anyone might be arrested) and technical violations (i.e., charges arising from nonadherence to the stipulations of probation and parole). A follow-up study was designed and funded to examine the role of psychiatric probation and parole in this further conceptualization of reincarceration for persons with mental illness. Currently, data from this study are being analyzed.

These examples show the extent to which research in a practice setting can contribute to a greater understanding of problems addressed and clients served. Results from the jail case management study challenged conventional assumptions about the effects of intensive services for mentally ill individuals in the criminal justice system. Thus, a reconceptualization of reincarceration provides an opportunity for further research and further knowledge development. Social workers always are conceptualizing problems, services, and outcomes. Extending these processes with more depth and systematic observation provides the basis for quantitative research methods as a natural extension of social work practice. Social work will benefit from continuing to integrate the development of these research skills into the training of social workers and the practice of social work. Engagement of social workers in researching their practice achieves a major aim of science—to build a knowledge base for social work practice.

REFERENCES

Babbie, E. (1998). *The practice of social research* (8th ed.). Belmont, CA: Wadsworth.

Cohen, P., & Cohen, J. (1984). The clinician's illusion. *Archives of General Psychiatry, 41,* 1178-1182.

Draine, J., & Solomon, P. (1994). Jail recidivism and the intensity of case management services among homeless persons with mental illness leaving jail. *Journal of Psychiatry and Law, 22,* 245-261.

Draine, J., Solomon, P., & Meyerson, A. (1994). Predictors of reincarceration among patients who received psychiatric services in jail. *Hospital and Community Psychiatry, 45,* 163-167.

Lam, D. (1991). Psychosocial family interventions in schizophrenia: A review of empirical studies. *Psychological Medicine, 31,* 423-441.

Lipsey, M. W., & Pollard, J. A. (1989). Driving toward theory in program evaluation: More models to choose from. *Evaluation and Program Planning, 12,* 317-328.

Nachmias, D., & Nachmias, C. (1987). *Research methods in the social sciences* (3rd ed.). New York: St. Martin's.

Reynolds, D. P. (1971). *A primer in theory construction.* New York: Macmillan.

Solomon, P., & Draine, J. (1995a). Issues in serving the forensic client. *Social Work, 40,* 25-35.

Solomon, P., & Draine, J. (1995b). Jail recidivism in a forensic case management program. *Health and Social Work, 20,* 167-173.

Solomon, P., & Draine, J. (1995c). One year outcomes of a randomized trial of case management with seriously mentally ill clients leaving jail. *Evaluation Review, 19,* 256-273.

Solomon, P. L., Draine, J. N., Marcenko, M. O., & Meyerson, A. T. (1992). Homelessness in a mentally ill urban jail population. *Hospital and Community Psychiatry, 43,* 169-171.

Solomon, P., Rogers, R., Draine, J., & Meyerson, A. (1995). Interaction of the criminal justice system and psychiatric professionals in which civil commitment standards are prohibitive. *Bulletin of the American Academy of Psychiatry and the Law, 23,* 117-128.

Thyer, B. (1999). The role of theory in research on social work practice. In T. Tripodi (Ed.), *Proceedings of the Eleventh National Symposium on Doctoral Research in Social Work* (pp. 1-25). Columbus: Ohio State University, School of Social Work.

CHAPTER THREE

Probability and Sampling

WILLIAM R. NUGENT

Probability theory concerns the relative frequency with which certain events occur. Probability is important in sampling because it is the vehicle that allows the researcher to use the information in a sample to make inferences about the population from which the sample was obtained. The purpose of this chapter is to give an overview of probability and sampling. The goals of this chapter are (a) to give the reader a brief introduction to probability and to the basis of sampling in probability, (b) to cover basic sampling methods with a focus on probability sampling, and (c) to illustrate these sampling methods by use of numerical examples that the reader can replicate.

PROBABILITY THEORY

Probability refers to the likelihood that an event will occur. The probability of an event is given by a number between 0 and 1, with probabilities closer to 0 indicating that the event is less likely and those closer to 1 indicating that it is more likely. A probability of 0 means that the event *never* will occur, whereas a probability of 1 means that it is *certain* to occur. The probability of Event A, symbolized as $p(A)$, is defined as the ratio of the number of "favorable" outcomes (i.e., the number of outcomes that count as the specific Event A) to the total number of outcomes:

$$p(A) = \text{(Number of Favorable Outcomes)}/$$
$$\text{(Total Number of Outcomes)}. \qquad (1)$$

For example, the probability of selecting an ace in a single draw from a deck of 52 cards is 4/52. There are 4 favorable outcomes—only one of the four aces— out of a total of 52 outcomes, so $p(\text{ace}) = 4/52$.

Now, suppose that we have a set of N "things" (N indicates that the number of things in the set is some arbitrary number) such as persons, objects, or phenomena. Probability theory tells us that if we want to select n of the things (where $n \leq N$) from the set of N things, then there are

$$\binom{N}{n} = N! / [n!(N-n)!] \qquad (2)$$

different combinations of n things that we can draw from the set of N things. The symbol $\binom{N}{n}$ is read as "N on n," and $N! = N \times [N-1] \times [N-2] \times \ldots \times 2 \times 1$ (where $N!$ is read "N factorial"). For example, $5! = 5 \times 4 \times 3 \times 2 \times 1$. The terms $n!$ and $(N-n)!$ are similarly defined (Ash, 1993).

For example, let the numbers 1, 2, 3, 4, and 5 constitute a set of numbers. We call this set a *population*. Suppose that we want to select $n = 2$ numbers from this population. We call the $n = 2$ numbers that we select a *sample*. There are

$$\binom{5}{2} = \frac{5!}{2!(5-2)!} = \frac{5!}{2!\,3!} = \frac{5 \times 4 \times 3 \times 2 \times 1}{(2 \times 1)(3 \times 2 \times 1)} = \frac{120}{12} = 10$$

possible samples of size $n = 2$ that we can select from this population: 1 and 2, 1 and 3, 1 and 4, 1 and 5, 2 and 3, 2 and 4, 2 and 5, 3 and 4, 3 and 5, and 4 and 5. If each of these samples of size $n = 2$ has the same probability of being selected, then the probability of any one of these 10 samples being selected will be 1/10. In general, if every sample of size n has the same probability of being selected from a population of size N, then the probability of any of the samples being selected is $\dfrac{1}{\binom{N}{n}}$. A sample selected from a population in such a manner that each sample of size n has the same probability of being selected is called a *simple random sample*.

Now, let us calculate the probability that, in a sample of $n = 2$ numbers from this population of $N = 5$ numbers, the number 3 is in the sample. There are two "slots" to be filled in our sample, and one of these must be filled by the number 3, so there is only one slot left to be filled, and because the number 3 can appear only once in a sample, there are only four numbers left to fill the remaining slot: 1, 2, 4, or 5. Thus, there are a total of four samples that contain the number 3: 1 and 3, 2 and 3, 4 and 3, and 5 and 3. If all samples of size $n = 2$ have the same probability of being selected, then the probability is 4/10 that the number 3 is in the sample (and this is true for any of the numbers in this population). In general, if all samples have the same probability of being selected, then the probability of a specific single thing in a population of N things appearing in a sample of size n will be

$$\frac{\binom{N-1}{n-1}}{\binom{N}{n}} = \frac{\frac{(N-1)!}{(n-1)![(N-1)-(n-1)]!}}{\frac{N!}{n!(N-n)!}} = \frac{n!(N-1)!}{N!(n-1)!} = \frac{n}{N}. \tag{3}$$

For example, if the population of the United States is about 250 million, and a sample of 1,000 persons is gathered from the U.S. population in such a manner that every sample of size $n = 1,000$ has the same probability of being selected, then the probability of a specific individual (say "Joe Smith") appearing in the sample is p(Joe Smith) = n/N = 1,000/250,000,000 = 1/250,000.

Any sample that is selected in such a way that each thing in the population has the same probability of being selected is representative of the population in a probabilistic sense. Thus, probability theory allows the researcher to select samples that are representative of the population in a special way (Rubin & Babbie, 1997).

SAMPLING

The term *sampling* refers to the methods that researchers use to select the groups of persons, objects, or phenomena that they actually observe. The very large set of persons, objects, or phenomena about which researchers wish to learn is called the *population,* and the individual persons, objects, or phenomena are referred to as the population *elements.* The group of persons, objects, or phenomena that they select from the population and observe is referred to as the *sample.* Most of the time, researchers wish to use the sample to make inferences about the population. *Sampling, then, concerns the methods used to obtain the samples of persons, objects, or phenomena from the population about which we wish to make inferences.*

Probability Samples

A very important type of sample is called a *probability sample.* Probability sampling is done in such a manner that we can compute probabilities for specific samples being obtained. A basic principle of probability sampling is that a sample will be representative of a population *if each member of a population has the same probability of appearing in the sample* (Rubin & Babbie, 1997). Probability samples have at least two advantages. First, they are unbiased and representative of the population. Second, we can estimate the amount of error involved in using the statistics we get from the sample as estimates of the values we would obtain if we observed the entire population. These population values are referred to as the *population parameters*. The more commonly used probability sampling methods are the *random sampling* methods consisting of simple random sampling, stratified random sampling, and systematic sampling.

Simple Random Sampling

A *simple random sample* of size *n* is defined as a sample obtained in such a manner that *every possible sample of size* n *has the same probability of being selected*. This sample is unbiased in that no population element or sample of size *n* has a greater or lesser probability of being selected than does any other element or sample of size *n*. A simple random sample of size *n* is obtained in the following manner. First, a list that identifies every element (e.g., a list of names) in the population is created. This exhaustive list is called the *sampling frame*. Each population element is given a numeric identifier, and then a random number table or computer is used to generate a list of *n* random numbers. These random numbers then are used to select the population elements that will be in the sample (Scheaffer, Mendenhall, & Ott, 1996).

Consider the population of scores shown in Figure 3.1. Suppose that the numbers in Figure 3.1 represent the attitudes of the persons constituting the population toward a proposed social policy (1 = *completely opposed,* 2 = *strongly opposed,* 3 = *moderately opposed,* 4 = *a little opposed,* 5 = *neither opposed nor in favor,* 6 = *a little in favor,* 7 = *moderately in favor,* 8 = *strongly in favor,* 9 = *completely in favor*). There are 900 scores in this population (for now, ignore the stratification and the portions of the population enclosed in boxes). The mean of this population of scores is 5.000, and the variance is 6.667. Let us imagine that we want a simple random sample of *n* = 15 scores from this population. We would assign a three-digit numeric identifier to each score in Figure 3.1. Because there are 900 scores in this population, we will need numeric identifiers that are three digits long. Thus, we would label the score in the first row of the first column in Figure 3.1 as 001, the score in the second row of the first column as 002, and so on down the first column to the final score, which would be labeled 025. The score in the first row of the second column would be labeled 026, the score in the second row of the second column would be labeled 027, and so on. This numeric labeling would continue through the final (36th) column. The score in

Stratum 1	Stratum 2	Stratum 3
1 1 1 1 2 2 2 2 3 3 3 3	4 4 4 4 5 5 5 5 6 6 6 6	7 7 7 7 8 8 8 8 9 9 9 9
1 1 1 1 2 2 2 2 3 3 3 3	4 4 4 4 5 5 5 5 6 6 6 6	7 7 7 7 8 8 8 8 9 9 9 9
1 1 1 1 2 2 2 2 3 3 3 3	4 4 4 4 5 5 5 5 6 6 6 6	7 7 7 7 8 8 8 8 9 9 9 9
1 1 1 1 2 2 2 2 3 3 3 3	4 4 4 4 5 5 5 5 6 6 6 6	7 7 7 7 8 8 8 8 9 9 9 9
1 1 1 1 2 2 2 2 3 3 3 3	4 4 4 4 5 5 5 5 6 6 6 6	7 7 7 7 8 8 8 8 9 9 9 9
1 1 1 1 2 2 2 2 3 3 3 3	4 4 4 4 5 5 5 5 6 6 6 6	7 7 7 7 8 8 8 8 9 9 9 9
1 1 1 1 2 2 2 2 3 3 3 3	4 4 4 4 5 5 5 5 6 6 6 6	7 7 7 7 8 8 8 8 9 9 9 9
1 1 1 1 2 2 2 2 3 3 3 3	4 4 4 4 5 5 5 5 6 6 6 6	7 7 7 7 8 8 8 8 9 9 9 9
1 1 1 1 2 2 2 2 3 3 3 3	4 4 4 4 5 5 5 5 6 6 6 6	7 7 7 7 8 8 8 8 9 9 9 9
1 1 1 1 2 2 2 2 3 3 3 3	4 4 4 4 5 5 5 5 6 6 6 6	7 7 7 7 8 8 8 8 9 9 9 9
1 1 1 1 2 2 2 2 3 3 3 3	4 4 4 4 5 5 5 5 6 6 6 6	7 7 7 7 8 8 8 8 9 9 9 9
1 1 1 1 2 2 2 2 3 3 3 3	4 4 4 4 5 5 5 5 6 6 6 6	7 7 7 7 8 8 8 8 9 9 9 9
1 1 1 1 2 2 2 2 3 3 3 3	4 4 4 4 5 5 5 5 6 6 6 6	7 7 7 7 8 8 8 8 9 9 9 9
1 1 1 1 2 2 2 2 3 3 3 3	4 4 4 4 5 5 5 5 6 6 6 6	7 7 7 7 8 8 8 8 9 9 9 9
1 1 1 1 2 2 2 2 3 3 3 3	4 4 4 4 5 5 5 5 6 6 6 6	7 7 7 7 8 8 8 8 9 9 9 9
1 1 1 1 2 2 2 2 3 3 3 3	4 4 4 4 5 5 5 5 6 6 6 6	7 7 7 7 8 8 8 8 9 9 9 9
1 1 1 1 2 2 2 2 3 3 3 3	4 4 4 4 5 5 5 5 6 6 6 6	7 7 7 7 8 8 8 8 9 9 9 9
1 1 1 1 2 2 2 2 3 3 3 3	4 4 4 4 5 5 5 5 6 6 6 6	7 7 7 7 8 8 8 8 9 9 9 9
1 1 1 1 2 2 2 2 3 3 3 3	4 4 4 4 5 5 5 5 6 6 6 6	7 7 7 7 8 8 8 8 9 9 9 9
1 1 1 1 2 2 2 2 3 3 3 3	4 4 4 4 5 5 5 5 6 6 6 6	7 7 7 7 8 8 8 8 9 9 9 9
1 1 1 1 2 2 2 2 3 3 3 3	4 4 4 4 5 5 5 5 6 6 6 6	7 7 7 7 8 8 8 8 9 9 9 9
1 1 1 1 2 2 2 2 3 3 3 3	4 4 4 4 5 5 5 5 6 6 6 6	7 7 7 7 8 8 8 8 9 9 9 9
1 1 1 1 2 2 2 2 3 3 3 3	4 4 4 4 5 5 5 6 6 6 6	7 7 7 7 8 8 8 8 9 9 9 9
1 1 1 1 2 2 2 2 3 3 3 3	4 4 4 4 5 5 5 5 6 6 6 6	7 7 7 7 8 8 8 8 9 9 9 9

Figure 3.1. A Population ($N = 900$) of Scores Ranging From 1 to 9 in Value

NOTE: The scores in the boxes constitute a sample of convenience (as described in the text).

the first row of the final column would be labeled 876, the score in the second row of the final column would be labeled 877, and so on to the score in the final row of this column, which is labeled 900.

We then would use a random number table, such as that found in Scheaffer et al. (1996) or Rubin and Babbie (1997), and select 15 different random numbers that are three digits long. Then, we would find the 15 scores in Figure 3.1 with the numeric identifiers that match the random numbers. The 15 elements selected in this manner would constitute our simple random sample.

Once we have obtained our simple random sample, we would compute a sample statistic that we wish to use as an estimate of a population parameter. One such sample statistic is the sample mean, $\bar{y}$, which serves as our estimate of the population parameter μ (i.e., the population mean),

$$\hat{\mu} = \bar{y} = [\sum_{i=1}^{n} y_i] / n, \tag{4}$$

where y_i = the value of the observed variable for the ith element in the sample, n = the sample size, and the $\wedge$ symbol over the μ indicates that Equation 4 estimates the population mean. We also compute the *error bound* (or sampling error) associated with the use of the sample statistic as an estimate of the population parameter. For the mean, we would compute the error bound, B,

$$B = \pm 2\sqrt{(\hat{s}^2 / n)[(N-n)/N]}, \tag{5}$$

where $\hat{s}^2$ = the sample estimate of the population variance given by

$$\hat{s}^2 = \frac{\sum_{i=1}^{n} y_i^2 - [(\sum_{i=1}^{n} y_i)^2 / n]}{n-1} \tag{6}$$

and N = the number of elements in the population. The term $(N - n) / N$ in Equation 5 [and in later equations] is called the finite population correction factor (FPC). Usually, if the FPC is equal to or greater than about .95, then it is dropped from the equation for the error bound. We can use the error bound to construct an approximate 95% confidence interval for the population mean by adding and subtracting B from the sample mean,

$$\bar{y} \pm B. \tag{7}$$

About 95% of all confidence intervals created using this method will encompass the true population mean (Scheaffer et al., 1996).

Let us obtain a simple random sample of $n = 15$ scores from the population in Figure 3.1. The random number table in Scheaffer et al. (1996) is used to obtain the following list of 15 random numbers: 104, 223, 241, 421, 375, 779, 895, 854, 289, 635, 094, 103, 071, 510, and 023. These 15 random numbers then are used to select the following scores from Figure 3.1: 2, 3, 3, 5, 4, 8, 9, 9, 3, 7, 1, 2, 1, 6, and 1. The estimate of the population mean based on this simple random sample is

$\hat{\mu} = [(2 + 3 + 3 + 5 + 4 + 8 + 9 + 9 + 3 + 7 + 1 + 2 + 1 + 6 + 1)/15] = 64/15 = 4.267 \approx 4.3.$

Furthermore,

$$\sum_{i=1}^{15} y_i^2 = [2^2 + 3^2 + 3^2 + 5^2 + 4^2 + 8^2 + 9^2 + 9^2 + 3^2 + 7^2 + 1^2 + 2^2 + 1^2 + 6^2 + 1^2] = 390,$$

and the sum of the scores in the sample is 64, so the sample estimate of the population variance is

$$\hat{s}^2 = [390 - (64^2/15)] / (15 - 1) = 8.3524.$$

For this simple random sample, $(N - n)/N = (900 - 15)/900 = .98 > .95$, so the FPC can be dropped and the error bound is

$$B = \pm 2\sqrt{8.3524/15} = \pm 1.49 \approx \pm 1.5.$$

The approximate 95% confidence interval for this estimate is 4.3 ± 1.5 or [2.8 to 5.8].

Stratified Random Sampling

A second form of random sampling is called *stratified random sampling*. This method allows us to use information that we already have about the population. For example, suppose that it is known that the population of persons whose attitude scores are shown in Figure 3.1 can be separated into three strata: the 300 persons in Stratum 1 who possess low levels of some variable x (e.g., level of education), the 300 persons in Stratum 2 who possess moderate levels of x, and the 300 persons in Stratum 3 who possess high levels of x. A stratified random sample of size n would be obtained from the population in Figure 3.1 by gathering simple random samples of size n_1, n_2, and n_3 from Strata 1, 2, and 3, respectively. The combined sample of size $n_1 + n_2 + n_3 = n$ elements would comprise the stratified random sample. Nugent and Paddock (1996) provide an example of stratified random sampling in social work research.

Once a stratified random sample has been obtained, the stratified random sample estimate of the total population mean will be given by

$$\hat{\mu} = \frac{1}{N} [\sum_{i=1}^{k} N_i \hat{\mu}_i], \tag{8}$$

where N_i = number of elements in Stratum i, $N = \sum N_i$ = total population size, and $\hat{\mu}_i$ = the simple random sample estimates of the stratum means, with i ranging from 1 to k (because there are k strata). The error bound on this estimate is given by

$$B = \pm 2\sqrt{1/N^2 \left\{ \sum_{i=1}^{k} N^2{}_i [(N_i - n_i)/N_i][s_i{}^2/n_i] \right\}} \ , \tag{9}$$

where $s_i{}^2$ = the simple random sample estimate of the variance of scores in Stratum i. Again, if FPC $\geq .95$, then it can be dropped.

Let us select a stratified random sample of $n = 15$ scores, with 5 scores randomly selected from each stratum, from the population in Figure 3.1. The random number table in Scheaffer et al. (1996) is used to obtain simple random samples of $n = 5$ scores from each stratum. The random numbers used to select the sample from Stratum 1 are 191, 196, 069, 210, and 114, and the scores 2, 2, 1, 3, and 2 are obtained. The estimated mean score in Stratum 1 is [(2 + 2 + 1 + 3 + 2)/5] = 10/5 = 2.0 (variance = 0.5). The random numbers obtained for selecting the simple random sample from Stratum 2 are 396, 443, 425, 337, and 306, and the scores 4, 5, 5, 4, and 4 are obtained. The estimated mean score in Stratum 2 is [(4 + 5 + 5 + 4 + 4)/5] = 22/5 = 4.4 (variance = 0.3). The random numbers obtained for selecting the simple random sample from Stratum 3 are 649, 781, 749, 898, and 696, and the scores 7, 8, 8, 9, and 7 are obtained. The estimated mean score in Stratum 3 is [(7 + 8 + 8 + 9 + 7)/5] = 39/5 = 7.8 (variance = 0.7).

The estimate of the overall population mean based on this stratified random sample is

$$\hat{\mu} = 1/900[300(2.0) + 300(4.4)] + 300(7.8) = (600 + 1{,}320 + 2{,}340)/900 = 4.73.$$

Because the FPC is greater than .95, it is dropped from Equation 9 and the error bound is

$$B = \pm 2\sqrt{\frac{1}{900^2}\left\{[300^2(\frac{.5}{5})] + [300^2(\frac{.3}{5})] + [300^2(\frac{.7}{5})]\right\}} = \pm .36 \ .$$

The approximate 95% confidence interval for the population mean is 4.73 ± 0.36 or [4.37 to 5.09].

Notice how much narrower this confidence interval is compared to the confidence interval from the simple random sample. This shows how much more efficient stratified random sampling can be relative to simple random sampling *if the within-stratum variances are less than the between-strata variance,* as is the case for the population in Figure 3.1. The variance of scores within each stratum is .667, whereas the between-strata variance is 6.000. Stratified random samples also are useful if estimates of stratum parameters, as well as estimates of the overall population parameters, are desired (Scheaffer et al., 1996).

Systematic Sampling

Systematic sampling sometimes is used in lieu of simple random sampling. First, we list each element in the population and assign the elements numeric identifiers, which will range in value from 1 to *n*. We then form the ratio $k = N/n$, where N = population size and n = sample size. The number k is the sampling interval (Rubin & Babbie, 1997). Next, we use a random number table and find a single random number between 1 and k and then find the element in the first k elements with the numeric identifier that matches this random number. Starting with this element, we go through the population and select every kth element until we have a sample of size n. A sample obtained like this is called a systematic sample. A good example of systematic sampling in social work research is provided by Glisson (1994).

Let us obtain a systematic sample of size $n = 15$ from the population in Figure 3.1. First, we compute the sampling interval k. Because there are 900 elements in this population,

$$k = N/n = 900/15 = 60. \qquad (10)$$

We then use the random number table in Scheaffer et al. (1996) to find a two-digit random number between 1 and k, in this case between 1 and 60. The random number we find is 10, so we select the 10th element in the population and every 60th element thereafter. Thus, the second element to be selected has the numeric identifier $10 + 60 = 70$, the third element has the numeric identifier $70 + 60 = 130$, the fourth element has the numeric identifier $130 + 60 = 190$, and so on. The 15 scores obtained in this manner are 1, 1, 2, 2, 3, 4, 4, 5, 5, 6, 7, 7, 8, 8, and 9. We then can use Equation 4 to compute our sample estimate of the population mean,

$$\hat{\mu} = [(1 + 1 + 2 + 2 + 3 + 4 + 4 + 5 + 5 + 6 + 7 + 7 + 8 + 8 + 9)/15] = 72/15 = 4.8.$$

One limitation with systematic sampling is that we can use Equation 5 to estimate the error bound *only* if the elements in the population are in random order. Such a population is called a *random population* (Scheaffer et al., 1996). If the elements in the population are *ordered* with respect to magnitude, then Equation 5 will overestimate the error bound. If the elements are *periodic*, showing some form of cyclic variation, then Equation 5 will underestimate the error bound (Scheaffer et al., 1996). Unless we know how the elements of the population are ordered in the sampling frame, we cannot use Equation 5 to estimate the error bound.

One way around this limitation is to use what is called *repeated systematic sampling*. This involves gathering n_s systematic samples simultaneously; that is, we systematically sample the population n_s times. When this is done, the error bound associated with use of the sample mean as an estimate of μ can be computed, regardless of whether the population is random, ordered, or periodic (Scheaffer et al., 1996). The following example shows how repeated systematic sampling is done. First, given the desired sample size ($n = 15$), the population size ($N = 900$), and the number of systematic samples to be obtained ($n_s = 5$), we compute the sampling interval for the repeated systematic samples, k',

$$k' = kn_s = (N/n)n_s, \tag{11}$$

which in this case will be $k' = (900/15)5 = (60)5 = 300$. This is the sampling interval that must be used in each of the five systematic samples so as to have an overall sample size of $n = 15$.

Next, we use the random number table in Scheaffer et al. (1996) to obtain $n_s = 5$ three-digit random numbers between 1 and $k' = 300$. We then add 300 to each of these random numbers to obtain the 15 numeric identifiers of the scores to be selected for each of the systematic samples. The first random number drawn is 163. Thus, the first systematic sample starts with the score in Figure 3.1 that has the numeric identifier 163. The other two scores selected for the first systematic sample are those with the numeric identifiers 463 (163 + 300) and 763 (463 + 300). The second random number drawn is 129, so the first score selected in the *second* systematic sample is the one with the numeric identifier 129. The other two scores in the second systematic sample are those with the numeric identifiers 429 (129 + 300) and 729 (429 + 300). The other three random numbers drawn from the table are 228, 185, and 035. The three numbers whose numeric identifiers match these random numbers are the starting points for the remaining three systematic samples, each of sample size $n_i = 3$. The five systematic samples obtained using these procedures are as follows (the reader should verify these samples): Sample 1 (2, 5, and 8), Sample 2 (2, 5, and 8), Sample 3 (3, 6, and 9), Sample 4 (2, 5, and 8), and Sample 5 (1, 4, and 7). The means of these systematic samples are 5, 5, 6, 5, and 4, respectively (the reader should verify these estimates using Equation 4).

The population mean then is estimated from the repeated systematic sample means by

$$\hat{\mu} = \frac{1}{n_s} \sum_{i=1}^{n_s} \bar{y}_i, \tag{12}$$

where $\bar{y}_i$ = the mean of the ith systematic sample. The error bound associated with use of the mean obtained from Equation 12 as an estimate of the population mean is given by

$$B = \pm 2 \sqrt{[(N-n)/N] \left\{ \left[\sum_{i=1}^{n_s} \bar{y}_i^{\,2} - 1/n_s (\sum_{i=1}^{n_s} \bar{y})^2 \right] / [n_s(n_s - 1)] \right\}}. \tag{13}$$

Thus, the repeated systematic sample estimate of the population mean, by Equation 10, is

$$\hat{\mu} = (5 + 5 + 6 + 5 + 4)/5 = 5,$$

and the error bound, using Equation 11 and omitting the FPC because $(N - n)/N \geq .95$), is

$$B = \pm 2 \sqrt{\left[(5^2 + 5^2 + 6^2 + 5^2 + 4^2) - \left\{ \frac{1}{5} (5+5+6+5+4)^2 \right\} \right] / 5(5-1)}$$

$$= \pm 2 \sqrt{[127 - (\frac{25^2}{5})] / 20} = \pm 2 \sqrt{[127 - 125]/20} = \pm.63.$$

Thus, the approximate 95% confidence interval is 5.00 ± 0.63 or [4.37 to 5.63].

Other Methods of Random Sampling

There are other random sampling methods, most notably *single-stage* and *multistage cluster sampling*. Cluster sampling is useful because in many circumstances it is logistically more practical than the random sampling techniques discussed previously. Scheaffer et al. (1996) discuss cluster sampling in some depth. A good example of the use of cluster sampling in social work research is provided by White (1998).

Nonprobability Sampling

Probability samples can be contrasted with *nonprobability* samples. When using nonprobability sampling methods, we cannot estimate the probabilities associated with selection of different samples of size *n*. This means that any of a plethora of biasing factors may be operative, leading some samples to have greater (or lesser) probabilities of being selected. The major consequences of this are that (a) the sample will most likely be biased in unknown ways and (b) we cannot estimate the error involved in our use of sample statistics as estimates of population parameters. Thus, inferences we make from nonprobability samples are very risky.

Perhaps the most commonly used nonprobability sampling method is *convenience* (or *accidental*) *sampling* (Cook & Campbell, 1979; Scheaffer et al., 1996). In convenience sampling, the researcher uses whomever he or she can find who meets the eligibility criteria for being involved in the research and who agrees to participate. The greatest advantage of convenience sampling is that it is easy to use. However, a convenience sample is not representative of the population, and if population estimates are made from the sample, then the researcher (or anyone else) is likely to reach erroneous conclusions (Scheaffer et al., 1996). Convenience samples can be very useful, however, in program evaluation and treatment outcome studies. The program evaluation done by Sprang (1997) makes good use of a convenience sample.

Convenience sampling can be illustrated as follows. Suppose that a politician, Generic Joe, represents the population of persons whose attitude scores are shown in Figure 3.1. Generic Joe tells a television reporter, "I have received 136 phone calls from my constituents, and the overall attitude in my district toward the proposed policy is one of 'strongly in favor.' This tells me that I absolutely must support this proposal." Let us suppose that the 136 calls that Generic Joe has received all have been made by the persons whose attitude scores are in the solid line boxes in Strata 2 and 3 of Figure 3.1. As can be verified from the scores in these boxes, the mean attitude toward the new policy held by the persons who called is 8.0, indicating that they strongly favor it (compare this estimate to the random sample estimates and to the true population mean of 5.0). Generic Joe is using this sample of convenience as if it is representative of his or her district when in fact it is not. Thus, the inferences that Generic Joe is making are incorrect.

There are other forms of nonprobability sampling including purposive sampling, sampling for heterogeneity, impressionistic modal sampling, quota sampling, and snowball sampling. These methods are discussed in Cook and Campbell (1979) and Scheaffer et al. (1996).

SAMPLING AND EXTERNAL VALIDITY

External validity concerns the extent to which research results can be generalized, and sampling is a critical issue in establishing the external validity of research results (Bracht & Glass, 1968; Cook & Campbell, 1979). Cook and Campbell (1979) make the important distinction between generalizing *to* a specific well-defined population and generalizing *across* specific subgroups of a population. Generalizing *to* a population involves making inferences about overall population parameters without any concern about parameter values for specific subgroups within the population. An example of this situation would be the researcher who is interested in the "typical" (i.e., mean) response to some treatment in a well-defined population of persons but who is *not* interested in knowing which subgroups within the population benefit, which are unaffected, and which get worse. By contrast, generalizing across specific subgroups involves making inferences about parameter values for specific subgroups without any concern about overall population parameters. An example of this situation would be the researcher who is interested *only* in showing that the treatment is beneficial for males of a certain age range in the population and is not interested in the typical effect of the treatment in the population. Random sampling is critical for generalizing *to* a well-defined population. However, it is *not* necessary for generalizing across subgroups. The replication of results across multiple nonprobability samples may, in fact, form a more sound basis for generalizing across subgroups than do results based on a large random sample. The reader is referred to Cook and Campbell (1979) and Johnston and Pennypacker (1993) for in-depth discussions of these issues.

CONCLUSION

The reader is encouraged to work through (and replicate) the examples given in this chapter and to select different random samples from the population in Figure 3.1 and compute sample estimates of the population mean as well as the associated error bounds. This practice can help the reader to develop a deeper understanding of the sampling methods presented in the chapter.

Probability and sampling are broad and complex topics, and this chapter only skimmed the surface of these important subjects. The reader is referred to the references cited for more detailed presentations. The text by Scheaffer et al. (1996) is recommended for a study of sampling theory, whereas Ash (1993) is an excellent (and understandable) treatment of probability theory.

REFERENCES

Ash, C. (1993). *The probability tutoring book.* New York: IEEE Press.

Bracht, G., & Glass, G. (1968). The external validity of experiments. *American Educational Research Journal, 5,* 437-474.

Cook, T., & Campbell, D. (1979). *Quasi-experimentation: Design and analysis issues for field settings.* Boston: Houghton Mifflin.

Glisson, C. (1994). The effect of services coordination teams on outcomes for children in state custody. *Administration in Social Work, 18,* 1-23.

Johnston, J., & Pennypacker, H. (1993). *Strategies and tactics of human behavioral research* (2nd ed.). Hillsdale, NJ: Lawrence Erlbaum.

Nugent, W., & Paddock, J. (1996). Evaluating the effects of a victim-offender reconciliation program on reoffense. *Research on Social Work Practice, 6,* 155-178.

Rubin, A., & Babbie, E. (1997). *Research methods for social work* (3rd ed.). Pacific Grove, CA: Brooks/Cole.

Scheaffer, R., Mendenhall, W., & Ott, R. (1996). *Elementary survey sampling* (5th ed.). New York: Duxbury.

Sprang, G. (1997). Victim impact panels: An examination of the effectiveness of this program on lowering recidivism and changing offenders' attitudes about drinking and driving. *Journal of Social Service Research, 22*(3), 73-84.

White, L. (1998). *An examination of quality of worklife in public service organizations.* Unpublished doctoral dissertation, University of Tennessee, Knoxville.

CHAPTER FOUR

Reliability and Validity in Quantitative Measurement

CATHELEEN JORDAN

RICHARD A. HOEFER

Is it possible to measure anything that exists? Quantitative measurement assumes that indicators may be found to represent the concepts of interest to social workers. It may be defined as the process of assigning numbers to the properties or attributes of client variables. For example, if a client is depressed and we want to know whether our intervention helps to alleviate that depression, then we might find a standardized questionnaire such as the Beck Depression Inventory (BDI; Beck, 1978) that asks for client self-reports of feelings of depression. We cannot actually see depression, nor can we touch it or feel it. But we can see its indicators, and we can design a questionnaire to measure it, or we might ask the client to track the specific symptoms of depression such as inability to sleep. Whatever method of measuring client problems that we choose, it is important to have the assurance that the measurement technique used is both valid and reliable.

Validity means that we are measuring what we think we are measuring and not some other concept or problem. With our depressed client, we want to measure depression and not self-esteem, anxiety, or some other concept. Reliability refers to the accuracy of the measure. Does it give us the same results each time that it is used? Measures can be reliable but not valid. The BDI may accurately measure anxiety every time we use it, making it a reliable and valid measure of anxiety rather than of depression. Valid measures always are reliable. If the BDI truthfully measures depression, then it also must be reliable.

The purpose of this chapter is to describe reliability and validity in quantitative measurement. Following a brief discussion of the purpose and levels of measurement, types of validity and reliability are described. This is followed by a description of sources of error in measurement.

PURPOSE OF MEASUREMENT

Measurement allows us to quantify, or represent numerically, concepts such as anxiety and depression that are of interest to helpers and their clients. Related to quantification is the development of standardized measurement instruments that ideally provide us with uniform and normative data. Standardized client data assure us that the data have been collected using a set of uniform procedures. For example, the BDI is a well-known standardized measure that gives us uniform questions to assess and measure clients' levels of depression. Concomitantly, the BDI also provides normative data so that we may compare our clients' scores on the questionnaire to the scores of normal nondepressed and clinically depressed individuals.

UNIFORMITY

Uniformity is established by detailing the guidelines for using a measurement instrument or procedure. For example, the BDI has specific guidelines for administering the measure as well as for scoring and interpreting it. A manual describing administration procedures usually accompanies measures that are standardized in this way. Uniform guidelines help to ensure the objectivity of measuring.

Normative Data

Data that are collected uniformly then can be administered to representative groups of individuals so as to develop normative scores. For example, when developing an instrument to measure depression, the instrument is administered to both clinical and nonclinical populations. Group norms or averages are developed, giving us information that allows us to compare any individual's scores to those of the normed reference group. Hudson (1982) developed a battery of standardized measures of inter- and intrapersonal issues such as self-esteem. These measures have a clinical cutting score used to differentiate between clinically significant and clinically nonsignificant scores. Hudson developed the cutting score by repeated testing of the measures on clinical and nonclinical populations.

LEVELS OF MEASUREMENT

During the measurement process, we may choose to define or operationalize a concept by looking at its indicators or attributes. For example, the concept of depression can be defined in terms of its variables and their attributes. Attributes are the characteristics of something, whereas a set of attributes make up a variable. Gender is a variable made up of two attributes: male and female. The nature or level of a variable's attributes determines the type of statistical analysis that may be done.

Nominal

Variables composed of attributes that vary according to category or type are said to be measured at the nominal level, the lowest level of measurement. Gender (male or female) is measured at the nominal level, as is eye color (e.g., green, blue, brown, hazel) and religious preference (e.g., Catholic, Protestant). Numbers may be assigned to the categories (e.g., male = 1, female = 2), but statistically, only descriptive techniques make any sense. For example, we might report that, in our sample of 10 high school students, 5 are male (Category 1) and 5 are female (Category 2).

Ordinal

Ordinal-level measurement is a higher level of measurement than the nominal level of measurement. The attributes of ordinal-level variables may be rank ordered. Examples include life satisfaction (scored from 1 = high satisfaction to 5 = low satisfaction) and degree of empowerment (scored from 1 = high empowerment to 3 = low empowerment). As with the attributes of nominal variables, numbers are assigned to each rank, and mathematical computations with ordinal-level data are limited. Although we might know that a score of 1 is better or higher than a score of 2, we cannot assume that there is an equal distance between categories. We do not know that a score of 4 is twice as good as a score of 2. For example, we might say that 6 of our 10 high school students reported that they were highly satisfied with life (Category 1), 3 reported that they were moderately satisfied with life (Category 3), and 1 reported that he or she had low satisfaction with life (Category 5). We can describe the rankings, but further statistical analysis makes no sense.

Interval

Interval-level measurement is a higher level of measurement than either the nominal or ordinal level of measurement. The attributes of the interval-level variables can be assigned numbers that do have some meaning in relationship to each other. That is, the intervals between the numbers may be assumed to be equal distances, although there is no absolute zero point. Examples include standardized measures of IQ and achievement motivation. Although no persons have zero IQs, we can say that an IQ of 90 is 10 points lower than 100, which is 10 points lower than 110. But we cannot say that a person with an IQ of 120 is twice as intelligent as a person with an IQ of 60.

Ratio

Ratio-level measurement is the highest level of measurement. It has all the missing properties of the previously described levels. Ratio-level measures have equal distance between attributes and are based on an absolute zero point. Examples include income, age, number of children, and number of times sent to the principal's office. Some persons have no children, whereas others have four children, which is twice as many as persons with two children. The most sophisticated types of statistical analyses may be used with ratio-level data.

The implications of level of measurement include types of statistical analysis that may be done with each, as mentioned previously. Another implication is whether to use single or composite indicators to measure client problems. Some information may be easily obtained by asking a single question such as "How many children do you have?" or "What is your income?" Other information is not so easy to operationalize with a simple question. Is the client depressed? Is the client anxious? Is the client experiencing marital problems? In these cases, composite indicators are necessary, so we may put together a 10-question instrument that measures all the variables necessary to understand life satisfaction. Most composite measures of client problems used by social workers are at the ordinal or interval level of measurement. When selecting a measuring instrument, it is important to consider the level of measurement in relationship to what statistical testing of its properties has been done. For example, has the author used the correct statistical procedure for the level of measurement to establish the measure's validity and reliability coefficients?

Questionnaires that measure nearly any construct of interest to social work practitioners have been developed (see, e.g., Corcoran & Fischer, 2000). With the plethora of available measurement instruments, social workers might find several questionnaires designed to measure the same problem or construct. The question then becomes, which is the better measure? Measurement selection is related to definition of the problem. Does the measure ask questions that are relevant to the specific client? Practitioners may define the same construct in different ways. For example, questionnaires to assess and measure marital problems may focus on communication, sexuality, child issues, money, or all of these. If the questionnaire is a good one, then it will have undergone testing to evaluate its validity or truth as well as its reliability or repeatability.

VALIDITY

Validity is an important component of quantitative measurement and means that the concept we think we are measuring (e.g., depression) is actually what we are measuring rather than some other concept (e.g., anxiety, anger). Validity of a written pencil-and-paper measure is established through the standardization process. "In order for a measure to be standardized, it must go through a rigorous process of research and development aimed at empirically verifying the measure's characteristics and usefulness" (Jordan & Franklin, 1995, p. 63). We have discussed the importance of establishing uniform procedures and norms to standardize a measure, and the three methods for establishing measurement validity are content, criterion, and construct validity.

Content or Face Validity

Face validity assumes that when we look at the questions included in a measuring instrument, it appears to measure the concept that it intends to measure. Face validity is, however, believed to be too subjective to be helpful. Content validity, which includes elements of face validity, is perhaps more helpful. It refers to evaluation of the items of a measure to determine whether they are representative of the domain that the measure seeks to examine (Anastasi, 1988). An example is a measure that seeks to assess behavioral disorders in children, a multidimensional concept (Jordan, Franklin, & Corcoran, 1992). To establish content validity, one would look for questions that reflect the multiple dimensions that make up child behavior disorders. For example, items might assess hyperactivity, depression, and anxiety. If only one dimension is reflected in the measure, then it would not be representative of the full range of possible child behavior problems and, therefore, would not have content validity. Two methods of determining the items to be included on a measure are (a) the rational-intuitive method or use of experts to choose items logically and (b) the empirical method or use of statistical methods such as factor analysis to choose items (Jordan, Franklin, & Corcoran, 1992).

A measure that reports good face validity is the Cognitive Triad Inventory (Beckham, Leber, Watkins, Boyer, & Cook, 1986). Its authors report that face validity was determined through high levels of agreement of 16 university faculty members.

Criterion Validity

Content validity is criticized because no clear rules exist for determining whether items in a measure have content validity. The second type of validity is criterion validity or establishing a correlation between the measure and an external criterion. Anastasi (1988) discusses five common criteria used to establish criterion validity: (a) performance measures in school such as grades, (b) contrasted groups assumed to be different from the group to be studied, (c) psychiatric diagnosis, (d) previously available measures with established validity, and (e) ratings by others such as teachers or parents (pp. 147-150). Researchers differentiate between two types of criterion validity: concurrent and predictive.

Concurrent validity. Concurrent validity refers to a measure being compared to an existing criterion. An example is the comparison of an instrument seeking to formulate a psychiatric diagnosis with the diagnosis of an expert mental health diagnostic team (Jordan & Franklin, 1995, p. 67). A measure reported to have excellent concurrent validity is the Center for Epidemiologic Studies–Depressed Mood Scale (Radloff, 1977). Its author reports that the scale was significantly correlated with a number of other depression and mood scales.

Predictive validity. Predictive validity refers to a measure's ability to predict a criterion in the future. For example, college entrance exams are assumed to have predictive validity and are validated by comparison to a person's later college grades. The Chinese Depressive Symptom Scale (Lin, 1989) reports good predictive criterion validity. The scale was correlated with four quality of life dimensions of a previously validated quality of life inventory.

Construct Validity

A third type of measurement validity is construct validity or the degree of measurement of a theoretical concept, trait, or variable. In establishing construct validity, we seek to satisfy our theory about the way in which our construct behaves or correlates with other related constructs. Construct validity is the highest type of validity and encompasses the others; if a measure has construct validity, then it also has content and criterion validity. Six criteria for establishing construct validity described by Anastasi (1988) are that (a) the measure is able to reflect clients' developmental changes, (b) the measure correlates with old measures that have proven construct validity, (c) the underlying dimensions or traits of the construct have been identified using factor analysis, (d) the measure's internal consistency has been demonstrated using statistical techniques such as biserial correlations, (e) the measure has convergent and discriminant validity, and (f) the construct is tested experimentally to see whether supposed interventions alter the construct in the hypothesized direction. Two types of construct validity are convergent and discriminant validity.

Convergent validity. Convergent validity assesses the degree to which the measure correlates with measures of like constructs. For example, a measure of depression should correlate highly with other known and valid measures of depression. The Conflict Tactics Scale (Straus & Gelles, 1990) reportedly is supported by extensive construct validity data including correlations with family violence risk factors, victims' antisocial behavior, and family members' affection levels and self-esteem.

Discriminant validity. Discriminant validity assesses the degree to which the measure accurately *does not* correlate with measures of dissimilar constructs. Our anxiety measure should not correlate with measures of life satisfaction or happiness. Hudson's (1992) Index of Family Relations reports good discriminant and convergent construct validity when compared to both dissimilar and similar measures.

STANDARDS: WHAT TYPES OF QUESTIONS EACH TYPE ANSWERS

Content, criterion, and construct validities are used to establish measurement validity when standardizing instruments for clinical practice. However, pencil-and-paper measures are not always used to study or assess client problems and behaviors. For example, a client might be asked to count numbers of specific problem behaviors rather than to fill out a self-report inventory about the problems (e.g., number of marital arguments, number of child's temper tantrums). In this case, validity issues may be addressed by using triangulated methods of data collection, that is, using more than one measure for each problem and/or having multiple respondents report. An additional technique is to use single-subject methodologies that stipulate the use of standardized and other systematic measurements of client problems, repeated measures, specification of the intervention, and posttreatment follow-up evaluations.

RELIABILITY

Reliability is the degree to which the same instrument provides a similar score when used repeatedly. A reliable bathroom scale, for example, will give a person a similar reading of his or her weight if the person steps off and then immediately steps back on the scale. A measurement instrument may be reliable without being valid. In the case of the bathroom scale, the number of pounds shown might not vary from one weighing to the next, but it could be off by a consistent amount, compared to a scale known to be accurate. The amount by which the scale is consistently wrong may be termed its *bias*. If a researcher knows by how much the scale is off (or how large its bias is), then he or she can correct the estimate to determine an accurate measure.

As another example, suppose that a rifle is aimed, bolted in place, and fired at a nonmoving target several times. If the sight on the rifle is good, then all the bullets should land near the bull's eye. That is, the sight is both valid (the bullets go into the center, where the rifle has been aimed) and reliable (the bullet holes are clustered together, being affected only by random things such as wind direction and speed). If the gun sight is reliable but not valid, then the bullet holes still would cluster closely, but in an area of the target away from the bull's eye. In this latter case, a skilled sharpshooter could correct for the sight's bias by aiming somewhere other than at the bull's eye.

If we looked at the target after several shots and found the bullet holes scattered all over, then we would believe that the sight was neither accurate nor reliable, and we likely would use a different sight. Similarly, when we use an instrument that gives us different scores when we do not believe that change has occurred, we should choose another instrument.

Of course, the issue of reliability in social work research is more complicated than the use of bathroom scales and rifle sights. Humans are complex actors, and they often do not react to measures in a consistent way. The effect of this inconsistency is to make it more difficult to determine whether social workers' efforts are having a significant effect. When we see change in the client outcomes that we measure, we must ask whether the change was the result of true change in the client, inconsistent responses by the client, or an unreliable instrument. Using an instrument with a known level of reliability allows us to be more certain that the client is the cause of the observed change. That is the reason for using instruments that have known reliability estimates and in conducting reliability tests in our own practice.

Whereas the basic notion of reliability is that a measure is consistent, there are three dimensions of reliability: stability, equivalence, and homogeneity. These are tested with different approaches to determine the reliability of a written instrument: test-retest, alternate forms, and split half. Each one has its advantages and disadvantages and should be chosen according to the situation at hand.

Test-Retest

In this type of reliability testing, the reliability of an instrument is calculated by determining how similar the results of repeated measures are. If the same individual's scores are stable when the instrument is administered a second or subsequent time and there is no reason to suspect client change on the variables being measured, then a researcher may believe that the instrument is reliable.

The advantage of this type of reliability testing is that it is easy to do. No additional questions need be developed, and there is no concern that using different (although seemingly equivalent) questions gives different results. It is well suited for paper-and-pencil types of measures. If the correlation of scores between one administration of the test and the next is above .70 (higher is better), then the test has acceptable reliability.

The main disadvantage of this type of testing is that people responding to the instrument might become acclimated to it. Thus, scores might be consistent because the individuals remembered their previous responses and then repeated them. Therefore, it is important to allow time between the repeated measures. No hard-and-fast rule exists as to how much time to allow. The basic principle is to wait long enough so that there is little chance of direct recall of questions but not so long that change in the client will occur. Thus, the nature of the variable being measured is important. Knowledge about current events can change quickly, but personality type is more stable.

It also is important to be consistent in the administration of the test from one time to the next. This includes having similar environmental conditions and administering the instrument at the same time of day, in the same place, and so on. The reason for this is to ensure that it is client change that causes changes in scores, not these types of extraneous factors.

An example of a scale with good test-retest reliability coefficients is the Spouse Enabling Inventory (Thomas, Yoshioka, & Ager, 1993). Its authors report that test-retest coefficients were computed over a 6-month period on nontreatment group participants.

Alternate Forms

In this type of reliability testing, the instrument has more than one version, but all the versions are considered to be equivalent. If a child takes a makeup test at school, for example, it is only fair that the test is as easy or as hard as the original test. In this way, it would not matter which version of the test was administered because the results should be the same. Both tests measure the same underlying knowledge to the same extent. Alternate forms reliability functions in the same way; one expects the results to be the same even when using different questions because the different forms of the test have been shown to provide similar results.

The advantage of alternate forms reliability is that it is not likely that clients' scores will change on the variables being measured simply because the clients have become used to the method of measurement (as in test-retest procedures). The main disadvantage is the difficulty and time-consuming nature of developing equivalent alternate measures. The instrument also must be administered on at least two separate occasions.

An example of a clinical social work scale that has alternate forms testing is the Environmental Assessment Index (Poresky, 1987). Its authors report that the correlation between the long and short forms was .93, indicating excellent alternate forms reliability.

Split Half

The third type of reliability is split half or internal consistency reliability. This type of reliability testing is similar to the alternate forms approach in that there are two sets of questions that are functionally equivalent. But it is different in that all the questions are given at the same time. The answers to the two sets of questions are compared to see how homogeneous the answers are across the halves of the instrument.

The main advantage of split half reliability is that it, like the alternate forms approach, eliminates the problem of having clients answer the same questions more than once. Unlike the alternate forms approach, however, it takes only one administration of the instrument to gather the necessary reliability data. Because there is only one administration, it reduces the problem of instability over multiple administrations of the measure.

Another advantage of this approach is that there are readily available computer programs that calculate the internal consistency statistic, coefficient alpha. The disadvantage of the split half approach (as is true of developing alternate forms) is the difficulty and time needed to ensure that the two halves of the test are in fact equivalent.

A scale with split half reliability is the Memory and Behavior Problems Checklist (Zarit & Zarit, 1985). Its authors report Guttman split half reliabilities of .65 for the problem checklist and .66 for the distress ratings, indicating fair reliability.

Determining Reliability in Other Situations

The preceding types of reliability testing are most appropriate for questionnaires or scales with multiple questions. Not all research uses this type of paper-and-pencil instrument. This section addresses ways of examining reliability in other situations.

Interrater reliability. Some research requires observers to look at and code behaviors of the target population. An example of this is a study of aggression by children on a playground. The researcher wishes to know whether training the children in mediation techniques lowers the numbers of "aggressive incidents" during recesses. She hires three assistants to be the data recorders. The obvious problem with this measurement approach is that the observers might not agree on how many incidents occurred. If this happens, then it might be difficult to draw any conclusions about the effectiveness of the program. Thus, testing interrater reliability establishes the degree to which different raters agree in their judgments of the phenomenon they are observing. Raters should be trained so that when different ones observe the same phenomenon, their ratings agree at least 70% to 80% of the time. (This is the same as an interrater reliability score of .70 to .80.).

Single-subject design measurement reliability. Social workers may conduct research using single-subject designs. Although it is advisable to use instruments with known reliability and validity in these situations, it might not be possible to assume that the standardization process used in large-scale studies transfers to single-subject designs. As noted by Rubin and Babbie (1993), clients who know that they are being tested repeatedly and who have close relationships with their service providers might be especially susceptible to providing what they know are "good" responses.

SOURCES OF ERROR

Earlier in the chapter, we introduced the idea of measurement inconsistency and how this is a problem for social work research. Another way in which to speak of inconsistency in results is to use the term *error.* Measurement error (or bias) has two sources: random error and systematic error.

Random (Variable) Error

As the name implies, the effect of random error cannot be predicted. It is caused by any number of factors that affect the measurement. Some factors may cause the score to be inflated, whereas others may cause the score to be deflated. Researchers can try to minimize random error by keeping conditions as similar as possible in the administration of measurement instruments, but some sources of random error are internal to the respondent. Blood sugar level or the amount of sleep the night before, for example, may affect the alertness of children taking achievement tests. Mood, personal antipathy toward the test giver, how well traffic flowed that morning, and countless other factors all can have a random impact on the scores achieved on any instrument. It is hoped that, over time and with repeated measures, the net effect of all random error approaches zero, but this is impossible to determine for certain.

Constant (Systematic) Error

Not all error associated with a particular use of a measurement instrument is random. Much work has gone into identifying potentially problematic situations that result in systematic measurement bias. Kyte and Bostwick (1997, p. 180) use two categories to discuss systematic error: errors due to the personal styles of the respondents and errors from the observers.

Errors due to personal styles of respondents. Kyte and Bostwick (1997) list three types of errors as being due to the personal styles of the respondents. The first error is known as *social desirability.* This type of error is caused by the desire of the respondents to "look good" to the person doing the measuring. It includes widely diverse responses such as falsely claiming to have voted in an election, denying the true extent of alcohol and other substance use, and downplaying prejudicial attitudes toward members of racial or ethnic minorities. Research techniques to minimize this type of error include making all questions neutral in tone and concealing the purpose of the study. Another approach is normalizing responses, for example, introducing the question by indicating that a wide range of replies are "good" answers or that there are no right or wrong responses.

The second error is called *acquiescence.* This is the tendency on the part of some people to agree with a statement, no matter what it says. The cultural norms of some populations indicate that it is rude to disagree with others, particularly those with a higher social standing such as social workers might have when compared to their clients. Other respondents might believe that it is better not to antagonize their case worker for fear of retribution. A good way in which to guard against this type of error is to vary the way in which statements are presented, using both negative and positive phrasings.

The third type of error is called *deviation.* It is essentially the opposite of acquiescence in that unusual and uncommon responses are given. An example is youths who exaggerate their use of alcohol, tobacco, and other drugs. Another example is the increasingly common reaction connected with exit polling during an election, where voters indicate that they have voted for a minor party candidate to protest being asked about what they consider a private matter. The major way in which to guard against this type of error is to build in "lie-detecting" questions that might indicate a pattern of answering questions falsely. An example would be to ask how often the client used a drug that did not exist. If respondents answer many of these questions as if they were real questions, then their entire instruments might need to be excluded from analysis. Another approach is to limit possible responses to "reasonable" answers. However, this will lead to truncated response sets, artificially limiting the answers provided.

Errors due to reactions of observers. Kyte and Bostwick (1997) list five types of errors as being due to the reactions of observers. The first is *contrast error.* This is the tendency of an observer to rate others as the opposite of himself or herself. That is, someone might indicate that others are lazy while thinking of himself or herself as hard-working.

The second error is known as the *halo effect,* which is the tendency to allow a general perception to affect the perception of individual traits or to allow the perception of one characteristic to affect the observer's perception of all other characteristics. An example of this is the common finding that attractive men and women are judged more competent on the job and more socially skilled than are less attractive people. This type of error can be in either a favorable or an unfavorable direction.

Third, *leniency* exists when an observer has a tendency to give overly favorable ratings or responses. Examples of this might occur in the classroom when students grade each other or when case managers using goal attainment scaling always rate their clients as achieving "much more" than expected. This error might be due to a desire to avoid being rated negatively by those being rated, not wanting to hurt anyone's feelings, or just wanting to "be supportive" of a client's progress, among other reasons.

Fourth, *severity* is the opposite of the error of leniency. In this situation, observers have a tendency to be overly harsh and critical in their ratings.

Finally, the error of *central tendency* occurs when the observer avoids extreme ratings, even when they are deserved. As an example, one may imagine a scale with many 5-point Likert items where the responses are *strongly agree, agree, neutral, disagree,* and *strongly disagree.* A person who usually answers *neutral* and never uses either the *strongly agree* or *strongly disagree* responses might be contributing to an error of central tendency.

Limited options exist for decreasing these types of errors. The most potent responses are (a) good training in using the chosen measures and (b) practice. Multiple observers with high interrater reliability also are useful in eliminating these errors.

SUMMARY

Quantitative measurement is the process of assigning numbers to the attributes of client variables. It serves the purpose of ensuring uniformity and objectivity in addressing client problems as well as providing normative data by which to set clients' problems in a larger context of clinical and nonclinical populations. Levels of measurement from lowest to highest are nominal, ordinal, interval, and ratio. Levels of measurement determine the sophistication of data analysis procedures to be used and also are important when designing or evaluating standardized composite measures of client characteristics or problems.

Good written measures are both valid and reliable. Three types of validity are content, criterion, and construct. Content validity establishes that all dimensions of the concept to be measured are included in the measure. Criterion validity uses an external criterion to establish measurement validity either in the present (concurrent validity) or in the future (predictive validity). Construct validity, the highest type of validity, assures us that the construct is like measures of other similar constructs (convergent validity) and different from dissimilar ones (discriminant validity). Other methods of establishing validity when no written measurement is used are triangulation in data collection, using multiple measures and data collectors, and single-subject methodologies.

Types of reliability are test-retest, alternate forms, and split half. Test-retest calculates reliability by determining how similar the results of repeated measures are. Alternate forms reliability tests different versions of the same measure to see whether the results are equivalent. Split half reliability (internal consistency) tests two equivalent halves of a measure, administered at the same sitting, to see whether the results are similar. Other methods of establishing reliability in situations when no pencil-and-paper measurement is used are interrater reliability and single-subject measurement reliability.

Measurement error or inconsistency comes from two sources. Random or variable error cannot be predicted and comes from variability in the setting, client, or researcher. Carefully controlled treatment conditions and use of repeated measures may minimize it. Constant or systematic error comes from the personal styles or reactions of respondents. Careful item construction, good training procedures in the use and administration of the measures, and use of multiple observers may be useful in minimizing these types of errors.

REFERENCES

Anastasi, A. (1988). *Psychological testing* (6th ed.). New York: Macmillan.
Beck, A. (1978). *Beck Depression Inventory.* San Antonio, TX: Psychological Corporation.

Beckham, E. E., Leber, W. R., Watkins, J. T., Boyer, J. L., & Cook, J. B. (1986). Development of an instrument to measure Beck's cognitive triad: The Cognitive Triad Inventory. *Journal of Consulting and Clinical Psychology, 54,* 566-567.

Corcoran, K., & Fischer, J. (2000). *Measures for clinical practice* (3rd ed.). New York: Free Press.

Hudson, W. (1982). *Clinical measurement package.* Chicago: Dorsey.

Hudson, W. W. (1992). *The WALMYR assessment scales scoring manual.* Tallahassee, FL: WALMYR Publishing.

Jordan, C., & Franklin, C. (1995). *Clinical assessment for social workers: Quantitative and qualitative methods.* Chicago: Lyceum.

Jordan, C., Franklin, C., & Corcoran, K. (1992). Standardized measures. In R. M. Grinnell, Jr. (Ed.), *Social work research and evaluation* (4th ed., pp. 198-219). Itasca, IL: Peacock.

Kyte, N. S., & Bostwick, G. J. (1997). Measuring variables. In R. M. Grinnell, Jr. (Ed.), *Social work research and evaluation: Quantitative and qualitative approaches* (pp. 161-183). Itasca, IL: Peacock.

Lin, N. (1989). Measuring depressive symptomatology in China. *Journal of Nervous and Mental Disease, 177,* 121-131.

Poresky, R. H. (1987). Environmental Assessment Index: Reliability, stability, and validity of the long and short forms. *Educational and Psychological Measurement, 47,* 969-975.

Radloff, L. S. (1977). The CES-D scale: A self-report depression scale for research in the general population. *Applied Psychological Measurement, 1,* 385-401.

Rubin, A., & Babbie, E. (1993). *Research methods for social work* (2nd ed.). Pacific Grove, CA: Brooks/Cole.

Straus, M. A., & Gelles, R. J. (1990). *Physical violence in American families: Risk factors and adaptations to violence in 8,145 families.* New Brunswick, NJ: Transaction Publishers.

Thomas, E. J., Yoshioka, M. R., & Ager, R. D. (1993). *The Spouse Enabling Inventory: Reliability and validity.* Unpublished manuscript, School of Social Work, University of Michigan.

Zarit, S. H., & Zarit, J. M. (1985). *The hidden victim of Alzheimer's disease: Families under stress.* New York: New York University Press.

CHAPTER 5

Locating Instruments

KEVIN CORCORAN

This chapter addresses how to locate instruments for social work research and practice. The task might not seem too challenging, but it is. Locating instruments includes being familiar with a number of sources and knowing what it is one wants to measure or observe.

To locate an instrument, the researcher must know what he or she intends to measure. This includes a well-defined construct or conceptual domain of study. The measurement tool is the operationalization of the variable, and it is impossible to locate an appropriate instrument unless the researcher is certain what is to be measured. Knowing what to observe includes precise definitions of the independent and dependent variables. Instruments often are associated with operationalizing the dependent variables (e.g., marital discord in a single system design of a couple in counseling, clinical depression in a controlled experiment or an epidemiological survey). As dependent variables, instruments chiefly ascertain the observations about one's own behavior or the behavioral observations by some relevant other such as a spouse or case manager. By design, instruments intend to systematically quantify some affect, cognition, or conduct in some environment or setting.

Instruments also are useful in operationalizing independent variables. In experimental designs, this is considered a manipulation check. The reason for using a measure of the independent variable, as the phrase suggests, is to determine whether the manipulation of the independent variable was successful. For example, assume that the researcher is conducting a study comparing in-home counseling services to case management services. The researcher would want to be reassured that the counseling group was actually getting "counseling" from the counselor and that the case management group was not also getting some form of counseling from the case managers. Without the former, the researcher would not be certain that the counseling groups actually had sufficient exposure to truly be considered under the treatment condition of counseling. By measuring the independent variable, the researcher also can determine whether exposure to some form of therapeutic relationship with the case manager contaminated the comparison group. To conduct a manipulation check like this, the researcher might decide to administer the Working Alliance Instrument (Horvath & Greenberg, 1989), which ascertains three elements of a therapeutic relationship: goal orientation, task directedness, and bonding. The researcher would expect or hypothesize that the research participants in the experimental condition would have strong indicators of a therapeutic relationship and that those in the control group would not.

In summary, the challenge of locating measures includes determining what well-defined construct or concept of either the independent or dependent variable is to be observed. Once that is determined, the challenge is to marshal through a number of sources of measures so as to find appropriate ones that are reliable and valid. This chapter provides a number of resources to locate instruments. The chapter does not promise to enable the reader to do a *complete* search for all existing instruments. That is becoming increasingly difficult with the development of more instruments and newer outlets of availability (e.g., the Internet). The scope of the resources in this chapter is, however, sufficiently broad to locate an adequate number of instruments for research and practice.

SOURCES FOR LOCATING INSTRUMENTS

There are a number of sources of instruments. This chapter considers four major sources: professional journals, books, commercial publishing houses specializing in marketing measurement tools, and the Internet.

Professional Journals

Instruments are of little value unless they are psychometrically sound (i.e., reliable and valid). Because the development of a good instrument itself involves research to estimate reliability and validity, professional journals often are the first outlets for new instruments. Journals also are one of the first outlets for normative data on more established instruments. Because of the rapid change in the knowledge base of the be-

TABLE 5.1   Selected Journals Frequently Publishing New Measurement Tools

American Journal of Psychiatry
Applied Behavioral Measurement
Behavior Assessment
Behavior Therapy
Behaviour Research and Therapy
Educational and Psychological Measurement
Family Process
Hispanic Journal of Behavioral Sciences
Journal of Behavioral Assessment and Psychopathology
Journal of Black Psychology
Journal of Clinical Psychology
Journal of Consulting and Clinical Psychology
Journal of Nervous and Mental Disease
Journal of Personality Assessment
Measurement and Evaluation in Counseling and Development
Psychological Assessment

SOURCE: Corcoran and Fischer (2000a).

havioral and social sciences, journals probably are the best way in which to keep up with the latest instruments.

There are many scholarly journals that are excellent sources of instruments. Some focus chiefly on measurement (e.g., *Journal of Personality Assessment, Psychological Assessment*). Other journals might publish instruments that are relevant to the professional or scholarly discipline of the readership (e.g., *Research on Social Work Practice, Family Process*). Table 5.1 contains a number of scholarly and professional journals useful in locating new instruments and published normative data.

Books

In addition to journals, there are numerous reference books available that describe instruments and about a dozen that actually reprint the instruments. Reference books for instruments review measurement tools and provide citations for further information on locating the actual measurement tools. Three widely noted examples are the *Mental Measurements Yearbook* (Conoley & Kramer, 1989, 1995), *Tests in Print* (Mitchell, 1983), and *Test Critiques* (Keyser & Sweetland, 1984-1991).

A number of books reference and actually reprint the instruments. Some are relevant to topics of social work practice (e.g., Corcoran & Fischer, 2000b; Schutte & Malouff, 1995), whereas others are more relevant to research (e.g., Robinson & Shaver, 1973). A couple are specific to certain populations (e.g., families [McCubbin, Thompson, & McCubbin, 1996]) and topics (e.g., stress [Cohen, Kessler, & Gordon, 1995]). Altogether, there are more than 100 reference books for instruments, al-

TABLE 5.2   Selected Books

Books that reprint and reference measurement tools
    Cautela (1977, 1981)
    Corcoran and Fischer (2000a, 2000b)
    Hudson (1982, 1992)
    McCubbin and Thompson (1991)
    McCubbin, Thompson, and McCubbin (1996)
    McDowell and Newell (1996)
    Robinson and Shaver (1973)
    Schutte and Malouff (1995)

Books that describe and reference measures
    Aiken (1996)
    Anastasi (1988)
    Bellack and Hersen (1988)
    Brodsky and Smitherman (1983)
    Ciarlo, Brown, Edwards, Kiresak, and Newman (1986)
    Conoley and Kramer (1989, 1995)
    Dana (1993)
    Fredman and Sherman (1987)
    Goldman and Busch (1982)
    Grotevant and Carlson (1989)
    Hammill, Brown, and Bryant (1989)
    Harrington (1986)
    Hersen and Bellack (1988)
    Holman (1983)
    Huber and Health Outcomes Institute (1994)
    Hunt and Lindley (1989)
    Kamphaus and Frick (1996)
    Kestenbaum and William (1988)
    Keyser and Sweetland (1984-1991)
    Kumpfer, Shur, Ross, Bunnell, Librett, and Millward (1992)
    McDowell and Newell (1987, 1996)

though a good university library might be needed. Table 5.2 lists several books for instruments, all published since 1980.

Commercial Publishing Houses

The researcher also may locate instruments from commercial publishing houses that specialize in marketing measurement tools. This outlet for instruments has a number of advantages including security from copyright infringement and access to established instruments and relevant normative data that might be available only from the stream of commerce. Examples of this last point include the Beck De-

TABLE 5.2 Continued

McReynolds (1981)
Mitchell (1983, 1985)
Olin and Keatinge (1998)
Sawin and Harrigan (1994)
Schutte and Malouff (1995)
Southworth, Burr, and Cox (1981)
Sweetland and Keyser (1991)
Thompson (1989)
Touliatos, Perlmutter, and Straus (1990)
van Riezen and Segal (1988)
Wetzler (1989)

Books that discuss measurement methods
Barlow (1981)
Butcher (1995)
Goldman, Stein, and Guerry (1983)
Hersen and Bellack (1988)
Jacob and Tennenbaum (1988)
Lambert, Christensen, and DeJulio (1983)
Lauffer (1982)
Mash and Terdal (1988)
Merluzzi, Glass, and Genest (1981)
Ogles, Lambert, and Masters (1996)
Ollendick and Hersen (1992)
Pecora (1995)
Reynolds and Kamphaus (1990)
Rutter, Tuma, and Lann (1988)
Sederer and Dickey (1996)
Streiner and Norman (1995)
Suzuki, Meller, and Ponterotto (1996)
Woody (1980)

pression Inventory, which is available through Psychological Corporation, and Hudson's popular clinical measurement package, which is available from WALMYR Publishing (Table 5.3). Most of the instruments marketed by publishing houses are available at a reasonable fee. Other instruments are available at no cost such as the widely used Physical and Mental Health Summary Scales, also known as the SF-36 (Ware, Kosinski, & Keller, 1994) and the SF-12 (Ware, Kosinski, & Keller, 1995). Both of these instruments are available through the Medical Outcomes Trust (Table 5.3).

Table 5.3 lists a variety of publishing houses providing instruments. It is far from a complete list given that there are nearly 1,000 publishing houses marketing assess-

TABLE 5.3   List of Selected Publishers Marketing Measurement Tools

Academic Therapy Publications, 20 Commercial Boulevard, Navato, CA 94947

Achenbach, Thomas M., Department of Psychiatry, University of Vermont, 1 S. Prospect Street, Burlington, VT 05401-3444

American Guidance Services, 4201 Woodland Road, P.O.B. 99, Circle Pines, MN 55014

Associates for Research in Behavior Inc., The Science Center, 34th and Market, Philadelphia, PA 19104

Biometrics Research, New York State Psychiatric Institute, 722 168th Street, Room 341, New York, NY 10032

California Test Bureau, 20 Ryan Ranch Road, Monterey, CA 93940

Center for Epidemiologic Studies, Department of Health and Human Services, 5600 Fishers Lane, Rockville, MD 20857

Consulting Psychologists Press Inc., 577 College Avenue, P.O.B. 11636, Palo Alto, CA 94306

Educational and Industrial Testing Services, P.O.B. 7234, San Diego, CA 92107

Institute for Personality and Ability Testing Inc., P.O.B. 188, 1062 Coronado Drive, Champaign, IL 61820

Medical Outcomes Trust, 20 Park Plaza, Suite 1014, Boston, MA 02116-4313

Multi-Health Systems Inc., 908 Niagara Falls Boulevard, North Tonawanda, NY 14120

NCS Assessments, 5605 Green Circle Drive, P.O.B. 1416, Minneapolis, MN 55440

Nursing Research Associates, 3752 Cummings Street, Eau Claire, WI 54701

Person-O-Metrics Inc., Evaluation and Development Services, 20504 Williamsburg Road, Dearborn Heights, MI 48127

Pro-Ed, 8700 Shoal Creek Boulevard, Austin, TX 78757

Psychodiagnostic Test Company, P.O.B. 859, East Lansing, MI 48823

Psychological Assessment Resources Inc., P.O.B. 998, Odessa, FL 33556

Psychological Corporation, 555 Academic Court, San Antonio, TX 78204

Psychological Publications Inc., 290 Conejo Ridge Road, Suite 100, Thousand Oaks, CA 91361

Psychological Services Inc., Suite 1200, 3450 Wilshire Boulevard, Los Angeles, CA 90010

Research Concepts, Test Maker Inc., 1368 East Airport Road, Muskegon, MI 49444

Research Press, Box 917760, Champaign, IL 61820

Science Research Associates Inc., 155 North Wacker Drive, Chicago, IL 60606

Scott, Foreman & Company, Test Division, 1900 East Lake Avenue, Glenview, IL 60025

Sigma Assessment Systems Inc., P.O.B. 610984, Port Huron, MI 48061-0984

SRA Product Group, London House, 9701 West Higgins Road, Rosemont, IL 60018

U.S. Department of Defense, Testing Directorate, Headquarters, Military Enlistment Processing Command, Attention: MEPCT, Fort Sheridan, IL 60037

U.S. Department of Labor, Division of Testing, Employment and Training Administration, Washington, DC 20213

WALMYR Publishing Company, P.O.B. 12217, Tallahassee, FL 32317-2217

Western Psychological Services, 12031 Wilshire Boulevard, Los Angeles, CA 90025

Wonderlic Personnel Test Inc., 1509 N. Milwaukee Avenue, Libertyville, IL 60048-1380 ment tools, not to mention a large number of presses that publish only a few specialized instruments. One of the most thorough lists is found in Conoley and Kramer (1995).

The Internet

The most recent source for locating instruments is the Internet. This remarkable source of information is truly a World Wide Web and provides access to actual measures from commercial Web sites, not-for-profit sites, research centers, and even individual authors who make their own published instruments available (e.g., Simpson & McBride, 1992 [http://www.ibr.tcu.edu]). Although the Internet provides seamless access to information, it is not without some limitations. One of the most critical ones is the exponential growth of information available. This rate of change often means that as Web sites come, so they may go. Unlike a library, the information retrieved might not continue to be available to others needing it in the future.

Although there are literally thousands of Web sites useful for locating instruments, the most useful ones are those that weave together a number of other sites. These are not simply "hot links" that are designed to provide access to other relevant Web sites. There are a number of sites designed as partnerships among various sources of information on instruments. One extremely useful example is ERIC/AE Test Locator (http://ericae.testcol.htm). Test Locator is a joint project of the ERIC Clearinghouse of Assessment and Evaluation of the Catholic University of America, the Educational Testing Services, the Buros Institute of Mental Measurement of the University of Nebraska, George Washington University, and the test publisher Pro-Ed. Each of these sponsors provides access to, and reviews of, instruments. For example, the Educational Testing Services page reviews more than 10,000 measurement tools. The combined sponsorship of Buros and Pro-Ed provides citations of publications using educational and psychological instruments as well as access to the three valuable reference books cited earlier: *Mental Measurements Yearbook, Tests in Print,* and *Test Critiques.* The site includes the names and addresses of nearly 1,000 commercial publishers of instruments. The scope of this Web site is broad, including information of qualitative research and measures, professional standards, and much more. It is an excellent initial step in locating instruments on the Internet.

Another particularly useful Web site is WWW Resources for Social Workers (http://nyu.edu/socialwork/wwwrsw/). This site was developed by Gary Holden and the Ehrenkranz School of Social Work at New York University and has been developed for more than 6 years (which is a long time in the history of the information highway). The goal of the Web site is to help social workers obtain relevant information on the Internet. This is accomplished by providing valuable information and hot links to more than 3,000 other sites. Navigation to and from these sites is facilitated by 16 topical categories including one on measurement.

Another way of locating instruments on the Internet is by joining a "listserv." A listserv is a service that, for a fee or for free, sends information on a specific topic via e-mail. A useful example of a listserv with information on instruments is the Managed Health Care listserv (mhcare-l@mizzoul.missouri.edu). To enroll in a listserv, one must be able to send and receive e-mail; one simply sends an e-mail message to the master listserv address and is automatically enrolled. One also may join listservs from Web sites that themselves are lists of listservs. One example from Drake University (http://soe.drake.edu/region7/rehabres/listservs/) provides access to enrolling in 30 different listservs relevant to rehabilitation and a link to other lists of listservs. When using the Web to find other listservs, it is easy to get lost. One very useful site is Liszt (http://www/liszt.com), which references nearly 100,000 listservs.

Another resource for using the Internet takes us back to where we began our search for instruments, that is, to professional and scholarly journals. With the advent of electronic information, many journals have begun to dedicate sections to the topic of electronic information and its access. This may include reviews of useful Web sites and publication of important Web site locations for special topics. One excellent example of this type of Web site citation is found in *Psychiatric Services,* which routinely publishes the Internet locations of a wide range of mental health information including instruments.

CONCLUSION

This chapter has attempted to show the reader how to locate instruments. What might have seemed like a rather simple task, it was shown, can actually be quite difficult. There are a number of sources of instruments to help with this challenge. This chapter considered four major ones: professional journals, books, commercial publishing houses, and the Internet. Each offers access to a wide range of measurement tools for multitudes of variables of study in social work research and practice.

The resources presented to help locate instruments are far from complete. Even if the resources presented are not complete, the outcome of a search for a relevant instrument is likely to produce more choices than expected rather than too few. This is due to the rapid growth of instruments, their use in an expanding number of social work research and practice settings, and the need for accountability by professionals. In the future, it is likely that even more and better measurement tools will become available. Because old instruments do not fade away (e.g., Beck Depression

Inventory [Beck, 1967]) and new ones emerge, the search for instruments will become increasingly challenging. It is hoped that the resources presented in this chapter will help the reader to navigate through this information and locate instruments for social work research and practice.

REFERENCES

Aiken, L. R. (1996). *Rating scales and checklists: Evaluating behavior, personality, and attitudes.* New York: John Wiley.

Anastasi, A. (1988). *Psychological testing* (6th ed.). New York: Macmillan.

Barlow, D. H. (Ed.). (1981). *Behavioral assessment of adult disorders.* New York: Guilford.

Beck, A. T. (1967). *Depression: Clinical, experimental, and theoretical aspects.* New York: Harper & Row.

Bellack, A. S., & Hersen, M. (Eds.). (1988). *Behavioral assessment: A practical handbook* (3rd ed.). New York: Pergamon.

Brodsky, S. L., & Smitherman, H. O. (1983). *Handbook of scales for research in crime and delinquency.* New York: Plenum.

Butcher, J. N. (Ed.). (1995). *Clinical personality assessment: Practical approaches.* New York: Oxford University Press.

Cautela, J. R. (1977). *Behavior analysis forms for clinical intervention.* Champaign, IL: Research Press.

Cautela, J. R. (1981). *Behavior analysis forms for clinical intervention* (Vol. 2). Champaign, IL: Research Press.

Ciarlo, J. A., Brown, T. R., Edwards, D. W., Kiresak, T. J., & Newman, F. L. (1986). *Assessing mental health treatment outcome measurement techniques* (DHHS Publication No. [ADM] 86-1301). Rockville, MD: National Institute of Mental Health.

Cohen, S., Kessler, R., & Gordon, L. U. (Eds.). (1995). *Measuring stress: A guide for health and social scientists.* New York: Oxford University Press.

Conoley, J. C., & Kramer, J. J. (1989). *The 10th mental measurements yearbook.* Lincoln, NE: Buros Institute of Mental Measurement.

Conoley, J. C., & Kramer, J. J. (1995). *The 12th mental measurements yearbook.* Lincoln, NE: Buros Institute of Mental Measurement.

Corcoran, K., & Fischer, J. (2000a). *Measures for clinical practice: A sourcebook: Vol. 1. Couples, families, and children* (3rd ed.). New York: Free Press.

Corcoran, K., & Fischer, J. (2000b). *Measures for clinical practice: A sourcebook: Vol. 2. Adults* (3rd ed.). New York: Free Press.

Dana, R. H. (1993). *Multicultural assessment perspectives for professional psychology.* Needham Heights, MA: Allyn & Bacon.

Fredman, N., & Sherman, R. (1987). *Handbook of measurement for marriage and family therapy.* New York: Brunner/Mazel.

Goldman, B. A., & Busch, J. C. (1982). *Directory of unpublished experimental mental measures* (Vol. 3). New York: Human Sciences Press.

Goldman, J., Stein, C. L., & Guerry, S. (1983). *Psychological methods of clinical assessment.* New York: Pergamon.

Grotevant, H. D., & Carlson, C. I. (Eds.). (1989). *Family assessment: A guide to methods and measures.* New York: Guilford.

Hammill, D. H. D., Brown, L., & Bryant, B. R. (1989). *A consumer's guide to tests in print.* Austin, TX: Pro-Ed.

Harrington, R. G. (Ed.). (1986). *Testing adolescents: A reference guide for comprehensive psychological assessment*. Austin, TX: Pro-Ed.

Hersen, M., & Bellack, A. S. (1988). *Dictionary of behavioral assessment techniques*. New York: Pergamon.

Holman, A. M. (1983). *Family assessment: Tools for understanding and intervention*. Beverly Hills, CA: Sage.

Horvath, A. O., & Greenberg, L. S. (1989). Development and validation of the Working Alliance Inventory. *Journal of Counseling Psychology, 36*, 223-233.

Huber, M., & Health Outcomes Institute. (Eds.). (1994). *Measuring medicine: An introduction to health status assessment and a framework for application*. New York: Faulkner & Gray.

Hudson, W. W. (1982). *The clinical measurement package: A field manual*. Chicago: Dorsey.

Hudson, W. W. (1992). *WALMYR assessment scales scoring manual*. Tempe, AZ: WALMYR Publishing.

Hunt, T., & Lindley, C. (1989). *Testing older adults*. Austin, TX: Pro-Ed.

Jacob, T., & Tennenbaum, D. L. (1988). *Family assessment: Rationale, methods, and future directions*. New York: Plenum.

Kamphaus, R. W., & Frick, P. J. (1996). *Clinical assessment of child and adolescent personality and behavior*. Needham Heights, MA: Allyn & Bacon.

Kestenbaum, C. J., & Williams, D. T. (Eds.). (1988). *Handbook of clinical assessment of children and adolescents*. Austin, TX: Pro-Ed.

Keyser, D. J., & Sweetland, R. C. (Eds.). (1984-1991). *Test critiques* (Vols. 1-8). Austin, TX: Pro-Ed.

Kumpfer, K. L., Shur, G. H., Ross, J. G., Bunnell, K. K., Librett, J. J., & Millward, A. R. (1992). *Measurements in prevention: A manual on selecting and using instruments to evaluate prevention programs* (CSAP Technical Report No. 8). Rockville, MD: U.S. Department of Health and Human Services, Center for Substance Abuse Prevention.

Lambert, M. J., Christensen, E. R., & DeJulio, S. S. (Eds.). (1983). *The assessment of psychotherapy outcome*. New York: John Wiley.

Lauffer, A. (1982). *Assessment tools for practitioners, managers, and trainers*. Beverly Hills, CA: Sage.

Mash, L., & Terdal, L. (Eds.). (1988). *Behavioral assessment of childhood disorders* (2nd ed.). New York: Guilford.

McCubbin, H. I., & Thompson, A. I. (Eds.). (1991). *Family assessment: Inventories for research and practice*. Madison: University of Wisconsin Press.

McCubbin, H. I., Thompson, A. I., & McCubbin, M. A. (1996). *Family assessment: Resilience, coping, and adaptation—Inventories for research and practice*. Madison: University of Wisconsin Press.

McDowell, I., & Newell, C. (1987). *Measuring health: A guide to rating scales and questionnaires*. New York: Oxford University Press.

McDowell, I., & Newell, C. (1996). *Measuring health: A guide to rating scales and questionnaires*. New York: Oxford University Press.

McReynolds, P. (Ed.). (1981). *Advances in psychological assessment* (Vol. 5). San Francisco: Jossey-Bass.

Merluzzi, T. V., Glass, C. R., & Genest, M. (Eds.). (1981). *Cognitive assessment*. New York: Guilford.

Mitchell, J. V. (Ed.). (1983). *Tests in print III*. Lincoln: University of Nebraska Press.

Mitchell, J. V. (Ed.). (1985). *The 9th mental measurement yearbook*. Lincoln: University of Nebraska Press.

Ogles, B. M., Lambert, M. J., & Masters, K. S. (1996). *Assessing outcome in clinical practice*. Needham Heights, MA: Allyn & Bacon.

Olin, J. T., & Keatinge, C. (1998). *Rapid psychological assessment*. New York: John Wiley.

Ollendick, T. H., & Hersen, M. (1992). *Handbook of child and adolescent assessment*. Needham Heights, MA: Allyn & Bacon.

Pecora, P. (1995). *Evaluating family-based services*. Hawthorne, NY: Aldine de Gruyter.

Reynolds, C. R., & Kamphaus, R. W. (Eds.). (1990). *Handbook of psychological and educational assessment of children*. New York: Guilford.

Robinson, J. P., & Shaver, P. R. (1973). *Measures of social psychological attitudes* (Rev. ed.). Ann Arbor, MI: Institute for Social Research.

Rutter, M., Tuma, A. H., & Lann, I. S. (Eds.). (1988). *Assessment and diagnosis in child psychopathology.* New York: Guilford.

Sawin, K. J., & Harrigan, M. (1994). *Measures of family functioning for research and practice.* New York: Springer.

Schutte, N. S., & Malouff, J. M. (1995). *Sourcebook of adult assessment strategies.* New York: Plenum.

Sederer, L. I., & Dickey, B. (Eds.). (1996). *Outcomes assessment in clinical practice.* Baltimore, MD: Williams & Wilkins.

Simpson, D. D., & McBride, A. A. (1992). Family, Friends, and Self (FFS) Assessment Scale for Mexican-American youth. *Hispanic Journal of Behavioral Sciences, 14,* 327-340.

Southworth, L. E., Burr, R. L., & Cox, A. E. (1981). *Screening and evaluating the young infant: A handbook of instruments to use from infancy to six years.* Springfield, IL: Charles C Thomas.

Streiner, D. L., & Norman, G. R. (1995). *Health measurement scales: A practical guide to their development and use* (2nd ed.). New York: Oxford University Press.

Suzuki, L. A., Meller, P. J., & Ponterotto, J. G. (Eds.). (1996). *Handbook of multicultural assessment: Clinical, psychological, and educational applications.* San Francisco: Jossey-Bass.

Sweetland, R. C., & Keyser, D. J. (1991). *Tests: A comprehensive reference* (3rd ed.). Austin, TX: Pro-Ed.

Thompson, C. (Ed.). (1989). *The instruments of psychiatric research.* New York: John Wiley.

Touliatos, J., Perlmutter, B. F., & Straus, M. A. (Eds.). (1990). *Handbook of family measurement techniques.* Newbury Park, CA: Sage.

van Riezen, H., & Segal, M. (1988). *Comparative evaluation of rating scales for clinical psychopharmacology.* New York: Elsevier.

Ware, J. E., Jr., Kosinski, M., & Keller, S. D. (1994). *SF-36 physical and mental health summary scales: User's manual.* Boston: Medical Outcomes Trust.

Ware, J. E., Jr., Kosinski, M., & Keller, S. D. (1995). *SF-12: How to score the SF-12 physical and mental health summary scales.* Boston: Medical Outcomes Trust.

Wetzler, S. (Ed.). (1989). *Measuring mental illness: Psychometric assessment for clinicians.* Washington, DC: American Psychiatric Association.

Woody, R. H. (Ed.). (1980). *Encyclopedia of clinical assessment* (Vols. 1-2). San Francisco: Jossey-Bass.

CHAPTER SIX

Statistics for Social Workers

J. TIMOTHY STOCKS

Statistics refers to a branch of mathematics dealing with the direct description of sample or population characteristics and the analysis of population characteristics by inference from samples. It covers a wide range of content including the collection, organization, and interpretation of data. It is divided into two broad categories: descriptive statistics and inferential statistics.

Descriptive statistics involves the computation of statistics or parameters to describe a sample[1] or a population.[2] All the data are available and used in computation of these aggregate characteristics. This may involve reports of central tendency or variability of single variables (univariate statistics). It also may involve enumeration of the relationships between or among two or more variables[3] (bivariate or multivariate statistics). Descriptive statistics are used to provide information about a large mass of data in a form that may be easily understood. The defining characteristic of descriptive statistics is that the product is a report, not an inference.

Inferential statistics involves the construction of a probable description of the characteristics of a population based on sample data. We compute statistics from a partial set of the population data (a sample) to estimate the population parameters. These estimates are not exact, but we can make reasonable judgments as to how precise our estimates are. Included within inferential statistics is hypothesis testing, a procedure for using mathematics to provide evidence for the existence of relationships between or among variables. This testing is a form of inferential argument.

DESCRIPTIVE STATISTICS

Measures of Central Tendency

Measures of central tendency are individual numbers that typify the total set of scores. The three most frequently used measures of central tendency are the arithmetic mean, the mode, and the median.

Arithmetic mean. The arithmetic mean usually is simply called the *mean*. It also is called the *average*. It is computed by adding up all of a set of scores and dividing by the number of scores in the set. The algebraic representation of this is

$$\mu = \frac{\sum X}{n},$$

where μ represents the population mean, X represents an individual score, and n is the number of scores being added.

The formula for the sample mean is the same except that the mean is represented by the variable letter with a bar above it:

$$\overline{X} = \frac{\sum X}{n}.$$

Following are the numbers of class periods skipped by 20 seventh-graders during 1 week: {1, 6, 2, 6, 15, 20, 3, 20, 17, 11, 15, 18, 8, 3, 17, 16, 14, 17, 0, 10}. We compute the mean by adding up the class periods missed and dividing by 20:

$$\mu = \frac{\sum X}{n} = \frac{219}{20} = 10.95.$$

Mode. The mode is the most frequently appearing score. It really is not so much a measure of centrality as it is a measure of typicalness. It is found by organizing scores into a frequency distribution and determining which score has the greatest frequency. Table 6.1 displays the truancy scores arranged in a frequency distribution.

Because 17 is the most frequently appearing number, the mode (or modal number) of class periods skipped is 17.

Unlike the mean or median, a distribution of scores can have more than one mode.

Median. If we take all the scores in a set of scores, place them in order from least to greatest, and count in to the middle, then the score in the middle is the median. This is easy enough if there is an odd number of scores. However, if there is an even number of scores, then there is no single score in the middle. In this case, the two middle scores are selected, and their average is the median.

TABLE 6.1   Truancy Scores

Score	Frequency
20	2
19	0
18	1
17	3
16	1
15	2
14	1
13	0
12	0
11	1
10	1
9	0
8	1
7	0
6	2
5	0
4	0
3	2
2	1
1	1
0	0

There are 20 scores in the previous example. The median would be the average of the 10th and 11th scores. We use the frequency table to find these scores, which are 14 and 15. Thus, the median is 14.5.

Measures of Variability

Whereas measures of central tendency are used to estimate a typical score in a distribution, measures of variability may be thought of as a way in which to measure departure from typicalness. They provide information on how "spread out" scores in a distribution are.

Range. The range is the easiest measure of variability to calculate. It is simply the distance from the minimum (lowest) score in a distribution to the maximum (highest) score. It is obtained by subtracting the minimum score from the maximum score.

Let us compute the range for the following data set:

$$\{2, 6, 10, 14, 18, 22\}.$$

The minimum is 2, and the maximum is 22:

$$\text{Range} = 22 - 2 = 20.$$

Sum of squares. The sum of squares is a measure of the total amount of variability in a set of scores. Its name tells how to compute it. *Sum of squares* is short for *sum of squared deviation scores*. It is represented by the symbol *SS*.

The formulas for sample and population sums of squares are the same except for sample and population mean symbols:

$$SS = \Sigma(X - \mu)^2 \qquad SS = \Sigma(X - \overline{X})^2.$$

Using the data set for the range, the sum of squares would be computed as in Table 6.2.

TABLE 6.2 Computing the Sum of Squares

X	X – m	(X – m)²
2	–10	100
6	– 6	36
10	– 2	4
14	+ 2	4
18	+ 6	36
22	+10	100

NOTE: $\Sigma X = 72$; $n = 6$; $\mu = 12$; $\Sigma(X - \mu)^2 = 280$.

Variance. Another name for variance is mean square. This is short for *mean of squared deviation scores.* This is obtained by dividing the sum of squares by the number of scores (n). It is a measure of the average amount of variability associated with each score in a set of scores. The population variance formula is

$$\sigma^2 = \frac{SS}{n},$$

where σ^2 is the symbol for population variance, SS is the symbol for sum of squares, and n stands for the number of scores in the population.

The variance for the example we used to compute sum of squares would be

$$\sigma^2 = \frac{280}{6} = 46.67.$$

The sample variance is *not* an unbiased estimator of the population variance. If we compute the variances for these samples using the SS/n formula, then the sample variances will average out smaller than the population variance. For this reason, the sample variance is computed differently from the population variance:

$$s^2 = \frac{SS}{n-1}.$$

The $n - 1$ is a correction factor for this tendency to underestimate. It is called degrees of freedom. If our example were a sample, then the variance would be

$$s^2 = \frac{280}{6-1} = \frac{280}{5} = 56.$$

Standard deviation. Although the variance is a measure of average variability associated with each score, it is on a different scale from the score itself. The variance measures average squared deviation from the mean. To get a measure of average variability on the same scale as the original scores, we take the square root of the variance. The standard deviation is the square root of the variance. The formulas are

$$\sigma = \sqrt{\sigma^2} \qquad\qquad s^2 = \sqrt{\sigma^2}.$$

Using the same set of numbers as before, the population standard deviation would be

$$\sigma = \sqrt{46.67} = 6.83,$$

and the sample standard deviation would be

$$s = \sqrt{56} = 7.48.$$

For a normally distributed set of scores, approximately 68% of all scores will be within ±1 standard deviation of the mean.

Measures of Relationship

TABLE 6.3 Frequency of Stressors and Use of Corporal Punishment

Stressors	Punishment
3	0
4	1
4	2
5	3
6	4
7	5
8	6
7	7
9	8
10	9

Table 6.3 shows the relationship between number of stressors experienced by a parent during a week and that parent's frequency of use of corporal punishment during the same week.

One can use regression procedures to derive the line that best fits the data. This line is referred to as a regression line (or line of best fit or prediction line). Such a line has been calculated for the example plot. It has a Y-intercept of –3.555 and a slope of +1.279. This gives us the prediction equation of

$$Y_{pred} = -3.555 + 1.279X,$$

where Y is frequency of corporal punishment and X is stressors. This is graphically predicted in Figure 6.1.

Slope is the change in Y for a unit increase in X. So, the slope of +1.279 means that an increase in stressors (X) of 1 will be accompanied by an increase in predicted frequency of corporal punishment (Y) of +1.279 incidents per week. If the slope were a negative number, then an increase in X would be accompanied by a predicted decrease in Y.

The equation does not give the actual value of Y (called the obtained or observed score); rather, it gives a prediction of the value of Y for a certain value of X. For example, if X were 3, then we would predict that Y would be –3.555 + 1.279(3) = –3.555 + 3.837 = 0.282.

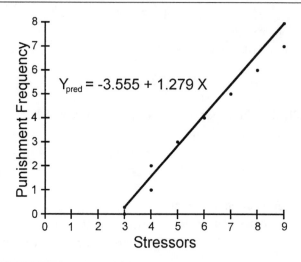

Figure 6.1. Frequency of Stressors and Use of Corporal Punishment

The regression line is the line that predicts Y such that the error of prediction is minimized. *Error* is defined as the difference between the predicted score and the obtained score. The equation for computing error is

$$E = Y - Y_{pred}.$$

When $X = 4$, there are two obtained values of Y: 1 and 2. The predicted value of Y is

$$Y_{pred} = -3.555 + 1.279(4) = -3.555 + 5.116 = 1.561.$$

The error of prediction is $E = 1 - 1.561 = -0.561$ for $Y = 1$, and $E = 2 - 1.561 = +0.439$ for $Y = 2$.

If we square each error difference score and sum the squares, then we get a quantity called the error sum of squares, which is represented by

$$SSE = \Sigma (Y - Y_{pred})^2 .$$

The regression line is the one line that gives the smallest value for *SSE*.

The *SSE* is a measure of the total variability of obtained score values around their predicted values. There are two other sums of squares that are important to understanding correlation and regression.

The total sum of squares (*SST*) is a measure of the total variability of the obtained score values around the mean of the obtained scores. The *SST* is represented by

$$SST = \Sigma(Y - \overline{Y})^2.$$

The remaining sum of squares is called the regression sum of squares (*SSR*) or the explained sum of squares. If we square each of the differences between predicted scores and the mean and then add them up, we get the *SSR*, which is represented by

$$SSR = \Sigma(Y_{pred} - \overline{Y})^2.$$

The *SSR* is a measure of the total variability of the predicted score values around the mean of the obtained scores.

An important and interesting feature of these three sums of squares is that the sum of the *SSR* and *SSE* is equal to the *SST*:

$$SST = SSR + SSE.$$

This leads us to three other important statistics: the proportion of variance explained (*PVE*), the correlation coefficient, and the standard error of estimate.

Proportion of variance explained. The *PVE* is a measure of how good the regression line predicts obtained scores. The values of *PVE* range from 0 (no predictive value) to 1 (prediction with perfect accuracy). The equation for *PVE* is

$$PVE = \frac{SSR}{SST}.$$

There also is a computational equation for the *PVE*, which is

$$PVE = \frac{(SSXY)^2}{SSX \bullet SSY},$$

where
  SSXY is the "covariance" sum of squares: $\Sigma(X - \overline{X})(Y - \overline{Y})$;
  SSX is the sum of squares for variable X: $\Sigma(X - \overline{X})^2$; and
  SSY is the sum of squares for variable Y: $\Sigma(Y - \overline{Y})^2$.

The procedure for computing these sums of squares is outlined in Table 6.4.

TABLE 6.4   Computation of r^2 (PVE)

Y	$Y - \overline{Y}$	$(Y - \overline{Y})^2$	X	$X - \overline{X}$	$(X - \overline{X})^2$	$(X - \overline{X})(Y - \overline{Y})$
3	−3.3	10.89	0	−4.5	20.25	+14.85
4	−2.3	5.29	1	−3.5	12.25	+ 8.05
4	−2.3	5.29	2	−2.5	6.25	+ 5.75
5	−1.3	1.69	3	−1.5	2.25	+ 1.95
6	−0.3	0.09	4	−0.5	0.25	+ 0.15
7	+0.7	0.49	5	+0.5	0.25	+ 0.35
8	+1.7	2.89	6	+1.5	2.25	+ 2.55
7	+0.7	0.49	7	+2.5	6.25	+ 1.75
9	+2.7	7.29	8	+3.5	12.25	+ 9.45
10	+3.7	13.69	9	+4.5	20.25	+16.65

NOTE: $\overline{Y} = 6.3$; $SSY = 48.1$; $\overline{X} = 4.5$; $SSX = 82.5$; $SSXY = +61.5$.

The proportion of variance in frequency of corporal punishment that may be explained by stressors experienced is

$$PVE = \frac{(+61.5)^2}{(48.1)(82.5)} = \frac{3782.25}{3968.25} = 0.953.$$

The *PVE* sometimes is called the coefficient of determination and is represented by the symbol r^2.

The correlation coefficient. A correlation coefficient also is a measure of the strength of relationship between two variables. The correlation coefficient is represented by the letter r and can take on values between −1 and +1 inclusive. The correlation coefficient always has the same sign as the slope. If one squares a correlation coefficient, then one will obtain the *PVE*. It is computed using the following formula:

$$r = \frac{SSXY}{\sqrt{SSX \bullet SSY}}.$$

For our example data, the correlation coefficient would be

$$R = \frac{+61.5}{\sqrt{(48.1)(82.5)}} = \frac{+61.5}{\sqrt{3968.25}} = \frac{+61.5}{62.994} = +0.976.$$

The standard error of estimate. The standard error of estimate is the standard deviation of the prediction errors. It is computed like any other standard deviation; the square root of the *SSE* divided by the degrees of freedom.

The first step is to compute the variance error ($s_E^{\,2}$):

$$s_E^2 = \frac{SSE}{n-2}.$$

Notice that the value for degrees of freedom is $n-2$ rather than $n-1$. The reason why we subtract 2 in this instance is that variance error (and standard error of estimate) is a statistic describing characteristics of *two* variables. They deal with the error involved in the prediction of Y (one variable) from X (the other variable).

The standard error of estimate is the square root of the variance error:

$$s_E = \sqrt{(s_E^2)}.$$

The standard error of estimate tells us how spread out scores are with respect to their predicted values. If the error scores ($E = Y - Y_{pred}$) are normally distributed around the prediction line, then about 68% of actual scores will fall between ± 1 s_E of their predicted values.

We can calculate the standard error of estimate using the following computing formula:

$$s_E = s_Y \sqrt{\left((1-r^2)\left(\frac{n-1}{n-2}\right)\right)},$$

where

s_Y is the standard deviation of Y;
r is the correlation coefficient for X and Y; and
n is the sample size.

For the example data, this would be

$$s_E = 2.311\sqrt{\left((1-.953)\frac{10-1}{10-2}\right)} = 2.311\sqrt{\left((.047)\frac{9}{8}\right)} = 2.311 \sqrt{0.053} = (0.230)(0.727) = 0.167.$$

INFERENTIAL STATISTICS: HYPOTHESIS TESTING

The Null and Alternative Hypotheses

Classical statistical hypothesis testing is based on the evaluation of two rival hypotheses: the *null hypothesis* and the *alternative hypothesis*.

We try to detect relationships by identifying changes that are unlikely to have occurred simply because of random fluctuations of dependent measures. Statistical analysis is the usual procedure for identifying such relationships.

The null hypothesis is the hypothesis that there is no relationship between two variables. This implies that if the null hypothesis is true, then any apparent relationship in samples is the result of random fluctuations in the dependent measure or sampling error.

Statistical hypothesis tests are carried out on samples. For example, in an *experimental two-group posttest-only design,* there would be a sample whose members received an intervention and a sample whose members did not. Both of these would be probability samples from a larger population. The intervention sample would represent the population of all individuals as if they had received the intervention. The control sample would be representative of the same population of individuals as if they had not received the intervention.

If the intervention had no effect, then the populations would be identical. However, it would be unlikely that two samples from two identical populations would be identical. So, although the sample means would be different, they would not represent any effect of the independent variable. The apparent difference would be due to sampling error.

Statistical hypothesis tests involve evaluating evidence from samples to make inferences about populations. It is for this reason that the null hypothesis is a statement about population parameters. For example, one null hypothesis for the previous design could be stated as

$$H_0: \mu_1 = \mu_2$$

or as

$$H_0: \mu_1 - \mu_2 = 0.$$

H_0 stands for the null hypothesis. It is a letter H with a zero subscript. It is a statement that the means of the experimental (Mean 1) and control (Mean 2) *populations* are equal.

To establish that a relationship exists between the intervention (independent variable) and the outcome (measure of the dependent variable), we must collect evidence that allows us to *reject* the null hypothesis.

Strictly speaking, we do not make a decision as to whether the null hypothesis is correct or not. We evaluate the evidence to determine the extent to which it tends to confirm or disconfirm the null hypothesis. If the evidence were such that it is unlikely that an observed relationship would have occurred as the result of sampling error, then we would reject the null hypothesis. If the evidence were more ambiguous, then we would fail to reject the null hypothesis. The terms "reject" and "fail to reject" carry the implicit understanding that our decision might be in error. The truth is that we never really know whether our decision is correct or not.

Situation: NULL HYPOTHESIS TRUE	
Decision	Result
Reject H_0	**Type I Error** α = the probability of rejecting the Null Hypothesis when it is true
Fail to Reject H_0	**Correct Decision** $1 - \alpha$ = the probability of not rejecting the Null Hypothesis when it is true.

Figure 6.2. The Null Hypothesis and Type I Error

When we reject the null hypothesis and it is true, we have committed a *Type I error*. By setting certain statistical criteria beforehand, we can establish the probability that we will commit a Type I error. We decide what proportion of the time we are willing to commit a Type I error. This proportion (probability) is called alpha (α). If we are willing to reject the null hypothesis when it is true only 1 in 20 times, then we set our α level at .05. If only 1 in 100 times, then we set it at .01.

The probability that we will fail to reject the null hypothesis when it is true (correct decision) is $1 - \alpha$ (Figure 6.2).

The following hypothesis would be evaluated by comparing the difference between sample means:

$$H_0: \mu_1 - \mu_2 = 0.$$

If we carried out multiple samples from populations with identical means (the null hypothesis was true), then we would find that most of the values for the differences between the sample means would not be zero. Figure 6.3 represents a distribution of the differences between sample means drawn from identical populations.

The mean difference for the total distribution of sample means is 0, and the standard deviation is 5. If the differences are normally distributed, then approximately 68% of these differences will be between –5 ($z = -1$) and +5 ($z = +1$). Fully 95% of the differences in the distribution will fall between the range of –9.8 ($z = -1.96$) and +9.8 ($z = +1.96$). If we drew a random sample from each population, it would not be unusual to find a difference between sample means of as much as 9.8, even though the population means were the same.

On the other hand, we would expect to find a difference more than 9.8 about 1 in 20 times. If we set our criterion for rejecting the null hypothesis such that a mean dif-

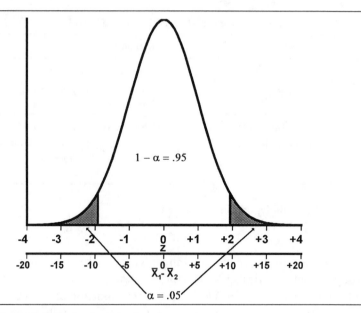

Figure 6.3. The Null Hypothesis and α Level

ference must be greater than +9.8 or less than –9.8, then we would commit a Type I error only 1 in 20 times (.05) on average. Our α level (the probability of committing a Type I error) would be set at .05.

The probability that a relationship or a difference of a certain size would be seen in a sample if the null hypothesis were true is represented by p. To reject the null hypothesis, p must be less than or equal to α. The probability of getting an effect this large or larger if the null hypothesis were true is less than or equal to the probability of making a Type I error that we have decided is acceptable.

> *Rejecting the* H_0: We believe that it is likely that the relationship in the sample is generalizable to the population.
> *Not rejecting the* H_0: We do not believe that we have sufficient evidence to draw inferences about the population.

For the previous example, let us imagine that we have set α = .05. Also, imagine that we obtained a difference between the sample means of 10. The probability that we would obtain a difference of +10 or –10 would be equivalent to the probability of a z score greater than +2.0 plus the probability of a z score less than –2.0 or .0228 + .0228 = .0456. This is our p value; p = .0456. Because $p < α$, we would reject the null hypothesis.

Some texts create the impression that the alternative (or research or experimental) hypothesis is simply the opposite of the null hypothesis. In fact, sometimes this naive alternative hypothesis is used. However, it generally is not particularly useful to researchers. Usually, we are interested in detecting an intervention effect of a particular size. On certain measures, we would be interested in small effects (e.g., death rate), whereas on others, only larger effects would be of interest.

When we are interested in an effect of a particular size, we use a specific alternative hypothesis that takes the following form:

$$H_1: \mu_1 - \mu_2 \geq |d|,$$

where d is a difference of a particular size. If the test is a nondirectional test, then the difference in the alternative hypothesis would be expressed as an absolute value, $|d|$, to show that either a positive or negative difference is involved.

It is customary to express the mean difference in an H_1 in units of standard deviation. Such scores are called z scores. The difference is called an effect size. Effect sizes frequently are used in meta-analyses of outcome studies to compare the relative efficacy of different types of interventions across studies.

Cohen (1988) groups effect sizes into small, medium, and large categories. The criteria for each are as follows:

Small effect size ($d = .2$): It is approximately the effect size for the average difference in height (i.e., 0.5 inches and $s = 2.1$) between 15- and 16-year-old girls.
Medium effect size ($d = .5$): It is approximately the effect size for the average difference in height (i.e., 1.0 inches and $s = 2.0$) between 14- and 18-year-old girls.
Large effect size ($d = .8$): This is the same effect size ($d = .8$) as the average difference in height for 13- and 18-year-old girls.

Intuitively, it would seem that we would want to detect even very small effect sizes in our research. However, there is a practical trade-off involved. All other things being equal, the consistent detection of small effect sizes requires very large ($n > 200$) sample sizes.

Because very large sample sizes require resources that might not be readily available, they might not be practical for all studies. Furthermore, there are certain outcome variables for which we would not be particularly interested in small effects.

If we reject the null hypothesis, then we implicitly have decided that the evidence supports the alternative hypothesis. If the alternative hypothesis is true and we reject the null hypothesis, then we have made a correct decision. However, if we fail to reject the null hypothesis and the alternative hypothesis is true, then we have committed a Type II error. A Type II error involves the failure to detect an existing effect (Figure 6.4).

Situation: ALTERNATIVE HYPOTHESIS TRUE	
Decision	Result
Reject H_0	**Correct Decision** $1 - \beta$ = the probability of rejecting the Null Hypothesis when the Alternative Hypothesis is true. The power of a test.
Fail to Reject H_0	**Type II Error** β = the probability of not rejecting the Null Hypothesis when the Alternative Hypothesis is true.

Figure 6.4. The Null Hypothesis and Type II Error

Beta (β) is the probability of committing a Type II error. This probability is established when we set our criterion for rejecting the null hypothesis. The probability of a correct decision $(1 - \beta)$ is an important probability. It is so important that it has a name—*power*. Power refers to the probability that we will detect an effect of the size we have selected.

We should decide on the power $(1 - \beta)$ as well as the α level before we carry out a statistical test. Just as with Type I error, we should decide beforehand how often we are willing to make a Type II error (fail to detect a certain effect size). This is our β level. The procedure for making such determinations is discussed in Cohen (1988).

Assumptions for Statistical Hypothesis Tests

Although assumptions are different for different tests, all tests of the null hypothesis share two related assumptions: randomness and independence.

The randomness assumption is that sample members must be randomly selected from the population being evaluated. If the sample is being divided into groups (e.g., treatment and control), then assignment to groups also must be random. This is referred to as *random selection* and *random assignment*.

The mathematical models that underlie statistical hypothesis testing depend on random sampling. If the samples are not random, then we cannot compute an accurate probability (p) that the sample could have resulted if the null hypothesis were true.

The independence assumption is that one member's score will not influence another member's score. The only common relationship among group scores should be the intervention. One implication of this is that members of a group should not have any contact with each other so as not to affect each other's scores.

Again, the mathematical models are dependent on the independence of sample scores. If the scores are not independent, then the probability (p) is, as before, simply a number that has little to do with the probability of a Type I error.

Parametric and Nonparametric Hypothesis Tests

Traditionally, hypothesis tests are grouped into parametric and nonparametric tests. The names are misleading given that one class of test has no more or less to do with population parameters than the other. The difference between the two tests lies in the mathematical assumptions used to compute the likelihood of a Type I error.

Parametric tests are based on the assumption that the populations from which the samples are drawn are normally distributed. Nonparametric tests do not have this rigid assumption. Thus, a nonparametric test can be carried out on a broader range of data than can a parametric test. Nonparametric tests remain serviceable even in circumstances where parametric procedures collapse.

When the populations from which we sample are normally distributed, and when all the other assumptions of the parametric test are met, parametric tests are slightly more powerful than nonparametric tests. However, when the parametric assumptions are not met, nonparametric tests are more powerful.

Specific Hypothesis Tests

We now investigate several frequently used hypothesis tests and issues surrounding their appropriate use. Where appropriate, parametric and nonparametric tests are presented together for each type of design.

Single-Sample Hypothesis Tests

These are tests in which a single sample is drawn. Comparisons are made between sample values and population parameters to see whether the sample differs in a statistically significant way from the parent population. Occasionally, these tests are used to determine whether a sample differs from some theoretical population.

For example, we might wish to gather evidence as to whether a particular population was normally distributed. We would take a random sample from this population and compare the distribution of scores to an artificially constructed, normally distributed set of scores. If there were a statistically significant difference, then we would reject the hypothesis that our sample came from a normally distributed population (the null hypothesis).

Typically, these tests are not used for experiments. They tend to be used to demonstrate that certain strata within populations differ from the population as a whole.

Here, we investigate two single-sample tests:

Single-sample t test (interval or ratio scale); and
χ^2 (chi-square) goodness of fit test (nominal scale).

The single-sample t *test.* This test usually is used to see whether a stratum of a population is different on average from the population as a whole (e.g., are the mean wages received by social workers in Lansing different from the mean for all social workers in Michigan?).

The null hypothesis for this test is that the mean wages for a particular stratum (Lansing social workers) of the population and the population as a whole (Michigan social workers) will be the same:

$$H_0: \mu_0 = \mu_1 \quad \text{or} \quad H_0: \mu_1 - \mu_0 = 0,$$

where μ_0 is the mean wage for the population and μ_1 is the mean wage for the stratum.

The assumptions of the single-sample t test are as follows:

Randomness: Sample members must be randomly drawn from the population.
Independence: Sample (X) scores must be independent of each other.
Scaling: The dependent measure (X scores) must be interval or ratio.
Normal distribution: The population of X scores must be normally distributed.

These assumptions are listed more or less in order of importance. Violations of the first three assumptions are essentially "fatal" ones. Even slight violations of the first two assumptions can introduce major error into the computation of p values.

Violation of the assumption of a normal distribution will introduce some error into the computation of p values. Unless the population distribution is markedly different from a normal distribution, the errors will tend to be slight (e.g., a reported p value of .042 actually will be a p value of .057). This is what is meant when someone says that the t test is a "robust" test.

The t statistic for the single-sample t test is computed by subtracting the null hypothesis (population) mean from the sample mean and dividing by the standard error of the mean.

The formula for t_{obt} (pronounced "t obtained") is

$$t_{obt} = \frac{\overline{X}_1 - \mu_0}{s_{\overline{x}}}.$$

As the absolute value of t_{obt} gets larger, the more unlikely it is that such a difference could occur if the null hypothesis is true. At a certain point, the probability (p) of obtaining a t so large becomes sufficiently small (reaches the α level) that we reject the null hypothesis.

The critical value of t (the value that t_{obt} must equal or exceed to reject the null hypothesis) depends on the degrees of freedom. For a single-sample t test, the degrees of freedom are $df = n - 1$, where n is the sample size.

Let us look at how to compute t_{obt}.

We know from a statewide survey that the average time taken to complete an outpatient rehabilitation program for a certain injury, X, is 46.6 days. We wish to see whether clients seen at our clinic are taking longer or shorter than the state average.

We randomly sample 16 files from the past year. We review these cases and determine the length of program for each of the clients in the sample. The mean number of days to complete rehabilitation at our clinic is 29.875 days. This is lower than the population mean of 46.6 days. The question is whether this result is statistically significant. Is it likely that this sample could have been drawn from a population with a mean of 46.6.

To determine this, we need to calculate t_{obt}. The first step in calculating t_{obt} was carried out when we computed the sample mean. The next step is to compute the standard error of the mean. We begin this by computing the standard deviation, which turns out to be $s = 11.888$.

The standard error of the mean is calculated by dividing the standard deviation by the square root of the sample size or

$$s_{\bar{x}} = \frac{s}{\sqrt{n}} = \frac{11.888}{\sqrt{16}} = \frac{11.888}{4} = 2.972.$$

We take the formula for t_{obt} and plug in our numbers to obtain

$$t_{obt} = \frac{\bar{X}_1 - \mu_0}{s_{\bar{x}}} = \frac{29.875 - 46.6}{2.972} = \frac{-16.725}{2.972} = -5.628.$$

We look up the tabled t value (t_{crit}) at 15 degrees of freedom. This turns out to be 2.131 for a nondirectional test at $\alpha = .05$ (see a table of the critical values for the t test, nondirectional, found in most statistics texts). The absolute value of $t_{obt} = 5.628$. This is greater than $t_{crit} = 2.131$, so we reject the null hypothesis. The evidence suggests that clients in our clinic average fewer days in rehabilitation than is the case in the statewide population.

The effect size index for a test of means is d and is computed as follows for a single-sample t test:

$$d = \frac{\bar{X}_1 - \mu_0}{s}.$$

The effect size for our example would be as follows:

$$d = \frac{29.875 - 46.6}{11.888} = \frac{-16.725}{11.888} = 1.4069,$$

which would be classified as a large effect.

The χ^2 goodness of fit test. The χ^2 goodness of fit test is a single-sample test. It is used in the evaluation of nominal (categorical) variables. The test involves comparisons between observed and expected frequencies within strata in a sample. Expected frequencies are derived from either population values or theoretical values. Observed frequencies are those derived from the sample.

The null hypothesis for the χ^2 test is that the population from which the sample has been drawn will have the same proportion of members in each category as the empirical or theoretical null hypothesis population:

$$H_0: P_{0k} = P_{1k} \qquad \text{or} \qquad H_0: P_{0k} - P_{1k} = 0,$$

where

P_{0k} is the proportion of cases within category k in the null hypothesis population (expected); and

P_{1k} is the proportion of cases within category k in the population from which the test sample was drawn (observed).

The assumptions for the χ^2 goodness of fit test are as follows:

Randomness: Sample members must be randomly drawn from the population.
Independence: Sample scores must be independent of each other. One implication of this is that categories must be mutually exclusive (no case may appear in more than one category).
Scaling: The dependent measure (categories) must be nominal.
Expected frequencies: No expected frequency within a category should be less than 1, and no more than 20% of the expected frequencies should be less than 5.

As with all tests of the null hypothesis, the χ^2 test begins with the assumptions of randomness and independence. Deriving from these assumptions is the requirement that the categories in the cross-tabulation must be *mutually exclusive* and *exhaustive*.

Mutually exclusive means that an individual may not be in more than one category per variable. *Exhaustive* means that all categories of interest are covered.

These assumptions are listed more or less in order of importance. Violations of the first three assumptions are essentially "fatal" ones. Even slight violations of the first two assumptions can introduce major errors into the computation of p values.

The χ^2 goodness of fit test is basically a large-sample test. When the expected frequencies are small (expected frequency less than 1 or at least 20% of expected frequencies less than 5), the probabilities associated with the χ^2 test will be inaccurate.

The usual procedure in this case is either to increase expected frequencies by collapsing adjacent categories (also called cells) or to use another test. Following is a concrete example.

The workers at the Interdenominational Social Services Center in St. Winifred Township wanted to see whether they were serving people of all faiths (and those of no faith) equally. They had census figures indicating that religious preferences in the township were as follows: Christian (64%), Jewish (10%), Muslim (8%), other religion/no preference (14%), agnostic/atheist (4%).

The workers randomly sampled 50 clients from those seen during the previous year. Before they drew the sample, they calculated the expected frequency for each category. To obtain the expected frequencies for the sample, they converted the percentage for each preference to a decimal proportion and multiplied it by 50. Thus, the expected frequency for Christians was 64% of 50 or $.64 \bullet 50 = 32$, the Jewish category was 10% of 50 or $.10 \bullet 50 = 5$, and so on. Table 6.5 depicts the expected frequencies.

TABLE 6.5   Expected Frequencies for Religious Preferences

	Christian	Jewish	Muslim	Other/ No Preference	Agnostic/ Atheist
Expected frequency	32	5	4	7	2

Two (40%) of our expected frequencies (Muslim and agnostic/atheist) are less than 5. Given that the maximum allowable is 20%, we are violating a test assumption. We can remedy this by collapsing categories (merging two or more categories into one) or by increasing the sample size. However, there is no category that we could reasonably combine with agnostic/atheist. It would not work to combine this category with any of the other categories because the latter are religious individuals, whereas atheists and agnostics are not religious.

However, we could increase the sample size. To get a sample in which only one (20%) of the expected frequencies was less than 5, we would need a sample large enough so that 8% (percentage of the population identifying as Muslim) of it would equal 5:

$$0.08 \bullet n = 5$$

$$n = \frac{5}{0.08} = 62.5 \sim 63.$$

So, our sample size would need to be 63, giving us the expected frequencies shown in Table 6.6. Only one of five (20%) of the expected frequencies is less than 5, and none of them is less than 1, so the sample size assumption is met.

TABLE 6.6   New Expected Frequencies for Religious Preferences

	Christian	*Jewish*	*Muslim*	*Other/No Preference*	*Agnostic/Atheist*
Expected frequency	40.32	6.30	5.04	8.82	2.52

The results of a random sample of 63 cases were as found in Table 6.7.

TABLE 6.7   Observed and Expected Frequencies for Religious Preferences

	Christian	*Jewish*	*Muslim*	*Other/No Preference*	*Agnostic/Atheist*
Expected frequency	40.32	6.30	5.04	8.82	2.52
Observed frequency	49	2	2	9	1

The null hypothesis for this example is that the proportion of people living in St. Winifred Township who identify with each religious category will be the same as the proportion of people who have received services at the Interdenominational Services Center in St. Winifred Township who identify with each religious category.

The null hypothesis expresses the expectation that observed and expected frequencies will not be different. Notice the similarity between the null hypothesis and the numerator of the χ^2_{obt} test statistic:

$$\chi^2_{obt} = \Sigma \frac{(f_O - f_E)^2}{f_E}.$$

The formula tells us to subtract the expected score from the observed score $(f_O - f_E)$ and then to square the difference $([f_O - f_E]^2)$ and divide by the expected score $([f_O - f_E]^2 / f_E)$ for each observed and expected score pair. When we are finished, we add the answers and obtain the χ^2_{obt} test statistic (Table 6.8).

The χ^2_{obt} is evaluated by comparing it to a critical value (χ^2_{crit}) that is obtained from a table of critical values of the χ^2 distribution. If χ^2_{obt} is greater than or equal to χ^2_{crit}, then we reject the null hypothesis.

TABLE 6.8   Computation of χ^2_{obt}

Observed (f_O)	Expected (f_E)	$f_O - f_E$	$(f_O - f_E)^2$	$\dfrac{(f_O - f_E)^2}{f_E}$
49	40.32	+8.68	75.3424	17.4404
2	6.30	−4.30	18.4900	2.9349
2	5.04	−3.04	9.2416	1.8337
9	8.82	+0.18	0.0324	0.0037
1	2.52	−1.52	2.3104	0.9168

NOTE: $\sum \dfrac{(f_o - f_o)^2}{f_E} = 17.4404 + 2.9349 + 1.8337 + 0.0037 + 0.9168 = \chi^2_{obt} = 23.1295$

For a χ^2 goodness of fit, the degrees of freedom are equal to the number of categories (c) minus 1 or $df = c - 1$. In our case, we have five categories (Christian, Jewish, Muslim, other/no preference, and agnostic/atheist), so $df = 5 - 1 = 4$.

The critical value for χ^2 at $\alpha = .05$ and $df = 4$ is $\chi^2_{crit} = 9.49$. We have calculated χ^2_{obt} as 23.1295. Because χ^2_{obt} is greater than χ^2_{crit}, we reject the null hypothesis. The evidence suggests that people of all faiths (and those of no faith) are not being seen proportionately to their representations in the township.

Earlier, we discussed the use of the effect size measure d for the t test. It is an appropriate measure of effect size for a test of means. However, the χ^2 test does not compare means. It compares frequencies (or proportions). Therefore, a different effect size index is used for the χ^2 test—w. This measure of effect size ranges from 0 to 1. Cohen (1988) classifies these effect sizes into three categories:

Small effect size: w = .10;
Medium effect size: w = .30; and
Large effect size: w = .50.

The effect size coefficient for a χ^2 goodness of fit test is computed according to the following formula:

$$w = \sqrt{(\chi^2 / N)},$$

where N = the total sample size.

For the St. Winifred Township example,

$$w = \sqrt{(23.1295 / 63)} = \sqrt{(0.3671)} = 0.6059,$$

which would be classified as a large effect.

Hypothesis Tests for Two Related Samples

These are tests in which either a single sample is drawn and measurements are taken at two times or two samples are drawn and members of the sample are individually matched on some attribute. Measurements are taken for each member of the matched groups.

We investigate three examples of two related sample tests in this section:

Dependent (matched, paired, correlated) samples *t* test (interval or ratio scale);
Wilcoxon matched pairs, signed ranks test (ordinal scale); and
McNemar change test (nominal scale).

Difference scores. The dependent *t* test and the Wilcoxon matched pairs, signed ranks test evaluate difference scores. These may be differences between scores from measurements taken at two different times on the same individual (pretest and posttest) or differences between scores taken on two different individuals who have been paired or matched with each other based on their similarity on some variable or variable cluster (e.g., gender, race/ethnicity, socioeconomic status). The formula for a difference score is

$$X_2 - X_1 = X_D,$$

where
 X_1 is the first of a pair of scores;
 X_2 is the second of a pair of scores; and
 X_D is the difference between the two.

The null hypothesis for all these tests is that the samples came from populations in which the expected differences are zero.

The dependent samples t *test.* This also is called the correlated, paired, or matched *t* test. The null hypothesis for this test is that the mean of the differences between the paired scores is zero:

$$H_0: \mu_{XD} - \mu_{0D} = 0,$$

where
 μ_{XD} = the mean difference between the populations from which the samples were drawn; and
 μ_{0D} = the mean difference between the populations specified by the null hypothesis.

Because the null hypothesis typically specifies no difference ($\mu_{0D} = 0$), the null hypothesis usually is written as

$$H_0: \mu_{XD} = 0.$$

The t statistic for the dependent t test is the mean of the sample differences divided by the standard error of the mean difference or

$$t_{\text{obt}} = \frac{X_D - \mu_{0D}}{s_{\overline{XD}}}.$$

As the absolute value of t gets larger, the more unlikely it is that such a difference could occur if the null hypothesis is true. At a certain point, the probability (p) of obtaining a t so large becomes sufficiently small (reaches the alpha level) that we reject the null hypothesis.

The assumptions of the dependent t test are as follows:

Randomness: Sample members must be randomly drawn from the population.
Independence: X_D scores must be independent of each other.
Scaling: The dependent measure (X_D scores) must be interval or ratio.
Normal distribution: The population of X_D scores must be normally distributed.

These assumptions are listed more or less in order of importance. Violations of the first three assumptions are essentially "death penalty" violations. Even slight violations of the first two assumptions can introduce major error into the computation of p values. Similarly, difference scores computed from two sets of ordinal data may incorporate major error.

Violation of the assumption of a normal distribution will introduce some error into the computation of p values. However, unless the population distribution is markedly different from a normal distribution, the errors will tend to be slight (e.g., a reported p value of .042 actually will be a p value of .057). This is what is meant when someone says that the t test is a "robust" test.

Still, even though the error is slight, the nonparametric Wilcoxon matched pairs, signed ranks test (discussed in the next section) probably will yield a more accurate test when there are violations of this normal distribution assumption.

Let us look at the procedure for computing the dependent groups t statistic. We use an evaluation of an intervention for individuals with depression problems. The dependent measure is the Beck Depression Inventory (BDI), a reliable and well-validated measure of depression.

Ten clients were randomly selected from clients seen for depression problems at a community center. They were pretested (X_1) with the BDI, received the treatment, and then were posttested (X_2) with the same instrument. The mean of the difference scores (X_D) was -1. This means that the average change in BDI scores from pretest to posttest was a decrease of 1 point. The standard deviation of the difference scores was 1.33.

The next step is the computation of the standard error of the mean. We divide the standard deviation by the square root of the sample size to get the standard error of the mean:

$$s_{\overline{XD}} = 1.33 / \sqrt{10} = 1.33 / 3.16 = 0.42.$$

We plug the values into the formula for t_{obt}:

$$t_{obt} = \frac{\overline{X}_D}{s_{\overline{XD}}} = \frac{-1}{0.42} = -2.38.$$

For $\alpha = .05$ and $df = n - 1 = 10 - 1 = 9$, $t_{crit} = 2.262$ (see a table of critical values for the t test, nondirectional, found in most statistics texts). Because $|t_{obt}| = 2.38$ is greater than or equal to the critical value, we reject the null hypothesis at $\alpha = .05$.

The effect size index for this test is d and is computed as follows:

$$d = \frac{\overline{X}_D - \mu_{0D}}{s}.$$

For the depression intervention example,

$$d = \frac{-1 - 0}{1.33} = \frac{-1}{1.33} = -0.752,$$

which would be classified as a medium effect.

The Wilcoxon matched pairs, signed ranks test. The Wilcoxon matched pairs, signed rank test is a nonparametric test for the evaluation of difference scores. The test involves ranking difference scores as to how far they are from zero. The difference score closest to zero receives the rank of 1, the next score receives the rank of 2, and so on. The ranks for difference scores below zero are given a negative sign, whereas those above zero are given a positive sign. The null hypothesis is that the sample comes from a population of difference scores in which the expected difference score is zero.

The assumptions for the Wilcoxon matched pairs, signed ranks test are as follows:

Randomness: Sample members must be randomly drawn from the population.
Independence: X_D scores must be independent of each other.
Scaling: The dependent measure (X_D scores) must be ordinal (interval or ratio differences must be converted to ranks).

TABLE 6.9   Computation of the Wilcoxon T_{obt}

| | | | | | Signed Ranks | |
ID Number	Pretest	Posttest	Difference	Rank	Positive	Negative
1	17	16	−1	3		3
2	19	18	−1	3		3
3	18	15	−3	9		9
4	18	17	−1	3		3
5	16	16	0			
6	16	17	+1	3	3	
7	18	16	−2	7		7
8	21	19	−2	7		7
9	18	19	+1	3	3	
10	18	16	−2	7		7

NOTE: Sum of ranks for less frequent sign = 6.

Let us look at the procedure for computing the Wilcoxon matched pairs, signed ranks test statistic. We use the same example as for the t test. The dependent measure is the BDI, a measure of depression. Scores on the BDI are not normally distributed, tending to be positively skewed.

Ten clients were randomly selected from clients seen for depression problems at a community center. They were pretested with the BDI, received the treatment, and then were posttested with the same instrument. We compute the difference scores (post − pre) for each individual. We assign a rank to each difference score based on its closeness to zero. Difference scores of zero do not receive a rank. Tied ranks receive the average rank for the tie.

So, if we look at Table 6.9, we see that there is one difference score of zero that goes unranked. There are five difference scores of either −1 or +1. These cover the first five ranks (1, 2, 3, 4, 5), giving an average rank of 3. There are three difference scores of −2 (and none of +2). These cover the next three ranks (6, 7, 8), giving an average rank of 7. The final score is −3, which is given the rank of 9.

The next step is to "sign" the rank. This means to place the rank in either the positive or the negative column in the table, depending on whether the difference score was positive or negative.

We then determine which sign (positive or negative) appeared less frequently and add up the ranks for this sign. Because the positive sign appeared only twice (compared to seven times for the negative sign), we add up the ranks in the positive column and obtain 6. This is the test statistic value for the Wilcoxon matched pairs, signed ranks test.

The test statistic is called T_{obt}. This is an uppercase T and is *not the same* as the statistic used with the (lowercase) t distribution.

There are two other issues with respect to the Wilcoxon T_{obt} that should be addressed:

1. The Wilcoxon T_{obt} is evaluated according to the number of nonzero difference scores. So, we should subtract 1 from the original n for each difference score that is zero to obtain a corrected n to use for the critical value table.
2. Unlike most other test statistics, the Wilcoxon T_{obt} must be *less than* or equal to the critical value to reject the null hypothesis.

We consult a table of critical values for the Wilcoxon T (see table of critical values for Wilcoxon T in any general statistics book) and see whether the result ($T_{obt} = 6$) was significant at $\alpha = .05$. Because there was one difference score equal to zero, the corrected $n = 9$. The critical value for the Wilcoxon T at $n = 9$ and $\alpha = .05$ is $T_{crit} = 5$. $T_{obt} = 6$ is *not* less than or equal to the critical value, so we fail to reject the null hypothesis at $\alpha = .05$.

There is no well-accepted post hoc measure of effect size for ordinal tests of related scores. One possible measure would be proportion of nonoverlapping scores as a measure of effect. Cohen (1988) briefly discusses this measure, called U.

The procedure begins with computing the minimum and maximum scores for each of the two related groups. We choose the least maximum and the greatest minimum. This establishes the end points for the overlap range.

We count the number of scores in both groups within this range (including the end points) and divide by the total number of scores. This gives a proportion of overlapping scores. Subtract this number from 1, and we obtain the proportion of nonoverlapping scores. This index ranges from 0 to 1. Lower proportions are indicative of smaller effects, and higher ones are indicative of larger effects.

Cohen (1998) calculates equivalents between U and d, which would imply the following definitions of strength of effect:

Small effect size:	$d = .2$	$U = .15$;
Medium effect size:	$d = .5$	$U = .33$; and
Large effect size:	$d = .8$	$U = .47$.

For the example data, the minimum score for the pretest was 16, and the maximum score was 21. The posttest minimum and maximum scores were 15 and 19, respectively. The greatest minimum is 16, and the least maximum is 19.

Of 20 total scores, 18 fall within this overlap range. The proportion of overlap is $18/20 = .90$. The proportion of nonoverlapping scores is $U = 1 - .90 = .10$, which would be a small effect.

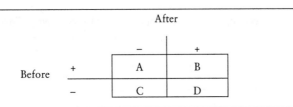

Figure 6.5. McNemar Change Test Layout

The McNemar change test. The McNemar change test is used for pre- and post-intervention designs where the variables in the analysis are dichotomously scored (e.g., improved vs. not improved, same vs. different, increase vs. decrease).

The layout for the McNemar change test is shown in Figure 6.5. Cell A contains the number of individuals who changed from + to –. Cell B contains the number of individuals who received + on both measurements. Cell C contains the number of individuals who received – on both measurements. Cell D contains the number of individuals who changed from – to +. The null hypothesis is expressed as

$$H_0: P_A = P_D \qquad \text{or} \qquad H_0: P_A - P_D = 0,$$

where

P_A is the proportion of cases shifting from + to – (decreasing) in the null hypothesis population; and

P_D is the proportion of cases shifting from – to + (increasing) in the null hypothesis population.

The assumptions for the McNemar change test are similar to those for the χ^2 test:

Randomness: Sample members must be randomly drawn from the population.
Independence: Within-group sample scores must be independent of each other (although between-group scores [pre- and posttest scores] will necessarily be dependent).
Scaling: The dependent measure (categories) must be nominal.
Expected frequencies: No expected frequency within a category should be less than 5.

A special case of χ^2_{obt} is the test statistic for the McNemar change test:

$$\chi^2_{obt} = \frac{(|f_A - f_D| - 1)^2}{f_A + f_D},$$

where

f_A = the frequency in Cell A; and
f_D = the frequency in Cell D.

TABLE 6.10   Observed and Expected Frequencies for the McNemar Change Test

	1999		Total
	None	Marijuana	
1997			
Marijuana	2 (Cell A)	21 (Cell B)	23
None	31 (Cell C)	11 (Cell D)	42
Total	33	32	65

This is a χ^2_{obt} test statistic with $df = 1$. For $df = 1$, we need to include something called the Yates correction for continuity in the χ^2_{obt} equation. This is –1, which appears in the numerator of the test statistic.

Let us imagine that we are interested in marijuana use among high school students. We also are interested in change in marijuana use over time. Imagine that we collected survey data on a random sample of ninth-graders in 1997. In 1999, we surveyed the same sample that had been in ninth grade in 1997. We found that 32 out of 65 students said that they used marijuana during the previous year, as compared to 23 out of 65 in 1999. The results are summarized in Table 6.10.

Cell A represents those students who had used marijuana in 1997 but who had not used it in 1999. Cell B shows the number of students who had used marijuana in both 1997 and 1999. Cell C shows the number of students who did not use marijuana either in 1997 or in 1999. Cell D shows the number of students who did not use marijuana in 1997 but who did use it in 1999.

So, the sum of Cells A and D is the total number of students whose patterns of marijuana use changed. The null hypothesis for the McNemar change test is that changing from nonuse to use would be just as likely as changing from use to nonuse.

In other words, of the 13 individuals who changed their pattern of marijuana use, we would expect half (6.5) to go from not using to using and the other half (6.5) to go from using to not using if the null hypothesis were true.

The calculation of the McNemar change test statistic is shown in Table 6.11.

For $df = 1$ and $\alpha = .05$, $\chi^2_{crit} = 3.84$ (see a table of critical values of χ^2 found in most statistics texts). Because $\chi^2_{obt} = 4.92$, we would reject the null hypothesis at $\alpha = .05$. We would conclude that there was in fact an increase in marijuana use between 1997 and 1999.

TABLE 6.11   Computation of the McNemar Change Test Statistic

Decrease (f_A)	*Increase* (f_D)	$|f_A - f_D| - 1$	$(|f_A - f_D| - 1)^2$	$\dfrac{(|f_A - f_D| - 1)^2}{f_A + f_D}$
2	11	8	64	4.9230767

NOTE: $\chi^2_{obt} = 4.923$.

The effect size coefficient for a McNemar change test is w and is computed according to the following formula:

$$w = \sqrt{(\chi^2 / N)}.$$

For the high school survey,

$$w = \sqrt{(4.923 / 65)} = \sqrt{0.0757} = 0.2752,$$

which would be classified as a medium effect.

Hypothesis Tests for Two Independent Samples

These are tests in which a sample is randomly drawn and individuals from the sample are randomly assigned to one of two experimental conditions.

We investigate three examples of two independent samples tests:

Independent samples (group) t test (interval or ratio scale);
Wilcoxon/Mann-Whitney (W/M-W) test (ordinal scale); and
χ^2 test of independence ($2 \times k$) (nominal scale).

The independent samples t *test.* This sometimes is called the group t test. It is a test of means whose null hypothesis is formally stated as follows:

$$H_0: \mu_1 - \mu_2 = 0.$$

Following are the assumptions of the independent t test:

Randomness: Sample members must be randomly drawn from the population and randomly assigned to one of the two groups.
Independence: Scores must be independent of each other.

Scaling: The dependent measure must be interval or ratio.

Normal distribution: The populations from which the individuals in the samples were drawn must be normally distributed.

Homogeneity of variances ($\sigma_1^2 = \sigma_2^2$): The samples must be drawn from populations whose variances are equal.

Equality of sample sizes ($n_1 = n_2$): The samples must be of the same size.

As before, these assumptions are listed more or less in order of importance. The first three assumptions are the "fatal" assumptions.

Violation of the normality assumption will make for less accurate p values. However, unless the population distribution is markedly different from a normal distribution, the errors will tend to be slight. Still, even though the error is slight, the nonparametric W/M-W test probably will be more accurate when the normality assumption is violated.

The independent groups t test also is fairly robust with respect to violation of the homogeneity of variances assumption and the equal sample size assumption. A problem may arise when both of these assumptions are violated at the same time.

If the smaller variance is in the smaller sample, then the probability of a Type II error (not detecting an existing difference) increases. If the larger variance is in the smaller sample, then the probability of a Type I error (rejecting the null hypothesis when it is true) increases.

If there is no association between sample size and variance, then violation of each of these assumptions is not particularly problematic. There may be fairly substantial discrepancies between sample sizes without much effect on the accuracy of our p estimates. Similarly, if every other assumption is met, then a slight difference in variances will not have a large effect on probability estimates.

The t statistic for the independent t test is the difference between the sample means divided by the standard error of the differences between means or

$$t_{obt} = \frac{\overline{X}_1 - \overline{X}_2}{s_{\overline{x}_1 - \overline{x}_2}}.$$

Because two sample means are computed, 2 degrees of freedom are lost:

$$df = n_1 + n_2 - 2,$$

where

n_1 = number of scores for the first group; and

n_2 = number of scores for the second group.

Following is an example of the use of the independent t test statistic. We wish to see whether there is a difference in level of social activity in children depending on whether they are in after-school care or home care. Because more children attended the after-school program, a proportionate stratified sample of 16 children in after-school care (Group 1) and 14 children in home care (Group 2) was drawn. The dependent measure was a score on a social activity scale in which lower scores represent less social activity and higher scores represent more social activity.

We evaluate this with an independent t test. The first step in calculating t_{obt} is to compute the sample mean for each group. The next step is to compute the standard error of the mean. However, the procedure for doing this is a little different from that used before. As you might recall, the standard error of the mean is the standard deviation divided by the square root of the sample size:

$$s_{\bar{x}} = \frac{s}{\sqrt{n}} = \sqrt{s^2 \frac{1}{n}}.$$

This also is equivalent to the square root of the variance times the inverse of the sample size ($1/n$).

Unfortunately, we cannot use this formula for the standard error of the mean. It is the standard error for a single sample. Because we have two samples in an independent groups test, the formula has to be altered a bit.

The first difference is in the formula for the variance. The variance is the sum of squares divided by the degrees of freedom. It is the same here except that we have two sums of squares (one for Group 1 and one for Group 2) and our degrees of freedom are $n_1 + n_2 - 2$. This gives us the following equation:

$$s_p^2 = \frac{SS_1 + SS_2}{n_1 + n_2 - 2},$$

where

s_p^2 is the pooled estimate of the variance based on two groups;
SS_1 is the sum of squares for Group 1;
SS_2 is the sum of squares for Group 2;
n_1 is the number of scores in Group 1; and
n_2 is the number of scores in Group 2.

Because there are two groups, we do not multiply s_p^2 times ($1/n$); rather, we multiply it by ($1/n_1 + 1/n_2$). We take the square root of this and obtain the pooled standard error of the mean:

$$s_{\bar{x}_1 - \bar{x}_2} = \sqrt{s_p^2 \left(\frac{1}{n_1} + \frac{1}{n_2} \right)}.$$

The means and sums of squares for our example are presented in Table 6.12. Now, let us try computing t_{obt}.

TABLE 6.12   Group Statistics

Group	Mean	Sum of Squares	n
After-school care	27.88	4330.40	16
Home care	21.36	1707.16	14

First, we compute the pooled standard error of the mean (also called the standard error of the mean difference). We begin by calculating the pooled variance:

$$S_p^2 = \frac{SS_1 + SS_2}{n_1 + n_2 - 2} = \frac{4330.40 + 1707.16}{16 + 14 - 2} = \frac{6037.56}{28} = 215.63.$$

From the estimate for the pooled variance, we may calculate the standard error of the mean difference:

$$s_{\bar{x}_1 - \bar{x}_2} = \sqrt{S_p^2 \left(\frac{1}{n_1} + \frac{1}{n_2}\right)} = \sqrt{215.63 \left(\frac{1}{16} + \frac{1}{14}\right)} = \sqrt{28.88} = 5.37.$$

We calculate t_{obt}:

$$t_{obt} = \frac{27.88 - 21.36}{5.37} = \frac{6.52}{5.37} = 1.213.$$

For $\alpha = .05$ and $df = n_1 + n_2 - 2 = 16 + 14 - 2 = 28$, $t_{crit} = 2.048$. Because $|t_{obt}| = 1.213$ is less than the critical value, we fail to reject the null hypothesis at $\alpha = .05$.

There are two post hoc effect size measures for an independent t test. The first of these (d) already has been discussed:

$$d = \frac{\overline{X}_1 - \overline{X}_2}{s_p}.$$

Note that the numerator is the difference between the two sample means and that the denominator is the pooled estimate of the standard deviation. The pooled standard deviation is the square root of the pooled variance that we calculated earlier:

$$s_p = \sqrt{s_p^2} = \sqrt{215.63} = 14.68.$$

The effect size for the example would be

$$d = \frac{27.88 - 21.36}{14.68} = \frac{6.52}{14.68} = 0.44,$$

which would be classified as a small to medium effect size.

The other measure is η^2 (eta-square). η^2 is the proportion of variance explained (*PVE*). This is equivalent to the squared point-biserial correlation coefficient and is computed by

$$\eta^2 = \frac{t_{\text{obt}}^2}{t_{\text{obt}}^2 + df}.$$

We were comparing social activity in children in after-school care versus those in home care. Children in after-school care scored higher on social activity than did children in home care. The difference was not statistically significant for our chosen $\alpha =$ .05.

t_{obt} was 1.213 with $df = 28$. Putting these numbers in the formula, we obtain the following:

$$\eta^2 = \frac{(1.213)^2}{(1.213)^2 + 28} = \frac{1.471}{29.471} = 0.0499.$$

So, a little less than 5% of the variability in social activity among the children was potentially explained by whether they were in after-school care or home care.

The Wilcoxon/Mann-Whitney test. Statistics texts used to refer to this test as the Mann-Whitney test. Recently, the name of Wilcoxon has been added to it. The reason that Wilcoxon's name has been added is that he developed the test first and published it first (Wilcoxon, 1945). Unfortunately, more folks noticed the article published by Mann and Whitney (1947) 2 years later.

The W/M-W test is a nonparametric test that involves initially treating both samples as one group and ranking scores from least to most. After this is done, the frequencies of low and high ranks between groups are compared.

The assumptions of the W/M-W test are as follows:

Randomness: Sample members must be randomly drawn from the population of interest and randomly assigned to one of the two groups.
Independence: Scores must be independent of each other.
Scaling: The dependent measure must be ordinal (interval or ratio scores must be converted to ranks).

When the assumptions of the *t* test are met, the *t* test will be slightly more powerful than the W/M-W test. However, if the distribution of population scores is even slightly different from normal, then the W/M-W test may be the more powerful test.

Let us look at the procedure for computing the W/M-W test statistic. We use the same example as we did for the independent *t* test. We evaluated level of social activity in children in after-school care and in home care. The dependent measure was a

TABLE 6.13 Summed Ranks for the Wilcoxon/Mann-Whitney Test

	After-School Care	Home Care
	$n_1 = 16$	$n_2 = 14$
Summed Ranks	$W_1 = 218$	$W_2 = 247$

score on a social activity scale in which lower scores represent less social activity and higher scores represent more social activity.

The first step in carrying out the W/M-W test is to assign ranks to the scores without respect to which group individuals were in. The rank of 1 goes to the highest score, the rank of 2 to the next highest score, and so on. Tied ranks receive the average rank. We then sum the ranks within each group. The summed ranks are called W_1 for Group 1 and W_2 for Group 2 and are found in Table 6.13.

The test statistic for the W/M-W test is U_{obt}. We begin by calculating U statistics for each according to the following equations:

$$U_1 = n_1 n_2 + \frac{n_1(n_1 + 1)}{2} - W_1$$

$$U_2 = n_1 n_2 + \frac{n_2(n_2 + 1)}{2} - W_2$$

$$U_1 = n_1 n_2 + \frac{n_1(n_1 + 1)}{2} - W_1 = (16)(14) + \frac{(16)(16 - 1)}{2} - 218 = 126$$

$$U_2 = n_1 n_2 + \frac{n_2(n_2 + 1)}{2} - W_2 = (16)(14) + \frac{(14)(14 - 1)}{2} - 247 = 224 + \frac{182}{2} - 247 = 224 + 91 - 247 = 68.$$

We choose the smaller U as U_{obt}. In this instance, $U_{obt} = U_2 = 68$.

U_{obt} must be *less than or equal to* the critical value to reject the null hypothesis. The critical value for the W/M-W U at $n_1 = 16$ and at $n_2 = 14$, and $\alpha = .05$ is $U_{crit} = 64$. $U_{obt} = 142$ is *not* less than or equal to the critical value, so we fail to reject the null hypothesis at $\alpha = .05$.

As before, there is no well-established effect size measure for the W/M-W test. The U measure of nonoverlap probably would be the best bet.

For our example data, the minimum and maximum for the after-school care group were 2 and 55, whereas they were 7 and 40 for the home care group. The greatest minimum is 7, and the least maximum is 40. All 14 scores in the home care group are within the overlap range, and 12 of 14 scores in the after-school care group are in the overlap range. This gives us a proportion of overlap of $26/30 = .867$. The proportion of nonoverlap is $U = 1 - .867 = .133$. This would be a small effect.

The χ^2 test of independence (2 × k). The assumptions for the χ^2 test of independence are as follows:

Randomness: Sample members must be randomly drawn from the population.

Independence: Sample scores must be independent of each other. One implication of this is that categories must be mutually exclusive (no case may appear in more than one category).

Scaling: The dependent measure (categories) must be nominal.

Expected frequencies: No expected frequency within a category should be less than 1, and no more than 20% of the expected frequencies should be less than 5.

As with all tests of the null hypothesis, the χ^2 test begins with the assumptions of randomness and independence. Deriving from these assumptions is the requirement that the categories in the cross-tabulation be *mutually exclusive* and *exhaustive*.

Mutually exclusive means that an individual may not be in more than one category per variable. *Exhaustive* means that all possible categories are covered.

Let us imagine that we are interested in marijuana use among high school students and specifically whether there are any differences in such use between 9th- and 12th-graders in our school district. We conduct a proportionate stratified sample in which we randomly sample 65 9th-graders and 55 12th-graders from all students in the district. The students are surveyed on their use of drugs over the past year under conditions guaranteeing confidentiality of response. Table 6.14 depicts reported marijuana use for the students in the sample over the past year.

A higher proportion of 12th-graders than 9th-graders in this sample used marijuana at least once during the past year. The question we are interested in is whether it is likely that such a sample could have come from a population in which the proportions of 9th- and 12th-graders using marijuana were identical.

TABLE 6.14   Marijuana Use

	Grade		
	9th	12th	Total
None	42	33	75
Marijuana	23	22	45
Total	65	55	120

The usual test used to evaluate such data is the χ^2 test of independence. The χ^2 test evaluates the likelihood that a perceived relationship between proportions in categories (called being dependent) could have come from a population in which no such relationship existed (called independence).

The null hypothesis for this example would be that the same proportion of 9th-graders as 12th-graders used marijuana during the past year. The null hypothesis values for this test are called the expected frequencies. These expected frequencies for marijuana are calculated so as to be proportionately equal for both 9th- and 12th-graders.

Because 45 out of 120 of the total sample (9th- and 12th-graders) used marijuana during the past year, the proportion for the total sample is 45/120 = .375. The expected frequency of marijuana use for the 65 9th-graders would be $.375(65) = 24.375$. The expected marijuana use for the 55 12th-graders would be $.375(55) = 20.625$. Table 6.15 shows the expected frequencies in parentheses.

The χ^2 test evaluates the likelihood of the observed frequency departing from the expected frequency. The null hypothesis is

$$H_0: P_{0k} - P_{1k} = 0,$$

where P_{0k} is the proportion of cases within category k in the null hypothesis population (expected) (in this case, this is the expected proportion of students in each of the two grade levels [9th and 12th] who fell into one or the other use category [marijuana use or no marijuana use]); and P_{1k} is the proportion of cases within category k drawn from the actual population (observed) (in this case, this is the observed [or obtained] proportion of students in each of the two grade levels (9th and 12th) who fell into one or the other use category [marijuana use or no marijuana use]).

TABLE 6.15   Observed and Expected Frequencies for Marijuana Use

	Grade		
	9th	12th	Total
None	42	33	75
	(40.625)	(34.375)	
Marijuana	23	22	45
	(24.375)	(20.675)	
Total	65	55	120

NOTE: Expected frequencies are in parentheses.

The χ^2_{obt} test statistic is

$$\chi^2_{obt} = \sum \frac{(f_O - f_E)^2}{f_E}.$$

Degrees of freedom for a χ^2 test of independence are computed by multiplying the number of rows minus 1 times the number of columns minus 1 or

$$df = (\text{Rows} - 1)(\text{Columns} - 1).$$

For our example, this would be

$$df = (2 - 1)(2 - 1) = (1)(1) = 1.$$

Recall from our discussion of the McNemar change test that we include the Yates correction for continuity in the formula for χ^2_{obt} when $df = 1$. The equation for the corrected χ^2_{obt} test statistic is as follows:

$$\chi^2_{obt} = \sum \frac{(|f_O - f_E| - 0.5)^2}{f_E}.$$

The form of the equation tells us to subtract the expected score from the observed score and take the absolute value of the difference (make the difference positive). Then, subtract 0.5 from the absolute difference ($|f_O - f_E| - 0.5$) and square the result. Next, divide by the expected score. This is repeated for each observed and expected score pair. When we are finished, we sum the answers and obtain the corrected χ^2_{obt} test statistic.

The reader might have noticed that the correction for the McNemar change test was 1.0, whereas the correction for the χ^2 test of independence (and the goodness of fit test) was 0.5. I will not go into any detail beyond saying that this is because the McNemar change test uses only half of the available cross-tabulation cells (two of four) to compute its χ^2_{obt}, whereas all cells are used to compute χ^2_{obt} in the independence and goodness of fit tests.

Table 6.16 shows how to work out the marijuana survey data.

TABLE 6.16 Computation of χ^2_{obt}

Observed (f_O)	Expected (f_E)	$\|f_o - f_E\| - 0.5$	$(\|f_o - f_E\| - 0.5)^2$	$\dfrac{(\|f_o - f_E\| - 0.5)^2}{f_E}$
42	40.625	.875	0.765625	0.019
33	34.375	.875	0.765625	0.022
23	24.375	.875	0.765625	0.031
22	20.625	.875	0.765625	0.037

NOTE: $\chi^2_{obt} = 0.019 + 0.022 + 0.031 + 0.037 = 0.109$.

For $df = 1$ and $\alpha = .05$, the critical value for χ^2 is 3.84. Our calculated value (χ^2_{obt}) was 0.109. Because the obtained (calculated) value did not exceed the critical value, we would not reject the null hypothesis at $\alpha = .05$.

As before, the effect size measure is w, which is computed as a post hoc measure by

$$w = \sqrt{(\chi^2 / N)}.$$

For a 2×2 table, w is equal to the absolute value of ϕ (phi), which is a true correlation coefficient. If we square w, then we obtain ϕ^2, which is the proportion of variance explained (*PVE*).

For our example,

$$w = \sqrt{(0.109/120)} = \sqrt{0.0009083} = 0.0301$$

and

$$w^2 = PVE = .0009.$$

This is an extremely small effect size.

For $2 \times k$ tabulation, we cannot convert w to PVE.

Hypothesis Tests for k > 2 Independent Samples

Imagine that we were interested in ageist attitudes among social workers. Specifically, we are interested in whether there are any differences in the magnitudes of ageist attitudes among (a) hospital social workers, (b) nursing home social workers, and (c) adult protective services social workers.

We could conduct independent group tests among all possible pairings: hospital (a) with nursing home (b), hospital (a) with protective services (c), and nursing home (b) with protective services (c).

This gives us three tests. When we conduct one test at the $\alpha = .05$ level, we have a .05 chance of committing a Type I error (rejecting the null hypothesis when it is true) and a .95 chance of making a correct decision (not rejecting the null hypothesis when it is true). If we conduct three tests at $\alpha = .05$, our chance of committing *at least one* Type I error increases to about .15 (the precise probability is .142625). So, we actually are testing at around $\alpha = .15$.

As the number of comparisons increases, the likelihood of rejecting the null hypothesis when it is true increases. We are "capitalizing on chance."

One way of dealing with capitalization on chance would be to use a stricter alpha level. For three comparisons, we might conduct our tests at $\alpha = .05/3 = .0167$. Unfortunately, if we do this, then we will reduce the power $(1 - \beta)$ of our test to detect a possible existing effect.

However, there are tests that allow one to detect whether there are any differences among groups without compromising power. This is done by simultaneously evaluating all groups for any differences. If no differences are detected, then we fail to reject the null hypothesis and stop. No further tests are conducted because we already have our answer. The differences among all groups are not sufficiently large that we can reject the notion that all of the samples come from the same population.

If significant differences are detected, then further pair comparisons are conducted to determine which pairs are different. The screening tests do not tell us whether only one pair, two pairs, or all pairs show statistically significant differences. Screening tests show only that there are some differences among all possible comparisons.

If we conduct our screening test at $\alpha = .05$, then we will carry out the pair comparisons when the null hypothesis is true 1 out of 20 times (commit a Type I error). By conducting the initial overall screening in a single test, we protect against the compounding of the alpha level brought on by multiple comparisons.

We look at three examples of screening tests for $k > 2$ independent samples:

One-way analysis of variance (ANOVA) (interval or ratio scale);
Kruskal-Wallis (K-W) test (ordinal scale); and
χ^2 test of independence ($k \times k$) (nominal scale).

One-way analysis of variance. The ANOVA is a test of means. The null hypothesis is

$$H_0: \mu_1 = \mu_2 = \ldots = \mu_k,$$

where k is the number of population means being estimated.

If all of the means are equal, then it follows that the variance of the means is zero or

$$H_0: \sigma_\mu^2 = 0.$$

The test statistic used in ANOVA is called F and is calculated as follows:

$$F_{\text{obt}} = \frac{ns_{\bar{x}}^2}{s^2},$$

where the numerator is the variance of the sample means multiplied by the sample size and the denominator is a pooled estimate of the score variances within the samples.

The assumptions underlying one-way ANOVA are as follows:

Randomness: Sample members must be randomly drawn from the population and randomly assigned to one of the k groups.
Independence: Scores must be independent of each other.
Scaling: The dependent measure must be interval or ratio.
Normal distribution: The populations from which the individuals in the samples were drawn must be normally distributed.
Homogeneity of variances ($\sigma_1^2 = \sigma_2^2 = \ldots = \sigma_k^2$): The samples must be drawn from populations whose variances are equal.
Equality of sample sizes ($n_1 = n_2 = \ldots = n_k$): The samples must be of the same size.

ANOVA involves taking the variability among scores and determining which is variability due to membership in a particular group (variability associated with group means or between-group variance) and which is variability associated with unexplained fluctuations (within-group variance).

The total variability of scores is divided into one component representing the variability of treatment group means around an overall mean (sometimes called a grand mean) and another component representing the variability of group scores around their own individual group means. The variability of group means around the grand mean is called between-group variance. The variability of individual scores around their own group means is called within-group variance. This division is represented by the following equation:

$$(X - \overline{\overline{X}}) = (X - \overline{X}) + (\overline{X} - \overline{\overline{X}}).$$

Total   Within   Between

The X with two bars represents the grand mean, which is the mean of all scores without respect to which group they are in. X is a particular score, and the X with one bar is the mean of the group to which that score belongs.

This equation illustrates that the deviation of the particular score from the grand mean is the sum of the deviation of the score from its group mean and the deviation of the group mean from the grand mean. This might be a little clearer if we look at a simple data set. Let us take the example about ageist attitudes among hospital social workers (Group 1), nursing home social workers (Group 2), and adult protective services social workers (Group 3). The dependent measure quantifies ageist attitudes (higher scores represent more ageist sentiment).

There are $k = 3$ groups, with each containing $n = 4$ scores. The total number of scores is $N = 12$. The group means are 3 (Group 1), 5 (Group 2), and 9 (Group 3), and the grand mean is 5.67.

There are three types of sum of squares calculated in ANOVA. The formulas for the sums of squares are derived from the deviation score equations.

SS_{total} is calculated by subtracting the grand mean from each score, squaring the differences, and adding up (summing) the squared differences:

$$SS_{total} = \Sigma(X - \overline{\overline{X}})^2 .$$

SS_{within} is calculated by subtracting the group mean from each score within a group, squaring the differences, and adding up (summing) the squared differences for each group. This gives us three sums of squares: $SS_{Group\ 1}$, $SS_{Group\ 2}$, and $SS_{Group\ 3}$. These are added up to give us SS_{within}:

$$SS_{within} = \Sigma(X - \overline{X}_1)^2 + \Sigma(X - \overline{X}_2)^2 + \Sigma(X - \overline{X}_3)^2.$$

$SS_{between}$ is calculated by subtracting the grand mean from each group mean, squaring the differences, and adding up (summing) the squared differences. Then, we multiply the total by the sample size. This is because this sum of squares needs to be weighted. Whereas $N = 12$ scores went to make up SS_{total}, and $(k)(n) = (3)(4) = 12$ scores went to make up SS_{within}, only the $k = 3$ group means went to make up $SS_{between}$. We multiply by $n = 4$ so that $SS_{between}$ will have the same weight as the other two sums of squares:

$$SS_{between} = n \, \Sigma(\overline{X} - \overline{\overline{X}})^2 .$$

The sums of squares are as follows:

$$SS_{within} = 20 + 20 + 20 = 60$$

$$SS_{between} = (4)18.667 = 74.667$$

$$SS_{total} = 134.667.$$

The total sum of squares (SS_{total}) is the sum of the within-group sum of squares (SS_{within}) and the between-group sum of squares ($SS_{between}$):

$$SS_{total} = SS_{within} + SS_{between}$$

or

$$134.667 = 60.00 + 74.667.$$

Each of these sums of squares is a component of a different variance. In ANOVA jargon, a variance is called a mean square. Each particular mean square (variance) has its own degrees of freedom.

Because the *total* sum of squares (SS_{total}) involves the variability of all scores around one grand mean, the degrees of freedom are $N - 1$. The within-groups sum of squares (SS_{within}) involves the variability of all scores within groups around k group means, where k is the number of groups. So, the within-groups degrees of freedom are $N - k$. The between-groups sum of squares ($SS_{between}$) involves the variability of k group means around the grand mean. So, the between-groups degrees of freedom are $k - 1$.

Because a variance (mean square) is a sum of squares divided by degrees of freedom, the formula for a mean square would be $MS = SS/df$.

Two mean squares are used to calculate the F_{obt} statistic: MS_{within} and $MS_{between}$. Their specific formulas are as follows:

$$MS_{between} = n s_{\overline{x}}^2 = \frac{SS_{between}}{k - 1} .$$

There are $k = 3$ groups, so $df_{between} = k - 1 = 3 - 1 = 2$. We may now compute

$$MS_{between} = 74.667 / 2 = 37.333 \text{ and}$$

$$MS_{within} = s^2 = \frac{SS_{within}}{N-k}.$$

There are a total of $N = 12$ scores within $k = 3$, so $df_{within} = 12 - 3 = 9$ and $MS_{within} = 60/9 = 6.667$.

These are the two variances used to make up the F ratio (F_{obt}): $MS_{between}$ and MS_{within}. The formula for F_{obt} is

$$F_{obt} = \frac{MS_{between}}{MS_{within}}.$$

If we plug in the values from our example, then we obtain

$$F_{obt} = \frac{MS_{between}}{MS_{within}} = \frac{37.333}{6.667} = 5.65.$$

This is a bit confusing when presented in bits and pieces. The ANOVA summary table is a way of presenting the information about the sums of squares, degrees of freedom, mean squares, and F statistics in a more easily understood fashion. Table 6.17 uses the example data.

TABLE 6.17   ANOVA Summary Table

Source	Sum of Squares	Degrees of Freedom	Mean Square	F_{obt}
Between	74.667	$3 - 1 = 2$	$74.67/2 = 37.333$	$37.333/6.667 = 5.65$
Within	60.00	$12 - 3 = 9$	$60.00/9 = 6.667$	
Total	134.667	$12 - 1 = 11$		

Once we have computed the F_{obt}, it is compared to a critical F. Because two variances were used to calculate our F_{obt}, there are two types of degrees of freedom associated with it: numerator degrees of freedom (between groups) and denominator degrees of freedom (within groups). These are used either to look up values in a table of the F distribution or by computer programs to compute p values.

For our example, the numerator degrees of freedom are $df = 2$ because 2 degrees of freedom were used in the calculation of $MS_{between}$. The denominator degrees of freedom are $df = 9$ because 9 degrees of freedom were used in the calculation of MS_{within}. The critical value for F at 2 and 9 degrees of freedom is $F_{crit} = 4.26$. Because $F_{obt} = 5.6$ is greater than the critical value, we reject the null hypothesis at $\alpha = .05$.

Based on these findings, it is likely that at least one pair of means come from different populations. Because we already have screened out other opportunities to commit Type I error, further testing would not be capitalizing on chance. Thus, we may carry out the following pair comparisons:

Group 1 versus Group 2;
Group 1 versus Group 3; and
Group 2 versus Group 3.

The individual pair comparisons may be carried out using any of a number of multiple comparison tests. One of the more frequently used is the least significant difference (LSD) test. The LSD test is a variant on the t test. However, the standard error of the mean is calculated from the within-groups mean square (variance) from the ANOVA:

$$s_{\bar{x}_i - \bar{x}_j} = \sqrt{MS_{within}\left(\frac{1}{n_i} + \frac{1}{n_{j,}}\right)},$$

where
n_i is the number of scores in Group i; and
n_j is the number of scores in Group j.

If the group n's are equal, then this becomes

$$s_{\bar{x}_i - \bar{x}_j} = \sqrt{(2\,MS_{within}\,/\,n)}\,.$$

For our example,

$$s_{\bar{x}_i - \bar{x}_j} = \sqrt{(2)(6.667)\,/\,4} = \sqrt{3.333} = 0.577.$$

We now may carry out our comparisons evaluating t at $df = N - k = 12 - 3 = 9$ (Figure 6.6).

In all three instances, we reject the null hypothesis at $\alpha = .05$.

There are a number of measures for effect size for ANOVA. For the sake of simplicity, we deal with two: Cohen's (1988) f and η^2.

The f effect size measure is equal to the standard deviation of the sample means divided by the pooled within-group standard deviation. It ranges from a minimum of zero to an indefinitely large upper limit. It may be estimated from F_{obt} by using the following formula:

$$f = \sqrt{nF_{obt}}\,.$$

Hospital (Group 1) vs. Nursing Home (Group 2)	$t_{obt} = \dfrac{3-5}{0.577} = -3.466$	$df = 9, \alpha = .05$ $t_{crit} = 2.262$ Reject H_0
Hospital (Group 1) vs. Adult Protective Services (Group 3)	$t_{obt} = \dfrac{3-9}{0.577} = -10.399$	$df = 9, \alpha = .05$ $t_{crit} = 2.262$ Reject H_0
Nursing Home (Group 2) vs. Adult Protective Services (Group 3)	$t_{obt} = \dfrac{5-9}{0.577} = -6.932$	$df = 9, \alpha = .05$ $t_{crit} = 2.262$ Reject H_0

Figure 6.6. Multiple Comparisons

η^2 earlier was discussed and defined as a proportion of variance explained. It is calculated by the following formula:

$$\eta^2 = \frac{SS_{between}}{SS_{total}}.$$

It also may be calculated from an F_{obt}:

$$\eta^2 = \frac{df_{between} \, F_{obt}}{df_{between} \, F_{obt} + df_{within}}.$$

Cohen (1988) categorizes these effect sizes into small, medium, and large categories. The criteria for each are as follows:

Small effect size: f = .10 $\eta^2 = .01$;
Medium effect size: f = .25 $\eta^2 = .06$; and
Large effect size: f = .40 $\eta^2 = .14$.

Using the example data, η^2 is

$$\eta^2 = \frac{SS_{between}}{SS_{total}} = \frac{74.667}{134.667} = 0.554,$$

which is a very large effect.

The Kruskal-Wallis test. The K-W test is the $k > 2$ groups equivalent of the W/M-W test. The test involves initially treating all samples as one group and ranking scores from least to most. After this is done, the frequencies of low and high ranks among groups are compared.

The assumptions of the K-W test are as follows:

Randomness: Sample members must be randomly drawn from the population of interest and randomly assigned to one of the k groups.
Independence: Scores must be independent of each other.
Scaling: The dependent measure must be ordinal (interval or ratio scores must be converted to ranks).

When the assumptions of ANOVA are met, the analysis of variance will be slightly more powerful than the K-W test. However, if the distribution of population scores is not normal and/or the population variances are not equal, then the K-W test might be the more powerful test.

The K-W test is a screening test. If there is no significant difference found, then we stop testing. If a significant difference is found, then we proceed to test individual pairs with the W/M-W test.

Our example involves the evaluation of three intervention techniques being used with clients who wish to stop making negative self-statements: (a) self-disputation, (b) thought stopping, and (c) identifying the source of the negative statement (insight). A total of 27 clients with this concern were randomly selected and assigned to one of the three intervention conditions. On the 28th day of the intervention, each client counted the number of negative self-statements that he or she had made.

The procedure for the K-W test is similar to that for the W/M-W test. We begin by assigning ranks to the scores without regard to which group individuals were in. We then sum the ranks within each group. The summed ranks are called W_1 for Group 1, W_2 for Group 2, and W_3 for Group 3 (Table 6.18).

TABLE 6.18   Summed Ranks for the Kruskal-Wallis Test

Group 1	Group 2	Group 3
Summed Rank$_1$ = W_1 = 89	Summed Rank$_2$ = W_2 = 122.5	Summed Rank$_3$ = W_3 = 166.5

The test statistic for the K-W test is H_{obt}, which is approximately distributed as χ^2 with $df = k - 1$. It is calculated according to the following equation:

$$H_{obt} = \frac{12}{N(N+1)} \cdot \Sigma \frac{(W_k)^2}{n_k} - 3(N+1),$$

where
  W_k is the sum of ranks for Group k;

n_k is the number of individuals in Group k; and
N is the total number of individuals in all groups.

From our example, we obtain the following:

$$H_{obt} = \frac{12}{27(27+1)} \bullet \frac{(89)^2}{9} + \frac{(122.5)^2}{9} + \frac{(166.5)^2}{9} - 3(27+1)$$

$$= \frac{12}{27(28)} \bullet \frac{7921+15006.25+27722.25}{9} - 3(28)$$

$$= \frac{12}{756} \bullet \frac{50649.5}{9} - 84 = (0.0159 \bullet 5627.7222) - 84 = 89.3289 - 84$$

$$= 5.3289.$$

This is the test statistic if there are no tied scores. However, if there are tied scores, then the K-W test statistic has a correction for ties, which is as follows:

$$C = 1 - \frac{\sum(t^3 - t)}{N^3 - N}.$$

The letter t refers to the number of tied scores for a particular tied group of numbers. In our example, the score of 4 occurred twice, so $t = 2$ for this group. The score of 5 occurred three times, so $t = 3$ for this group. There were seven groups for which $t = 2$ and two groups for which $t = 3$.

The correction is calculated as follows:

$$C = 1 - \frac{(2^3-2)+(2^3-2)+(2^3-2)+(2^3-2)+(2^3-2)+(2^3-2)+(2^3-2)+(3^3-3)+(3^3-3)}{27^3-27}$$

$$= 1 - \frac{(8-2)+(8-2)+(8-2)+(8-2)+(8-2)+(8-2)+(8-2)+(9-3)+(9-3)}{19,683-27}$$

$$= 1 - \frac{6+6+6+6+6+6+6+6+6+}{19,656} = \frac{54}{19,656} = 1 - 0.0027$$

$$= 0.9973.$$

We divide H_{obt} by the correction factor (C) to obtain the corrected test statistic H':

$$H' = \frac{H_{obt}}{C} = \frac{5.3289}{0.9973} = 5.3434.$$

H'_{obt} is approximately distributed as χ^2 with $k - 1$ degrees of freedom. The critical value for χ^2 at $df = 2$ and $\alpha = .05$ is $\chi^2_{crit} = 5.99$ (see a table of critical values of χ^2 found in most statistics texts). $H'_{obt} = 5.34$ is *not* greater than or equal to the critical value, so we fail to reject the null hypothesis at $\alpha = .05$.

TABLE 6.19   Reported Frequencies of Marijuana Use

| | Grade | | | |
	10th	11th	12th	Total
None	30	28	33	91
Marijuana	30	37	22	89
Total	60	65	55	180

Based on these results, we would *not* carry out multiple pair comparisons. Because the K-W test did not find any significant differences among the three groups, retesting the same null hypothesis by a series of pair comparisons would not be justified.

The χ^2 test of independence $(k \times k)$. The test statistic is the same for a $k \times k \, \chi^2$ test of independence as for a $2 \times k$ test. The assumptions are as follows:

Randomness: Sample members must be randomly drawn from the population.
Independence: Sample scores must be independent of each other. One implication of this is that categories must be mutually exclusive (no case may appear in more than one category).
Scaling: The dependent measure (category) must be nominal.
Expected frequencies: No expected frequency within a category should be less than 1, and no more than 20% of the expected frequencies should be less than 5.

Let us imagine that we still are interested in marijuana use among high school students. We are interested in the marijuana use differences (if any) among 10th-, 11th-, and 12th-graders in our school district. A proportionate stratified random sample was drawn of 60 10th-graders, 65 11th-graders, and 55 12th-graders from all students in the district. The students were surveyed on their use of drugs over the past year under conditions guaranteeing confidentiality of response. Table 6.19 shows reported marijuana use for the sampled students.

The null hypothesis for this example would be that the same proportions of 10th-, 11th-, and 12th-graders used marijuana during the past year. The null hypothesis values for this test are the expected frequencies. These expected frequencies are calculated in the same way as for a $2 \times k \, \chi^2$.

Table 6.20 shows the cross-tabulation with the expected frequencies.
Table 6.21 shows the procedure for calculating χ^2_{obt}.

TABLE 6.20   Observed and Expected Frequencies for Marijuana Use

	Grade			
	10th	11th	12th	Total
None	30	28	33	91
	(30.33)	(32.86)	(27.81)	
Marijuana	30	37	22	89
	(29.67)	(32.14)	(27.19)	
Total	60	65	55	180

NOTE: Expected frequencies are in parentheses.

TABLE 6.21   Computation of χ^2_{obt}

Observed (f_O)	Expected (f_E)	$f_O - f_E$	$(f_O - f_E)^2$	$\dfrac{(f_O - f_E)^2}{f_E}$
30	30.33	−0.33	0.1089	0.00359050
28	32.86	−4.86	23.6196	0.71879489
33	27.81	+5.19	26.9361	0.96857605
30	29.67	−0.33	0.1089	0.00367037
37	32.14	+4.86	23.6196	0.73489732
22	27.19	−5.19	26.9361	0.99066201

NOTE: χ^2_{obt} = 0.00359050 + 0.71879489 + 0.96857605 + 0.00367037 + 0.73489732 + 0.99066201 = 3.42019114.

For $df = 2$ and $\alpha = .05$, the critical value for χ^2 is 5.99 (see a table of critical values of χ^2 found in most statistics texts). Our calculated value (χ^2_{obt}) was 3.420. Because the obtained (calculated) value did *not* exceed the critical value, we would *not* reject the null hypothesis at $\alpha = .05$. Because the screening test results were not statistically significant at $\alpha = .05$, we do not carry out the pair comparisons (10th with 11th grades, 10th with 12th grades, and 11th with 12th grades).

CONCLUSION

This chapter has discussed some of the more frequently used statistical hypothesis tests and their associated measures of effect size. Of course, there are many other important statistical hypothesis tests that were not discussed. These include tests of correlation coefficients, multiple regression analysis, and factorial and block design ANOVAs, among many others. The reader who wishes to learn more should consult one of the recommended further readings at the end of the chapter.

Similarly, the discussion of statistical power in this chapter was necessarily limited due to space constraints. I strongly urge the reader to become more deeply acquainted with power analysis.

Finally, the reader should recognize that statistical hypothesis tests provide evidence only for relationships between independent and dependent variables. They do not provide evidence that such relationships are functional ones. This is the more difficult task of accounting for or controlling extraneous variables that is discussed in other chapters of this handbook.

NOTES

1. A sample is a subgroup from a population.
2. A population is all that there is of a particular thing.
3. A variable is a characteristic that may assume more than one value. It varies. Some examples of variables include number of people living in a household, score on the Index of Family Relations, length of time engaged in cooperative play, and self-rating of anxiety.

REFERENCES

Cohen, J. (1988). *Statistical power analysis for the behavioral sciences* (2nd ed.). Hillsdale, NJ: Lawrence Erlbaum.

Mann, H. B., & Whitney, D. R. (1947). On a test of whether one of two random variables is stochastically larger than the other. *Annals of Mathematical Statistics, 18,* 50-60.

Wilcoxon, F. (1945). Individual comparisons by ranking methods. *Biometrics, 1,* 80-83.

RECOMMENDED READINGS

Cohen, J., & Cohen, P. (1983). *Applied multiple regression/correlation analysis for the behavioral sciences* (2nd ed.). Hillsdale, NJ: Lawrence Erlbaum.

Siegel, S., & Castellan, N. J. (1988). *Nonparametric statistics for the behavioral sciences* (2nd ed.). New York: McGraw-Hill.

Stevens, J. (1986). *Applied multivariate statistics for the social sciences.* Hillsdale, NJ: Lawrence Erlbaum.

C H A P T E R   S E V E N

Descriptive Studies

B A R B A R A   T H O M L I S O N

Descriptive research studies generate information that is situated at the midpoint of the knowledge spectrum between exploratory and explanatory designs. Perhaps more than any other research method, social work researchers and practitioners rely on descriptive studies to provide a wealth of information about people, their circumstances, and their environments. The social worker is likely to participate in and consume the results of descriptive studies if he or she is interested in improving practice, policy, and program services.

WHAT ARE DESCRIPTIVE STUDIES?

Descriptive studies intend to describe or explain relationships among phenomena, situations, and events as they occur. The major purpose of descriptive research is to provide an overall "picture" of a population or phenomenon by describing situations or events (Rubin & Babbie, 1997). Although the level of knowledge generated from descriptive studies is less than ideal, it provides data that identifies variables, describes relationships, and contributes to increasing our understanding of the question being asked. The impacts of a phenomenon or an intervention are not studied. Therefore, descriptive studies do not explain or confirm the relationship between the inde-

131

pendent and dependent variables. The primary task is aimed at describing a social phenomenon when it is relatively new or simply needs to be described. Research questions that describe the extent of a specific problem, the number of referrals to a service, or the characteristics and problems of a group are best suited for descriptive research designs.

Descriptive studies may be designed as a qualitative strategy such as ethnographic approaches in which examination of cases, records, other materials, or participants' experiences provides a description of a phenomenon through interpretive methods. Identifying themes and patterns using words can produce rich interpretations of the phenomenon. If the intention is to generalize to other populations, then quantitative strategies, using numbers to provide descriptions of the qualities of participants being served in a program, are more useful. Survey research that describes characteristics of a group (e.g., the number of children living below the poverty line) is useful for improving or developing services. Both approaches can lead to a description of the needs of consumers and practice activities and can initiate a change in services or facilitate further research.

Descriptive research can be designed to answer questions by describing one variable, comparing the variable to another standard, or summarizing a relationship between or among two or more variables (Bickman & Rog, 1998). Understanding what it is that needs to be studied assists in creating theories and hypotheses for future research such as explanatory studies.

FEATURES OF DESCRIPTIVE STUDIES

A review of descriptive studies or research entails the following elements: (a) type of research question, (b) literature review, (c) study rationale, (d) source of data, (e) time frame, (f) type of design, and (g) unit of analysis.

Descriptive Research Questions

Descriptive studies inquire about the *what* of a given phenomenon without attempting to explain *why* it happened. It is an attempt to find answers to the questions "What is happening?" and "What would the researcher like to know about clients, services, groups, communities, problems, or specific needs?" Therefore, research at the descriptive level has as its purpose the systematic description of the phenomenon and the factors that influence it (Palsy, 1992).

As an example, you might want to know about the characteristics and service needs of women who seek emergency shelter who have been physically abused by their partners (Tutty & Rothery, 1998), the perceptions of African American foster parents' satisfaction with fostering children (Denby & Rindfleisch, 1996), or the needs of family caregivers of terminally ill persons (Cheng et al., 1994). The questions for these descriptive designs emerged from the practice experiences of social workers who wanted to plan services for abused women, enhance the recruitment and training needs of African American foster parents, and understand the psychosocial needs of caregivers of terminally ill persons, respectively. Although a central line of inquiry was identified in each of these examples, the studies attempted to address several questions and describe in more detail, and identify and classify relationships among variables (persons, groups, situations, and problems), that were not well understood.

What Type of Question?

The purpose of the question is to refine and clarify the nature of the problem. Remember, this is not the same as developing a hypothesis. It will not state what is known or what can be expected. Marlow (1998, p. 35) identifies three types of questions for descriptive studies:

1. Questions used in needs assessments describing the extent of a problem

   Question: How often do the phenomena occur?
   Example: How many times do women seek emergency shelter before deciding to separate from an abusive relationship? (Tutty & Rothery, 1998)

   Question: When does it happen?
   Example: When do women who have been physically abused by their partners decide not to return to their partners? (Tutty & Rothery, 1998)

2. Questions used to evaluate practice

   Question: How long does it last?
   Example: How long do African American families provide foster care services? (Denby & Rindfleisch, 1996)

   Question: How pervasive is it?
   Example: What are the disciplinary styles of African Americans? (Denby & Alford, 1996)

   Question: How are important variables distributed throughout the population?
   Example: What are African Americans' foster parenting experiences? (Denby & Rindfleisch, 1996)

3. Questions used to evaluate services or programs

   Question: What are the basic characteristics?

Example: What are the psychosocial needs of family caregivers of terminally ill persons? (Cheng et al., 1994). What are the service needs of women in shelters who have been physically abused by their partners? (Tutty & Rothery, 1998)

Question: Who is involved?

Example: Are caregivers sufficiently supported by other helpers so that their own health does not deteriorate under continuous caregiving? (Cheng et al., 1994)

Generating the *what* question helps the researcher to begin to think about what the literature says about the problem area. Conducting a review of the literature will inform the researcher further and will refine the research question as he or she attempts to develop an understanding of a situation or an event.

Reviewing the Literature

The purpose of the literature review is to determine the quality of available information about the researcher's topic. What has been studied? What have other researchers said about the subject? What theories are used to describe the topic? What are the findings of research related to the topic including the strengths and limitations of previous studies? Two types of literature may be reviewed: the theoretical literature and the empirical literature.

Reviewing the theoretical literature may help to clarify several issues. It may help the researcher to understand the conceptual framework underlying the problem or topic. The theories or constructs inform the researcher about how the problem has been defined, and they provide a potential understanding of the behavior or problem for study. The literature includes the historical context of the problem and any debates. From this literature review, the researcher is in a better position to provide the rationale or arguments for the position taken in his or her proposed study.

Organizing the findings of empirical literature within a framework assists the researcher in understanding similarities and differences of prior research. It also facilitates classification, comparisons, and connections at this stage and will assist in the findings and discussion phase of the proposed study. "Reviewing the literature is not simply a recounting of what has been done in a long list of studies. It requires you to put them together in unique ways that reflect your critical thinking abilities and highlight the patterns that you have noticed across studies" (Szuchman & Thomlison, 2000, p. 45). For example, in summarizing the literature of the previous 15 years in the area of tribal child welfare, MacEachron (1994) concludes that some organizational information is available but that little is known about certain variables (e.g., ethnicity, training needs, job satisfaction) related to tribal child welfare personnel. Lindsey (1998) concludes that the literature on homeless families has not previously described factors related to the "process by which families are able to emerge from homelessness" (p. 160). Each example illustrates the researcher's critical thinking based on a review of the literature.

If prior research has been conducted on the variable, then examining the variable in another population, other than those already in the literature, might be of interest to the investigator. For example, Aguilar and Williams (1993) note, "Although a number of studies have examined variables that lead to women's achievement and success, the literature on minority women and success is sparse" (p. 410). These examples indicate that there is existing information about the area to be studied but that more is needed to fully understand the problem or topic.

A good literature review requires the researcher to assess, organize, and synthesize a wide range of retrieved information. It presents a state of the knowledge related to the topic of interest and gives direction to the design strategy.

Rationale for the Study

Strong rationales distinguish a quality descriptive study. Because descriptive studies frequently lack a conceptual framework and do not produce data leading to conclusive findings, the rationale and objectives for the study become critical. In the example by Cheng et al. (1994), the rationale for studying the needs of family caregivers indicates that "medical advances have meant that terminally ill persons may live longer and require more care. Measures of cost containment have shortened hospitalizations, shifting more of the burden to family caregivers" (p. 1243). In the Lindsey (1998) study, there was a gap in the literature on homeless families, and the objective was to look at service providers' perceptions of factors associated with families emerging from homelessness. Citing certain facts (e.g., the growing numbers of homeless children) established importance to the study and set the stage for discussing implications for policy or practice decisions.

Explaining how the research might promote the development of social work knowledge for practice and how the results might lead to further research is important as well. In the study of characteristics of tribal child welfare personnel, MacEachron (1994) provides the rationale for studying certain characteristics as critical information to guide decision making about recruitment and training programs "as well as [to] provide insight about the effect of cultural auspice on expectations for supervisory roles and job attitudes in child welfare organizations" (p. 118).

There may be a theoretical or conceptual framework underlying the study, as in the case of a known concept being studied with a new population. An example of this occurs in the Aguilar and Williams (1993) study to identify the variables that lead to women's success and achievement and to examine these variables in minority populations. Prior research is used to provide the rationale for systematically examining the variables in another population by the question, "How are the variables that were identified as important distributed in the minority population?" Perhaps the most important point about the rationale for the study is to appraise and synthesize the key literature pertaining to the problem area and, based on that literature, develop the rationale and question for the study. Without strong rationales, descriptive studies tend to appear immaterial, are unlikely to be funded by granting agencies, and are unlikely to be published once completed.

Data Sources

Although the type of research question distinguishes a descriptive design, the manner in which the data sources are selected also is notable. Often, it is not realistic to study the entire population, and a sample is selected. Random sampling is the best way in which to ensure that the study has a representative sample to adequately describe some situation or group with accuracy. This procedure for selecting the sample gives every element of the population an equal chance of being selected to the sample. A sample selected in this way tends to be representative of the population. It minimizes bias and other systemic factors that might make the sample different from the population from which it was drawn (Rubin & Babbie, 1997). Ensuring that the selection of participants is representative of the population and is free of bias relating to gender, race, and class also is important. Language and culture may be an unintentional source of making one group of participants different from another. In addition to obtaining a representative sample of the population through random selection, random assignment to two or more groups is done to improve reliability and validity of the study. Often, descriptive research designs lack random selection of the participants from a population, so the type of design chosen attempts to compensate for this in various ways by using comparison groups.

All sampling methods can be divided into two major categories: nonprobability samples (those that do not use random sampling) and probability samples (those that use random sampling in at least one part of the sampling plan). If the purpose of the study is to describe population characteristics, then probability sampling techniques are necessary to ensure external validity (i.e., generalizability). External validity refers to the extent to which the observations or characteristics of the participants or settings are valid and generalizable. Frequently, however, population parameters are not available and probability sampling cannot be used, thereby creating problems for external validity. Internal validity is less of an issue in descriptive designs because no attempt is made to examine causal relationships among variables (Rubin & Babbie, 1997). If the focus of the study is an in-depth description, then the design is improved by setting up some type of comparison group. For example, a study might wish to determine differences between males and females, among ethnic groups, or among income groups.

It is clear that randomness and representativeness are two important characteristics of samples. Another anticipated source of bias in the data can be in the measures or instruments used to collect data. Reliability of measures for descriptive studies varies by situation, purpose, and characteristics of a sample or population (Bickman & Rog, 1998).

The major methods of data collection or measuring instruments are observation, questionnaires, scales, use of secondary data (data already collected), interviews, logs, and journals. Interviews, questionnaires, and scales are the most frequently used forms of data collection in descriptive studies. Reliance on interviews and questionnaires where reliability has not been established may limit decision making. Use of measures with low reliability (e.g., unstructured interviews) leaves descriptive studies open to acquiescent response set, a form of bias in which people tend to agree with the interviewer. Bias also may result from social desirability responses when people tend to answer according to what they think are the socially correct answers rather than the actual answers. The use of reliable and valid measures allows the investigator to have some measure of control over the data insofar as questions are standardized and asked in a standardized order (Rubin & Babbie, 1997).

Studies may use a single in-depth method (e.g., interviewing, questionnaires), but combinations of semistructured and structured methods frequently are used. Survey designs using questionnaires or interview schedules to collect data from a sample or population are one of the most rigorous methods for conducting needs assessment. Use of structured questions (e.g., multiple-choice options, Likert scaling, ranking items) are good options for data collection procedures that have higher reliability. The use of repeated interviews over time on the same respondent also is a way in which to test the stability of informants' statements and, therefore, the reliability of data (Brink & Wood, 1995).

Whether questions are structured or semistructured, the purpose is to be as standardized as possible at this stage of research so as to analyze the answers to each individual question as a unit in and of itself using tests of association or correlation.

Time Frame

Descriptive studies can be designed to take observations at one point in time or over a period of time. Studies examining phenomena at one point in time by gathering information from a cross section of the population are cross-sectional studies. Studies in which observations and information are taken over a period of time are longitudinal studies. A census survey, for example, analyzes the population at one point in time by going to each household for descriptive information. Many characteristics of the population are observed (e.g., number of children, number of males and females, income level, race, age). This provides a one-time picture of the population and, thereby, contributes useful information for many aspects of planning and decision making. It does not help to explain what is learned from the study, only that the characteristics exist. When the census is repeated over time, more insights are obtained about the changing nature and characteristics of the population. Growth or decline of the population and other changes (e.g., shifts in specific minority population characteristics) may be noted.

Longitudinal information provides a better understanding of needs and can assist in projecting what these trends imply for planning and decision making. It will not explain causal relationships, only that a relationship is present. Longitudinal studies have many advantages over the cross-sectional design, but they have disadvantages as well (e.g., requiring more resources and money). Longitudinal studies are prone to threats of reliability and validity including historical events, attrition or mortality, and maturation. People move, get married, change their names, and change their telephone numbers, all of which make it difficult to locate participants. Cross-sectional designs, on the other hand, are more economical and manageable while providing immediate information.

DESCRIPTIVE RESEARCH DESIGNS

Descriptive studies are designed to address one variable, to compare variables to other standards or populations, or to summarize the relationship between or among two or more variables.

Unit of Analysis

There is a wide variation in *what* and *who* social work researchers study. Individuals, groups, and social aspects usually are studied as the unit of analysis. The individual is the most common unit of analysis. Factors such as age, gender, religion, and health are examples of what may be studied about individuals. When these characteristics are aggregated as the unit of analysis, a picture is obtained of the population made up of those individuals. This may be a descriptive analysis of an agency program such as abused women seeking shelter. It is not a complete picture of the problem, and generalizations cannot be made about abusive relationships based solely on the observations of the abused women. There may be gender and cultural biases as well as policy bias operating. Caution is needed in characterizing individuals and the populations they constitute. Groups (e.g., youth gangs, social work managers in child welfare settings) may be studied.

Another unit of analysis often studied is known as social qualities. Social workers often study the relationship or interaction between partners or between children and parents (e.g., the impact on children of witnessing family violence). Many different units of analysis may be studied for information about the same problem. It is important that the unit of analysis be clearly identified before the study.

Methods of analysis will differ according to the type of study, the sampling procedures, and the degree of complexity of data collection methods. Qualitative data analysis involves content analysis of semistructured or structured data collection. Categories and subcategories are gleaned from the answers provided by participants. Eventually, the frequency of responses can be tabulated for each category/subcategory (Brink & Wood, 1995).

Descriptive statistics (frequency, percentages, means, medians, and modes) are basic to descriptive analyses. In studies of population characteristics, sample statistics are used to predict population parameters and, therefore, the ability to estimate the incidence of problems in the population from data collected from a random sample. Depending on sampling procedures and the level of data available, nonparametric and simple tests of association can be helpful in indicating whether further research might be warranted (Brink & Wood, 1995).

Strengths and Limitations

Descriptive studies are extremely useful in evaluating programs and can serve as a means for reporting problems, needs, and patterns of service use. This information is relevant for improving service or establishing needs. Descriptive studies usually do not cost a great deal and can be implemented with relative ease in short periods of time. Although surveys can involve considerable expense and resources, findings are readily available for immediate use. In this way, descriptive studies contribute to the development of further research relatively quickly.

Case Example 1

Cheng, W., Schuckers, P., Hauser, G., Burch, J., Emmett, J., Walker, B., Law, E., Boyle, D., Lee, M., & Thyer, B. (1994). Psychosocial needs of family caregivers of terminally ill patients. *Psychological Reports, 75,* 1243-1250.

The researchers identified that medical advances promote the longevity of terminally ill patients, while managed care has shortened hospitalizations. However, there is little known about the needs of family caregivers of terminally ill patients. Five questions were developed. First, do caregivers know enough about the expected course of the patient's illness to be prepared for the increasing demands that might be placed on them? Second, have they been trained to perform the tasks required to care for the patient's physical needs? Third, are they sufficiently supported emotionally to bear the twin burdens of anticipatory grief and of actively giving care to a physically and mentally deteriorating loved one? Fourth, are they sufficiently supported by other helpers so that their own health does not deteriorate under continuous caregiving? Fifth, what are the needs of family caregivers of terminally ill persons? These represent good questions that can potentially contribute to our understanding of the causes of stress in caregivers.

The limitation of this study is the small convenience sample, making the representativeness of the caregiver population unknown. The strengths of the study include the excellent job of describing the needs of the family caregivers using a two-part survey. Part 1 was a structured interview regarding basic demographic characteristics of the caregivers and the terminally ill patients. Part 2 used four previously validated and published self-report scales given to the caregivers: the Beck Depression Inventory to assess clinical depression, the Life Satisfaction Index, the Provision of Social Relations to measure social support, and the Burden Inventory to assess burdensomeness (Cheng et al., 1994, p. 1245).

A profile of the terminally ill patients revealed that all of them were male and that all of the caregivers were female. The usual caregiving relationship was that of a terminally ill husband being cared for by a wife as the primary caregiver ($n = 22$, 79% of the 28 cases). Based on the data collection measures, the researchers were able to rank order caregivers' concrete and psychosocial needs. The study added to the literature on the psychosocial needs of caregivers of the terminally ill, assisting hospital social workers in responding to needs of caregivers and in exploring the quality of the patient-caregiver relationship as an essential component of the situation. This study supported some prior research, thereby adding to the knowledge, using a one-group practice posttest-only approach to understanding needs of caregivers (the unit of analysis).

This study used a descriptive strategy to investigate a known concern in an understudied population. Important information for establishing and developing social work programs (e.g., extent of support needed, numbers and types of services needed, type of service) was determined in the study.

Case Example 2

Wright, B., Thyer, B. A., & DiNitto, D. (1985). Health and social welfare needs of the elderly: A preliminary study. *Journal of Sociology and Social Welfare, 12,* 431-439.

From the literature review, these authors identified that the perceived needs of the elderly were omitted from research and that a random probability approach would help to achieve a more accurate model of service use. Participants were selected by random addresses within a north Florida community from the telephone directory. Using each address, the interviewer selected the household immediately to the left of the starting address, canvassing this household and every third household until three elderly participants had completed interviews. This study illustrates solid attempts to obtain a representative sample and an effort to build on a prior set of questions using trained interviewers.

REFERENCES

Aguilar, M. A., & Williams, L. P. (1993). Factors contributing to the success and achievement of minority women. *Affilia, 8,* 410-424.

Bickman, L., & Rog, D. (Eds.). (1998). *Handbook of applied social research methods.* Thousand Oaks, CA: Sage.

Brink, P. J., & Wood, M. J. (1995). Descriptive designs. In P. J. Brink & M. J. Wood (Eds.), *Advanced design in nursing research* (pp. 123-139). Thousand Oaks, CA: Sage.

Cheng, W., Schuckers, P., Hauser, G., Burch, J., Emmett, J., Walker, B., Law, E., Boyle, D., Lee, M., & Thyer, B. (1994). Psychosocial needs of family caregivers of terminally ill patients. *Psychological Reports, 75,* 1243-1250.

Denby, R., & Alford, K. (1996). Understanding African American discipline styles: Suggestions for effective social work intervention. *Journal of Multicultural Social Work, 4,* 81-98.

Denby, R., & Rindfleisch, N. (1996). African Americans' foster parenting experiences: Research findings and implications for policy and practice. *Children and Youth Services Review, 18,* 523-551.

Lindsey, E. W. (1998). Service providers' perception of factors that help or hinder homeless families. *Families in Society, 79,* 160-172.

MacEachron, A. E. (1994). Supervision in tribal and state child welfare agencies: Professionalization, responsibilities, training needs, and satisfaction. *Child Welfare, 73,* 117-128.

Marlow, C. (1998). *Research methods for generalist social work* (2nd ed.). Pacific Grove, CA: Brooks/Cole.

Palsy, T. S. (1992). *Research decisions: Quantitative and qualitative perspectives.* Toronto: Harcourt Brace Jovanovich Canada.

Rubin, A., & Babbie, E. (1997). *Research methods for social work* (3rd ed.). Pacific Grove, CA: Brooks/Cole.

Szuchman, L., & Thomlison, B. (2000). *Writing with style: APA style for social work.* Pacific Grove, CA: Brooks/Cole.

Tutty, L. M., & Rothery, M. A. (1998, June). *Women who seek shelter from wife assault: Risk assessment and service needs.* Paper presented at the Fifth International Family Violence Research Conference, Durham, NH.

Wright, B., Thyer, B. A., & DiNitto, D. (1985). Health and social welfare needs of the elderly: A preliminary study. *Journal of Sociology and Social Welfare, 12,* 431-439.

CHAPTER EIGHT

Surveys

CAROL T. MOWBRAY
MIEKO YOSHIHAMA

A survey is a method of systematically asking people questions and recording their answers to produce information that is difficult or impossible to obtain through observation. Surveys are conducted by interviewers in person (group or individually based) or over the telephone, or they are self-administered (delivered in person or through the mail). Surveys collect information on attitudes, knowledge, beliefs, values, and past or current behaviors, and they may include factual data as well as subjective states. In social work research, the survey is a mainstay for a wide variety of data collection purposes. Surveys have been used for needs assessment (prevalence of health problems in a sample of homeless adults [Harris, Mowbray, & Solarz, 1994]), epidemiological research (on the incidence of domestic violence in recently immigrated and acculturated Japanese American women [Yoshihama, 1999]), and treatment effectiveness research (outcomes from a randomized trial of supported educational services for adults with psychiatric disabilities [Mowbray, Collins, & Bybee, 1999]).

High-quality survey data are produced by minimizing error variance and eliminating bias. Groves (1989, cited in Braverman, 1996) categorizes components of survey error and bias into errors of nonobservation and errors of observation. Errors of nonobservation are caused by failure to include eligible persons in the survey due to coverage/sampling errors or nonresponse errors. The latter occur when eligible participants refuse or cannot be located and are of most concern when they involve systematic bias such as failure to include individuals with the most problems. There is a growing literature on techniques to maximize participation of eligible respondents. The reader is referred to Couper and Groves (1996) and Ribisl and colleagues (1996). For issues concerning coverage/sampling errors, consult the chapter by Nugent on probability theory and sampling methods in this volume (Chapter 3).

Errors of observation are due to measurements that do not reflect the true value of the variables they represent. They stem from interviewer errors, instrument errors, and respondent errors. Instrument errors are produced from uncertainties in the comprehension and meaning of items due to vagaries of question wording, structure, sequencing, and the like. Respondent errors involve processes or characteristics of the respondents that produce inconsistent or unreliable answers or reports that are systematically biased (e.g., due to cognitive problems, lower educational levels, or social desirability effects). This chapter focuses on instrument and respondent errors as two major problems for survey construction. We first provide an overview of the knowledge base on methods to reduce these errors. Next, we focus particularly on the validity of self-report, providing more detail on methods to increase accurate recall of distant events and valid answers to questions on sensitive topics. Subsequently, we briefly discuss choices in the mode of survey administration (e.g., mail vs. telephone vs. in person). The chapter ends with a brief overview of ethical issues.

WHAT IS KNOWN ABOUT SURVEY CONSTRUCTION?

The use of surveys and polls has increased exponentially during the past 20 years. A number of large national databases are available to monitor societal trends and cross-cultural differences in medical and social science research, from the worldwide prevalence of mental illness, to crime and unemployment rates, to prejudicial attitudes and discriminatory behaviors. Despite this expansion, there is limited scientifically based knowledge about survey methods. Most of what is written is derived from experience and common sense; survey construction still is as much an art as a science. In this short chapter, it would be impossible to describe and address all the multiple considerations involved in producing the best survey. Here, we can only provide overall guidance and specific answers to some of the most commonly asked questions.

The knowledge base relevant to survey question construction has been derived from experiments and theory, particularly from the field of cognitive psychology (Krosnick, 1999; Schwarz, 1999). We know that respondents handle survey questions as they do normal conversation; that is, they try to cooperate with the researcher and make their answers clear. We also know that respondents are active in trying to clarify the meanings of questions asked in surveys. Finally, although we would like respondents to optimize their efforts to answer survey questions, they often instead engage in satisficing, that is, expending the minimum effort necessary to provide satisfactory answers. Based on this knowledge, some general principles of survey construction have been derived:

1. Minimize respondent burden in terms of the length of the survey, tedium of question format and demands, boredom, and the effort that the respondent must expend in answering questions. Satisficing is more likely to occur when respondent burden is high (e.g., at the end of an interview).

2. Make sure that the questions asked and the response alternatives provided are clear and unambiguous to all survey respondents. In concrete terms, this means using standard English, avoiding double negatives and hypothetical questions, and realizing that abstractions usually are difficult for many respondents to grasp.

3. To get clear responses, be explicit about the purpose of each question. For example, asking about income could provide information on social status, resources available, or personal earnings.

In addition to this general guidance, some advice is available regarding specific issues.

Use of Established Instruments

Using established instruments usually is a good idea, but it will not necessarily solve all problems. For some topics (e.g., drug use), terminology and attitudes may change quickly, outdating scales in a few years. Also, established scales might not have been used with the target population; scales often are constructed with white, middle class college students and might be inappropriate for diverse populations (e.g., older, poor, multicultural).

Length of Questions

Questions should be short and simple. However, question wording might need to be extended to provide a common definition for ambiguous terms (e.g., "employment" refers to having a regular paid position). Terms that frequently need definitions include *unemployment, ethnicity, neighborhood,* and *community.* If a question requires a complex definition, such as income, then it is usually more desirable to substitute the general question with a list of its components (e.g., money from entitlement programs, welfare, paid employment, self-employment, resources provided by other household members, money from odd jobs, illegal income). Other frequently used terms that should be assessed by listing components are *criminal victimization, domestic abuse, sexual abuse, community, health,* and *medical care.*

Open-Ended Versus Closed-Response Questions

Closed-response questions might fail to provide an appropriate set of alternatives for the respondent, particularly when individuals of diverse cultures are being studied. Adding an "other" response category does not solve this problem because respondents usually confine their answers to the choices offered (Krosnick, 1999). Closed-response questions also might promote guessing as to what is the "right" or expected answer. However, answers to open-ended questions are also problematic in that they sometimes are ambiguous or overly affected by the respondent's education or articulateness or by the interviewer's skills at probing. For example, when asked the most important thing about a job, a respondent who says "the pay" could mean either the amount of pay or getting paid regularly. The best advice is to pretest, using open-ended questions in focus groups with heterogeneous composition. This allows construction of response alternatives to closed-ended questions with some confidence. Alternatively, pilot testing could be used to identify the ambiguous answers to open-ended questions that need to be followed up by interviewer probes. A final alternative would be to ask an open-ended question first, followed by the closed-response version. Interviews always need *some* open-ended questions, however, to vary the response format—for sensitive topics, when not enough is known about expected responses, when rapid changes in response categories might be expected, or to pick up on emergent issues.

Question Order Effects

Although many survey designs assume that there are no effects from the order in which questions are asked, preceding questions have been found to affect responses, especially in attitude measurement (Schwarz, 1999). Ordering can produce "assimilation effects" (when a previous question provides a positive frame that enhances positive judgments about a target) or "contrast effects" (when a previous question provides a positive standard of comparison against which the target is evaluated more negatively). Question order effects do not appear to be pervasive; however, they are not rare either. Unfortunately, there still is insufficient information to predict whether and how such effects will appear. The researcher should review questionnaire construction and be sensitive to these possibilities. When contrasting responses across populations or over time, items should be presented in the same order.

Question Wording

Participant responses definitely can be affected by question tone, the classic example being that Americans are much more willing to "not allow" something than to "forbid" it (Schuman & Presser, 1996). Small wording changes, especially those using "prestige symbols," can affect responses, especially for respondents with less education. The researcher should be aware of this and avoid emotionally "loaded" words. A related issue is balanced versus unbalanced wording, for example, the unbalanced question "Do you favor the death penalty?" versus the balanced wording "Do you favor or oppose the death penalty?" In general, attempts to achieve balance have little effect. However, adding substantive counterarguments to questions can produce directional shifts in the range of 4% to 13% (Schuman & Presser, 1996).

Question Format

Two of the most common formats are ratings and agree-disagree statements. The latter format is most appropriate for attitude questions and is more problematic for factual questions. Thus, although commonly used, an agree-disagree format might be inappropriate for product/service satisfaction or academic course evaluations addressing specific performance topics (Lyons, 1998). Frequently, surveys ask respondents to compare various objects, for example, the importance of aspects of the work environment. Question formats for this purpose sometimes use forced-choice (e.g., pay level vs. job stability), rankings, and ratings of each dimension on a common metric. The latter is more common. However, for valued objects, where all ratings are likely to be high and thus indistinguishable, the first author of this chapter has employed rankings to differentiate responses (so long as not more than six to eight objects are ranked [Converse & Presser, 1986]). Krosnick (1999) concludes that rankings yield higher quality data, especially when satisficing is likely to occur.

Number and Type of Response Alternatives

Closed questions in surveys use different numbers of response choices. More usually is better, up to a limit. With only 2 or 3 choices, response distributions often are skewed and provide little differentiation of respondents. However, respondents do not appear able to process more than 10 choices. Usually, 5 to 7 alternatives are optimal, depending on the type of questions. When more than 3 response options are available, they should be written out on response cards and provided to the respondent. Another choice is whether each response alternative has an adjectival label (e.g., strongly disagree) or a numerical label (e.g., 1 to 10, –5 to +5). The use of adjectives is preferred by respondents (Krosnick, 1999) and promotes more consistent interpretation of scale points because the midpoints on numerical scales often have different interpretations (e.g., neutrality vs. degrees of positiveness; Fowler, 1998). However, it is very difficult to find ordered adjectives for more than 7 scale points, and for cross-cultural research, exact translations of adjectives are nearly impossible.

The Effects of Response Alternatives

The survey researcher is advised to avoid vague quantifiers in response alternatives (e.g., frequently). Objective choices are preferred (e.g., the number of times in a day, week, or month that a behavior occurred). Schwarz (1999) describes how the set of responses offered can produce context effects. If response alternatives contain low-frequency categories (e.g., once a year) or cover a lengthy time frame (e.g., last year), then the respondent is likely to infer that the question concerns *more severe* episodes, whereas for higher frequency responses (e.g., once a day or more), the respondent probably will conclude that *less severe* states or problems are the focus. The researcher must know what he or she wants to measure (e.g., rage and aggressive outbursts or minor irritable behaviors) and must frame the questions and responses accordingly. Schwarz (1999) suggests that for many studies measuring response frequencies, open-ended questions with terms clearly specified (e.g., number of times during the past month) might be the best alternative.

Including a *Don't Know* Option

Standard questionnaires usually do not include a *don't know* option to a question because such an answer counts as missing data and decreases power. However, the reader should be advised that forcing respondents to answer all questions can increase error variance and probably systematic bias as well (because not knowing often relates to lower educational levels). About 30% of the public will provide opinions on a topic they know nothing about when the question is asked without a *don't know* filter, and the percentages are higher for less educated populations. The recommendation is that if an informed opinion is sought on a particular issue, then a *don't know* filter should be added (e.g., "Do you have an opinion on . . .? If so, do you agree . . .?"). However, if the intent is to tap a general attitude or an underlying disposition, then it is fine to omit the *don't know* option (Schuman & Presser, 1996).

Measuring a Middle Position

Whether or not to include a middle position in surveys appears to be of less consequence than the *don't know* option. That is, although inclusion of a middle category increases the number of people in the middle (by 10% to 20%), the same conclusions usually are drawn with or without it; declines in polar positions occur proportionally (Schuman & Presser, 1996).

Acquiescent Response Sets

Acquiescence bias, or the tendency of respondents to agree with attitude statements, seems to have a consistent effect (estimated at about 10% [Schuman & Presser, 1996]), but its origins and solutions have not been resolved. Acquiescent tendencies are more common in people with limited cognitive capabilities and also may reflect personality orientations, status deference, or satisficing tendencies (Krosnick, 1999). Equalizing the numbers of positive and negative statements usually is the solution, but the researcher needs to avoid question rewording that produces double negatives or obscures meaning. Another solution is to use forced-choice rather than agree-disagree versions of items when possible (Schuman & Presser, 1996).

Response Order Effects

This topic has to do with whether there may be a systematic bias for respondents to pick responses listed first (primacy effect) or last (recency effect) in closed-response questions. Although systematic study has produced mixed results, Krosnick (1999) indicates that a theory of satisficing provides a heuristic explanation: Primacy effects can be expected when response options are presented visually, whereas recency effects can be expected when they are presented orally. Furthermore, these effects will be exacerbated for more difficult questions and as respondents become more fatigued (in addition to other conditions related to satisficing).

Formatting and Question Flow

There seems to be consistent agreement that respondent burden is decreased when surveys vary their format to keep the respondent's attention and interest (e.g., using different types of questions and tasks, different responses, or response cards). Transitions between sections are necessary, but they should be brief and simple. Surveys should begin with questions that are interesting and not too taxing or discouraging. For an in-person interview, sometimes simple demographic questions may be a good place to start, although some sources suggest that such questions might be too boring to start the interview. Income and other sensitive questions definitely should be asked later in a questionnaire after rapport is established. Surveyors are advised not to use too many open-ended questions at the beginning because this sets the tone and expectations for the format throughout. In a long interview, questions at the end should be either simple or interesting to compensate for respondent and interviewer energy levels. When longer surveys are necessary in face-to-face interviews, there should be a break with refreshments provided. Following interviews of a highly personal and sensitive nature, debriefing is recommended.

Pretesting

The importance of this activity cannot be overemphasized, yet ironically, there is little detailed information about pretesting methods. Fowler (1998) notes that investigators should pay attention to this topic because improving questions is a cost-effective approach to improving the quality and, hence, the power of research (in contrast to increasing sample size, response rates, etc.). Identifying problematic questions before the survey begins will help to increase the validity of respondents' answers and, hence, the validity of the study findings. Knowing the type/source and degree of response error can inform analyses and interpretation of results (e.g., limitations in the data). The recommended steps (Converse & Presser, 1986) in pretesting are to (a) use exploratory inquiry with cultural insiders to construct a draft questionnaire; (b) read the questionnaire out loud and listen for flow and naturalness; (c) conduct a first pretest on the most problematic sections of the survey (usually closed-response questions) and combine with extensive use of probes and respondent debriefing on reactions to and validity of the questions; and, after making revisions, (d) conduct a second pretest on the final draft to polish it before data collection. Feedback should be sought from interviewers on questionnaire length, respondent reactions, and perceptions of problems. Interviewers should be asked to write extensive comments in the margins of interviews and to participate in oral debriefings. Converse and Presser (1986) recommend doing at least 25 of each pretest, with a minimum of 5 per interviewer. We advise that established instruments also need to be pretested because their uses can differ substantially across diverse populations. Krosnick (1999) notes new methods in pretesting to detect respondent difficulties and interviewer problems: (a) behavior coding in which an observer monitors pretest interviews, noting interviewing interactions and significant deviations from the protocol; and (b) cognitive interviews in which respondents are asked to "think aloud," verbalizing what comes to mind in formulating responses, or are asked how they interpreted a question or went about answering it. Both of these methods purportedly are more reliable in detecting problems than is conventional pretesting. Because interpretations of questions vary across population subgroups, it is important to use these pretest methods with respondents who represent backgrounds as diverse as those of respondents for the actual survey (Johnson et al., 1996).

THE VALIDITY OF SELF-REPORT

Surveys involve self-report data of individuals' own past behavior, perceptions, feelings, and/or opinions. These reports are assumed as valid at face, and many times they cannot be corroborated easily from other sources. Although self-report data are a valuable, and often the only feasible, way in which to collect data in which researchers are interested, they can be subject to multiple errors. Survey questions that require respondents to retrieve memory about personally experienced events are particularly susceptible to errors because they often reconstruct or infer details based on partial, and often fuzzy and faulty, memory (Bradburn, Rips, & Shevell, 1987; Braverman, 1996). Also, respondents may edit their responses to create positive images of themselves or to conform, consciously or unconsciously, to the perceived expectations of the interviewer or researcher. Underreporting, especially in questions involving socially undesirable behavior or attitudes, is common. So is overreporting, although to a lesser degree. Another common error is misplacing the timing of an event's occurrence; salient personal events are likely to be reported as having occurred more recently than they actually did (forward telescoping; Thompson, Skowronski, & Lee, 1988).

An assessment of the accuracy/validity of self-report is difficult because frequently there is no one else or no other record to validate it. Over the past several decades, however, an increasing volume of research has been conducted to examine the type and size of response errors, and a number of innovative approaches have been developed to both measure and minimize (or even eliminate) response effects. In what follows, we discuss research findings about and strategies to deal with response errors in two major task areas: memory retrieval and responses to sensitive questions.

Memory Retrieval

Survey research methodologies have benefited tremendously from research in cognitive psychology, especially concerning memories of personally experienced events (autobiographical memories). Due to space constraints, details of findings from this growing field cannot be presented here. The interested reader may consult reviews by Bradburn et al. (1987) or Jobe, Tourangeau, and Smith (1993). Briefly put, these research findings cast doubt on the reliability of respondents' self-reports of autobiographical events. People quickly forget details associated with particular events, and the quality of self-reports declines as the length of the recall period increases (Bradburn et al., 1987; Thompson et al., 1988). The extent of remembering or forgetting depends on the nature of the events and the degree of salience to the respondent (Bradburn et al., 1987). Although critical details might be better remembered

(Thompson, Skowronski, Larsen, & Betz, 1996), 20% of critical details fade away after 1 year and 60% fade away after 5 years (Bradburn et al., 1987).

Strategies to increase retrieval and recall. Matching the structure of a survey questionnaire to the respondent's memory structure (i.e., how memory is stored) facilitates efficient memory retrieval and increases the completeness and accuracy of recall and self-report of personal events (Belli, 1998). The conventional practice of asking general questions (e.g., use of health care) before more specific ones (e.g., number of hospitalizations, number of visits to a physician's office) is a way in which to match the survey structure to the general-to-specific, top-down structure of recall. However, researchers have found that autobiographical memories are stored in a far more complex manner in which events that are of similar thematic or temporal nature are stored together (Bradburn et al., 1987). These thematically and/or temporally connected periods are referred to as autobiographical sequences (e.g., during my M.S.W. training, when I was working at a homeless shelter). Autobiographical sequences anchor events onto a personal time frame that contains additional cues, such as likely location and participants, that facilitate retrieval of events occurring during that period (Bradburn et al., 1987).

The complex ways in which autobiographical memories are stored necessitate multiple retrieval approaches (e.g., sequencing, parallel retrieval). Sequencing retrieval refers to tracing events in a chronological sequence, backward or forward, within a specific thematic domain (e.g., retrieving a husband's violence from the first episode to the most recent episode, obtaining information about the housing histories of individuals who are homeless [Mowbray & Bybee, 1998]). Parallel retrieval involves interconnected events across domains that are thematically connected (e.g., a woman tracing back episodes of her partner's violence using easily remembered events in other aspects of her life such as pregnancies and her husband's unemployment).

Unless individuals make conscious efforts to remember the timing of events, no time trace is automatically encoded in autobiographical memories, making time (dates) an unreliable cue for memory retrieval (Bradburn et al., 1987; Thompson et al., 1996). The use of a salient time frame (e.g., a period since a holiday, a personally important landmark event) generally works better than using a time frame based on the calendar (e.g., during the past 3 months; Loftus & Marburger, 1983). Also, more time spent attempting to recall memories results in more accurate reporting (Sudman, Bradburn, & Schwarz, 1996). Thus, asking as many questions as possible within a limited time frame probably increases the risk of collecting low-quality data.

The effectiveness of memory cues varies depending on the type of information to be recalled. Memory cues of a personal nature (e.g., schools attended, places of residence) facilitate recall of personal events (Sudman et al., 1996). Because the salience of public events varies across groups, it can be important to tailor landmarks to respondents' cultures or other reference groups. For example, with immigrants, events in their countries of origin (e.g., natural disasters) might be very salient. Consulting pertinent records (e.g., health insurance reimbursement forms, bank statements) may serve as additional recall aides (Bradburn et al., 1987). However, the use of records does not necessarily eliminate errors (Sudman et al., 1996). Surveyors also should keep in mind that the respondent's current psychological distress may influence the recall and appraisal of past and current events (Eich, Macaulay, & Ryan, 1994).

Life history calendar method. The types of cues identified as effective in enhancing the accuracy and completeness of recall may be systematically incorporated into a survey's design. One example of such an approach is the Life History Calendar (LHC) method (Freedman, Thornton, Camburn, Alwin, & Young-DeMarco, 1988). As its name indicates, the LHC uses a calendar format to organize personal events in chronological order. The respondent first is asked to remember and report events in more easily recalled domains (e.g., marriages, births of children) or other domains, depending on the topic of a study. Using this information as recall cues, the respondent then is asked about events that are less salient and/or more difficult to recall (e.g., job histories). The structure of the LHC, both theme based and temporal based, fits the structures of individuals' autobiographical memories. As a result, it provides multiple timing cues to maximize recall, encouraging top-down, sequencing, and/or parallel retrieval pathways (Belli, 1998). In addition, the information laid out in a calendar format allows the interviewer to detect discrepancies between answers.

Self-report data obtained through the LHC method have been found to be highly reliable. A comparison of the data obtained through the LHC to those originally obtained 15 years earlier found low error rates (0% to 4%) for events in the family domain (e.g., divorce, separation, marriage, births of children), somewhat higher error rates in the employment domain (19%), and little sociodemographic bias (Ensel, Peek, Lin, & Lai, 1996). One distinct advantage of the LHC is that it can expand the recall period while maintaining the quality of data (e.g., instead of collecting data every year in a longitudinal panel study, researchers may collect data every other year or every third year).

Bounded recall. This technique also is useful for both increasing memory retrieval and reducing errors in placing the timing of events (Nater & Waksberg, 1964). In bounded recall, data from a previous interview serve as recall cues during the next time period, and the previous interview also serves as a landmark as the respondent is asked to report new events since the previous interview. The respondent's report of events in the new time period can be checked against data from the previous period. Bounded recall is highly effective for reducing telescoping errors (i.e., wrongly placing an event that occurred in the previous period in the present period), but its high cost has precluded widespread use.

Responding to Sensitive Questions

Social work researchers frequently inquire about sensitive topics such as sexual behavior, use of contraception, reproductive histories, substance use/abuse, history of victimization and perpetration, criminal activities, and mental illness. These types of questions may be particularly susceptible to social desirability bias. First identified by Crowne and Marlowe (1964), social desirability bias now is considered a multidimensional construct, involving self-deception (the tendency to provide favorably biased but honestly held self-descriptions) and impression management (the tendency to give favorable self-descriptions). Studies indicate that impression management, rather than self-deception, is the major source of response error and needs to be controlled (Paulhus, 1984). In a meta-analysis of studies of domestic violence, the effect of social desirability was relatively small but varied by the respondent's role (perpetrator vs. victim) and not by gender (Sugarman & Hotaling, 1997). Social desirability bias in surveys may be less prevalent than has been assumed (Krosnick, 1999), although research remains inconclusive.

In general, with sensitive questions or those associated with a high degree of social desirability, the more anonymous methods of administration appear to work somewhat better (e.g., lower degrees of under- or overreporting). A recent study by Roffman, Picciano, Wickizer, Bolan, and Ryan (1998) illustrates an innovative use of the telephone as a medium to reach out to a subgroup of gay and bisexual men who otherwise would not have participated in a survey that required disclosure of their identities. However, the superiority of telephone interviews cannot be assumed across various settings and research topics; telephone interviews yielded underreporting compared to face-to-face interviews in some studies (Tourangeau & Smith, 1996). Another method that allows high degrees of anonymity is computer-assisted administration.

Also in general, it is recommended that sensitive questions be placed in the latter parts of a survey to allow rapport to develop between the respondent and the interviewer. However, when the survey is long, respondent fatigue is likely to decrease the quality of self-report for questions placed at the end of the survey. Another way in which to minimize underreporting of socially undesirable behavior or attitudes is to provide an introduction to normalize answers that might be considered deviant. Interestingly, interviewers' expectations about difficulties in obtaining sensitive information have a small but significant effect on responses (Bradburn, 1983). Adequate pilot testing to identify these effects may address this problem. Researchers then can provide extra training or decide not to use the items or the interviewers.

CHOICE OF SURVEY MODE

The decision as to whether a survey should be self-administered, conducted over the telephone, or administered in person is based on a number of factors—type of information to be obtained, characteristics of the target population, logistics, and resources. Some information can be obtained only by a trained interviewer, for example, contingency questions and questions with more complicated formatting (e.g., diagnostic assessments, social networks, social support, the LHC). Computer-assisted telephone interviewing (CATI) can address much of this complexity, with the exception of lengthy or numerous response alternatives. The first author has administered long follow-up surveys over the phone when necessary. However, each respondent is sent a packet of response cards in the mail in advance and has a preestablished rapport with an assigned interviewer.

Mail surveys usually have much lower participation rates than do telephone or in-person interviews in the general population, although rates can be increased by using motivational letters and endorsements, incentives, and multiple reminders. However, if respondent burden is too high, then these already low rates might be reduced below an acceptable level (50%). Thus, when a questionnaire appears to be too long, too detailed, too hard to understand, too intrusive, and the like, the respondent may simply throw it away. Telephone interviews can be somewhat more complex, except that they will suffer when questions require rapport with the interviewer. For sensitive questions, phone surveys often are inappropriate; face-to-face interviews or even anonymous mail surveys might be preferable. Telephone interviews must be considerably shorter than in-person interviews and will produce fewer and less detailed responses to open-ended questions. Studies also suggest that telephone interviews are more subject to acquiescence and social desirability effects than are mail interviews (Dillman, Sangster, Tarnai, & Rockwood, 1996).

Participant characteristics are a second significant consideration in determining survey mode. Although about 95% of U.S. households now have telephones, there still are certain subgroups whose consistent access to phones is unlikely (Lavrakas, 1998). These often are the target groups for social work research, that is, individuals with social problems such as drug and alcohol addictions, homelessness, mental illness, and severe and chronic health problems (e.g., HIV/AIDS). Even if recruited in face-to-face contacts, these populations often have residential or economic instability, so that the researcher's ability to access them via their previous phone numbers is limited. The same limitations apply to these populations completing mail surveys. Even if not affected by unstable housing, other populations also might have difficulty with phone or mail surveys, for example, those with cognitive deficits (e.g., mental retardation, Alzheimer's disease, paranoid beliefs). Mangione (1998) advises that mail surveys are a good and inexpensive choice when the research sample has a moderate to high investment in the survey topic and that, in terms of demographics, nonresponders to mail surveys are likely to be less educated, elderly, unmarried, and male.

Finally, even if in-person interviews are desirable, the researcher might be limited by resources or logistics. In-person interviews have the most expensive interviewer costs; interviews usually are longer, and additional time is required for training, travel, missed interviews, and the like. However, when considering mail interviews to a preselected sample, costs also might be high (e.g., postage and copying expenses for repeated mailings, clerical support for mailings and for dealing with address changes, expenses of data coding and data entry). Many phone surveys now are routinely administered through CATI techniques, which can minimize interviewer errors (e.g., in skip patterns) and increase efficiency (e.g., through direct and accurate data entry). Some in-person interviews now are using computer-assisted technology on laptop computers that interviewers bring with them to the interviews, called computer-assisted personal interviewing (CAPI). Computer-assisted interviewing technology also has been applied to having respondents complete self-administered surveys using on-site computers, called computer-assisted self-interviewing (CASI) and audio computer-assisted self-interviewing (ACASI) (for details, see Tourangeau & Smith, 1996). Interestingly, this technology appears to have promise for decreasing systematic bias in response to sensitive questions.

ETHICAL ISSUES

As with many other methods of social research, the use of surveys requires careful consideration of safety and ethical issues. For example, in studies of violence perpetrated by family members, randomly selecting respondents might place current or former victims at risk of further victimization because perpetrators could become suspicious that selection was the result of the victims' reporting the violence to outside agencies. Or, when respondents are selected based on having a certain condition (e.g., HIV-positive status, prior psychiatric hospitalizations), contacting participants through mail, telephone, or in-person visits might expose their condition to family members. Researchers must establish and follow precautionary protocols to ensure confidentiality.

Researchers also need to be sensitive to potential negative effects from participating in surveys, especially those on sensitive topics such as past traumatic experiences. It is important that interviewers be trained to detect emotional distress in respondents and to be able to make referrals to appropriate professionals and organizations if necessary. Providing participants with a list of assistance programs is recommended. If respondents are likely to encounter barriers when accessing help, then additional efforts might be required (e.g., making prior arrangements with service providers, providing a toll-free telephone number).

In an increasingly diverse society such as the United States, conducting surveys requires researchers to develop culturally relevant study designs and to ask questions (in terms of both content and methods) that reflect the diverse experiences and perceptions of participants. Toward this end, conducting thorough preliminary studies, using focus groups, consulting with community members and professionals, and conducting sufficient pilot tests are critical to producing a survey that is valid and reliable across multiple contexts.

APPENDIX

Exemplars of Social Work Research Using Survey Methods

Mowbray, C. T., & Bybee, D. (1998). The importance of context in understanding homelessness and mental illness: Lessons learned from a research demonstration project. *Research on Social Work Practice, 8,* 172-199.

Interviews were conducted with adults who were homeless, mentally ill clients of an outreach linkage project at program entry and at 4 and 12 months following program completion. Changes in housing status and in number of days housed in institutional versus independent living settings were used as outcome measures. Housing histories were obtained through a flexible, sequential retrieval approach that allowed respondents to report residences back in time from the present or forward in time from a past landmark, dependent on the method that was easiest for them.

Roffman, R. A., Picciano, J., Wickizer, L., Bolan, M., & Ryan, R. (1998). Anonymous enrollment in AIDS prevention telephone groups counseling: Facilitating the participation of gay and bisexual men in intervention and research. *Journal of Social Service Research, 23*(3/4), 5-22.

This study illustrates the feasibility of survey methods in studies of sensitive topics with difficult-to-reach populations. Through the use of telephone contacts and mailing written materials to post office boxes, both of which allowed participants to remain anonymous, the investigators were able to reach out to those individuals who otherwise would not have participated in the intervention (group counseling regarding risk reduction for HIV transmission) or in a survey that required disclosure of their identities.

Yoshihama, M. (1999). Domestic violence among women of Japanese descent in Los
   Angeles: Two methods of estimating prevalence. *Violence Against Women, 5,*
   869-897.

This face-to-face interview study of a community-based random sample of
women used a series of behavior-specific questions, rather than a broad screener, to
examine respondents' experiences of a wide range of domestic violence. A brief introduction, intended to normalize experiences, preceded the questions about domestic violence victimization. The study was conducted in both English and Japanese and used 4- or 5-point Likert-type scales. It was based on extensive preliminary
studies indicating that a Likert-type scale with more than 5 points for frequencies or
degrees of agreement cannot be adequately translated into Japanese.

REFERENCES

Belli, R. F. (1998). The structure of autobiographical memory and event history calendar: Potential improvements in the quality of retrospective reports in survey. *Memory, 6,* 383-406.
Bradburn, N. M. (1983). Response effects. In P. H. Rossi, J. D. Wright, & A. B. Anderson (Eds.), *Hand-
   book of survey research* (pp. 289-328). San Diego: Academic Press.
Bradburn, N. M., Rips, L. J., & Shevell, S. K. (1987). Answering autobiographical questions: The impact
   of memory and inference on survey. *Science, 236,* 157-161.
Braverman, M. (1996). Sources of survey error: Implications for evaluation studies. In M. T. Braverman &
   J. K. Slater (Eds.), *Advances in survey research* (pp. 17-28). San Francisco: Jossey-Bass.
Converse, J. M., & Presser, S. (1986). *Survey questions: Handcrafting the standardized questionnaire.*
   Beverly Hills, CA: Sage.
Couper, M. P., & Groves, R. M. (1996). Household-level determinants of survey nonresponse. In M. T.
   Braverman & J. K. Slater (Eds.), *Advances in survey research* (pp. 63-80). San Francisco: Jossey-Bass.
Crowne, D. P., & Marlowe, D. (1964). *The approval motive.* New York: John Wiley.
Dillman, D. A., Sangster, R. L., Tarnai, J., & Rockwood, T. H. (1996). Understanding differences in peo-
   ple's answers to telephone and mail surveys. In M. T. Braverman & J. K. Slater (Eds.), *Advances in sur-
   vey research* (pp. 45-62). San Francisco: Jossey-Bass.
Eich, E., Macaulay, D., & Ryan, L. (1994). Mood dependent memory for events of the personal past. *Jour-
   nal of Experimental Psychology, 123,* 201-215.
Ensel, W. M., Peek, M. K., Lin, N., & Lai, G. (1996). Stress in the life course: A life history approach. *Jour-
   nal of Aging and Health, 8,* 389-416.
Fowler, F. J., Jr. (1998). Design and evaluation of survey questions. In L. Bickman & D. J. Rog (Eds.),
   Handbook of applied social research methods (pp. 343-376). Thousand Oaks, CA: Sage.
Freedman, D., Thornton, A., Camburn, D., Alwin, D., & Young-DeMarco, L. (1988). The Life History
   Calendar: A technique for collecting retrospective data. In C. C. Clogg (Ed.), *Sociological methodol-
   ogy* (Vol. 18, pp. 37-68). San Francisco: Jossey-Bass.
Groves, R. M. (1989). *Survey errors and survey costs.* New York: John Wiley.
Harris, S. N., Mowbray, C. T., & Solarz, A. (1994). Physical and mental health problems of Detroit shelter
   users. *Health and Social Work, 19*(1), 37-45.
Jobe, J. B., Tourangeau, R., & Smith, A. F. (1993). Contributions of survey research to an understanding of
   memory. *Applied Cognitive Psychology, 7,* 723-738.
Johnson, T. P., O'Rourke, D., Chavez, N., Sudman, S., Warnecke, R. B., Lacey, L., & Horm, J. (1996). Cultural variations in the interpretation of health survey questions. In R. Warnecke (Ed.), *Health Survey*

Research Methods Conference proceedings (pp. 57-62). Washington, DC: U.S. Department of Health and Human Services.

Krosnick, J. A. (1999). Survey research. *Annual Review of Psychology, 50,* 537-567.

Lavrakas, P. J. (1998). Methods for sampling and interviewing in telephone surveys. In L. Bickman & D. J. Rog (Eds.), *Handbook of applied social research methods* (pp. 429-472). Thousand Oaks, CA: Sage.

Loftus, E. F., & Marburger, W. (1983). Since the eruption of Mount St. Helens, has anyone beat you up? Improving the accuracy of retrospective reports with landmark events. *Memory and Cognition, 11,* 114-120.

Lyons, W. (1998). Beyond agreement and disagreement: The inappropriate use of Likert items in the applied research culture. *International Journal of Social Research Methodology, 1*(1), 75-83.

Mangione, T. W. (1998). Mail surveys. In L. Bickman & D. J. Rog (Eds.), *Handbook of applied social research methods* (pp. 399-428). Thousand Oaks, CA: Sage.

Mowbray, C. T., & Bybee, D. (1998). The importance of context in understanding homelessness and mental illness: Lessons learned from a research demonstration project. *Research on Social Work Practice, 8,* 172-199.

Mowbray, C. T., Collins, M. E., & Bybee, D. (1999). Supported education for individuals with psychiatric disabilities: Long-term outcomes from an experimental study. *Social Work Research, 23*(2), 89-100.

Nater, J., & Waksberg, J. (1964). A study of response errors in expenditures data from household interviews. *Journal of the American Statistical Association, 59,* 18-55.

Paulhus, D. (1984). Two-component models of socially desirable responding. *Journal of Personality and Social Psychology, 46,* 598-609.

Ribisl, K. M., Walton, M. A., Mowbray, C. T., Luke, D. A., Davidson, W. S., & BootsMiller, B. J. (1996). Minimizing participant attrition in panel studies through the use of effective retention and tracking strategies: Review and recommendations. *Evaluation and Program Planning, 19*(1), 1-25.

Roffman, R. A., Picciano, J., Wickizer, L., Bolan, M., & Ryan, R. (1998). Anonymous enrollment in AIDS prevention telephone groups counseling: Facilitating the participation of gay and bisexual men in intervention and research. *Journal of Social Service Research, 23*(3/4), 5-22.

Schuman, H., & Presser, S. (1996). *Questions and answers in attitude surveys: Experiments on question form, wording, and context.* Thousand Oaks, CA: Sage.

Schwarz, N. (1999). Self-reports: How the questions shape the answers. *American Psychologist, 54,* 93-105.

Sudman, S., Bradburn, N. M., & Schwarz, N. (1996). *Thinking about answers: The application of cognitive processes to survey methodology.* San Francisco: Jossey-Bass.

Sugarman, D., & Hotaling, G. (1997). Intimate violence and social desirability: A meta-analytic review. *Journal of Interpersonal Violence, 12,* 275-290.

Thompson, C. P., Skowronski, J. J., Larsen, S. F., & Betz, A. (1996). *Autobiographical memory: Remembering what and remembering when.* Hillsdale, NJ: Lawrence Erlbaum.

Thompson, C. P., Skowronski, J. J., & Lee, D. J. (1988). Telescoping in dating naturally occurring events. *Memory and Cognition, 16,* 461-468.

Tourangeau, R., & Smith, T. W. (1996). Asking sensitive questions: The impact of data collection mode, questions format, and question context. *Public Opinion Quarterly, 60,* 275-304.

Yoshihama, M. (1999). Domestic violence among women of Japanese descent in Los Angeles: Two methods of estimating prevalence. *Violence Against Women, 5,* 869-897.

CHAPTER NINE

Needs Assessments

LESLIE M. TUTTY
MICHAEL A. ROTHERY

Needs assessments are studies conducted to gather information about the needs of populations or groups in communities. One of the more practical types of research, needs assessments are used to develop new services or to evaluate the relevance of existing programs. They also may be used to establish a need to revise or create policy.

Kuh (1982, cited in Stabb, 1995) lists five general purposes commonly served by needs assessment research:

1. Monitoring stakeholders' perceptions of various issues that can guide the development of new programs or policies
2. Justifying existing policies or programs
3. Assessing client satisfaction with services
4. Selecting the most desirable program or policy from several alternatives
5. Determining whether needs have been met, a purpose closely akin to program evaluation

Two key questions are addressed as needs assessment research is undertaken: *who?* and *how?* The *who?* question requires the researcher to be clear about the membership of the group whose needs are to be assessed. Often, a given study will entail gathering information from various respondents ranging from individuals who might never have been clients to those receiving multiple services. However, in nearly every case, at least one set of respondents will be those citizens who are most immediately affected by gaps in services or supports rather than relying too much on the opinions of service providers, academics, or funders.

The *how?* question addresses the methods used to gather information from the group whose needs are of interest. These are not unique; needs assessments borrow familiar techniques such as surveys, interviews, and focus groups, some of which are highlighted in other chapters in this handbook. Quantitative methods (e.g., surveys, standardized measures) may be used, as may qualitative methods (e.g., exploratory interviews). Combinations of both are increasingly popular given that each method has its advantages and limitations.

This chapter begins with a discussion of how we define *needs* and how we determine who to ask about them. Common methodological approaches are described and evaluated using examples from the social work literature. The benefits of triangulation, or using more than one source or method of gathering information, are presented first, followed by a discussion of who should digest and weigh information about needs once it is gathered. Finally, we consider the importance of developing a plan to implement recommendations, so that the work of assessing needs is used to clients' benefit, not relegated to the shelves occupied by other dusty neglected reports.

DEFINING *NEED*

When we invoke the concept of needs, we may easily assume that we share with others a common understanding of what we are talking about. However, it is worthwhile to look more closely at the definition of the term because useful characteristics and distinctions are highlighted when we do so.

Lenning (1980) distinguishes between met and unmet needs: "Met needs are necessary or desirable conditions that already exist in actuality. Unmet needs arise when there is a discrepancy between desirable conditions and current actuality" (cited in Stabb, 1995, p. 52). Both met and unmet needs could conceivably be the focus of needs assessment research, although unmet needs will be the main concern in the vast majority of cases.

A different distinction (perhaps more useful for our purposes) is taken by Witkin and Altschuld (1995), who define a need as "a discrepancy or gap between 'what is,' or the present state of affairs, and 'what should be,' or a desired state of affairs" (p. 4). In this analysis, needs equate with Lenning's (1980, cited in Stabb, 1995) unmet needs, the most common focus for needs assessment research.

Revere, Berkowitz, Carter, and Ferguson (1996) add the suggestion that need is defined by "community values [and is] amenable to change" (p. 5). From these perspectives, and with reference to considerations introduced earlier, a needs assessment gathers information about gaps between real and ideal conditions, the reasons these gaps exist, and what can be done about them, all within the context of the beliefs of the community and available resources for change.

Another distinction introduces the question of degree; some needs are stronger or more important than others. Fundamental needs that have relevance to people's survival, safety, or basic comforts are not the same as "wants" or less compelling needs. A social work professor's desire for a week in Mexico as a break from winter is qualitatively very different from a homeless person's need for food and shelter in the face of the same cold conditions. Although it is not possible to be declarative regarding where the line between relatively important needs and less important wants is to be drawn, it still is an important issue. Needs assessments are focused on needs that affect individuals' abilities to function well in important areas of their lives. Wants associated with perceived quality of life (but not to the same extent as with life's real essentials) are more the purview of market research.

Maslow's (1970) hierarchy of needs has proven useful to social workers for thinking about the needs and priorities of their clients, and it also is a framework that can inform needs assessments. Maslow's five levels of needs are physical and life-sustaining needs (e.g., air, water, food, warmth, elimination of bodily wastes), physical safety (e.g., protection from physical attack and disease), love and support, self-esteem and self-worth, and self-realization (e.g., needs to be productive and creative). Maslow contends that the more basic needs must be attended to before attempting to address higher level needs (or wants). Needs assessments can gather information relevant to any one or more of these five levels, but the hierarchy of priorities provides useful criteria for deciding what to focus on first in data collection and for recommending changes.

Finally, some authors argue that once an "expressed need" is verbalized, it becomes a want or a demand (Lenning, 1980, cited in Stabb, 1995). This is distinct from differentiating needs from wants on the basis of the strength of their potential impact on someone's well-being, and it probably is less useful for our purposes. However, there is a related point that is noteworthy: Verbal demands are not always the direct expression of need. Thus, in needs assessments, it is important to gather information from members of a population beyond those publicly advocating specific demands.

WHOM TO ASK ABOUT NEEDS

The popular term *stakeholders* often refers to clients (or potential clients) or the people who actually experience the need that is being studied. However, Revere and colleagues (1996) suggest broadening the definition to mean "service providers and management, community members, certain politicians, the funding source, business/trade associations, and the actual research workers" (p. 7) because each of these has a vested interest in the study and its outcomes. This flexible use of the term is helpful, suggesting a range of potential sources of data and recognizing that needs assessments have ramifications for people beyond those normally surveyed.

Needs assessments traditionally look to three groups as sources of data: the target group (i.e., clients, potential clients), key informants (e.g., community leaders, service providers), and a sample of all members of the relevant community.

First, the *target group or population* comprises the very individuals with whom we are concerned and whose needs we wish to assess. Common sense suggests that this is the voice we are most interested in hearing if we want the best current information possible. However, the issue can be more complicated than it appears on the surface. Highly disadvantaged, socially marginalized groups are not always accustomed to having their voices heard and might not easily articulate their needs to a researcher when invited to do so. Consider the homeless as an example, especially the subpopulation within their ranks who are psychiatrically disadvantaged. With any such group, the researcher cannot simply approach the individuals and ask that they enumerate their needs. Strategies (and time) for building trust and rapport and for encouraging engagement in the research process are prerequisites for successful data gathering.

Second, McKillip (1998) defines another group serving as a common source of data, *key informants,* as "opportunistically connected individuals with the knowledge and ability to report on community needs. Key informants are lawyers, judges, physicians, ministers, minority group leaders, and service providers who are aware of the need and services perceived as important by a community" (pp. 272-273). An advantage of gathering data from key informants is that such individuals often have a broader knowledge than do target population members of services that are available in the community; they also may be more skilled at articulating needs that remain to be effectively addressed. One disadvantage is that key informants sometimes have a vested interest in developing new services or in preserving established resources, even though they are less than adequate (we all develop loyalties, and these can affect our judgment). McKillip also notes that key informants may underestimate the willingness of members of the target population to participate in programs while overestimating the extent of problems.

The third group, *community members,* comprises the entire citizenry of a community, which may include members of the target population as well as others unaffected by the same needs. Approaching community members for information has the advantage of potentially learning how broadly based needs are rather than assuming that they are restricted to the target population. It also offers the opportunity to learn about how needs (and measures to ameliorate them) are perceived in the community at large and to think about how that will affect efforts to implement changes. However, a disadvantage is that community members might remain relatively unaware of the needs of some of the community's more marginalized subgroups.

In summary, each of these groups may be the focus of the variety of needs assessment methods documented in the next several sections.

METHODS OF NEEDS ASSESSMENT

As mentioned previously, there are many ways to conduct needs assessments. We discuss methods in two broad categories: quantitative and qualitative. Quantitative methods gather data that are translated into numerical form and are described using statistics. Using such methods, for example, it is possible to conclude that in a sample of 102 shelter residents, 70.5% of these women abused by intimate partners were abused themselves as children and described 73.7% of their partners as also having been abused (Tutty & Rothery, 1997). Such high proportions may be interpreted as suggesting the need for early intervention with children in shelters in the hope of preventing the cycle of violence from affecting a new generation.

Providing statistics about the extent of a need can be a powerful way to raise awareness of the severity of gaps in services. The section on quantitative needs assessment describes three such methods: surveys, standardized needs assessment measures, and using existing statistical databases.

By contrast, qualitative needs assessments ask questions that tend to be more open-ended and allow the research informant to describe in detail the complexities of the issues at hand. For example, a qualitative needs assessment conducting interviews with another group of 63 abused women residing in a shelter noted that providing for their basic needs for safety and food was of great importance (Tutty, Weaver, & Rothery, 1999). However, some women expressed concern that a few residents were difficult to live with and that some mothers did not manage their children's aggressive behavior or ignored it. These results suggest a somewhat different focus for intervention by crisis counselors and the need to provide parenting programs for some residents.

Results from qualitative needs assessments often lack statistical data that could convey the extent of the problem, but they tend to be rich in detail that conveys the complexities and uniqueness of the experiences of different individuals. The qualitative needs assessment methods described in this chapter include interviews (either face-to-face or by telephone), focus groups, nominal groups, and town hall meetings.

Quantitative Methods of Needs Assessment

Surveys. Although surveys may ask open-ended qualitative questions, the great majority are developed for quantitative analysis. Quantitatively oriented surveys, particularly those employing questionnaires, are the most frequent method of assessing needs. The tasks involved in developing a survey to assess needs are identical to those undertaken when surveys are developed for other purposes, so they are not detailed here. The major steps involve the following:

- Deciding whom to survey (e.g., target groups, key informants)
- Selecting a method of sampling (e.g., random sample, systematic sample)
- Determining the content of items (through examination of the literature or through focus groups with key informants)
- Choosing what type of question to use (e.g., open-ended, multiple choice, scaled with respect to the extent of agreement)
- Selecting a method of distribution (e.g., mail, telephone)

Advantages of surveys include the ease and flexibility with which they can be administered compared to other methods and the relative lack of expense with which a considerable amount of data can be collected. Disadvantages include the extent to which a set questionnaire can predetermine the issues that respondents address and the consequent danger of not hearing about needs that would emerge in a more open-ended process.

With such risks in mind, Witkin and Altschuld (1995) recommend caution in accepting the easy assumption that a written questionnaire is the most appropriate tool when a needs assessment is contemplated. Although a questionnaire can be important to a needs assessment, they suggest that it should not be used until more exploratory methods have been employed to ensure that the factors measured by questionnaire items are as well chosen as possible.

Furthermore, some cultural groups might find surveys to be strange or difficult and respond negatively to them. Weaver (1997), for example, describes a questionnaire developed to assess the needs of an off-reservation Native American community in an urban area. A large number of questionnaires were mailed out, with virtually no returns. The alternative of a qualitative approach, including focus groups and individual interviews, was adopted with considerably greater success.

An example of needs assessment research employing survey methods more appropriately is offered by Rosenthal, Groze, and Morgan (1996). These social workers were interested in identifying the needs of families who adopt children with special needs, both before and after placement. They developed a questionnaire asking parents about the adequacy of the following:

- The background information on the child that had been provided to parents
- Information that had been shared with the parents by the social worker
- The adequacy of postadoptive services provided

The survey was mailed to 906 families in three states, with a response rate of 62% ($n = 562$). The results supported the utility of counseling and education around adoption issues and child development, with more than 60% of families stating that these services were *very helpful*. The need for opportunities for respite from parenting for people adopting a child with major behavioral difficulties was identified as a significant gap.

Standardized needs assessment measures. A relatively new needs assessment methodology uses standardized measures developed to assess the needs of a specific population group. For example, Cummings, Kelly, Holland, and Peterson-Hazan (1998) developed the Needs Inventory for Caregivers of Hospitalized Elders (NICHE) to measure the perceived needs of familial caregivers of elderly patients and the impact of hospitalization on those needs. The tool was developed using clinical knowledge regarding caregivers' stresses (derived from focus groups with professional social workers experienced in working with the population) and a review of the relevant literature. The questionnaire asks informants to identify the extent to which each of 17 needs is a concern on a 5-point Likert scale. Needs assessed include information regarding the doctor's diagnosis, emotional support for self or family members, and advice for coping with problem behaviors.

Using such a measure in needs assessment research has the advantage of building on the work that has gone into identifying and conceptualizing potentially important needs and of using a measure for which reliability and validity have been established. A possible disadvantage is that needs that have proved to be relevant to familial caregivers of hospitalized elderly patients in one location might not have the same importance in other locations. Conversely, items about other needs that are important in a new locale might be missing from the standardized measure.

Using existing statistical information. Another quantitative method of conducting needs assessments is to use data that have been collected previously. Existing data might be available, for example, in agency files or in government data banks. Such secondary analyses have the advantage of sparing the researcher the time and expense of gathering new data. A disadvantage is that the researcher is limited to data that someone else considered worth gathering. Potentially important variables might be absent or might need to be inferred indirectly from the data that were recorded.

Tracy, Green, and Bremseth (1993) reviewed case records of supportive services for abused and neglected children in one state. A total of 500 child welfare cases were sampled to explore factors associated with the decision of whether to offer one of two services: family preservation (if children at risk still were at home) or reunification (for families with children who had been placed). Information was collected regarding demographic variables, presenting problems, service history, service needs, services planned and provided, service characteristics, and service outcomes (an enterprise that, Tracy et al. note, consumed thousands of hours).

Tracy et al.'s (1993) analysis uncovered significant stresses affecting the children sampled—parental substance abuse, economic difficulties, and poor living conditions—that were infrequently addressed in case plans and emphasized indications of child abuse. The authors conclude that "there was little one-to-one direct correspondence between the service need and the service offered" (p. 26), raising serious questions about the quality of service planning (and the training of child welfare workers).

Qualitative Methods of Needs Assessment

Qualitative needs assessment research may be conducted via individual interviews, small group discussions, or even large town hall meetings that allow for more open exploration of issues than do the quantitative methods discussed previously. Such studies tend to involve a greater time commitment from respondents but offer much more opportunity to identify and discuss issues in depth.

Individual interviews. Face-to-face and telephone interviews are one method of gathering in-depth information about the needs of particular groups. Preparation involves thinking through the purpose of the interview, constructing an interview schedule, and training interviewers (Witkin & Altschuld, 1995).

When a good rapport develops between the interviewer and the respondent, the result can be disclosure of information and ideas about sensitive issues that would not emerge when more formal structured approaches are used. Also, in a more open-ended process, the respondent may identify needs that no one had anticipated. Disadvantages of this approach include the fact that it is notoriously labor intensive; interviews are time-consuming (so that relatively small samples might be all that realistically can be used), training interviewers takes time, and the transcription and analysis of interviews typically is a lengthy and complex task.

Singer, Bussey, Song, and Lunghofer (1995) interviewed 201 randomly chosen female inmates, identifying numerous needs relevant to their time in jail and post-release rehabilitation. Many of the women became very distressed discussing issues about their children and about violence they had experienced during their lives. Many shared details about abusive relationships with partners or "johns," and several had been sexually abused as children and adults.

Singer and colleagues (1995) used their data to raise daunting program and policy issues. The practice of incarcerating nonviolent female offenders was questioned. Most of the research participants had committed only petty crimes, and their being jailed, being separated from their children, and facing serious needs on release for housing and drug and mental health counseling all were seen as requiring a fundamental rethinking of policy and practice.

Focus groups. Focus groups are relatively unstructured exercises with small groups (usually 8 to 12 participants). Membership usually is homogeneous in that members share a particular experience or interest such as the members of what we described earlier as the target population. Focus group interviews typically take from 1.5 to 2.5 hours, and several may be conducted for a given study.

Witkin and Altschuld (1995) summarize the process that a focus group typically follows. Initially, members hear a general statement of the purpose of the session and are given a question related to this purpose designed to elicit perceptions about important needs. Often, participants are asked to write down the ideas that the question stimulates and then to share these ideas with the group. The leader typically writes ideas as they are shared, summarizing them and making sure that there is agreement among members with what is being recorded. This process is repeated with other predetermined questions.

Leadership is important to the success of a focus group, especially because there is not a highly structured agenda (except for the posing and answering questions aspect). According to Witkin and Altschuld (1995), "The leader must be nonjudgmental, create a supportive group atmosphere, be able to keep the interview process going, be a good listener, and be alert to sense when a group is deviating from the prescribed question route in meaningful and nonmeaningful directions" (pp. 172-173). These are not easy demands.

One advantage of group approaches over individual interviews also can be a disadvantage. Whereas participants do not have the same opportunity to explore their own perceptions or experiences in depth as in individual interviews, a group approach can elicit information that would not emerge without the stimulus of interacting with others and reacting to their ideas. When group discussions detour in innovative ways, this may lead to original and creative ideas. Brainstorming, or encouraging members to present any solution to a problem without prejudging it, is one way in which to encourage such innovation. Alternatively, without effective facilitation, the group may pursue unproductive tangents, and there is a heightened risk of interpersonal conflict detracting from the effectiveness with which research goals are pursued.

Lyman, Pulice, and McCormick (1993) used focus groups composed of service providers from mental health and alcohol and substance abuse agencies to assess needs of individuals with dual diagnoses of mental illness and substance abuse. Group members were asked to estimate the extent and clinical complexity of this problem and to think about how well substance abuse and mental health agencies serving such clients were collaborating. Their responses were analyzed using content analysis, resulting in important themes being identified. For example, definitional problems resulted in diagnostic inconsistencies among agencies. Access to financial support for incapacitated clients was another critical issue identified, as was a need for cross-training for mental health and substance abuse counselors.

These themes were presented at a 1-day conference offered to the original focus group members along with additional service providers. The focus group process was used once again to develop ideas about solutions to the problems that had been identified during the first round.

Nominal groups. An alternate group approach to needs assessment has been developed by Delbecq (1986, cited in McKillip, 1998). Nominal groups are more structured than focus groups. The agenda allows group discussion but with more consistent attention to the goal of achieving consensus about needs.

Gerdes and Benson (1995) used a nominal group process to assess the problems of inner-city African American schoolchildren. The goal was to identify the most serious problems faced by students. A stratified random sample of students from the first to ninth grades was assigned to groups based on whether they were from primary grades (first to third grades), middle grades (fourth to sixth grades), or junior high grades (seventh to ninth grades). Ninth-grade students experienced with the nominal group process were used as facilitators.

Group members first were asked to list the problems they faced at school on a sheet of paper. Using a round-robin format, each student identified one problem, adding a new item to a list being kept on a flip chart until it was agreed that the list was complete. From this list, each student identified the seven most serious problems and rated their severity. The facilitator then calculated a group ranking for the items.

The rankings of concerns were different among the various age groups. Fighting and problems with teachers were priority issues for students in the primary grades; fighting and drugs were the most serious for students in the middle grades; and pregnancy, drugs, and drug deals were the strongest concerns for students in the junior high grades.

Teachers from the students' schools also participated in nominal groups. They registered more concern about issues for students such as low parental support, parental problems, and lack of motivation. Both students and teachers expressed a sense of powerlessness in addressing the problems that they were identifying. Although the nominal group identified needs very effectively (and in a way that encouraged partnership), it was but the first step in the process of change.

Community forum approach. Large open public hearings or community forums often are used to gather information from the diverse individuals who make up a community for which needs are being assessed (McKillip, 1998). Similar to a town hall meeting lasting several hours with large numbers of participants (sometimes 50 or more), this method aims to ensure that the broadest possible sampling of opinions results in a data set reflecting a community consensus respecting the issues being scrutinized. Clearly, this approach aims to give a voice to all community members including many who are immediately affected by the problems of interest.

Witkin and Altschuld (1995) note that special leadership skills are vital to the success of this approach. Not everyone is able to facilitate large meetings that encourage group members to participate actively and to feel that they can openly share ideas that might be different from those of the majority.

Advantages of community forums include the fact that they are a relatively inexpensive way in which to hear from large numbers of interested individuals. Another advantage is that public meetings serve to sensitize the general public to the problems and to highlight potential resistance to proposed solutions. Also, engaging a cross section of community members may have valuable secondary benefits. For example, when the time comes to implement recommendations, important people might have bought into the changes being suggested.

A primary disadvantage of this method is that there is no means of ensuring that the participants are a representative sample of their community. Indeed, they normally are not; the ideas and perceptions collected typically will be those of people who, for some reason, are motivated to influence what happens. Citizens who are less interested will not attend and will not be heard, even though they might have reactions to the needs being assessed and the eventual recommendations for dealing with them.

A midwestern university offers an example of a community forum that employed contemporary technology in a highly effective fashion. The goal was to develop recommendations for an overhaul of the undergraduate curriculum, so the purpose of the research was to document perceptions of students' learning needs across a broad range of disciplines. An "electronic" town hall meeting was held over a period of several days. The meeting was widely publicized, and the need for input from all interested stakeholders was emphasized. The committee overseeing the process identified a number of key areas about which decisions would have to be made. These areas were presented to the community in turn, with questions and preliminary ideas posed through e-mail and on the university's Web site. Students, academic staff, support staff, and administrators all read and responded to these initial stimuli and then responded to each other's responses. Thus, a very rich data set was compiled comprising perceptions about students' learning needs, ideas about how to meet them, and obstacles to the changes being considered.

TRIANGULATION OF NEEDS ASSESSMENT INFORMATION

To obviate risks of bias from using limited sources of information, Yegidis, Weinbach, and Morrison-Rodriguez (1999) recommend "triangulating" or collecting data from three (or more) sources, with each having a different perspective. Witkin and Altschuld (1995) argue more strongly for this step, suggesting that studies using only one method should be considered seriously flawed.

To illustrate, suppose that one was researching the need in a community for a shelter for women. The researcher could conduct a survey of key informants (e.g., social workers, police, women's organizations, self-help group leaders), host a community forum, and perform a secondary analysis of existing data in police and social service agency files about the incidence of women requiring shelter. Congruence in the perceptions obtained in this way clearly would represent a stronger case than if only one source was accessed. However, if the results contradict each other, then the researcher has the difficult task of assessing which set of perceptions enjoys the greatest credibility.

A number of the examples provided in this chapter illustrate the use of more than one method of data collection. Weaver's (1997) needs assessment of off-reservation Native Americans was cited earlier and is a case in point. In this study, focus groups were used, but there also were individual interviews and a mailed questionnaire. Each of these methods was used with three constituents: agency staff, clients, and individuals with no agency involvement. This complex data-gathering strategy is notable for its sensitivity and inclusiveness.

It is not uncommon for various constituents to have different views about needs. As Revere et al. (1996) note,

> It is relatively easy to decide that a starving man needs food or [that] a homeless person needs shelter. But what if an assessment points to areas of need that are not acknowledged by the individuals themselves, who may believe they need something else altogether? What if the target population and the service providers in the community recognize different areas of need or disagree as to what will best meet that need? (p. 4)

For example, a needs assessment standardized instrument was developed by Carter, Crosby, Geertshuis, and Startup (1996) to assess the needs of people with chronic mental illness. A total of 32 questions measured perceptions as to whether clients needed assistance with a variety of tasks and issues such as shopping and cooking, family relationships, making use of spare time, and motivation.

Two forms were developed—one for clients and one for staff—so that the perceptions of the clients and of the key informants could be triangulated. The results showed poor agreement between workers and clients on many items, suggesting critical differences in perceptions. The issue in such a case is not who to believe but rather how to address the discrepancies so that they do not negatively affect services.

Another sense in which discrepancies can be problematic has to do with who prioritizes needs once they are identified. Whether and how research results get used often are political decisions, and different social issues are given importance at various times. For example, child abuse has existed throughout recorded history, but its perceived importance as a problem has varied considerably over time and place, and the resources available to reduce it and ameliorate its effects have fluctuated as well.

Over the past several decades, we have come to recognize the surprisingly large number of children who have been sexually abused. Identifying this problem entailed measuring its prevalence, clarifying the needs of child victims for child welfare intervention and psychotherapeutic help, and the like. Because these efforts absorbed scarce research resources, some have argued that our push to assist sexual abuse victims has been given such a strong priority that we have not attended sufficiently well to the needs of other mistreated children, for example, those who are neglected or who witness violence between their parents.

IMPLEMENTING THE RESULTS OF NEEDS ASSESSMENTS

Although needs assessments are, by definition, research with practical implications, ensuring that the results are implemented frequently is challenging. Several issues are part of this general problem. First, the results must be presented in a form where the suggestions and how to implement them are clearly outlined. This has been problematic in the past, as Carter (1996) notes in her review of needs assessments from the late 1970s through 1989. She found that, although authors usually detailed the research process, they offered few suggestions about how to carry out the required changes.

Second, Carter (1996) observes that researchers often write for other academics. Important as the academic audience is, with needs assessments, the people we want to influence with our work include service providers, policymakers, and the target population. These groups might require a different report from that for professors and their students. The organization of material and the style of presenting findings and recommendations should be sensitive to the likely interests and priorities of nonacademic readers. Researchers might even consider writing more than one report in the interest of effective communication with diverse audiences.

Amodeo and Gal (1997) recommend another strategy for facilitating the use of needs assessment research, namely, to involve the sponsor organizations in all steps of the study. This ensures that the sponsor is knowledgeable about the research and committed to following it up effectively. In their discussion of this theme, Amodeo and Gal propose that researchers should allot a generous amount of time after data collection to help the sponsor agency digest the findings and plan a response to them.

CONCLUSIONS

The examples we have offered in this chapter illustrate that needs assessments are a practical research method with vast potential usefulness to social work. The results can be especially meaningful in our work because they document the needs of people experiencing problems rather than addressing the more esoteric interests of social scientists bent on testing or developing theory. Needs assessment can raise important questions, identify what aspects of services or policies are useful, indicate what needs to be improved, and highlight gaps or misapplications of services. The results can challenge us in the same ways as all good research does, inviting us to test our assumptions against evidence gathered from the clients and communities we serve and changing our beliefs and interventions in beneficial ways as a result.

REFERENCES

Amodeo, M., & Gal, C. (1997). Strategies for ensuring use of needs assessment findings: Experiences of a community substance abuse prevention program. *Journal of Primary Prevention, 18,* 227-242.

Carter, C. (1996). Using and communicating findings. In R. Revere, S. Berkowitz, C. Carter, & C. Ferguson (Eds.), *Needs assessment: A creative and practical guide for social scientists* (pp. 185-201). Washington, DC: Taylor & Francis.

Carter, M., Crosby, C., Geertshuis, S., & Startup, M. (1996). Developing reliability in client-centered mental health needs assessment. *Journal of Mental Health, 5,* 233-243.

Cummings, S. M., Kelly, T. B., Holland, T. P., & Peterson-Hazan, S. (1998). Development and validation of the Needs Inventory for Caregivers of the Hospitalized Elderly. *Research on Social Work Practice, 8,* 120-132.

Delbecq, A. L. (1986). *Group techniques for program planning: A guide to nominal groups and Delphi processes.* Middleton, WI: Green Briar.

Gerdes, K. E., & Benson, R. A. (1995). Problems of inner-city schoolchildren: Needs assessment by nominal group process. *Social Work in Education, 17,* 139-147.

Kuh, G. D. (1982). Purposes and principles for needs assessment in student affairs. *Journal of College Student Personnel, 23,* 202-209.

Lenning, O. T. (1980). Assessment and evaluation. In U. Delworth & G. R. Hanson (Eds.), *Student services: A handbook for the profession* (pp. 232-266). San Francisco: Jossey-Bass.

Lyman, S. R., Pulice, R. T., & McCormick, L. L. (1993). Developing strategies for providing services to the mentally ill chemically abusing population. *Administration in Social Work, 17,* 97-108.

Maslow, A. (1970). *Motivation and personality.* New York: Harper & Row.

McKillip, J. (1998). Needs analysis: Process and techniques. In L. Bickman & D. Rag (Eds.), *Handbook of applied social research methods* (pp. 261-284). Thousand Oaks, CA: Sage.

Revere, R., Berkowitz, S., Carter, C., & Ferguson, C. (1996). Introduction. In R. Revere, S. Berkowitz, C. Carter, & C. Ferguson (Eds.), *Needs assessment: A creative and practical guide for social scientists* (pp. 1-12). Washington, DC: Taylor & Francis.

Rosenthal, J. A., Groze, V., & Morgan, J. (1996). Services for families adopting children via public child welfare agencies: Use, helpfulness, and need. *Children and Youth Services Review, 18,* 163-182.

Singer, M., Bussey, J., Song, L., & Lunghofer, L. (1995). The psychosocial issues of women serving time in jail. *Social Work, 40,* 103-113.

Stabb, S. (1995). Needs assessment methodologies. In S. D. Stabb, S. M. Harris, & J. E. Talley (Eds.), *Multicultural needs assessment for college and university student populations* (pp. 51-115). Springfield, IL: Charles C Thomas.

Tracy, E. M., Green, R. K., & Bremseth, M. D. (1993). Meeting the environmental needs of abused and neglected children: Implications from a statewide survey of supportive services. *Social Work Research & Abstracts, 29*(2), 21-26.

Tutty, L. M., & Rothery, M. (1997, July). *Women who seek shelter for wife assault: Risk assessment and services needs.* Paper presented at the Fifth International Family Violence Research Conference, Durham, NH.

Tutty, L. M., Weaver, G., & Rothery, M. A. (1999). Residents' views of the efficacy of shelter services for abused women. *Violence Against Women, 5,* 869-925.

Weaver, H. W. (1997). The challenges of research in Native American communities: Incorporating principles of cultural competence. *Journal of Social Service Research, 23,* 1-15.

Witkin, B. R., & Altschuld, J. W. (1995). *Planning and conducting needs assessments: A practical guide.* Thousand Oaks, CA: Sage.

Yegidis, B. L., Weinbach, R. W., & Morrison-Rodriguez, B. (1999). *Research methods for social workers* (3rd ed.). Needham Heights, MA: Allyn & Bacon.

CHAPTER TEN

Randomized Controlled Trials

RAM A. CNAAN

GUY ENOSH

Science is concerned with understanding variability in nature, statistics is concerned with making decisions about nature in the presence of variability, and experimental design is concerned with reducing and controlling variability in ways that make statistical theory applicable to decisions made about nature.

—*Winer, Brown, and Michels (1991, p. 1)*

I was struck by the power of this novel technique [experimentation] to cut through the clouds of confusing correlations that make the inference of causality so hazardous. . . . With experimental data, one could state with measurable confidence whether a particular public policy affected a particular outcome. I have never quite lost my sense of wonder at this amazing fact.

—*Orr (1999, p. xi)*

The purpose of this chapter is twofold. The first purpose is to acquaint the reader with the experimental design called *randomized controlled trial* (RCT) in biomedical research and *field experiments* in social policy/program evaluation. These two terms are used interchangeably throughout the chapter. The second purpose is to identify ways in which the researcher can reduce and control biases (systematic errors) that may affect the validity and generalizability of evaluation research. The role of experimental design is to enable the researcher to control for various biases or alternative hypotheses to the studied intervention.

The natural and behavioral sciences have long used an experimental approach to research (Boruch, 1997). Unlike laboratory experiments, these experiments are conducted in naturalistic contexts (Boruch, 1997; Orr, 1999) such as clinics, welfare agencies, and schools. The advantage of this type of experiment is that findings are more realistic and can be generalized. The disadvantage is that the nonlaboratory setting makes it more difficult to control for confounding variables. In this context, the RCT, although costly in terms of time and money in its more complex form, is important because its design makes it possible to control for biases that may affect the validity and generalizability of the study.

This chapter starts with a presentation of the basic experimental design and the ways in which it deals with possible biases to the validity of conclusions. The chapter continues with the more elaborate forms of RCTs developed in the biomedical sciences and the possible drawbacks associated with those. A section titled "Issues of Assignment and Analysis" deals with various problems related to the randomization process as well as possible design variations and statistical procedures that were developed to handle those issues. Then, the application of RCT to social work research is discussed, leading to a discussion of ethical issues and their methodological implications.

THE EXPERIMENTAL DESIGN

Field experiments became popular when it became clear that inferences about effective treatment for a patient population could not be generalized from a single case study. Furthermore, many non-RCT studies that reported therapeutic success later proved to be inaccurate due to selection bias. Therefore, researchers have concluded that only a planned field experiment based on carefully selected cases (i.e., those who meet well-defined inclusion/exclusion criteria) is sufficient to elucidate the most appropriate treatment for future patients with a given medical or social condition (Pocock, 1983).

The basic experimental design is a field experiment that has a treatment group and a control group. Unlike other group comparisons, experimental designs (a) compare those receiving a new treatment to those receiving no treatment or an existing treatment, (b) randomly assign participants to either the treatment group or the control group, and (c) take relevant measurements of both groups when treatment is complete. For a truly randomized trial, a before-treatment assessment is optional but not necessary (for a discussion of this point, see Campbell & Stanley, 1963, p. 25). Lack of one or more of those characteristics does not necessarily render the study improper but might confound the results.

Issues of Bias and Validity in Evaluation Research

Bias is defined as systematic error introduced into sampling or testing that influences outcome. In general terms, *validity* refers to the extent to which the conclusions about the effects of the intervention are well founded. Threats to internal validity may be conceived as alternative hypotheses to the explanation of the results of an intervention, whereas threats to external validity are threats to the generalizability of the results beyond the specific study (Kazdin, 1992). In the following section, we discuss biases that may invalidate results and the ways in which the experimental design attempts to control for them.

Bias and Internal Validity

Internal validity is concerned with the demonstrated correlation between the intervention and the changes observed. In their seminal work on experimental and quasi-experimental designs, Campbell and Stanley (1963) identify a number of biases that may confound the results of the experiment and lead the researcher to conclude erroneously that the intervention is responsible for the results. These biases, which may interact with one another, are defined as follows:

History: This is bias due to the influence of events that may be responsible for the results measured.

Maturation: This is bias due to the effect of developmental processes on changes being measured in the experiment.

Testing: This is bias due to repeating the same measurement several times.

Instrumentation: This is bias due to poorly standardized measurements, changes in the measurement instrument over time, influence of the testers, or use of subjective norms to judge the efficacy of an intervention.

Statistical regression to the mean: This is bias associated with the selection of participants based on a certain scale. For example, if the inclusion criteria for a new therapeutic intervention define eligible participants as those with acute symptoms, then a natural process of "recovery" may occur. This, in turn, would confound findings regarding the effects of the intervention.

Selection: This is bias due to a systematic difference between the control and treatment groups or to self-selection. Selection may combine with other threats, especially history and maturation, to create inequality between the experimental and control groups. Such inequality might influence the results, leading the researcher to wrong conclusions concerning the intervention.

Attrition/"experimental mortality": This is bias due to client dropout from the program. If the dropout rates between the treatment and control groups are balanced, and if the reason for dropping out is unrelated to the intervention, then this bias may be controlled by using statistical techniques such as survival analysis (Allison, 1995; Greenhouse, Stangl, & Bromberg, 1989).

Lack of compliance: Similar to attrition but much more severe (because it is less salient), this bias is a major threat to the internal validity of experimental design, especially field experiments. For example, if, as part of the intervention, clients are supposed to keep diaries, attend a series of meetings, take medication, and the like, then not fulfilling those demands might bias the results of the intervention and the conclusions drawn based on the results.

Crossover: This bias refers to the threat to internal validity that emanates from the switching of clients between experimental groups or between experimental and control groups.

To control for biases to internal validity, important steps must be taken in the experimental design. First, the use of random assignment to control and experimental groups enables the researcher to minimize the threat emanating from possible biases such as history, testing, regression toward the mean, and selection. Randomized assignment creates an "equal chance" for each individual to belong to either of the groups. Having two (or more) groups that are equivalent and that exist at the same point in time minimizes the threats of selection, history, maturation, and the interaction between them. Second, by combining the design with a process evaluation and qualitative methods, it is possible to record and account for various biases and threats to validity including history, maturation, crossover, lack of compliance, testing, and instrumentation. Process evaluation is important in ruling out alternative explanations to the results. It also can help to identify possible new hypotheses that may lead to further research. Third, use of advanced statistical procedures (e.g., event-history analysis) can minimize the threats emanating from attrition. Fourth, to avoid or minimize crossover and attrition, suitable incentives and controls should be implemented (e.g., material incentives, explanation of the importance of the study and its design). Such incentives are meant to deter clients from leaving the program and from sharing information or materials (e.g., medications) that might jeopardize the study. Similar procedures should be taken with the staff of the program. Attrition and crossover may be the result of attitudes and behaviors of workers as well as clients. The use of more elaborate forms of RCTs that are designed to control for such threats is the focus of later sections of this chapter.

Bias and External Validity

External validity relates to the degree to which the results can be generalized beyond the study population to the general population. Biases that may compromise the generalizability of evaluation experiments have been widely discussed in the literature. In what follows, based mostly on Kazdin's (1992) excellent summary, we discuss the most common biases (for a more detailed discussion, see Bracht & Glass, 1968; Campbell & Stanley, 1963):

Characteristics of the sample: This is bias occurring when the sample is (a) not characteristic of the population for whom the new intervention is intended, (b) not representative of the general population demographically, or (c) not representative in terms of the clinical or social problems that the intervention is meant to alleviate.

Stimulus characteristics: This is bias due to (a) differences between the experimental setting and the setting for which the intervention ultimately is intended, (b) effects related to researcher characteristics, or (c) setting characteristics. This threat is especially important in social work research as compared to biomedical research. Biomedical research is based mostly on easily measurable interventions such as drugs. Social work interventions, on the other hand, consist mostly of interaction between the worker and participants. Thus, such interventions are more prone to bias emanating from possible reactivity of participants to characteristics of the setting or the worker.

Reactivity of experimental arrangements: This is bias due to participants' awareness that they are part of an experiment. Participants may develop an attitude toward the experiment and their role in it, thus compromising the impact of the intervention and the ability to generalize from the results. Possible reactions might include trying hard to "succeed," developing negative attitudes, and the like.

Reactivity of assessment: This is bias due to participants' awareness that they are being assessed during the experiment. The assessment procedure becomes a major part of the intervention instead of having a marginal role.

Contamination: This is bias that occurs when the experimental and control interventions are carried out within the same site and controls are influenced by what they learn about the experimental group. This bias is related to the crossover threat to internal validity discussed earlier. Like the crossover threat to internal validity, contamination may emanate from the staff of the program as well as from interactions between members of the experimental and control groups.

Multiple treatment interference: This is bias due to participants' exposure to prior treatment that may confound the results of the new trial. This may be especially important when the design includes different stages with different interventions or when clients come from diverse backgrounds with extremely different prior interventions and experiences. The results of the intervention may be due to an interaction between prior interventions and the current one and not from each of them separately.

Test sensitization: This is bias due to repeated testing during the experiment.

Novelty/Hawthorn effects: This is bias due to participants' reactions to having any type of intervention, regardless of its content.

Time effects: This is bias due to lack of follow-up to determine whether effects measured shortly after treatment are valid over time.

To control for external biases that can invalidate the generalizability of the findings, two important steps are required. First, the experiment should be replicated in different contexts of time, sites, and clients. Basing a new intervention policy on one trial may be justified in biomedical research, where physiological and medical knowledge enables the researcher to reach definite conclusions based on a comparatively limited sample (Brody, 1998). However, in the behavioral and social sciences, it is imperative to use multiple trials and comparisons to substantiate a claim for definitive and generalized results (Campbell & Rouso, 1999). Second, the design of the intervention must provide for ongoing monitoring and process evaluation, using in-depth interviews and systematic observation whenever possible (Rossi & Freeman, 1993). This will enable the researcher to (a) ascertain that the intervention was carried out according to the intervention protocol and that randomization was not compromised and (b) assess the reactions of the clients to the intervention, the setting, and the clinicians or professionals involved.

DESIGN OF RANDOMIZED CONTROLLED TRIALS

The design of RCTs used in biomedical research has become increasingly complex, compared to the design of the basic randomized field experiment that uses one experimental group and one control group. The elaborated RCT format developed for biomedical research may be categorized by four phases:

- A Phase 1 (initial) trial generally is performed when a new treatment method is proposed. The sample size is limited, and the frequency of data collection is high. The purpose is to detect any negative or side effects to the treatment that might occur over short-term use. Typically, this phase requires about 20 participants.
- A Phase 2 trial involves a larger sample (20 to 100 participants). The purpose is to provide preliminary information regarding the efficacy of the new treatment versus other modes of treatment. Phase 2 studies are used to identify therapies that should be tested in a large-scale clinical trial.
- A Phase 3 trial, often the final and largest phase, compares the new treatment to the standard treatment, other experimental treatments, or a "no treatment" option to determine its efficacy among certain subgroups. The minimum sample size usually is 100 participants and at times will be much higher.
- A Phase 4 trial is used to follow up the long-term effects and safety of a treatment that has been approved for public use. (Meinert & Tonascia, 1986)

The basic characteristics of any controlled clinical trial are that (a) it is carried out on humans, (b) it is designed to assess the effectiveness of one or more modes of intervention, (c) it is preceded by the preparation of a very detailed protocol, (d) clients are randomly selected for one of the relevant study groups, (e) blind treatment is provided if possible, (f) the study is preferably done in a multicenter arrangement so as to accrue a large enough number of participants, (g) pretreatment data are carefully selected and collected for each client for as long as possible, (h) response data are collected for as long as the study is under way, and (i) clients are carefully and randomly selected for the study so that generalization will be feasible.

Stability of Change and Replication

An important design aspect of an RCT is the repetition of measurements over time (Phase 4 trial). By following up on clients for an extensive period after the study, researchers can ascertain not only the degree of change but also the stability of the change. As important as short-term randomized trials are in proving the effectiveness of a new intervention, the generalizability and long-term effectiveness of the study might be in doubt if clients are not followed up.

To assess the effects of the study treatment, one or more observations/measurements are recorded for each client during each trial phase. Pretreatment assessment includes the client's condition prior to treatment, personal characteristics, and clinical history (i.e., duration of the problem, previous care, and severity of the problem). To ensure reliability, the client's condition is measured one or more times prior to treatment. During treatment, measurements specified in the study protocol are taken on a regular basis. Finally, side effects may be monitored by using a preapproved checklist or through systematic open-ended questioning (Meinert & Tonascia, 1986).

Replication is essential for demonstrating the generalizability of research findings. Replication is defined as examining change over different sites, sample populations (as defined by eligibility criteria), and time. One way in which to achieve generalizability is by using multiple replications or by summing results over several studies with the use of meta-analysis (Mulrow & Cook, 1998). Another way is to use multiple sites, connected and coordinated by one center, all participating in the randomized trials (Meinert & Tonascia, 1986). A multiple-site RCT, as with any RCT, requires a very explicit protocol that details the criteria for eligibility and randomization. This ensures that replication can be carried out, either synchronically or diachronically, with minimum risk of biased results (Cnaan, 1991).

In a multiple-site trial, collaborating practitioners give treatment in various settings. The names of all clients who meet the study criteria and who are willing to participate are reported to the coordinating center. To ensure that the sample is representative of the client population for whom the new treatment is intended, the coordinating center must adhere strictly to the eligibility criteria so as to avoid any selection biases (Pocock & Lagakos, 1982). Those meeting the study criteria are randomly assigned to a treatment or control group. It is important to note that, in many RCTs, the control group may be receiving an alternate intervention rather than no intervention.

Allocation of responsibility. To reduce bias, responsibilities for carrying out RCTs are best divided among three units: service providers, data analysts, and study managers (McDill, 1979). This is necessary due to the level of sophistication required for this type of study. In addition, major RCTs require a coordinating center to handle administrative matters such as approving new studies, registering and randomizing new clients, collecting and processing client records, monitoring protocol procedures, and developing policy in collaboration with other participants (Meinert, Heintz, & Forman, 1983; Meinert & Tonascia, 1986). Usually, an RCT has a steering committee that meets periodically to assess the overall progress of the study. It is the responsibility of the statisticians to determine the number of clients required in each trial and the method of randomization as well as to conduct the data analysis. Finally, institutions that have agreed to participate in the study have the responsibility of sharing their results with the principal investigator(s).

Issues of Assignment and Analysis

Extreme care must be taken in the selection of the sample to ensure that those in the experimental and control groups are representative of the population for whom the new treatment/intervention is intended. The reader should keep in mind the difference between random sampling (which rarely is feasible in intervention studies) and random assignment (which is the defining feature of experimental designs). Random assignment theoretically gives the greatest likelihood that the experimental and control groups will be similar.

Blind assignment. One way in which to control for bias that may compromise internal/external validity is by assigning participants to experimental and control groups so that they are not aware to which groups they belong. This is called *blind assignment.* In *double-blind assignment,* neither the clinicians nor the clients know which is the experimental group and which is the control group. Double-blind assignment generally is used in pharmaceutical research. However, it should be noted that over the course of a trial, clients may become aware of whether they are in the experimental or control group.

Matched control and experimental groups. Despite randomization, chance alone could lead to differences between groups that later might be interpreted as due to the experimental intervention (Kazdin, 1992). To control for this possibility, researchers should match clients on characteristics known or suspected to be related to the outcome variables. The matched groups then are randomized so that the experimental and control groups will be similar.

Matching can be done in several ways. The simplest way is to create a list of relevant variables and then split the original pool of clients according to their scores on the variables. This approach is not always feasible due to the difficulty of finding clients who match each other on all relevant variables. One alternative is to calculate a statistical profile of the matching variables in the original group and to match clients according to their profile scores. This approach is known as *propensity score matching* (Boruch & Terhanian, 1998; Rosenbaum & Rubin, 1983).

Group-randomized trials. Group-randomized trials are comparative studies in which (a) the units of assignment are identifiable groups and (b) the units of observation are members of those groups (Murray, 1998, p. 3). In such designs, the groups are not formed at random but rather are clustered according to some connection among their members. The groups may be schools, agencies, clinics, hospitals, and the like. The groups may be defined according to geographic location (e.g., block, neighborhood, city), social connection (e.g., families, members of a congregation), and the like. The sets of groups are randomly assigned, but the members are not. The units of observation are the members of the groups, not the groups. Usually, the number of groups in such a design is limited and rarely exceeds 10 to 15 groups. Such a design creates hierarchical nesting of the units of observation (individuals) within the units of assignment (groups) (Murray, 1998).

A group-randomized trial has several advantages. First, it may be easier to divide experimental and control groups along group lines than within groups. For example, different social welfare agencies could be used as control and experimental groups for a new job training program. This would enable the investigator to compare and evaluate the impact of natural clustering on the results of the intervention. Second, the researcher would need only the consent of the agencies involved rather than the consent of every individual. Third, this design is useful in minimizing biases due to clients' reactions to an experimental setting. On the other hand, because the number of groups usually is small, bias is nearly inevitable. Nevertheless, it is important to note that potential sources of bias are compounded by the use of groups as the units of assignment. For example, group rivalry, due to reactions of clients and/or professionals to being assigned to either the experimental or control group, may distort the results, and instrumentation differentials between the groups may yield different results that might be interpreted as related to the intervention (Murray, 1998).

The researcher also must consider the process of change with regard to group randomization. Explaining individual change differs from explaining group change in that group processes differ from individual processes. When conducting any type of field experiment or RCT, the researcher should take into account the influence of contextual variables such as the influence of belonging to a certain community or agency and even being treated by a certain therapist rather than another. Because the use of group comparisons creates natural clustering of the individuals into groups and, with large-scale and multisite RCTs, creates clustering of groups into "meta-groups," the influence of the group-related variables should be accounted for or controlled. Although this might justify using naturally occurring groups as the unit of assignment, understanding the contextual influences should be integrated into the therapeutic or social theory of change guiding the research project (Murray, 1998).

The use of multiple sites in individual- or group-randomized controlled trials, as well as the comparison of multiple replications (meta-analysis), raises several methodological questions. Do the sites themselves have an impact beyond the intervention? Are the sites equivalent to each other in their impact? Answers to these questions are crucial in interpreting results. If the sites themselves create a result beyond the intervention, then they cannot be regarded as equivalent, and randomization might be skewed due to clustering within individual sites. Moreover, even within the same site, each worker may implement the intervention in a slightly different way, creating biased results for the clients served by the worker.

As noted previously, one way in which to approach this problem is to assign the unit of analysis at the site or group level, but such a method has its own disadvantages. An alternative approach is to use statistical procedures known as multilevel analysis (or sometimes as *hierarchical linear modeling* [Bryk & Raudenbush, 1992; Kreft & de Leeuw 1998]). These procedures enable the researcher to differentiate between the impact of the intervention itself and the impact of contextual variables. These statistical models are quite complex and require the assistance of an experienced statistician.

Randomization and bias. Randomization in RCTs is not a foolproof solution for selection bias. Although randomized assignment of intervention at the site level is one way in which to control for this bias, this approach has drawbacks, as discussed earlier. Furthermore, if clients have alternatives available to them other than those at the agency, then the group that is examined will be representative of those willing to try new approaches or disappointed with existing ones, but it will not be representative of the general population. Thus, the ability to generalize to the general population would be questionable, and the external validity of the experiment would be jeopardized.

One famous case in which clients' preferences and intentional lack of compliance influenced the results is that of an AIDS randomized control clinical trial. Not trusting the pharmaceutical industry, AIDS patients met and shared their medications regardless of group assignment and study participation. The end result was the discovery of the cocktail of medications as an effective treatment. However, the study's ability to generate valid results was compromised. In social and human trials, clients can meet and discuss their experiences to pose similar threats to study validity. This threat is a form of the lack of compliance threat to validity discussed earlier.

Randomization and client preference. Randomization can cause bias when the procedure ignores the preferences of clients and professionals. As discussed earlier, blinding and double-blinding seldom are possible within the context of psychosocial intervention or policy change. Unless there is a "captive" clientele, clients' willingness to participate in an experiment will be influenced by their personal evaluation of existing treatments and by the persuasive powers of the staff. The end result is that those who choose to participate might be biased in their assessments of existing treatments. Whereas those in the treatment group might be influenced by the novelty effect, those in the control group might be disappointed in not receiving the new treatment.

Another source of bias due to client preferences is dropout of clients whose preferences were not met by the randomization procedure. Statistical procedures such as survival analysis are useful in controlling for the effect of dropout only when the dropout is not related to the treatment itself (Greenhouse et al., 1989).

An alternative solution to the problem of bias in randomization is to use a research design known as *partial randomization preference trials* (Bradley, 1997). In this approach, clients are presented with various options and asked whether they have any preference. Those who report no preference are assigned randomly, and those who have preferences are assigned to their preferred intervention approaches. This design uses four groups: two RCT groups (treatment and control) and two quasi-experimental groups. Analysis of the differences among the groups enables the researcher to measure the effects of preferences on outcome and reduces the problems related to dropout/experimental mortality.

Similar problems and concerns are encountered with regard to professionals' preferences. Many clinicians prefer their own modes of operation. Forcing them to try a new approach might bias their implementation of an intervention, either consciously or unconsciously. In medical research, for example, the literature has found intentional subversion of randomization procedures and medication schedules by practitioners participating in RCTs (Bradley, 1997).

USE OF RANDOMIZED CONTROLLED TRIALS IN SOCIAL WORK RESEARCH

The use of RCTs in social work generally follows the same phases as those in biomedical research. As noted earlier, Phase 1 is concerned with safety of the treatment, whereas Phase 2 identifies whether the treatment merits further study. A Phase 3 trial that investigates relative efficacy of treatments to various subgroups is particularly appropriate for social work because it can yield significant results with minimum investment. A Phase 4 trial, which measures long-term effects, can easily be incorporated into social work research because, by the nature of most social work interventions, clients continue to receive interventions long after the study is over.

The choice of experimental and control treatment/nontreatment is crucial given the many types/varieties of treatments used in social work practice. As a guideline, it is suggested that the most frequently used mode of practice in the participating agencies be chosen. Other major decisions (e.g., outcome measures, randomization, sample size, forms, data analysis, length of follow-up) should be based on the means and designated problem of the trial.

Selecting the Research Problem

A major issue in applying RCTs to social work practice is determining the problem on which to focus. Areas in social work best suited for RCTs include (a) emerging problems, that is, newly identified problems for which there is no tradition of care (e.g., comparing modes of treatment for chronically mentally ill homeless persons); (b) lack of successful treatment outcomes (e.g., comparing several methods of drug rehabilitation); (c) preventive measures in mental health (e.g., comparing programs to prevent sexual abuse of children); and (d) implementation of new policies (e.g., implementing innovations in a foster care program). Decisions as to the specific focus of any RCT in social work must necessarily be based on available resources and on the joint interests of collaborating agencies and political decision makers. An additional criterion is proposed by Hanrahan and Reid (1984), who state, "It makes sense to give more weight to studies dealing with problems of considerable importance to clients rather than problems of minor concern" (p. 248).

In this context, one caveat should be added. Because social work and social welfare research is embedded within a context of organizational and political decision making and power relations, such experiments can be carried on by an agency or at the county, state, or national level. Nevertheless, decision makers who decided to test a new program are much more likely to be interested in quick results than in waiting for results of a well-designed RCT that can take much longer. Thus, researchers should be watchful for the trade-off between satisfying organizational and political goals and satisfying research criteria.

ETHICAL CONSIDERATIONS

Research with humans involves three basic principles that are operationalized through the issues discussed in this chapter: respect for humans, beneficence (benefits exceed risks/disadvantages involved in the study), and justice (equal and fair distribution of the research benefits/burdens) (Lo, Feigal, Cummings, & Hulley, 1988). In any research concerning humans, one cannot separate ethical issues from pragmatic concerns. In other words, ethical considerations have an immediate impact on the methodology of research. Because ethical considerations always should take precedence, the following discussion relates each ethical concern to ethical solutions that were offered in the literature and to the impact that those solutions have on the methodology to be used.

Consent

The first and foremost ethical concern in any research involving humans is informing the participants in the research of the advantages and risks involved in the study and obtaining their consent to participate in the study. The participants should be informed of the treatment options and the randomization, and consent should be given to both (Lo et al., 1988). Because participants may object to randomization, several procedures to address this issue have been discussed in the biomedical literature. One alternative is to prerandomize the clients and ask their consent only for the particular intervention to which they are assigned. This approach, although used, raises ethical doubts because it implies manipulation and lack of respect (Brody, 1998). Another alternative is to randomize at the unit level (e.g., agency, clinic, school). This approach requires the consent of the agency management but bypasses the need for individual consent. A third approach is to include in a clinical trial only clients who agree *prior to* random assignment to be randomly assigned to a particular condition. For the participating individuals, agency policy is finite, as would be any other agency policy with which they might or might not agree. Methodologically, the result is group randomization, with all the advantages and drawbacks discussed earlier.

Equipoise

Randomized trials include a control group or groups that receive a placebo intervention or no intervention. The question that often arises is whether it is ethical to give controls no treatment or an alternative treatment that might be considered inferior. Two issues must be considered in attempting to answer this question. First, is it known that the experimental intervention is superior to the control intervention or no intervention? If we possess such knowledge, then there is no need for the experiment. In medical research, this principle was framed under the concept of *equipoise* by Charles Fried. Equipoise is defined as "a state of uncertainty [that] must exist for a concurrently controlled trial to be justified" (Brody, 1998, p. 145). The responsibility of the researcher is to routinely monitor the results of the RCT and stop the trials at the point at which conclusive results can be determined, either for or against the intervention under study.

Independent Review

Any RCT includes an independent review board. It is the board's responsibility to review (a) the proposed intervention, (b) the advantages expected to accrue for the clients, (c) inherent/possible risks involved, (d) possible injustices in the study, and (e) safeguards against exploitation of participants, especially vulnerable ones (Brody, 1998; Lo et al., 1988). For a detailed discussion of the composition and functions of review boards, the interested reader should consult relevant sources (e.g., Brody, 1998, pp. 41-43).

SUMMARY

Conducting a randomized field experiment is a tedious and expensive endeavor, enabling the researcher to control for potential biases that may be involved in evaluating program efficacy and efficiency while demanding a huge investment in terms of time and human and fiscal resources. The major justification for such an endeavor is the immense potential it holds for substantiating the effectiveness and efficacy of social interventions.

This chapter started with a presentation of the basic experimental design and a discussion of its potential for controlling possible biases to validity in the inferences drawn by researchers when they come to evaluate social interventions. It continued by describing the more elaborate form of RCTs developed in the biomedical field and different variations on those designs such as group-randomized design and partial randomization preference design. All of these designs have one common goal: to minimize and control for possible sources of bias. Each design poses a solution to a possible threat discussed previously and raises its own problems.

The fields of social work, psychosocial intervention, and social policy historically have been guided by practices based on personal and professional belief systems. By using experimental designs, those fields are presented with the potential to establish the effectiveness of their interventions. This opportunity defines the subtle division between practice as art and practice as science. The experimental design creates the bridges between personal and professional beliefs and the actual reality of outcomes and between theory-based practice and its impact. Using the experimental design, and especially the variety of elaborate forms discussed in this chapter, is not a foolproof path to "the truth." These are, however, the best available means that researchers have in their search for better solutions to social problems.

Case Example 1

Hogarty et al. (1986) studied 103 persons diagnosed with schizophrenia or schizoaffective disorder who lived in high-expressed emotion households. They randomly assigned the participants to after-hospital care of four treatments: family treatment and medication, social skills training and medication, their combination, or a drug-treated condition. Follow-up 1 year later indicated higher rates of relapse among the fourth group (medication only) and no relapse in the third group (both social treatment and medication), suggesting that social care in addition to medication is effective in preventing relapse after hospitalization.

Case Example 2

Solomon, Draine, Mannion, and Meisel (1998) examined the effects of family intervention on help-seeking behavior of families of adults with severe mental illness. A total of 225 family members were randomly assigned to one of three conditions: a 10-week group workshop, individual family consultation, or a waiting list (control group). Family members were interviewed about the extent of their contact with three help sources: mental health professionals, providers, and community resources. Interviews were conducted at baseline (before the intervention), at termination of the intervention, and at 6 months after termination. No differences were found among the three groups in the extent of family members' contact with three types of services: conventional, psychosocial, and ancillary mental health services.

REFERENCES

Allison, P. (1995). *Survival analysis using the SAS system: A practical guide*. Cary, NC: SAS Institute.

Boruch, R. F. (1997). *Randomized experiments for planning and evaluation: A practical guide*. Thousand Oaks, CA: Sage.

Boruch, R. F., & Terhanian, G. (1998). Cross-design synthesis. In A. J. Reynolds (Ed.), *Evaluation methods for educational productivity* (pp. 59-85). Greenwich, CT: JAI.

Bracht, G. H., & Glass, G. V. (1968). The external validity of experiments. *American Educational Research Journal, 5*, 437-474.

Bradley, C. (1997). Psychological issues in clinical trial design. *Irish Journal of Psychology, 18*(1), 67-87.

Brody, B. A. (1998). *The ethics of biomedical research*. New York: Oxford University Press.

Bryk, A. S., & Raudenbush, S. W. (1992). *Hierarchical linear models: Applications and data analysis methods*. Newbury Park, CA: Sage.

Campbell, D. T., & Rouso, M. J. (1999). *Social experimentation*. Thousand Oaks, CA: Sage.

Campbell, D. T., & Stanley, J. C. (1963). *Experimental and quasi-experimental designs for research*. Chicago: Rand McNally.

Cnaan, R. A. (1991). Applying controlled clinical trials in social work practice. *Research on Social Practice, 1*, 139-161.

Greenhouse, J. B., Stangl, D., & Bromberg, J. (1989). An introduction to survival analysis: Statistical methods for analysis of clinical data. *Journal of Counseling and Clinical Psychology, 57,* 536-544.

Hanrahan, P., & Reid, W. J. (1984). Choosing effective intervention. *Social Service Review, 58,* 244-258.

Hogarty, G. E., Anderson, C. M., Reiss, D. J., Kornblith, S. J., Greenwald, D. P., & Javna, C. D. (1986). Family psychoeducation, social skills training, and maintenance chemotherapy in the aftercare treatment of schizophrenia: One-year effects of a controlled study on relapse and expressed emotion. *Archives of General Psychiatry, 43,* 633-642.

Kazdin, A. E. (1992). *Research design in clinical psychology.* Needham Heights, MA: Allyn & Bacon.

Kreft, I., & de Leeuw, J. (1998). *Introducing multilevel modeling.* Thousand Oaks, CA: Sage.

Lo, B., Feigal, D., Cummings, S., & Hulley, S. B. (1988). Addressing ethical issues. In S. B. Hulley & S. R. Cummings (Eds.), *Designing clinical research* (pp. 151-159). Baltimore, MD: Williams & Wilkins.

McDill, M. (1979). Activity analysis of data coordinating centers. In *Coordinating Center Model Project: A study of coordinating centers in multicenter clinical trials XVI* (pp. 105-125). Bethesda, MD: National Heart, Lung and Blood Institute.

Meinert, C. L., Heintz, E. C., & Forman, S. A. (1983). Role and method of the coordinating center. *Controlled Clinical Trials, 4,* 355-375.

Meinert, C. L., & Tonascia, S. (1986). *Clinical trials: Design, conduct, and analysis.* New York: Oxford University Press.

Mulrow, C., & Cook, D. (1998). *Systematic reviews: Synthesis of best evidence for health care decisions.* Philadelphia: American College of Physicians.

Murray, D. M. (1998). *Design and analysis of group-randomized trials.* New York: Oxford University Press.

Orr, L. L. (1999). *Social experiments.* Thousand Oaks, CA: Sage.

Pocock, S. T. (1983). *Clinical trials: A practical approach.* New York: John Wiley.

Pocock, S. T., & Lagakos, S. W. (1982). Practical experience of randomization in cancer trials: An international survey. *British Journal of Cancer, 46,* 368-375.

Rosenbaum, P. R., & Rubin, D. B. (1983). The central role of the propensity score in observational studies for causal effects. *Biometrika, 70,* 41-55.

Rossi, P. H., & Freeman, H. E. (1993). *Evaluation: A systematic approach* (5th ed.). Newbury Park, CA: Sage.

Solomon, P., Draine, J., Mannion, E., & Meisel, M. (1998). Increased contact with community mental health resources as a potential benefit of family education. *Psychiatric Services, 49,* 333-339.

Winer, B. J., Brown, D. R., & Michels, K. (1991). *Statistical principles in experimental design.* New York: McGraw-Hill.

CHAPTER ELEVEN

Program Evaluation

T. K. LOGAN

DAVID ROYSE

For social problems such as drug addiction, homelessness, child abuse, domestic violence, illiteracy, and poverty, programs have been designed to directly attack either the problems' origins or to ameliorate their effects on individuals, families, and communities. These programs are what attract many social workers to the profession; we want to be part of the mechanism through which society provides assistance to those most in need. Despite low wages, bureaucratic red tape, and routinely uncooperative clients, we tirelessly provide our best services that are, at various times, insufficient, inappropriate, and (quite often) invaluable. But without conducting evaluation, we do not know whether our programs are helping or hurting, that is, whether they are postponing the hunt for real solutions or truly constructing new futures for our clients.

There are two major types of evaluation: informal and formal. We all are consumers and constantly are evaluating products, services, and information supplied to us. For example, we may choose not to return to a store or an agency again if we do not believe that the staff were helpful. We may mentally file a handful of unsolicited comments from clients and draw unwarranted conclusions about a program. Anecdotal and informal approaches such as these generally are not regarded as carrying scientific credibility.

By contrast, formal evaluation systematically examines data from and about programs and their outcomes so that better decisions can be made about the interventions designed to address the related social problem. Thus, program evaluation involves the use of social research methodologies to appraise and improve the ways in which human services, policies, and programs are conducted. Formal evaluation, by its very nature, is applied research.

Program evaluation attempts to answer questions such as the following. Do our clients get better? How does our success rate compare to those of other programs or agencies? Can the same level of success be obtained through less expensive means? What is the experience of the typical client? Should this program be terminated and its funds applied elsewhere?

Formal program evaluations can be found on just about every topic including the following examples. Fraser, Nelson, and Rivard (1997) examine the effectiveness of family preservation services. Kirby, Korpi, Adivi, and Weissman (1997) evaluate an AIDS and pregnancy prevention middle school program. Morrow-Howell, Becker-Kemppainen, and Judy (1998) evaluate an intervention designed to reduce the risk of suicide in elderly adult clients of a crisis hotline. Richter, Snider, and Gorey (1997) use a quasi-experimental design to study the effects of a group work intervention on female survivors of childhood sexual abuse. Leukefeld and colleagues (1998) examine the effects of an HIV prevention intervention with users of injected drug and crack.

ESSENTIAL EVALUATION PRECURSORS

Program evaluators can be categorized as being either internal or external. An *internal evaluator* is someone who is a program staff member or regular agency employee, whereas an *external evaluator* is a professional on contract hired for the specific purpose of evaluation. There are advantages and disadvantages at times in either role. For example, the internal evaluator probably will be very familiar with the staff and the program. This may save a lot of planning time. The disadvantage is that evaluations completed by an internal evaluator may be considered less valid by outside agencies such as the funding source. The external evaluator generally is thought to be less biased in terms of evaluation outcomes because he or she has no personal investment in the program. One disadvantage is that an external evaluator frequently is viewed as an "outsider" by the staff within an agency. This may affect the amount of time necessary to conduct the evaluation or cause problems in the overall evaluation if staff are reluctant to cooperate. Regardless of whether internal or external, the evaluator is well advised not only to keep agency staff informed but also to ask for their input at appropriate times.

There are six basic questions that guide and shape the design of any program evaluation effort that must be given thoughtful and deliberate consideration. These essential questions that must be asked prior to the planning of any formal evaluation effort are as follows:

1. What is the purpose of the evaluation?
2. What information is needed from the evaluation?
3. What is the best way in which to measure the target variables?
4. What is the unit of analysis?
5. How will the results be used and presented?

1. What Is the Purpose of the Program Evaluation?

It is essential that the evaluator has a firm understanding of the short- and long-term objectives of the evaluation. Imagine being hired for a position but not being given a job description or informed about how the job fits into the overall organization. Without knowing why an evaluation is called for or needed, the evaluator might attempt to answer a different set of questions from those of interest to the agency director or advisory board. The management might want to know why the majority of clients do not return after one or two visits, whereas the evaluator might think that his or her task is to determine whether clients who received group therapy sessions were better off than clients who received individual counseling. If the future funding of the program rises or falls on the findings of the evaluation, then a lot more importance will be attached to it than if a new manager simply wants to know whether clients were satisfied with services. The more that is riding on an evaluation, the more attention will be given to the methodology and operationalization of variables and the more threatened staff can be, especially if they think that the purpose of the evaluation is to downsize and trim excess employees.

In clarifying the overall purpose of the evaluation, it is critical to talk with different program "stakeholders." Scriven (1991) defines a program stakeholder as "one who has a substantial ego, credibility, power, futures, or other capital invested in the program. . . . This includes program staff and many who are not actively involved in the day-to-day operations" (p. 334). Stakeholders include both supporters and opponents of the program, and the evaluator needs to obtain all the different views about the program. By listening and considering stakeholder perspectives, the evaluator can potentially ascertain the most important aspects of the program to target for the evaluation by looking for overlapping concerns, questions, and comments from the various stakeholders. It also is critical that the evaluator works closely with whoever initiated the evaluation to set priorities for the evaluation.

Once the overall purpose and priorities of the evaluation are established, the rest of the evaluation plan can be addressed, but first it is important to develop a written agreement, especially if the evaluator is an external one. Misunderstandings can and will occur months later if things are not written in black and white.

2. What Information Is Needed From the Evaluation?

This second question requires the evaluator to develop good researchable questions. A good rule to follow is to focus the evaluation on one or two key questions. Too many questions can lengthen the process and overwhelm the evaluator with too much data that, instead of facilitating a decision, might produce inconsistent findings. Sometimes, funding sources require only that some vague undefined type of evaluation is conducted. The funding sources might neither expect nor desire dissertation-quality research; they simply might expect "good faith" efforts when beginning evaluation processes. Other agencies may be quite demanding in the types and forms of data to be provided. Obviously, the choice of methodology, data collection procedures, and reporting formats will be strongly affected by the purpose, objectives, and questions examined in the study. It is important to note the difference between general research and evaluation. In research, the investigator often focuses on questions based on theoretical considerations or hypotheses generated to build on research in a specific area of study. Although program evaluations may focus on an intervention derived from some theory, the evaluation questions should, first and foremost, be driven by the program's objectives. The evaluator is less concerned with building on prior literature or contributing to the development of practice theory than with determining whether a specific program worked in a specific community or location.

After deciding what general information is needed from the evaluation, it is important to define the specific target variables. These will vary from evaluation to evaluation, depending on the questions being asked. In one project, the focus might be on the variable of arrests (or rearrests) so as to determine whether the program reduced criminal justice involvement. In another project, the target variable might be number of hospitalizations or days of hospitalization. Both of these evaluations would be attempting to answer the question, "What impact did the program have?" The variables of interest would be those that could show whether there were any posttreatment effects (also known as outcome evaluation). However, if the question posed to the evaluator was "Did the program achieve its goals?" or "What was learned in operating this program?," then the evaluator would look at another whole set of variables dealing with how well the program was implemented.

Process Evaluation

Narrative in nature, process evaluation describes the day-to-day program efforts; program modifications and changes; outside events that influenced the program; people and institutions involved; culture, customs, and traditions that evolved; and sociodemographic makeup of the clientele (Scarpitti, Inciardi, & Pottieger, 1993). Process evaluation is concerned with identifying program strengths and weaknesses so that other agencies or localities wishing to start similar programs can benefit without having to make the same mistakes. For example, Bentelspacher, DeSilva, Goh, and LaRowe (1996) conducted a process evaluation of the cultural compatibility of psychoeducational family group treatment with ethnic Asian clients.

Researchers often have relied only on program outcomes such as termination and graduation rates or number of rearrests to determine effectiveness. However, to better understand how and *why* a program such as Drug Court is effective, an analysis of how the program was conceptualized, implemented, and revised is needed. A process evaluation, in contrast to an examination of program outcome only, can provide a clearer and more comprehensive picture of how Drug Court affects those involved in the treatment program process (e.g., prosecutors, judges, staff, defendants, defense attorneys).

More specifically, a process evaluation can provide information about program aspects that need to be improved and those that work well (Scarpitti et al., 1993). Finally, a process evaluation may help to facilitate replication of the Drug Court program in other areas. This often is referred to as technology transfer.

A different but related process evaluation could be a description of the failures and departures from the way in which the intervention originally was designed. How were the staff trained and hired? Did the intervention depart from the treatment manual recommendations? Influences (e.g., delayed funding or staff hires, changes in policies or procedures) that shape and affect the intervention that clients receive need to be identified because they affect the fidelity of the treatment program. When program implementation deviates significantly from what was intended, this might be the logical explanation as to why a program is not working.

Outcome or Impact Evaluation

This type of evaluation focuses on the targeted objectives of the program such as behavior change. Outcomes usually are the after-treatment or postintervention effects. These effects may be either short term or long term. Immediate outcomes, or those generally measured at the end of the treatment or intervention, might or might not be the same results as one would get later in a 6- or 12-month follow-up. For example, immediately after an intensive drug education program for children, negative attitudes about using drugs might be observed. However, 1 year later, the children's attitudes toward drug use might have become favorable. Interpreting whether or not the program "worked" or whether the program had positive, negative, or no impact on attitudes toward drug use can depend on when measurements are obtained. It is not unusual for some evaluation questions to need a combination of both process and impact evaluation methodologies. For example, if it turned out that results of a particular evaluation showed that the program was not effective (impact), then it might be useful to know why it was not effective (process). In such cases, it would be important to know how the program was implemented, what changes were made in the program during the implementation, what problems were experienced during the implementation, and what was done to overcome those problems.

Evaluators also must consider costs as outcome and process considerations. Although the full cost of the program usually is easily computed, benefits are more difficult to convert into dollars. For example, Anderson, Bowland, Cartwright, and Bassin (1998) developed a methodology for estimating costs of delivering specific substance abuse treatment services. They collected data from 13 programs and found that the mean cost of residential treatment was $2,773 per patient per month and that outpatient treatment costs averaged $636 per patient per month. The benefit in terms of the monetary cost of someone abstaining from substance use is more difficult to estimate. With cost effectiveness, the evaluator divides the total program cost by the number of "successes" that the program has produced. This allows comparisons among programs in terms of something similar in concept to a "unit cost" or cost per program graduate.

3. What Is the Best Way in Which to Measure the Target Variables?

Determining the best way in which to measure the evaluation objectives and the target variables is the next important decision. Actually, there are a number of decisions that need to be made under this topic in evaluation planning. Measurement does not occur in a vacuum but rather might require data gathering in several locations over an extended length of time. Thus, the overall cost of the evaluation always surfaces as a prime consideration when planning how to measure the variables of interest.

Cost

All costs must be considered when thinking about needed financial resources. These include staff time to design and plan; availability of staff for collecting data and entering them into the computer; as well as supplies, photocopying, and time for analysis and report writing. In brief, the evaluator must ensure that there are funds to carry out all components of the evaluation and should not overlook the need to purchase psychological tests, drug testing kits, and/or technical assistance (e.g., statistical consultation).

Several options can be used to decrease the costs of evaluation. First, the evaluator can look to see whether there has been a similar study that could be replicated. A simple review of such a study might provide answers to particular measurement problems at hand. Replicating a similar study also can cut down on the time needed for planning and instrument development and may save time by eliminating thorny issues that inevitably arise during an evaluation. Second, the evaluator might determine whether there are data already available (collected and ready for analysis) that can be used to answer some of the questions of interest, as opposed to collecting new original data. Many agencies have a wealth of data that go unanalyzed.

Measurement

The evaluator must ponder issues such as the following. Is one instrument or scale better than another for measuring depression? What are the trade-offs relative to shorter or longer instruments? (For example, the most valid instrument might be so long that clients will get fatigued and refuse to complete it.) Is it better to measure a reduction in symptoms associated with a standardized test or to employ a behavioral measure (e.g., counting the number of days that patients with chronic mental illness are compliant with taking their medications)? Is measuring attitudes about drug abuse better than measuring knowledge about the symptoms of drug addiction? Evaluators frequently have to struggle with decisions about whether it is better to use instruments that are not "perfect" or to go to the trouble of developing and validating new ones.

When no suitable instrument or available data exist for the evaluation, the evaluator might have to create a new scale or at least modify an existing one. If an evaluator revises a previously developed measure, then he or she has the burden of demonstrating that the newly adapted instrument is reliable and valid. Then, there are issues such as the reliability of data obtained from clients. Will clients be honest in reporting actual drug and alcohol use? How accurate are their memories?

Evaluators use a multitude of methods and instruments to collect data for their studies. Interviews are good for collecting qualitative or sensitive data such as values and attitudes. This method requires an interview protocol or questionnaire. These usually are structured so that respondents are asked questions in a specific order, but they can be semistructured so that there are fewer topics and the interviewer has the ability to change the order based on a "reading" of the client's responses. Surveys can request information of clients by mail, by telephone, or in person. They may or may not be self-administered. So, besides considering what data are desired, evaluators must be concerned with pragmatic considerations regarding the best way in which to obtain or approximate the desired data.

One option for obtaining needed data is to use existing data. Collecting new data often is more expensive than using existing data. Examining the data at hand and already available always is a good first step. However, the evaluator might want to rearrange or reassemble the data, for example, dividing it by quarters or combining it into 12-month periods that help to reveal patterns and trends over time.

Existing data can come from a variety of places including the following:

Client records maintained by the program: These may include a host of demographic data about the population served.

Program expense and financial data: These can help the evaluator to determine whether one intervention is much more expensive than another.

Agency annual reports: These can be used to identify trends in service delivery and program costs. The evaluator can compare annual reports from year to year and can develop graphs to easily identify trends with clientele and programs.

Databases maintained by state health departments and vital records bureaus: Public data on births, deaths, and people served by public agencies can provide valuable information.

State and local population statistics: State and city planning offices maintain census data that may be helpful in targeting special services or outreach.

The federal government: The federal government collects and maintains a large amount of data on many different issues and topics. State and national data provide benchmarks for comparing local demographic or social indicators to national-level demographic or social indicators.

If existing data cannot be used or cannot answer all of the evaluation questions, then original data must be collected. There are many types of evaluation designs from which to choose, and no single one will be ideal for every project. The specific approach chosen for the evaluation will depend on the purpose of the evaluation; the research questions to be explored; the hoped-for or intended results; the quality and volume of data available or needed; and staff, time, and resource constraints. The next section presents a brief overview of the major types of evaluation designs. For a fuller discussion of these topics, refer to Royse, Thyer, Padgett, and Logan (2000).

4. How Will the Data Be Analyzed?

Numerous research designs and countless data collection procedures exist and can be used in a nearly infinite variety of ways to structure and accumulate the information needed in a program evaluation. Although there has been some solid movement toward mixed-methods evaluation, discussion of research designs traditionally has focused on those that could be classified as being chiefly qualitative or quantitative.

Qualitative Evaluation Designs

Qualitative evaluations are largely descriptive and rely primarily on interviews and observations. Sample sizes tend to be small, and little use (or no use) is made of procedures that attempt to quantify (count) or measure dependent variables. Qualitative evaluation designs include case studies, focus groups, and observational techniques. Case studies include comprehensive narrative descriptions of events or programs. These descriptions may use one or all of the following techniques: in-depth interviews, observation, content analysis of documentation, and focus groups. Case studies may be used to help develop the questions for a larger evaluation. Qualitative studies of this type can be very comprehensive, but they do not generalize to other situations. In addition, causal relationships usually cannot be determined through case studies.

Focus groups typically are small informal groups of persons asked a series of questions that starts out very general and then becomes more specific. Focus groups are increasingly being used to provide evaluative information about human services. They work particularly well in identifying the questions that might be important to ask in a survey, in testing planned procedures or the phrasing of items for the specific target population, and in exploring possible reactions to an intervention or a service.

All of the qualitative approaches can yield strong data for decision makers. At the same time, these approaches can produce findings that are not all that accurate. A lot depends on how participants are selected to be interviewed, the number of observations or focus groups, and even subtleties in the questions asked. With qualitative approaches, the evaluator nearly always has much less ability to account for alternative explanations because he or she has much less control than when a quantitative evaluation strategy is used.

Quantitative Evaluation Designs

Quantitative designs include surveys, pretest/posttest studies, quasi-experiments with nonequivalent control groups, longitudinal designs, experiments, and needs assessments. Quantitative approaches transform answers to specific questions into numerical data. Outcome and impact evaluations nearly always are based on quantitative evaluation designs.

Cross-sectional surveys. A survey is limited to a description of a sample at one point in time and provides us with a "snapshot" of a group of respondents and what they were like or what knowledge or attitudes they held at a particular point in time. If the survey is to generate good generalizable data, then the sampling procedures must be carefully planned and implemented. A cross-sectional survey requires rigorous random sampling procedures to ensure that the sample closely represents the population of interest. A repeated survey is similar to a cross-sectional study but collects information at two or more points in time from the same respondents. A repeated (longitudinal) survey is effective at measuring changes in facts, attitudes, or opinions over a course of time.

Pretest/posttest designs (nonexperimental). Perhaps the most common quantitative evaluation design used in social and human service agencies is the pretest/posttest. In this design, a group of clients with some specific problem or diagnosis (e.g., depression) is administered a pretest prior to the start of intervention. At some point toward the end or after intervention, the same instrument is administered to the group a second time (the posttest). The one-group pretest/posttest design can measure change, but the evaluator has no basis for attributing change solely to the program. Confidence about change increases and the design strengthens when control groups are added and when participants are randomly assigned to either a control or experimental condition.

Quasi-experimental designs. Also known as nonequivalent control group designs, quasi-experiments generally use comparison groups whereby two similar groups are selected and followed for a period of time. One group typically receives some program or benefit, whereas the other group (the control) does not. Both groups are measured and compared for any differences at the end of some time period. Participants used as controls may be clients who are on a waiting list, those who are enrolled in another treatment program, or those who live in a different city or county. The problem with this design is that the control or comparison group might not, in fact, be equivalent to the group receiving the intervention. Comparing Ocean View School to Inner City School might not be a fair comparison. Even two different schools within the same rural county might be more different than similar in terms of the learning milieu, the proportion of students receiving free lunches, the number of computers and books in the school library, the principal's hiring practices, and the like. With this design, there always is the possibility that whatever the results, they might have been obtained because the intervention group really was different from the control group. This type of study does not provide proof of cause and effect, and the evaluator always must consider other factors that could have affected the study's outcomes.

Longitudinal designs. Longitudinal designs are a type of quasi-experimental design that involves tracking a particular group of individuals over a substantial period of time to discover potential changes due to the influence of a program. It is not uncommon for evaluators to want to know about the effects of a program after an extended period of time has passed. The question of interest is whether treatment effects last. These studies typically are complicated and expensive in time and resources. In addition, the longer a study runs, the higher the expected rate of attrition from clients who drop out or move away. High rates of attrition can bias the sample.

Experimental designs. In a *true experimental design,* participants are randomly assigned to either the control or treatment group. This design provides a persuasive argument about causal effects of a program on participants. The random assignment of respondents to treatment and control groups ensures that both groups are equivalent across key variables such as age, race, area of residency, and treatment history. Therefore, any observed differences at the end of the experiment can be attributed to the intervention.

One word of warning about random assignment is that staff in social service agencies sometimes find it very difficult to randomly assign program participants. Especially if they view the treatment program as beneficial, staff might have problems not giving the intervention to specific needy clients or to all of their clients instead of just to those who were randomly assigned. If they do succumb to this temptation, then the evaluation effort can be unintentionally sabotaged. The evaluator must train and prepare all of those individuals involved in the evaluation to help them understand the purpose and importance of the random assignment—that it, more than any other procedure, provides the evidence that the treatment really does benefit the clients.

Needs assessment. Needs assessment is a special form of evaluation (sometimes called a front-end evaluation) designed to establish that a proposed program really is needed before resources are expended. Or, if there is little doubt about the need, then a needs assessment can be used to fine-tune and position the intervention exactly as it is needed using precise population demographics. Sometimes, needs assessments are done to examine the gap between the services currently being delivered and unidentified needs in the underserved portions of the population. Needs assessments have been called feasibility studies and can be conducted using demographic, social indicator, or survey data.

The evaluation design is a critical decision for a number of reasons. Without the appropriate evaluation design, confidence in the results of the evaluation might be lacking. A strong evaluation design minimizes alternative explanations and assists the evaluator in gauging the true effects attributable to the intervention. In other words, the evaluation design directly affects the interpretation that can be made re-garding whether an intervention should be viewed as the reason for change in clients' behavior.

5. What Is the Unit of Analysis?

The unit of analysis refers to the person or things being studied or measured in the evaluation of a program. Typically, the basic unit of analysis consists of individual cli-ents but also may be groups, agencies, communities, schools, or even states. For ex-ample, an evaluator might examine the effectiveness of a drug prevention program by looking for a decrease in drug-related suspensions or disciplinary actions in high schools in which the program was implemented across the country; in that instance, schools are the primary unit of analysis. Another evaluator might be concerned only with the attitudes toward drugs and alcohol of students in one middle school; in that situation, individuals would be the unit of analysis. The smallest unit of analysis from which data are gathered often is referred to as a *case*. The unit of analysis is critical for determining both the sampling strategy and the data analysis.

Sampling Strategies and Considerations

When the client population of interest is too large to obtain information from each individual member, a sample is drawn. Sampling allows the evaluator to make pre-dictions about a population based on study findings from a sample of cases. Sampling strategies can be very complex. If the evaluator needs the type of precision afforded by a probability sample in which there is a known level of confidence and margin of error (e.g., 95% confidence ±3 percentage points), then he or she might need to hire a sampling consultant. A consultant is particularly recommended when the decisions about the program or intervention are critical such as in drug research or when treat-ments could have potentially harmful side effects. However, recognize the trade-offs that are made when determining sampling strategy and sample size. Large samples can be more accurate than smaller ones, yet they usually are more expensive. Small samples can be acceptable if a big change or effect is expected. As a rule, the more crit-ical the decision, the larger (and more precise) the sample should be.

There are two main categories of sampling strategies from which the evaluator can choose: probability sampling and nonprobability sampling. Probability sampling im-poses statistical rules to ensure that unbiased samples are drawn. These samples nor-mally are used for impact studies. Nonprobability or convenience sampling is less complicated to implement and is less expensive. This type of sampling often is used in process evaluations.

With probability sampling, the primary idea is that every individual, object, or institution in the population under study has a chance of being selected into the sample, and the likelihood of the selection of any individual is known. Probability sampling provides a firm basis for generalizing from the sample to the population. Nonprobability samples severely reduce the evaluator's ability to generalize the results of the study to the larger population.

The evaluator must balance the need for scientific rigor against convenience and often limited resources when determining sample size. If a major decision is being based on data collected, then precision and certainty are critical. Statistical precision increases as the sample size increases. When differences in the results are expected to be small, a larger sample guards against confounding variables that might distort the results of a treatment.

6. How Will the Results Be Used and Presented?

Lastly, before launching an evaluation, it is essential to identify the intended uses of its findings. The planned use of the results will, to some extent, determine the evaluation questions, suggest specific methodologies, and even direct the allocation of resources. Programs are evaluated for very practical reasons. Besides overall performance improvement and monitoring, the chief executive officer of an agency might wish to use the evaluation as part of a request for increased funding. Similarly, program evaluations are useful for strategic planning; required reports to sponsoring private, state, or federal agencies; professional staff development; and the pilot testing and development of new interventions. Needs assessments can help an agency's administration with general planning and budgeting.

An evaluation that does not meet the needs of the organization might be ignored or overlooked by program planners, policymakers, and/or funding agencies. By designing the evaluation with the use of the results in mind from the very beginning, greater use of the findings will occur. This consideration also affects the reporting format and style, even the amount of statistical material presented.

It often is a good idea for the evaluator to incorporate an executive summary or a one- or two-page summary of the results into his or her report. This might be the only part of the evaluation report that will be read by the majority of the stakeholders. Also, presenting results verbally, either individually or in a group, is a good idea. In this way, questions can be addressed, and the important information regarding the evaluation results will be communicated. In addition, including tables and charts to summarize large amounts of information or critical points is a useful tool in communicating results.

By being mindful of the audience for whom the evaluator is writing the evaluation report, he or she will be aided in making important decisions about how much detail (e.g., statistical tests used) to place in or omit from the presentation of findings. An evaluation report that is easily understood can make a big difference.

REFERENCES

Anderson, D., Bowland, B., Cartwright, W., & Bassin, G. (1998). Service-level costing of drug abuse treatment. *Journal of Substance Abuse Treatment, 15,* 201-211.

Bentelspacher, C., DeSilva, T., Goh, T., & LaRowe, K. (1996). A process evaluation of the cultural compatibility of psychoeducational family group treatment with ethnic Asian clients. *Social Work With Groups, 19,* 41-55.

Fraser, M. W., Nelson, K. E., & Rivard, J. C. (1997). Effectiveness of family preservation services. *Social Work Research, 21,* 138-153.

Kirby, D., Korpi, M., Adivi, C., & Weissman, J. (1997). An impact evaluation of project SNAPP: An AIDS and pregnancy prevention middle school program. *AIDS Education and Prevention, 9,* 44-61.

Leukefeld, C., Logan, T., Dennis, M., Hoffman, J., Wechsberg, W., Desmond, D., Cottler, L., Inciardi, J., & Rasch, R. (1998, November). *Changes in HIV-related sexual behaviors among out-of-treatment drug abusers in the 1993-1997 NIDA Cooperative Agreement Cohort.* Paper presented at the annual meeting of the American Public Health Association, Washington, DC.

Morrow-Howell, N., Becker-Kemppainen, S., & Judy, L. (1998). Evaluating an intervention for the elderly at increased risk of suicide. *Research on Social Work Practice, 8,* 28-46.

Richter, N. L., Snider, E., & Gorey, K. M. (1997). Group work intervention with female survivors of childhood sexual abuse. *Research on Social Work Practice, 7,* 53-69.

Royse, D., Thyer, B. A., Padgett, D. K., & Logan, T. K. (2000). *Program evaluation: An introduction* (3rd ed.). Belmont, CA: Wadsworth.

Scarpitti, F. R., Inciardi, J. A., & Pottieger, A. E. (1993). Process evaluation techniques for corrections-based drug treatment programs. *Journal of Offender Rehabilitation, 19*(3/4), 71-79.

Scriven, M. (1991). *Evaluation thesaurus* (4th ed.). Newbury Park, CA: Sage.

CHAPTER TWELVE

Using Cost → Procedure → Process → Outcome Analysis

BRIAN T. YATES
PETER J. DELANY
DOROTHY LOCKWOOD DILLARD

*M*oney matters, always, and especially during this era of managed care, limited resources, and constrained budgets. Social workers, whether they practice in a public or private setting, are confronted daily with the reality of competition for increasingly limited service resources. But it is not only money that matters, of course. What is accomplished with that money—the *outcomes* of social work—matter too. Given the extensive involvement in funding and oversight of human services by government agencies, private foundations, consumer groups, and taxpayers, it is not surprising that everyone in human services is being asked whether the money is being spent in the best way. One result is that we all are looking more closely at how we can measure and maximize the impact of resources available for our services. One tool that is useful in responding to concerns about money *and* outcomes is a form of

AUTHORS' NOTE: This chapter was prepared while the second author was partially supported by a subcontract through American University for NIDA Grant R01 DA10705-01A2.

cost-effectiveness analysis called cost $\rightarrow$ procedure $\rightarrow$ process $\rightarrow$ outcome analysis (CPPOA; Yates, 1996). CPPOA is designed to help social workers transform often conflicting concerns about cost, outcomes, and cost-effectiveness into a concrete approach to optimize cost-effectiveness in a service system. Because the cost-effectiveness analysis of interventions and service programs rarely is addressed in courses in schools of social work, by in-service workshops, or through continuing education programs, we thought that a chapter on the subject could be helpful.

We begin with definitions of costs, outcomes, cost-benefit analysis, cost-effectiveness analysis, and CPPOA. Next, we present two case studies to demonstrate how CPPOA works when applied to an individual client and to a program servicing many clients. Between these case study presentations, we discuss practical techniques for measuring costs, tracking the implementation of service procedures, detecting client processes that might be modifiable, and measuring program outcomes.

DEFINITIONS

Cost Analysis

In the simplest terms, *cost analysis* is a thorough description of the type and amount of all resources used to produce program services. These resources include the time invested by social workers in direct treatment of a client as well as the time spent in activities related to a particular client and time spent managing the program. Time often is spent in direct or indirect service activities by professionals from a variety of disciplines including physicians, nurses, counselors, and psychologists. Other resources used by programs commonly include space, furniture, supplies, equipment, transportation services, and communication and information services (e.g., phone, fax, e-mail, Internet access), vendor services (e.g., drug testing, accounting, security), insurance, financing, and marketing. We use *resources* rather than *payment* or *money* to highlight the difference between the economic approach that we are advocating and an accounting approach. Many social services use resources that are not reflected in their accounting records such as volunteers' time and donated facilities. An accounting approach that focuses on dollars expended rarely reflects the complete measure of total treatment costs. An economic approach that emphasizes the costs of each component of a treatment program provides a better picture of current program operations and also is able to predict how total costs would be affected by different combinations of existing components and additions of new components.

Outcomes

Measuring *outcomes* can include both objective and subjective measurement strategies. In the field of drug abuse treatment, most programs describe their effectiveness in terms of drug use, HIV serostatus, and arrests and convictions. These measures are important not only because they are acceptable to a variety of stakeholder groups but also because of their high level of validity and reliability. Other objective measures that are of equal importance but are reported less often include program retention and compliance with treatment, both of which are critical indicators of later success. Self-report information on changes in drug use, depression, legal status, family and employment, and physical and mental health should not be overlooked as potential sources of information.

There also are outcomes that can be expressed in monetary terms such as increased contributions to the tax base and reductions in health care and welfare costs as the client returns to work. Monetary benefits also occur in the form of avoided costs such as medical care (e.g., for HIV/AIDS as the client modifies drug-using and sexual behaviors) and reductions in criminal justice expenditures (e.g., as the client avoids future drunken driving and/or drug purchasing). These benefits often are included in cost-benefit analyses.

Cost-Benefit Analysis

Cost-benefit and *cost-effective* often are used as if they mean the same thing. They do not. The *benefit* in cost-benefit analysis means that outcomes are measured in monetary units. Cost-benefit analysis shows how the costs of a program compare to the benefits of the program. The "program" being analyzed can be a clinic that serves hundreds, a treatment plan for an individual client, or an entire approach to solving a social problem. For example, the CALDATA study found that for every $1 spent on drug treatment, California taxpayers saved an average of $7 in terms of criminal justice costs and costs to the victims (including replacing material losses and expenses for medical and mental health services related to being victims of crimes [Gerstein et al., 1994]). Clearly, cost-benefit analysis can demonstrate the impact of a program to politicians and other stakeholders in a manner that often does not require additional explanations.

Monetary Benefits

Social service programs produce a variety of measurable monetary outcomes (e.g., increased days of employment) that lead to increased tax revenues and reduced costs to employers for employee replacement. Treatment programs also create monetary benefits when clients reduce their use of food stamps, access fewer or less costly health care services, and reduce their dependence on public assistance. Eventually, use of health and other services can be brought to normal levels. For example, a study of insurance costs and health care use by Lennox, Scott-Lennox, and Holder (1992) found that health expenditures for employees with drug and alcohol problems in one company rapidly increased during the year prior to treatment. However, these costs decreased steadily after treatment over a period of 2 years for both the clients and their families. After 2 years, no statistically significant differences could be found in individual and family health care costs when compared to non-substance use cases. In some cases, costs may *increase* temporarily as clients begin to use needed services more effectively and more assertively. For these and other reasons, a positive net benefit for treatment might not occur for 1 or more years following the start of treatment.

Cost-Benefit Calculations

The most common ways of quantifying the cost-benefit relationship include calculating the *net benefit* of a program (by subtracting total program costs from total program benefits) and calculating the *ratio of benefits to costs* (by dividing total program benefits by total program costs). These calculations can be performed at the level of the individual client (cf. Table 12.1) and then averaged for the entire program in which clients are participating. Total costs of the program can be subtracted from total benefits of the program to describe the total net benefit of the program.

Calculating net benefits and benefit/cost ratios generates numbers that are easy to remember but that also can mislead. Of course, some benefits of programs cannot be monetized in a reliable and valid manner. Also, the difference or ratio throws away potentially important information, particularly the amount of investment required (i.e., the cost). After all, a ratio of 7/1 does not tell us whether $100 or $10,000 needs to be paid per client to achieve a return of $700 or $70,000. Furthermore, a ratio of 7/1 suggests to some decision makers that they can keep adding (or subtracting) money to (or from) a program's budget and keep getting the same rate of return. Although this might be the case, the changes that a program must go through to handle large increases (or decreases) in the number of clients seen might alter the benefit/cost ratio, possibly enhancing it but more likely diminishing it.

Finally, it is tempting but sometimes incorrect to say that all programs with higher benefits than costs should receive funding. That decision rule ignores the all too frequent reality that, whether private or public, budgets for most social services are terribly limited. There hardly ever is enough money to fund all the programs whose

TABLE 12.1 Cumulative Cost-Benefit Analysis and Running Calculation of Net Benefit: Individual Level

A	B	C	D	E	F
Time	*Investment*	*Return on Investment*	*Cumulative Investment*	*Cumulative Return on Investment*	*Net Benefit (cumulative return minus cumulative investment)*
Date	Cost of Treatment Services Delivered	Benefit (to society, client, or other individual)	Running Total of All Treatment Costs	Running Total of All Benefits of Treatment	(subtract entry in this row in column D from entry in same row in column E)
January 3 (start)	$376 (screening, session)		$376	$0	−$376 ($0 − $376)
January 5	$145 (session)		$521 ($376 + $145)	$0	−$521 ($0 − $521)
January 5		$21 (drug-free day)	$521	$21 ($21 + $0)	−$500 ($21 − $521)
January 6		$21 (drug-free day)	$521	$42 ($21 + $21)	−$479 ($42 − $521)
January 8		$21 (drug-free day)	$521	$63 ($42 + $21)	−$458 ($63 − $521)
January 8	$95 (group)		$616 ($521 + $95)	$63	−$553 ($63 − $616)
January 8	$145 (session)		$761 ($616 + $145)	$63	−$698 ($63 − $761)
January 9		$124 (income for employed day)	$761	$187 ($63 + $124)	−$574 ($187 − $761)
January 9		$21 (drug-free day)	$761	$208 ($187 + $21)	−$553 ($208 − $761)

benefits exceed costs. More useful indicators of cost-benefit analysis are how *quickly* benefits exceed costs (e.g., during the 1st year after the client begins treatment or only after 5 years). These indexes of *time to return on investment* can be complex to calculate accurately. For example, if some benefits are delayed by several years, then they might need to be adjusted using *present value* calculations (cf. Yates, 1996). In sum, when data are available for cost-benefit analysis, some very powerful but potentially oversimplifying statistics can be produced.

Cost-Effectiveness Analysis

Calculating Cost-Effectiveness

Cost-effectiveness analysis examines the relationship between the cost of a given program and the objectives of that program. For example, social work evaluators might want to compare the costs of providing relapse prevention training to a specific program objective, such as the cost of producing a drug-free month for the average client (e.g., $355 per drug-free month). In this chapter, we focus more on cost-effectiveness analysis than on cost-benefit analysis for two reasons. First, many social workers and social work programs work very hard to achieve a mixture of outcomes that cannot be readily expressed in the monetary units that would allow cost-benefit analysis. Second, many social work program managers and evaluators are given fixed budgets within which they must work. Considering how much additional benefit may be achieved by investing more resources might be irrelevant if no additional resources are available.

Evaluating and Improving Cost-Effectiveness

In contrast to cost-benefit analysis, cost-effectiveness analysis can be used by social workers to evaluate the relative values of different interventions. This can help managers to both understand the current performance of their program and determine whether and how to enhance program performance and client outcomes (Gold, Siegel, Russell, & Weinstein, 1996; Kee, 1994). Gaining experience in the use of cost-analytic tools such as cost-effectiveness analysis can help social work professionals to demonstrate to funding sources, policymakers, and other service professionals the very real value of investing in social work programming.

Improving the cost-effectiveness of a program starts with finding which components of a program contribute most to effectiveness and proceeds to finding which of those components have the lowest cost. This is not always easy. Social service programs, such as drug treatment, are complex enterprises. Administrators may improve the overall cost-effectiveness by enhancing the use of more effective or less costly components while decreasing the use of less effective or more costly components. Alternatively, it might be more cost-effective in the long term to implement new intervention technologies that have demonstrated effectiveness. Of course, costs of training staff in new interventions, and possibly increased supervision costs, must be taken into account as well.

Also, indicators of intervention effectiveness usually vary over time and from client to client in ways that are not entirely the result of any one program component. Moreover, although the cost-effectiveness analyst usually can identify differences in the cost-effectiveness of a particular program and in the cost-effectiveness of different interventions within a program, it is not so easy to show conclusively that those differences are reliable, valid, and clinically or socially meaningful. These criteria need to be met before changes in program components can be implemented with confidence, even on a trial basis.

Cost-Effectiveness Analysis Versus Cost-Benefit Analysis

There are some limitations in cost-effectiveness analysis relative to cost-benefit analysis. One is that the former does not provide a single number or "bottom line" indicating whether benefits exceed costs or vice versa. This, however, may be less important in social work practice, where the goals are less likely to be turning a profit and more likely to be improving the health and well-being of clients, their families, and their communities. Furthermore, cost-effectiveness ratios do provide the social work practitioner with specific information on the amount of effectiveness attainable per dollar spent. With a cost-effectiveness ratio, the units in which effectiveness is measured are not forgotten; rather, they are incorporated with monetary units to express a quantitative relationship between the value of resources invested in treatment and the effects of treatment on measures that matter professionally and socially. Interventions, program components, and entire programs that use the same measures of effectiveness can be compared objectively using statistical tests on cost-effectiveness ratios calculated for each client. A degree of subjectivity certainly enters into the choice of measures of effectiveness and into the ways in which different interventions, components, or groups of programs are defined. However, these choices tend to keep cost-effectiveness analysis focused on improving program operations (*formative* evaluation) rather than on judging the "worth" of a program (*summative* evaluation). As Gold et al. (1996) state, cost-effectiveness analysis generally *informs* the decision making rather than making the decision.

Cost → Procedure → Process → Outcome Analysis

To help program managers use cost-effectiveness analysis more systematically to improve their treatment programs, CPPOA was developed (cf. Yates, 1998). CPPOA collects and analyzes data on program operations to examine the strength of relationships that are supposed to exist among the (a) *resources* (e.g., personnel, space, furniture, equipment, supplies, vendor services) that make possible the (b) *procedures* (e.g., interview simulations and role-playing, resume preparation) that were designed to remove, reduce, or instill or enhance specific (c) *processes* (e.g., expectancies of being able to spontaneously answer questions in a job interview) that are hypothesized to increase the chances of (d) *outcomes* (e.g., getting interviews, getting and keeping a job).

In CPPOA, *outcomes* are defined as changes in or achievement of specific variables such as substance abuse, employment, health, mental health, and whatever the program views as its final results. Many programs distinguish between long-term outcomes (e.g., employment) and shorter term outcomes (e.g., actively looking for a job by sending out resumes). CPPOA uses theory and prior research to hypothesize the *processes* that should lead to those outcomes. (Program staff usually are consulted as well because they often focus their efforts on very specific processes with the intent of achieving specific outcomes.) Processes that might increase the probability of getting a job could include development of interview skills and positive expectancies. CPPOA measures and tests the strength and consistency of relationships between the processes and outcomes of a program. This usually is done by collecting data on processes and outcomes for each client at different points in treatment and by statistically analyzing these data to show which processes are significantly related to which outcomes.

In turn, CPPOA examines the possible linkages between program procedures and client processes. The processes that lead to desired outcomes are supposed to be achieved, in most programs, by conducting specific *procedures* (sometimes called *interventions* or, if more general, *program components*). Procedures generally are what program staff do when working directly with staff. Role-playing and getting the client to develop and commit to specific plans are among the many procedures that could contribute to employment-related processes. CPPOA measures and statistically tests the strength and consistency of relationships between the procedures implemented in a program and those processes that were found to be strongly and consistently related to outcomes. For these analyses, data on procedures and processes are collected for each client periodically throughout treatment. In this way, CPPOA empirically discovers which procedures lead most consistently to the changes in client processes that produce the goal outcomes.

Finally, the amount and value (*cost*) of each resource used to implement each procedure are measured for each client regularly throughout treatment. The amount of time devoted by staff to treatment of each client, as well as "overhead" time spent by staff, is recorded. Time of administrators and others not directly working with staff is allocated to specific clients according to the relative amounts of time spent by direct service staff on the client. Resources such as office space and supplies used in treatment of the client are recorded as well. Overhead resources, such as space used by administrators and their staff as well as hallways and reception areas, also are allocated among clients in proportion to the relative amounts of what might be called "direct service" resources used in treatment of those clients. The monetary value of these resources is determined so that the overall cost of specific procedures can be compared to budget limits as well as outcomes. This allows the manager to estimate what the cost-effectiveness of the program would be if different components were removed or added. The original units of the resources used are retained so that the amounts of each resource available can be compared to the amounts that would be used by different combinations of program procedures or components. Special mathematical techniques can be used to find the amount of each procedure that clients should receive so that outcomes are maximized within the constraints of the amounts available for each type of resource (e.g., linear programming, other operations research methods [cf. Yates, 1980]). This brief definition of CPPOA is elaborated in what follows and is illustrated with case examples at two levels: an individual client and a program.

COST → PROCEDURE → PROCESS → OUTCOME ANALYSIS: USE AT THE INDIVIDUAL CLIENT LEVEL

As shown in the logic model in Figure 12.1, CPPOA offers a framework for programming treatment and guiding data collection to improve existing programming. CPPOA also can show where to change programming to improve outcomes at the client and program levels. Although this model and associated methods of measuring costs, procedures, processes, and outcomes are applicable to private and public sector programs, we illustrate its application with a complex drug abuse treatment case drawn from the public sector.

Case Essentials: Individual Client Level

Mr. E. is a 44-year-old white man referred to an outpatient substance abuse treatment facility by his lawyer following an arrest for DWI/DUID (driving while intoxicated/driving under the influence of drugs) 1 month before the initiation of CPPOA.

RESOURCES	→	PROCEDURES	→	PROCESSES	→	OUTCOMES
DIRECT, INDIRECT		*Therapeutic procedures:*		*Incentives* (e.g., for maintaining current processes and deficits as well as current levels of outcome)		(short- and long-term)
Time		• Education				Employment: Maintain current job
• of change agent(s)		• Training		*Social support* (e.g., natural social support)		Drug use. Attend and participate in education, counseling, Alcoholics Anonymous, and Narcotics Anonymous
• in program		• Counseling, individual therapy		*Knowledge* (e.g., how to access social services)		
• extra-program						
• of administrator(s)		*Delivery systems:*		*Social skills* (e.g., how to keep a job, self-advocacy skills)		
• of office staff		• Office		*Addiction physiology* (e.g., types of addiction, presence of nonremediable changes in neurochemistry)		Family relationships (e.g., with spouse and children)
• of consultants		• Mobile (e.g., van, mobile home)				Social relationships (e.g., with friends who support sobriety)
• of client		• Home/work visits		*Health status* (e.g., knowing one's HIV status, understanding the primary determinants of physical health [including HIV infection] and dental health)		HIV-risk behaviors (e.g., no injecting drug use, no unprotected sex)
• of third parties (e.g., family, employer)		• Telecommunications (e.g., telephone, computer)				Health (e.g., physical, dental, HIV status)
Space				*Mental health status* (e.g., lithium levels)		Mental health (e.g., attend one session per month with psychiatrist, attend dual diagnosis education group)
Equipment		*Therapeutic action steps for each process:*		*Self-management skills* (e.g., being able to honestly identify deficits in knowledge and behavior, remove those deficits, and continue or modify self-management heuristic [including being able to accurately and readily identify the need for professional assistance])		Legal affairs: No new charges
Supplies						Financial affairs (e.g., work with credit counselor
Telecommunications services		a. Assess current level of process				Use of natural *recovery* systems
Transportation		b. Identify processes to change				Mobilization of natural *support* systems
Advertising/marketing		c. Change processes		*Psychological issues* (e.g., being dually diagnosed, parent of teenager)		Self-referral when appropriate (e.g., enter treatment to avoid relapse or rehospitalization)
Security		• *Instill or enhance constructive processes*		*Expectancies* (e.g., self-efficacy expectancies for securing and performing the above to achieve the outcomes)		
Financial resources		• *Mitigate or eliminate destructive processes*				
Other						

Figure 12.1. Cost → Procedure → Process → Outcome Analysis Model for the Individual Client

During two previous assessment sessions, Mr. E. freely admitted being addicted to heroin for the past 10 years and to alcohol for at least 12 years. He reports 4 years of abstinence prior to this latest relapse after a previous inpatient treatment for heroin and alcohol dependence in which he was diagnosed with bipolar affective disorder. This is his third treatment episode. He reports using both heroin and alcohol during the 2 weeks before his arrest, following alterations in his prescribed medications for bipolar affective disorder. Mr. E. states that he started feeling "a little crazy," began drinking, and then ran into an old "dope" friend who offered to share some heroin with him. Subsequently, he used every day until his arrest. Mr. E. also reports that his 18-year-old daughter came to live with him 2 weeks ago after her mother (the patient's ex-wife, divorced 10 years earlier) moved her boyfriend into her home. Mr. E. says that there are ongoing problems with his ex-wife and their daughter.

Mr. E. states that he regularly attended Alcoholics Anonymous (AA) and Narcotics Anonymous (NA) before this relapse and has since returned. He says that he has been abstinent since the night of his arrest. He has an active NA sponsor who is very supportive. He reports that his employer also is supportive of him so long as he follows treatment recommendations and resolves his legal problems. He has regularly scheduled visits with the health maintenance organization psychiatrist to monitor "blood work and medications." He signed a release allowing program staff to have ongoing communication with the psychiatrist about progress, participation, and presentation.

Using the Cost → Procedure → Process → Outcome Analysis Logic Model for an Individual Client

Costs

Costs are the values of resources consumed in activities. In the case of Mr. E., this is the third visit being made to his social worker, so considerable resources already have been spent. The time spent with the social worker—about 4 hours so far—includes (a) three 50-minute sessions meeting with the client, (b) 20 minutes spent opening up the case file in the computer system, and (c) phone calls and a case meeting. Additional resources expended include office space used for the meetings and calls as well as office supplies, telecommunications (phone) services, computer hardware and software, liability insurance, and administrative and other overhead services. Those are the resources consumed so far from the provider's perspective. From the client's perspective, the resources used for treatment are transportation including time spent in transit from his job as well as time he had to take off from work to get to the sessions. From the funders' perspectives, considerable paperwork resources already have been devoted to this case.

Costs can be assigned to each of these provider, client, and funder resources. That actually is the easy part. The major challenge in assessing costs is to include all of the major resources that are used in providing the service and to represent the different perspectives fairly so that CPPOA produces a complete picture of the types and amounts of resources needed to provide each treatment procedure. Forgetting the paper clips but measuring the volunteered time and donated facilities can be exceptionally important when measuring the resources that make programs possible.

Outcomes

On the other end of the CPPOA model are, of course, outcomes. A crucial part of CPPOA, as well as cost-effectiveness analysis and cost-benefit analysis, is measuring the degree to which intervention procedures used by social work practitioners actually achieve treatment goals. For example, Mr. E. states that his top priority is to avoid going to jail. However, during the initial treatment planning meeting, he notes that his court date is 3 months away. Mr. E. also notes that his attorney has suggested that the first priority should be to demonstrate that he is attending and participating in treatment for addiction and mental health problems. In addition, Mr. E. needs to avoid further legal entanglements. In a session with his social worker, Mr. E. decides that he needs to develop a stronger recovery program addressing *both* his drug use and his mental health problems. He believes that this is the best way in which to achieve his immediate goal of avoiding jail and his long-term goal of maintaining sobriety.

Pursuing a stronger recovery program also should stabilize his employment situation in the immediate future (another priority), but Mr. E. says that part of his problem in that regard is getting his boss to realize that when he needs to go to a meeting or to see his psychiatrist, he is *not* "slacking off." Together, he and the social worker identify the goal of assertive behavior in dealing with his health needs in work and other environments.

Other short-term goals include (a) increasing appropriate use of mental health services to stabilize psychotropic medication, (b) arranging a physical examination to determine his current health status, (c) counseling and testing for HIV, (d) getting dental work done to improve his appearance and what he can eat, (e) being referred to a credit counseling service, and (f) identifying and using natural support and natural recovery systems that will help him to avoid relapse long after formal treatment is concluded. Each of these goals builds on the others to achieve an ultimate goal of abstinence and improved functioning within the community. Progress toward each of these goals can be measured at regular intervals (e.g., each meeting) in any number of ways including the degree to which each goal is approximated.

What Goes On Between Costs In and Outcomes Out: Treatment Procedures and Internal Processes

Although costs and outcomes used to be all that one measured before comparing them in traditional cost-effectiveness and cost-benefit analyses, there are two additional sets of variables that can be examined to understand the service system: (a) the treatment *procedures* performed when providing the service and (b) the cognitive, affective, and even biological *processes* that (hopefully) change within the client as a result of those treatment procedures.

Processes

For each of the outcome goals identified by the client or another interested party, the social worker and client identify internal psychological or biological processes that, when changed, would produce the outcomes desired. These processes are listed in Figure 12.1 with examples. They include incentives, improved social support, increased knowledge related to accessing social services (e.g., understanding what credit counseling can and cannot do for one's financial situation), addiction physiology, health and mental health status, and self-management skills and efforts.

Procedures

To modify these processes so as to produce the targeted outcomes, the social worker uses counseling, training, and educational *procedures*. These procedures are activities that anyone watching and listening could see and hear the social worker doing with the client. For example, the social worker may teach the client about the treatment program through an orientation lecture. The social worker also may help the client learn more about treating two chronic disorders—drug abuse and mental health problems—through drug education and dual diagnosis groups. The social worker might need to show the client which social services he could receive and how to apply for them. This also will require Mr. E. (and the social worker) to follow up on the application until those services are received.

Mr. E. might find assertiveness training helpful in dealing with his employer, his psychiatrist, and the program in that it could increase the likelihood that he will be able to meet his needs proactively rather than after yet another relapse. Counseling procedures also might help the client to clarify and address psychological issues (additional *processes*) related to being dually diagnosed, being the father of a teenager, and needing to have increased self-efficacy expectancies for securing support to maintain sobriety from his daughter, employer, AA/NA members, and others.

To perform these procedures, the social worker uses a variety of *service delivery systems* (e.g., individual and group sessions at the office, over the phone, and when meeting at the client's home or place of employment). There also is a temporal dimension to performance of the procedures that will change the processes that, in turn, can enhance Mr. E.'s ability to function. These include assessing the current level of each process in the client (e.g., knowledge and expectancy of HIV status, current self-efficacy expectancies for being assertive), working with the client to identify which processes need to be changed, and implementing agreed-on interventions to (a) install or enhance processes identified as *constructive* (e.g., remedy skills deficits by teaching self-advocacy skills) and to (b) mitigate or eliminate *destructive* processes (e.g., remove social or financial incentives that might maintain current harmful levels of processes).

Cost → Procedure → Process → Outcome Analysis: Client Level

When meeting with the individual client, the social worker can assess and optimize the cost-effectiveness of specific intervention procedures explicitly or intuitively. The primary concerns are, naturally, whether the client is moving toward attainment of the most important goals identified at the start of treatment and what resources are being used to get there. Knowing the contribution of specific procedures to the attainment of those goals, and understanding the routes by which those procedures move the client closer to treatment goals, could be useful in future work with Mr. E. and in work with similar clients. Knowing the resources required by the most effective procedures would help move clients toward their goals more quickly while keeping within budgets and limitations on other resources.

At 4 weeks, an analysis of relationships among costs, procedures, processes, and outcomes indicated that Mr. E. was able to do the following:

1. Show up for work on time and provide his employer with a schedule when he had to be at treatment
2. Maintain abstinence and attend all scheduled counseling, education, and AA/NA meetings (natural recovery system)
3. Decrease his HIV risk status to zero
4. Stabilize on his medication and meet with his psychiatrist as required

The preceding *outcomes* occurred because there were real changes in these key *processes:*

Incentives: Mr. E. perceived a real benefit from following a treatment plan that he helped to develop to stay out of jail and keep his job.

Physiology: As Mr. E. continued to be abstinent and stabilize on his medications, this helped to improve how he used services as well as how he made decisions regarding choices for following treatment recommendations.

Knowledge and self-management: Mr. E. gained a great deal of information regarding his addiction, mental illness, and managing his own care.

Health status: Mr. E. changed his drug use and improved his choices regarding sexual behavior.

Mental health status: As lithium levels stabilized, Mr. E.'s mood stabilized.

However, Mr. E. continued to have difficulty at home with his daughter, he had not seen the doctor for a physical examination and HIV testing, and he had not seen a dentist. His legal and financial status remained unstable. Mr. E.'s lawyer was able to obtain a continuance for 6 months so that Mr. E. could attend treatment and keep working to support his daughter. Mr. E. himself continued to have serious financial problems that appeared to be growing with the additional costs of treatment and legal bills. At this point, referrals to health care and financial counseling were made by the social worker but were seen as a lower priority than stabilizing his recovery program for addiction and mental illness.

Furthermore, despite faithful performance of the individual therapeutic procedures, the goal of improving relationships between Mr. E. and his daughter and ex-spouse had not been approximated to any degree. Analysis of session notes and some reflection suggested that the relationship outcomes had not been attained because the assumed linkages between individual counseling and the processes of increased social support for recovery and improved social (parenting) skills did not appear to exist yet for Mr. E. Current efforts in this case focus on creating these linkages and, if that fails, finding what specific internal processes *will* lead to the desired outcomes and what specific procedures will induce those processes while staying within the limitations of time, money, and other resources available to the client and social worker.

COST → PROCEDURE → PROCESS → OUTCOME ANALYSIS: USE AT THE PROGRAM LEVEL

Whereas the preceding case study showed how CPPOA can be applied at the level of individual clients, the most common application is at the program level. Even here, however, the measurements of costs, of procedures, of processes, and of outcomes all begin at the level of individual clients but for the purpose of describing the least costly paths through treatment procedures and internal processes to achievement of outcome goals.

Considerations for Measuring Costs

A traditional economic definition of cost is the amount that the consumer is willing to pay for a good or service, but this definition is less useful in human services, the consumers of which are able to pay little or nothing. Furthermore, the fragmentation of services and the economic context in which many clients find themselves combine to prevent clients and social workers from making informed service selections. Because reasonably informed decisions are necessary for market forces to drive costs down (or up) to values that closely reflect the actual worth of resources required for treatment, the "going price" of treatment rarely is a valid (or even an available) measure of the cost of treatment.

Cost conceptualization. Our approach to cost measurement is to conceptualize costs as the value of resources (e.g., time, labor) expended to perform a specific treatment procedure. The treatment procedure is performed with the intent of changing certain processes that will, in turn, achieve one or more specific outcomes. A comprehensive description of resources used by a program also allows the program to be funded more accurately in the future and to be replicated with more fidelity elsewhere. Conducting an accurate and thorough cost analysis means considering donated resources (e.g., volunteered time), which do not appear in most program accounting records, as well as overhead costs.

Overhead costs. Overhead costs may be standardized within a program as a particular percentage of direct service costs (e.g., for each $1.00 of service delivered, funders may be charged an additional $0.47 to cover overhead expenses). Many programs define *direct costs* as provision of services "face-to-face" with the client but ignore phone calls to clients or case meetings with other service providers. Yet, many of these services are essential components of social work treatment plans. The resources that make these important non-face-to-face activities possible should be included in the direct costs for the client and not considered overhead because they do not involve the client and provider being in close physical proximity. Drawing on Yates (1999), we now present strategies for enumerating resource costs within a program and for translating that information into a form that can then be used to develop a cost-effectiveness analysis.

Direct personnel costs. Direct service costs in treatment settings can be assigned to each client according to time spent by staff (paid and volunteer) providing services to that client. Direct service costs include the value of time spent by personnel in direct contact with the client (e.g., intake assessment, testing, counseling, education) and time spent in other services directly related to helping that specific client (e.g., calling an attorney to discuss progress in treatment and recovery, making a connection with a referral agency to transfer information and confirm entry). Volunteer time is collected in the same way and valued at the same rate as that of the paid staff who deliver the same service. For example, when an unpaid intern or extern is a co-counselor in a group therapy session, his or her time should be valued at the same rate as the paid staff that the intern or extern is replacing (minus, perhaps, the value of educational supervision that he or she receives without pay). Also, the value of time devoted to treatment of a specific client by paid staff would be based on time actually spent, not on time planned or on a "standard" (e.g., 35-hour) work week. For all personnel, hours spent working with a client or in directly related activities are multiplied by the hourly pay rate for personnel of that level of education and experience. An example of how to calculate this pay rate for salaried personnel is provided later in this chapter.

Overhead personnel costs. Overhead personnel costs include all other activities conducted by direct service personnel and administrative and support service personnel. Examples of indirect service activities include paperwork, case conferences, staff meetings, supervision, training workshops, reception, preparing budgets, and other services that are related to operating the program. Depending on the purposes of the CPPOA, administrative and support staff may be asked to record the activities they perform just like direct service staff do, or the cost of administrative and support staff may be assigned entirely to the category of overhead costs.

Other direct costs. We favor allocating the cost of resources, such as space and transportation, to each client according to his or her use of those resources rather than simply dividing the total cost of facilities or all transportation expenses by the number of clients seen. Our preference is based on the observation that some clients use these supposed nonpersonnel overhead resources much more than do others. For example, some clients attend group counseling once a week, whereas others might attend group and individual counseling sessions, educational meetings, and medication monitoring several times each week. The latter clients use facilities (and very likely transportation) substantially more than do the former clients. Cost data, if not charges to clients, should reflect this differential use to be accurate and useful for CPPOA.

Collecting Cost Data

At some point, it is necessary to stop enumerating specific costs and to get on with the business of measuring them. Yates (1999) suggests this rule of thumb: If the person providing the service cannot easily enter it on a standard form in a few minutes, then it might not be worth considering. Much of the data that one will need to measure costs, and to actually conduct a whole CPPOA, might already be available in the information system used by the program to monitor client progress and social worker activity and to submit and process bills. The remaining information for cost assessment and the rest of CPPOA may be gathered with some simple forms. In some format, the following information needs to be gathered and placed in a database or on a spreadsheet (Yates, 1999):

Date and time the service was delivered

Identifying code (or name, if confidentiality is not an issue) of the client(s) who received the service

Provider of the service procedure

Nature of the service producer (which can be precoded, e.g., 01: individual counseling, 02: group counseling, 06: paperwork, M: medications, T1: one-way transportation, T2: round-trip transportation)

Amount of each resource used (e.g., provider minutes, space description [e.g., "individual office, Room 204"])

When beginning to develop forms and codes for cost and other CPPOA data collection, the advice of program staff can be invaluable. They can identify and operationalize treatment activities for reliable and valid recording. Staff reactions to mock-ups of forms can show how to make them user-friendly.

Experience has shown that, after the researcher and staff are satisfied that the forms allow the necessary cost data to be collected, the forms do not fill themselves out. It is essential to work with staff to develop procedures so that the forms are completed in an accurate and timely manner. One strategy is to ensure that staff have time each day to complete all the forms for that day and that their supervisor has time to review that work on a regular basis, ideally each day before staff leave.

Ensuring that the data on resources and procedures are collected is one thing; maintaining the reliability and validity of the data is another. Both need to be assessed regularly, and the findings need to be fed back to staff and supervisors. Reliability can be measured by comparing records for the same client over weeks for the same staff member and for the same types of clients following similar treatment plans with different staff. Validity of cost-related data can be assessed regularly by comparing information on the forms (e.g., days and hours clients were seen according to the forms) to information in clinical case notes and to billing records (if available).

Analyzing Costs to Prepare for Cost →
Procedure → Process → Outcome Analysis

The next step is to find the cost for the resources that make possible the procedures used to service program clients. The first step is to establish regular time cycles for collecting, analyzing, and reporting cost and procedure data. Accumulating cost data for a week is a good period for piloting data collection forms and procedures. After several weeks of collecting cost and procedure data and quickly analyzing and reporting it (and revising data collection forms), a monthly cycle might work better.

Resource Use Spreadsheet

To organize data on time spent by each staff member on each procedure for each client, a computer spreadsheet or database works best. (Although most data compilation can be done by hand, computer spreadsheets such as Excel will save time in terms of copying, manipulating, and calculating, and computer databases such as Access are even easier to work with once one is familiar with database commands.) A spreadsheet of columns and rows helps to visualize the data needed. This cost-procedure or *resource use spreadsheet* lists all the resources in rows (e.g., direct service personnel, indirect service personnel, other services), all the clients in columns, and all the procedures in columns repeated within each client's column. Using data on forms submitted by staff, the time (hours and fractions of hours) spent by each service provider implementing each treatment procedure for each client is entered in the cell on the worksheet that corresponds to that provider, that client, and that procedure. Not surprisingly, perhaps, some cells will show no time because that provider did not implement that procedure with that client during a particular time cycle of data collection. For example, a social worker might provide counseling but not psychological testing or medication management to a client during a particular month. For procedures such as group counseling and education, it might be necessary to divide the time equally among all clients who actually attended the meeting. Whenever possible, indirect service time devoted by providers to particular clients should be entered in the same manner.

Cost per Unit Resource Spreadsheet

The next step is to create a new spreadsheet that records the cost per unit of resource used. It looks exactly like the resource use spreadsheet except that the *cost per unit resource spreadsheet* lists the pay rate per hour for each staff member for each direct and indirect service procedure implemented. Direct service costs may be set by contract as so many dollars per hour, or there may be different rates of pay to the same person for providing different services. For example, a social worker might be paid $25 for a 45-minute individual session, $50 for a 1.5-hour group session, and $35 for a 1-hour drug education course. A counselor with an M.Ed. might be paid at different rates. For salaried employees, hourly rates can be calculated using the following steps (cf. Yates, 1999):

Step 1: Multiply the number of work days per week times the number of weeks (e.g., 5 days × 52 weeks = 260 work days per year).

Step 2: Subtract the total number of days of allowed leave, vacation, and non-work activity from the total number of work days per year (e.g., 25, so 260 work days − 25 days leave and vacation = 235 workdays).

Step 3: Multiply the work days times the work hours per day (e.g., 235 work days × 8 hours = 1,880 work hours per year).

Step 4: Add the annual fringe benefits to the annual salary (e.g., $40,000 annual salary + $4,000 for 10% fringe benefits = $44,000).

Step 5: Divide the total of salary and fringe benefits by the work hours to obtain the hourly rate (e.g., $44,000/1,880 = $23.40 per hour).

These pay rates need to be calculated and entered into the spreadsheet for direct service staff, for indirect service staff, and for volunteers whose time is treated as a resource and whose costs are assessed at the same rate as those of paid staff who would assume those jobs if the volunteers were not performing those activities. Once the cost per unit spreadsheet is complete, entries in each cell of the resource use spreadsheet are multiplied by entries in the cost per unit spreadsheet for the same provider, client, and procedure to produce a third *resource cost spreadsheet* that provides the cost per client per procedure.

Incorporating Other Resources Into the Cost per Unit Resource Spreadsheet

Just as with the time taken by personnel to perform direct and indirect service procedures, the time spent using other resources (e.g., space) to implement a particular procedure for a particular client needs to be recorded in the resource use spreadsheet. Also just as for personnel resources, the cost of the space per hour should be calculated and entered into the cost per unit resource spreadsheet. Space cost rates per hour can be calculated using the following steps (adapted from Yates, 1999):

Step 1: Find the total annual cost of the entire facility (lease payment or equivalent; utilities; maintenance; and prorated furniture, equipment, and renovations; e.g., $180,000 [lease] + $20,000 [utilities/maintenance] + $18,000 [furniture, equipment, and renovations] = $218,000 total annual cost).

Step 2: Determine the number of hours that the facility is open during the year (hours per day per year; e.g., 6, so 6 [hours per day] × 7 [days per week] × 52 [weeks per year] − 2 [holidays] = 5,822 hours per year).

Step 3: Divide the total annual cost by the total hours open per year to obtain the cost per hour (e.g., $218,000/5,822 hours = $37.44 per hour).

Step 4: Determine the proportional share of the total space (e.g., 8 feet × 10 feet [80 square feet]/total office space [800 square feet] = 10% of total area).

Step 5: Multiply the cost per hour by the proportion of the total space used to deliver the procedure to the client (e.g., $37.44 × 10% = $3.74).

Including Indirect Costs in Cost Analyses

After distributing personnel and space costs to specific clients and procedures, there might be significant additional resources to allocate to individual clients and to the procedures that they receive. Some of these can be assigned to specific clients and procedures (e.g., costs of therapeutic drugs prescribed for a particular client). Other resources, such as administrators' time and their office space, cannot be readily assigned to any one client or procedure because administrators' work indirectly serves all clients and makes possible all procedures. One strategy for assigning the value of these overhead resources to individual clients and the procedures in which they participate is to add the costs of all overhead resources and simply divide that sum by the number of clients and then by the number of procedures performed on each client. This works well if each client uses the same amount of all those overhead resources, but that rarely is the case. Some clients consume extraordinary amounts of time even though they are in treatment for only a few weeks, whereas other clients require expenditure of minor amounts of resources.

A more accurate method of distributing costs of overhead resources among clients and their procedures is to find the total of resources known to be consumed by a client (e.g., direct and indirect service time, session space) and determine what percentage those "known" resources are of all known resources for *all* clients. For example, if there are just three clients in a clinic and one spends twice as much time receiving services at the clinic as do the other two clients, then the percentages of total resources for the three clients would be 50%, 25%, and 25%. These percentages then would be used to distribute overhead costs among clients. These calculations and distributions are relatively easy to conduct using the resource cost, cost per unit resource, and resource cost spreadsheets developed previously to allocate services costs among clients and procedures.

The final step in the cost analysis procedure is to combine all of these specific costs for each procedure for each client. Costs themselves can be added in various ways so as to provide program managers with an overview of program operations (e.g., average cost for each of several common procedures, average cost for all procedures for a client for a month). (This is where computer spreadsheets really pay off.) More important for CPPOA, once cost data are available for individual clients and procedures, that information can be combined with information on how much of each procedure was received by each client, what processes changed how much for the client, and what outcomes were achieved for the client. Statistical analyses that actually are fairly quick and simple to perform can digest these data in ways that show which paths lead most often from resources through procedures and processes to outcomes. Rather than explaining how to do this with detailed statistical analyses, we decided to use data collected in a more subjective fashion to illustrate CPPOA in a decidedly nonstatistical (although still quantitative) manner.

Case Example: Cost → Procedure → Process → Outcome Analysis at the Program Level

CPPOA can be much more than just keeping track of resources while determining whether clients are making satisfactory progress under current treatment plans. In the following case study, we show how CPPOA can create a feedback process that can enhance program management by showing where resources are going and what they are being used to do with clients, to change in clients, and to achieve for clients.

Case Essentials: The Program

This case study examines the specific resources, procedures, processes, and outcomes of an entire therapeutic community aftercare program, working with costs for a 1-month period. The costs of each resource and of each procedure implemented, process changed, and outcome achieved were estimated and then analyzed for specific cost → procedure, procedure → process, and process → outcome linkages. This aftercare program was required of clients as part of their probation. It usually occupied the final 3 months of participation in a work release therapeutic community. The aftercare component was administered in an office of the therapeutic community facility. A single counselor ran the aftercare component with minimal support from a secretary and oversight from the director of the program. The caseload was about 30. Each week, clients attended group counseling and relapse prevention sessions. Clients also participated in individual counseling on a monthly basis. The counselor provided case management services such as referrals, employment monitoring, and coordination with probation and parole officers.

Selecting and Defining Resources, Procedures, Processes, and Outcomes

The resource and procedure variables were easy to select and are shown in the CPPOA model in Figure 12.2. After some discussion, the program director and the aftercare worker described three types of processes that were the focus of treatment procedures: self-efficacy expectancies, the acquisition of necessary skills, and bond-

RESOURCES

Direct Service Staff
Administrative Staff
Facilities
Utilities
Support Staff
Supplies
Urine Testing

PROCEDURES

Group Counseling
Relapse Prevention
Individual Counseling
Case Management

PROCESSES

Self-Efficacy Enhancement
Skill Acquisition for Relapse
  Prevention
Skill Acquisition for Support Access
Skill Acquisition for Service Access
Bonding With Addicts and
  Ex-Offenders
Bonding With Counselors

OUTCOMES

Drug Free
Stable Employment
Crime Free
Compliance With Probation
  and Parole

Figure 12.2. Cost → Procedure → Process → Outcome Analysis Model for Program

ing. Three skills were focused on in particular: (a) *relapse prevention,* (b) *accessing social and financial support,* and (c) *accessing public and private services* for health, mental health, vocational training, and employment and related opportunities.

These processes, in turn, were supposed to increase the likelihood that a client would achieve four primary outcomes:

Being drug free (i.e., abstaining from drugs for 1 month according to urine tests, self-report, and peer-report or from other former users)
Having stable employment (i.e., having a legal full-time job for the past month)
Being crime free (i.e., avoiding all criminal behavior for the past month according to self and peers as well as reports from family and probation officers)
Complying with probation and parole (according to the probation officer who met weekly with the aftercare worker)

After defining the essential resource, procedure, process, and outcome variables of the drug treatment program, the program director and the aftercare worker estimated, rather than measured, the relative strength of each possible relationship between each resource, procedure, process, and outcome. The existence and strength of these resource → procedure, procedure → process, and process → outcome relationships were estimated, rather than measured empirically, to save time and money. The strength of these links need not be expressed in monetary units or percentages, but staff of this program were comfortable doing this. The result carried forward costs from resources all the way through outcomes, making for a subjective but quantitative cost → outcome analysis. (It would be fascinating, and important for future applications of CPPOA, to examine the extent to which these estimations of relation existence and strength resembled empirically observed relationships.)

Analyzing Resource → Procedure Relationships

Costs for each major resource type are listed following the resource name in the resource→procedure matrix (Figure 12.3). Total program cost for the month was the sum of resource costs: $2,500 + $250 + $500 + $150 + $500 + $500 + $1,000 = $5,400. Total costs of a procedure are shown in the lowest row, in the column with the label of the procedure in the top row, and are the sums of the values of each resource expended to implement the procedure. The value of each resource spent in each procedure is shown in the cells of the matrix. The time of direct service staff, the time of support staff, and the costs of supplies and of urine testing were distributed among procedures according to staff estimates of how much of each resource was used in each procedure.

Often, these estimates were percentages, which we then multiplied by the total value of the resource to calculate how much of the resource was spent on each proce-

		Procedures			
		Group Counseling	Relapse Prevention	Individual Counseling	Case Management
Resources	Direct Service Staff ($2,500) / Administrative Staff ($250) / Facilities ($500 rent) / Utilities ($150)	18% = $612	23% = $782	23% = $782	36% = $1,224
	Support Staff ($500)		50% = $250		50% = $250
	Supplies ($500)	$100	$150	$100	$150
	Urine Testing ($1,000)		$1,000		
Total Procedure Cost		$712	$2,182	$882	$1,624

Figure 12.3. Resource → Procedure Matrix

dure. For example, based on estimates made by the program administrator, costs of the remaining resources (facilities at $500, utilities at $150, administrative staff at $250, and direct service staff at $2,500, summing to $3,400) were allocated among all four treatment procedures according to the percentage of time that direct staff spent on each procedure: 18% of $3,400 = $612 for group counseling, 23% of $3,400 = $782 for relapse prevention, again 23% of $3,400 = $782 for individual counseling, and 36% of $3,400 = $1,224 for case management. Sometimes, an actual monetary value was associated with the resource →procedure combination. For example, the distribution of supplies among different procedures was based on estimated use for each procedure: $100 for group counseling, $150 for relapse prevention, $100 for individual counseling, and $150 for case management. The entire $1,000 cost of urine testing was allocated to relapse prevention because it was not used in any other treatment procedures. Because support staff assisted primarily with relapse prevention and case management, support staff costs were divided equally between these two procedures ($250 each).

Analyzing Procedure → Process Relationships

To quantify relationships between treatment procedures implemented and internal processes changed, staff also estimated the percentage of time that a given treatment procedure focused on modifying specific processes. These percentages then were used to distribute the total cost of each procedure (which was calculated in the preceding section) among the processes, as detailed in the procedure →process matrix shown in Figure 12.4. These costs were totaled for each process to arrive at the costs shown in each process square in the bottom row.

Procedures typically contributed to changes in several, but not all, processes. Specifically, according to staff estimates, group counseling focused 33% on self-efficacy enhancement, 33% on bonding with addicts and ex-offenders, and 33% on bonding with counselors. Relapse prevention focused 20% on self-efficacy enhancement, 20% on skill acquisition for relapse prevention, 20% on skill acquisition for support access, 20% on bonding with addicts and ex-offenders, and 20% on bonding with counselors. Individual counseling focused 50% on self-efficacy enhancement and 50% on bonding with counselors. Finally, case management focused 75% on skill acquisition for service access, with half of the remaining 25% (12.5%) contributing to bonding with addicts and ex-offenders and the other half (12.5%) contributing to bonding with counselors.

Analyzing Process → Outcome Relationships

Staff were asked to estimate how much each process determined each of the four types of program outcomes. Several hours of discussion were required to obtain these estimates. The results are detailed in the process →outcome matrix shown in Figure 12.5, with monetary values assigned to each process → outcome relationship using the same multiplication procedure as used for other matrices. Staff estimated that 40% of the self-efficacy enhancement was focused on being drug free, 20% was focused on helping clients to get and retain employment, and 40% was focused on helping clients to avoid criminal behavior. Staff viewed relapse prevention skills as entirely (100%) focused on being drug free. Staff also reported that equal proportions of skill acquisition for support access affected the outcomes of being drug free, getting and retaining employment, avoiding criminal behavior, and complying with probation and parole (25% each). In addition, staff estimated that skill acquisition for service access contributed primarily to stable employment (80%) and somewhat to compliance with probation and parole (20%). Bonding with addicts and ex-offenders contributed in different degrees to all four outcomes: 32% to drug abstinence, 4% to stable employment, 32% to avoidance of criminal behavior, and 32% to compliance with probation and parole. Finally, bonding with counselors also contributed in varying degrees to all four outcome types: 10% to drug abstinence, 40% to stable

		Processes					
			Skill Acquisition			Bonding	
		Self-Efficacy Enhancement	Relapse Prevention	Support Access	Service Access	With Addicts and Ex-Offenders	With Counselors
Procedures	Group Counseling ($712)	33% = $237				33% = $237	33% = $237
	Relapse Prevention ($2,182)	20% = $436	20% = $436	20% = $436		20% = $436	20% = $436
	Individual Counseling ($882)	50% = $441					50% = $441
	Case Management ($1,624)				75% = $1,218	12.5% = $203	12.5% = $203
Total Procedure Cost		$1,115	$436	$436	$1,218	$877	$1,318

Figure 12.4. Procedure → Process Matrix

employment, 10% to avoidance of criminal behavior, and 40% to compliance with probation and parole.

Analyzing Cost → Outcome Relationships

The totals in the final row of Figure 12.5 show how costs of resources transferred to outcomes. These costs sum to $5,400, the total cost of the program for the month. This does not, of course, reflect the total cost of achieving these outcomes. The total cost per outcome achieved per client must include the cost of participating in the therapeutic community for 6 to 9 months plus 3 months of the aftercare program. Unfortunately, data were not available for the therapeutic community program. Although it is tempting to assign a cost to these outcomes of three times the monthly cost and then to divide the cost by the proportion of clients attaining the outcome to arrive at a cost/outcome ratio, this would seriously underestimate the cost of attaining these

			Outcomes			
			Drug Free (complete drug abstinence)	*Stable Employment*	*Crime Free (avoidance of all criminal behavior)*	*Compliance With Probation and Parole*
Procedures		Self-Efficacy Enhancement ($1,115)	40% = $446	20% = $223	40% = $446	
	Skill Acquisition	Relapse Prevention ($436)	100% = $436			
		Support Access ($436)	25% = $109	25% = $109	25% = $109	25% = $109
		Service Access ($1,218)		80% = $974		20% = $244
	Bonding	With Addicts and Ex-Offenders ($877)	32% = $281	4% = $34	32% = $281	32% = $281
		With Counselors ($1,318)	10% = $132	40% = $527	10% = $132	40% = $527
Total Outcome Cost			$1,404	$1,867	$968	$1,161

Figure 12.5. Process → Outcome Matrix

outcomes. That ratio would completely omit the costs of the therapeutic community, which necessarily occurred before the program was evaluated.

Subjective Quantitative Analysis of Costs of Procedures, Processes, and Outcomes

By constructing bar graphs of the amounts of resources focused on each procedure, process, and outcome in the program, it is easy to see where the costs are and what outcomes they make possible. For example, it is evident that the most costly procedures are relapse prevention and case management (see top bar graph in Figure 12.6). In addition, some processes absorb far more resources than do others. As shown in the second bar graph in Figure 12.6, self-efficacy enhancement, skill acquisition for service access, and both types of bonding are particularly large investments of potentially therapeutic resources. However, the outcomes associated with these procedures and processes differ in both the costs of resources devoted to them and the degree to which clients achieved what was desired. The outcome toward which the

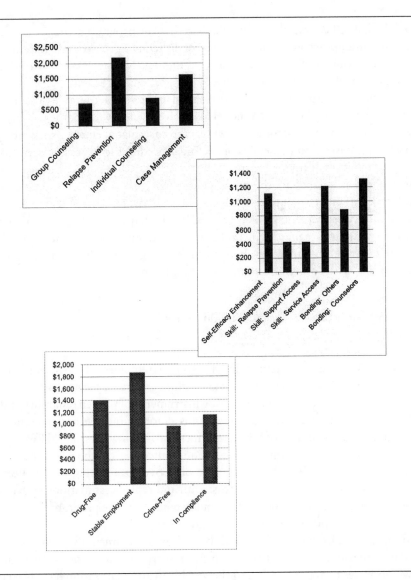

Figure 12.6. Estimated Costs of Procedures, Processes, and Outcomes
NOTE: See text for important qualifications.

least amount of resources was directed, being crime free, was the most likely to be achieved (by 100% of clients). The outcome toward which the *most* resources were directed (stable employment) was the least likely to be achieved (by a relatively low

65% of clients). Of course, these costs likely reflect the program manager's expectation that stable employment would be the most difficult to achieve and, therefore, deserved more resources. Nevertheless, the cost findings for each class of variables in the CPPOA model are of potential value in program management.

Most of the relapse prevention efforts resulted in the very acceptable outcome of a 90% abstinence rate. The CPPOA model also shows that several of the other procedures contribute to this outcome. However, the case management procedure produced a less impressive outcome. By connecting procedures to processes to outcomes in the sort of diagram provided earlier, it becomes clear that much of the case management effort is related to the employment outcome. Yet, stable employment (steady work sufficient to support the client and dependents) is the outcome that is attained by the lowest percentage of clients (65%). Perhaps this outcome would have been worse without case management, but it does call into question the value of this procedure for program outcomes. It also is interesting to note how much staff estimated bonding with counselors contributes to outcomes.

Integrating Subjective and Quantitative Models for Formative Cost → Procedure → Process → Outcome Analysis

The preceding model and its associated costs and outcomes (and cost/outcome ratios) are, of course, based on estimated relationships generated over a matter of hours rather than on objective data collected using instruments of proven reliability and validity over several months or years. The result is a more subjective and uncertain but still intriguing understanding of how a treatment program works. The CPPOA logic model and its associated estimates of costs and outcomes can be used as a sort of "baseline" against which to compare more objective data during data collection. Regular updates of the model can contrast with and replace estimations with observations, showing staff how closely their understanding of the program matches the understanding provided by more objective measures.

In sum, CPPOA begins to get into that black box of treatment that none of us has opened up well using traditional approaches to research and to economic evaluation. The two obstacles to applying CPPOA thoroughly in an organization have been time and money. A possible solution outlined earlier is to pursue both paths:

1. To start with the qualitative understanding of program operations provided by a CPPOA logic model developed through conversations with staff (and potentially clients)
2. To generate quick subjective estimates of the values of resource → procedure, procedure → process, and process → outcome linkages and to analyze these estimates via simple calculations, as illustrated earlier

3. To then collect objective data on the same relationships and to analyze those relationships statistically
4. To compare the findings of the quick subjective CPPOAs and the more time- and resource-consuming objective CPPOAs to contrast "understood" models with "real" models of the treatment program

Using Cost → Procedure → Process → Outcome Analysis to Make Decisions About Program Operations

With this information, the CPPOA model then can be used to make decisions about program changes or developments. Using the previous example, it seems reasonable to keep intact the procedures and processes related to the abstinence outcome. In fact, the model affirms staff efforts in assisting clients in maintaining abstinence. For example, some staff questioned the efficacy of urine testing. For the program analyzed here, it appears that urine testing actually is an important part of the procedures that are most likely to produce the desired processes that, in turn, lead to the achievement of the hoped-for outcomes.

Examining the "slices" of the CPPOA logic model reflected in the separate resource → procedure, procedure → process, and process → outcome *matrices* (Figures 12.3, 12.4, and 12.5), staff can see that the case management efforts aimed at improved employment status might not be producing the desired outcomes. Seeing that a different approach (aimed at skill acquisition and self-efficacy enhancement) was more productive in maintaining abstinence, staff might decide to decrease some of the time devoted to case management to allow for a more focused skill-building and problem-solving employment group.

This is just a brief description of how the CPPOA model can be used to make decisions about program changes and expansions. Many other program descriptions are embedded in the preceding sample. From these descriptions and connections between costs and outcomes, a variety of additional informed program decisions can be made.

CONSIDERATIONS FOR THE RESEARCHER'S NEXT COST ANALYSIS, COST-EFFECTIVENESS ANALYSIS, COST-BENEFIT ANALYSIS, OR COST → PROCEDURE → PROCESS → OUTCOME ANALYSIS

Cost-benefit analysis, cost-effectiveness analysis, and CPPOA are important tools that can be used to evaluate the performance of an existing program and to determine whether and how it can be modified to enhance program and client outcomes. By gaining experience in the use of cost analysis, social work professionals can demonstrate to funding sources, policymakers, and other service professionals the value of investing in social work programming. It also makes it more difficult to dismiss requests for program funding. We encourage the researcher to use the methods outlined in this chapter to begin cost-effectiveness, cost-benefit analysis, and CPPOA of his or her own programs. And, we ask that the researcher let us know how they work in his or her community—and how much these analyses cost.

REFERENCES

Gerstein, D. R., Johnson, R. A., Harwood, H., Fountain, D., Suter, N., & Malloy, K. (1994). *Evaluating recovery services: The California Drug and Alcohol Treatment Assessment (CALDATA)*. Sacramento: California Department of Alcohol and Drug Programs.

Gold, M. R., Siegel, J. E., Russell, L. B., & Weinstein, M. C. (1996). *Cost-effectiveness in health and medicine*. New York: Oxford University Press.

Kee, J. E. (1994). Benefit-cost analysis. In J. S. Wholey, H. P. Hatry, & K. E. Newcomer (Eds.), *Handbook of practical program evaluation*. San Francisco: Jossey-Bass.

Lennox, R. D., Scott-Lennox, J. A., & Holder, H. D. (1992). Substance abuse and family illness: Evidence from health care utilization and cost-offset research. *Journal of Mental Health Administration, 19*, 83-95.

Yates, B. T. (1980). *Improving effectiveness and reducing costs in mental health*. Springfield, IL: Charles C Thomas.

Yates, B. T. (1996). *Analyzing costs, procedures, processes, and outcomes in human services*. Thousand Oaks, CA: Sage.

Yates, B. T. (1998). Formative evaluation of costs, cost-effectiveness, and cost-benefit: Toward cost → procedure →process →outcome analysis. In L. Bickman & D. Rog (Eds.), *Handbook of applied social research methods* (pp. 285-314). Thousand Oaks, CA: Sage.

Yates, B. T. (1999). *Measuring and improving cost, cost-effectiveness, and cost-benefit for substance abuse treatment programs* (NIH Publication No. 99-4518). Rockville, MD: National Institute on Drug Abuse.

CHAPTER THIRTEEN

Single-System Designs

BRUCE A. THYER

Single-system research designs (SSRDs) are investigatory methodologies intended to help the social worker answer two questions of fundamental importance to practice: "Have things changed?" and "Have things changed *because* of social work intervention?" The first of these can be deemed the *evaluation* question and is easy to answer relative to the second, which can be called the *causal* question. The undertaking of a SSRD has only two essential steps:

1. Locate a reliable and valid outcome measure (dependent variable) that can be repeatedly assessed.
2. Actually assess this outcome measure repeatedly over time.

The term *single-system* does not mean that SSRDs are limited to studies involving given individuals. Rather, it means that some single unit of analysis is repeatedly measured over time. The unit of analysis in an SSRD can be an individual, a couple, a small group, a family, a community, or society as a whole. At the level of an individual, it could be some measure of a client's alcohol consumption. With a couple, it could be a measure of discord such as weekly arguments or abusive episodes. With a community or society as a whole, it could be some social indicator such as monthly reports of a particular type of crime, out-of-wedlock births, or high school dropouts (all reported over some time period). Thus, SSRDs lend themselves to evaluation research at all levels of social work practice, micro through macro.

MEASUREMENT ISSUES

When choosing an outcome measure, it is important to ascertain that the variable possesses adequate reliability and validity. Jordan and Hoefer's chapter on reliability and validity in quantitative measurement (Chapter 4) and Corcoran's chapter on locating instruments (Chapter 5) in this volume provide guidelines in this regard, as do some other texts such as Corcoran and Fischer (2000) and Royse, Thyer, Padgett, and Logan (2000). Rarely is it a good idea to invent a questionnaire designed to assess some construct for use in one's own research purposes. For nearly everything the researcher is interested in measuring, prior authors already have undertaken the intensive labor required to demonstrate the reliability and validity of some appropriate measure and have published it in a journal or book. Before undertaking such a task (i.e., creating a new measure) himself or herself, the researcher should complete a thorough literature review to be sure that a suitable measure does not already exist. It is a sign of a novice researcher to conduct a study using a "homemade" instrument of unknown reliability and validity and to attempt to publish findings derived from this measure when appropriate outcome measures already are established. This caveat applies only to the development of some quantitative measure of an "attitude" (e.g., racism, self-esteem), emotional state (e.g., worry, love), or indicator of psychopathology (e.g., paranoia, depression, mania). In the case of conducting a survey study of some sort, it is very common (and legitimate) to construct a series of questions designed to systematically elicit information from respondents.

In attempting to choose one or more outcome measures, the social work researcher has only three major categories from which to select:

1. The researcher can choose to measure *observable behavior.*
2. The researcher can choose to measure respondents' reports of *affect or thoughts* (these cannot be assessed directly, of course, only via self-reports).
3. In selected instances, the researcher can choose to measure some relevant *physiological indicator.*

Most psychosocial issues of concern to the social worker can be assessed by using outcome measures derived from one or more of these domains. Domestic violence can be researched using actual episodes of abuse as an outcome measure as well as through rapid assessment instruments designed to quantify the attitudes of the victims or perpetrators of abuse. Alcohol or other drug abuse can be assessed by measuring consumption; by reports of "cravings"; and by breath, urine, or saliva tests that report the amount of substances in the body. Clients' "phobias" can be assessed by behavioral avoidance, self-reports of anxiety, and heart rate. It is not possible to provide definitive instructions regarding what needs to be measured—and how—in every possible instance where a social worker would be interested in making use of an SSRD. Indeed, each major field of social work practice has a highly specialized literature describing various outcome measures, and a social work practitioner or researcher focusing on a given area is expected to become thoroughly familiar with the most scientifically substantiated measures relevant to that area.

Although it is not possible to recommend specific outcome measures for all problem areas, one piece of sound advice for the researcher is to consider measures from *different domains* (e.g., self-reports, direct measures of behavior, physiological indicators) given that each possesses certain strengths and limitations. By using measures from two or more of these domains, it is possible to obtain a clearer picture of any changes that may occur than is the case when only one mode of response is used. If the researcher has three measures capturing change—one self-report, one measure of behavior, and one physiological indicator—and all three change in a positive (or negative) direction, then the researcher has stronger evidence that changes occurred than he or she would if only one response domain were measured.

ANALYZING SSRD DATA

The most useful approach to analyzing data obtained in the context of an SSRD is through visually inspecting the data once they are presented graphically. This is in contrast to data obtained from research using group research designs, where the primary method of analysis relies on the use of inferential statistics. We make use of visual analysis in everyday life to answer simple but important questions. A glance at the daily newspaper can inform the reader how the stock market has performed for the past month, quarter, or year. There is no need to apply a statistical test to answer the question, "Has the stock market gone up, gone down, or stayed pretty much the same?" Similarly, in a patient's hospital record, a graph will depict the patient's temperature and blood pressure over time, and clinically significant rises and falls can be seen simply by looking at the results over time.

Using visual analysis of graphically presented data makes it difficult to detect small or unreliable changes, and this failure to detect small effects (i.e., failing to "find" a "real" change) is called a *Type II error*. In research on practice outcomes, the social worker usually is concerned with finding strong and powerfully effective treatments—those that exert very clear and compelling beneficial effects—hence Type II errors are not as crucial as they may be in other forms of inquiry such as theory-testing studies. Most types of inferential statistics that have been advocated for use in analyzing SSRD data present serious limitations in their applicability, and in practice they rarely are used by researchers who employ SSRDs.

TYPES OF SSRDS

Like the group or nomothetic research designs, SSRDs can be reviewed in order of their increasing complexity or ability to yield conclusions of high internal validity. I use this approach to provide an overview and case illustrations of SSRDs, first by examining designs suitable for answering the *evaluative question* and then by looking at designs that have the potential to answer the *causal question*. Whereas group designs usually are symbolically depicted using the letters O (for observation) and X (for intervention), SSRDs make use of a different yet analogous approach—using the letters A (indicating a time when data are collected and no formal intervention occurred) and B (indicating a time when intervention was undertaken). In SSRDs, the A phase is called a *baseline,* and the B phase is called a *treatment phase.*

Most social work interventions contain multiple elements and are delivered in a "package deal," but they still are referred to as a B phase. However, if discrete and legitimately discriminable interventions are sequentially applied, then further treatments can be labeled as C, D, and so forth.

If the researcher fulfills the two prerequisites of conducting an SSRD—finding a suitable measure and then graphing the repeatedly collected data over time—then he or she has completed an A design. This can be a highly useful method for the purposes of completing a needs assessment. For example, community advocates can obtain police records of the numbers of crimes per month reported in a given neighborhood, graph these data month by month, and make their case more powerfully to the mayor that additional police patrols are needed in this neighborhood. Remember, a picture is worth a thousand words. A picture also is easier to interpret and yields more accurate conclusions. Which is more comprehensible, a column of numbers or a line graph showing those numbers ascending or descending?

Suppose that the researcher does not opt to take a baseline; rather, the researcher begins the reliable and valid measurement of the client's problem at the same time that formal social work intervention starts. This can be a good idea, and if continued periodically throughout treatment, it results in a B SSRD, a practical design that is very helpful in credibly answering the vital question, "Did my client get better over the course of social work intervention?"

Taking the earlier example a bit further, the researcher should imagine that the community organizers were successful in getting augmented police patrols for the targeted neighborhood. If they then continued to obtain the same crime statistics as before (during the A phase) while the police patrols were in force, then they have the makings of an A-B SSRD—data graphically recorded before and during an intervention. If the implementation of the additional policing was immediately followed by a reduction in criminal activity, then the line connecting the data points during the B phase should clearly reflect this. By visually comparing the descending B phase line to the ascending A phase data, a clear inference can be made regarding the question, "Did change occur?"

The baseline data may be obtained prospectively (in a planned manner before intervention begins) or retrospectively (in some circumstances). For certain problems, retrospective data already are available and can be used in lieu of prospective baselining. Some problems or events occur so infrequently or are so significant that clients can reliably recall them. Governmental and private agencies keep abundant data on various issues—accidents, child abuse, domestic violence, recidivism, drunken driving, school attendance, numbers of psychiatric hospitalizations, and so forth—all of which are grist for the retrospective baseline phase of a study of the potential effects of some large-scale intervention.

With the simple A-B SSRD, it usually is not legitimate to conclude that the treatment *caused* any observed changes. There may be a host of rival explanations to account for the improvements, rival explanations that are collectively known as the *threats to internal validity*. For example, perhaps it got colder, and criminals remained at home. Perhaps the augmented police patrols coincided with other community members organizing a "neighborhood watch" program. Perhaps school began, diverting juvenile delinquents from the streets and into the classroom. For most social problems or interpersonal concerns, the data obtained in an A-B study usually do not permit us to confidently rule out all of these rival explanations; therefore, the A-B design, like the B design, is referred to as an *evaluation design*. We can evaluate whether change really occurred (and this is a good and valuable thing to do) even if we cannot be certain as to what caused these changes. Usually in a successful A-B study, the most generous and legitimate conclusion to make is something such as, "The data are consistent with the hypothesis that Treatment B reduced the problem."

Suppose that the preceding really happened. Baseline (A phase) data were collected and showed that crime was increasing. Augmented policing was implemented (B phase), and for a number of months the data showed that crime began to decrease. But then the thrifty mayor decided to cut back the police budget, resulting in a return to the level of patrolling found during the original baseline phase. This unfortunate circumstance can result in an A-B-A SSRD. Although not desirable from a public policy point of view, if crime went way back up during the second A phase, then this would strengthen the confidence the researcher can have that the police patrols were genuinely responsible for the original decrease in crime seen during the B phase. Logically, it is less likely that two concomitant events occurred that just happened to coincide with the introduction and removal of the intervention (augmented police patrols). With the A-B-A design, we have begun to move toward the more "experimental" SSRDs or those that permit some degree of causal inference, namely evidence supporting the hypothesis that augmented policing was causally responsible for the observed reduction in crime and that the elimination of augmented policing "caused" crime to increase. Designs that involve the intentional or unintentional removal of an intervention are called *withdrawal designs* (not reversal designs, which are an entirely different concept and very rarely used in social work research).

Continuing with this example, the community organizers returned to the city council with their big graph depicting the preceding A-B-A SSRD, with the data clearly demonstrating that crime had increased greatly following the reduced policing. They obtained a sympathetic hearing, largely engendered by their careful presentation of factual data, and augmented policing was restored. This sets the stage for the A-B-A-B study, an experimental SSRD that is capable of controlling or eliminating most rival threats to internal validity. Here, the skeptic would have to contend that on *three* successive occasions—the initial addition of augmented police patrols, the removal of augmented police patrols, and the second addition of augmented police patrols—some external factors intervened at just about the same point in time as the intentionally contrived changes in policing, and that it was these external factors, not the policing, that caused alterations in crime. This usually is a difficult argument to make, with the result that a stronger causal conclusion often can be drawn regarding the effects of the B intervention.

SSRDs can be used creatively to *compare* the possible levels of effectiveness of different treatments. We could complete the effectiveness of augmented police patrols with the results of a neighborhood watch program by using an A-B-A-C design, with A indicating a time period when nothing unusual was undertaken, B indicating a time period when augmented police patrolling occurred, and C indicating a time period when the neighborhood watch program was instituted. If crimes were curtailed more strongly during B than during C, then such a result would be consistent with the hypothesis that police patrols are a more effective deterrent than neighborhood patrols (or vice versa). Unfortunately, this approach usually does not control for the possibility of *sequencing* effects (e.g., C might work *only after* being preceded by B).

Another form of SSRD with potentially high internal validity is the *multiple baseline* (MBL) design. Suppose that the researcher wanted to design a study that would really (i.e., causally) determine whether augmented police patrols reduced crime. One approach would be to find two communities (let us call them Rubinville and Grinnell City) that afforded access to reliable and valid crime data separately for each one. The researcher would begin baselining (this could be done using retrospective or archived data) the crimes of interest in each community. After suitable baseline data were gathered, the researcher would begin the augmented police patrols in one community only (say, Rubinville). The researcher would continue baseline data (A phase) collection in Grinnell City while gathering B phase data in Rubinville. After a proper amount of time has passed and the researcher (hopefully) sees a meaningful reduction in crime in Rubinville and *no* change in Grinnell City, the researcher would implement the *same* intervention in the second community. If the researcher sees changes in Grinnell City similar to those seen in Rubinville *only after* the intervention is begun, then the researcher has strong causal evidence that the police patrols really do reduce crime. This example makes use of an MBL design across clients/systems variation on a macro scale.

Another example of this variant of the MBL design, drawing from interpersonal practice, was used by Maeser and Thyer (1990) to evaluate intervention with three young men with severe developmental disabilities. The outcome measure was a reliable and valid determination of their ability to display appropriate table manners, tested several times a day across a number of weeks, before and during the social worker's providing the teenagers with skills training in selected table manners. But the social worker trained one youth first, trained the second some days later, and trained the third some days after that. The baselines for the three clients were of uneven lengths—shortest for the first youth trained, next longest for the second youth trained, longest for the third youth trained. Improvements in table manners were observed only following social work intervention. The staggered baselines of uneven length, coupled with finding improvements only after intervention began, results in a graphically powerful display of the effectiveness of intervention in causing improvements.

A second variation of the MBL is called the *MBL across problems* design. This requires one client with two or more problems to be sequentially treated in the same way. Suppose that a disadvantaged youth has difficulties in reading, writing, and arithmetic. The outcome measures are his scores on daily or weekly quizzes at school on each subject. The researcher would baseline his grades in all three subjects beginning at the same time. Presumably, the grades are both low and stable. The researcher would begin intervention (say, a peer tutoring program) for one subject only (say, reading). Reading scores now fall into a B phase, whereas writing and arithmetic scores remain in their A phases. It is hoped that reading scores will improve following the initiation of tutoring while reading and arithmetic scores remain stable. Now, the researcher would add tutoring in writing (which now enters a B phase) while continuing the baseline data collection in arithmetic. It is hoped that writing scores now will improve while arithmetic scores stay stagnant. Finally, the researcher would implement tutoring for arithmetic. Once again, logic suggests that if scores improved only after tutoring in each subject began, then one may conclude that tutoring *caused* the observed academic improvements. In this example, it is highly unlikely that other explanations (i.e., threats to internal validity) can account for the results.

A third variant of the MBL is called the *MBL across settings* design. This requires one client who displays a problem in several different settings, a problem that is treated in the same manner, sequentially, in each of these contexts. For example, a boy displays aggression at home (with siblings), at school (with peers), and in the car (with any youthful passengers, siblings, or peers). The occurrence of aggression is validly recorded (frequency measures would be a good option) separately in each setting over an appropriate time period. Then, an intervention (B) is employed in one setting only (say, school) while baseline (A) conditions are maintained at home and in the car. Assume that aggression soon decreases dramatically at school but continues unabated at home and in the car. The same intervention then is applied at home and continued at school while baseline measures are continued in the car. If aggression now declines at home and continues in the car and is reduced only after the same intervention is lastly applied while driving, then the social worker has gathered very compelling evidence that the intervention *caused* aggression to decline.

Again, the experimental logic involved in MBL designs is the same as that when using withdrawal designs; that is, see whether an apparent effect can be replicated two or more times on different occasions. Each successful replication increases confidence that the improvements were caused by the treatment and not by some potentially confounding threat to internal validity. This logic has been called the *principle of unlikely successive coincidences* and is the foundation of all potentially experimental SSRDs. There are some additional variations in the composition of SSRDs, but for most practice evaluation circumstances, the general designs outlined in this chapter will suffice. In the next section, I provide some illustrations of actually using SSRDs in the evaluation of social work practice.

Using a B Design

Social worker Betsy Vonk was employed as a clinical social worker at a university student counseling center. She had a new client whose presenting problem was a severe fear of vaginal penetration, a fear of such magnitude that she had avoided pap smears, pelvic examinations, and vaginal intercourse—all sources of great distress for her. Omitting much clinical detail here, Vonk provided the client with a social work intervention called *exposure therapy,* an evidence-based intervention well documented as effective in helping people with phobias. The client was asked to privately practice gradually increasing fear-evoking exposure tasks several times each week. These tasks consisted of activities such as touching the opening to her vagina and resting her finger there for several minutes at a time and then, when this became less upsetting, inserting the tip of her finger and leaving it there, and so forth. The outcome measure was her own self-report of the greatest level of fear she experienced during each home exercise, rated on a scale of 0 (*no fear at all*) to 10 (*maximum fear or panic*). After several weeks, she involved her cooperative boyfriend in these exercises, and during one session they got carried away and actually had vaginal intercourse. Nothing untoward happened, and indeed, she soon experienced a complete resolution of her fears. Greater details of this case, and of its evaluation using a B SSRD, can be found in Vonk and Thyer (1995). The graph of the data is depicted in Figure 13.1.

The A-B Design

Hospital social worker Lisa Baker worked on a neonatal intensive care unit, caring for premature infants at high risk for sudden infant death syndrome (SIDS). When an infant was discharged home, the attending pediatrician usually prescribed that the caregiver (typically the mother) make daily use of a home infant apnea monitor. The baby would wear a gentle elastic band around its chest, and if the baby's heart rate or breathing abnormally slowed or stopped, then an alarm would sound, startling the infant (often restoring normal breathing and heart rate) and alerting the mother to render assistance.

Sometimes, the mothers did not use the monitor, and this placed the infants more at risk for SIDS and made it difficult for the pediatricians to determine the babies' health. In such circumstances, Baker would receive referrals to work with these families to get them to make more consistent use of the apnea monitor.

One such case is depicted in Figure 13.2. The vertical axis depicts the hours per day that the monitor was used (i.e., when the mother placed it properly around the infant's chest). The data were gathered electronically by the monitor itself and are assumed to be both reliable and valid. As can be seen, monitor use was very rare during the 39 days prior to Baker's consultation but increased dramatically during the month after she began working with the family, eventually providing the physician with enough information to safely discontinue the monitor use. For further information on this case and its evaluation, see Baker and Thyer (1999). Do the data in Figure 13.2 permit an unambiguous conclusion that the intervention *caused* the improvements during the B phase? No, not in any conservative interpretation. However, the consistency of the baseline, coupled with the rapidity and magnitude of the improvements, certainly suggests this to be true.

The A-B-A-B Design

Thyer and Geller (1987) used an A-B-A-B design to see whether automobile dashboard stickers reading "Safety Belt Use Required in This Vehicle" had any appreciable effect on automobile passenger use of safety belts. A class of M.S.W. students were recruited to record the spontaneous use of safety belts on a daily basis for any passengers who happened to drive with them in the students' own automobiles. Al-

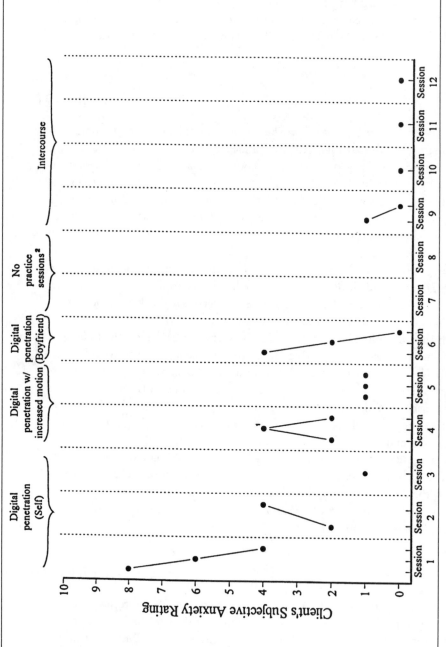

Figure 13.1. Client's Maximum Reported Anxiety (0 = *no anxiety*, 10 = *panic-like anxiety*) Evoked During Self-Exposure Homework Exercises During 12 Treatment Sessions

SOURCE: Reprinted from *Journal of Behavior Therapy and Experimental Psychiatry, 26*, Vonk, M.E., & Thyer, B.A., Exposure therapy in the treatment of vaginal penetration phobia, pp. 359-363, copyright 1995, with permission from Elsevier Science.

1. At this point, the client became aware of arousal. Subsequent sessions included arousal.

2. The client's boyfriend was out of town. The client focused on ambivalence about her relationship.

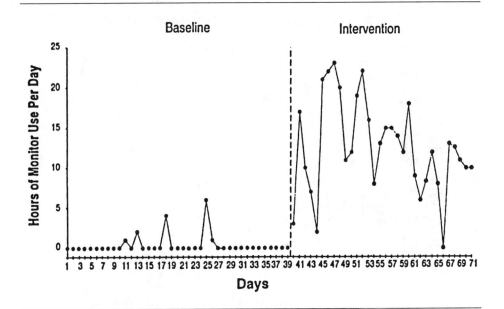

Figure 13.2. Daily Home Use (in hours) of the Infant Apnea Monitor, Pre- and Post-Family Social Work Intervention
SOURCE: Reprinted from Baker and Thyer (1999) with the permission of the publisher.

though a varying number of passengers were given rides each day, by using the *percentage* of passengers who buckled up, a standard outcome measure could be determined. For 2 weeks, baseline (A_1 phase) data were gathered (the student drivers always wore their safety belts, so this possible confound was kept constant). Then, at the beginning of the third week, the students were given professionally prepared stickers to apply to the passenger sides of their car dashboards, prompting passengers to buckle up (the state did not require safety belt use when this study was undertaken). The next 2 weeks constituted the first intervention phase (B_1). After 2 weeks, the stickers were removed for 14 days (A_1) and then replaced for a final 2-week period (B_2).

The data are presented in Figure 13.3. They indicate that safety belt use approximately *doubled* above baseline levels when the stickers were used. Although large variations in the data are present, the data during each phase are relatively stable in the sense of not obviously ascending or descending. The effects of introducing or removing the prompting stickers were immediate and obvious, and the three iterations of an effect effectively serve to remove most common threats to internal validity (e.g., regression, mortality, concurrent history, instrumentation, testing effects). The data

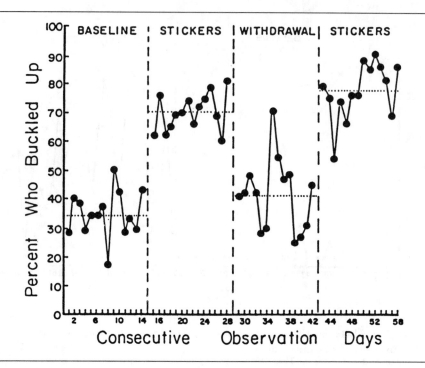

Figure 13.3. Percentages of Passengers Who Buckled Up Over 58 Consecutive Observation Days, 2 Weeks per Consecutive Baseline, Intervention, Withdrawal, and Intervention Phase
SOURCE: Reprinted from Thyer and Geller (1987) with the permission of the publisher.

are so compelling that one can have great confidence in the *causal* relationship between sticker use and safety belt use.

An MBL Design

Social worker Paul Gallant used an MBL across clients design to examine the effects of using a bug-in-the-ear (BITE) device in clinical supervision. The BITE is a small wireless earphone worn by a clinician during therapy sessions with clients while receiving supervisory comments from a supervisor who watches the session from behind a one-way mirror. Although widely touted as an effective tool for clinical supervision, the BITE suffers from a lack of empirical evidence that it really does influence clinician behavior during therapy. Gallant wanted to see whether it really did.

The outcome measures were reliable and valid assessments of the extent to which the two therapists used a key clinician skill—supportive statements. Baseline measures of the two clinicians' (let us call them Allen and Rick) use of supportive statements were made for 4 sessions in the case of Allen and for 9 sessions with Rick's supervision. Use of actual BITE feedback began in Session 5 during Allen's work with clients but not until Session 10 during Rick's live supervision. The results are displayed in Figure 13.4. Both Allen and Rick demonstrated low use of supportive statements. Allen's use of supportive statements obviously went up only after BITE feedback began, whereas Rick's remained low, only to increase after BITE feedback was provided to Rick. The results are visually compelling, strongly corroborating the hypothesis that BITE feedback can affect clinicians' behavior during therapy (for more details on the project, see Gallant, Thyer, & Bailey, 1991).

SOME TECHNICAL MATTERS

How long must a baseline be? How long must an intervention phase be? How many data points are needed? What if I cannot make any sense of the data? These are questions that often trouble the social worker attempting to use SSRDs for the first time. But the researcher should have no fear, keeping in mind the idea that these research methods are intended to assist in the evaluation of practice, not to dominate how it is undertaken.

In general, *the researcher should seek enough data points over a long enough period of time to obtain stable data.* Stable data are those that allow a conclusion regarding directionality. Are the data clearly going up? Are the data clearly going down? Are the data clearly stable? Are the data clearly unstable? Keeping in mind that any two data points can form a line, the researcher needs at least three to infer the beginnings of a *trend.* The length of time depends on the problem and outcome measures. Evaluations of public policy changes might require monthly data collected over several years or a longer period of time, whereas the effects of certain interpersonal skill-building or psychoeducational interventions can be detected in a single session of treatment with a given client. There are no simple answers to these questions beyond recognizing in the abstract that more data points usually are better than fewer data points and that longer phases are better than shorter phases. But in the world of practice, the social worker needs to temper such ideals with clinical realities and the needs of clients.

Does the researcher need the same number of data points per phase to conduct an SSRD? No. Does the researcher need phases of equal duration? No. Must the researcher begin a SSRD with a baseline? No, the researcher can begin one at the same time as he or she begins treatment, as in a B design, a B-A-B design, and so forth. The

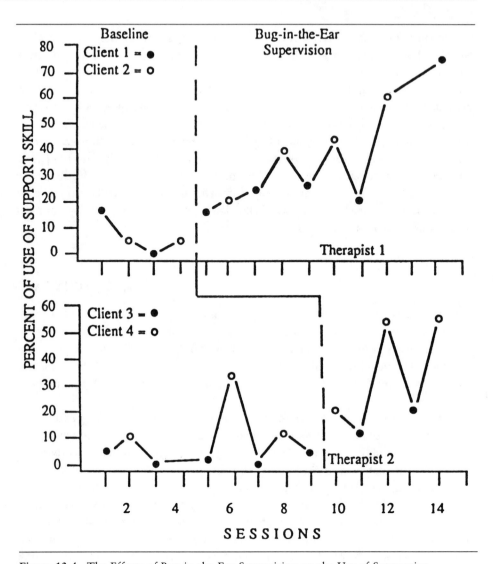

Figure 13.4. The Effects of Bug-in-the-Ear Supervision on the Use of Supportive Statements by Therapists 1 and 2
SOURCE: Reprinted from Gallant, Thyer, and Bailey (1991) with the permission of the publisher.

researcher should take advantage of whatever evaluation opportunities practice affords him or her. However, the researcher should not wring his or her hands over the failure to conduct a perfectly controlled study.

How to Graph SSRD Data

Either freehand or using a computer, the researcher should draw a big bold L shape, with the bottom axis about twice as long as the vertical axis. The vertical line represents the outcome measure, and the horizontal line represents the dimension of time. The researcher should insert suitable tic marks and numbers on these two axes indicating the possible values of the outcome measure and of time. The researcher also should insert suitable descriptive words under the horizontal axis (e.g., Beck Depression Inventory scores, numbers of reported crimes per month) and under the vertical axis (e.g., hours, days, sessions, weeks, months). The researcher should use big solid dots to depict each data point during each phase and should use a thinner line to connect the data points *within* each phase. The data points should be three to four times as thick as the line connecting them. The researcher should not connect data points between phases. He or she should use a dashed vertical line to distinguish between phases, being careful not to draw these lines through a data point or through a tic mark on the horizontal axis. If the researcher has two different outcome measures that he or she wants to display on the same graph, then the researcher should use solid and open circles to denote the data points. Additional simple symbols (e.g., squares, triangles) should be used as needed to depict additional different dependent variables, but the researcher should be careful not to clutter the graph to the point of illegibility. More than one graph may be used, if necessary. Only black ink should be used; color never should be used to depict important information because it reproduces poorly. Carr and Burkholder (1998) provide simple instructions for creating SSRD graphs using *Microsoft Excel*. Conboy, Auerbach, Beckerman, Schnall, and LaPorte (2000) describe some inexpensive software specifically created for this purpose. The reader may consult any recent issue of the *Journal of Applied Behavior Analysis* or Mattaini (1993) to find numerous examples of properly constructed graphs.

A Word About Causation

In outcome studies using SSRDs and group research designs, the language of *causation* sometimes is tossed about freely. In a well-crafted A-B-A-B study with strong changes observed each time the intervention is introduced or removed, the social worker might be tempted to state that the intervention caused these changes. This is permissible if such a statement is made with a vivid awareness of its limitations. What often actually is implied is that a compelling *functional relationship* has been observed between some independent variable and some outcome. We do this all the time in our everyday lives and in our professional lives—"Poverty causes homelessness," "Genetic anomalies cause Down's syndrome," "Smoking causes cancer," "Drinking causes more automobile accidents," and so forth. Indeed, such statements are true if we are referring to functional relationships between variables. But there is no implication intended that we have a complete understanding of the causal "mechanisms" of *why* and *how* things work. We do not really know how aspirin works, much less how the Head Start program does. Such questions relating to some sort of ultimate causation have troubled scientists for decades and philosophers for millennia, and we do not seem to be particularly closer to sound answers to such questions, dealing as perhaps they do with issues such as determinism and the nature of reality itself. So, for social work research, and especially for research on the outcomes of practice, we must be content with a far less comprehensive meaning of the word *cause*. "Intervention B caused positive outcomes for clients with Problem X" might well be a provisional conclusion limited to these particular clients at this point in time, but such knowledge is precisely what social work is all about—finding practical solutions to social problems. SSRDs are ideally suited to this task.

Many years ago, one of the founders of social work, Mary Richmond, told social workers, "Special efforts should be made to ascertain whether abnormal manifestations are *increasing* or *decreasing* in number and intensity, as this often has a practical bearing on the management of the case" (Richmond, 1917/1935, p. 435, italics in original). SSRDs are one way in which to follow this recommendation. Virtually *any* social work intervention (irrespective of the theory or model on which it is based), applied at virtually *any* level of practice (micro through macro), can be evaluated using SSRDs (see also Thyer, 1998). The Council on Social Work Education currently requires that M.S.W. students be taught to "conduct empirical evaluations of their own practice interventions and those of other relevant systems" (Council on Social Work Education, 1999, Standard M5.7.11), and a similar standard has been in place for nearly 20 years.

SSRDs are a useful way in which to complete what has been labeled *Level 1 research,* defined as "systematically monitoring clinical outcomes—one's effects on client behavior—without any need to scientifically prove what is causing those effects" (Hawkins & Mathews, 1999, p. 117). Doing so is a very constructive approach to bridging the often commented on and much lamented gap between research and practice in social work.

REFERENCES

Baker, L. R., & Thyer, B. A. (1999). Family social work intervention to increase parental compliance with infant apnea monitor use in the home. *Journal of Family Social Work, 3*(3), 21-27.

Carr, J. E., & Burkholder, E. O. (1998). Creating single-subject design graphs with Microsoft Excel. *Journal of Applied Behavior Analysis, 31,* 245-251.

Conboy, A., Auerbach, C., Beckerman, A., Schnall, D., & LaPorte, H. H. (2000). M.S.W. student satisfaction with using single system designs software to evaluate social work practice. *Research on Social Work Practice, 10,* 126-137.

Corcoran, K., & Fischer, J. (2000). *Measures for clinical practice* (3rd ed.). New York: Free Press.

Council on Social Work Education. (1999). *Curriculum policy statement for master's degree programs in social work education*. Alexandria, VA: Author. Available: www.cswe.org

Gallant, J. P., Thyer, B. A., & Bailey, B. A. (1991). Using bug-in-the-ear feedback in clinical supervision: Preliminary evaluations. *Research on Social Work Practice, 1,* 175-187.

Hawkins, R. P., & Mathews, J. R. (1999). Frequent monitoring of clinical outcomes: Research and accountability for clinical practice. *Education and Treatment of Children, 22,* 117-135.

Maeser, N., & Thyer, B. A. (1990). Teaching boys with severe mental retardation to serve themselves during family-style meals. *Behavioral Residential Treatment, 5,* 239-246.

Mattaini, M. A. (1993). *More than a thousand words: Graphics for clinical practice*. Washington, DC: National Association of Social Workers Press.

Richmond, M. (1935). *Social diagnosis*. New York: Russell Sage. (Originally published in 1917)

Royse, D., Thyer, B. A., Padgett, D., & Logan, T. K. (2000). *Program evaluation: An introduction (3rd ed.)*. Belmont, CA: Wadsworth.

Thyer, B. A. (1998). Promoting research on community practice: Using single-system designs. In R. H. MacNair (Ed.), *Research strategies in community practice* (pp. 47-61). New York: Haworth.

Thyer, B. A., & Geller, E. S. (1987). The "Buckle-Up" dashboard sticker: An effective environmental intervention for safety belt promotion. *Environment and Behavior, 19,* 484-494.

Vonk, M. E., & Thyer, B. A. (1995). Exposure therapy in the treatment of vaginal penetration phobia: A single-case evaluation. *Journal of Behavior Therapy and Experimental Psychiatry, 26,* 359-363.

PART II

Qualitative Approaches

Qualitative inquiry is enjoying something of a renewal of interest within academic and practice social work. This renewal is spurred by the development and expansion of qualitative methods of study within related fields such as education, sociology, and education—developments with obvious and direct implications for research on social work practice. However, it must be clearly stated from the outset that qualitative methods always have enjoyed a prominent role as a major approach to social work research. This makes sense given that qualitative methods always have been part-and-parcel of mainstream science.

Barker (1999) provides a succinct definition of qualitative research as "systematic investigations that include inductive, in-depth, nonquantitative studies of individuals, groups, organizations, or communities. Examples include field study, ethnography, and historiography" (p. 393). A somewhat more elaborate definition is given by McCoy (1995):

Qualitative research is concerned with nonstatistical methods of inquiry and analysis of social phenomena. It draws on an inductive process in which themes and categories emerge through analysis of data collected by such techniques as interviews, observations, videotapes, and case studies. Samples are usually small and are often purposively selected. Qualitative research uses detailed descriptions from the perspective of the research participants themselves as a means of examining specific issues and problems under study. (p. 2009)

A number of recent social work textbooks have been devoted to qualitative research methods (e.g., Padgett, 1998b; Rodwell, 1998; Sherman & Reid, 1994), and most generalist research methods books include substantial content related to qualitative methods. The Society for Social Work and Research (SSWR) contains a strong contingent of members interested in qualitative research methods, and the SSWR conference is emerging as the major venue for the presentation of studies using these approaches. Qualitative methods generally seek to discover, not to test. They are an important part of the hypothetico-deductive process constituting much of conventional scientific inquiry in that they can be very useful in helping researchers to learn more about a given problem area or about the perspectives and experiences of clients. A rough but approximately valid statement would be that qualitative methods help researchers to develop hypotheses, whereas quantitative methods help researchers to test hypotheses. Qualitative methods are ideal for beginning investigations where little already is known. The lengthy case histories of Freud come to mind as early examples of using qualitative methodologies, as do many early social work practice textbooks that contained numerous case studies.

Qualitative research always has been accepted by mainstream science. Sometimes, one reads that conventional research dismisses qualitative methods or that qualitative research is somehow discriminated against within the social work academy. It is difficult to understand where such erroneous views come from given that actual examples or quotations never are given to illustrate these contentions. It is tempting to conclude that those advocating the adoption of qualitative methods believe that it is necessary to criticize quantitative methods so as to strengthen their argument regarding the possible value of the former approaches. This clearly is not true. Qualitative methods possess sufficient virtue to stand on their own without having to be placed on a fallacious deconstruction of conventional scientific practices. Both can happily exist parallel to, and indeed can support, each other.

Psychologist David Rosenhan conducted a marvelously designed and widely cited pseudo-patient study in which graduate students sought admission to psychiatric hospitals by feigning fairly benign symptoms and then recorded their experiences. Rosenhan (1973) published this qualitative work in the journal *Science,* arguably one of the most respected research journals in the world. More recently (in 1999), an M.S.W. was employed by the television news program *60 Minutes* to gain access to a private psychiatric hospital as an employee. The patient abuses and fraud uncovered and videotaped by this social worker were instrumental in the closure of a number of private psychiatric facilities run by this particular behavioral health care firm. As this introduction is being written, scientists have released a report on the discovery of water on the planet Mars. The method of research? Qualitative analysis of photographs. Last week (as of this writing), a new fossil was announced, one that supposedly possessed feathers millions of years prior to the emergence of dinosaurs, throwing on its head the hypothesis that birds developed from dinosaurs. The method of research? Qualitative analysis through visual inspection of the fossil itself. How did physicist Richard Feynman illustrate to Congress the origins of the *Challenger* space shuttle disaster? Did he stand before a chalkboard and draw mathematical equations? No, he dunked a flexible rubber O-ring in ice water and showed the legislators how brittle it became when subjected to cold, a qualitative illustration.

Rudolph Carnap was one of the founders of logical positivism, the approach to scientific inquiry sometimes (and not quite accurately) equated with mainstream conventional research approaches. He addressed the issue of qualitative data in his landmark monograph, *The Unity of Science,* as follows:

> Quantitative determination can also be replaced by qualitative [determination], as is usual in science as well as in everyday life, for reasons of brevity and ease of understanding. Qualitative determinations can, therefore, be included . . . , provided rules are set up for translating all such quantitative determinations so that, e.g., the statement "It is rather cool here" might be translated into the statement "The temperature here is between 5 and 10 degrees Centigrade." (Carnap, 1934/1995, p. 53)

Thus, if we are investigating the subjective experiences of clients through the analysis of videotapes or written transcripts, then clear rules need to be established at some point to aid in the reliable categorization of statements as, for example, positive, negative, or neutral. These rules need to be "teachable" (communicable) to others, must be explicit, and must result in reliable categorizations of statements. In this manner, all types of qualitative data become accessible to scientific study.

Depending on the research issue being addressed, either qualitative or quantitative methods may be most appropriate, and sometimes both can be profitably used together, resulting in a so-called "mixed-methods" study. The late feminist and social work qualitative researcher Liane V. Davis illustrates this process of using the research method best suited to the task at hand:

> On behalf of NASW's [National Association of Social Workers] National Committee on Women's Issues, I had taken on the task of looking anew at the issue of gender disparities in our own profession. I had obtained a large data set and was cranking out statistic after statistic on my office computer. Using this quantitative research method, I was once again demonstrating that female social workers earn less than male social workers. . . . Clearly, this is a task that can only be accomplished with quantitative methodology. (Davis, 1994, p. 73)

But if Davis's (1994) task had been to understand the subjective perspectives of hard-working female social workers who actually experienced salary discrimination, then a qualitative method would have been more appropriate.

Michael Holosko (Chapter 14), a distinguished Canadian scholar, has written the introductory chapter for this part of the handbook including a brief history of qualitative research, some definitions and descriptions, and its underlying philosophy.

Cynthia Franklin and Michelle Balan (Chapter 15) discuss how qualitative researchers attempt to establish the reliability and validity of their findings, a central area of concern shared by quantitative and qualitative scholars alike.

Jerry Brandell and Theodore Varkas (Chapter 16) describe the use of the narrative case study as a qualitative research tool within a study undertaken in the context of Brandell's clinical practice. Such studies can yield rich insights into clients' lives, but as Padgett (1998a) cautions, the goodness of fit between qualitative research methods and clinical work is by no means perfect.

Harriet Goodman (Chapter 17) describes how qualitative researchers make use of in-depth interviews as a research tool, a method that permits a greater analysis of client subjective responses than does direct observation or videotaping. The extensive training in interviewing skills enjoyed by many social workers makes this approach to research fairly familiar territory for most readers.

As a Native American social worker, Christine Lowery (Chapter 18) is well positioned to author a chapter on ethnographic methods. Lowery illustrates the early use of these approaches by Jane Addams and other participants in the Hull House neighborhood center during the early part of the 20th century and with a more contemporary example involving the well-known organization Alcoholics Anonymous.

Although presently a senior medical college administrator, Kevin Grigsby (Chapter 19) draws on his many years of practice experience to discuss the use of participant observation as a qualitative research tool. (Participant observation was the approach used by Rosenhan's [1973] students described earlier.) Grigsby presents the strengths and weaknesses of this approach and also provides a nice discussion of the ethical issues related to social workers unobtrusively recording information from possibly unwitting research participants.

Jane Gilgun's chapter (Chapter 20) on grounded theory closes out this part of the handbook devoted to qualitative research. Grounded theory is one of the more widely known conceptual models underlying some types of qualitative research, and Gilgun skillfully presents the depth of this inductive approach to inquiry.

REFERENCES

Barker, R. L. (Ed.). (1999). *The social work dictionary* (4th ed.). Washington, DC: NASW Press.

Carnap, R. (1995). *The unity of science.* Bristol, UK: Thoemmes Press. (Originally published in 1934)

Davis, L. V. (1994). Is feminist research a fundamentally different approach? In W. W. Hudson & P. S. Nurius (Eds.), *Controversial issues in social work research* (pp. 63-74). Needham Heights, MA: Allyn & Bacon.

McCoy, R. G. (1995). Qualitative research. In R. L. Edwards (Ed.), *Encyclopedia of social work* (19th ed., pp. 2009-2015). Washington, DC: NASW Press.

Padgett, D. K. (1998a). Does the glove really fit? Qualitative research and clinical social work practice. *Social Work, 43,* 373-381.

Padgett, D. K. (1998b). *Qualitative methods in social work research*. Thousand Oaks, CA: Sage.

Rodwell, M. L. (1998). *Social work constructivist research*. New York: Garland.

Rosenhan, D. L. (1973). On being sane in insane places. *Science, 179*, 250-258.

Sherman, E., & Reid, W. J. (Eds.). (1994). *Qualitative research in social work*. New York: Columbia University Press.

CHAPTER FOURTEEN

Overview of Qualitative Research Methods

MICHAEL J. HOLOSKO

Qualitative research has a long history in the social and behavioral sciences. In social work, it has evolved from the previously deemed "other method" of empirical research to the "alternative method." This represents a considerable shift in how social work has come to accept, use, teach, and embrace it as a bona fide research method. This chapter is organized according to (a) a brief history of qualitative research, (b) definitions, (c) beyond the qualitative-quantitative debate, (d) research roles and responsibilities, and (e) steps in conducting qualitative social work research.

A BRIEF HISTORY OF QUALITATIVE RESEARCH

The use of qualitative research in the social sciences can be traced back to Frederick LePlay's 19th-century observational study of European families, kinship, and communities titled *The European Working Class* (Bogdan & Taylor, 1975; Nesbit, 1966). LePlay's study predated Emile Durkheim's *Suicide*, considered by many in the

Western world to be the first scientific research work in the social sciences (Durkheim, 1951).

Although qualitative research had its formal beginnings in sociology during the late 19th and early 20th centuries, it was anthropologists studying so-called primitive societies who successfully embraced the method. After the turn of the 20th century, North American sociologists reclaimed the method and began popularizing it at the hotbed of American sociology, the "Chicago School" (Bogdan & Taylor, 1975). Thomas and Znaniecki (1927), two of the more influential sociologists at the school during the late 1920s, wrote,

> We are safe in saying that personal life-records [personal documents] constitute the perfect type of sociological material and that if social science has to use other materials at all, it is only because of the practical difficulty of obtaining at the moment [a] sufficient number of such records to cover the totality of sociological problems. (p. 1832)

Following the Great Depression and two world wars during the period 1930-1950, as North American society evolved from a primary economy (e.g., farming, fishing) to a more technologically advanced secondary one (e.g., manufacturing), qualitative research lost much of its early appeal to social researchers who now were smitten by quantitative research and its methods. However, during the 1960s and 1970s, a group of sociologists and anthropologists persevered and would not let the method die. These included Herbert Gans, Fred Davis, Howard Becker, Blanche Geer, Alvin Gouldner, Barney Glaser, Anselm Strauss, Robert Park, Jack Douglas, Laud Humphreys, Margaret Mead, Oscar Lewis, Erving Goffman, and others, many of whom were affiliated with the Chicago School. Thus, qualitative research became more readily accepted as the "other research method" of social science.

From the 1980s until the present day, a proliferation of qualitative studies and methodological texts emerged across the allied disciplines of sociology, educational psychology, business, public health, anthropology, nursing, and social work. During the past 20 years, in all of the aforementioned disciplines, qualitative methods evolved from the previously described "other research method" to the presently deemed "alternative research method."

DEFINITIONS OF RESEARCH, SOCIAL RESEARCH, AND QUALITATIVE RESEARCH

The definitions of research, social research, and qualitative research offered here are in a conceptual hierarchy, with the elements of one being incorporated into the elements of the one before. Thus, qualitative research is a part of social research, which is a part of research. *Research* is the systematic investigation of a phenomenon. It is the process of searching, investigating, and/or discovering facts through scientific inquiry. *Social research* is that research germane to the social or behavioral sciences. All social research includes the following four elements to varying degrees: (a) observation, (b) questioning, (c) collecting information, and (d) analysis.

The philosophers of science remind us that, ideally, research produces knowledge through the discovery of new facts, theories, methods, and ideas. In this regard, research is the fuel that drives the engine of knowledge acquisition. Thus, the central concern of researchers is to conduct "good" research that duly incorporates all four of the elements just listed.

Filstead's (1970) text puts forward a simple definition of *qualitative research*: "firsthand involvement with the social world." As analyzed by Goldstein (1991), "firsthand" implies the context of investigation or the immediate on-site setting in which qualitative methods are employed, and "involvement" refers to the actual participation of the researcher in the social world that is being studied. The researcher is not an attached observer; rather, the researcher is *in* and, as such, becomes *an active part of* the event that he or she is investigating (p. 103).

Despite the fact that professional social work has employed qualitative methods in practice since its inception, it was not until the 1980s (when qualitative research was more accepted by other disciplines) that social work fully embraced the method. Thus, North American schools of social work began including its content in their accredited B.S.W. and M.S.W. curricula. In addition, mainstream academic social work journals began publishing more qualitative studies than ever before, numerous methods texts appeared almost overnight, and (since about 1990) Ph.D. programs began to regularly teach and promote it as an acceptable method for fulfilling the thesis requirement.

BEYOND THE QUALITATIVE-QUANTITATIVE DEBATE: SOME SELECTED DIFFERENCES

The allied social science disciplines that teach and use qualitative research have matured significantly beyond the debate as to whether qualitative or quantitative methods are better. This is because the debate often polarizes these methods when, in many instances, they often overlap and complement each other. Comparing selected differences between quantitative and qualitative research in a positive way without disparaging either method at the expense of the other has been shown to be an appropriate way of clarifying research concepts, ideas, and assumptions (Cassel & Symon, 1994).

In social work, the profession has incorporated its principles into one of its research mainstays, single-system design (Bloom, Fischer, & Orme, 1999), shown its applicability to diverse social work theories such as feminism (Davis & Marsh, 1994), demonstrated its applicability to practice knowledge in general (Goldstein, 1991), demonstrated its teaching appeal to social work academics (Roberts, 1989), maximized its data utility and accountability (Beeman, 1995; Harold, Palmiter, Lynch, & Freedman-Doan, 1995), touted its statistical application and relevance (Rosenthal, 1996), informed professionals about how to get their qualitative studies published (Gilgun, 1993), and written practitioner-oriented methods texts on how to conduct qualitative research (Tutty, Rothery, & Grinnell, 1996).

Table 14.1 presents some of the selected differences from primarily a social work research perspective. It is important to note that there are areas of overlap between quantitative and qualitative research in each of the selected criteria listed in the table. For example, both may produce descriptive data (Criterion 1), and both may incorporate aspects of phenomenology and positivism (Criterion 2). So, for each criterion listed, these differences are true in most circumstances but not absolutely.

Purpose. Qualitative social work research has as its expressed purpose to produce descriptive data in an individual's own written or spoken words and/or observable behavior. Whether the topic of study is the client, individual, family, event, behavior, agency, organization, and/or culture, all qualitative research yields descriptive data foremost. Quantitative social work research, however, also may produce descriptive data, but these normally are in quantitative-descriptive (numeric or statistical) form. Its purpose also can be to explore a phenomenon; test ideas, assumptions, or variables; or assess/evaluate something (e.g., a practice intervention, a human service program or policy).

Philosophical perspective. Also referred to as epistemology, qualitative research (social work or otherwise) is primarily phenomenological. Quantitative research is primarily positivistic. The former is defined as being concerned with understanding the human experience from the individual's own frame of reference (Bogdan & Taylor, 1975, p. 2). The latter, commonly referred to in social work as logical positivism or logical empiricism (Thyer, 1993), seeks the facts or causes of social phenomena based on experimentally derived evidence and/or valid observations (p. 16).

Logical orientation. Qualitative social work research primarily works from an inductive point of view or a general perspective that does not require rigorously defined questions and hypotheses. As such, a study evolves from the "facts up" and logically proceeds from a general point of view to a specific conclusion, set of questions, hypotheses, or grounded theory (Tutty et al., 1996). Quantitative social work research, for the most part, works from the problem question, or "theory down," to a generalizable conclusion. In this hypothetico-deductive process, testable assump-

TABLE 14.1   Selected Differences Between Qualitative and Quantitative
Social Work Research

Selected Criteria	Qualitative	Quantitative
Main purpose	To describe individuals and events in natural settings	To explore, describe, test, or assess phenomena
Philosophical perspective	Phenomenology	Positivism
Logical orientation	Inductive (G → S)	Hypothetico-deductive (S → G)
Dynamism	Process oriented: experiential and systemic	Deterministic: linear and prescribed
Theory use and generation	Integrated throughout; requisite grounded theory	To justify hypothesis questions and to validate
Researcher's role	Active (immersion)	Passive (immersion optional)
Problem specification	May emerge at the end	Early on
Method	Create as one evolves	Predetermined
Generalizability	Low	High

tions or hypotheses are determined and then operationalized, data are collected, and the assumptions or hypotheses are assessed for their validity (Thyer, 1993, p. 9).

Dynamism. Qualitative social work research, by its very nature, is process oriented, whereby the researcher enters the natural setting and touches, feels, lives, and observes the subject of study (e.g., the individual behavior, family, group, agency, or community). This experiential perspective is a requisite for collecting rich, contextual, and complete descriptive data. Thus, one observation shapes the perception of the other and vice versa. Quantitative social work research typically follows a more deterministic lock-step process: from problem statement, to literature review, to testable assumptions/hypotheses, to data collection, to analysis. Although some quantitative social work research methods allow for the researcher to be more experientially and actively involved in his or her study (e.g., single-system designs), the researcher's role still is detached and is oriented toward following the linear steps described previously.

Theory use and generation. Qualitative social work researchers may or may not use theory to assist them in the subjects of their investigations, and some argue that rigorously defined questions or hypotheses emanating from theory delimit such research. Concepts, ideas, and questions that guide their work often emerge during the course of their study in response to what they are observing, not to preordained theories or beliefs (Tutty et al., 1996, p. 12). Furthermore, it is an implicit requirement of qualitative research that the conclusions of their studies result in simple explanatory or middle-range theory, referred to as *grounded theory* (Schatzman & Strauss, 1973). Theory in quantitative social work research first is used to derive the testable assumptions/hypotheses of the study. It then is used during the data analysis or end stage of the study, whereby the data collected are used to verify or negate the theory from which the testable assumptions/hypotheses were formulated. The push to grounded theory to explain findings is not a requisite of this method, and as a result, many social work researchers do not generate any theory per se from their studies.

Researcher's role. All qualitative research requires the researcher to be actively immersed in the natural environment that he or she is observing. The subjective lens that the researcher brings to the subject of study is an important and integral part of such research. Quantitative research does not require this, and for the most part, the researcher has a passive and detached role. However, some social work research (e.g., practice or program evaluation) requires the researcher to be more involved in the setting in which his or her investigation takes place. But even in such cases, the researcher generally assumes a value neutral and objective role during the course of the study.

Problem specification. Qualitative research avoids specifying the problem of study early on. Indeed, the actual phenomenon being studied might not be apparent until the very end of the investigation. Conversely, quantitative research requires clear problem specification and operationalization of study variables from the onset (Thyer, 1993).

Method. This term generally encompasses the study design, sample selection, study procedure, and data collection. Qualitative social work research allows the method to unfold during the course of the investigation. The researcher then flexibly crafts the method to suit the evolving study requirements (Fischer, 1993; Holosko & Leslie, 1998). So, questions such as how many observations should be made, how many interviews should take place, and what questions the researcher should ask respondents usually are not addressed until the researcher gets to that step in the investigation. Quantitative social work research, however, usually predetermines the method by planning it carefully, ideally pretesting aspects of it (e.g., its feasibility, length of time for data collection, and instrumentation), and describing it in detail.

Generalizability. Generalizability is attributed to two components of the research process: the method and the findings. In qualitative social work research, because methods often use biased or purposive samples, abnormal events, and/or anomalies, findings are targeted not to precise conclusions but rather to more general conclusions. As such, their generalizability is deemed low. Quantitative research, however, strives for more precise measurement and findings. For example, psychometrically standardized instruments are encouraged, random samples that can generalize to populations often are selected, and parametric statistics often are used to promote generalizability. Findings normally are answers to the questions posed at the beginning of the study and are stated in precise and qualified ways to enhance their overall generalizability.

Overall, Table 14.1 outlines a number of selected differences between qualitative social research and quantitative social research. Social work has been highly successful in using both types of research and lately has encouraged the use of both methods concurrently. As indicated previously, some social work research (e.g., case analyses, policy analyses, practice and program evaluations) often incorporate both qualitative and quantitative elements in their designs, and as a result, many of the previously described differences of these approaches overlap, even in areas otherwise deemed to be vastly different. As such, some social work research has assisted in integrating aspects of the principles and procedures of these two approaches, and future projections about social work practice and research suggest that this trend will continue.

RESEARCH ROLES AND RESPONSIBILITIES

In an effort to more fully describe the roles and responsibilities for conducting qualitative social work research, Neuman (1994) describes 10 roles that the researcher must employ:

1. Observe ordinary events and everyday activities as they happen in natural settings in addition to any unusual occurrences.
2. Become directly involved with the people being studied and personally experience the process of daily social life in the natural setting.
3. Acquire an insider's point of view while maintaining an analytic perspective or distance of an outsider.
4. Flexibly use a variety of techniques or social skills as the situation demands.
5. Produce extensive data in the form of written notes, diagrams, maps, sketches, and/or pictures to provide detailed descriptions.
6. Study events holistically (e.g. systemically as things relate to each other) and individually within their social context.
7. Understand and develop empathy for individuals in the field setting, and do not just record "cold" objective facts.

8. Notice both explicit (e.g., recognized, conscious, spoken) and tacit (e.g., less recognized, implicit, unspoken) aspects of the setting and culture.

9. Observe ongoing process without upsetting, disrupting, or imposing an outsider's point of view.

10. Be capable of coping with high levels of personal stress, time demands, uncertainty, ethical dilemmas, and ambiguity.

Taken as a whole, the preceding roles and their responsibilities not only are carried out in qualitative social work research studies but also are required for good social work practice (Tutty et al., 1996, p. 5).

STEPS IN CONDUCTING QUALITATIVE SOCIAL WORK RESEARCH

Only recently have so-called methods textbooks about how to conduct qualitative social work research been published. Two fine examples are Sherman and Reid (1994) and Tutty and colleagues (1996). Prior to this, many of us who taught qualitative research to social work students used well-worn "how to" books written by sociologists (e.g., Schatzman & Strauss, 1973; Wiseman & Aron, 1970). An examination of the differences between the current social work texts and others in the allied fields reveals that (a) the basic steps of the method are the same, (b) the subjects of the investigations are slightly different in that social workers produce client-centered research (Holosko & Leslie, 1998), and (c) the previously described "goodness of fit" between what social workers do (their day-to-day practice) and qualitative methods makes for a nice blend between the method and social work practice.

Finally, the main steps in conducting qualitative research are summarized by Denzin (1989) with some elaboration:

1. Learn to prepare oneself, read the literature, and focus.
2. Select a field site and gain access to it. Get formal permission in writing.
3. Prepare for more time to do the study than one thinks is needed.
4. Adopt a social role, learn the ropes, and get along with members in the setting.
5. Watch, listen, and collect quality data.
6. Take careful notes of all observations.
7. Focus on specific aspects of the setting and use theoretical sampling.
8. Begin to analyze data, generate working hypotheses, and evaluate the hypotheses.
9. Conduct field interviews with selected individuals.
10. Physically learn the field setting.
11. Complete the analyses.
12. Develop grounded theory to explain one's findings.
13. Write the final research report and disseminate one's findings.

Tutty et al. (1996) use these steps as a template for their text, *Qualitative Research for Social Workers,* and collapse them into four simple phases: (a) planning the study, (b) collecting the data, (c) analyzing the data, and (d) writing the report. These then are presented in "user-friendly" ways in their text.

In conclusion, qualitative social work research is a viable method for producing practice knowledge for the profession. Foremost, it involves the researcher starting from "where the study is at" and then using the steps described here to conduct the investigation. By continuing to strive for conducting "good" research through this method, the profession not only will enhance its credibility within its own professional parameters (e.g., by producing relevant knowledge to enhance its practitioners) but also will reaffirm its claim to the "scientific-practitioner" model that has been touted as the profession's research paradigm for the past 20 years.

REFERENCES

Beeman, S. (1995). Maximizing credibility and accountability in qualitative data collection and analysis: A social work research case example. *Journal of Sociology and Social Welfare, 22*(4), 99-114.

Bloom, M., Fischer, J., & Orme, J. (1999). *Evaluating practice: Guidelines for the accountable professional* (3rd ed.). Needham Heights, MA: Allyn & Bacon.

Bogdan, R., & Taylor, S. (1975). *Introduction to qualitative research methods.* New York: John Wiley.

Cassel, C., & Symon, G. (Eds.). (1994). *Qualitative methods in organizational research: A practical guide.* London: Sage.

Davis, L., & Marsh, J. (1994). Is feminist research inherently qualitative, and is it a fundamentally different approach to research? In W. Hudson & P. Nurius (Eds.), *Controversial issues in social work research* (pp. 63-74). Needham Heights, MA: Allyn & Bacon.

Denzin, N. K. (1989). *The research act: A theoretical introduction to sociological methods* (3rd ed.). Englewood Cliffs, NJ: Prentice Hall.

Durkheim, E. (1951). *Suicide: A study in sociology* (G. Simpson, Ed. and Trans.). New York: Free Press.

Filstead, W. J. (1970). *Qualitative methodology: Firsthand involvement with the social world.* Chicago: Markham.

Fischer, J. (1993). Empirically-based practice: The end of an ideology? *Journal of Social Service Research, 18*(1), 19-64.

Gilgun, J. (1993). Publishing research reports based on qualitative methods. *Marriage and Family Review, 18,* 177-181.

Goldstein, H. (1991). Qualitative research and social work practice: Partners in discovery. *Journal of Sociology and Social Welfare, 18*(4), 101-109.

Harold, R., Palmiter, M., Lynch, S., & Freedman-Doan, C. (1995). Life stories: A practice-based research technique. *Journal of Sociology and Social Welfare, 22*(2), 23-43.

Holosko, M., & Leslie, D. (1998). Obstacles to conducting empirically based practice. In J. Wodarski & B. Thyer (Eds.), *Handbook of empirical social work practice* (Social Problems and Practice Issues, Vol. 2, pp. 433-453). New York: John Wiley.

Nesbit, R. (1966). *The sociological tradition.* New York: Basic Books.

Neuman, W. L. (1994). *Social research methods: Qualitative and quantitative approaches* (2nd ed.). Newbury Park, CA: Sage.

Roberts, C. (1989). Research methods taught and utilized in social work. *Journal of Social Service Research, 13*(1), 65-86.

Rosenthal, J. (1996). Qualitative descriptors of strength of association and effect size. *Journal of Social Service Research, 21*(4), 37-59.

Schatzman, L., & Strauss, A. (1973). *Field research: Strategies for a natural sociology.* Englewood Cliffs, NJ: Prentice Hall.

Sherman, E., & Reid, W. (Eds.). (1994). *Qualitative research in social work.* New York: Columbia University Press.

Thomas, W. I., & Znaniecki, F. (1927). *The Polish peasant in Europe and America.* New York: Knopf.

Thyer, B. (1993). Social work theory and practice research: The approach of logical positivism. *Social Work and Social Sciences Review, 4,* 5-26.

Tutty, L., Rothery, M., & Grinnell, R. (1996). *Qualitative research for social workers.* Needham Heights, MA: Allyn & Bacon.

Wiseman, J., & Aron, M. (1970). *Field projects for sociology students.* Cambridge, MA: Schenkman.

CHAPTER FIFTEEN

Reliability and Validity in Qualitative Research

CYNTHIA FRANKLIN

MICHELLE BALLAN

It is important for qualitative studies to emulate the scientific method in striving for empirical groundedness, generalizability, and minimization of bias (Hammersly, 1992). Reliability and validity depend on the skills of the researcher. Questions concerning reliability and validity are associated with how reliable and valid the researcher's data collection and analysis are. Using research methods that ensure that the data recording is accurate and the interpretations of data are empirical and logical is important to increasing reliability and validity in qualitative studies.

This chapter defines reliability and validity in the context of qualitative research. Methods are suggested for helping researchers to increase the reliability and validity of qualitative studies. A case example is presented illustrating how one social work researcher combined methods to increase reliability and validity in a qualitative research study.

RELIABILITY

In science, reliability is concerned with the replicability and consistency of findings (Kirk & Miller, 1986; Rafuls & Moon, 1996). LeCompte and Goetz (1982) define reliability in qualitative research as the extent to which the set of meanings derived from several interpreters are sufficiently congruent. Reliability refers to the degree to which other researchers performing similar observations in the field, and analysis such as reading field notes transcribed from narrative data, would generate similar interpretations and results. From this viewpoint, reliability is the extent to which a data collection procedure and analysis yield the same answer for multiple participants in the research process (Kirk & Miller, 1986).

Intersubjective agreement, consensus between two or more observers, is necessary for establishing reliability in any scientific study. Confirmation checks by more than one observer also are important for establishing reliability in qualitative studies. The cross-checking process is the reliability check of choice for most researchers (Brink, 1989, as cited in Newfield, Sells, Smith, Newfield, & Newfield, 1996). Although some qualitative researchers do calculate interrater reliability, most do not. Instead, qualitative researchers use different observers to check interpretations and to help them question differing observations, with a goal of achieving a higher continuity and dependability of observations across different settings and time periods.

For this reason, in qualitative research, reliability also is called dependability. Dependability involves researchers' attempts to account for changing conditions in their observations as well as changes in the design that may occur once they are collecting data in the field (Marshall & Rossman, 1995). Recall from Holosko's chapter in this handbook (Chapter 13) that qualitative research designs often evolve once researchers begin collecting data. It is important for researchers to carefully document how their design decisions are made and how their methods and interpretations evolved. This type of documentation is called an audit trail and provides a basis for checking the researchers' methods and interpretations to see whether they are dependable from the perspective of other collaborators or independent researchers. The audit trail is discussed in more detail later.

Synchronic reliability refers to the similarity of observations within the same time period. Synchronic reliability is most useful to qualitative researchers when it fails to yield similar results because a disconfirmation of synchronic reliability forces researchers to imagine how multiple, but somehow different, observations might simultaneously be true (Kirk & Miller, 1986). Therefore, it promotes both critical and creative thinking aimed at reaching resolutions to the differences in observations. Such resolutions require researchers to find empirical answers that include or exclude the differing interpretations based on various evidence that is compiled.

Internal and External Reliability

Reliability is dependent on the resolution of both internal and external research design issues (Hansen, 1979, as cited in LeCompte & Goetz, 1982). Internal reliability refers to the degree to which other researchers given a set of previously generated constructs would match them with data in the same way as did the original researcher

(LeCompte & Goetz, 1982). External reliability addresses the issue of whether independent researchers would discover the same truth or generate the same constructs in the same or similar setting.

Threats to internal and external reliability can be circumvented by providing the reader with explicit details regarding researchers' theoretical perspective and the research design being used. Explication of data collection may include selection criteria of participants, interview guide questions, description of researchers' roles, and the methods of analysis (e.g., explaining coding procedures, development of categories and hypotheses) (Rafuls & Moon, 1996).

Criteria for Assessing Reliability

To assess reliability in qualitative research, Miles and Huberman (1994) suggest that the following should be applied:

1) Are the research questions clear, and are the features of the study design congruent with them? 2) Is the researcher's role and status within the site explicitly described? 3) Do findings show meaningful parallelism across data sources? 4) Are basic paradigms and analytic constructs clearly specified? 5) Were data collected across the full range of appropriate settings, times, respondents, and so on suggested by research questions? 6) If multiple field-workers are involved, do they have comparable data collection protocols? 7) Were coding checks made, and did they show adequate agreement? 8) Were data quality checks made? 9) Do multiple observers' accounts converge in instances, settings, or times, when they might be expected to? 10) Were any forms of peer or colleague review in place? (p. 278)

Methods for Increasing Reliability

Examining Informant Responses Across Alternate Form Questions

Equivalence of responses to various forms of the same question provides a useful reliability check. Using a questioning process that requires informants to provide in-depth explorations of their perspectives guards against a socially desirable response set because informants must expand on their responses to questions in ways that help researchers to examine the internal consistency. When informants are interviewed only once, identical and alternate form questions within that interview may be used to test informants' reliability (Brink, 1989, as cited in Newfield et al., 1996).

Establishing Recording Procedures for Field Notes

When completing field notes, greater reliability can be established if researchers keep four separate types of field notes: (a) a condensed (verbatim) account that serves as an immediate recording of what happened; (b) an expanded account that serves as a log of events and should be recorded as soon as possible after each field session; (c) a "field work journal" that contains more reflective experiences such as ideas, emotions, mistakes, and concerns that may be noted as memos to oneself about the field work process; and (d) a running record of the analysis and interpretations that researchers perform while in the field work process (Kirk & Miller, 1986, p. 55).

Procedures must be documented with meticulous detail and behavioral descriptions so that all the internal workings of research projects are made apparent to those examining the findings. Researchers should take thorough notes and keep logs and journals that record each design decision and the rationale behind it to allow others to inspect their procedures, protocols, and decisions. Researchers can improve reliability by keeping all collected data in a well-organized and retrievable format that makes it easy for other researchers to retrieve and reanalyze (Marshall & Rossman, 1995). The maintenance of a research database is highly recommended. A database can be established using qualitative software, database systems, or even old-fashioned notebooks and files. We discuss qualitative software later.

Some data collection circumstances yield more dependable information than do others, so researchers may choose to rank their interviews and observation time points according to how closely their codebooks and procedures were followed in different situations. Data collected later in the study might be more relevant than data collected early in the study because the procedures will have been worked out to be more uniform across informants. Also, data provided voluntarily might be more consistent across accounts than data collected from individuals whose participation was mandatory. Lying and falsifying information is an ongoing issue that must be evaluated during researchers' interactions with participants in field work.

Cross-Checking

Qualitative researchers use multiple team members and research participants to confirm their observations in the field, interpretations, and transcriptions. Cross-checking coding and findings usually is built into qualitative studies to improve reliability because humans are subject to numerous judgment errors (Franklin & Jordan, 1997). Some research teams use second coding of the data. Second coding data means that two researchers working independently of one another code the data. This method allows researchers to develop an interobserver reliability coefficient for the data in the same manner as in a quantitative study. Miles and Huberman (1994) suggest that 70% is an acceptable level of agreement for qualitative data. In addition, it is possible for researchers to calculate an agreement rate between the sources of data and to use multiple researchers in the field so that their observations can be confirmed. Some researchers even have all the data coded by one or more independent coders who are not involved with the research process. These coders serve like copy editors who can check the logic and assignment of meanings to the text (Hill, Thompson, & Williams, 1997). Other researchers use members of their teams to confirm part of their coding or to check their observations in the field.

Most qualitative researchers do not calculate reliability statistics for second coding but do use this procedure to improve the consistency of their data analyses. For example, these researchers would note every discrepancy between coders and use team meetings to discuss these discrepancies and to make decisions about which way the data should be coded. Through this process, researchers hope to improve the consistency of the coding, and if this is the case, then there likely will be fewer discrepancies over time. Researchers also vary on how much of the data should be second coded. Some settle for portions of the data, whereas others insist on most or all of the data being second coded.

Staying Close to the Empirical Data

Qualitative researchers often speak of staying close to their data. What is meant by this statement varies across researchers, but in general, researchers mean staying close to the descriptive verbatim accounts and subjective meanings of the research participants. Researchers do not move to a higher level of inference without first thoroughly testing those assumptions against the descriptive data and the interpretations of the participants. In qualitative research, problems with internal reliability are resolved by providing the verbatim accounts of participants. For example, descriptions phrased precisely and with good definitions of constructs under study help to improve interrater reliability and yield consistent coding (Rafuls & Moon, 1996).

To stay close to the empirical data, qualitative researchers usually support their inferential statements about the data with exact quotes from research participants. They also establish a chain of evidence that is linked with different data sources and might even be represented pictorially as one would do in a path analysis diagram. Another method used to establish internal reliability of narrative data is to calculate the number of statements made across cases that support the inferential conclusion. This simple descriptive statistical account keeps researchers from making too much out of one compelling statement. Grigsby, Thyer, Waller, and Johnston (1999), for example, used this method when verifying the statements from medical patients who were found to have a culturally bound syndrome of chalk eating.

Using Homogeneous Samples

As one makes samples more homogeneous, the reduced variability generally tends to increase reliability (Zyzanski, McWhinney, Blake, Crabtree, & Miller, 1992). Hill et al. (1997) recommend randomly selecting the small samples used in qualitative research based on homogeneous characteristics as a first method for sample selection. In general, qualitative researchers do not use random selection because they use purposive samples as exemplars that illustrate their points. Hill and colleagues, however, believe that by using some random selection within homogeneous samples, researchers can increase consistency and transferability of their findings. For example, Hill, Gelso, Mohr, Rochlen, and Zack (1997, cited in Hill et al., 1997), in a study investigating the resolution of transference in psychotherapy, randomly selected their sample from a professional directory of therapists who self-identified themselves as being psychoanalytic and proceeded to further screen and include only those therapists who met all the criteria they had set for the study.

Hill et al. (1997) also believe that it is important to sample enough cases to allow across-case comparisons and a thorough testing of one's findings. They recommend 8 to 15 cases for establishing consistency in findings and providing examples to initially hypothesize about the limits of those findings.

Developing an Audit Trail

According to Tutty, Rothery, and Grinnell (1996), a process audit conducted by a researcher's peers may provide additional evidence of an effort to maintain consistency throughout one's study. The researcher should develop an audit trail in the form of documentation and a running account of the process throughout the study. After the study is completed, the researcher can arrange for an external auditor or researcher to examine the audit trail and to verify whether procedures were followed and interpretations were reasonable (Guba, 1981).

Applying a Consistent Analytic Method

An analytical approach is a set of methods that researchers use to interpret and make sense of the data. Analytical approaches to qualitative data analysis consist of a theoretical framework and a set of methods for gathering and interpreting data. The grounded theory method of data analysis provides an approach that is helpful for understanding the essence of structured qualitative data analysis (Glaser & Strauss, 1967; Strauss & Corbin, 1999). Grounded theory is an approach to qualitative research that emphasizes discovering theories, concepts, propositions, and new hypotheses from the data sources collected in the field instead of relying on already existing theories. Chapter 19 in this handbook explains more about this research.

Using Computer Software

Qualitative researchers use multiple methods for data management, ranging from color coding schemes, folders, and word processing programs to computer data analysis programs developed especially for managing this type of narrative data. The computer approaches are highlighted here because they have potential for helping researchers to develop a consistent method for handling their data. Computer programs such as ETHNOGRAPH, HYPERQUAL, ATLASti, NUDIST, and NVIVO make the coding and data analysis process easier to manage. Computer programs can (a) serve as a database for researchers' mountains of narrative data, (b) allow researchers to code the data in a computer program, (c) sort the narrative data by codes and categories for researchers' viewing, (d) give researchers frequency counts of codes, (e) test hypotheses using different systems of logic, (f) provide technical aids to help in theorizing and concept building, and (g) provide graphic representations of data that build schematics demonstrating how researchers' variables or ideas are connected (these schematics look like path models or structural equation diagrams). Programs are available for both IBM-compatible and Macintosh computer systems (Fielding & Lee, 1991; Miles & Huberman, 1994; Miles & Weitzman, 1999; Richards & Richards, 1992; Tesch, 1990).

All data management and analysis software programs have strengths and weaknesses. For a recent comprehensive review of the specific features of qualitative data analysis software, see Miles and Weitzman (1999).

VALIDITY

In science, "validity is concerned with the accuracy of findings" (Rafuls & Moon, 1996, p. 77). Reliability is a precondition for validity (Guba, 1981). For example, in quantitative studies, it is easy to show that the validity of a measurement cannot exceed the square root of its reliability (Gulliksen, 1950). In other words, if observations are not consistent and dependable, then they are not likely to be accurate. Validity in qualitative research addresses whether researchers see what they think they see (Kirk & Miller, 1986). Validity in qualitative research also is referred to as credibility (Guba, 1981). Credibility involves the "truthfulness" of study findings, and it is researchers' responsibility to provide chains of evidence and sets of narrative accounts that are plausible and credible (Hammersly, 1992).

Qualitative researchers are most concerned with testing the credibility of their findings and interpretations with the various sources (audiences or groups) from which data were collected (Guba, 1981). According to Padgett (1998), most threats to validity fall under one of three broad headings: reactivity, researcher biases, or respondent biases. Reactivity refers to the potentially distorting effects of qualitative researchers' presence in the field. Researchers' biases may distort the findings. For example, according to Schacter (1999), numerous studies demonstrate that bias is one of the major attributes of human cognition and memory.

Memory, encoding, and retrieval of memories are highly contingent on preexisting beliefs and knowledge. For this reason, it is easy for researchers to ignore information that does not support their conclusions. Humans also experience consistency bias, which is a tendency for people to recall and report past events in the same way as they feel in the present instead of the manner in which they experienced them in the past. This type of bias makes it especially important to use various sources of information instead of relying exclusively on the subjective accounts of participants.

There is an equal threat due to respondents' biases. Respondents may withhold information or present facts differently from how other observers may perceive them. In addition, respondents may forget, experience recall or temporary amnesia, or consider it necessary to present themselves in a positive manner to enhance their self-portraits. Researchers always should assess the rewards for giving differing answers as well as the threat of socially desirable responses. Lying or malingering also might come into play in some qualitative studies, and researchers may guard against fraudulent data by including diverse data sources and increasing their sample sizes.

There are a number of threats to the credibility and trustworthiness of qualitative research. Similar to the issues covered in reliability, qualitative researchers have to be concerned with both internal and external validity in their research designs.

Internal and External Validity

"Internal validity refers to the extent to which researchers' observations and measurements are accurate representations of some reality. Are researchers actually observing or measuring what they think they are observing or measuring?" (LeCompte & Goetz, 1982, p. 43). To achieve internal validity using narrative data, researchers must demonstrate that data collection was conducted in such a manner as to ensure that the subjects under study were identified and described accurately. In other words, the observations and interpretations must be "credible" to the participants as well as to those who are involved in reading and checking the study results (Marshall & Rossman, 1995).

External validity, or transferability, is dependent on the degrees of similarity (match) between one sample and its setting events (Guba, 1981). Most qualitative researchers follow in the scientific tradition of Cronbach (1975), who explains that multiple contingencies and historical constraints limit generalizations. Cronbach argues that all generalizations "decay" like radioactive substances with their half-lives so that, after a time, every generalization is "more history than science."

Qualitative researchers rely on analytic generalization (which focuses on the generalizability of findings from one case to the next) rather than on probabilistic generalization used in quantitative studies (which focuses on generalizing findings from a sample to a population). Researchers are responsible for the provision of sufficiently descriptive data that will enable the reader to assess the validity of these analyses and the transferability to his or her own situation (Firestone, 1993). Therefore, qualitative researchers do not attempt to form generalizations that will hold at all times and in all places; rather, they try to form working hypotheses that may be transferred from one context to another depending on the degree of match between the contexts (Guba, 1981).

Criteria for Assessing Validity

Eisner (1979, as cited in Phillips, 1987, p. 18) provides three criteria for assessing the validity of qualitative research: structural corroboration, referential adequacy, and multiplicative replication. Structural corroboration is the process by which various parts of the account, description, or explanation give each other mutual support. It is a process of "gathering data or information and using it to establish links that eventually create a whole that is supported by the bits of evidence that constitute it" (p. 18). According to Eisner (1979, as cited in Phillips, 1987), a work has referential adequacy when it enables us to see features that it refers to but that we might not ourselves have noticed.

Relevant questions that help researchers to assess internal validity in qualitative studies include the following (Miles & Huberman, 1994, p. 279). How context rich and meaningful ("thick") are the descriptions (Denzin, 1989; Geertz, 1973)? Does the account "ring true," seem convincing, make sense, or enable a "vicarious presence" for the reader? Did triangulation among complementary methods and data sources produce generally converging conclusions? Are the presented data well linked to the categories of prior or emerging theory? Are the findings internally coherent (Eisner, 1991)? Are areas of uncertainty identified? Was negative evidence sought? Have rival explanations been actively considered? Have findings been replicated in different parts of the database? Were the conclusions considered to be accurate by original informants? Were any predictions made in the study, and how accurate were they?

Relevant questions pertaining to external validity include the following (Miles & Huberman, 1994, p. 279). Are the characteristics of the original sample of persons, settings, processes, and the like fully described to permit adequate comparisons with other samples? Does the report examine possible threats to generalizability? Is the sampling theoretically diverse enough to encourage broader applicability? Does the researcher define the scope and the boundaries of reasonable generalization from the study (McGrath & Brinberg, 1983)? Do the findings include enough thick description for the reader to assess the potential transferability, or appropriateness, for his or her own setting? Do a range of readers report the findings to be consistent with their experiences? Are the findings congruent with, connected to, or confirmatory of prior theory? Are the processes and outcomes described in conclusions generic enough to be applicable in other settings, even those of a different nature? Have narrative sequences been preserved unobscured? Does the report suggest settings in which the findings could be fruitfully tested further? Have the findings been replicated in other studies to assess their robustness?

Methods for Increasing Validity

Using Prolonged Engagement

To increase the likelihood of attaining credibility, qualitative researchers should use prolonged engagement at a site or a field setting so that distortions produced by their presence can be overcome. Prolonged engagement also provides researchers with the opportunity to test their own biases and perceptions as well as those of their respondents (Guba, 1981). Extended time is used to reflect on journals and field notes and to test how their perceptions changed over the extended time frame. Researchers need to be able to show that sufficient time was spent in the field setting to justify their characterization of it, whereas their journals will reflect their questioning of their interpretations and findings (Guba, 1981).

Purposive Sampling

Qualitative researchers should demonstrate how the samples they selected are governed by emergent insights about what is important and relevant to the research questions and emerging findings. Being able to demonstrate emergent findings and important insights sometimes is called catalytic validity (Reason & Rowan, 1981). Interest in a specific question and the need for across-case analysis to test findings is the basis for most purposive sampling techniques. This means that researchers must intentionally select a few cases and proceed to select additional cases so that they can test the findings of the cases they have analyzed. Researchers also may first select similar cases and then proceed to collect divergent cases to further test the limits of their findings. For example, if transferability depends on a match of characteristics, then it is incumbent on researchers to provide the information necessary to test the degree of match between cases.

Purposive sampling also can mean that successive interview respondents were selected by asking each respondent to suggest someone whose point of view is as different as possible from his or her own so as to test findings (Guba, 1981). Purposive sampling guides researchers to think in terms of replicating their findings. If a researcher can reproduce his or her findings in a new context or in another case, then the hypothesis gains more credibility. If someone else can reproduce the findings, then the hypothesis becomes even more persuasive. Researchers should be replicating findings as they collect data from new participants, settings, and events. "Doing replication at the very end of the fieldwork, during final analysis and write-ups, is very difficult and less credible" (Miles & Huberman, 1994, p. 274).

Using Triangulation

Triangulation can be used for the purpose of achieving confirmation of constructs using multiple measurement methods (Campbell, 1956) or as a method to gain comprehensive information about a phenomenon (Fielding & Fielding, 1986; Jick, 1983). Qualitative researchers seek trustworthiness in data collection by using multiple methods and divergent data sources. Through cross-checking observations among divergent data sources, apparent differences eventually may resolve themselves, and a favored interpretation may be constructed that coheres with all of the divergent data sources and that itself accounts for the differences observed earlier (Brody, 1992).

Denzin (1994, as cited in Padgett, 1998) identifies four types of triangulation relevant to a qualitative study:

1. Theory triangulation: the use of multiple theories or perspectives to interpret a single set of data. The goal is not to corroborate study findings, but to analyze them in different ways and through different theoretical lenses. 2. Methodological triangulation: the use of multiple methods to study a single topic, for example, combining quantitative and qualitative methods in a single study. Methodological triangulation can also be accomplished by using the methods of different disciplines. 3. Observer triangulation: the use of more than one observer in a single study to achieve intersubjective agreement. Qualitative researchers may use multiple observers in the field during data collection (see Snow and Anderson's 1991 study of the urban homeless) or may use multiple coders (analytic triangulation) to ensure that the categories and themes that emerge are confirmed by intercoder consensus. 4. Data triangulation: the use of more than one data source (interviews, archival materials, obser-

vational data, etc.). This refers to the use of different types of data as a means of corroboration. When data from fieldnotes, interviews, and archival materials are convergent and support each other, we can be more confident of our observations and study conclusions.
Triangulation helps to counter all threats to trustworthiness (reactivity, researcher bias, and
respondent bias). When there is disagreement among data sources, researchers are faced
with a decision about which version to rely on or might view the discrepancies as an opportunity to explore new insights. (pp. 97-98)

Using Measurement Instruments to Corroborate Findings

In verifying constructs in a qualitative study, some researchers recommend using
standardized measurement instruments to test the observations of the researcher
or as a method of triangulation (Hill et al., 1997). This method is similar to the way
in which a clinician might use a psychosocial measure to assess a client on characteristics that the clinician has observed, thus allowing for a corroboration of one's
perceptions.

Using Structured Codebooks

Qualitative data analysis requires the categorization of narrative data into themes.
Qualitative researchers use codebooks not only to sort and organize the data but also
as a means of developing useful schemata for understanding the data. Codebooks allow data to be sorted into meaningful codes (descriptive narrative labels) and linked
in categories (conceptual narrative labels) so that researchers can begin to make sense
of the data. Using a codebook serves a function similar to the statistical techniques
(e.g., cluster analysis, factor analysis) used in quantitative research.

A codebook can be constructed prior to data collection (a priori codebook) or in
the process of data analysis and interpretation (priori codebook). If researchers begin
with a codebook, then they are more likely to achieve greater construct validity. But if
they wait and develop the codebook in the field, then they may gain more representativeness. Some researchers use both approaches, starting with a codebook but also
modifying it while in the field. This might be the best approach for achieving internal
and external validity.

The validity of the coding process is important to qualitative research designs, and
some cognitive researchers have tried to determine the best and worst cognitive strategies used by studying coding using experimental research methods (Chwalisz,
Wiersma, & Stark-Wroblewski, 1996). Findings suggest that in the best cognitive
strategies, data are grouped together into coherent and consistent categories of
meaning and then are further linked into higher order inferences that explain different clusters. Findings also suggest that familiarity with the data is important and that

there is no advantage to using simple descriptive units, pointing to the necessity of being able to see the larger connecting themes.

Peer Debriefing

Peer debriefing serves a function similar to that of peer supervision in clinical practice. It provides researchers with the opportunity to test their growing insights and to expose themselves to critical questions and feedback (Guba, 1981). Researchers select one or more peers to serve as guides and discuss interpretations and concerns with those colleagues. Researchers should regularly detach themselves from the field and seek out the counsel of other professionals who are willing and able to perform the debriefing function. Researchers' journals and field activities need to indicate that they acted on critical reflections and timely redirection by the peer debriefers and to show that their analyses changed due to the critiques obtained during the debriefings (Guba, 1981).

Using Negative Case Analysis

To increase the likelihood of attaining credibility, researchers should use negative case analysis, which involves "revising your analysis until it accounts for all the findings of all of your cases" (Tutty et al., 1996, p. 126). To perform negative case analysis, researchers must look for contrasting cases and be able to increase the number of cases if needed to resolve questions. Stratification and randomization methods used by experimental researchers also may enhance internal validity in negative case analysis. Qualitative researchers use experimental methods as verification devices to guard against sampling and measurement error (Miles & Huberman, 1994).

Using a Guiding Theory to Verify Findings

To counter challenges to transferability and construct validity in qualitative research studies, researchers can refer back to the original theoretical framework to show how data collection and analysis are guided by concepts and models (Marshall & Rossman, 1995). For example, individuals who design research studies within the same parameters of another study can determine whether the cases described can be transferred to other settings, and the reader can see from the findings how the research ties in to the development of a theory or other empirical findings.

Leaving an Audit Trail

Audit trails, or meticulous logs and records concerning one's research methods and decisions, ensure that every aspect of the data collection and analysis can be traced and verified by others. Audits were discussed earlier in relationship to reliability, but they also are an important method for validity. Chwalisz et al. (1996) suggest that qualitative researchers consider combining "think aloud" techniques with keeping journals during their analyses, thus producing a protocol of cognitive strategies for analysis that other researchers could examine subsequently. Thus, the spirit of the audit trail is captured in this method. An audit trail allows research teams and outside researchers to reconstruct the work of the original researcher. This method may be used to critically investigate or cross-check the data collection and analysis.

Using Reflexivity

Reflexivity is the "ability to examine one's self" (Padgett, 1998, p. 21). To ensure reflexivity, open disclosures of preconceptions and assumptions that might have influenced data gathering and processing become an important part of the research method (Brody, 1992). Franklin (1996) provides an example of how reflexivity was used by a doctoral student whom she was supervising during a qualitative study. The student, a feminist activist, was doing a study on the effects of taking a polygraph test on female rape victims. The person conducting the research had a strong bias and set of theoretical assumptions that assumed that being exposed to the polygraph test was disempowering to women. However, the interview data she collected did not support this conclusion; instead, the researcher found that the women felt vindicated by the positive results of the test. It was an emotional struggle for the researcher to give up her biases in favor of the empirical data from the women. But through careful examination of her beliefs and biases, she finally was able to do so.

Using Member Checks

Obtaining feedback from research participants is an essential credibility technique that is unique to qualitative methods. Although feedback from research participants should be part of the ongoing process of the qualitative research study, it is particularly useful when the analysis and interpretations have been made and conclusions have been drawn (Tutty et al., 1996). Researchers should work out a method for documenting member checks as well as the interpretations that were changed as a result of the member feedback (Guba, 1981).

Establishing Structural Corroboration and Referential Adequacy

Establishing structural corroboration, or coherence, is essential to hermeneutics and other forms of narrative analysis. This method involves testing every data source and interpretation against all others to be certain that there are no internal conflicts or contradictions (Guba, 1981). Interpretations also should take into account possible rival explanations and negative or deviant cases (Patton, 1980). Establishing referential adequacy also involves testing analyses and interpretations made after completion of the field study against other research, theories, and data sources (Guba, 1981).

Establishing Causal Network

Miles and Huberman (1994) invented an approach for testing the validity of findings by predicting what will happen in the case after a period of 6 months or 1 year has elapsed. The basic idea for establishing the causal network involves obtaining feedback from informants to verify the causal explanations that researchers conclude. The result is qualitative researchers' version of predictive validity, where researchers can verify that their predictions hold true based on future sets of evidence. For example, will it hold true that grades predict later job success (Miles & Huberman, 1994)?

Checking the meaning of outliers. Researchers should take a good look at the exceptions, or the ends of a distribution, because they can test and strengthen the basic findings. Researchers need to find the outliers and then verify whether what is present in them is absent or different in other, more mainstream examples. Extreme cases can be useful in verifying and confirming conclusions. When researchers take the time and do the critical thinking necessary to rule out spurious relations between variables, many outliers are explained. A spurious relation exists when two variables appear to be correlated, especially when the researcher thinks that they are causally associated, but they are not. Usually, a third variable of interest can explain the differences (Miles & Huberman, 1994).

Making "if-then" tests. Using basic algebraic logic can help us to test our notions. The use of the conditional future tense in "if-then" statements helps to remind us that we have to look to see whether the "then" happened. If-then statements are a way in which to formalize "propositions" for testing causal statements implying that explanations are different (Miles & Huberman, 1994). Computer programs mentioned previously (e.g., NUDIST) provide software functions for testing these hypotheses in the data and may aid analysis of causal explanations.

Using Thick Descriptions in Write-Up

After their studies are completed, qualitative researchers can develop thick descriptions of the content. This helps the reader to make judgments about how transferable the findings are from one case to next. Researchers should make available appendixes to their studies providing full descriptions of all contextual factors impinging on the studies (Guba, 1981). The typical final qualitative research report, as Carney (1990) notes, normally will contain a mixture of full-scale narrative text where thoroughly thick description is needed, displays, and associated analytic text. As Krathwohl (1991) suggests, the reader can "reconstruct how an analysis developed, check the translation fidelity of constructs, and [check] the logical validity of conclusions" (p. 243).

QUALITATIVE CASE EXAMPLE

Beeman (1995) conducted a qualitative study to better understand the concept of social support as it relates to parenting and child neglect. Based on gaps in previous research, Beeman identified a clear need for research that (a) differentiated among social relationships, social interaction, and social support; (b) identified the characteristics and dimensions of social relationships and social interactions that the individual himself or herself perceived as "supportive"; and (c) compared and contrasted these characteristics for parents who have neglected their children and for parents who have not (p. 102).

According to Beeman (1995), there were several qualitative methods used that enhanced validity and reliability in the study. First, a guiding theoretical concept of the social network and social network analysis were used to operationalize the distinctions among social relationships, social interaction, and social support as well as to explore the importance of characteristics of social relationships as described in the social network literature. Second, a type of comparative analysis was used to compare social network characteristics of a group of mothers who had neglected their children to those of a group of sociodemographically similar mothers who were identified as key community contacts successfully raising their children in a high-risk environment—in this case, low-income, single, African American mothers living in the same inner-city neighborhood.

Thus, Beeman's (1995) study allowed for excellent across-case comparisons and for the testing of divergent cases. Finally, qualitative data collection and data analysis methods were used, and these allowed for the discovery of important aspects of social relationships and social interaction from the respondents' perspectives using member checks as a method of increasing validity of the researcher's interpretations.

The main method of data collection chosen for the Beeman (1995) study was repeated semistructured interviewing. An interview guide consisting of open-ended questions was developed with input from other researchers experienced in interviewing mothers living in high-risk environments and with extensive piloting and pretesting with representatives of both groups of mothers. Therefore, the qualitative researcher maximized the internal validity of the study by using a structured interview guide developed from theory and advisement of participants. The interview guide was based on past theory and research and, therefore, made use of sensitizing concepts.

Repeated interviews contributed to the building of rapport between the interviewer and respondents, and they prolonged engagement in the field. Data collection and data analysis ran concurrently. During the interview process, the researcher recorded emerging insights, data themes, and patterns in a field journal. The emerging insights and themes, along with portions of the transcripts that represented those themes, were discussed at regular meetings with the external case reviewers. This helped to improve reliability of coding (Beeman, 1995, pp. 104-105).

Data credibility and accountability, characteristics guided by past research and theory and, therefore, anticipated in advance, were systematically recorded on data matrices during the interview process. These data matrices served as a structured method for coding that aided the analysis of the data. After the interview tapes were transcribed, data on the matrices were rechecked against the transcripts for verification (Beeman, 1995, p. 108).

The second part of data analysis took an inductive approach to understanding the data and involved the following five stages. First, the raw field material was prepared for content analysis. Interview tapes were transcribed verbatim. Second, a general scheme for categorizing field data was developed. Thus, the researcher made use of an a priori codebook. At this step, open coding is used involving the identification of themes or categories in the data and placing a preliminary label on them. Themes are identified through a process in which the analyst alternates between asking questions about the data and returning to the data to verify and compare (Beeman, 1995, pp. 108-109).

Third, the researcher also made use of multiple case and across-case analyses, first analyzing a subset of four cases. Two cases were chosen from the sample of neglecting mothers, as well as two from the sample of non-neglecting mothers, on which to focus the initial comparative analysis. Homogeneity was a principle guiding case analysis in that cases were chosen that did not seem atypical of other cases in their group and for which a large amount of data were available to maximize the possibility of discovering important differences. Fourth, grouping by similar characteristics helped the researcher to compare the subsets and to preliminarily identify dimensions of similarity and differences (Beeman, 1995, p. 110).

During the process and summarizing of the four cases, key areas of differences were noted in a summary form and disseminated in a memo to two external advisers and reviewers. This memo served as a record of the process of analysis and provided a means by which external reviewers could review case material and provide feedback on the credibility and interpretation. Memos, the reduction forms, data matrices, and the field journal provided a chronology of the identification and evolution of data collection themes, and they served as documentation of the process of data collection and data analysis. Fifth, working the existing set of themes and codes, the researcher proceeded to add the remaining cases into the analysis. To increase the consistency and validity of the coding ethnograph, a computer software program developed for qualitative analysis was used (Beeman, 1995, p. 110).

According to Beeman (1995), the study example involves a process of research that left "footprints" (thus maximizing accountability) at the same time that it enabled the researcher to discover and identify meaning from the respondents' perspectives (thus maximizing credibility) (p. 112). The process of data analysis also used methods of documentation and external reviews of case materials to maximize intersubjectivity and accountability (p. 113).

SUMMARY

This chapter defined reliability and validity in the context of qualitative research. Several steps were discussed that can help the social work researcher to increase the reliability and validity of qualitative studies. Although it is not possible for the researcher to include every method discussed in this chapter, it is important to combine as many diverse methods as is feasible. By doing so, the researcher will increase the reliability and validity of his or her studies. The chapter ended by presenting a case example illustrating one qualitative research study in which a social work researcher combined different methods to increase reliability and validity.

REFERENCES

Beeman, S. K. (1995). Maximizing credibility and accountability in qualitative data collection and data analysis: A social work research case example. *Journal of Sociology and Social Welfare, 22*, 99-114.

Brink, P. (1989). Issues in reliability and validity. In J. Morse (Ed.), *Qualitative nursing research: A contemporary dialogue*. Rockville, MD: Aspen.

Brody, H. (1992). Philosophic approaches. In B. F. Crabtree & W. L. Miller (Eds.), *Doing qualitative research: Research methods for primary care* (Vol. 3, pp. 174-185). Newbury Park, CA: Sage.

Campbell, D. T. (1956). *Leadership and its effects upon the group*. Columbus: Ohio State University Press.

Carney, T. F. (1990). *Collaborative inquiry methodology*. Windsor, Ontario: University of Windsor, Division for Instructional Development.

Chwalisz, K., Wiersma, N., & Stark-Wroblewski, K. (1996). A quasi-qualitative investigation of strategies used in qualitative categorization. *Journal of Counseling Psychology, 43,* 502-509.

Cronbach, L. J. (1975). Beyond the two disciplines of scientific psychology. *American Psychologist, 30,* 116-127.

Denzin, N. K. (1989). *Interpretive interactionism.* Newbury Park, CA: Sage.

Denzin, N. K. (1994). The art and politics of interpretation. In N. K. Denzin & Y. S. Lincoln (Eds.), *Handbook of Qualitative Research.* Thousand Oaks, CA: Sage.

Eisner, E. W. (1979). *The educational imagination.* New York: Basic Books.

Eisner, E. W. (1991). *The enlightened eye: Qualitative inquiry and the enhancement of educational practice.* New York: Macmillan.

Fielding, N., & Fielding, J. (1986). *Linking data.* Beverly Hills, CA: Sage.

Fielding, R., & Lee, R. (Eds.). (1991). *Using computers in qualitative analysis.* Newbury Park, CA: Sage.

Firestone, W. A. (1993). Alternative arguments for generalizing from data as applied to qualitative research. *Educational Researcher, 22*(4), 16-23.

Franklin, C. (1996). Learning to teach qualitative research: Reflections from a quantitative researcher. *Marriage and Family Review, 24,* 241-274.

Franklin, C., & Jordan, C. (1997). Qualitative research methods. In R. M. Grinnell (Ed.), *Social work research and evaluation: Quantitative and qualitative approaches* (5th ed., pp. 106-140). Itasca, IL: Peacock.

Geertz, C. (1973). *The interpretation of culture.* New York: Basic Books.

Glaser, B. G., & Strauss, A. L. (1967). *The discovery of grounded theory.* Chicago: Aldine.

Grigsby, R. K., Thyer, B. A., Waller, R. J., & Johnston, G. A. (1999). Chalk eating in middle Georgia: A culture-bound syndrome of pica? *Southern Medical Journal, 92,* 190-192.

Guba, E. G. (1981). Criteria for assessing the trustworthiness of naturalistic inquiries. *Educational Communication and Technology Journal, 29,* 75-91.

Gulliksen, H. (1950). *Theory of mental tests.* New York: John Wiley.

Hammersly, M. (1992). *What's wrong with ethnography.* New York: Routledge.

Hansen, J. F. (1979). *Sociocultural perspectives on human learning: An introduction to educational anthropology.* Englewood Cliffs, NJ: Prentice Hall.

Hill, C. E., Gelso, J., Mohr, J., Rochlen, A., & Zack, J. (1997). *The qualitative study of a successful long-term therapy.* Unpublished manuscript.

Hill, C. E., Thompson, B. J., & Williams, E. N. (1997). A guide to conducting consensual qualitative research. *The Counseling Psychologist, 25,* 517-527.

Jick, T. (1983). Mixing qualitative and quantitative methods: Triangulation in action. In J. Van Maanen (Ed.), *Qualitative methodology* (pp. 135-148). Beverly Hills, CA: Sage.

Kirk, J., & Miller, M. L. (1986). *Reliability and validity in qualitative research.* Beverly Hills, CA: Sage.

Krathwohl, D. (1991). *Methods of educational and social science research: An integrated approach.* New York: Longman.

LeCompte, M. D., & Goetz, J. P. (1982). Problems of reliability and validity in ethnographic research. *Journal of Educational Research, 52,* 31-60.

Marshall, C., & Rossman, G. B. (1995). *Designing qualitative research* (2nd ed.). Thousand Oaks, CA: Sage.

McGrath, J. E., & Brinberg, D. (1983). External validity and the research process: A comment on the Calder-Lynch dialogue. *Journal of Consumer Research, 10,* 115-124.

Miles, M., & Weitzman, E. (1999). *Computer programs for qualitative data analysis* (2nd ed.). Thousand Oaks, CA: Sage.

Miles, M. B., & Huberman, A. M. (1994). *An expanded sourcebook: Qualitative data analysis* (2nd ed.). Thousand Oaks, CA: Sage.

Newfield, N., Sells, S. P., Smith, T. E., Newfield, S., & Newfield, F. (1996). Ethnographic research methods: Creating a clinical science of the humanities. In D. H. Sprenkle & S. M. Moon (Eds.), *Research methods in family therapy* (pp. 25-63). New York: Guilford.

Padgett, D. K. (1998). *Qualitative methods in social work research: Challenges and rewards.* Thousand Oaks, CA: Sage.

Patton, M. Q. (1980). *Qualitative evaluation methods.* Beverly Hills, CA: Sage.

Phillips, D. C. (1987). Validity in qualitative research: Why the worry about warrant will not wane. *Education and Urban Society, 20,* 9-24.

Rafuls, S. E., & Moon, S. M. (1996). Grounded theory methodology in family therapy research. In D. H. Sprenkle & S. M. Moon (Eds.), *Research methods in family therapy* (pp. 64-80). New York: Guilford.

Reason, P., & Rowan, J. (1981). Issues of validity in new paradigm research. In P. Reason & J. Rowan (Eds.), *Human inquiry: A sourcebook of new paradigm research* (pp. 239-262). New York: John Wiley.

Richards, L., & Richards, T. J. (1992). Analyzing unstructured information: Can computers help? *Library Hi-Tech, 10,* 95-109.

Schacter, D. L. (1999). The seven sins of memory: Insights from psychology and cognitive neuroscience. *American Psychologist, 54,* 182-203.

Snow, D. A., & Anderson, L. (1991). Researching the homeless: The characteristic features and virtues of the case study. In J. R. Feagin, A. M. Orum, & G. Sjoberg (Eds.), *A case for the case study* (pp. 148-173). Chapel Hill: University of North Carolina Press.

Strauss, A., & Corbin, J. (1999). *Basics of qualitative research: Techniques and procedures for developing grounded theory* (3rd ed.). Thousand Oaks, CA: Sage.

Tesch, R. (1990). *Qualitative research: Analysis types and software tools.* New York: Falmer.

Tutty, L. M., Rothery, M. A., & Grinnell, R. M. (1996). *Qualitative research for social workers.* Needham Heights, MA: Allyn & Bacon.

Zyzanski, S. J., McWhinney, I. R., Blake, R., Crabtree, B. F., & Miller, W. L. (1992). Qualitative research: Perspectives on the future. In B. F. Crabtree & W. L. Miller (Eds.), *Doing qualitative research: Research methods for primary care* (pp. 231-248). Newbury Park, CA: Sage.

CHAPTER SIXTEEN

Narrative Case Studies

JERROLD R. BRANDELL
THEODORE VARKAS

The narrative case study is a research instrument that is used for the in-depth study of various social and clinical problems, to understand stages or phases in processes, and to investigate a phenomenon within its environmental context (Gilgun, 1994). The case study method, which has been termed "the only possible way of obtaining the granite blocks of data on which to build a science of human nature" (Murray, 1955, p. 15), has been used in fields such as clinical psychoanalysis, human behavior theory, and Piagetian cognitive development theory. Case studies also have been used to advantage in diverse professions such as medicine, law, and business, where they hold a time-honored role in both research and teaching (Gilgun, 1994). One popular writer, the neurologist Oliver Sacks, has received critical acclaim for his richly detailed and compelling case studies of patients with various types of brain diseases and syndromes, ranging from postencephalitis to autism. In its simplest form, the case study is a story told for the purpose of understanding and learning. It captures essential meanings and qualities that might not be conveyed as forcefully or as effectively through other research media. Fundamentally, the narrative case study provides entrée to information that might otherwise be inaccessible. It makes possible the capture of phenomena that might not be understood as readily through other means of study.

The narrative case study has been a tradition in social work that spans several generations of social work theorists. Authors such as Mary Richmond, Annette Garrett, Helen Harris Perlman, Florence Hollis, and Selma Fraiberg have, inter alia, used case exemplars to illustrate a range of issues and problems in diagnosis and intervention. Case studies continue to hold a prominent role in the dissemination of clinical knowledge in social work education. Although somewhat less common today, the use of casebooks to augment textual and other didactic materials in the clinical instruction of social work graduate students historically was a common practice. Spence (1993) observes that the traditional case report remains the "most compelling means of communicating clinical findings, and the excitement attached to both reading and writing case histories has lost none of its appeal" (p. 37). The value of the case study, it might be argued, lies in its experience-near descriptions of clinical processes. Such descriptions are phenomenologically distinctive and permit the student to identify with the experience of the worker and the reality of the clinical encounter, albeit vicariously. Case studies provide examples of what already has been encountered and how difficult situations were handled. Narrative case studies have been used extensively in several different social work literatures including child and family welfare, family therapy, individual therapy, group work, cross-cultural studies, and practice evaluations.

THE CASE STUDY DEFINED

The narrative case study is defined as the intensive examination of an individual unit, although such units are not limited to individual persons. Families, treatment teams, clinical interview segments, and even whole communities are legitimate units for investigation (Gilgun, 1994). It also can be argued that a defining characteristic of the case study in social work is its focus on environmental context, although certain exceptions may exist (e.g., single-case experimental research designs, where context is either not emphasized or deemed to be irrelevant). Case studies are held to be *idiographic* (which means that the unit of study is the single unit); multiple variables are investigated; and generalization is fundamentally analytic, inferential, and impressionistic rather than statistical and probabilistic. When generalization takes this form, the findings extrapolated from a single case subsequently are compared for "goodness of fit" with other cases and/or patterns predicted by extant theory or prior research (Gilgun, 1994). *Nomothetic* research, by contrast, systematically investigates a few variables using groups of subjects rather than individual units. Nomothetic research, currently the dominant mode of investigation in the social and behavioral sciences, attempts to distill general laws from its findings. Large probability samples are especially valued inasmuch as they permit the use of powerful statistics. These, in turn, strengthen the claim of probabilistic generalizability (Gilgun, 1994).

POSTMODERNISM AND THE NARRATIVE CASE STUDY

Although many journals in social work continue to place an emphasis on nomothetic research, clinical social work, psychology, and other human services appear to be in a transitional period where basic assumptions about what constitutes science and scientific inquiry are being challenged. The positivist worldview, which has exerted a powerful and pervasive influence on modern scientific thought, also has imposed significant restraints on the nature of research within the clinical professions (Howard, 1985; Mahoney, 1991; Niemeyer, 1993; Polkinghorne, 1988). As theorists have become increasingly aware of such restrictions, efforts to cultivate and distill methods of investigation that are less bound by the assumptions of positivist science have increased (Niemeyer, 1993). Consequently, clinical scholars have begun to consider issues or approaches such as self-agency, hermeneutics, semiotics, and theories that emphasize intentional action and narrative knowing. Anderson (1990) even goes so far as to declare, "We are seeing in our lifetimes the collapse of the objectivist worldview that dominated the modern era" and that it is being supplanted by a *constructivist* worldview (p. 268). This position seems rather extreme, although there clearly has been a sustained transdisciplinary interest in constructivism over the past 20 years or so. The common assumption shared by all constructivist orientations has been described in the following manner: No one has access to a singular, stable, and fully knowable reality. All of our understandings, instead, are imbedded in social and interpersonal contexts and are, therefore, limited in perspective, depth, and scope. Constructivist approaches appear to have a common guiding premise that informs all thinking about the nature of knowing. In effect, constructivist thinking assumes that all humans (a) are naturally and actively engaged in efforts to understand the totality of their experiences in the world, (b) are not able to gain direct access to external realities, and (c) are continually evolving and changing (Niemeyer, 1993). Therefore, constructivism and the study of case narratives are the study of meaning making. As social workers and as humans, we are compelled to interpret experience, to search for purpose, and to understand the significance of events and scenarios in which we play a part. Although incompatible with the aims of nomothetic research investigation, the narrative case study might prove to be especially well suited for the requirements of a postmodern era.

LIMITATIONS OF THE NARRATIVE CASE STUDY

Several significant limitations of the narrative case study have been identified in both the clinical social work and psychoanalytic literatures. One of these is the heavy reliance placed on anecdote and narrative persuasion in typical case studies, where a favored or singular explanation is provided (Spence, 1993). In effect, the story that is being told often has but one ending. In fact, the narrative case study might "function best when all the evidence has been accounted for and no other explanation is possible" (Spence, 1993, p. 38). Spence (1993) also believes that the facts presented in typical case studies almost invariably are presented in a positivist frame. In other words, a somewhat artificial separation occurs between the observer/narrator and the observed. Although clinical realities are inherently ambiguous and subject to the rule of multideterminism (a construct in which any psychic event or aspect of behavior can be caused my multiple factors and may serve more than one purpose in the psychic framework and economy [Moore & Fine, 1990, p. 123]), "facts" in the case narrative are presented in such a manner as to lead the reader to a particular and, one might argue, inevitable solution.

Another criticism of the narrative case study has been what Spence (1993) terms the "tradition of argument by authority." The case narrative has a "closed texture" that coerces the reader into accepting at face value whatever conclusions the narrator himself or herself already has made about the case. Disagreement and alternative explanations often are not possible due to the fact that only the narrator has access to all of the facts and tends to report these selectively. In Spence's view, this "privileged withholding" occurs for two interrelated reasons: (a) the narrator's need to protect the client's confidentiality by omitting or altering certain types of information and (b) the narrator's unintended or unconscious errors of distortion, omission, or commission. The effect, however, is that the whole story is not told. Sigmund Freud, whose detailed case studies of patients with obsessive-compulsive, phobic, hysterical, and paranoid disorders are recognized as exemplars of the psychoanalytic method, appears to have anticipated this limitation. Freud (1913/1958) remarked, "I once treated a high official who was bound by his oath of office not to communicate certain things because they were state secrets, and the analysis came to grief as a consequence of this restriction." Freud reasoned,

> The whole task becomes impossible if a reservation is allowed at any single place. But we have only to reflect what would happen if the right of asylum existed at any point in a town;

how long would it be before all the riff-raff of the town had collected there? (p. 136, as cited in Spence, 1993)

USING THE NARRATIVE CASE STUDY AS A QUALITATIVE RESEARCH TOOL

Although some authors have observed that case studies are not limited to qualitative research applications, the basic focus in the remainder of this chapter is on the narrative case study in the context of qualitative research. The case study allows for the integration of theoretical perspective, intervention, and outcome. In an effort to establish a link between a unique clinical phenomenon and its context where one might not be immediately evident, the case study can be used to hypothesize some type of cause and effect. In clinical work, case studies often are the only means by which to gain entrée to various dimensions of therapeutic process and of certain hypothesized aspects of the complex treatment relationship between the social worker and the client (e.g., the transference-countertransference axis). The dissemination of such data thus becomes an important method both for theory building and as a vehicle for challenging certain assumptions about treatment process, diagnosis, and the therapeutic relationship, inter alia. Despite the limitations noted earlier and the fact that there appears to be little uniformity in the structure of published case studies, the narrative case study, nevertheless, continues to make significant (some would argue seminal) contributions to social work practice theory and clinical methods.

GUIDELINES FOR DETERMINING GOODNESS OF FIT

It first must be determined whether the narrative case study is the most appropriate research tool for the theme or issue that is being explored. Narrative case studies should be written so that it is possible to make useful generalizations. It should be possible to use the case study as the basis for additional research, an important point that argues against the closed texture issue identified by Spence (1993). For example, in hypothesizing that a particular variable or a specific sequence of events is responsible for a particular outcome, the structure of the case study should permit the subsequent testing of such a hypothesis via additional qualitative or quantitative means.

One might consider the case of a man who has developed a fear of riding in cars following an automobile accident in which another motorist was killed. In his case, he eventually becomes fearful not only of riding in cars but also of being near streets or, perhaps, even of seeing films of others riding in cars. These, as well as other phenomena associated with automobiles and accidents, eventually lead to states of nearly incapacitating anxiety. The clinician might hypothesize that, following a traumatic experience such as a serious automobile accident, the development of acute anxiety might not be limited solely to driving in cars but might extend or generalize to other, nominally more benign stimuli (e.g., pictures of cars, engine sounds). One might design another study to determine the statistical probability of developing such symptomatology following a serious auto accident by interviewing a large sample of accident victims to determine how similar their experiences were. However, suppose that in our case, the man developed not only a fear of cars and associated phenomena but also a fear of leaving his house or of being around unfamiliar people. This might be somewhat more difficult to explain without obtaining additional data. One might wish to have further information regarding whether there is a history of emotional problems or other traumata predating the most recent traumatic experience, the individual's physical health status, current or past use of drugs and/or alcohol, and quality of current interpersonal relationships including those with family members. It also might be helpful to have more remote data such as early life history and history of losses. In effect, as more variables are added to the equation, the narrative case study becomes that much more attractive as a basic research instrument, uniquely equipped to identify an extensive range of variables of interest.

In such an instance, the narrative case study permits the researcher to "capture" exceedingly complex case situations, allowing for a considerable degree of detail and richness of understanding. Elements of the recent and remote past can be interwoven with particular issues in the present, thereby creating a rich tapestry and an equally sound basis for additional investigation. In fact, the narrative case study is especially useful when complex dynamics and multiple variables produce unusual or even rare situations that might be less amenable to other types of research investigations.

SPECIFIC GUIDELINES FOR PRACTICE UTILIZATION

One very common type of case study is chronological in nature, describing events as they occur over a period of time. Making inferences about causality, or about the linkage between events and particular sequelae, may be enhanced by the use of such an organizing framework. A second type of structure for organizing the narrative case study is the *comparative structure,* in which more than a single commentary is provided for the case data. Such an organizing framework may be a method for combating the problem of the narrator's tendency to arrive at a singular explanation for the clinical facts and their meaning.

One somewhat more complex sequence for the structure of the narrative case study might consist of the following components: (a) identification of the issue, problem, or process being studied; (b) review of relevant prior literature; (c) identification of methods used for data collection such as written process notes, progress notes, other clinical documentation, archival records, client interviews, direct observation, and participant observation; (d) description of findings from data that have been collected and analyzed; and (e) development of conclusions and implications for further study.

Certainly, other frameworks also exist inasmuch as case studies are heterogeneous, and serve a variety of purposes. Runyan (1982) observes that case studies may be descriptive, explanatory, predictive, generative, or used for hypothesis testing. Furthermore, case narratives may be presented atheoretically or within the framework of particular developmental or clinical theory bases.

CLINICAL CASE ILLUSTRATION

The case study method was selected in this instance for two reasons. First, this case was deemed by the therapist (the first author) to have a highly unusual and complex clinical profile. Second, there is a paucity of clinical and theoretical literature focusing generally on countertransference issues and reactions in the treatment of children and adolescents. The case is described in the first person by the first author (for a more detailed discussion of this case, see Brandell, 1999).

Dirk was not quite 20 years old when he first requested treatment at a family service agency for long-standing insomnia and a "negative outlook on life." He often felt as though he might "explode," and he suffered from chronic anxiety that was particularly pronounced in social situations. He reluctantly alluded to a family "situation" that had exerted a dramatic and profound impact on his life, and as the early phase of his treatment began to unfold, the following account gradually emerged. When Dirk was perhaps 13 years of age, his father (who shall be referred to as Mr. S.) was diagnosed with cancer of the prostate. Unfortunately, neither parent chose to reveal this illness to Dirk, his two older brothers, or his younger sister for nearly 1½ years. Mr. S., an outdoorsman who had been moderately successful as a real estate developer and an entrepreneur, initially refused treatment, and his condition gradually worsened. By the time he finally consented to surgery some 18 months later, the cancer had metastasized and his prognosis was terminal. A prostatectomy left him impotent, increasing the strain in a marriage that already had begun to deteriorate.

Within several months of his father's surgery, when Dirk was perhaps 14 or 15 years old, Ms. S. (Dirk's mother) began a clandestine affair with a middle-aged man who resided nearby. The affair intensified, and presumably as a consequence of Ms. S.'s carelessness, Mr. S. learned of the affair. He also learned that she was planning a trip around the world with her lover. Although narcissistically mortified and enraged, he chose not to confront his wife right away, instead plotting secretly to murder her. On a weekday morning when Dirk and his younger sister were at school (his older brothers no longer resided in the family home), Mr. S. killed his wife in their bedroom with one of his hunting rifles. He then carefully wrapped her body up, packed it in the trunk of the family car, and drove to a shopping center, where he took his own life. The news was, of course, devastating to Dirk and his siblings, and it was made even more injurious due to the relentless media coverage that the crime received. Every conceivable detail of the murder-suicide was described on television and in the local press. Suddenly, Dirk and his siblings were completely bereft of privacy. Nor was there any adult intercessor to step forward and protect them from the continuing public exposure, humiliation, and pain.

These traumatic injuries were compounded by the reactions of neighbors and even former family friends, whose cool reactions to Dirk and his siblings bordered on social ostracism. The toll on Dirk's family continued over the next several years. First, the elder of Dirk's two brothers, Jon, committed suicide at the age of 27 years in a manner uncannily reminiscent of Mr. S.'s suicide. Some months later, Dirk's surviving brother, Rick, a poly-substance abuser, was incarcerated after being arrested and convicted of a drug-related felony. Finally, Dirk and his sister became estranged from each other, and by the time he began treatment, they were barely speaking to one another. Dirk, in fact, had little contact with anyone. After his parents' deaths, he spent a couple of years in the homes of various relatives, but eventually he decided to move back into his parents' house, where he lived alone. Dirk had been provided for quite generously in his father's will. He soon took over what remained of the family business, which included a strip mall and a small assortment of other business properties. At the time when he began weekly therapy, Dirk had monthly contact with some of his tenants when their rents became due and made occasional trips to the grocery store. He had not dated since high school and had only episodic contact with his paternal grandmother, whom he disliked. He slept in his parents' bedroom, which had not been redecorated after their deaths. There even was unrepaired damage from the shotgun blast that had killed his mother, although he did not at first appear discomfited by this fact and maintained that it was not abnormal or even especially noteworthy. He explained that he was loath to change or repair anything in the house, which he attributed to a tendency toward "procrastination." People were unreliable, but his house, despite the carnage that had occurred there, remained a stabilizing force. Change was loathsome because it interfered with the integrity of important memories of the house and of the childhood lived within its walls.

Dirk was quite socially isolated and had a tremendous amount of discretionary time, two facts that were alternately frightening and reassuring to him. Although he wanted very much to become more involved with others and eventually to be in a serious relationship with a woman, he trusted no one. He believed others to be capable of great treachery, and from time to time, he revealed conspiratorial ideas that had a paranoid, if not psychotic, delusional resonance to them. He lived in a sparsely populated semirural area, and for the most part, he involved himself in solitary pursuits such as stamp collecting, reading, and fishing. He would hunt small game or shoot at targets with a collection of rifles, shotguns, and handguns that his father had left behind, and at times he spoke with obvious pleasure of methodically skinning and dressing the small animals he trapped or killed. There was little or no waste; even the skins could be used to make caps or mittens. He maintained that hunting and trapping animals was by no means unkind; indeed, it was far more humane than permitting the overpopulation and starvation of raccoons, muskrats, opossums, foxes, minks, and the like. Occasionally, he would add that he preferred the company of animals, even dead ones, to humans. They, unlike people, did not express jealousy and hatred.

As the treatment intensified, Dirk began to share a great deal more about his relationships with both parents. Sometimes, he would speak with profound sadness of his staggering loss. Needing both to make sense of the tragedy and to assign responsibility for it, he then would become enraged at his mother's lover. It was *he* who was to blame for everything that had happened, Dirk would declare. At other times, he described both of his parents as heinous or monstrous, having total disregard for the rest of the family's welfare.

Things never had been especially good between Dirk and his mother. She had a mild case of rubella during her pregnancy with Dirk, which he believed might have caused a physical anomaly as well as a congenital problem with his vision. Perhaps, he thought, she had rejected him in his infancy when the anomaly was discovered. The manner in which his mother described the anomaly, which later was removed, made him feel as though his physical appearance displeased, and perhaps even disgusted, her. Although he spent a great deal of time with her growing up, he recalled that she often was emotionally distant or upset with him.

From this time onward, he had gradually become less trusting of his mother and grew closer to his father, whom he emulated in a variety of ways. He often had noted that he and his father were very much alike. He had thought the world of this strong "macho" man who demanded strict obedience but also was capable of great kindness, particularly in acknowledgment of Dirk's frequent efforts to please him. It was quite painful for Dirk to think of this same strong father as a cuckold. It was even more frightening to think of him as weakened and castrated, and it was profoundly traumatic to believe that he could have been so uncaring about Dirk and his siblings as to actually carry out this unspeakably hateful crime of vengeance.

Early in his treatment, Dirk was able to express anger and disappointment with his mother for her lack of warmth and the painful way in which she avoided him, even shunned him. She had made him feel defective, small, and unimportant. This material was mined for what it revealed of the nature of Dirk's relational (selfobject) needs. We gradually learned how his mother's own limited capacity for empathy had interfered with the development of Dirk's capacity for pleasure in his own accomplishments, for healthy self-confidence and the indefatigable pursuit of important personal goals. In fact, Dirk avoided virtually any social situation where he thought others might disappoint him, where his mother's inability to mirror his boyhood efforts and accomplishments might be traumatically repeated. This was an important theme in our early explorations of Dirk's contact-shunning adaptation to the world outside his family home. However, this dynamic issue was not at the core of the transference-countertransference matrix that gradually evolved in my work with Dirk.

During the early spring, about 5 months into his treatment, Dirk gradually began to reveal more details of his relationship with his father. His father, he observed, was really more like an employer than a parent, forever assigning Dirk tasks, correcting his mistakes, and maintaining a certain aloofness and emotional distance from him. Although up until this point Dirk had tended to place more responsibility for the murder-suicide on the actions of his mother and her lover, he now began to view his father as having a greater role in the family tragedy. For the first time, he sounded genuinely angry. However, awareness of this proved to be exceedingly painful for him, and depressive thoughts and suicidal fantasies typically followed such discussions: "My father could have shot me. . . . In fact, sometimes I wish he had blown me away."

During this same period, burglars broke into the strip mall that Dirk had inherited from his father's estate. This enraged Dirk, almost to the point of psychotic disorganization. He reacted to it as though his personal integrity had been violated, and he reported a series of dreams in which burglars were breaking into homes or he was being chased with people shooting at him. His associations were to his father, whom he described as a "castrating" parent with a need to keep his three sons subservient to him. Dirk observed, for perhaps the first time, that his father might have been rather narcissistic, lacking genuine empathy and interest in his three boys. He was beginning to think of himself and his two older brothers as really quite troubled, although in different ways. He then recounted the following dream:

> [A man who looked like] Jack Benny was trying to break into my house to steal my valuables. He wanted me to think that he had rigged some electrical wire with a gas pipe to scare me and, thereby, force me to disclose the hiding place where my valuables were. . . . He was a mild-mannered man.

We hypothesized that Benny, a mild-mannered Jewish comedian whose initials were identical to my own, also might represent me or, in any event, aspects of Dirk's experience of the treatment process. In an important sense, I was asking Dirk to reveal the hidden location of treasured memories, feelings, and fantasies that he had worked unremittingly to conceal not only from others but also from himself. These interpretations seemed to make a good deal of sense to both of us, yet my recollection at the end of this hour was that I somehow was vaguely troubled. It also was approximately at this point in Dirk's treatment that I began to take copious notes. I rationalized that this was necessary because I felt unable to reconstruct the sessions afterward without them. However, I now believe that this note taking also was in the service of a different, fundamentally unconscious motive. From time to time, Dirk would complain that I was physically too close to him in the office or that I was watching him too intently during the hour, which made him feel self-conscious and ashamed. On several occasions, I actually had moved my chair farther away from him at his request. Again, in response to his anxiety, I had made a point of *looking away* from him precisely during those moments when I ordinarily would want to feel *most* connected to a client (e.g., when he had recalled a poignant experience with his father or was talking about the aftermath of the tragedy). I also noted that it was following "good" hours—hours characterized by considerable affectivity and important revelations—that he would request that our meetings be held on a biweekly basis. When this occurred, probably a half dozen times over the 2 years he was in treatment with me, I recall feeling both disappointed and concerned. My efforts to convince him of the therapeutic value in exploring this phenomenon rather than altering the frequency of our meetings were not simply fruitless; they aroused tremendous anxiety, and several times Dirk threatened to stop coming altogether if I persisted. In effect, my compulsive note taking represented an unconscious compliance with Dirk's articulated request that I titrate the intensity of my involvement with him. At times, our interaction during sessions bore a marked similarity to his interactions with both parents, particularly his father. Like his father, I had become increasingly distant and aloof. On the other hand, Dirk exercised control over this relationship, which proved to be a critical distinction for him as the treatment evolved.

It was during a session in late July, some 9 months into treatment, that I reminded Dirk of my upcoming vacation. As we ended our hour, he remarked for the first time how similar we seemed to each other. I did not comment on this observation because we had reached the end of the hour. However, I believe that I felt rather uneasy about it. During the next session, our last hour prior to my vacation, Dirk reported that he was getting out more often and had been doing a modest degree of socializing. He was making a concerted effort to be less isolated. At the same time, he expressed a considerable degree of hostility when speaking of his (then-incarcerated) brother, whom he described as "exploitative" and deceitful. Toward the end of this hour, he asked where I would be going on vacation. On one previous occasion, Dirk had sought extra-therapeutic contact with me; that had been some months earlier when he called me at home, quite intoxicated, at 2 or 3 a.m. However, during his sessions, he rarely had asked me questions of a personal nature. I remember feeling compelled to answer this one, which I believed represented an important request. It was while I was on vacation some 800 miles away, in a somewhat isolated and unfamiliar setting, that I experienced a dramatic countertransference reaction inextricably linked to my work with Dirk. Although space does not permit a more detailed discussion here, at its core, this reaction faithfully reproduced two important elements of our work: Dirk's paranoia and the highly significant and traumatogenic elements of his relationship with both parents.

Although Dirk was not an easy client to treat, he was likeable. I felt this way from our first meeting, and I believe that this basic feeling for him permitted our work to continue despite his paranoia and a number of disturbing developments along the transference-countertransference axis. During the first weeks of therapy, I recall that although I found his story fully believable, I also felt shocked, overwhelmed, and at times even numbed by it. It was difficult, if not impossible, to conceive of the impact of such traumas occurring seriatim in one family.

Although I felt moved by Dirk's story and wished to convey this to him, his manner of narrating it was a powerful signal to me that he would not find this helpful, at least for the time being. It was as though he could not take in such feelings or allow me to be close in this way. I was not especially troubled by this, and I felt as though my principal task was simply to listen, make occasional inquiries, and provide a climate of acceptance. Although I believe that my discomfort with Dirk cumulated silently during those first few months of treatment, an important threshold was crossed with Dirk's revelation that he continued to sleep in his parents' bedroom. I found this not only bizarre but also frightening. When we attempted to discuss this, he was dismissive. I, on the other hand, was quite willing to let the matter rest, and it was only much later in his treatment that we were able to return to this dialogue. This fact, in combination with my awareness of Dirk's nearly obsessive love of hunting and trapping, led me to begin to view him not so much as a victim of trauma as a heartless and potentially dangerous individual. It did not occur to me until months later that each time he killed a muskrat or a raccoon, it might have served as a disguised reenactment of the original trauma and simultaneously permitted him to identify with an admired part of his father, who had taught him how to hunt and trap. Dirk, after all, had observed in an early session that he and his father were really quite similar. It may, of course, be argued that his paranoia and penchant for hunting, trapping, and skinning animals, in combination with my knowledge of the frightening traumas he had endured, might have helped to shape my countertransference-driven withdrawal and compulsive note taking. He also had requested, somewhat urgently, that I exercise caution lest he feel "trapped"; I was to pull my chair back, not make eye contact, and the like. But soon I felt trapped as well; I had altered my therapeutic modus operandi, and I became aware of experiencing mild apprehension on those days when Dirk came in for his appointments. Some of Dirk's sessions seemed interminable, and if I was feeling this way, then I think it likely that he was feeling something similar. Perhaps in this additional sense, *both* of us were feeling trapped.

As Dirk became increasingly aware of the depth of the injury that he believed his mother had caused him and of the rage he felt toward his father, the extent of his developmental arrest became more comprehensible. I had noted to myself at several junctures that Dirk spoke of his father, in particular, as though he still were alive. In an important sense, Dirk had been unable to bury either parent. Haunted by them, he was unable to relinquish his torturous ties to them. Eventually, the house came to symbolize not only the family tragedy that had begun there but also his relationship with both parents.

As Dirk developed greater awareness of the rage he felt for his father, a feeling that he had worked so hard to project, dissociate, and deny, he seemed to demonstrate greater interest in me and in our relationship. When he commented with some satisfaction that the two of *us* seemed to be similar, I suddenly recalled Dirk's earlier comment about how similar he and his father were. His associations to dream material as well seemed to equate me with his father. Like his father, I might attempt to trick him into a relationship where he was chronically exploited and mistreated and was reduced to a type of helpless indentured servitude. Although the oedipal significance of this dream was not inconsequential, with its reference to hidden valuables, I do not believe that this was the most salient dynamic issue insofar as our relationship was concerned. As mentioned earlier, I ended that hour feeling vaguely troubled in spite of Dirk's agreement that the interpretation was helpful. Although the dream was manifestly paranoid, an important truth about the asymmetry of the therapeutic relationship also was revealed. I was apprehensive because Dirk's associations had signaled the presence of a danger, and that danger now was perceived in some measure as coming from me.

Dirk's report that he was "getting out more" and was less reclusive should have been good news, although I recall reacting with but mild enthusiasm when he informed me of this shortly before my vacation. Dirk was just fine to work with so long as his paranoid fears prevented him from venturing out very far into the world of "real" relationships. However, the thought of Dirk no longer confined to a twilight existence, coupled with his increasing capacity both to feel and express rage, was an alarming one. What ultimately transformed my countertransference fantasies into a dramatic and disjunctive countertransference reaction was the haunting parallel—partially transference based, partially grounded in reality—that had emerged in Dirk's view of me as fundamentally similar to both him and his father. I now believe that my intensive countertransference reaction while on vacation had accomplished something that had simply not been possible despite careful introspection and reflection. I finally came close to experiencing Dirk's terror, although in my own idiosyncratic way. Like Dirk, I felt small, vulnerable, and alone. I was isolated and helpless, in unfamiliar surroundings, and cut off from contact with reality and the intersubjective world. Dirk was frightening, but it was even more frightening to *be*

Dirk. As his therapist, I had been the hunter; suddenly, I was the hunted. I was convinced that I had betrayed Dirk in much the same way as his father had betrayed him, the trauma reenacted in his treatment. In effect, in this extra-therapeutic enactment, I felt not only as Dirk felt but also as I believe he might wish his father to feel—the dreaded and hated father against whom he sought redress for his grievances. Dirk, of course, had enacted both roles daily for well over 5 years; I had enacted them but for a single night.

DISCUSSION

The narrative case illustration used here highlights the complexity of the intersubjective milieu surrounding this young man's treatment and the relationship of past traumata to the evolving therapeutic relationship. The case study method permitted an examination of various historically important dynamic issues that might have relevance to the client's presenting symptomatology. It also revealed important parallels between features of the client's transference relationship and various unresolved issues between the client and his parents. Finally, reasons for the powerful countertransference reactions of the clinician were suggested and explored. This narrative case study is principally generative. It focuses on an exceptional case, addressing particular issues germane to the transference-countertransference matrix in adolescent treatment for which there is little antecedent clinical or theoretical literature. A range of researchable themes and issues (e.g., the impact of severe childhood trauma on personality development, handling of transference, recognition and use of disjunctive countertransference reactions) can be identified for subsequent investigation.

REFERENCES

Anderson, W. T. (1990). *Reality isn't what it used to be.* New York: Harper & Row.

Brandell, J. (1999). Countertransference as communication: Intersubjectivity in the treatment of a traumatized adolescent patient. *Smith College Studies in Social Work, 69,* 405-427.

Freud, S. (1958). On beginning the treatment. In J. Strachey (Ed.), *Standard edition of the complete psychological works of Sigmund Freud* (Vol. 12, pp. 123-144). London: Hogarth. (Originally published in 1913)

Gilgun, J. (1994). A case for case studies in social work research. *Social Work, 39,* 371-380.

Howard, G. (1985). Can research in the human sciences become more relevant to practice? *Journal of Counseling and Development, 63,* 539-544.

Mahoney, M. (1991). *Human change processes.* New York: Basic Books.

Moore, B., & Fine, B. (1990). *Psychoanalytic terms and concepts.* New Haven, CT: Yale University Press.

Murray, H. (1955). Introduction. In A. Burton & R. Harris (Eds.), *Clinical studies of personality* (Vol. 1, pp. 4-17). New York: Harper & Row.

Niemeyer, G. (1993). Constructivist assessment. In G. Niemeyer (Ed.), *Constructivist assessment: A casebook* (pp. 1-30). Newbury Park, CA: Sage.

Polkinghorne, D. (1988). *Narrative knowing and the human sciences.* Albany: State University of New York Press.

Runyan, W. M. (1982). *Life histories and psychobiography: Explorations in theory and method.* New York: Oxford University Press.

Spence, D. (1993). Traditional case studies and prescriptions for improving them. In N. E. Miller, L. Luborsky, J. Barber, & J. Docherty (Eds.), *Psychodynamic treatment research: A handbook for clinical practice* (pp. 37-52). New York: Basic Books.

CHAPTER SEVENTEEN

In-Depth Interviews

HARRIET GOODMAN

Qualitative studies use three types of data collection: content analysis, observation of events in the real world, and interviews (York, 1998). These types frequently are woven together in a single study, whether it is ethnographic, participant observation, or grounded theory research, discussed elsewhere in this handbook. However, content analysis and observation alone do not allow the researcher to explore the thoughts, experiences, and feelings of people who have direct experiences with the issue under study (Patton, 1990). While observing, the researcher may question participants about events that occur naturalistically over the course of a study, and spontaneous responses to questions asked on the spot can augment the researcher's understanding of participants' thoughts about events in progress.

However, in a naturalistic setting, questioners cannot probe extensively beyond what they observe. The constraints are both practical and conceptual. Impromptu questioning does not give researchers a chance to select particular subjects or time to explore how their views buttress or challenge existing empirical or theoretical models. Qualitative studies often require planned interviews so that the researcher can design the format in advance. This method, the in-depth interview, is one of the most powerful tools in qualitative research (McCracken, 1988), and it certainly is the most used one (Tutty, Rothery, & Grinnell, 1996).

This chapter presents elements of thoughtful, empirically based, research-driven in-depth interviews for various applications in qualitative studies. First, the researcher who employs in-depth interviews considers the advantages and disadvantages of interviews and decides whether they are an appropriate observation method for his or her study. The researcher also determines the appropriate level of structure for interviews for a particular study or study phase and how it relates to the overall knowledge-building plan. An informed methodology requires identification of domains to explore, or specific questions, and probes in a more structured format. The researcher must choose whom to interview and how to recruit knowledgeable participants.

In-depth interviews in social work research require special consideration in two areas. Threats to internal validity, as commonly described in social research literature (Grinnell & Unrau, 1997; Yegidis, Weinbach, & Morrison-Rodriguez, 1998), are threaded throughout nearly all phases of studies that involve in-depth interviews. In addition, in-depth interviews in social work research present unique human subjects issues. The intimate nature of the interview format means that sensitive material and, consequently, strong emotional responses may erupt, presenting special dilemmas for social work research practitioners. This chapter proposes practical solutions in both areas.

ADVANTAGES AND DISADVANTAGES OF THE IN-DEPTH INTERVIEW

When selecting in-depth interviews for a qualitative study, the researcher assumes that the perspectives of people who have personal experiences with the issue under investigation are a vital source of information. Language is the data of in-depth interviews (Patton, 1990), enabling the researcher to capture the complexity of individuals' feelings, thoughts, and perceptions. What people have to say reveals their mental worlds and the logic they bring to experiences. A skilled researcher-interviewer can penetrate the words that people employ as personal symbols for life events. In-depth interviews provide a spontaneous and flexible opportunity for them to achieve this.

At first blush, the fact that social workers are skilled interviewers by training seems to be an undiluted advantage. After all, social workers receive extensive supervision in interviewing techniques as a part of their education that includes the observational aspects of assessment. Workers enter professional life with confidence in their interviewing skills, and this confidence grows through experience and career advancement. However, clinical and research interviews are very different. The purpose of clinical interviewing is to help clients, whereas in-depth interviewing for research is an observational method to develop empirical knowledge or theoretical models (Padgett, 1998).

Gilgun (1994) proposes that certain qualitative research methods are natural to social work practitioners, "like sliding a hand into a well-made glove" (p. 115). In her view, the procedures of grounded theory, in particular, and direct social work practice are parallel. The "hand-in-glove" assertion of multiple parallels between the processes of direct practice and research is controversial, resulting in contention about the relationship between clinical practice and in-depth interviews. Issues include the tension between professional ethics and scientific rigor (Pieper & Tyson, 1999) contrasted with the advantage of qualitative research perspectives in applied work as a tool for client empowerment (Bein & Allen, 1999). Hartman's (1990) view that exploring clients' worlds through in-depth interviews "gives voice" to their life experiences, providing entrée into cultures beyond our own, suggests a research technology that enhances practice across culture, race, and ethnicity. In other words, in-depth interviews provide an authentic path to understanding diversity, with important implications for practice among underserved and oppressed populations (DePoy, Hartman, & Haslett, 1999).

Research practitioners attempt to shift authority away from themselves to their informants when they use in-depth interviews. Clients come to social workers because the latter are "experts" who can help the clients. However, when a researcher recruits people to interview, the informants become the experts. The interviewer's ability to transfer authority to them is essential to produce credible and trustworthy information about a social problem, at least from the perspectives of particular interviewees. The researcher seeks to uncover and amplify study participants' perspectives in an in-depth interview (Rapp, Kisthardt, Growdy, & Hanson, 1994). When Spradley (1979) rejects the terms *subject* and *respondent* in qualitative interviewing and says that *informants* is the preferred label for people interviewed by the researcher, he is advocating an idealized shift in status, authority, and expertise.

On a more practical note, in-depth interviews are much less standardized than other data collection methods because of interview variability and interactive effects between interviewers and informants. Conducting interviews is expensive, particularly if a design requires hiring interviewers, training, and paying for their time and travel. Interviewing is labor intensive. Recording, transcribing, and coding data are time-consuming, complex, and often painfully slow. Furthermore, even a small sample of informants might be difficult to find.

DETERMINING THE DEGREE OF STRUCTURE FOR THE INTERVIEW

In a study that uses in-depth interviews, the researcher decides how structured the interview will be in advance. Typically, the qualitative researcher (Patton, 1990; Tutty et al., 1996) differentiates among three structural types based on their predetermined levels of organization and construction: structured, unstructured, and in-depth interviews. With structured interviews or "standardized open-ended interviews" (Patton, 1990, p. 284), the researcher decides what questions will be asked and the order in which the interviewer will ask them. The structured format imposes the researcher's "template" about a problem on the interview. The more structured the interview, the closer the method of observation to quantitative study, providing a narrow platform for participants to respond in their own words (York, 1998). Although a high level of structure might be appropriate when different people are conducting interviews or with novice interviewers (Tutty et al., 1996), flexibility and spontaneity are compromised to collect systematic data across variables from each respondent (Patton, 1990).

Unstructured interviews are at the other end of the continuum. Sometimes called "open-ended interviews," many consider them the best method for delving into the ways in which other people experience and view the world (Tutty et al., 1996). The interviewer does not use a preestablished interview schedule. Instead, before interviews begin, the researcher assumes that the interviewer does not know what variables are important to the informants or even how informants define or operationalize significant variables through language or experience. This stance is more symmetrical and democratic and, therefore, is more likely to provide informants with a more dominant status.

Essentially, interviews vary according to whether the interviewer or the informant guides the direction of the interview, and in an unstructured interview, the informant is more likely to be the guide. The unstructured format relies heavily on the skill of the interviewer to construct questions in situ. The interviewer must have a comprehensive knowledge of the existing literature about the study problem coupled with an underlying willingness to reject any or all prior theories or research findings. Decisions about what to ask informants are made reflectively during the interview, based on fluent knowledge of the topic (Kvale, 1996).

Most in-depth interviews use at least some predetermined system that places them between the extremes of structured and unstructured formats. A degree of instrumentation prevents the interviewer from collecting superfluous or irrelevant information and avoids overlooking important questions. Specific techniques enable the interviewer to maintain control over the interview with minimum instrumentation. Checklists, such as the one developed in Poindexter and Linsk's (1999) study of HIV-related stigma among older African American caregivers, can ensure that the interviewer will cover all desired topics. Specific questions or key words developed in advance can accomplish the same objective. With some minimal prompts, the sequencing of questions can flow naturally from material that informants present. Another guide that provides a structural aid in grounded theory studies is examples from previous interviews for the informant to confirm, elaborate, or discard.

QUESTIONS, PROBES, AND SEQUENCING
IN THE IN-DEPTH INTERVIEW

Unarmed with a conventional data collection instrument and faced with the task of entering the worldview of another person can be a daunting experience. A major concern for novice interviewers and human subjects committees alike is the content of the in-depth interview itself. However, the interviewer has an opportunity (and a responsibility) from the start to tell the informant the purpose of the interview. Generally, human subjects committees request a "script" for their review process to make certain that participants understand the nature of the study and any risks involved in their participation. The scripts contain assurances about anonymity, how the findings will be used, discussion about the limits of confidentiality, and how the researcher intends to protect the participants' confidentiality.

Although the idea of a scripted beginning for an in-depth interview might seem to contradict the purpose of selecting this approach in the first place, it allows the interviewer to accomplish several important things. First, a good script is written as it would be spoken in a conversational style, appropriate to the context and in language easily understood by the particular informants. It shows the interviewer's respect for informants' special knowledge about an issue and appreciation for what might become a conversation about a difficult subject. It suggests that the interviewer wants to listen. The script should establish the boundaries of the relationship to those of researcher and informant. If the researcher wants the interview to be audiotaped or videotaped, then this is the point at which the interviewee may be asked to sign a consent form.

Besides managing the tasks required for protecting the participant, the first minutes of the interview set the ground rules and tone for participants to guide the direction of the in-depth discussion. Ideally, the script should lead seamlessly into a "grand tour" question that gives the informant the opportunity to provide wide-ranging information and a platform from which to go forward. An example of a grand tour question that bridges a scripted beginning and elicits the informant's story might be the following: "As I said when we began, I want to hear about the ways in which caring for your granddaughter has affected you. Could you tell me about a typical day with her?"

Grand tour questions are 1 of some 30 types of questions that Spradley (1979) identifies for ethnographic interviewing. Questions can be distilled into four broad types: grand tour, example, structural, and contrast questions (Franklin & Jordan, 1997). With example questions, the interviewer asks the informant to provide an instance of a single act, event, or category. Continuing with the previous example, following an informant's description of a caregiving day, the questioner might ask, "You said you take your granddaughter outside depending on how poorly she looked that day. Can you tell me about a time when you thought she looked too bad to go out?" Structural questions ask the informant to group items into particular sets. Contrast questions ask about the similarities and differences in actual events or symbols that the person uses, for example, "You said there weren't a lot of people you told about your granddaughter's AIDS. What words would you use to describe a person you might tell? What words would you use to describe a person you would be unlikely to tell?"

Patton (1990) adds affective-type questions to these categories. Opinion or value questions are aimed at understanding how a person thinks about and interprets his or her experiences. Feeling questions determine the emotional reactions of the informant. Knowledge questions ask what information a person has. The interviewer also can ask about the sensory experiences of the informant, for example, "When you have to take your granddaughter out on a day when she looks bad, what do people say to you?"

Probes are simply follow-up questions that help the interviewer to go deeper into the interviewee's responses. Although the word *probe* might sound invasive, probes are ideally offered in a natural conversational style to give the informant cues to give more information or to continue talking in more depth. Probes can be nonverbal or verbal so that simply leaning forward or nodding one's head slightly can convey a desire to hear more. The interviewer might need more information because he or she cannot understand what an informant is communicating. This can be resolved by asking the interviewee to restate what he or she said or by seeking additional information or a clarifying example (Patton, 1990).

Although no fixed rules exist about the sequencing of questions in the body of the interview itself, beginning with descriptive questions is useful. Grand tour questions are an excellent way in which to begin the interview. What follows can fill out the initial picture that the informant presents. As is often suggested with survey questionnaires, demographic questions are best introduced at the end of the interview.

SAMPLING AND RECRUITING RESPONDENTS FOR THE IN-DEPTH INTERVIEW

In-depth interviews in qualitative studies involve nonprobability sampling. External validity, or the ability to generalize study findings beyond study participants using inferential statistics, is not the objective of in-depth interviews. Sample specificity, rather than a representative sample, is the important factor. Determining the important characteristics of informants and locating people who match them is important, not developing a large sample size.

However, in these studies, research participants must have specific characteristics. They should be able to provide useful and reliable information about the problem under study. Therefore, sampling decisions are purposive and specific to each study. The only regulation is that informants are able to know the problem under study from personal experiences. They also have the capacity and willingness to express those experiences to another person. Standards for the selection process reflect prior scholarship and practical considerations. Usually, the researcher establishes specific criteria generated from study of the particular issue at hand. From a practical point of view, the researcher must consider how to find informants. By necessity, recruitment strategies generally involve convenience sampling.

Other sampling strategies used to identify informants are accidental and snowball sampling in which the researcher finds informants through referrals from other informants. Many qualitative studies attempt to retrieve information from oppressed groups, that is, people who are participating in illicit or illegal behavior or who might have other reasons why they do not want to be identified. If a research practitioner has access to such groups as a part of his or her work, then the problem of access is mitigated but raises ethical flags such as the suggestion of coercion. The problems with informant recruitment are reflected in small samples, sample attrition, and the frequent need to expand inclusion criteria in studies using in-depth interviews. For example, in Poindexter and Linsk's (1999) study, the dearth of volunteer informants resulted in the researchers modifying their sampling criteria to a comparable but available sample.

THE ISSUE OF VALIDITY

The notion of validity as applied in inferential research has little application in qualitative research. The objective of in-depth interviewing for qualitative study is to illuminate experience or generate hypotheses and not to test them. The generalizability of study findings, or external validity, is not a consideration. Instead, the qualitative researcher seeks to transfer his or her study results to similar contexts (Reese, Ahern, Nair, O'Faire, & Warren, 1999).

Reese and colleagues (1999) propose that rigor in qualitative study aims for trustworthiness and credibility. The most obvious threat to trustworthy and credible data is the observation method itself. In-depth interviews are subject to distortion, either because informants are reluctant to reveal information or because the interviewer interjects his or her own perspective. One reason given for asking specific questions and establishing preexisting categories in an in-depth interview is to remove human error. However, too much structure can compromise credibility and trustworthiness if researcher bias already is imbedded in predetermined instrumentation.

The best solution is the interviewer's self-monitoring activities. First, questions should be open-ended, neutral, singular, and clear to the informant. Because the objective is to reduce predetermined responses, any questions that influence or program responses need to be avoided. For example, dichotomous questions result in binary responses; they give "either-or" choices, neither of which might express the informant's sentiments. The interviewer must learn the argot of the people interviewed. Sometimes, the interviewer is able to know the language of the informant in advance. Even so, asking for examples of what people mean when they use particular terms is useful. Besides confirming what the interviewer thinks that people mean when they use a particular expression, developing a deeper knowledge of language use can create opportunities to understand content during analysis (Patton, 1990). Another technique to employ during the interview is to seek disconfirming evidence of an initial impression. Self-monitoring includes giving the informant an opportunity to validate notes or transcriptions of taped interviews. The interviewer should show these materials to the informant, who should be able to correct these materials. In particular, this is an opportunity in which the informant can be encouraged to use his or her own words to enhance clarity.

Triangulation is a technique that uses different sources of data to confirm or disconfirm consistency with what people say during the interview. This provides another route to establishing trustworthy and credible information. However, inconsistent or contradictory responses from one individual or among individual cases can advance knowledge. Contradictions between what people say and information from other empirical or scholarly sources is potentially informative. On the one hand, they might reveal internal conflicts or true inconsistencies in perception. For example, the behavior of respondents in Poindexter and Linsk's (1999) study showed that people change their behavior according to the contexts in which they find themselves. Here, the women were very particular about those to whom they would disclose their caregiver status. More significantly, however, contradictions might reveal a need for further, more focused study.

ETHICAL ISSUES IN THE IN-DEPTH INTERVIEW

In-depth interviews have the potential to elicit strong feelings in informants. They may involve asking people to share critical events in their lives so that it is possible for informants to become overwhelmed with emotion. As pointed out earlier, this reinforces a perceived dilemma for research practitioners and the need to separate therapeutic objectives from the research objectives of the interview. Even in exemplary studies that use in-depth interviews, researchers report problems in maintaining their role. As eloquently expressed by Burnette (1994), "Emotional proximity to interviewees grew considerably over the course of the study. An articulated personal and professional commitment to understand their experiences, to assist when possible . . . , did pose substantial problems" (p. 10).

The desire to reach out to help informants seems to be a reasonable response for people trained as helpers. Social worker practitioners might feel as though they are competent clinicians, but their relationship as researchers needs to focus on gathering data, not on therapeutic intervention. It is unethical for a research interviewer to try to modify change or justify an informant's feelings (Tutty et al., 1996). Also, anticipating such events, or anticipating special needs that might affect such events, is important. A requisite part of voluntary participation in a study is that a participant may withdraw from the study at any point in time. In addition, consistent with social work ethics, the researcher needs to be prepared in advance with referral resources and remember the scope of the relationship established at the start of the interview.

CONCLUSION

The in-depth interview is a widely used observation method in many types of qualitative studies. This chapter reviewed key decision points for the researcher who uses this method, beginning with whether in-depth interviews are consistent with the overall research objectives of a given study. It also discussed interview format, sampling techniques, and participant recruitment. The chapter proposed practical ways in which to manage the issue of internal validity in these observations and special ethical issues in conducting in-depth interviews—both thorny problems for the research practitioner.

Case Example

Poindexter, C. C., & Linsk, N. L. (1999). HIV-related stigma in a sample of HIV-affected older female African American caregivers. *Social Work, 44,* 46-61.

Poindexter and Linsk (1999) conducted a qualitative study of HIV-related stigma among older African American women who were informal caregivers for children or adults with AIDS. These authors made exemplary use of in-depth interviews. First, they framed their methodology around the extensive literature on "AIDS-related stigma" that reflects a deeper level of discrimination and prejudice conferred on AIDS than on other types of illnesses and social problems. They developed the following three broad research questions. What was the evidence of HIV-related stigma among these caregivers? How did this experience affect the caregivers? What are the connections among disclosure of HIV-related status, support, and stigma? The interviews were open-ended but used a checklist as a guide to ensure content comparability.

Poindexter and Linsk (1999) established initial inclusion criteria based on the caregiver's age and self-identification as nonwhite. They sought informants currently caring for their HIV-infected children or grandchildren. They used a convenience sampling method, recruiting study participants by distributing fliers through HIV service agencies. Family members or case managers made referrals. However, the researchers ultimately eased the inclusion requirements. On the one hand, they found recruitment difficult, but they also received "eager" calls from younger or older people caring for persons with AIDS or caring for people who were not their children or grandchildren. The authors' need to expand criteria foreshadowed findings on interviewing participants. Only 1 person who disclosed her role as an HIV caregiver did not experience stigma. The other 18 informants either did not disclose, selectively disclosed, or did not disclose to anyone that they were caring for persons with AIDS. They either feared stigma or had experienced it when they disclosed this status to friends or family. The respondents were very aware of HIV-related stigma, which they expressed when interviewed. This was underscored when, at the start of the interview, one woman expressed concern about using the term *AIDS* in a public place and another initiated the issue of confidentiality even before the interviewer could raise it.

Why did this study make exemplary use of the in-depth interview? First, elderly women of color are an essentially "voiceless" group in our society, and for these women who chose to be caregivers for people with AIDS, the stigma attached to this role suppressed their ability to be heard or their willingness to speak out. Simply put, using in-depth interviews was an effective way in which to understand the worldview of these women and, consequently, to refine the understanding of both their need for services and the apparent reasons why those needs were not addressed—the meticulous avoidance of stigma that the women maintained so as to continue their difficult caregiving role.

The researchers were rigorous in recording the women's responses in their own language. The interviews were recorded on audiotape and transcribed verbatim. The researchers "tried to be true to the words, phrases, styles, and pronunciations of the interviewees to convey the tone and affect of their statements and to preserve the elegance of their expression" (Poindexter & Linsk, 1999, p. 49). Their clarity about the purpose of the interviews and presentation about human subjects issues may be inferred from the findings themselves. The strictness with which the researchers communicated their commitment to maintaining confidentiality enabled participation. It also provided behavioral findings that provided an unanticipated opportunity for triangulation and, consequently, a means of addressing threats to internal validity.

REFERENCES

Bein, A., & Allen, K. (1999). Hand in glove? It fits better than you think. *Social Work, 44,* 274-277.

Burnette, D. (1994). Managing chronic illness alone in late life: Sisyphus at work. In C. K. Riessman (Ed.), *Qualitative studies in social work research* (pp. 5-27). Thousand Oaks, CA: Sage.

DePoy, D. J., Hartman, A., & Haslett, D. (1999). Critical action research: A model of social knowing. *Social Work, 44,* 560-570.

Franklin, G., & Jordan, C. (1997). Qualitative approaches to the generation of knowledge. In R. M. Grinnell, Jr. (Ed.), *Social work research and evaluation: Quantitative and qualitative approaches* (5th ed., pp. 106-140). Itasca, IL: Peacock.

Gilgun, J. F. (1994). Hand into glove: The grounded theory approach to social work practice research. In E. Sherman & W. J. Reid (Eds.), *Qualitative research in social work* (pp. 115-125). New York: Columbia University Press.

Grinnell, R. M., & Unrau, Y. A. (1997). Group designs. In R. M. Grinnell, Jr. (Ed.), *Social work research and evaluation: Quantitative and qualitative approaches* (5th ed., pp. 259-311). Itasca, IL: Peacock.

Hartman, A. (1990). Many ways of knowing. *Social Work, 35,* 3-4.

Kvale, S. (1996). *InterViews: An introduction to qualitative research interviewing.* Thousand Oaks, CA: Sage.

McCracken, G. (1988). *The long interview.* Newbury Park, CA: Sage.

Padgett, D. K. (1998). Does the glove really fit? Qualitative research and clinical social work practice. *Social Work, 43,* 373-381.

Patton, M. Q. (1990). *Qualitative evaluation and research methods* (2nd ed.). Newbury Park, CA: Sage.

Pieper, M. H., & Tyson, K. (1999). Response to Padgett's "Does the Glove Really Fit?" *Social Work, 44,* 278-299.

Poindexter, C. C., & Linsk, N. L. (1999). HIV-related stigma in a sample of HIV-affected older female African American caregivers. *Social Work, 44,* 46-61.

Rapp, C. A., Kisthardt, W., Growdy, E., & Hanson, J. (1994). Amplifying the consumer voice: Qualitative methods, empowerment, and mental health research. In E. Sherman & W. J. Reid (Eds.), *Qualitative research in social work* (pp. 381-395). New York: Columbia University Press.

Reese, D. J., Ahern, R., Nair, S., O'Faire, J. D., & Warren, C. (1999). Hospice access and use by African Americans: Addressing cultural and institutional barriers through participatory action research. *Social Work, 44,* 549-559.

Spradley, J. P. (1979). *The ethnographic interview.* New York: Harcourt Brace Jovanovich.

Tutty, L. M., Rothery, M. A., & Grinnell, R. M., Jr. (1996). *Qualitative research for social workers.* Needham Heights, MA: Allyn & Bacon.

Yegidis, B. L., Weinbach, R. W., & Morrison-Rodriguez, B. (1998). *Research methods for social workers* (3rd ed.). Needham Heights, MA: Allyn & Bacon.

York, R. O. (1998). *Conducting social work research.* Needham Heights, CA: Allyn & Bacon.

CHAPTER EIGHTEEN

Ethnographic Research Methods

CHRISTINE T. LOWERY

*H*umans are striking in their diversity, and ethnography is based on the assumption that "knowledge of all cultures is valuable" (Spradley, 1979, p. 10). Cultural diversity and cultural competence are valued in statements of the National Association of Social Workers and the Council of Social Work Education, and they are essential components of social work practice in a multicultural world. Leigh (1998) uses the ethnographic interview as a process of discovery in social work "to learn about the cultural behavior, values, language, and worldviews of the person" and to inform the process of treatment planning and intervention "congruent with the cultural demands of the person" (p. 79).

Elements of ethnography and ethnographic research methods are braided into social work values and practice. Common to both social work and ethnography are use of self, awareness of biases, exploration of context (person in environment), native's or client's perspective, acknowledgment of different cultural realities and patterns, nonjudgmental attitude, reflection, and process of self-monitoring. Likewise, addiction and recovery are braided into the lives of people with whom social workers collaborate and work. To support the intersections among culture, ethnographic study, and addiction, excerpts from *The Alcoholic Society: Addiction and Recovery of the Self* (Denzin, 1993) provide case examples for this chapter.

The basic purpose for qualitative research is a process of "how best to describe and interpret the experiences of other peoples and cultures" (Lincoln & Denzin, 1994, p. 577). Spradley (1979) describes culture as "the acquired knowledge that people use to interpret experience and generate social behavior" (p. 5). Ethnography is a methodology used to scientifically describe individual cultures and the people-hood within these cultures. Ethnography contributes to social work, among other culture-bound disciplines, for this work of "discovery and description" (p. 17) documents alternative cultural realities of people in their own terms using their own concepts. Agar (1996) explains the ethnographic perspective as (a) "because it is unknown, it must be learned," and (b) "it has a pattern that must be discovered and interrelated with other patterns" in the culture (p. 243).

> Guards and prisoners in jails, patients and physicians in hospitals, the elderly, the various religious groups—all have cultural perspectives. . . . As people move from one cultural scene to another in complex societies, they employ different cultural rules. Ethnography offers one of the best ways to understand these complex features of modern life. It can show the range of cultural differences and how people with diverse perspectives interact. (Spradley, 1979, p. 12)

Ethnography focuses on the "predictable patterns of human thought and behavior" and on the routine patterns of everyday life (Fetterman, 1998, p. 1). Weisner (1996) unabashedly asserts that, in human development, a "cultural place" is the most significant element in the development of a child. Ethnography incorporates a cultural place and, therefore, becomes the "most important method in the study of human development" (p. 306). At a mezzo level, ethnography can describe institutions or organizations and social life within them. Goffman (1961) examines the concept of the "total institution, symbolized by the [physical] barrier to social intercourse with the outside and [barriers to] departure" (p. 4). This concept frames meaning and relevance in his study of social life in a mental hospital. At a macro level, ethnography is a tool for social justice that informs social change in multicultural societies, as discussed later in the chapter.

ETHNOGRAPHY DURING THE PAST CENTURY

From the turn of the 20th century to World War II, ethnography traditionally was associated with the mythical "lone ethnographer" (Rosaldo, 1989, cited in Lincoln & Denzin, 1994) doing years of anthropological fieldwork in native villages. Classical ethnographic texts demonstrated four beliefs: "a commitment to objectivism, a complicity with imperialism, a belief in monumentalism (the ethnography would create a museum-like picture of the culture studied), and a belief in timelessness (what was studied never changed)" (Lincoln & Denzin, 1994, p. 7). In the global arena of the 21st century, beliefs have changed markedly. "Ethnographies do not produce timeless truths. The commitment to objectivism is now in doubt. The complicity with imperialism is openly challenged today, and the belief in monumentalism is a thing of the past" (p. 7).

Writing in 1979, Spradley describes the "ethnographic revolution" overflowing the banks of anthropology "like a stream that rises slowly, then spills over its banks, sending rivulets of water in many directions" (Spradley, 1979, p. iii). During the modernist phase (postwar to the 1970s), social realism produced sociological stories extracted from lives and social problems. Although the researcher as author gained power as a representative of the participant's narrative, the voice of the underclass found potential power (Lincoln & Denzin, 1994, p. 8). Theories from symbolic interactionism to feminism, a diversity of qualitative methods and research strategies, and data collection and analyses, including computer programs, set the context for the next phase of ethnography (1970-1986) or "blurred genres" (p. 9). Geertz (1973) defines this period, including "thick description" anthropological writings, as "interpretations of interpretations" and with a new emphasis on the cultural meanings of the local situation, the usurpation of the role of the researcher as the privileged voice (p. 9). Spradley (1979) gives three examples of ethnography in multicultural societies: the special language and culture of a junior high school in St. Paul, Minnesota; the culture and life view of men who were quadriplegic; and his own ethnographic study, the complex culture of the "skid row alcoholic" (p. iii). More recently, Agar (1996) refers to the "ethno-boom" from nursing, education, and cultural studies to administrative studies, child and family development, and speech communication.

ELEMENTS OF ETHNOGRAPHY

Spradley (1979) suggests that, in multicultural complex societies, ethnography offers a strategy for what Glaser and Strauss (1967) call grounded theory, the "development of theories grounded in empirical data of cultural description" (p. 11). From this perspective, ethnography is "grounded" in that observations in the social context are thought through before existing theory enters the picture. However, grounded theory focuses on coding conditions and concepts and on constant comparison. Ethnography focuses on description; on context; and on comparisons among actors, settings, specificities, and the explanation of the patterns of behavior and relationships among the actors in the culture (Stewart, 1998). Likewise, ethnography is not naturalistic inquiry (Lincoln & Guba, 1985). Participant observation and fieldwork are central in ethnography and are peripheral in naturalistic inquiry.

Participant observation, holism, context sensitivity, sociocultural description, and theoretical connections all are characteristics of ethnography (Stewart, 1998). Components of an ethnographic study require the participation of the researcher in some facet of the culture. For example, Denzin (1993) followed a cohort of clients through a 4-week treatment cycle as one facet of extended fieldwork on alcoholism and recovery. Despite multicultural contexts, narrowly focused research, and a diversity of academic specialties, there is a persistent holism requiring depth, breadth, and comprehensiveness in ethnographic data (Stewart, 1998).

Farella (1996) marks this cultural holism in his ethnography and synthesis of Navajo philosophy and distinguishes between the tasks of fieldwork and ethnography. Farella's premise is that cultural synthesis is accessed through key symbols or unifying themes and concepts. "The task of fieldwork, then, is to seek these key concepts, and the task of ethnography is to explain one's understanding of them" (p. 15). Who in the society (informants) knows these concepts, and how and to whom are concepts transmitted? Within this thematic understanding lies the understanding of the whole of the culture. Without thematic understanding, worldview is treated encyclopedically or anecdotally, a list of detail without unifying themes (p. 15). Holism is present once more in the transformation of data, a process that Wolcott (1994) summarizes as description ("What is going on here?"), analysis ("How do things work?"), and interpretation ("What does it all mean?") (p. 12).

Research is shaped by the professional, personal, and ethnic perspectives of different ethnographers; perspective and orientation shape discovery (Fetterman, 1998). For example, indigenous ethnographers have exposed Western assumptions in anthropological research of previously studied groups. Researchers who are guided by ideational theories explore the world through "ideas, cognitive maps, beliefs, and knowledge" (p. 6). Researchers who use materialist theories see the world through observable behavior patterns (Fetterman, 1998). Theoretical considerations vary depending on the tradition of the researcher. For example, ethnography helps to reconstruct sociological theory; in the anthropological tradition, ethnography is expected to create new concepts (Agar, 1996).

The worlds that ethnographers study change, and so do ethnographers and the authority and responsibility that they must accept. In a world of global business, migration, tourism, and ethnic wars, ethnographers carry additional responsibility for what they say and write, for "politically active 'others' and their enemies now read what we produce" (Agar, 1996, p. 3).

Ethnography can inform opportunities to make social change. Early in the 20th century, ethnographers from the "Chicago school" used social disorganization as their "metaphor." They provided evidence that poverty in the city contributed to "socially disorganized areas that had fewer informal mechanisms for social control" and allowed increased criminal activity. "The social milieu was sick, not the offender" (Thomas, 1993, p. 20). When Spradley (1979) was conducting his study on the social structure of an alcoholism treatment center, his informants asked why he did not study what happened to them in jail, and Spradley broadened his study to include oppression in the jails.

During their first 5 years of work in Chicago, Jane Addams and Hull-House participants developed descriptive and investigative works such as *Hull-House Maps and Papers*. These facts and reflections on poverty and neighborhood broadly informed work on social problems—child labor, working conditions for women, and reforms of juvenile law (Addams, 1910/1990, p. 91). From the Henry Street Settlement House in New York, *The Addict in the Street* (Larner, 1965) exposed the drug culture as seen through the eyes and experiences of neighborhood heroin addicts during the 1950s. This person-in-environment description forced an unaware public to acknowledge the turmoil caused by addiction for humans, their relationships, and their communities (Hall, 1971).

It is imperative that social workers understand the sociopolitical contexts within which social service delivery is organized. After a brief period of systemic community treatment (particularly methadone intervention for heroin addiction) under President Nixon during the 1970s (Massing, 1998), the country moved toward severe law enforcement of drug abuse—the "war on drugs"—during the 1980s. Looking back, Agar (1996) realizes that the ethnographies on the drug world up to that time targeted "junkies." "Nothing in the ethnographies showed how personal-identity struggles might suggest different interventions, not much about how the drug field might rethink its own assumptions, [and] not much about how we might fix policies or institutions rather than individual addicts" (p. 6).

Agar (1996) gives credit to younger ethnographers such as Bourgois (1995), Hamid (1996a, 1996b), and Waterston (1993). These ethnographers demonstrated the role of the chemical within the contextual power of the political economy and the "unholy alliances with criminal and legitimate markets and governments in ways that us old-timers never noticed with our focus on the streets" (Agar, 1996, p. 5).

DOING ETHNOGRAPHY

How does one do ethnography? Where does one start? For the novice, Spradley wrote two overlapping texts that include site selection, data collection, and domain analysis: *The Ethnographic Interview* (Spradley, 1979) and *Participant Observation* (Spradley, 1980). (Spradley's ethnographic interview is summarized in the next section.) The more advanced researcher should consider Agar's (1996) *The Professional Stranger*, which includes a short section on funding for research. Detail on personal experience in fieldwork is found in *Journeys Through Ethnography: Realistic Accounts of Fieldwork*, edited by Lareau and Shultz (1996). The epilogue includes recommended literature including the *Journal of Contemporary Ethnography* and *An-*

thropology and Education Quarterly, which carry high-quality ethnographic articles.

Learning the Culture

If ethnographic purpose is to learn and understand the culture, then the ethnographer needs good informants and ethnography requires the commitment of both. Spradley (1979) describes the process of establishing rapport as apprehension, exploration, cooperation, and participation (p. 79). A respectful balance of "a thoroughly enculturated informant and a thoroughly unenculturated ethnographer" is recommended (p. 50). First, informants must currently be part of the culture and must have been part of the culture for a long enough time to know the "culture so well [that] they no longer think about it" (p. 47). Because ethnography requires hours of interviews over a period of time, informants' ability to provide the time is critical. Tandem informants who know the same cultural situations might be considered, for example, multiple caregivers of an elderly patient who work different shifts or work in different capacities. Informants can use their cultural knowledge and language to describe events and actions, or they can use "folk theory" to offer analyses and interpretations of these events (p. 52). Spradley cautions the novice ethnographer about informants who use analytical insights from social science and psychology to give meaning to their behavior. It is the insider's perspective that is the focus in ethnography, not a theoretical overlay or explanation drawn from the outside.

Spradley's (1979) ethnographic interview is more formal than informal. Both researcher and informant understand that there is intent and purpose in talking with one another. Whereas the informant is the teacher, the ethnographer directs the course of the interview toward discovery of the cultural knowledge that the informant holds. Explanations from the first interview through the last one are necessary. From informant to ethnographer, cultural explanations (teaching) are required. From ethnographer to informant, project explanations and recording explanations are necessary ("I want to study _____ from your point of view"; "I'm going to write this down"). Interview explanations are required when the informant is asked to draw maps or sort terms written on cards. Critical to an ethnographer's understanding are native language explanations ("If you were talking to a customer, what would you say?"). No analysis or ability to translate was requested (translation competence), only samples of the language (pp. 58-60).

Spradley (1979) identifies more than 30 types of ethnographic questions. Three specific types and their functions are summarized. Descriptive questions are the most common ("Could you describe _____?"). One specific type of descriptive question is the "grand tour" question, a broad description of a cultural situation, for example, an alcoholism treatment center or a series of events. The grand tour question expands on a basic question, allowing the informant time to think (p. 62). Spradley gives an example of the grand tour question from a study of the culture of cocktail waitresses in a college bar:

> Could you start at the beginning of an evening, say a typical night at Brady's Bar, and describe to me what goes on? Like, what do you do when you first arrive, [and] then what do you do next? What are some of the things you would have to do on most nights, and then go on through the evening right up until you walk out the door and leave the bar? (p. 62)

Looking for Patterns and Interrelationships

Ethnographic analysis is a search for the parts of a culture, the relationships among the parts, and their relationships to the whole (Spradley, 1980, p. 116). For example, without understanding the relationship among the stars that form the Big Dipper, the uninformed might see random stars. Although there are many ways in which to analyze data (Agar, 1996), Spradley's domain analysis—"a relational theory of meanings" (p. 97)—is briefly described. What are the native terms used in the field notes? What are the relationships among these terms? What can be hypothesized from these relationships? Semantic relationships begin to address the question, "What are the patterns that form the system of symbols that constitute a culture?" (p. 97). Spradley (1979) emphasizes a related principle in the ethnographic interview: "Don't ask for meaning, ask for use":

> When I asked tramps to give me examples of how they used the term "days hanging," they revealed relationships between this term and others like "suspended sentence," "dead time," "beating a drunk charge," "rabbit," etc. Listen for use, not meaning; this principle leads directly to decoding the full meaning of symbols in any culture. (p. 97)

Domains are the first unit of analysis. The domain structure includes cover terms, included terms, and semantic relationships. First, the ethnographer examines a sample of verbatim notes from an ethnographic interview, looking for folk terms that name things (Spradley, 1979, p. 104). Folk terms may be used to name more than one thing; for example, trees include pines, aspens, and oaks. These equivalents would be identified as cover terms (types of trees). Next, the ethnographer returns to the data and searches for other terms that could be included as types of trees. This process is repeated until domains in the culture have been tentatively identified. Structural questions are used to confirm or disconfirm the domains hypothesized ("Are there other types of trees?"). Spradley cautions the ethnographer to consistently use folk terms for the entire analysis rather than switching to analytic terms that could produce a "shallow analysis" (p. 102).

Domain analysis identifies categories of native thought to produce a basic overview of the cultural scene under study (Spradley, 1979, p. 117). This process is similar to identifying domains but incorporates semantic relationships. Strict inclusion and means-end are two of the nine universal semantic relationships that are useful in domain analysis. Strict inclusion (X is a type of Y) focuses on nouns, and means-end (X is a way in which to do Y) focuses on verbs. In reviewing the ethnographic interview, the search now is for cover terms and included terms that fit the semantic relationship. For example, hitting someone is a type of aggression (X is a kind of Y). Included terms are discovered with the structural question, "Are there different types of aggression?" A range of behaviors, from cursing at someone to different forms of aggressive driving, may be included. In a means-end example, walking is a way in which to get exercise (X is a way in which to do Y; "Are there different ways in which to get exercise?"). Again, a list of domains and their semantic relationships are made. The process is repeated until domains are exhausted. Spradley (1979, 1980) is recommended reading for further exploration of componential analysis (contrasting domains), taxonomy, and theme analysis.

ETHNOGRAPHY: CASE STUDY

Lofland and Lofland (1995) suggest that the goal in naturalistic research is to collect the "richest possible data . . . a wide and diverse range of information collected over a relatively prolonged period of time" (p. 16). Wolcott (1994) takes a stance at the other end of the continuum: "The critical task in qualitative research is not to accumulate but to winnow. What is the essence? How can one reveal those essences with sufficient context?" (p. 35). Denzin's (1993) ethnography on the cultures of addiction and recovery and Alcoholics Anonymous (AA) accomplishes both. Denzin's fieldwork is broad and meets Lofland and Lofland's (1995) requirements for face-to-face interaction to explore the minds of the participants in their settings and "intimate familiarity" with the settings (p. 17). Denzin's (1993) analysis also finds the essence with sufficient context to meet Wolcott's (1994) requirements.

As a beginning point in an ethnography, Spradley (1979) poses the question, "What are the cultural meanings people are using to organize their behavior and interpret their experience?" (p. 93). Denzin (1993) specifically asks, "How do ordinary men and women live and experience the alcoholic self [that] active alcoholism produces? How is the recovering self lived into existence?" (p. xxix). Denzin describes his work as ethnographic including participant observation, open-ended interviewing, triangulation, and the study of biographical and autobiographical accounts of the recovery process. Denzin's goal was to discover the "universal or generic structures" of recovery. He asks his audience to evaluate his interpretations. Do the interpretations explain and reveal recovery as a lived experience? Are the interpretations based on "thickly contextualized materials" that are grounded in time, history, and biographical material (triangulation)? Do the interpretations make use of previous understandings of the recovery process? Do the interpretations make meaning that contributes to understanding (p. 11)?

Fieldwork is the essence of ethnography and employs "two interrelated methods most closely associated with the naturalistic preference for direct apprehension: participant observation and intensive interviewing" (Lofland & Lofland, 1995, p. 17). From 1980 to 1985, Denzin (1993) observed more than 2,000 open and closed AA meetings in a medium-sized community in the eastern part of the country. In 1985, AA, a worldwide organization of recovering alcoholics, had an estimated membership of more than 1 million in some 58,000 groups in 110 countries (p. 7). The social world of alcoholics that Denzin observed included more than 200 regular members who reported near or continuous sobriety over different lengths of time. Members participated in a variety of groups—two women's groups, one gay and lesbian group, a young people's group, and seven Narcotics Anonymous groups. Denzin included description from "stories of self that active and recovering alcoholics bring to [AA]" (p. 7) and discussions with alcoholics and their families in Al-Anon and Alateen.

Denzin (1993) interviewed a broad range of treatment personnel and professionals working with alcoholics. He also observed process in three substance abuse treatment centers and detoxification programs. At each center, the treatment interventions were multimodal, abstinence was the treatment goal, and the "Twelve Steps" of AA were used, taking clients through the first five steps. Each center treated both males and females, had a three-to-one staff-to-client ratio, and had 20 to 60 beds. The two smaller programs were observed for 4 years, and a cohort of clients was followed through a 4-week treatment cycle in the largest treatment center. Denzin's study of published material on alcoholism and AA rounded out his fieldwork.

Description, Analyses, and Meaning

Denzin (1993) synthesized his data into multiple analytical and descriptive themes and processes, from lay theory and temporality to slips and relapses. Three broad interpretive frameworks are summarized as examples: the six theses of alcoholism and recovery, the paradoxes of treatment, and the three languages of treatment. The six theses of alcoholism and recovery defined the alcoholic's relationship to the world. The premise for the theses is instability and inner emptiness of the alcoholic self, a self that reflects early family experiences of loss, abuse, and addiction:

1. *Thesis of temporality of self:* The alcoholic is out of synchronization with others. Alcohol dulls or speeds the emotional and thought processes. Alcoholism is a disease of time.

2. *Thesis of relational structures of self:* Alcohol is that which "joins interactants in combative, competitive, negative, hostile relationships" or "ressentiment."
3. *Thesis of emotionality of self:* Painful and negative feelings experienced on a daily basis are filtered through the "altered temporal consciousness [that] alcohol creates."
4. *Thesis of bad faith:* "Structures of denial, self-deception, lying, and bad faith thus lie at the heart of the alcoholic's alcoholism."
5. *Thesis of self-control:* To prove self-control, the alcoholic drinks.
6. *Thesis of self-surrender:* Recovery begins when the alcoholic "surrenders to false self-pride, breaks through systems of bad faith, and comes to accept his or her alcoholism." (pp. 6-7)

Denzin (1993) identifies the paradoxes of treatment, which form the culture of treatment centers in his ethnography of the treatment process:

1. Alcoholism is an illness—physical, mental, and spiritual—that cannot be cured.
2. The alcoholic and his or her relationship with the world is at the center of the alcoholic's illness. The alcoholic drinks to be able to confront the world in which he or she lives.
3. If the alcoholic is at the center of his or her illness, then only the alcoholic can treat his or her illness. The alcoholic is the patient and the therapist.
4. The alcoholic's illness is emotional. The alcoholic lives within an emotional prison that must have expression, and yet he or she lacks the language of emotion. To become healthier, the alcoholic must "undergo painful exposure of the buried structures of self that [he or] she has kept hidden from [himself or] herself and from others." (p. 190)
5. The paradox of uniqueness is stripped away to recover the self that has been given away to alcohol. "The recovery of self through emotionality is the underlying premise of treatment. . . . Treatment provides the context of discovery for the recovery of the self" (pp. 189, 191).

Denzin (1993) analyzes the language of treatment focusing on key terms. A sample of key terms is taken from the client's workbook at the northern treatment center: communication, addiction, aftercare, Alcoholics Anonymous, blackout, chemical dependency, congruence, confronting, treatment plan, and the like. Although the language of emotion—blaming, placating, distracting, acceptance, denial, and the like—was not defined, it "established a context for an emotional language of self" through which the clients had to feel their way:

Two languages of emotionality exist side by side in treatment. The first is the meta-language of emotionality, a language about the language of emotions and treatment [technical language of treatment]. This language includes such terms as head-tripping, leveling, and confronting. Second, there is the language of direct and indirect emotionality, expressed in the phrase "learn to communicate on a feeling level." At this feeling level, terms require no definition[s]. At the meta level, definitions are required and are given. (p. 195)

How are these two languages interrelated? The technical language provides the framework within which the emotional work takes place. The emotional language is further reduced to language about feelings (metaphors) and language of feelings (hurt, anger, guilt, and resentment—emotions that are likely to lead to relapse; Denzin, 1993, p. 196). Finally, the language of AA is the third language of treatment, with terms such as "our lives have become unmanageable," "a power greater than ourselves," "personal inventory," and "making amends" (p. 197).

It is the framework of language (meta-language, emotionality, and AA) that permits the work of socialization and identity construction starting in treatment groups:

1. Naming the alcoholic self or "I am an alcoholic"
2. Learning the language of emotion
3. Forming the alcoholic bond with others in the group
4. Starting a reverse stigmatization process

All of these solidify a collective identity (Denzin, 1993, p. 239).

When the alcoholic leaves the safety and timelessness of the treatment center and steps into a social void armed only with a new vocabulary and a new sense of self, AA offers a fellowship in which the primary identity is "being an alcoholic" (Denzin, 1993, p. 243). Here, emotional understanding through shared experiences supports sobriety. However, failure is not a return to drinking. Failure, essentially, is the loss of the collective identity.

This is the work that ethnography can do. Social workers must then serve as the conduit for bringing this knowledge to social work education and practice.

REFERENCES

Addams, J. (1990). *Twenty years at Hull-House.* Chicago: University of Illinois Press. (Originally published in 1910)

Agar, M. (1996). *The professional stranger* (2nd ed.). San Diego: Academic Press.

Bourgois, P. (1995). *In search of respect.* Cambridge, UK: Cambridge University Press.

Denzin, N. K. (1993). *The alcoholic society: Addiction and recovery of the self.* New Brunswick, NJ: Transaction Publishers.

Farella, J. R. (1996). *The main stalk: A synthesis of Navajo philosophy.* Tucson: University of Arizona Press.

Fetterman, D. M. (1998). *Ethnography: Step by step* (2nd ed.). Thousand Oaks, CA: Sage.

Geertz, C. (1973). *The interpretation of cultures.* New York: Basic Books.

Glaser, B. G., & Strauss, A. L. (1967). *The discovery of grounded theory: Strategies for qualitative research.* Chicago: Aldine.

Goffman, E. (1961). *Asylums: Essays on the social situation of mental patients and other inmates.* New York: Anchor Books.

Hall, H. (1971). *Unfinished business: In neighborhood and nation.* New York: Macmillan.

Hamid, A. (1996a). *The political economy of drugs: Vol. 1. Ganja and the Rastafarians in San Fernando, Trinidad—A precapitalist mode of production.* New York: Guilford.

Hamid, A. (1996b). *The political economy of drugs: Vol. 2. The cocaine smoking epidemic of 1981-1991 in New York City's low-income neighborhoods.* New York: Guilford.

Lareau, A., & Shultz, J. (Eds.). (1996). *Journeys through ethnography: Realistic accounts of fieldwork.* Boulder, CO: Westview.

Larner, J. (Ed.). (1965). *The addict in the street.* New York: Grove Press.

Leigh, J. W. (1998). *Communicating for cultural competence.* Needham Heights, MA: Allyn & Bacon.

Lincoln, Y. S., & Denzin, N. K. (1994). The fifth moment. In N. K. Denzin & Y. S. Lincoln (Eds.), *Handbook of qualitative research* (pp. 7-8, 575-586). Thousand Oaks, CA: Sage.

Lincoln, Y. S., & Guba, E. G. (1985). *Naturalistic inquiry.* Beverly Hills, CA: Sage.

Lofland, J., & Lofland, L. H. (1995). *Analyzing social settings: A guide to qualitative observation and analysis.* Belmont, CA: Wadsworth.

Massing, M. (1998). *The fix.* New York: Simon & Schuster.

Rosaldo, R. (1989). *Culture and truth: Renewing the anthropologist's search for meaning.* Boston: Beacon.

Spradley, J. P. (1979). *The ethnographic interview.* New York: Holt, Rinehart & Winston.

Spradley, J. P. (1980). *Participant observation.* New York: Holt, Rinehart & Winston.

Stewart, A. (1998). *The ethnographer's method.* Thousand Oaks, CA: Sage.

Thomas, J. (1993). *Doing critical ethnography.* Newbury Park, CA: Sage.

Waterston, A. (1993). *Street addicts in the political economy.* Philadelphia: Temple University Press.

Weisner, T. S. (1996). Why ethnography should be the most important method in the study of human development. In R. Jessor, A. Colby, & R. A. Shweder (Eds.), *Ethnography and human development: Context and meaning in social inquiry* (pp. 305-326). Chicago: University of Chicago Press.

Wolcott, H. F. (1994). *Transforming qualitative data: Description, analysis, and interpretation.* Thousand Oaks, CA: Sage.

CHAPTER NINETEEN

Participant Observation

R. KEVIN GRIGSBY

$\mathbf{A}$ ll research involves observation, whether before, during, or after an event or events. The scope of observation in social work research ranges from the passive viewing of everyday social behavior to observation during the active participation of the researcher in real-life situations. Becker and Geer (1957) define participant observation as "that method in which the observer participates in the daily life of the people under study, either openly in the role of researcher or covertly in some disguised role" (p. 28). Engaging in participant observation requires the researcher to (a) engage in activities appropriate to the situation and (b) observe the activities, people, and physical aspects of the situation (Spradley, 1980, p. 54).

MORE THAN OBSERVATION, MORE THAN PARTICIPATION

Observation is essential to science. Observation from an objective perspective is a basic tenet of the scientific method in that it is essential to control for the subjective experience of the researcher having undue influence on the outcome of hypothesis testing. The participant observer does not deny the importance of objectivity in the logical positivist paradigm. Rather, participant observation uses the subjective experience of the researcher to gain a better understanding of social phenomena. It is anything but "objective," whereas observation (alone) could take place with a very high degree of objectivity. A researcher might conceal himself or herself so as to observe the behavior of persons in public places. A behavior or set of behaviors might be observed, be counted, be measured in duration, and have some meaning ascribed to them. Participant observation would differ markedly in that the subjective experience of the researcher not only would be encountered but also would be explored. In other words, the researcher works to maintain the role of being "inside and outside" the experience simultaneously.

To participate is to "take part" (join or share) with others. In some situations, only the researcher is aware of the role that he or she plays beyond that of participant when other research participants assume that the researcher is genuine in the participation behavior. The researcher may be genuine in participation but is actively observing at the same time. Unlike other participants in the activities and situation, the "researcher as observer" is active in a cognitive process of recording events, behaviors, and consequences with the intention of analyzing context, significance, and implications.

Observation of social phenomena, such as human behavior in a social/cultural context, is only the beginning of coming to an understanding of the phenomenon being studied. Observation may be combined with in-depth interviewing. Typically, those persons being observed are asked to account for or to explain their behavior and/or the behavior of other participants. Interviewing participants is one way of accessing information beyond what has been observed, and that is related to the "meaning" of the experience or the purpose of the behavior. Participant observation does not exclude direct interviewing of participants and may make extensive use of interviewing as a means for data collection. The process of interviewing in participant observation is within the experiential context, allowing for a more in-depth understanding of how what has been communicated is related to what has been observed. Becker and Geer (1957) state, "This wealth of information and impression sensitizes him to subtleties which might pass unnoticed in an interview and forces him to raise continually new and different questions" (p. 32).

Participant observation is a type of field research or "fieldwork." Fieldwork is the study of "persons or groups in their own environment and without manipulation for research purposes" (U.S. Department of Health and Human Services, 1993, p. 4-4). It is important to note that "all participant observation is fieldwork, but not all fieldwork is participant observation (Bernard, 1988, p. 148). For example, going from door to door to survey residents of a neighborhood is field research, but it is not participant observation—unless the researcher is studying the process of surveying and is participating as a surveyor so as to observe the survey process firsthand. Gold (1958) describes a continuum of roles in fieldwork consisting of the "complete observer," the "observer as participant," the "participant as observer," and the "complete participant."

In relation to the individuals being studied, the *complete observer* consciously takes on a passive role as a data collector. If the participants are aware of the presence of the researcher, then their view is that the researcher is participating as an observer only. However, the observer also may employ covert methods (observing surreptitiously) to collect data. The complete observer may employ the use of audio or video recording of an event or events, either with the knowledge and informed consent of the participants or covertly without their consent or knowledge. One advantage of audio or video recording is that the researcher has a permanent record that can be revisited (ex post facto) for continued data analysis. Of course, recording of participants, especially in a covert manner (as "an eavesdropper with a camera"), raises a number of ethical issues related to the "informed consent" of the participants. (Ethical issues are addressed later in this chapter.)

The *observer-as-participant* role typically is used in studies where the researcher has contact with participants that is of a time-limited nature. The researcher is constrained in the depth of relationship that can be formed with participants. However, in-depth interviewing often is employed in collecting data. Although there are limits to the value of information collected using this role, the findings might be of great utility in understanding social phenomena. However, the researcher must be cautious in interpreting data. By having limited contact with participants and forming relationships that are somewhat superficial, there is a much greater chance of overlooking important data or of misinterpreting data. A good example of using this role to study "hustling" (prostitution by young males) in Times Square in New York City can be found in McNamara (1994). Ware, Tugenberg, Dickey, and McHorney (1999) describe the use of this role in their study of continuity of care in mental health services.

The *participant-as-observer* role describes studies in which the researcher participates with the other participants while observing firsthand. The researcher is immersed in the activities of the participants, usually through adoption or assignment of some role. Typically, participants are aware that the researcher is "more than a participant" and that the researcher will be working to record and understand what is "going on." Snow, Benford, and Anderson (1986) offer an explicit discussion of the roles that might be adopted by the researcher including that of "credentialed expert." (See the case example at the end of this chapter, or Grigsby, 1992, for a description of how this role was used in a study of homeless and runaway children in shelter care.)

Adoption of the role of *complete participant* often is used in studying more controversial topics. In this role, the identity of the participant as researcher is concealed from the other participants, whose expectation is that the participant as researcher is more or less "the same" as they are—an ordinary person engaging in similar behavior. This role often is used in studying social deviance because it might be the only means for observing the phenomenon without having an effect on the phenomenon under consideration. The sociologist Laud Humphreys was honored with the C. Wright Mills Award from the Society for the Study of Social Problems for his study of impersonal sexual behavior between men in public places (Humphreys, 1975). In this very controversial research study, Humphreys posed as a "lookout" in a public restroom known as a *tearoom*. In this role, he was a voyeur but also served the function of alerting the men engaged in sexual behavior if a police officer or another authority figure was in view and was likely to enter the public restroom. Humphreys comments on his role as being "a natural one in those settings" and states that he was "a true participant" but did not engage in sex with the participants (p. 227).

PARTICIPANT OBSERVATION IN ETHNOGRAPHY

Participant observation describes one of the techniques used in ethnographic research. However, ethnography goes beyond the scope of participant observation in that "ethnography is the work of describing a culture. The central aim of ethnography is to understand another way of life from the native point of view" (Spradley, 1980, p. 3). Typically, the researcher is immersed in the culture for "a long period of intimate study and residence in a small, well-defined community, knowledge of the spoken language, and the employment of a wide range of observational techniques including prolonged face-to-face contacts with members of the local group" (Conklin, 1968, p. 172). The researcher uses participant observation to truly understand "what the world is like to people who have learned to see, hear, speak, think, and act in ways that are different" (Spradley, 1980, p. 3). (See Lowery's chapter in this handbook [Chapter 17] for an in-depth discussion of ethnographic research methods in social work.)

A STRATEGY FOR LEARNING ABOUT BEHAVIOR

By immersing himself or herself in an environment and a situation, the researcher is better able to have experiences similar to the experiences of the persons native to the environment and situation. Reactivity is reduced as well because the researcher is less "out of place" and is, in a sense, camouflaged in the role that has been adopted. Experiencing the environment and situation as a native leads to better and more refined research questions. When describing an experience that was comical or humorous, one might find that the humor is lost in relating the story to others who were not present for the initial event. "I guess you had to be there" is used to explain that the humor was implicit in the observer's experience. The meaning of social phenomena often is implicit in the experience of the participant observer. To communicate the meaning to others, the researcher must develop a means for capturing and describing the experience so that it makes sense to others who were not present.

Participant observation allows the researcher to experience events and situations over time. This allows the researcher to identify patterns or, conversely, anomalies that might be necessary for understanding a series of events. In fact, the researcher might be a "credentialed expert" on a topic yet lack experience within the social environment.

STRENGTHS OF PARTICIPANT OBSERVATION

One of the greatest strengths of participant observation is the comprehensive nature of its perspective. As the researcher "lives" the experience, the richness of the data can be captured in the description of the experience as well as in the identification of discrete variables and their relationships. Becker (1958) suggests that participant observation is used when the researcher is "interested in understanding a particular organization or substantive problem rather than demonstrating relations between abstractly defined variables" (p. 653). In other words, participant observation lends itself to the study of events or behaviors that are best understood within their natural setting. Oversimplification of complex social realities is avoided by the researcher's exposure to "the whole" of the data.

Participant observation is particularly useful for studying events over time or studying a process rather than studying an isolated event or behavior. If the researcher is interested in understanding a problem but is not yet able to pose hypotheses, then participant observation should be considered as a research approach that might help to reveal or generate hypotheses. Bosk (1985) describes the researcher as a "watcher and witness" with two objectives: (a) to provide "an empirically thick description of what happened" (p. 10) and (b) to analyze and interpret this description. Muller (1995) describes five characteristics of the participant observation method that were particularly useful to her in understanding the experiences of physicians in training and their interaction with dying patients. Flexibility, the view of the insider, the context, the process, and what she describes as the "quality of being there," were beneficial in the collection of detailed information of the phenomenon under investigation. Flexibility allows for the constant refinement of questions, changes in observational techniques, and other "midcourse" adjustments that are made on the basis of the subjective participation experience. The view of the insider is used to gain insight into the nature and structure of social reality from the participants' perspective.

The emphasis on context is useful in that it allows the researcher to have a better understanding of the "meaning" of events or behaviors within the social setting. In fact, context often defines the meaning of behaviors and is a necessary data element for truly understanding behaviors. Likewise, the emphasis on process allows for developing an understanding of the meaning of behavior over time. Rather than looking at any particular event in isolation, sustained contact over time allows the researcher to look at a series of events and to understand their interrelatedness. The "quality of being there" over time is related to the emphasis on process but also is useful in improving the quality of data in terms of participants' reactivity. Participants are less likely to change behaviors because of the researcher's presence if the researcher spends a sustained amount of time in the social milieu. As the researcher "blends into the background," participants minimize his or her presence and sometimes forget that a researcher is present.

DRAWBACKS TO THE USE OF PARTICIPANT OBSERVATION

Participant observation might not be appropriate when clearly defined hypotheses have been formed, discrete variables have been defined, or the relationships between discrete variables are in question. External validity (generalizability) might be limited because rigorous sampling approaches cannot be used due to the unique social construction of the "natural setting." Although samples of participants sometimes are used in participant observation, those samples typically are prospective rather than randomly selected and representative of a larger population.

Potential biases of the researcher might represent problems in participant observation. Observation from an external point of view is difficult when the researcher is immersed in the situation as a participant. Participation might require so much time and energy that there is not enough time for the researcher to really explore the experience from the observer's point of view. In some cases, the role of the researcher actually is lost to that of the total participant. At other times, the researcher may assume such a strong role as an advocate that any objectivity that might be considered in the role of observer is lost.

Another drawback to the use of participant observation is best described as the problem of "risk" to the researcher. This is particularly true for the researcher studying behaviors that are illegal or may be seen as immoral. Managing danger in violent social contexts (Sluka, 1990) requires energy and investment of the researcher, and this might detract from the overall quality of the experience and the quality of the data collected. The researcher's attention on avoiding danger disallows the appropriate focus of attention on what is happening in the social environment. The subjective experience of the researcher might be influenced too strongly by the threat of bodily harm to yield meaningful findings. Lee (1995) describes research efforts involving participant observation with substance abusers, gangs, and other populations or situations that might present imminent physical danger to participant observers.

ETHICAL DILEMMAS IN PARTICIPANT OBSERVATION

As with any research approach, ethical dilemmas are likely to arise as the researcher participates with the research participants. Strictly maintaining the anonymity of participants might be impossible if the researcher is truly immersed in the milieu of the study in the role of participant as observer or total participant (Gold, 1958) because the researcher will come to know the identities of individuals and, at times, intimate details of their lives.

On the other hand, anonymous observation does not imply the same level of risk for research participants. Federal standards regulating research with human subjects exempt the anonymous observation of persons in public places:

> Where the subjects are adults, research of this type is exempt from IRB [institutional review board] review unless the information obtained is recorded in such a manner that subjects can be identified, and the information obtained could reasonably place the subjects at risk of criminal or civil liability or be damaging to the subjects' financial standing, employability, or reputation. (U.S. Department of Health and Human Services, 1993, p. 4-7)

In most cases, it would be difficult, if not impossible, to engage in participant observation and simultaneously maintain the anonymity of research participants, at least to the researcher. A researcher proposing the use of participant observation should understand that his or her presence alone would present some risk for research participants in most situations pertinent to social work research. One of the inherent problems of participant observation is that the researcher might observe illegal acts taking place (e.g., prostitution, use of intravenous drugs, domestic violence). As a witness to a crime, the researcher may be asked to testify as to what he or she observed. The researcher, under the power of a subpoena, may be asked to produce research records including field notes. In most cases of this type, maintenance of confidentiality of participants would be impossible unless the researcher had been guaranteed confidentiality and immunity from prosecution for refusing to testify beforehand. An arrangement of this type is unusual, but the researcher can obtain protection against a subpoena for research data in specific cases as outlined in Section 301(d) of the Public Health Service Act (U.S. Department of Health and Human Services, 1993, pp. 3-32). Even without the threat of having to testify in court, social work researchers are likely to feel obligated to protect the identities of research participants. Section 5.02 of the *Code of Ethics* of the National Association of Social

Workers (NASW, 1996, p. 25) is explicit in statements about the obligations of the social work researcher to participants in research or evaluation in requiring the researcher to follow guidelines for protection of research participants. In most types of research, the researcher is required to engage participants in the process of obtaining informed consent. However, the *Code of Ethics* does allow for "certain forms of naturalistic observation" if "rigorous and responsible review of the research has found it to be justified because of its prospective scientific, educational, or applied value" (p. 25), and there are no feasible alternative procedures that would allow for the research to be done with informed consent of the participants. Humphreys's (1975) study of anonymous sex between adult males was critically acclaimed but also was attacked on the basis that it was not ethically sound. In a revised edition of his book, Humphreys and others respond to the criticism that was generated in relation to his research. A social worker considering the use of overt deception of research participants should carefully consider the potential consequences of his or her actions for both the participants and the researcher.

DATA COLLECTION AND ANALYSIS

Collection of data that are of such a comprehensive nature (sometimes described as "thick and rich") requires a means for organization. If a systemic method for collection and organization of data is not in place at the outset of the study, then the result might be a morass of data that are incomprehensible. Although videotaping or audiotaping might offer the advantage of creating a more permanent record of events, there are many disadvantages, especially if the topic of research involves deviance. Participants might "react" to the presence of a camera or tape recorder by behaving very differently from how they would without the presence of a recording device. In most participant observation research efforts, field notes are the means employed by the researcher to record observations. Simply put, the researcher commits his or her experience to paper in an ongoing organized fashion. Bernard (1988) describes three types of field notes: substantive, methodological, and analytic. Substantive notes represent a sequential account of the researcher's experience including situations, conversations, and activities. Methodological notes consist of the researcher's subjective personal account of the experience. Analytic notes represent the field analysis of data, often leading to other questions or preliminary hypotheses. As data collection proceeds, rudimentary data analysis occurs simultaneously. In some cases, a midcourse adjustment in data collection might be necessary based on preliminary findings.

Yin (1989) offers three principles that are particularly relevant to the data collection process in participant observation. First, the participant observer should use multiple sources of evidence. For example, the researcher should consider speaking with more than one participant or examining documents for content rather than relying on information that comes from one source. Second, the participant observer should work to create a database consisting of notes, copies of documents, narrative accounts, and tables of relevant quantitative data. Third, to increase the reliability of information, a chain of evidence should be constructed as data are collected. Although this is not as important to data collection in isolation, the chain of evidence helps the researcher to understand the continuity of data, especially as data are analyzed post hoc.

Although data collected via participant observation may be qualitative for the most part, quantitative data often are collected as well. For example, data documenting the rate of unplanned discharge from a youth shelter (as in the case study that follows) clearly are quantitative in nature (Grigsby, 1992). Likewise, the amount of money earned through hustling on a given night (McNamara, 1994) and the incidence of physical abuse in an institution for the mentally retarded (Taylor, 1997) are other examples of making use of quantitative data collected during a period of participant observation.

PARTICIPANT OBSERVATION IN SOCIAL WORK RESEARCH

The participant observer role may be well suited for research on a number of topics related to social work including child welfare, family incest treatment (Gilgun, 1992), social interaction in adult day care (Williams & Roberts, 1995), care of the dying (Muller, 1995), rural battering (Websdale, 1998), and psychiatric comorbidity (Padgett & Johnson, 1990).

Case Example

A youth shelter in an urban area provided temporary safe shelter for 13 male and female adolescents between 11 and 17 years of age who had no alternative other than living on the street. During a 1-year period, 44% of those served at the shelter were black and 11% were Hispanic, suggesting that this shelter served a greater percentage of minority youths than did other shelters in the state. Statewide, during one period of 12 months, 49% of the youths entering shelter care had histories of psychiatric hospitalization or residential mental health placement. Not surprisingly, more than 43% of the children discharged during a 1-year period were described as "unplanned" in that youths leaving the shelter either ran away, entered a psychiatric hospital on an emergency basis, or entered a juvenile detention facility.

A team of three experienced mental health professionals (two licensed clinical social workers and a master-level public health professional) was assigned to provide mental health consultation to the shelter. The team members recognized that they had a good understanding of child welfare services and of child mental health services, but they were not familiar with the day-to-day details of shelters for children and youths. The group members agreed that the shelter represented a "culture" of which they had little knowledge or familiarity. To gain an understanding of shelter culture would require one of the consultants to enter as a participant observer to learn directly from the children, youths, and staff through participation in shelter activities, extensive interviewing, and investigation of cultural "artifacts" such as case records, program policies and procedures, and a program logbook.

One consultant (the author of this chapter) entered the shelter for a period of "intimate study" in the role of a "credentialed expert" (Snow et al., 1986). The on-site consultant was introduced as an "expert" from the child guidance clinic with expertise in the areas of mental health and child welfare. In turn, staff members were introduced to the consultant as "experts" on the shelter. Professional literature suggested that problems might be encountered if child care workers perceived researchers as only interested in meeting their own needs and not genuinely interested in the program, its participants, or its staff (Eisikovits, 1991). It was decided that the consultant would remain in the role of participant observer until the staff at the shelter requested assistance.

To process the vast amount of information encountered, the participant observer met with the other consultants on a routine scheduled basis so as to debrief. To avoid creating an atmosphere of mistrust, field notes were written by the consultant only outside of the shelter. Debriefing with the other consultants and reviewing field notes led to an understanding of the shelter culture. In turn, specific suggestions for changes in the shelter program were implemented. Over a period of months, the rate of unplanned discharge was reduced from 43% to 18%. Shelter staff became much more sensitive to the "meaning" of behavior and much more attuned to the needs of shelter residents.

In a typical study of this type, understanding the shelter culture from the "native point of view" (Spradley, 1980, p. 3) would represent the findings of the study. This project applied the findings to the situation at hand. By using the participant observer role to understand the shelter culture, a shift to mental health consultation occurred. Schein (1987) describes this process as the "clinical perspective in fieldwork" (p. 24), where an organization is studied with the goal of applying the knowledge gained to help the organization in some way.

REFERENCES

Becker, H. S. (1958). Problems of inference and proof in participant observation. *American Sociological Review, 23,* 652-660.

Becker, H. S., & Geer, B. (1957). Participant observation and interviewing: A comparison. *Human Organization, 16,* 28-32.

Bernard, H. R. (1988). *Research methods in cultural anthropology.* Newbury Park, CA: Sage.

Bosk, C. (1985, June). The fieldworker as watcher and witness. *Hastings Center Report,* 10-14.

Conklin, H. C. (1968). Ethnography. In D. Sills (Ed.), *The International Encyclopedia of Social Science* (Vol. 14). New York: Crowell, Collier, & Macmillan.

Eisikovits, R. A. (1991). The child care worker as ethnographer. In J. Beker & Z. Eisikovits (Eds.), *Knowledge utilization in residential child and youth care practice* (pp. 275-290). Washington, DC: Child Welfare League of America.

Gilgun, J. F. (1992). Observations in a clinical setting: Team decision-making in family incest treatment. In J. F. Gilgun, K. Daly, & G. Handel (Eds.), *Qualitative methods in family research* (pp. 236-259). Newbury Park, CA: Sage.

Gold, R. L. (1958). Roles in sociological field observations. *Social Forces, 36,* 217-223.

Grigsby, R. K. (1992). Mental health consultation at a youth shelter: An ethnographic approach. *Child & Youth Care Forum, 21,* 247-261.

Humphreys, R. A. L. (1975). *Tearoom trade: Impersonal sex in public places* (Rev. ed.). Hawthorne, NY: Aldine.

Lee, R. M. (1995). *Dangerous fieldwork.* Thousand Oaks, CA: Sage.

McNamara, R. P. (1994). Earning a place in the hustler's world. In C. D. Smith & W. Kornblum (Eds.), *In the field: Readings on the field research experience* (2nd ed., pp. 51-58). Westport, CT: Praeger.

Muller, J. H. (1995). Care of the dying by physicians-in-training: An example of participant observation research. *Research on Aging, 17,* 65-88.

National Association of Social Workers. (1996). *Code of Ethics of the National Association of Social Workers.* Washington, DC: Author.

Padgett, D., & Johnson, R. M. (1990). Somatizing distress: Hospital treatment of psychiatric co-morbidity and the limitations of biomedicine. *Social Science and Medicine, 30,* 205-209.

Schein, E. H. (1987). *The clinical perspective in fieldwork.* Newbury Park, CA: Sage.

Sluka, J. A. (1990). Participant observation in violent social contexts. *Human Organization, 49,* 114-126.

Snow, D. A., Benford, R. D., & Anderson, L. (1986). Fieldwork roles and informational yield. *Urban Life, 14,* 377-408.

Spradley, J. P. (1980). *Participant observation.* New York: Holt, Rinehart & Winston.

Taylor, S. J. (1997). Observing abuse: Professional ethics and personal morality in field research. *Qualitative Sociology, 10,* 288-302.

U.S. Department of Health and Human Services. (1993). *Protecting human research subjects: Institutional review board guidebook.* Washington, DC: Government Printing Office.

Ware, N. C., Tugenberg, T., Dickey, B., & McHorney, C. A. (1999). An ethnographic study of the meaning of continuity of care in mental health services. *Psychiatric Services, 50,* 395-400.

Websdale, N. (1998). *Rural woman battering and the justice system: An ethnography.* Thousand Oaks, CA: Sage.

Williams, B., & Roberts, P. (1995). Friends in passing: Social interaction at an adult day care center. *International Journal of Aging & Human Development, 41,* 63-78.

Yin, R. K. (1989). *Case study research: Design and methods* (Rev. ed.). Newbury Park, CA: Sage.

Grounded Theory and Other Inductive Research Methods

JANE F. GILGUN

The purpose of this chapter is to show that grounded theory, a form of inductive re-search, has many qualities that suggest its potential significance to social work. Grounded theory can provide social work with important types of knowledge such as the development of theories of human development and change, descriptions of clients' subjective points of view, and identification of the multiple social forces that affect client functioning and opportunity. Grounded theory lends itself to research that begins where clients are.

GROUNDED THEORY AS A GOOD FIT WITH EVERYDAY PRACTICE

Social workers experienced in direct practice on the individual level already are using many skills that also are procedures of grounded theory and other types of inductive research (Gilgun, 1994a, 1994b). Intuitively, then, most social workers recognize the value not only of how grounded theory research is done but also of how the knowl-edge generated applies to practice. Furthermore, with additional training, direct practitioners who are so inclined are positioned to do grounded theory and other types of inductive research.

The primary unit of analysis is the case, the level at which direct practitioners work. Like social work practice, grounded theory and other forms of inductive research focus on the complex social and personal forces that shape individual lives. Besides starting where clients are, the procedures of grounded theory also begin where practitioners are.

Many of the procedures of grounded theory are procedures used in other forms of inductive research such as analytic induction (Bogdan & Biklen, 1998; Gilgun, 1995, 1999e; Znaniecki, 1934), pattern matching (Gilgun, 1994a), narrative analysis (Riessman, 1993), critical theory (Morgaine, 1994), and interpretive phenomenology (Benner, 1994). Thus, with training in the specifics of various approaches, social work researchers can develop and test theories using analytic induction, analyze client stories using narrative approaches, present the lived experiences of clients through phenomenological methods, and analyze data sets using assumptions and conceptual grids that are linked to theoretical perspectives, as Sherman (1994) does when he matches the patterns of the Experiencing Scale with transcripts from therapy sessions.

Grounded Theory in Social Work

Grounded theory, however, has a long way to go to catch up to the survey, the most frequently used method in the social sciences. A search of the database *Social Work Abstracts* in July 1999 located 2,180 citations with *survey* in the title or abstract. By contrast, the database located only 49 citations with *grounded theory* as key words. Yet, the number of citations of grounded theory is increasing. The database identified 43 citations for the 1990s, 6 for the 1980s, and 2 for the 1970s. Doctoral dissertations accounted for more than half of the citations, and their numbers are increasing over time. For example, 9 dissertations used the term *grounded theory* in their titles or abstracts in 1997, 2 in 1996, 5 in 1995, 3 in 1994, and so on. Many social workers with doctorates become researchers and instructors in research methods. It is likely that the use of grounded theory and other inductive approaches will increase in the new millennium.

Because grounded theory is a type of inductive research, it is logical to think that the key words *inductive analysis, inductive research,* and *analytic induction* would have far more citations in the *Social Work Abstracts* than would *grounded theory*. In other words, the class should be larger than one of its types. This is not the case. These key words yielded a total of six articles and dissertations. Although there could be many possible reasons for this paucity of citations, a plausible explanation is the popularization of the term *grounded theory* by Glaser (1978, 1992), Glaser and Strauss (1967), Strauss (1987), and Strauss and Corbin (1998).

When researchers want to undertake inductive research, they might rely on the grounded theory version because of its current saliency. They might not realize that many of the procedures that Strauss and colleagues label as *grounded theory* actually are methods of data collection, analysis, and interpretation that have been used in social science research for more than 100 years (Gilgun, 1999e). As pointed out by grounded theorist Phyllis Stern, a former graduate student of Glaser and Strauss, grounded theory sometimes becomes muddled with other inductive methods such as ethnography and phenomenology. Stern advocates much more clarity about both the procedures of grounded theory analysis and the nature of its products (Gilgun, 1992b).

UNIQUE AND COMMON FEATURES
OF GROUNDED THEORY

Grounded theory has some characteristics that are unique and some that it holds in common with other inductive approaches. The unique features are theoretical sampling and the gentle directives to identify social processes and elaborate on them in terms of their "conditions, consequences, dimensions, types," and causes (when applicable), ideas based on Lazarfeld's elaboration analysis (Glaser & Strauss, 1967, p. 104). The term *constant comparison* also is associated with grounded theory (cf. Belcher, 1994). These elements are integral to the most recent versions of the doing of grounded theory (e.g., Strauss & Corbin, 1998).

Grounded theory's theoretical perspectives make it unique, just as the theoretical perspectives of other types of inductive research make them unique. A graduate of the University of Chicago's sociology department during the 1940s, Strauss was trained in pragmatist and interactionist perspectives that led him to be especially aware of social processes, the social contexts in which they take place, the advantages of direct contact with informants in their own contexts, and the importance of developing explicit social theory that has clear links to data (Corbin, 1991). Glaser, a graduate of Columbia University's sociology department, was trained by Lazarfeld and Merton, who emphasized theory development. Both Strauss and Glaser were concerned with the state of sociological theory and took the study of social processes as the focus of their research.

How Glaser and Strauss analyzed data, however, can be applied to a wide range of types of inductive research. The titles or subtitles of three major texts (Glaser & Strauss, 1967; Strauss, 1987; Strauss & Corbin, 1998) contain terms such as "strategies for qualitative analysis," suggesting the generic nature of aspects of the method they call grounded theory. In his neglected classic, *Theoretical Sensitivity,* Glaser (1978) called the products of these strategies *grounded theory,* but the ideas and procedures Glaser explicated are applicable to a wide range of types of inductive research. For example, Glaser built on Lazarfeld's (1959) discussion of the concept-indicator model, in which a set of empirical instances are identified, compared, and then named (or coded) as a concept. This process is called *constant comparison*. Strauss (1987) also used the concept-indicator model in his discussion of coding, but he made no attributions as to its origins. An understanding of the concept-indicator model facilitates the understanding of inductive research in general and in grounded theory in particular.

The uniqueness of other inductive approaches also stems from their theoretical and methodological perspectives. For example, Morgaine (1994) used critical theory and inductive methods to develop a theory of the formation of self-concept. She used generic inductive procedures as well as procedures drawn from assumptions of critical theory such as looking at ideologies, dialoguing about them, and then reflecting on them. Among the generic procedures were identifying emergent themes and developing an understanding of the perspectives and circumstances of her sample. The research reports in Benner's (1994) edited collection also used generic inductive procedures in doing interpretive research based on Heideggerian phenomenology. Inductive researchers, then, can apply a wide range of perspectives to their studies, perspectives that make their studies unique, whereas their approaches to data analysis and interpretation are generic.

In its purposes, grounded theory is not unique. In the words of Strauss and Corbin (1998), its purposes are to "build rather than test theory" and to "identify, develop, and relate the concepts that are the building blocks of theory" (p. 13). Other approaches to inductive analysis seek to both test and build theory, such as analytic induction (Gilgun, 1995, 1999e), whereas most forms of inductive analysis identify and build concepts or typologies (cf. Benner, 1994; Gilgun, Daly, & Handel, 1992; Riessman, 1994).

The generalizability of grounded theory findings is similar to the generalizability of the findings of other forms of inductive analysis. In addition, inductive researchers typically code, make comparisons of coded data between and within cases (e.g., constant comparisons [Glaser & Strauss, 1967]), diagram, memo, and link previous research and theory to emerging findings. Finally, processes such as researcher immersion in the field and the gradual emergence of themes and patterns are generic.

Unique Features of Grounded Theory

Theoretical sampling, theoretical saturation, open coding, selective coding, axial coding, basic social processes, conditions, and consequences are original to grounded theory. *Theoretical sampling* involves selecting informants and/or settings so that the developing concepts and theories are elaborated to as full an extent as possible. When researchers are learning nothing new within a delimited set of informants and settings, a state called *theoretical saturation* (Glaser, 1978), they seek informants and/or settings that vary slightly from those already sampled. In that way, variables are observed under a range of conditions.

For example, in a comparative study of five adult male child sexual abusers and their wives, Gilgun (1987) identified the presence of confidant relationships in childhood and adolescence, linked to gender-based socialization, as a major differentiating factor between men who sexually abuse children and the women they married who do not. After interviewing two more couples, Gilgun thought that she had reached theoretical saturation, where she was learning little new about confidant relationships. Thus, Gilgun (1992c) expanded her sample to include men who had risks for sexual abuse of children but who did not sexually abuse children. She found that these men had confidant relationships.

As Gilgun achieved theoretical saturation with a delimited set of informants, she purposefully expanded the sample to include informants who differed on a significant variable. By doing this, Gilgun began accounting for variations associated with relationships between risks for perpetrating child sexual abuse, gender, and confidant relationships. She was building theory based on procedures of theoretical sampling. Today, Gilgun (1999d) has a general theory on the development of violent behaviors. Accounting for variations and the conditions and consequences under which they exist is a central goal in grounded theory research (Glaser, 1978, 1992; Glaser & Strauss, 1967; Strauss, 1987; Strauss & Corbin, 1998) and in other types of inductive analysis.

Although the terms *theoretical sampling* and *theoretical saturation* are part of grounded theory, Gilgun (1995) found that she used similar procedures in a study of the moral discourse of male incest perpetrators, where her goal was to test and modify theories derived from the concepts of justice and care. Gilgun called her method *analytic induction,* based on the writings of Znaniecki (1934) and Bogdan and Biklen (1998), among others. Gilgun actively sought to disconfirm her emerging understandings so as to account for as many variations as possible in the empirical instances of how the men used concepts of justice and care. In analytic induction, seeking to disconfirm emerging findings is called *negative case analysis* (Bogdan & Biklen, 1998). Emerging concepts and hypotheses are modified to fit the instances that disconfirm previous findings, just as they are modified using theoretical sampling.

The terms *open coding* and *selective coding* were present in the first formulation of grounded theory (Glaser, 1978; Glaser & Strauss, 1967), whereas *axial coding* appears to have originated with Strauss (1987), who also used it in his co-authored text with Corbin (Strauss & Corbin, 1998). Open coding often is done line by line, where researchers name the processes and situations that they identify within transcripts or other data. Open coding leads to the identification of possible central or core concepts on which the analysis begins to build.

Axial coding, which comes after open coding, is the process by which researchers discover whether a variable can become a core concept. Sometimes, researchers run into a "dead end," where they find that what might have been a promising variable peters out. This part of the analysis is like finding a vein of gold and following it, hoping to discover the "mother lode" (Phyllis Stern, personal communication, October 1992). Examples of core concepts include confidant relationships (Gilgun, 1992c, 1996, 1999d), women's perceptions of risk (Gregg, 1994), and identity loss in Alzheimer's patients (Orona, 1997).

Selective coding increases the density of core variables and is done after open and axial coding. Researchers comb the data for empirical instances that they might have overlooked so as to be as thorough as possible about the dimensions, conditions, and consequences associated with core variables. Selective coding, then, is focused on particular concepts. Additional data collection and analysis can be done to reach saturation (Strauss, 1987; Strauss & Corbin, 1998).

Processes, conditions, and consequences are key terms in grounded theory. Although the identification and elaboration of core categories are essential to research called grounded theory, a focus on basic social processes is not necessary (Glaser, 1978). Rather basic social processes are simply one type of core variable (or category). Conditions and consequences are part of Glaser's (1978) "Six C's"—"Causes, Contexts, Contingencies, Consequences, Covariances, and Conditions"—that he called the " 'bread and butter' theoretical code of sociology" and the first codes to "keep in mind when coding data" (p. 74). He pointed out that most theories fit a causal, conditional, or consequence model, and grounded theories can be any of these.

To summarize, grounded theory is a particular style of inductive analysis that, in Glaser's (1978) words, "is based on the systematic generating of theory from data" that are themselves "systematically obtained from social research" (p. 2). Grounded theory is both a process and an outcome. Developed by two sociologists with complementary but not identical interests, grounded theory has unique qualities related to the theoretical and methodological perspectives of its originators. At the same time, grounded theory shares several features with other inductive methods. These other inductive methods also have unique features that derived from researchers' methodological and theoretical perspectives.

Features That Grounded Theory Has in Common With Other Inductive Approaches

Inductive research is a way of thinking. As Strauss (1991) pointed out, grounded theory "is a general way of thinking about analysis" (p. 2), an idea present in his other work (e.g., Strauss, 1987; Strauss & Corbin, 1998) and the work of researchers who do not consider themselves grounded theorists. For example, Bogdan (Bogdan & Biklen, 1998; Taylor & Bogdan, 1998) said the following about his training with one of Strauss's collaborators, Blanche Geer (Becker, Geer, & Hughes, 1968; Becker, Geer, Hughes, & Strauss, 1961): "Blanche modeled how to think conceptually. What I got out of her seminar was not the content. She was teaching a way of thinking" (quoted in Gilgun, 1992a, p. 9). Glaser (1978) saw ideas as central: "Good ideas contribute the most to the science of sociology" (p. 8).

Inductive researchers use open-ended approaches to develop findings. In general, inductive researchers, including grounded theorists, approach their data with minds as open as possible; immerse themselves in data; watch for the emergence of patterns and processes; identify core variables; and then gradually develop hypotheses, typologies, and/or detailed descriptions of their observations. Glaser (1992) stated that grounded theory is not about types of data but rather about how researchers approach data analysis and interpretation. Thus, the data to be analyzed can be qualitative, quantitative, or both (Glaser, 1992; Glaser & Strauss, 1967).

Findings of inductive research are linked closely to the empirical world. Inductive researchers pay heed to Blumer's (1969) thinking on the link between theory and the empirical world: "Theory is of value in empirical science only to the extent to which it connects fruitfully to the empirical world" (p. 143). Such thinking is of high relevance to social work, in which the task is to understand social conditions and, when conditions are unjust, to develop strategies for managing them and/or changing them. Social work very much needs well-delineated concepts and theories that are closely tied to the worlds of clients and that help us to see these worlds more clearly.

Inductive researchers do not enter the field as "blank slates." Glaser and Strauss (1967) have been interpreted as advising researchers to enter the field with no preconceived ideas. Yet, their advocacy of Lazarfeld's elaboration analysis involves using a set of preconceived ideas that directs researchers to observe "conditions, consequences, dimensions, types, processes," and causes when applicable (p. 104) during data analysis and interpretation. In addition, more than 20 years ago, Glaser (1978) advised staying sensitive to basic social processes, which are "fundamental patterned processes in the organization of social behaviors which occur over time and go on irrespective of the conditional variation of place" (p. 100). Thus, the originators of the term *grounded theory* provide instruction on the importance of preconceived categories and ideas. At the same time, they advise researchers to "stay sensitive to all possible theoretical relevances" (p. 194).

It may be an act of genius for researchers to see phenomena with completely fresh eyes. Einstein may have done so with his theory of relativity, and Curie may have done so as well when she discovered radium and its properties. In general, a researcher cannot enter the field with a completely open mind. What a researcher can do is be open to what informants are saying or, if using documents or quantitative data, to what data are telling the researcher.

Inductive researchers attempt to be open-minded, ready to set aside their own ideas when evidence presents itself, but they are not empty-headed. Thus, when entering the field, grounded theorists guard against imposing preconceived ideas on the phenomena of study while recognizing that they have them. Glaser (1992) advised researchers to trust the processes of doing grounded theory and not to let impatience and anxiety lead to forcing ideas on data. Rather, researchers should be patient and let emergence occur.

Gregg's (1994) research is an example of these processes. In her study of women's decisions about their pregnancies, Gregg began with theory-laden questions such as "Do they use a rational costs-benefits model of decision making?" Yet, she also consciously kept herself open to the stories that the women told her. She let the women's concerns guide research processes. As Gregg noted, the procedures of grounded theory, procedures held in common with other inductive approaches, allowed her to do this. By so doing, she "transformed women's initial answers to my original research questions into important research questions in their own right" (p. 64). She found that although she did not use the word *risk* in her questions, the women frequently did. Furthermore, the women had concerns about many more issues than she had anticipated and saw many parts of their lives at risk (e.g., changing roles and identities, impact of pregnancy on family and work relationships).

The findings of inductive analysis are generalizable in the analytic sense but not probabilistically. Inductive researchers rarely have random samples. Therefore, findings usually are not generalizable in the probabilistic sense. The generalizability of grounded theory's hypotheses lies in their application, that is, how well they aid in understanding other situations, a form of analytic rather than probabilistic generalizability. In terms of application, the hypotheses developed from inductive research are no different from hypotheses developed through probabilistic studies. Any hypothesis, from whatever source (including armchair reflection), is useful in applied situations only to the extent that it illuminates the social and individual processes of new settings. This principle has been well known in social research for decades (Cronbach, 1975).

Researchers link findings to previous research and theory. Whereas Gregg's (1994) research is an example of setting aside theory to grasp what informants tell us, previous research and theory are important both to sensitize researchers to the meanings they can identify in their data and to enlarge the significance and applicability of their own findings. Schatzman provided an example of sensitization (cited in Gilgun, 1993). In their field study of a psychiatric hospital, Strauss, Schatzman, and other members of the research team used the concepts of rules and norms from organizational theory in combination with their field observations to develop the theory of negotiated order (Strauss, Schatzman, Bucher, Ehrlich, & Sabshin, 1962), the idea that, in Schatzman's words, "there are rules, but rules are negotiated, rules are bent, broken, ignored, [and] argued over, all within the negotiation process" (quoted in Gilgun, 1993, p. 5). The use of sensitizing concepts does not rule out the identification of new concepts (Blumer, 1969). When they began their research, Strauss, Schatzman, and other team members did not know that they would discover the concept of negotiated order. They might not have identified the idea, however, had not notions of rules and norms been part of their analysis.

In Gilgun's (1995) research on the moral discourse of incest perpetrators, the concepts of justice and care, two fundamental ideas in moral philosophy, served as sensitizing concepts in Gilgun's analysis of the perpetrators' discourse and helped her to identify processes and assumptions she otherwise would have missed. Furthermore, these ideas gave Gilgun a vocabulary with which to discuss what she found. The meaning and significance of some perpetrators' experiences of incest as love were enhanced by research on therapists' accounts of their sexual relationships with clients. Both types of perpetrators invoked discourses of caring as the reason for their abusive behaviors, behaviors they did not regard as abusive.

To summarize the place of previous research and theory in inductive research, sometimes previous research and theory is set aside to hear what informants tell us, sometimes they help to sensitize us to what to look for and thus guide research, sometimes they help to interpret data not only in terms of concepts and ideas but also in terms of vocabulary, and sometimes they help to expand the meanings and applicability of our findings.

Inductive approaches produce hypotheses, grounded concepts, typologies, and descriptions. Hypotheses are abstractions from the data, abstractions are represented by concepts, and concepts are set in relationship to each other. Concepts are the defining elements of hypotheses, and hypotheses are the elements of theory. Blumer (1969) wrote that concepts are the only means for establishing connections between theory and the empirical world. Concepts point to "empirical instances about which a theoretical proposal is made" (p. 143). Blumer probably was building on a concept-indicator model, as Glaser (1978) did in explicating grounded theory, as discussed earlier.

Hypotheses can be written in many different forms (e.g., "if-then" or cause-effect hypotheses), and at various levels of abstraction, so long as their links to data are clear. Sometimes, the conceptual products are a set of descriptive statements that are further described through excerpts from field notes, transcripts, or other forms of data.

Few reports of grounded theory research summarize in one section the hypotheses that the research has identified, even reports that Strauss and Corbin (1997) collected to show "grounded theory in practice." In analytic induction, however, the defining product is a theory that has guided the research, been tested on data, and been modified to fit the data. Other forms of induction also may produce a theory, such as Morgaine's (1994) application of critical theory cited earlier.

More commonly, researchers who call their studies *grounded theory* have as their goals not hypothesis development but rather the identification and description of core categories. For example, Parker (1997) identified "strategies of broaching power issues" (p. 9) that clinicians use to address gender inequity issues in treatment, and she presented descriptions of each. Orona (1997) identified "four major 'themes' or categories" that "emerged from the data" (p. 182) in her research on the loss of identity in Alzheimer's patients, and she elaborated on one of them.

Inductive research typically invites the reader into vicarious experiences and, therefore, is positioned to give voice to the voiceless. The findings of inductive research typically are presented in such a way that the reader can experience for himself or herself the bases on which the hypotheses were developed. Glaser and Strauss (1967) advised researchers to present findings in such a way that the reader is "sufficiently caught up in the description so that he [or she] feels vicariously that he [or she] was also in the field" (p. 230). Glaser (1978) later called this quality "grab" (p. 4), which is a marker of trustworthy grounded theory research and of qualitative research in general.

Daly's (1999) work on the meanings of infertility to heterosexual couples illustrates a grounded theory study in which the hypotheses and supporting data have "grab." The report begins with a statement of Daly's perspectives on infertility:

> The language of infertility stands in sharp contrast to the tall, living regenerative tree of genealogy. "Barren," "fruitless," and "sterile" shift the focus from the lush foliage of the tree to the hot, rocky ground where nothing grows. Infertility represents a crisis of genealogy. Infertility precipitates a crisis of belonging, rootedness, and growth. (p. 2)

Multiple presentations of supporting data bring this perspective to further life. The following is one example in which a man talks about his crisis of belonging related to infertility in his marriage:

"People ask whether I have kids and how long have I been married. Then they look at me funny when I say I don't after having been married for 13 years. After that, I feel like I'm not like everyone else, and I feel less of myself." (quoted in Daly, 1999, p. 16)

Daly (1999) interpreted quotes such as these as evidence for hypothesizing that infertility also is a crisis of identity including a crisis in perceptions of the self as having power and control over when to have children and how many to have, among many other issues.

Inviting the reader into the vicarious experiences of informants is a vehicle for giving voices to the voiceless. Social work is concerned with vulnerable, oppressed people who seldom influence social policy with consequences for the distribution of wealth and opportunity in this country. Inductive research can play a role in righting this serious imbalance. As Denzin (1989) pointed out, "*The perspectives and experiences of those persons who are served by applied programs must be grasped, interpreted, and understood if solid, effective applied programs are to be created*" (p. 12, italics in original).

Seccombe's (1999) study of welfare reform from the perspectives of recipients is an example of this type of research. Combining ethnographic interviewing with a personal concern for social justice and the theoretical perspectives of critical feminist theory, Seccombe documented the effects of social policy on individual lives. Recipients also had insight into further reform:

People need to think about investing in women and children. Give people the opportunity to work or give them an education. . . . Help them make the transition from being on welfare to getting off [welfare]. We need to make sure that people are living in decent, clean housing, with clean water, and [with] decent air and good food. (p. 179)

Seccombe put a human face on the effects of welfare reform and brought the perspectives of clients to wider attention.

Some grounded theory reports do not invite the reader into vicarious experiences. For example, Konecki's (1997) study of recruiting by headhunting companies, included in Strauss and Corbin's (1997) *Grounded Theory in Practice,* contains no quotes from informants, thereby preventing the reader from experiencing what it meant to be in the field. Glaser's (1964) study of careers of organizational scientists also does not invite the reader into the experience.

Inductive researchers attempt to present major patterns and their exceptions. In presenting findings, grounded theorists and many other inductive researchers not only present the major patterns they identified but also present any exceptions to these patterns. There are many reasons to do so. One reason is accuracy. Another is that researchers have no idea which patterns are dominant in actuality. Dominant patterns in nonrandom samples could be minor in random samples, and qualitative researchers rarely have random samples. Therefore, in Gilgun's (1990, 1991, 1992c) research on the development of sexually abusive behaviors toward children, she could make no statements about the percentages of men and women with risks for sexual abuse of children who are likely to abuse children sexually. What Gilgun could do was show the variations in the relationships among risks, protective factors, and outcomes.

Furthermore, the goal of inductive research is application to particular settings. It matters not one bit that a particular pattern *is* dominant in a random sample because what is true for a group usually is not true in the same way for an individual. Thus, grounded theory has built-in safeguards against the ecological fallacy, which is the application of aggregate findings to individuals (Rubin & Babbie, 1997). The ecological fallacy leads to stereotyping clients.

These ideas are familiar to practitioners who are trained to enter the field with many ideas about what possibly could be going on in particular cases but who begin to hypothesize only after they have begun their assessments.

The data of inductive analysis come from many sources such as interviews, observations, documents of various types, and primary and secondary quantitative sources. Interviews are particularly amenable to obtaining points of view of informants and provide opportunities to develop theories based on informants' perspectives. In addition, as informants talk about their lives, the influences of multiple social forces can be observed. Often, clients are unaware of how classism, sexism, and gender role socialization have affected their lives. Furthermore, what is "everyday" for informants might be extraordinary for researchers. For example, Gilgun was absolutely shocked when a convicted rapist told her, "Rape is not personal." He did not bat an eye when he said this.

The use of multiple methods is common. Murphy (1992), who did doctoral work with Strauss, Corbin, and Schatzman at the University of California, San Francisco, used multiple sources of data in her grounded theory study of sibling relationships including interviews with parents, interviews with school-aged children, videotapes of the first time that school-aged children saw their newborn siblings, videotapes of everyday interactions in the family home, and children's drawings of their relationships with newborn siblings. The result was a multifaceted study of important family phenomena that yielded grounded theories.

Documents can be a source of data for researchers. For example, Gilgun (1999c) developed a set of social action principles based primarily on analyses of newspaper articles and Internet postings on former professional wrestler Jesse Ventura. Gilgun focused her analysis on Ventura's strategies for winning the governorship of Minnesota in 1998 and then maintaining himself as a high-profile newsmaker since his election. Goldstein (1996) used archival records, interviews, and his own memories to compose an ethnographic social history of a Jewish children's home, where many of the residents were childhood friends of Goldstein, who as a child lived across the street from the home.

An example of a grounded theory study using quantitative data is Glaser's (1964) grounded theory of survey findings, although Glaser was not explicit about his methods of data analysis and interpretation. Glaser also wrote a chapter in *The Discovery of Grounded Theory* (Glaser & Strauss, 1967) on the analysis of quantitative data using grounded theory procedures.

Researchers learn by doing. Schatzman wondered how anyone can learn to do grounded theory from a book (Gilgun, 1993). "Quarter after quarter, our students worked with Strauss, Glaser, and me, and after all of that, some of them still struggled. How can anyone learn to do this from a book?" (p. 7). Such a perspective originates not only from Schatzman's (1991) experience as a professor and dissertation adviser but also from the pragmatist tradition of learning by doing within grounded theory and inductive research in general. Schatzman was Strauss's first graduate student, and the two men worked together as faculty colleagues and co-researchers for more than 30 years at Indiana University, the University of Chicago, and the University of California, San Francisco (Gilgun, 1993). For many years, Schatzman taught an introductory field methods course at San Francisco, and then Strauss and Glaser taught the procedures of grounded theory.

Strauss was a graduate of the University of Chicago during the 1940s, when pragmatist philosophies were influential. Among many other pragmatist principles is the idea of the importance of firsthand experience and immersion in phenomena of interest. For generations, starting during the first part of the 20th century, social science professors urged Chicago graduate students to go into the field and get the seats of their pants dirty in their efforts to understand social processes (Robert Park, quoted in McKinney, 1966, p. 71).

Not only grounded theorists but also other researchers influenced by University of Chicago pragmatism taught research through seminars that involved group analysis of data that students gathered through document analysis, observations, and interviews. Such analysis of data for teaching purposes is traditional in qualitative research. During the 1920s and early 1930s, Robert Park, Ernest Burgess, and Vivian Palmer at the University of Chicago used these methods in teaching field research (Bulmer, 1984). This approach was similar to the data analysis sessions that Booth conducted to analyze multiple types of data collected during studies of the London poor (Webb & Webb, 1932).

Strauss, Glaser, Schatzman, and Corbin also used this approach, which remains how qualitative research is taught today at the University of California, San Francisco (Olesen, Droes, Hatton, Chico, & Schatzman, 1994), and at Syracuse University, which is a major center of teaching and learning qualitative approaches but not necessarily approaches that practitioners would call *grounded theory* (Gilgun, 1992a).

In seminars, the usual method is for students to provide copies of their field notes to other participants in the seminar at least 1 week beforehand. Each week, participants discuss field notes so that multiple perspectives are brought to bear on what the notes might mean.

Unfortunately, many researchers have learned qualitative methods from books because their training did not include opportunities to learn qualitative research in such seminars. Ralph LaRossa, a well-known qualitative researcher, sat on the floor with field notes for his dissertation while he read *The Discovery of Grounded Theory* (Glaser & Strauss, 1967). "They told me I was supposed to look for concepts," he said, and that is what he did (quoted in Gilgun, 1999e, p. 249). Some not only rely on books but also contact practitioners of qualitative researchers. Isabelle Baszanger, a French scholar who is an editor and translator of some of Strauss's books, "spent many hours talking with him [Strauss] during several visits to America" (Strauss & Corbin, 1998, p. 2). Strauss advised researchers whose only access to procedures of qualitative analysis is through books to form groups of three or four researchers to do group analysis of data ("Symposium on Grounded Theory," 1993).

PRACTICE EVALUATION AND INDUCTIVE METHODS

The Council on Social Work Education requires that accredited social work programs teach both methods of practice evaluation and qualitative research. Inductive methods, which now are widely known as grounded theory, have great potential in evaluating practice. Procedures for combining inductive methods and practice evaluation already exist in the form of change process research, discourse analysis (Nye, 1994; Sherman, 1994), and task analysis (Berlin, Mann, & Grossman, 1991). Task analysis involves prior development of a theory of client change and then testing the theory on the change processes that clients undergo over the course of treatment. Researchers/clinicians modify the theory in response to their observations of client change processes.

Discourse analysis begins with a preconceived theory or with sensitizing concepts. Its purpose is to track processes of client change. For example, Sherman (1994) used the Experiencing Scale as a framework for analyzing a client's movement from a remote to an immediate experiencing and expressions of feelings, with immediacy being the treatment goal. Sherman's data were the transcripts of therapy sessions. Through his analysis, he demonstrated that the client made gains in connecting with his emotions. Nye (1994) used a framework adapted from Labov and Waletsky (1967) and Garvey (1986) to analyze therapeutic talk. Presently, there are few examples in social work of inductive approaches to practice evaluation. As we become more knowledgeable about qualitative methods, we will devise increasingly useful ways of evaluating practice.

DEVELOPING ASSESSMENT AND EVALUATION TOOLS USING INDUCTIVE METHODS

Inductive research leads to the amassing of multiple empirical instances of core concepts. Such material is readily transferable to the development of assessment and evaluation tools. Gilgun developed the Clinical Assessment Package for Assessing Client Risks and Strengths (CASPARS; Gilgun, 1998, 1999a, 1999b; Gilgun, Keskinen, Marti, & Rice, 1999) based on life history interviews she did with adults with childhood and adolescent risks for violence and on related research on risk and resilience. Focus group material also is a potentially rich source of items for instruments. Developing items and core concepts from data gathered inductively results in instruments that are more likely to reflect the perspectives and concerns of clients and are in a language that clients already use.

DEVELOPING RESEARCH PROPOSALS BASED ON INDUCTIVE PROCEDURES

Not only is the term *induction* rarely found in searches of research databases, but proposals based on induction are a challenge to get funded. Understandably, funding agencies do not want to sponsor projects that do not have concise conceptual frameworks from which proceed clear, logical plans for data collection, analysis, interpretation, and application. To state that the research questions and the design will evolve as research proceeds asks funders to have faith. Unless the researchers are very well known and their work is impeccable, their projects will not be funded. Also, dissertation committees rarely (if ever) accept proposals that are vague in their essentials. Therefore, the preliminary work of finding a focus (i.e., of choosing core concepts and hypotheses) is best done prior to submitting the proposal to funders and committees. The use of analytic induction and sensitizing concepts permits the development of conceptual frameworks prior to entering the field. If researchers use this approach, then qualitative proposals are more likely to be funded. To be convincing, however, researchers must satisfy the following criteria:

- Have a clear and thorough initial conceptual framework that includes hypotheses
- Show the logical links between the conceptual framework and the design of the research
- State clearly that the purpose of the research is to modify the initial hypotheses
- State the procedures to be used in modifying the initial hypotheses

When the research is concluded, the reports that have authority will satisfy the following criteria:

- Present the findings with such clarity that the core concepts, hypotheses, and supporting data are obvious (i.e., the reader should not be forced to comb the findings for these products)
- Have "grab" and findings that are important to social work
- Situate findings within the research and theory to which they are linked
- Show how findings are applicable to other cases and situations

DISCUSSION

To meet the demands for knowledge that effective practice requires, social workers must continue to expand our repertoire of research methods. The complex social issues that we confront require methodological pluralism. Inductive methods, now commonly known as grounded theory, may become an increasingly important method of knowledge development.

Many of the procedures of inductive research parallel procedures of social work practice. Therefore, social workers have a built-in understanding and appreciation of how researchers arrive at their products. In addition, the products themselves are easily transferable to practice. Social workers already know that individual cases have both unique and common properties in relationship to similar cases. Therefore, when an inductive study comes to a conclusion about one case or several cases, social workers already know what to do with these findings. They know to take the findings into consideration when approaching a similar case and to wait and see whether these findings are relevant. Relevant findings help social workers to see processes that they might otherwise have missed. Thus, findings of inductive studies can serve sensitizing functions.

Furthermore, findings of inductive studies do not preclude discovery of new aspects of client situations. An appreciation of uniqueness allows for the identification of dimensions of client situations that previous research and theory might not have anticipated. Inductive research and practice, then, fit well.

Practice evaluation methods using inductive approaches are not yet widely used, nor are they well developed in social work. Routinely, however, practitioners informally test their theories of client change every time they implement an intervention, and they use conceptual frameworks to analyze practice situations. Thus, to do more formal hypothesis testing, or to use explicit preconceived frameworks to analyze social worker-client interactions, is not a big leap from everyday practice.

Social workers who are inclined to do research that involves immersion in the field (i.e., intensive interactions with informants) might enjoy doing inductive research. Not only does such immersion call on social workers to think deeply about what they are observing and experiencing and to make sense of it, but inductive research usually involves the whole self—heart, values, and mind.

To show funders and dissertation committees that inductive research is of high merit, researchers must present their initial conceptual frameworks and hypotheses as clearly as possible and explain in detail how the research is to be done. They should not expect funders and committees to go on faith.

Inductive methods provide forms of knowledge that focus on client perspectives. Thus, social work researchers can take leadership in bringing the voices of clients into debates and decision making about policies and programs that affect them. Interviews, observations, and document analysis can provide a rich store of knowledge on social forces that affect individual and community life. Finally, inductive approaches can become a primary source of items and concepts for assessment and evaluation instruments that are much needed in contemporary practice.

Inductive methods are one of many approaches to research that will advance knowledge needed for practice effectiveness. Today, inductive methods are underused in social work. Glaser (1978) recognized the importance of methodological pluralism more than two decades ago when he said that grounded theory is only one of many styles of sociological research and that the field needs *all* perspectives. This thought applies to social work as well.

REFERENCES

Becker, H. S., Geer, B., & Hughes, E. (1968). *Making the grade: The academic side of college life.* New York: John Wiley.

Becker, H. S., Geer, B., Hughes, E. C., & Strauss, A. L. (1961). *Boys in white: Student culture in medical school.* Chicago: University of Chicago Press.

Belcher, J. R. (1994). Understanding the process of social drift among the homeless: A qualitative analysis. In W. J. Reid & E. Sherman (Eds.), *Qualitative methods and social work practice research* (pp. 126-134). New York: Columbia University Press.

Benner, P. (Ed.). (1994). *Interpretive phenomenology: Embodiment, caring, and ethics in health and illness.* Thousand Oaks, CA: Sage.

Berlin, S. B., Mann, K. B., & Grossman, S. F. (1991). Task analysis of cognitive therapy for depression. *Social Work Research and Abstracts, 27,* 3-41.

Blumer, H. (1969). What is wrong with social theory? In H. Blumer, *Symbolic interactionism: Perspective and method* (pp. 140-152). Berkeley: University of California Press.

Bogdan, R., & Biklen, S. K. (1998). *Qualitative research for education: An introduction to theory* (3rd ed.). Needham Heights, MA: Allyn & Bacon.

Bulmer, M. (1984). *The Chicago School of Sociology: Institutionalization, diversity, and the rise of socio-logical research.* Chicago: University of Chicago Press.

Corbin, J. (1991). Anselm Strauss: An intellectual biography. In D. R. Maines (Ed.), *Social organization and social process: Essays in honor of Anselm Strauss* (pp. 17-42). Hawthorne, NY: Aldine.

Cronbach, L. (1975). Beyond the two disciplines of scientific psychology. *American Psychologist, 30,* 116-127.

Daly, K. J. (1999). Crisis of genealogy: Facing the challenges of infertility. In H. I. McCubbin, E. A. Thompson, A. I. Thompson, & J. A. Futrell (Eds.), *The dynamics of resilient families* (pp. 1-39). Thousand Oaks, CA: Sage.

Denzin, N. K. (1989). *Interpretative interactionism.* Newbury Park, CA: Sage.

Garvey, C. (1986, April). *Discourse analysis.* Paper prsented at a colloquium of the Department of Psychology, Wayne State University.

Gilgun, J. F. (1987). *The transformation from victim to perpetrator in child sexual abuse.* Final report to the Family Sexual Abuse Project of the Saint Paul Foundation, St. Paul, MN.

Gilgun, J. F. (1990). Factors mediating the effects of childhood maltreatment. In M. Hunter (Ed.), *The sexually abused male: Prevalence, impact, and treatment* (pp. 177-190). Lexington, MA: Lexington Books.

Gilgun, J. F. (1991). Resilience and the intergenerational transmission of child sexual abuse. In M. Q. Patton (Ed.), *Family sexual abuse: Frontline research and evaluation* (pp. 93-105). Newbury Park, CA: Sage.

Gilgun, J. F. (1992a). Field methods training in the Chicago School tradition: The early career of Bob Bogdan. *Qualitative Family Research, 6*(1), 8-12.

Gilgun, J. F. (1992b, November). *Grounded theory analysis and its influence on family scholarship.* Paper presented at the Symposium on Grounded Theory Methodology: Historical, Theoretical, and Clinical Perspectives, National Council on Family Relations, Orlando, FL.

Gilgun, J. F. (1992c). Hypothesis generation in social work research. *Journal of Social Service Research, 15,* 113-135.

Gilgun, J. F. (1993). Dimensional analysis and grounded theory: Interviews with Leonard Schatzman. *Qualitative Family Research, 7*(1/2), 1-2, 4-7.

Gilgun, J. F. (1994a). A case for case studies in social work research. *Social Work, 39,* 371-380.

Gilgun, J. F. (1994b). Hand into glove: The grounded theory approach and social work practice research. In W. J. Reid & E. Sherman (Eds.), *Qualitative methods and social work practice research* (pp. 115-125). New York: Columbia University Press.

Gilgun, J. F. (1995). We shared something special: The moral discourse of incest perpetrators. *Journal of Marriage and the Family, 57,* 265-281.

Gilgun, J. F. (1996). Human development and adversity in ecological perspective, Part 2: Three patterns. *Families in Society, 77,* 459-576.

Gilgun, J. F. (1998). Clinical instruments for assessing client assets and risks. *Medical Journal of Allina, 7,* 31-33.

Gilgun, J. F. (1999a). CASPARS: Clinical assessment instruments that measure strengths and risks in children and families. In M. C. Calder (Ed.), *Working with young people who sexually abuse: New pieces of the jigsaw puzzle.* Dorset, UK: Russell House.

Gilgun, J. F. (1999b). CASPARS: New tools for assessing client risks and strengths. *Families in Society, 80,* 450-459.

Gilgun, J. F. (1999c, May). *If Jesse Ventura can be elected governor of Minnesota, just think what the actions of a few social workers can do.* Keynote address delivered at the Conference on Social Action and Research, Rhode Island College, Providence, RI.

Gilgun, J. F. (1999d, November). *In their own words: Men talk about their violence.* Paper presented at the Pre-Conference Workshop on Theory Construction and Research Methodology, National Council on Family Relations, Irvine, CA.

Gilgun, J. F. (1999e). Methodological pluralism and qualitative family research. In M. Sussman, S. Steinmetz, & G. Peterson (Eds.), *Handbook of marriage and the family* (2nd ed., pp. 219-261). New York: Plenum.

Gilgun, J. F., Daly, K., & Handel, G. (Eds.). (1992). *Qualitative methods in family research.* Newbury Park, CA: Sage.

Gilgun, J. F., Keskinen, S., Marti, D. J., & Rice, K. (1999). Clinical applications of the CASPARS instruments: Boys who act out sexually. *Families in Society, 80,* 629-641.

Glaser, B. (1964). *Organizational scientists: Their professional careers.* Indianapolis, IN: Bobbs-Merrill.

Glaser, B. (1978). *Theoretical sensitivity.* Mill Valley, CA: Sociology Press.

Glaser, B. (1992). *Basics of grounded theory analysis: Emergence vs. forcing.* Mill Valley, CA: Sociology Press.

Glaser, B., & Strauss, A. (1967). *The discovery of grounded theory: Strategies for qualitative research.* Chicago: Aldine.

Goldstein, H. (1996). *The home on Gorham Street and the voices of its children.* Tuscaloosa: University of Alabama Press.

Gregg, R. (1994). Explorations of pregnancy and choice in a high-tech age. In C. K. Riessman (Ed.), *Qualitative studies in social work research* (pp. 49-66). Thousand Oaks, CA: Sage.

Konecki, K. (1997). Time in the recruiting search process by headhunting companies. In A. Strauss & J. Corbin (Eds.), *Grounded theory in practice* (pp. 131-145). Thousand Oaks, CA: Sage.

Labov, W., & Waletsky, J. (1967). Narrative analysis: Oral versions of personal experience. In J. Helm (Ed.), *Essays on the verbal and visual arts* (pp. 12-44). Seattle: University of Washington Press.

Lazarfeld, P. F. (1959). Problems in methodology. In R. K. Merton, L. Broom, & L. S. Cottrell, Jr. (Eds.), *Sociology today* (pp. 47-67). New York: Basic Books.

McKinney, J. C. (1966). *Constructive typology and social theory.* New York: Appleton-Century-Crofts.

Morgaine, C. A. (1994). Enlightenment for emancipation: A critical theory of self-formation. *Family Relations, 43,* 325-335.

Murphy, S. O. (1992). Using multiple forms of family data: Identifying pattern and meaning in sibling-infant relationships. In J. F. Gilgun, K. Daly, & G. Handel (Eds.), *Qualitative methods in family research* (pp. 146-171). Newbury Park, CA: Sage.

Nye, C. (1994). Discourse analysis methods and clinical research: A single case study. In E. Sherman & W. J. Reid (Eds.), *Qualitative research in social work* (pp. 216-227). New York: Columbia University Press.

Olesen, V., Droes, N., Hatton, D., Chico, N., & Schatzman, L. (1994). Analyzing together: Recollections of a team approach. In A. Bryman & R. G. Burgess (Eds.), *Analyzing qualitative data* (pp. 111-128). London: Routledge.

Orona, C. J. (1997). Temporality and identity loss due to Alzheimer's disease. In A. Strauss & J. Corbin (Eds.), *Grounded theory in practice* (pp. 171-196). Thousand Oaks, CA: Sage.

Parker, L. (1997). Unraveling power issues in couples therapy. *Journal of Feminist Family Therapy, 9,* 3-18.

Riessman, C. K. (1993). *Narrative analysis.* Newbury Park, CA: Sage.

Riessman, C. K. (Ed.). (1994). *Qualitative studies in social work research.* Thousand Oaks, CA: Sage.

Rubin, A., & Babbie, E. (1997). *Research methods for social work* (3rd ed.). Pacific Grove, CA: Brooks/Cole.

Schatzman, L. (1991). Dimensional analysis: Notes on an alternative approach to the grounding of theory in qualitative research. In D. R. Maines (Ed.), *Social organization and social process: Essays in honor of Anselm Strauss* (pp. 303-314). Hawthorne, NY: Aldine.

Seccombe, K. (1999). *"So you think I drive a Cadillac?" Welfare recipients' perspectives on the system and its reform.* Needham Heights, MA: Allyn & Bacon.

Sherman, E. (1994). Discourse analysis in the framework of change process research. In E. Sherman & W. J. Reid (Eds.), *Qualitative research in social work* (pp. 228-241). New York: Columbia University Press.

Strauss, A. (1987). *Qualitative analysis for social scientists.* New York: Cambridge University Press.

Strauss, A. (1991). A personal history of the development of grounded theory. *Qualitative Family Research, 5*(2), 1-2.

Strauss, A., & Corbin, J. (Eds.). (1997). *Grounded theory in practice.* Thousand Oaks, CA: Sage.

Strauss, A., & Corbin, J. (1998). *Basics of qualitative research: Techniques and procedures for developing grounded theory* (2nd ed.). Thousand Oaks, CA: Sage.

Strauss, A., Schatzman, L., Bucher, R., Ehrlich, D., & Sabshin, M. (1962). *Psychiatric ideologies and institutions.* Chicago: University of Chicago Press.

Symposium on grounded theory generates excitement. (1993). *Qualitative Family Research, 7*(1/2), 13-16.

Taylor, S. J., & Bogdan, R. (1998). *Introduction to qualitative research methods: A guidebook and resource* (3rd ed.). New York: John Wiley.

Webb, S., & Webb, B. (1932). *Methods of social study.* London: Longman, Green.

Znaniecki, F. (1934). *The method of sociology.* New York: Farrar & Rinehart.

PART III

Conceptual Research

This part of the handbook, devoted to conceptual research, contains the fewest number of chapters. Nevertheless, these research methods can be among the most intensely interesting types of inquiry that one can undertake. Space permitted the inclusion of only four methods of conceptual research: theory development, historical research, literature reviews, and critical analyses.

Within social work, we usually are interested in two major types of theory: theories about the causes of psychosocial problems and theories about how particular psychosocial interventions may work. The issue of causation is central to both concerns. It frequently is assumed, if not explicitly asserted, that to effectively intervene we must know the underlying causes of a problem. It also is a common reading that the development of an intervention or treatment is incomplete until we have come to a clear understanding about how the treatment actually exerts its presumably beneficial influences on clients or larger systems. Until such causal mechanisms are arrived at, it can be said that we lack a good theoretical understanding of an issue. As stated explicitly by Kerlinger (1977), the author of an influential psychology research text, "The basic purpose of scientific research is theory" (p. 5). A contemporary social work research text echoes this view:

> Some studies make no use of theory at all. . . . Of course, conducting such atheoretical studies that have little or no relevance outside of their pragmatic purposes for a particular agency does little to build social work knowledge. Consequently, some do not call such studies "scientific research," preferring instead to label them with terms like "administrative data gathering." (Rubin & Babbie, 1997, p. 55)

Similar sentiments are widespread within social work. But they are not uniform. Thyer (in press) points out that many valuable forms of scientific inquiry make little use of theory; they do not draw on it in formulating a particular study, and few or no implications to theory are derived from the results. Examples of such studies might include purely descriptive studies, needs assessments, epidemiological studies, cross-cultural investigations, risk assessments, predictive studies, and evaluation research. Some forms of qualitative research specifically avoid basing their investigations in theory, believing that adopting theoretical blinders might bias a study. Michael Scriven, past president of the American Evaluation Association, categorizes evaluation work as falling into three broad categories: so-called black box evaluations (outcomes are empirically determined, but the evaluator has virtually no idea as to how the intervention works), gray box evaluations (some causal mechanisms are established), and clear box evaluations (the causal mechanisms are clearly established) (Scriven, 1994). Frankly I am not aware of any example of clear box studies within social work, and gray box appraisals also are quite rare.

The reality is that very often in social work, we advocate for intervening even when the causes/etiologies of psychosocial problems remain indeterminate. Domestic violence and child protective services are but two common examples. Once a person has been identified as at risk, social workers have little hesitancy to initiate sometimes powerful interventions (e.g., placement of a woman in a battered women's shelter, placement of a child in foster care) without much in the way of careful analysis of the cause of the problem. For many areas of applied work, in fact, the causes are simply irrelevant. We do not completely know the real causes of alcoholism, schizophrenia, major depression, and obsessive-compulsive disorder, yet we have forged ahead with the development of sometimes very effective interventions. And many interventions have been well established as effective (Thyer & Wodarski, 1998; Wodarski & Thyer, 1998), even though the causal mechanisms responsible for their efficacy remain similarly unknown.

But this clearly is not a satisfactory state of affairs. A correct etiological understanding of psychosocial problems certainly is desirable, just as an accurate delineation of how effective treatments affect clients' lives certainly is a worthwhile goal. But these noble purposes need not be said to characterize all legitimate scientific research, only some of it.

Given the preceding caveats, it is worth reiterating that conceptual work devoted to the advancement of etiological or interventive theory is a terrifically interesting endeavor. And we are fortunate that one of social work's most profound thinkers in the field of theory development, Francis Turner (Chapter 21), has prepared a chapter on the topic for this handbook. In keeping with most authorities on the topic, Turner advocates a strong linkage between practice and theory. Theory development is a largely conceptual activity; it depends more on careful thinking, analysis, and synthesis—activities from which subsequent data-based research may be derived. Jerome Wakefield is one of social work's most thoughtful theoreticians, and his insightful contributions have focused largely on the theory of mental disorders (e.g., Buss, Haselton, Shackelford, Bleske, & Wakefield, 1998; Wakefield, 1997, 1999a, 1999b, 1999c). Individuals interested in reviewing superlative examples of theory development work are urged to examine Wakefield's contributions in this area.

Historical research is another largely conceptual research activity, and having accurate knowledge of the historical antecedents of any area of scientific inquiry can be seen as an essential element in a thorough conceptual grounding of a contemporary study. Social work historians John Graham and Alean Al-Krenawi (Chapter 22) have written a fine chapter on the value and conduct of historical studies. The Social Welfare History Group (SWHG) is loosely affiliated with the Council on Social Work Education (CSWE), and social workers with an interest in such work are urged to attend sessions sponsored by the SWHG as a part of the CSWE's annual program meeting.

A third form of conceptual research consists of conducting literature reviews in particular areas of social work. These help us to assimilate, to digest, and to summarize what initially might appear to be an overwhelmingly large body of literature. Karen Sowers, Rodney Ellis, and Nancy Meyer-Adams (Chapter 23) describe the design and conduct of literature reviews, viewing these studies as reservoirs of knowledge, as a tool for study development, and as an "atlas of error." They discuss methods of conducting a literature review, how to develop inclusionary and exclusionary criteria (necessary to keep from being swamped by too many studies), and how to write up a report. Literature reviews can be primarily quantitative or qualitative or can combine both elements. These can be very valuable publications and are particularly useful forms of research that can be published by social work doctoral students.

William Epstein's chapter (Chapter 24) on critical analyses as a form of conceptual research closes this part of the handbook. Epstein (1990) himself is the author of a widely discussed and cited critical piece looking at the quality of the social work journal publication system. Critical analysis refers to iconoclastic inquiry, studies that critique widely assumed perspectives and challenge accepted practice. Among other well-crafted examples of this type of study in social work are Eysenck's (1952) classic analysis of the effects of psychotherapy; Segal's (1972) and Fischer's (1973) reviews of the (lack of) effectiveness of social casework; Prioleau, Murdock, and Brody's (1983) analysis of psychotherapy versus placebo studies; and Wakefield's (1996) critique of general systems theory. The shattering of shibboleths enjoys a long and respected tradition as a research method, although the purveyors of unwelcome news often suffer for their efforts.

REFERENCES

Buss, D. M., Haselton, M. G., Shackelford, T. K., Bleske, A., & Wakefield, J. C. (1998). Adaptations, exaptations, and spandrels. *American Psychologist, 53,* 533-548.

Epstein, W. M. (1990). Confirmational response bias among social work journals. *Science, Technology, & Human Values, 15,* 9-38.

Eysenck, H. (1952). The effects of psychotherapy: An evaluation. *Journal of Consulting Psychology, 16,* 319-324.

Fischer, J. (1973). Is social work effective? A review. *Social Work, 18,* 5-20.

Kerlinger, F. (1977). *Foundations of behavioral research* (3rd ed.). New York: Harcourt, Brace, Jovanovich.

Prioleau, L., Murdock, M., & Brody, N. (1983). An analysis of psychotherapy versus placebo studies. *Behavioral and Brain Sciences Review, 6,* 275-310.

Rubin, A., & Babbie, E. (1997). *Research methods for social work* (3rd ed.). Pacific Grove, CA: Brooks/Cole.

Scriven, M. (1994). The fine line between evaluation and explanation. *Evaluation Practice, 15,* 75-77.

Segal, S. P. (1972). Research on the outcome of social work interventions: A review of the literature. *Journal of Health and Social Behavior, 13,* 3-17.

Thyer, B. A. (in press). The role of theory in research on social work practice. *Journal of Social Work Education.*

Thyer, B. A., & Wodarski, J. S. (Eds.). (1998). *Handbook of empirical social work practice* (Vol. 1). New York: John Wiley.

Wakefield, J. C. (1996). Does social work need the eco-systems perspective? I. Is the perspective clinically useful? *Social Service Review, 70,* 1-32.

Wakefield, J. C. (1997). When is development disordered? Developmental psychopathology and the harmful dysfunction analysis of mental disorder. *Development and Psychopathology, 9,* 269-290.

Wakefield, J. C. (1999a). The measurement of mental disorder. In A. V. Horwitz & T. L. Scheid (Eds.), *A handbook for the study of mental health* (pp. 29-57). New York: Cambridge University Press.

Wakefield, J. C. (1999b). Mental disorder as a black box essentialist concept. *Journal of Abnormal Psychology, 108,* 465-472.

Wakefield, J. C. (1999c). Philosophy of science and the progressiveness of the DSM's theory-neutral nosology. *Behaviour Research and Therapy, 37,* 963-999.

Wodarski, J. S., & Thyer, B. A. (Eds.). (1998). *Handbook of empirical social work practice* (Vol. 2). New York: John Wiley.

CHAPTER TWENTY-ONE

Theory Development

FRANCIS J. TURNER

*H*ow is theory developed in social work? Certainly, such a question has an essential place in a handbook of social work research methods. However, although the number of research texts in social work is expanding, a development that bodes well for the profession, few have addressed this question of how theory is developed.

I begin with a statement that I used to present to my students when I was teaching research. "Theory," I would say, "is not developed the way research texts say it is developed." This perhaps sounds too cynical and unfairly critical of those colleagues who write such texts. I did not mean it as such. I used it to make a point that the development of theory for a profession such as ours is a much more complex process than the traditional formulation of null hypotheses and the subsequent testing of them.

Before we look at the issue of how I believe theory develops and how I have observed it developing, I think that we should be clear as to what is meant by the term *theory*. By theory, we mean those organized bodies of testable explanations of phenomena that are the bases of our professional activities for and with clients to whom we are prepared to be accountable.

Following this, we also need to examine the question of why theory is developed. To put such a question to a group of colleagues or to our social work students at every level would, hopefully, elicit responses related to our ethical responsibility to build our interventions on sound knowledge. This would include the underlying premise that knowledge emerges from theory. Of course, this is correct and probably helps to explain, at least in part, the unprecedented expansion of bodies of theory in social work during the past three decades.

Those of us who entered the profession during the 1950s and now are nearing the ends of our careers have seen us move from a practice base driven by only two or three theories to today's reality in which we have available to us more than 30 theories or models of practice, with new ones in various stages of emergence. Some might see this as a sign of conceptual uncertainty and a lack of a solid knowledge base. Before we are quick to view this from a negative perspective, we need to remind ourselves that this same phenomenon is taking place in other disciplines. Astronomy and medicine are two good examples.

Like many other helping professions, in a very short time, our profession has moved from a position where we were criticized for having a very thin theory base to one where our current challenge is how to best make use of our abundance of interlocking theories. That this has happened and continues to happen is an exciting prospect for us. Indeed, it is a phenomenon of sufficient interest and importance that it is in itself an area deserving of research. If we can begin to understand how and why sound theory develops, then we can facilitate the process and better serve our clients.

Because this topic of how theory develops is not one to which we have devoted much attention, especially that of a formal research nature, this chapter does not constitute an analysis of the literature or a body of data. Rather, it reflects that preliminary stage of research discussed in other chapters in this handbook in which the researcher begins by exploring the body of "practice wisdom" related to a specific topic and deliberates on it. It is out of such processes that hypotheses are formulated and ultimately tested. Because this is a topic in which I have had considerable interest and about which I have long pondered, I present ideas and observations I have made over the decades, fully aware that others might well see this process differently. Therefore, these comments are a form of rough-and-ready impressionistic research rather than a more structured examination of available data. But I hope that such a process will lead to more refined conceptualizing and testing in the future.

We begin with the premise that responsible practice needs to be based on sound theory and that quality responsible practice is based on richly developed and tested theory. This theme, in one way or another, underlies the structure of all curricula of schools and faculties of social work. It is particularly reflected in the expansion in number, quality, and diversity of research courses at all levels of social work education as well as in our rich growing tradition of practice-based research.

However, even though I am a committed optimist convinced that sound practice is based on sound theory, as a researcher I have to accept the fact that this is, for the most part, only a supposition. This is because the amount of research related to testing various aspects of the relationship of theory to practice is sparse. What we do know is that our cadre of theories has expanded dramatically. What we want to consider in this chapter is what variables appear to have influenced this expansion. That is, how is theory developed in a profession such as ours? We leave to others the task of addressing the impact of this rich development on our practice.

Although a variety of non-research-based sociological factors that greatly influence how theory is developed in our profession are discussed later in the chapter, my first proposition is that theory is formulated in our profession in the same way as it is developed in other professions. *Theory develops by the slow, steady, multitargeted, broadly focused accumulation of observations in a humble, patient, open, disciplined way from which hypotheses about their interconnection are formed.* Such hypotheses then are variously tested by means of a broad range of strategies. It is within the rubric of this classical perspective of knowledge building that we have seen the dramatic increase in such activities in social work.

Indicators of this greatly expanded traditional research activity are numerous. In a few short years, we have seen a dramatic increase in the number of scholarly refereed journals in our field where the articles reflect a broad range of research-based projects. In a few decades, we have moved from a situation where there were only some 30 or 35 refereed journals in our profession to the present where the number is approaching 200.

Indeed, such has been the extent of this expansion that it has been necessary to develop journals that seek only to gather and abstract the research that is being reported in other journals. The former include *Research on Social Work Practice, Social Work Research, Journal of Social Service Research,* and *Social Services Review,* among others.

I am not suggesting that, within this expansion of literature, every article in every journal can be called a theory-developing, research-based article in a classical sense. Nevertheless, each article represents an effort on the part of a colleague or colleagues to advance our knowledge in some particular aspect of the profession, and this indeed is a step in the way to the development of theory. This is done by focusing particular attention in a disciplined, peer-reviewed way on some aspect of practice so as to better understand it.

Why this dramatic explosion of research in our profession? I believe that this must be answered in the plural because the reasons are varied. One factor that needs to be considered, and I think is not fully appreciated, is the way in which social work education emerged on this continent early in the 20th century. As the profession took shape late in the 19th century, formal social work education moved very quickly into the universities, and this was at a graduate level. This means that from the very earliest days of the profession, our knowledge base was developing within the climate of academe where the value system demanded that a discipline needed to demonstrate its scientific legitimacy within the ethos of research. This partially manifested itself in the tradition of the master's thesis, which was an integral part of most graduate social work programs for many decades. Here, we are discussing not the level or quality of these theses but rather the fact that they were required of all students. As an aside, it would be interesting to randomly sample these master's theses over the decades from the viewpoint of their theory-developing quality. (I would support such research so long as my own thesis was not included in the sample.)

This requirement of formal research projects by all social work students served several functions. It sought to establish within the students an interest in, and a commitment to, the process of evaluation and testing of knowledge as a part of practice. It also provided a basic skill set to operationalize practice-based research. Whether or not it succeeded in doing this is not the question here. What is important was the effort to put into practice within the profession a value set that the ongoing testing of knowledge from which theory is derived was an essential component of any practitioner in particular and of the profession as a whole.

One of the critical developments emerging from the master's base of the profession that I believe further contributed to the building of theory was the very rapid development of doctoral programs. Because initially the basic programs for social work education were at the master's level rather than at the baccalaureate level as in most professions, very bright and inquiring students, able to meet the general universities' requirements for graduate students, were attracted to these programs. These persons quickly internalized the values of and excitement about the quest for knowledge. Many of the early graduates, either immediately following their master's degrees or a few years later, sought opportunities to search further and to expand our knowledge and theory base at the doctoral level.

Out of this interest in further knowledge, the demand for doctoral studies quickly developed among students. There also were pressures within the university world, related to its mores, to move to the doctorate. In North America, a discipline was not viewed as fully respectable and established within the university if it was not engaged in postgraduate work, and this provided a further thrust to the need for doctoral programs.

As these two processes developed, and as the number of schools of social work expanded on this continent, the need for social work professors also expanded. This was happening during a time when, as now, a relevant doctorate was considered to be the basic entrée to the professorate in the academic world. As more and more social workers entered the professorate within the university, the pressure to demonstrate academic acumen on the road to promotion further contributed to the development of theory. This was done, for the most part, through publication in "refereed journals."

With this expansion of the number of social work doctorates, of course, came an expanded cadre of colleagues with a much higher level of research expertise, experience, and theory development interest than had ever existed within the profession. I believe, but cannot offer substantive data to confirm, that because we had more and more doctorate-level people teaching in master's programs, the quality and level of research done at the master's level also improved.

Fortunately, not all of our doctorate-level people went, nor do they go today, into the university world. Many took, and still take, positions in government, research centers, foundations, agencies, lobbying groups, and direct practice settings in which their knowledge, interest, and skills in theory-building research were, and still are, greatly needed, used, respected, and demanded.

Thus, in a very short time in North America, we moved from a profession that depended much more on charismatically driven practice wisdom than on theory to a profession that had internalized the responsibility to build our practice on a much stronger knowledge base. At the same time, we had equipped ourselves with the skills knowledge, personnel, and experience to take responsibility for our own theory development and testing of practice.

Although valid in itself, the preceding description of our movement into the theory-building phase of the profession is a naive one if taken on its own. The process and variables involved were, and still are, much more complex than the preceding discussion reflects. Several other factors need to be noted to fully understand not only how we build theory but also which theories we build.

During the 1960s and 1970s, several things were happening within the profession and external to it that influenced the development of theory. Externally, as the ever-present struggle for funding of programs continued, the theme of accountability and evaluation began to take on a very high profile. Over and over again, funding bodies were wondering, then asking, and then demanding that the seekers of funds, whether the funds be private or public, needed to demonstrate that the programs for which dollars were being sought were achieving their established goals. Out of this emerged a dramatic increase of interest in and demands for accountability. The basic and driving question was, "Do you social workers know what you are doing, and can you demonstrate this to us?" Interest in this question raised many queries, discussions, and indeed acrimonious debates as to the theoretical bases of practice and the existence, or lack thereof, of empirical evidence that would validate the theory or theories driving the practice.

At the same time as external demands for demonstration of empirically supported evidence of competence came to the fore within the profession, we were needing to come to terms with the reality of a multi-theory-based body of knowledge. Inevitably, as new theories emerged and were incorporated into the profession in various ways, rivalries between and among the adherents and supporters of various theories emerged. Understandably, because theories have different value bases and have emerged from different sources and traditions, they will differentially appeal to individuals and groups. An ever-changing hierarchy of theories in vogue at different times develops as well. Space does not permit an analysis of how and when various theories moved up and down on the charts of desirability and fashionablness except to note that this phenomenon has long marked our profession—as, of course, it has marked other professions.

One of the aspects of rivalries between theories was, and still is, to use available empirical evidence in support or criticism of a particular theory's efficacy. However, different theories lend themselves more readily to empirical investigation than do others and, therefore, have stronger research bases. This, in turn, helps them to achieve a stronger position in the theory hierarchy. This factor also strengthens interest in, and support for, research into the particular theory's applicability and effectiveness. Thus, one of the important ways in which theory is developed in our profession relates to the support or popularity that a particular theory enjoys and, hence, the resources available to further develop it.

A THEORY'S STATUS: INFLUENCING FACTORS

But the popularity of a theory, or its social status and ongoing development within a profession such as ours, is not fixed only by the extent of its research base and its ability to be researched. There are other important factors that need to be mentioned. As I have become more and more aware of such factors, I have identified eight that should be considered in looking at this question of how theory develops.

1. Charisma

One of the things that has greatly interested me as I watched the process of theory development in our profession is the role that individuals have played in legitimizing or greatly influencing the acceptance and popularity of particular theories through their ability to influence others. This is important because, as just mentioned, when a particular theory is in the limelight, there is both a high level of interest in examining it from a research perspective and the concomitant aspect of the higher availability of resources to study it further. An interesting study could be done of how some theories have achieved high popularity based on the renown or charismatic qualities of the persons supporting them regardless of the theories' empirical bases or lack thereof.

This is not necessarily a bad thing. It might well be that having the endorsement of high-profile people in the profession of some new or emerging idea might ensure that it is given the attention needed to properly assess it and evaluate its potential for practice or some aspect of practice. For a long time, such charismatic persons were of influence only if they were members of other professions. I think a great mark of our own maturity came as we began to find our charisma bearers from within.

Of course, what is dangerous about what I call the "charismatic factor" is that often some of the supporters of the "theory gurus" begin to view a particular theory from a dogma or cult-like perspective. Thus, rather than viewing the theory as a body of concepts that need to be studied and evaluated on an ongoing basis, some subscribe to a quasi-belief system in which those who might question or challenge are viewed as biased and prejudiced. I suggest that one of the important roles of professors and other leaders in the field is to legitimize the search for new approaches to practice and to examine them in as objective a manner as possible rather than pushing people into particular directions viewed as "the canon."

2. Economics

A further contributing factor in the development of theory is the role played by economics. The provision of interventions in our society by the human service professions is a matter of considerable interest to individuals and society in general both as recipients and as funders of services. Thus, such services are continually under the scrutiny of the professions involved as well as other societal groups that pose legitimate questions about costs and alternative strategies to deliver what are viewed as the same services in other less expensive ways.

In this vein, one of the current highly fashionable approaches to social work treatment is the emphasis on providing very short term interventions. Thus, theories and models such as task-centered, crisis, and problem solving are very much to the fore and, with others, are labeled under the general rubric of "solution-focused intervention." It is understandable that research into the development and effectiveness of such theories is popular. Such research is much more likely to be funded than is theory-based research that, for example, might look at some aspect of a more traditional longer term intrapsychically oriented style of treatment. Because research is expensive, it is understandable that many researchers will go where the resources are. This, in turn, will expand the research base of some theories over others, and this further increases the prominence of such theories.

Another spin-off of the increased connecting of funding to ability to demonstrate effectiveness has been the way in which this has carried down to frontline agencies. With increasing frequency, even the smallest of our service centers are being asked to demonstrate the impact, or lack thereof, of services in general as well as in particular. One of the very positive aspects of this is an expansion of basic frontline research, especially of an outcome nature. Because our theory is practice oriented, and because (for the most part) practice theory ultimately emerges from practice, this dramatic increase in direct practice research undoubtedly will further contribute to the enhancement of our theory base, even if, at the present, it might focus too much on particular theories to the exclusion of others.

3. Cultural Values

A further important contributing factor in the development of theory within a profession relates to the cultural milieu in which research and practice is carried out. As mentioned earlier, one of the important insights emerging from the study of the impact of a pluralistic theory base on our profession has been the understanding that theories need to be viewed as dynamic developing systems, each of which carries with it a particular value set. These value sets relate to, for example, views of the world, of human potential, and of the nature of growth and responsibility for change. Thus, it is not surprising that, at different times and in different milieus, different theories will be more acceptable and fit better with the existing value sets of relevant culture than will others.

In such situations, some theories will receive more research attention than will others more distant from surrounding worldviews. I remember well the strong negative reaction I received from several significant quarters of the profession when I first introduced a chapter on meditation theory in a book on differential theories. The argument put forward by my critics related to a mistaken perceived contradiction between the origins of meditation and the value basis of social work. Interestingly, as the research evidence has grown—research that has taken place, for the most part outside of social work—as to the efficacy and utility of this body of thought for treatment, we are becoming more interested in it. I have not had any questioning of its relevance for contemporary practice for several years.

In my travels, I have noted a very strong interest in existential theory among colleagues in both France and Spain, a theory that has just gained some importance in North America. Although of long interest to some in this part of the world, it would not be viewed as a high-status practice theory and still is perceived by many as a bit on the fringe side of practice. In the most recent edition of a theory book, I had considerable difficulty in finding someone to write about hypnosis as a component of contemporary practice, even though I was aware of a large number of persons who did make use of the theory and practice of hypnosis in their clinical work. The reason often given for declining was these people's fear that their views on this theory would be considered out of step with what currently was acceptable in practice and that they would be subject to suspicion by others in the profession. A similar example relates to the use of Marxist theory as a basis for practice, a theory that underlies the practice of many of our colleagues in other parts of the world. In this instance, our publisher would not agree to my titling one of the chapters in the book as Marxist, and we were able to include the chapter only by calling it by another name.

Thus, a critical area of examination that needs to be addressed in looking at how theory is developed in social work is to ask which theories are permitted to develop, which are encouraged to develop, and which are prohibited from developing either within the profession or in the broader community based on a presumed value fit or lack thereof.

4. Interest in Outcomes

A further factor that has influenced the development of theory in our profession has been a renewed enthusiasm about our demonstrated efficacy mentioned earlier. During the past decade, we have come far from a position of discouragement and bitterness as to whether, in fact, our interventions were helpful or not. During the 1970s and 1980s, there had been strong allegations both within and outside the profession that there was little evidence that our therapeutic interventions were effective. This often was backed up with data that seemed to support such allegations.

There were two very positive outcomes that came out of this "time of disillusionment." First, there was a marked commitment to hone our research skills and abilities so as to authoritatively critique research and defend ourselves when necessary. In so doing, it frequently was found that the research that allegedly criticized our therapeutic endeavors was itself flawed and had little validity. Second, beyond being defensive, we began to put increased efforts and competencies into the challenge of evaluating the outcome of various interventions and their relationship to the knowledge on which they were based. Over and over again, the findings indicated, and continue to indicate, that we were, and still are, not only effective but highly effective and that we were, and still are, helpful to most of the people we serve.

I do not think that the importance of this shift from a defensive attitude about our theories and their usefulness to a more positive one in which we became much more skilled and comfortable in examining practice has been fully appreciated within the profession. Now, we are increasingly looking at questions of how we differentially affect persons and situations rather than asking the more politically driven questions about our utility or lack thereof. It is this latter type of research that will help us to expand our knowledge about the differential impact of various theories.

If, indeed, we have reached this stage of theory maturity, then I suggest that we now need to start emphasizing not only what we know but also what we do not know. I believe that it is time that we start capitalizing on areas of our ignorance as befits our stature. I thought of this on the subway the other day in observing an advertisement sponsored by our medical colleagues that showed a picture of a very pretty little girl whom the ad said would be dead in 2 years if we did not find a cure for her particular disease. To carry out the needed research would require many millions of dollars, which we were being asked to contribute. I suggest that it is time that we also identify those areas in which we are continually ineffective and seek interventions that will help.

Another outcome of our growing comfort with competence is the realization and acceptance that advancements in knowledge and theory are going to take place in minute steps. I believe that one of the very serious mistakes we have made in the past was to ask large and difficult research questions and attempt to answer them with minimal resources. This seemed to stem from both a combination of naïveté and a strong desire to play "catch-up." Much greater progress will be made in the development of theory and its differential utility when we become more comfortable with asking small—indeed, very small—and manageable theory questions rather than the large questions that are doomed to insignificant findings before they start, such as "Does Theory A cure substance abuse?" and "Does Theory B stop spousal abuse?" Knowledge will advance when we find that many small, well-designed projects have found similar results that help us to shed light on some minuscule area of practice. This will be more fruitful than trying to ask all-encompassing questions.

Related to our increased skill and comfort in learning to ask very precise but manageable questions is the realization that much of the change in clients and their life situations that we affect in our practice is not going to be dramatic. For example, we are not going to change someone's personality totally; rather, we are going to help someone to enhance his or her self-image slightly so as to live more comfortably. We are not going to cure schizophrenia; rather, we are going to develop strategies that help persons with schizophrenia to learn to live in a more comfortable and less troubled lifestyle.

With much more restricted research goals, we need to learn to identify and then recognize small movements in our clients and learn to connect these to the theories we have used. I am quite certain that many clients are helped much more than we realize by having the opportunity to sit with skilled, understanding, patient, empathic persons who let them look at themselves in a more positive way that will have payoffs in many aspects of their lives. This is true, even though at the ends of our relationships with them, these clients' original problems or situations that brought them to us in the first place still exist. Our challenge as theory builders is to seek to identify what types of changes occurred in their situations and to connect these to our input that we have selected based on our theory repertoire.

5. Enhanced Technology

A further factor that has assisted, and is going to increasingly assist, us in the development of theory is the ready availability of resources, the powers of which are beyond our wildest dreams of only a few years ago. I speak here of the dramatic availability of communications and data manipulation technology. If it is true that much of the impact we have on clients in various situations is small but cumulative, then to tease these out and examine them from a theoretical perspective will require both highly sensitive instruments of analysis and much larger samples and populations than we have had access to in the past.

We are making tremendous progress in learning to identify small but significant areas of change in large populations. As our statistical skills improve, we are learning how to quantify the various effects of many factors that will permit us not only to observe change but also to more clearly identify which factors influenced the change and by how much. That is, not only can we now gather much larger bodies of information in a variety of formats, but we have the know-how to "squeeze" such data for information in ways that were not possible a short time ago.

I find it almost unbelievable to recall that one of the accomplishments of which I was quite proud as a doctoral student was learning to use a slide rule to analyze data collected on punched McBee cards. I now find myself writing this chapter on a computer that can link me to colleagues, libraries, and databases all over the world and can permit me to carry out sophisticated data analyses quickly, sensitively, and accurately without ever leaving my home-based study. However, for a complex set of factors, there still is a reluctance among many social workers to draw on the potentials of available and affordable communications technology to begin more sensitive testing of our theories.

6. Theoretical Rivalries

There is a further factor that has contributed to the growth of research in our profession, one alluded to earlier that, I believe, needs to be explicated. I mentioned that one source of increased theory building that emerges from research has stemmed from the rivalry that sometimes exists among the espousers of various theories. Such rivalries put pressure on the holders of theory to demonstrate the efficacy of the theory and its ongoing development that they are championing. The extent that a theory is well developed from a base of well-designed research, of course, greatly enhances its position on the hierarchical ladder of theories. Indeed, as suggested earlier, this type of rivalry is not necessarily a bad thing if it fosters efforts to test theories as a way of expanding them or as a way of challenging theories to enhance the position of another theoretical body. Such rivalries serve the function of "Her Majesty's Loyal Opposition" in the British Parliament. In a profession such as ours, the task of the opposers is to critique the soundness of research related to theoretical propositions and to ensure that they are sound and valid.

In summary, I am suggesting that theory develops partially through competition among persons, institutions, and strong adherents to particular bodies of theory. Such competition goes far in ensuring that the quality of research will be maintained as various theory fans carefully scrutinize the findings of groups in camps other than their own.

7. Theory Superstars

A further way in which theory is developed is through the directed efforts of individuals. In a profession such as ours, we have had, and continue to have, persons whose intellectual curiosity and commitment drives them to pursue the development of particular theories. Unlike the charismatic figures mentioned earlier, these colleagues often are not in the limelight of the profession, and their work frequently is unrecognized. In looking at other disciplines, in addition to the professional and intellectual satisfactions that come with the process of theory building, there often are other tangible rewards such as honors and prizes. Unfortunately, one thing that we do not have to the extent that colleagues in some other disciplines do is a structure of processes through which we can award recognition to those colleagues who make major theoretical advances. There is no Nobel Prize-like structure to recognize and reward advances in theory.

Because we proudly proclaim that we are a highly person-oriented profession, we should build on our knowledge of ego-enhancing strategies to foster the development of theory. I believe that we get caught up in some sense of false humility that social work, as a profession, does not need such incentives and rewards. Once again, this seems to be an example of our failure to make use of our own wealth of knowledge about the things that help to motivate all persons including ourselves.

8. Politics

The factor of politics also has to be considered in this discussion as a further facet of the sociology of theory development. I mentioned earlier that although it has long been overlooked, an important component of theory is that, as dynamic systems, each is built on a value set. Therefore, sometimes theories fit well with the value sets and resultant political climates of the countries or cultures in which they are being practiced, and sometimes they do not. Clearly, when a particular theory is out of synchronization from a value perspective with an important aspect of the society in which it is being practiced, it will be very much in a less favored position. Such a position can well affect the number of persons who still will find it attractive or acceptable; the extent to which it is a part of the profession's general practice base; and (perhaps most important) the resources available to the theory's adherents for its ongoing use, testing, and development. A part of this less-than-favored position is that such theories also probably will play a minimal role in the theory sets of many practitioners, agencies, and curricula of social work education centers, again resulting in a lower level of development and interest.

There are two groups of theories that can fall into this type of nonattention or minimal attention. The first are those that are viewed in a negative manner as being out of step with a particular value set of some or many significant societal groups. The second is, in some ways, a more subtle situation, and that is where we have theories that are not actively in conflict in any way with a dominant value set, but neither are they particularly congruent with it. Such theories are in a state where there are few people who speak against them but, at the same time, also few people who are particularly interested in them. Often, such theoretical systems languish in situations of disinterest or very low interest except perhaps on the part of a few devotees. These theories stay that way until they either drift into total obsolescence, as has happened in the past, or some societal change or some shifts in the professional culture bring them off the shelf into a position of high attention and fashionability.

THEORY AND PRACTICE

The preceding sections have been devoted to discussions of some of the political and sociological factors that effect the development of theory. Important as these are, I believe that they all pale into the background to the principal manner in which theory is built. I speak here of the day-to-day, case-by-case, colleague-by-colleague development of theory as a part of the service-giving function of the profession.

I believe that this aspect of theory development has been greatly overlooked. This is partially due to the unfortunate misperceived and falsely maintained alleged schism between research and practice. My thesis here is that every act of responsible social work practice is a process of theory testing and theory building. Therefore, theory is being developed with every interventive act of a social worker. What is meant here is that the process of social work intervention, regardless of what theory or theories drive it, can and should be seen as the same process of formal hypothesis testing of the researcher. Our task as researchers is to learn how to tap this process in a much more effective way than we currently tap it.

In social work treatment, a situation is examined, conclusions are drawn about its significant components, judgments are made about its essential factors, and decisions are made about what are perceived to be responsible and helpful forms of intervention. That is, hypotheses are formulated in the diagnostic process, and based on such hypotheses, decisions are made as to what types of interventions will bring about what types of changes. As with all research, these processes are not initially sequential but rather begin and proceed simultaneously from the first interest in the case or, for the researcher, the topic of study.

Just as our diagnoses change as the process with the client continues sometimes several times, even in our first contact, so too does our process of hypotheses reformulation and refinement change. The judgments that we make about a client are based on the body or bodies of theory that drive our practice. In each intervention, what we are saying to ourselves directly, and to the profession indirectly, is, "Here is how I view this situation based on my present knowledge base, and hence, this is how I propose to interact with this client. I do so with a particular level of comfort as to my certainty and with a concept of what should happen if I am correct." That is, "I am in an ongoing process of formulating a prognosis." For the researcher, this is the equivalent of asking, "What do I think I should find if my formulations are correct?" Obviously, there are differences, most particularly in the time frames in which these processes occur. However, they are identical conceptually.

If there is merit in viewing the treatment process as an ongoing process of theory-driven hypotheses testing, then it becomes imperative that we devote much more attention to developing strategies of tapping this mine of practitioner-driven theory development.

It might be that we have spent much too much time and effort on criticisms of frontline practitioners and their perceived lack of a sufficiently rich and articulated theory base and have spent too little time on finding ways of learning from their practice. As mentioned earlier, the evidence continues to grow that our interventions are, for the most part, effective. What we need to do now, as researchers, is to find better ways of assessing which theoretical concepts lead practitioners to formulate particular diagnoses and interventions with which clients and with what levels of success. This would be more effective than our continuance of a haughty tradition emerging from the summits of academe that drives us to imply that practice is not theory driven.

Our challenge, then, is to find better ways of learning from practice. We now have the research tools (both quantitative and qualitative), a rapidly expanding sophisticated level of statistical competence, and the technology that permits us to do this. As mentioned earlier, if we move in this direction, then it ought be from a position that takes as given that the type of changes we bring about are, for the most part, minuscule. This is not to minimize their importance for clients. Their importance for theory building is in their accumulation within and across cases. Thus, for example, we need to understand and be able to measure that a particular client has been able to reduce his or her anger outbursts by 8% rather than try to establish that the client has totally mastered anger control. We will advance when we can find ways in which to increase this 8% positive change to 12% and see this as a dramatic step forward in our efficacy.

As mentioned earlier, our challenge in research now is to find ways of gathering bodies of homogeneous data in a manner that permits us to abstract the very sparse but rich indicators of successful intervention they contain and seek to tie these into differential theory outcomes. That is, we need to know which theories have which effects with which clients when and in which situations. This will be done by long, tedious, and undramatic research, but it is and shall be the way in which theory develops in our profession. I think that by going in this direction, we will truly and responsibly serve the clients in whose lives we involve ourselves.

Certainly, we should continue to look for and welcome new theories and theoretical insights, but we should temper these with the knowledge that there probably is not going to be some all-powerful theory that will tie all aspects of our practice together in a readily understood manner. This, of course, does not mean that we should not be alert to concepts and theoretical bodies that indeed are major breakthroughs, but we need to be aware that such things rarely happen.

I began this chapter by quoting myself from some of my research teaching. As I conclude the chapter, I do so with an awareness that, in my oft-stated dictum about theory not being developed the way in which teachers of research say it is developed, I have been wrong. There are, and will continue to be, many extraneous influences on the way in which theory develops that need to be understood. In the end, however, theory is going to continue to develop in that slow but responsible formulation of theory-grounded hypotheses that are then tested and the findings analyzed. This needs be done whether this takes place in the use of a multi-million-dollar research grant or it takes place through the efforts of one of our hard-driven frontline colleagues who asks himself or herself after a session with a client, "Now, what was that all about? I wonder if . . . ?"

RECOMMENDED READINGS

Burghardt, S. (1997). A materialist framework for social work theory and practice. In F. Turner (Ed.), *Social work treatment* (4th ed., pp. 409-433). New York: Free Press.

Curnock, L., & Hardicker, S. P. (1974). *Towards practice theory.* London: Routledge and Keagan Paul.

Goldstein, H. (1990). The knowledge base of social work practice: Theory, wisdom, analogue, craft? *Families in Society, 71,* 32-43.

Imre-Wells, R. (1984). The nature of knowledge in social work. *Social Work, 29,* 51-56.

Keefe, T. (1997). Meditation and social work treatment. In F. Turner (Ed.), *Social work treatment* (4th ed., pp. 434-460). New York: Free Press.

Kendall, P. C., & Butler, J. N. (Eds.). (1982). *Handbook of research methods in clinical psychology.* New York: John Wiley.

Latting, J. K. (1990). Identifying the "isms": Enabling social work students to confront their biases. *Journal of Social Work Education, 26,* 36-44.

Lewis H. (1982). *The intellectual base of social work practice.* New York: Haworth.

Merton, R. K. (1957). *Social theory and social structure.* Glencoe, IL: Free Press.

Mishne, J. M. (1993). *The evolution and application of clinical theory.* New York: Free Press.

Reid, W. J. (1984). Treatment of choice or choices of treatment: An essay review. *Social Work Research and Abstracts, 20,* 33-38.

Rubin, A. (1985). Practice effectiveness: More grounds for optimism. *Social Work, 30,* 469-476.

Shulman, L. (1993). Developing and testing a practice theory: An interactional perspective. *Social Work, 38,* 91-93.

Siporin, L. (1993). Metamodels, models, and basics: An essay review. *Social Service Review, 63,* 474-480.

Specht, H. (1990). Social work and popular psychotherapies. *Social Service Review, 64,* 345-357.

Thomlison, R. J. (1984). Something works: Evidence from practice effectiveness studies. *Social Work, 29,* 51-56.

Thyer, B. A. (1993). Social work theory and practice research: The approach of logical positivism. *Social Work and Social Science Review, 4,* 5-26.

Turner, F. J. (1995). Social work practice: Theoretical base. In R. Edwards (Ed.), *Encyclopedia of social work* (19th ed., pp. 2258-2265). Washington, DC: National Association of Social Workers Press.

Turner, F. J. (1997). *Social work theories and models: A chart comparing 27 theories by fifty variables.* Toronto: Author.

Turner, F. J. (1997). *Social work treatment* (4th ed.). New York: Free Press.

Turner, F. J. (1998). Theories of practice with vulnerable populations. In D. Biegel & A. Blum (Eds.), *Innovations in practice and service delivery across the lifespan.* New York: Oxford University Press.

Turner, F. J. (1999). The theoretical base of practice. In F. J. Turner (Ed.), *Social work practice: A Canadian perspective.* Englewood Cliffs, NJ: Prentice Hall.

CHAPTER TWENTY-TWO

Historical Research

JOHN R. GRAHAM
ALEAN AL-KRENAWI

More than 60 years ago, American historian Carl Becker made two critical points about historical research. The first was his insistence that historical writing must be useful; it must have some application to better our understanding of our world. The second was that historical writing invariably reflected the needs of those who wrote it (cited in Nord, 1998). These observations probably are as true today as they were then, and they are as relevant to our profession as they are to many others.

Social work, as well as sister disciplines such as economics, political science, religious studies, sociology, and theology, has widely incorporated historical research into its knowledge base. Historians are well aware of the inevitability of competing visions of the past, and the perennial evolution of these interpretations. History's principal contribution to social work is to provide context to our understanding: greater depth and breadth to what we know as well as assistance in further sharpening those questions that we pose for analysis. To these ends, as this chapter also points out, historical research can be an emancipatory tool for social workers and for peoples affected by social issues of interest to our profession. The chapter presents an overview of the range of historical issues of interest to social workers that have been examined to date, commonly referred to as *social welfare history*. Then, the chapter briefly considers major points of methodology, substance, and several fallacies that may impede effective research. A historical case example, elaborating history's potential as a social change agent, follows. A short concluding section considers the future of historical research relevant to social work.

SOCIAL WORK, SOCIAL POLICY, AND SOCIAL WELFARE HISTORY

In the English-speaking world, the terms *social welfare* and *social service* came into currency shortly before the outbreak of World War I, succeeding earlier notions of *charity and correction, philanthropy,* and *poor relief* (Leiby, 1985, p. 323). *Social welfare history,* the subject of this chapter, is a comprehensive term. It includes, but is not limited to, the history and antecedents of the social work profession, social policies, different fields of practice, social work research, and the lives of people concerned (Chambers, 1986a). The earliest pioneers of our profession were deeply aware of the importance of history and the relationship of our profession to the past. For example, in the United States, Karl de Schweinitz argued persuasively that social policies harkened back to the English labor legislation of 1349 (de Schweinitz, 1943). In Canada, John S. Morgan insisted that the post-World War II universal welfare state was the result of gradually emerging policies and changes in consciousness over the course of many decades (Morgan, 1948). Contrary to what some conservative critics might have inferred, these scholars maintained that the welfare state was not a serendipitous happening or a historical aberration. Rather, it was a logical and natural extension of our historical traditions.

Edith Abbott, professor of social work at the University of Chicago and one of the leading lights in early social work education, insisted in 1928 that only "by building knowledge of the past" would the profession "be able to go forward and not backward" (quoted in Breul & Diner, 1980, p. 2). Likewise, Jane Addams's pioneering settlement house work (Addams, 1930) and Mary Richmond's early pathbreaking theories of social casework (Richmond, 1917, 1922) were firmly anchored to historical memory. All three writers believed that the professional social worker was expected to provide assistance that was even more helpful, systematic, and efficient than before. But the predominantly religious values orientations that had so influenced social work's immediate precursors—members of the late 19th- and early 20th-century charity organization movement (Leiby, 1984)—never could be forgotten. Small wonder, then, that in our own time, social work, perhaps more than any other discipline, is so profoundly values driven in its own now secular way.

HISTORICAL METHODS

The historian's chief task, as Chambers (1992) perceptively argues, is "to tell stories of the past as accurately, honestly, and fairly as possible." In this process, the historian will "bring forward people telling their own stories and . . . provide plausible explanations of the course events took over time" (p. 493). What one generation (or person) thinks about the past may differ markedly from what the next generation (or person) thinks. Any historical account, then, will be provisional. At best, historians strive to produce prose that is clear, precise, graceful, and jargon free; analysis that is judicious, is always striving for deeper connections, and is ever mindful of nuances, patterns, exceptions, and paradoxes; and evidence that is accurate, balanced, and comprehensive.

Historiography

Good history starts with the available secondary literature produced by historians and allied disciplines. From it, a writer may consider issues related to major analytical themes—"sources, methods, competing interpretive schemes, the kinds and range of questions to be asked, and the appropriate processes for seeking tentative answers" (Chambers, 1992, p. 494). Historiographical articles—literature reviews of recently published works—are a superb vehicle for an overview of major recent developments in analysis and methodology (Chambers, 1986a, 1992; Graham, 1996; Martin, 1992). An annual bibliography of social welfare historical research also is published by the Social Welfare History Group, a member organization of the Council of Social Work Education in the United States (Wilk, 1998). In addition, there are helpful overview secondary research resources such as chapters on history and biographical sketches in the National Association of Social Workers' *Encyclopedia* and *Yearbook* series as well as social welfare historical dictionaries (Greve, 1998).

Context

Also important, to turn to a related area, are the major social, political, cultural, and economic issues of the day that profoundly influence the range of questions historians pose for analysis as well as the subjects and sources they use. Social movements, such as the civil rights initiatives of the 1960s, likely inspired the liberal left writings of Piven and Cloward. Their book, *Regulating the Poor,* indicted the welfare state's social control function—its ability to avert civil chaos during economic downturns and to exert pressure on the workforce during periods of stability (Piven & Cloward, 1971). To turn to a second example, feminist thinking has motivated some of the current writing of social welfare history. We now know much about the patriarchal basis of social policies (Gordon, 1994) and social work practice and theories (Gordon, 1988), the nature of particular social problems such as family violence (Pleck, 1987), and the enduring efforts of women social workers to develop meaningful professional lives and social justice for their clients—despite the barriers imposed from within and outside the profession (Chambers, 1986b).

Particular public issues certainly instigate historical writing. The contemporary tendency to download fiscal and administrative social welfare responsibilities from higher levels of government to municipal jurisdictions inspired several scholars to point out the obvious connection to the 1930s. During the Great Depression of that decade, the historical precedent of administrative and financial obligations for many of the most essential social programs could not be sustained at the local level. Indeed, one of many major reasons for the establishment of a more comprehensive welfare state involving the participation of higher levels of government was the municipal fiscal crisis of the 1930s and the manifest failure of local governments to sustain basic social programs such as unemployment relief. In our time, it seems, by downloading greater responsibilities to local governments, we are quickly moving back to the practices of the Depression era without particular reference to why they were abandoned some 70 years ago (Fuchs, 1998; Graham, 1995).

Historical Sources

Perhaps the most important criterion of historical research is the sources, or primary materials, that its practitioners consult. Historical data may be derived from oral historical interviews (Martin, 1995). Indeed, in efforts to preserve ethno-specific cultures, recent social work research has used oral historical data to recover the lived histories of elderly women in Hawaii (Mokuau & Browne, 1994) and in Afro-American communities (Carlton-LaNey, 1992). In other instances, primary materials are found in hard copy form derived from newspapers and electronic media, published books and journals, surveys, opinion polls, public records, private papers, and governmental reports. These primary sources often are found in archives and other repositories of historical records. The Social Welfare History Archives at the University of Minnesota is the locus of many primary documents relating to American social welfare history. Particular institutions, possibly the subject of historical inquiry, also may have their own formal archives. In other instances, materials of interest to social welfare historians may be in municipal archives, national archives, state or provincial archives, university archives, and various media archives.

Potentially valuable materials might well remain in the possession of individuals or institutions rather than archives, and it sometimes is the case that those with proprietorship might not appreciate the value of what they have. Historians, then, have a responsibility to assist people in identifying and donating these materials to archives, where trained staff can ensure storage and preservation for ongoing use.

Experienced historians well appreciate the declining quality of paper production since the 1890s; the inevitability of deterioration of all print, photograph, video, and film materials; and the importance of storing, handling, and preserving these under optimal conditions. Good archival practices include storage under constant temperature and humidity levels as well as in nonacidic boxes and file folders, the handling of fragile documents only when wearing cotton gloves, minimal exposure of materials to direct sunlight, and (where possible) duplication of a copy of fragile documents by a restoration specialist (Pickford, Rhys-Lewis, & Weber, 1997).

THE SCOPE OF RESEARCH

The most frequently cited and read social welfare history has appeared during the past 40 years and is, necessarily, broad. In the English-speaking world, two major areas of concentration have evolved. The first is the history of the welfare state (Bremner, 1956; Bruce, 1961), and the second is the history of the social work profession (Lubove, 1965; Woodroffe, 1962). Much of the literature since then has elaborated particular nuances on either topic and also involves major analytical differences in making sense of them. As a source of better conceptualizing our knowledge base, the historical method is virtually limitless in potential including, but not limited to, examining the specifics of the following:

1. The moral foundations of the profession (Leiby, 1985)
2. Social work theories such as functionalism (Dore, 1990)
3. Research approaches such as positivism (Tyson, 1992)
4. Trends in practice such as deinstitutionalization (Dore & Kennedy, 1981)
5. Types of practice such as community organization (Betten & Austin, 1990) or casework (Lubove, 1965)
6. Public issues such as social perceptions of disabilities (Covey, 1998)
7. Social policies such as adoption (Carp, 1998), day care (Rose, 1998), and income security programs (Sass, 1997)
8. Particular racial and ethnic communities with which social workers could interact (Chavez, 1998)
9. Ways in which social work has interacted with ethnoracial and other minority communities (Iacovetta, 1992).

Social welfare history may be considered closely allied to, and sometimes under the broader rubric of, social history, with the latter's commitment to understanding the lives of ordinary people, not just society's political, economic, social, religious, and cultural elites. Writing nearly 15 years ago, Chambers (1986a) rightly insisted that social welfare historians had "pursued traditional lines of inquiry and employed traditional methods of analysis," remaining "largely untouched by the dramatic shifts in perspective, perception, and method that marked the work of their colleagues in other divisions of social history" such as cliometrics, labor history, and women's history (p. 407). But in our time, the questions posed for analysis, as well as the subjects and sources of history, have changed. Gordon's (1988) book, noted in the annotated bibliography at the end of this chapter, is an excellent example of the social historical imperative of including the perspectives of ordinary people. A small but significant literature also has sought to understand the complex interplay of civil society and family structures in the welfare process (Frank, 1998). Turning to a different methodology, historians, inspired by a cliometric tradition of quantitative analysis, have begun to quantify levels of poverty and social need (Di Mateo, 1996; Di Mateo & George, 1992).

Above all else, historical research is in a constant state of evolution, and the questions that it raises invariably lead to further questions and qualifications of previous answers. For example, the 1940s, conventionally perceived as a period of welfare state advancement in industrialized countries, have been portrayed recently as a decade of austerity and minimalist social welfare structures in the United Kingdom (Tomlison, 1998) and in the United States (Amenta, 1988). Turning to a second example, that of diversity, recent research explores the contributions of women (as mentioned previously), of gays and lesbians (Gordon, 1994), of ethnoracial and religious communities (Ilchman, Katz, & Queen, 1998), and the way in which social policies and social work have oppressed disempowered minority communities (Covey, 1998; Quadagno, 1994), moving well beyond previous generations' range of analytical assumptions.

HISTORIANS' FALLACIES

As in all forms of academic research, it is important to avoid fallacies or illogical arguments that pose as logical. Several of the more common fallacies are as follows:

1. *The atheoretical fallacy.* This is the wrongful assumption that a historian selects and analyzes data without preconceived questions, hypotheses, prejudices, presuppositions, assumptions, and/or theory (Fischer, 1970, p. 4). But as one famous adage has it, there are no neutral facts in history, only interpretations.

2. *The fallacy of poorly framed questions.* One such variant poses questions that have false presumptions or that beg other questions that might go unanswered (Fischer, 1970, pp. 8-9). An example might be "Why was President Kennedy more sympathetic toward social welfare than was President Carter?" That question has presuppositions that may be challenged; Carter, in fact, might have been more sympathetic than Kennedy.

3. *The fallacy of false dichotomies.* A historian may ask whether Lord Beveridge, who wrote the famous 1942 report ushering in a universal welfare state in Great Britain, was a genius or painfully naive. In truth, he may have been both, neither, or somewhere in between. But the question, as currently posed, might not allow such nuances to be appreciated (Fischer, 1970).

4. *The fallacy of one-dimensionality.* A scholar interested exclusively in intellectual history may overlook the connections of late 19th-century social surveys to the generation of class consciousness among trade unionists. Conversely, a historian interested exclusively in the class assumptions of members of the charity organization movement may overlook some of the intellectual/theological assumptions governing their work (Fischer, 1970).

5. *Post hoc ergo propter hoc (i.e., because this happened after that, it happened because of that).* The stock market crashes of October 1929 did precede the 1930s Great Depression. However, it is a distortion to claim that the crashes *caused* the Depression given that many intervening variables also were at play including a lack of consumer confidence, a modest social and interventionist state, and nascent transnational structures of international finance (Marius, 1995, p. 71).

6. *The fallacy of indiscriminate pluralism.* This is the mistake of inadequately defining, or ascribing relative weight to, causal explanations (Fischer, 1970, p. 175). In the preceding example, a historian might want to prioritize the various factors that contributed to the 1930s Great Depression.

7. *The antiquarian fallacy.* This is the refusal to use present theoretical or values assumptions as a basis for illuminating the past. For example, if historians assumed the value positions of the periods under study, then they might overlook many social problems of the past (e.g., child abuse, violence against women) as worthy topics of historical scrutiny (Fischer, 1970).

8. *The fallacy of presentism.* This is the opposite to the preceding fallacy. It is the inability to analyze historical data from the perspective of a given time period and to thereby impose different value assumptions of a different era. For example, it might be problematic to dismiss entirely the social action initiatives of some well-to-do 19th-century child welfare crusaders merely because they held then common assumptions about socioeconomic class distinctions (Fischer, 1970).

9. *The fallacy of composition.* This occurs when the characteristics of one individual or of a small number of people are applied as attributes of the group itself

(Fischer, 1970, p. 219). For example, it is erroneous to assume that all Victorians were not disturbed by the presence of children working in factories, even though some factory owners at the time evidently were undisturbed.

CASE EXAMPLE

In Canada, as in other countries such as the United States, treaties were struck between Aboriginal peoples and the colonizing government. Between 1871 and 1921, the Canadian federal government negotiated what became known as "numbered treaties," Treaties 1 to 11, on which the government intended to extinguish Aboriginal claim to most of western and northern Canada east of the Rocky Mountains (Bercuson & Granatstein, 1988, p. 101). The treaties were significant factors in the deterioration of Aboriginal culture and society. Aboriginal peoples were to live on reserves of land, set aside by the Crown, and the federal government pursued implicit and explicit policies of assimilation. For the past 30 years, Aboriginal leaders have become increasingly active politically, rejecting notions of assimilation and challenging the unconscionably high levels of unemployment, poverty, and other social problems on and off the reserves. As part of this effort, Treaty 7 Elders and Tribal Council, with the assistance of three writers, published a landmark book of historical scholarship and contemporary social activism (Treaty 7 Elders and Tribal Council, Hildebrandt, First Rider, & Carter, 1996). The result is an interpretation of history markedly different from Ottawa's and from many previous academic and public interpretations outside Aboriginal communities. As the book's foreword mentions, "In the past we have heard about treaties from legal experts, politicians, anthropologists, and historians, but we have never heard from the elders of Treaty 7 in a comprehensive way" (p. vii).

Treaty 7 was concluded during the summer of 1876 following negotiations between the Crown and Aboriginal peoples occupying present-day southern Alberta. The 1996 research is based on the testimony of more than 80 elders from the five First Nations tribes involved in Treaty 7—the Blood, Peigan, Siksika, Stoney Nakoda, and Tsuu T'ina—and was undertaken in elders' language in accordance with culturally appropriate methods of ethnographic and oral historical research. Also as part of the research, the book provides a historical overview of Treaty 7 and an analysis of the literature on treaties in general and Treaty 7 in particular, highlighting the different worldviews affecting each side's interpretation of the events. As elders point out, there were grave misconceptions and misrepresentations due, in part, to inadequate interpretation and to deliberate attempts to mislead. Elders consistently insist that the treaty, as their community always understood it, was to share the land with European newcomers in exchange for resources to establish new economies including education, medical assistance, and annuity payments. Aboriginal peoples never intended to surrender land. Indeed, the Aboriginal worldview understands occupancy, as distinct from ownership. As another historian argues, there is no evidence, on these grounds alone, of informed consent to relinquish lands (Dempsey, 1987). The implications of such research are many:

1. Dialogue between Aboriginal and Euro-Canadian society, which has been so damaging to Aboriginal peoples on the basis of previously held assumptions, now can be carried forward with greater sensitivity to Aboriginal understanding.
2. Previous Euro-Canadian and governmental claims to truth, as manifested by treaties and official government opinion, and as reinforced by previous academic scholarship, are appropriately challenged by an Aboriginal perspective.
3. Further negotiations on land agreements, self-government, and Aboriginal autonomy in social service and other spheres of life can be influenced by the findings of such research.
4. The research itself further empowers and legitimates the community.
5. The elders convey to and beyond the Aboriginal community a capacity to influence Aboriginal peoples and Canadian society.
6. Other Aboriginal communities within and outside Canada can replicate the research and benefit from its findings.

CONCLUSION

Many scholars lament the lack of reference to history in contemporary life during an era of television, the "global village," and geographic mobility (Harlan, 1997; Schorske, 1998). As Reisch (1988) bluntly puts it, "Because they have grown up in an ahistorical culture, many of today's social work students"—and, one might add, practitioners and scholars—"do not challenge prevailing myths about our past, and consequently, dissociate present problems from their historical antecedents" (p. 3). But in our time, perhaps more than at any other point in our profession's short life, history provides much-needed points of illumination. It allows us to appreciate that, during an age of seemingly insurmountable obstacles (e.g., dismantling of welfare states, destruction of physical ecologies, ascendancy of global finance and its liberal ideologies), there is hope nonetheless. History provides role models of people and institutions that have triumphed over issues of comparable magnitude during different ages, be they the heroes of the Victorian-era settlement houses, the rank-and-file progressive social workers of the 1930s and 1940s, or the members of ethnoracial minority communities who provided mutual support and assistance to society's most marginalized during any era. Similarly, we might need to return to certain traditions in our past that have been forfeited in the present. For example, some historians advocate our profession's recovery of a commitment to social change (Reeser & Leighninger, 1990).

Likewise, history can provide manifest insight into the genuine shortcomings that constitute our past. Social work, like welfare states, sometimes has tended to reinforce oppression on the basis of socioeconomic class, gender, age, ethnicity, sexual orientation, and range of ability, among other parameters. This is not to suggest an incapacitating shame; rather, it is to invoke a considered awareness of the full extent of our capacity for good and bad as well as a commensurate humility and constant questioning in our own time to minimize the probability of oppressing and doing wrong in the present and future. Finally, and along similar lines, history can encourage us not to repeat past mistakes in public policy. To cite one example, previous experiences can show how current trends to relinquish government social welfare responsibility to civil society may hurt society's most vulnerable and create inordinate pressure on women as caregivers and on social service organizations with limited funds. Indeed, philosopher George Santayana remarked earlier in the 20th century that those who do not remember their history are condemned to repeat it. This adage, as one historian wisely comments, "does not promise that knowledge will transform, only that lack of it dooms us" (Gordon, 1994, p. 305).

SELECT ANNOTATED BIBLIOGRAPHY

Gordon, L. (1988). *Heroes of their own lives: The politics and history of family violence, Boston, 1880-1960*. New York: Viking.

This is a masterful study based on rich and detailed casework records of three child welfare agencies in Boston and one of the earlier works to comprehensively capture the perspectives of consumers of social service agencies. Gordon brilliantly outlines how socioeconomic class strongly influenced which families were selected for intervention, how family violence is politically constructed, how the state and the social work profession have variously intervened, and how clients themselves ask for and attempt to influence the nature of interventions and the definitions of family violence.

Lees, L. H. (1998). *The solidarities of strangers: The English poor laws and the people, 1700-1948*. New York: Cambridge University Press.

Individual stories and official actions are conveyed in accessible prose. A judicious analysis points out the cycles of generosity and unkindness that affected men and women unequally. Beneficiaries and amounts were determined more by cultural definitions of entitlement than by available resources. The long-term history of English welfare is one of ebbs and flows rather than continued progress. This is an important work that will provide many opportunities for further refinement of fundamental policy questions in historical and social policy literatures.

Leiby, J. (1984). Charity organization reconsidered. *Social Service Review, 58,* 523-538.

Prior to Leiby's work, historical references to the late 19th-century charity organization movement (COS), a key historical phenomenon giving rise to the development of a social work profession, tended to have presentist assumptions; the literature emphasized how the COS contributed to the rise of the welfare state and a scientific knowledge base for social work. But Leiby points out how charity organizers regarded themselves, first and foremost, as religious people working in a religious tradition and elegantly elaborates their theological assumptions about love and community. This is an essential article on the history of social work values.

REFERENCES

Addams, J. (1930). *The second twenty years at Hull-House, September 1909 to September 1929: With a record of a growing world consciousness.* New York: Macmillan.

Amenta, E. (1988). *Bold relief: Institutional politics and the origins of modern American social policy.* Princeton, NJ: Princeton University Press.

Bercuson, D. J., & Granatstein, J. L. (1988). *The Collins dictionary of Canadian history.* Toronto: Collins.

Betten, N., & Austin, M. J. (1990). *The roots of community organizing, 1917-1939.* Philadelphia: Temple University Press.

Bremner, R. H. (1956). *From the depths: The discovery of poverty in the United States.* New York: New York University Press.

Breul, F. R., & Diner, S. J. (1980). Introduction. In F. R. Breul & S. J. Diner (Eds.), *Compassion and responsibility: Readings in the history of social welfare policy in the United States.* Chicago: University of Chicago Press.

Bruce, M. (1961). *The coming of the welfare state.* London: Batsford.

Carlton-LaNey, I. (1992). Elderly black farm women: A population at risk. *Social Work, 37,* 517-523.

Carp, E. W. (1998). *Family matters: Secrecy and disclosure in the history of adoption.* Cambridge, MA: Harvard University Press.

Chambers, C. A. (1986a). Toward a redefinition of welfare history. *Journal of American History, 73,* 407-433.

Chambers, C. A. (1986b). Women in the creation of the profession of social work. *Social Service Review, 60,* 1-33.

Chambers, C. A. (1992). "Uphill all the way": Reflections on the course and study of welfare history. *Social Service Review, 66,* 492-504.

Chavez, J. R. (1998). *East landmark: A history of the East Los Angeles Community Union, 1968-1993.* Stanford, CA: Stanford University Press.

Covey, H. S. (1998). *Social perceptions of people with disabilities in history.* Springfield, IL: Charles C Thomas.

Dempsey, H. A. (1987). *Treaty research report: Treaty Seven.* Ottawa: Treaties and Historical Research Centre.

de Schweinitz, K. (1943). *England's road to social security.* Philadelphia: University of Pennsylvania Press.

Di Mateo, L. (1996). Wealth of the Irish in nineteenth-century Ontario. *Social Science History, 20,* 209-234.

Di Mateo, L., & George, P. J. (1992). Canadian wealth inequality in the late nineteenth century: A study of Wentworth County, Ontario, 1872-1902. *Canadian Historical Review, 73,* 453-483.

Dore, M. M. (1990). Functional theory: Its history and influence on contemporary social work practice. *Social Service Review, 64,* 358-374.

Dore, M. M., & Kennedy, K. G. (1981). Two decades of turmoil: Child welfare services, 1960-1980. *Child Welfare, 60,* 371-382.

Fischer, D. H. (1970). *Historians' fallacies: Toward a logic of historical thought.* New York: Harper & Row.

Frank, S. M. (1998). *Life with father: Parenthood and masculinity in the nineteenth-century American North.* Baltimore, MD: Johns Hopkins University Press.

Fuchs, E. R. (1998). The permanent urban fiscal crisis. In A. J. Kahn & S. B. Kamerman (Eds.), *Big cities in the welfare transition.* New York: Columbia University, School of Social Work.

Gordon, L. (1988). *Heroes of their own lives: The politics and history of family violence, Boston, 1880-1960.* New York: Viking.

Gordon, L. (1994). *Pitied but not entitled: Single mothers and the history of welfare.* New York: Free Press.

Graham, J. R. (1995). Lessons for today: Canadian municipalities and unemployment relief during the 1930s Great Depression. *Canadian Review of Social Policy, 35,* 1-18.

Graham, J. R. (1996). An analysis of Canadian social welfare historical writing. *Social Service Review, 70*(1), 140-158.

Greve, B. (1998). *Historical dictionary of the welfare state.* Lanham, MD: Scarecrow.

Harlan, D. (1997). *The degradation of American history.* Chicago: University of Chicago Press.

Iacovetta, F. (1992). Making "new Canadians": Social workers, women, and the reshaping of immigrant families. In F. Iacovetta & M. Valverde (Eds.), *Gender conflicts: New essays in women's history* (pp. 261-303). Toronto: University of Toronto Press.

Ilchman, W. F., Katz, S., & Queen, E. L. (Eds.). (1998). *Philanthropy in the world's traditions.* Bloomington: Indiana University Press.

Lees, L. H. (1998). *The solidarities of strangers: The English poor laws and the people, 1700-1948.* New York: Cambridge University Press.

Leiby, J. (1984). Charity organization reconsidered. *Social Service Review, 58,* 523-538.

Leiby, J. (1985). Moral foundations of social welfare and social work: A historical view. *Social Work, 30,* 323-330.

Lubove, R. (1965). *The professional altruist: The emergence of social work as a career, 1880-1930.* Cambridge, MA: Harvard University Press.

Marius, R. (1995). *A short guide to writing about history.* New York: HarperCollins.

Martin, E. W. (1992). Themes in a history of the social work profession. *International Social Work, 35,* 327-345.

Martin, R. R. (1995). *Oral history in social work: Research, assessment, and intervention.* Thousand Oaks, CA: Sage.

Mokuau, N., & Browne, C. (1994). Life themes of native Hawaiian female elders: Resources for cultural preservation. *Social Work, 39,* 43-49.

Morgan, J. S. (1948). The break-up of the Poor Law in Britain, 1907-47: An historical footnote. *Canadian Journal of Political Science and Economics, 14,* 209-219.

Nord, D. P. (1998). The uses of memory: An introduction. *American Historical Review, 85,* 409-410.

Pickford, C., Rhys-Lewis, J., & Weber, J. (1997). *Preservation and conservation: A guide to policy and practices in the preservation of archives.* London: Society of Archivists.

Piven, F. F., & Cloward, R. A. (1971). *Regulating the poor: The functions of public welfare.* New York: Vintage.

Pleck, E. (1987). *Domestic tyranny: The making of American social policy against family violence from colonial times to the present.* New York: Oxford University Press.

Quadagno, J. S. (1994). *The color of welfare: How racism undermined the war on poverty.* New York: Oxford University Press.

Reeser, L. C., & Leighninger, L. (1990). Back to our roots: Towards a specialization in social justice. *Journal of Sociology and Social Welfare, 17*(2), 69-87.

Reisch, M. 1988. The uses of history in teaching social work. *Journal of Teaching in Social Work, 2,* 3-16.

Richmond, M. (1917). *Social diagnosis.* New York: Russell Sage.

Richmond, M. (1922). *What is social case work?* New York: Russell Sage.

Rose, E. (1998). *A mother's job: The history of day care, 1890-1960.* Oxford, UK: Oxford University Press.

Sass, S. A. (1997). *The promise of pensions: The first hundred years.* Cambridge, MA: Harvard University Press.

Schorske, C. E. (1998). *Thinking with history: Explorations in the passage to modernism.* Princeton, NJ: Princeton University Press.

Tomlison, J. (1998). Why so austere? The British welfare state of the 1940s. *Journal of Social Policy, 27,* 63-77.

Treaty 7 Elders and Tribal Council, Hildebrandt, W., First Rider, D., & Carter, S. (1996). *The true spirit and original intent of Treaty 7.* Montreal: McGill-Queen's University Press.

Tyson, K. B. (1992). A new approach to relevant scientific research for practitioners: The heuristic paradigm. *Social Work, 37,* 541-556.

Wilk, R. J. (Ed.). (1998). *Annual bibliography of scholarship in social welfare history* (Social Welfare History Group, No. 94). Minneapolis: University of Minnesota, School of Social Work.

Woodroffe, K. (1962). *From charity to social work in England and the United States.* Toronto: University of Toronto Press.

CHAPTER TWENTY-THREE

Literature Reviews

KAREN SOWERS

RODNEY A. ELLIS

NANCY MEYER-ADAMS

The literature review is a foundational stage in the development of any research project. During this stage, researchers gain information regarding the current knowledge base in their areas of interest, refine their conceptualizations and operationalizations, and identify problems that are likely to arise during their studies.

The literature review is an important step in the research process. Its results provide a foundation for every other stage of the study. It helps the researcher to anticipate and avoid problems, define concepts, identify measures, and select design. The literature review is equally important to the reader of the research report because it helps him or her to understand the researcher's decisions and choices.

This chapter discusses the use of the literature review in social work research. First, it describes the reasons why literature reviews are conducted. Second, it offers an overview of the review process. Third, it examines several specific aspects of review including identification of inclusionary and exclusionary criteria, methods of calculating interrater agreement, and principles of reporting the results. Finally, it examines two types of literature reviews (qualitative and quantitative) and describes a specific type of review, the meta-analysis.

PURPOSES OF LITERATURE REVIEWS

A literature review serves three important purposes. First, it constitutes a reservoir of knowledge for planning and understanding research. Second, it affords a tool for conceptualization and operationalization. Third, it provides an atlas of potential error, facilitating the identification of potential problems in the research process.

The Literature Review as a Reservoir of Knowledge

The literature review serves primarily as a reservoir of knowledge, first for the researcher and then for those who may read his or her published report. For the researcher, this reservoir has several functions. It helps to deepen the researcher's understanding of the history of the problem, its origin, and its scope (Yegidis & Weinbach, 1996). It also helps the researcher to connect his or her study to others in the area (Creswell, 1994). Furthermore, it helps the researcher to determine what answers already exist regarding the problem as well as what potential answers have not been supported (Yegidis & Weinbach, 1996). It also highlights the avenues taken by previous research and may offer insight into promising new directions (Neuman, 1997). Finally, it helps to establish the importance of the study (Creswell, 1994) and to facilitate the summary and integration of available knowledge (Neuman, 1997).

For the reader of the published research report, the literature review has at least three functions. It helps to establish the credibility of the researcher and his or her background work. It helps the reader to gain a basic understanding of the findings of other researchers as a foundation for evaluating the results of the current study (Neuman, 1997). Finally, it may form a source for additional information if the reader desires to learn more about the research problem.

The Literature Review as a Tool for Study Development

The literature review also is an important tool for the development and design of the research project. It can be used to identify methodologies that have been effective (or ineffective) for other researchers (Yegidis & Weinbach, 1996). It can facilitate the development of measures or help in the identification of measures that have been developed previously (Rubin & Babbie, 1997; Yegidis & Weinbach, 1996). It also can help the researcher to shape his or her research question, refine his or her operational definitions, and identify alternative hypotheses (Creswell, 1994; Yegidis & Weinbach, 1996).

The Literature Review as an Atlas of Error

The final function of the literature review is as an atlas of potential error (Rubin & Babbie, 1997; Yegidis & Weinbach, 1996). Publications of previous studies often report limitations, problems, and paradoxes experienced by the authors. By becoming aware of and planning for these situations, the researcher can greatly improve the quality of his or her study.

CONDUCTING A LITERATURE REVIEW

Each year, the number of studies available increases in many fields, and new fields of study are developed. In addition, the potential sources of publications and types of publications become increasingly diverse. These conditions have important implications for at least two aspects of the literature review process. The first, the methods used in conducting a review, are described in this section. The second, the importance of specific inclusionary and exclusionary criteria, are described in a later section.

The abundance of both publications and sources makes careful planning and method selection vital in the review process. The researcher must plan a search that is sufficiently comprehensive, that includes a plan for adequately tracking the publications that have been received and reviewed, and that uses clear and consistent research paths.

Identifying Potential Sources of Publications

The first step in acquiring publications for inclusion in the literature review is identifying potential sources. Potential sources include library catalogs, CD-ROM databases, the Internet, government agencies, local funding agencies, and other researchers. The first step that the prospective reviewer should make is to develop a checklist of resources that are likely to have relevant material. For example, a researcher intending to conduct an evaluation of a substance abuse treatment program for women might want to check his or her own and other library catalogs as well as CD-ROM databases such as PSYCHLIT, Social Work Abstracts, SOCIOFILE, MEDLINE, and ERIC. The researcher also might search the Internet using several of the available search engines, place telephone calls to agencies such as the National Institute on Drug Abuse, and call colleagues at other universities who have conducted research on substance abuse treatment. She then would record these resources on a checklist of potential publication sources. A partial checklist for this review is illustrated in Table 23.1.

TABLE 23.1   Partial Sample Checklist of Sources of Publications

Substance abuse treatment evaluation: Females

___ University library
___ Colorado Association of Research Libraries
___ PSYCHLIT
___ Social Work Abstracts
___ SOCIOFILE
___ MEDLINE
___ ERIC
___ National Institute on Drug Abuse
___ Other researchers
    ___ John Smith
    ___ Susan Williams

Preparing to Review

Preparing to review includes two additional important steps: (a) developing a list of descriptor words and (b) preparing a tracking form. Descriptor words are key words and phrases that may be entered into a search field on a computer. This enables the computer to scan its records to determine whether any publications exist in its database that use that word or phrase. For example, the researcher who is interested in theoretical material regarding delinquency prevention might include words such as *delinquency, prevention, adolescent, problem behavior,* and *treatment* on his or her list. The researcher then could use each descriptor word as he or she searches each computerized resource listed on the checklist of potential publication sources. A sample list of descriptor words is shown in Table 23.2.

The researcher also may choose to prepare a publication tracking form (PTF), a page containing columns for authors, date of publication, date ordered, resource used, date received, and additional comments. The PTF is a simple method for keeping an inventory of the publications ordered and received. Using a PTF helps the researcher to be assured that no important materials are inadvertently omitted.

Developing a Research Path

Once descriptor words have been identified, the researcher can proceed to distinguish and follow research paths. The term *research path* refers to a specific order that may be consistently followed in identifying publications. A research path contains three stages: identify, locate, and obtain.

Identify refers to the process of determining what publications exist that may be of interest to the researcher. This stage frequently is accomplished by the use of

TABLE 23.2 Partial Sample Checklist of Descriptor Words

Prevention of delinquency

___ Delinquency
___ Prevention
___ Adolescent
___ Problem behavior
___ Teen/teenager
___ Treatment

descriptor words. For example, the researcher mentioned earlier looking for material on prevention programming might use the descriptors *adolescent problem behavior and prevention.* In the PSYCHLIT database, this would identify several publications, some theoretical and some empirical. If the researcher were interested in model programs, then he or she could peruse an abstract of an article by Ellis (1998) titled "Filling the Prevention Gap: Multi-Factor, Multi-System, Multi-Level Intervention." If the researcher were interested in the full article, then he or she also could learn that the article was published in the Fall 1998 issue of the *Journal of Primary Prevention.*

Having identified the article, the researcher could progress to the second stage: locate. To locate the article just mentioned, the researcher would need to find a library that carried the *Journal of Primary Prevention.* One way in which the researcher might accomplish this is by searching the catalog of the university library and those of related institutions. The researcher would conduct this search by using the journal's title as the descriptor. Once the researcher had determined what resource carried the journal, he or she could progress to the third stage.

The third stage of the research path is *obtain.* During this stage, the researcher actually acquires the desired publication. The method of acquisition will vary depending on where the publication is located. In the preceding example, the researcher might have located the journal in his or her own university library. In this case, the researcher might simply locate and photocopy the article. If the library did not carry the journal, then the researcher could order a copy of the article through interlibrary loan. Information obtained at each of the stages would be recorded on the PTF.

Research Paths and Other Sources of Publications

The stages of the research path are accomplished differently depending on the resources from which they are obtained. For example, an article might be identified through a Web page or through a conversation with a colleague. In the first case, the article might be downloaded from the Web page (locate and obtain). In the latter case, the colleague might simply be asked for a copy or for information on where the publication might be obtained. Once a path has been identified for each type of resource, it may be repeated with other similar resources. For example, the path used for PSYCHLIT might be repeated for other CD-ROM databases such as Social Work Abstracts and SOCIOFILE.

DETERMINING INCLUSIONARY AND EXCLUSIONARY CRITERIA

Once the publications have been obtained, it is necessary to determine which will be included in the review. This is accomplished by developing specific inclusionary and exclusionary criteria. Yegidis and Weinbach (1996) list three standards for including literature. First, it should provide both researcher and reader with needed information. Second, it should allow both researcher and reader to draw conclusions regarding the proposed research. Third, the source should be trustworthy and believable. These criteria clearly are essential to any literature review. Other criteria might be necessary, however, depending on the nature and purpose of the review and on the quantity and quality of available publications.

Criteria Based on the Nature and Purpose of the Review

The nature and purpose of the review may greatly influence its contents. One important factor affecting selection is whether the review is to inform a qualitative or quantitative study. Qualitative studies are best informed by studies that use an inductive approach, consistent with the goals of the study itself (Creswell, 1994). This would suggest that the primary content of a literature review for a qualitative study would be qualitative literature. Similarly, quantitative reviews would be composed predominantly of quantitative studies. Additional considerations in qualitative and quantitative reviews are discussed later in this chapter.

Another important factor affecting literature selection is whether the study will be exploratory or experimental. In the former, the review often is used to explore alternative theoretical perspectives. Such a review would attempt to include as many perspectives as possible and examine each for its explanatory power, its logical consistency, the strength of its assumptions, and its scope (Neuman, 1997). Criteria would focus selection on theoretical explanations and studies that support or fail to support each theory.

In an experimental study, the literature review focuses on the empirical outcomes of previous studies. The emphasis is on summarizing what others have found and on determining how that information will inform the current study. Selection criteria may include study design, relevance of the variables, and the nature of the population studied.

A final essential factor is whether the literature reviewed is intended to inform a study or to be the object of the study. Literature becomes the object of the study in at least two instances: content analysis and meta-analysis. In content analysis, a body of literature is examined to determine the frequency with which specific topics and ideas are presented and to trace the development of those ideas. Clearly, literature for a content analysis would need to be drawn specifically from that body.

Literature also is the object of the study in meta-analysis. For meta-analysis, empirical studies are collected and their outcomes are integrated and compared by statistically analyzing their reported results. In this case, the literature obtained should include only empirical studies concerning a specific topic. An additional factor to consider in meta-analysis is whether any study should be excluded on the basis of its methodological limitations. This issue relates to the quality of available publications and is discussed in the next section.

Criteria Based on Available Publications

The quality and quantity of available publications also may strongly affect selection. Neuman's (1997) third criterion is credibility, and credibility may be negatively affected by methodological limitations. Such limitations might lead the researcher to draw strict guidelines excluding quasi-experimental designs or studies in which mortality seemed particularly high. Low availability of studies, however, might induce the researcher to loosen those criteria. In fact, Hunter, Schmidt, and Jackson (1982) argue that studies should not be excluded due to methodological limitations. They contend that a priori exclusion of such studies is itself a bias because it cannot be known whether the studies were affected by their limitations. The point at which the researcher elects to exclude due to methodological limitations must be left to each individual. However, the criteria and basis for developing it should be clearly stated in the researcher's report.

Additional Considerations in Developing Criteria

Under certain conditions, the reviewer might wish to exclude studies conducted prior to a specified date. For example, the reviewer might elect to exclude gang intervention literature written prior to 1970 because of the tremendous social and cultural differences that exist between today's gangs and those existing before that date. The researcher's decision could both limit the tremendous volume of material in the area and help to exclude irrelevant information.

Another important consideration is relevance of the variables in a publication. For example, a study might report only distal outcomes, whereas the researcher is interested only in proximal measures. A study of social skills training for delinquents might report improvements in peer interactions, and this might be of little interest to the researcher who is concerned with recidivism rates among offenders.

Some publications may exclude data or information that is crucial to the purpose of the review. This sometimes happens in meta-analysis when specific statistics necessary to calculate effect sizes are omitted from a published report. It might be possible to obtain such statistics by contacting the author directly. If this cannot be done, then it might be necessary to exclude the study.

Another method of making inclusionary decisions is the use of independent raters. This system follows the method for determining interrater reliability suggested by Bloom, Fischer, and Orme (1999). To use this system, the researcher first would identify two experts willing to review a group of articles. The researcher then would send all of them publications that met basic inclusionary criteria. The experts would review each publication and make recommendations as to which should be included. Agreement, or reliability, between the two could be calculated as described in Bloom and colleagues (1999).

Regardless of their source, the criteria should be written clearly and concisely prior to the initiation of the review. Although it might be necessary to modify the criteria as the study progresses, the reasons should be compelling and explained in the researcher's report. A sample list of criteria for a study is included in Table 23.3.

REPORTING THE RESULTS OF LITERATURE REVIEWS

When the literature has been collected and integrated, a report must be prepared. The report should be prepared in accordance with several specific guidelines. These guidelines can be grouped into two major categories: the structure of the report and the content of the report.

The Structure of the Report

A well-written literature review is clear, concise, and well organized. Experts recommend the development of a specific outline (Pyrczak & Bruce, 1992), careful organization of notes (Neuman, 1997), and an ample amount of rewriting (Neuman, 1997). Pyrczak and Bruce (1992) also suggest that critiques of initial drafts by colleagues and friends may be useful.

TABLE 23.3   Sample Literature Inclusion/Exclusion Criteria

1. The literature must help to answer the question, "Do female adolescent substance abusers differ from male adolescent substance abusers in ways that are likely to affect treatment?"
2. Theoretical literature must be related to gender schema theory or social learning theory.
3. Empirical literature must focus on gender differences among adolescent or adult substance abusers.
4. Empirical literature must include only articles that report studies using equivalent or nonequivalent control group designs.

Organizationally, a review should move from more general topics toward more specific ones (Yegidis & Weinbach, 1996). It should begin by describing the problem and then introduce research hypotheses, purposes, and/or questions. Information gleaned from the literature should be presented as an integrated essay, not as an annotated list. The researcher should point out themes in the literature, note the presence of any gaps, and use quotations only when they are essential. Only the most salient details of the included studies should be reported. This means that the review should focus on findings rather than on methods and variables.

The Contents of the Report

Most important, the review should contain only articles that meet the inclusionary/exclusionary criteria of the researcher. The review should contain articles that demonstrate the need for the current study, that relate directly to the research question, and that will contribute substantively to the reader's understanding (Creswell, 1994). Every effort should be made to make the review comprehensive while ensuring that no peripheral material is included.

Yegidis and Weinbach (1996) raise important points regarding the role of the author in communicating the content. They indicate that the thought processes of the researcher should be made clear to the reader. The researcher should function as a guide, assimilating the literature for the reader but allowing the reader to think for himself or herself. This feature, Yegidis and Weinbach argue, will help to unify the review that provides the reader with structure and direction.

Pyrczak and Bruce (1992) add that the researcher should feel free to use the first person when it contributes to the review. They also indicate that the reviewer should express opinions about the research being cited if this facilitates understanding by the reader.

TYPES OF LITERATURE REVIEWS

Literature reviews often are a part of a larger article or research report. Some, however, constitute articles in themselves. Three types of literature reviews are particularly distinctive and are discussed here: qualitative reviews, quantitative reviews, and meta-analyses.

Qualitative Reviews

Qualitative reviews collect and assimilate the results of qualitative studies, that is, studies that have used the inductive method of reasoning. Typically, these studies (a) are conducted in natural settings, (b) involve variables that cannot be controlled and often are not reduced to numbers, (c) include data the nature of which is heavily influenced by the progressive experience of the researcher rather than by predetermined instrument items, and (d) involve methods for extracting information from the data that typically are more familiar and natural than those used in other methods. Sometimes, research questions are not clearly specified at the study's conception but develop along with the researcher's experiences (Rothery, Tutty, & Grinnell, 1996).

Qualitative review articles have characteristics similar to field research. They primarily include qualitative articles such as ethnographies, case studies, narratives, and discourse analyses (Grinnell, 1997). They rely on induction so that questions asked by the researcher grow out of the literature itself (Creswell, 1994). They are used to prepare a researcher for a given field of study, to initiate an exploration that leads to the formulation of hypotheses and qualitative research, and to gain a broad understanding of the object of study. An example of a qualitative review article is "Marriage and Family Therapy: A Decade Review" (Piercy & Sprenkle, 1990).

Quantitative Reviews

Quantitative review articles summarize the findings of empirical research projects. Their focus is on data and the analysis of data that has been reduced to numbers. The literature within them is used deductively. Quantitative reviews often are used to summarize extant knowledge as a foundation for hypothesis development and future research (Creswell, 1994). An example of a quantitative review article is "Teaching Social Work Practice: A Review and Analysis of Empirical Research" (Sowers-Hoag & Thyer, 1986).

Meta-Analyses

The meta-analysis is a special case of the quantitative literature review. In meta-analysis, statistical formulas are used to convert the results of the collected studies into standardized numbers called effect sizes. These effect sizes are then compared. From the process, a matrix is derived that allows the effects of various variables to be analyzed among multiple studies. Meta-analyses are very valuable because they provide simple but effective comparisons of multiple studies and outcomes. For an example of a meta-analysis of selected social work literature, see Gorey, Thyer, and Pawluck (1998). For a more in-depth discussion of the methods of conducting a meta-analysis, see Hunter and colleagues (1982).

CONCLUSION

The literature review is a crucial and foundational stage in planning any research project. This chapter has discussed several aspects of the literature review. It summarized the reasons for conducting a literature review. It described specific methods used in conducting the review. It also discussed inclusionary/exclusionary criteria, interrater reliability, and three types of reviews. Finally, it offered instruction on how to write a successful literature review.

REFERENCES

Bloom, M., Fischer, J., & Orme, J. G. (1999). *Evaluating practice: Guidelines for the accountable professional*. Needham Heights, MA: Allyn & Bacon.

Creswell, J. W. (1994). *Research design: Qualitative and quantitative approaches*. Thousand Oaks, CA: Sage.

Ellis, R. A. (1998). Filling the prevention gap: Multi-factor, multi-system, multi-level intervention. *Journal of Primary Prevention, 19*, 57-71.

Gorey, K. M., Thyer, B. A., & Pawluck, D. E. (1998). Differential effectiveness of prevalent social work practice models: A meta-analysis. *Social Work, 43*, 269-278.

Grinnell, R. M. (1997). *Social work evaluation and research: Quantitative and qualitative approaches*. Itasca, IL: Peacock.

Hunter, J. E., Schmidt, F. L., & Jackson, G. B. (1982). *Meta-analysis: Cumulating research findings across studies*. Beverly Hills, CA: Sage.

Neuman, W. L. (1997). *Social research methods: Qualitative and quantitative approaches*. Needham Heights, MA: Allyn & Bacon.

Piercy, F. P., & Sprenkle, D. H. (1990). Marriage and family therapy: A decade review. *Journal of Marriage and the Family, 52*, 1116-1126.

Pyrczak, F., & Bruce, R. R. (1992). *Writing empirical research reports: A basic guide for students of the social and behavioral sciences*. Los Angeles: Pyrczak Publishing.

Rothery, M. A., Tutty, L. M., & Grinnell, R. M. (1996). Introduction. In L. M. Tutty, M. A. Rothery, & R. M. Grinnell, Jr. (Eds.), *Qualitative research for social workers: Phases, steps, and tasks* (pp. 2-22). Needham Heights, MA: Allyn & Bacon.

Rubin, A., & Babbie, E. (1997). *Research methods for social workers* (3rd ed.). Pacific Grove, CA: Brooks/Cole.

Sowers-Hoag, K. M., & Thyer, B. A. (1986). Teaching social work practice: A review and analysis of empirical research. *Journal of Social Work Education, 21,* 3-15.

Yegidis, B. L., & Weinbach, R. W. (1996). *Research methods for social workers* (2nd ed.). Needham Heights, MA: Allyn & Bacon.

CHAPTER TWENTY-FOUR

Critical Analyses

WILLIAM M. EPSTEIN

All research begins either explicitly or implicitly with the analysis of a problem, hopefully at its critical branching points. By its very nature, the scientific analysis of social problems, especially with an eye to social policy, must be critical given that it assesses alternatives against objective criteria and, necessarily, rejects all but one candidate for policy adoption. Critical analysis is, in a sense, a redundancy—analytic analysis. However, the flourishing demand in the social services for unquestioning belief and self-certification commands attention to its research, even at the risk of a bleak assessment. Critical analysis engenders the promise of science in society— objectivity, coherence, and social relevance—in rejection of obedient research tamed by political convenience, social favor, and professional ambition.

There are three critical branching points for research in the social services. These opportunities for appraisal define the willingness to challenge orthodoxy, the essential mood of science and democracy at the heart of the Enlightenment legacy. Consequently, the analysis of branching point choices measures the importance of the social services scholarship, that is, its ability to maintain congruence between scientific practice (objectivity and coherence), on the one hand, and social relevance, on the other. Yet, social services scholarship typically sacrifices science to the politically ascendant, but at the price of both true benefits for lower status groups and intellectual probity. Therefore, critical analysis becomes a crucial professional commitment in the social services.

Science is intellectually coherent; the rest is not. The evocative, personally meaningful, transcendental, spiritual, godly, religious, intuitive, artistic, and otherwise riotous emotional floribunda of culture are incapable of establishing reliable cause, the prime task that moves critical analysis. Whatever the inspiration—bathtub epiphany or patterned discovery—critical analysis gains a powerful ability from science to create reliable and effective services.

Scientific credibility is achieved through randomized controlled trials, the objective criteria of critical analysis (Epstein, 1993b). Where they are impractical, unethical, or otherwise impossible to apply—and often for substantial reasons—the outcomes of research are necessarily uncertain proportionate to the violations of the rational canons of science. Nevertheless, the social services rarely apply randomized controlled trials, and in all cases where they have been applied to clinical practice, their methodological pitfalls vitiate their conclusions. The failure to provide reliable social services, or at least to prove that they are reliable and effective, has been coincidental with the failure to conduct scientifically credible research. The communal enterprise of scholarship in the social services has been sidetracked by a concern for "practical" research and other postmodern oddities.

Of course, there are numerous noncritical decisions that are important for the construction of credible research—initial explorations of social problems and possible solutions, development of instruments and measures, and the conduct and interpretation of pilot tests. However, the contributions of the noncritical tasks relate to the major themes of critical analysis in the social services—effectiveness, social role, and social motive.

EFFECTIVENESS

The effectiveness of the social services is a key question and the first branching point of critical analysis. The dignity of social work and the other semiprofessions of the welfare state is ostensibly predicated on production functions of cure, prevention, and rehabilitation in the same manner as any industrial enterprise assesses its effectiveness and efficiency in the explicit terms of a specific product. In the absence of a true production function, the persistence of social welfare programs can be explained only in political terms. A social welfare program demonstrates its production function through credible research and demonstrates its political utility through popularity. Therefore, a social service that fails to cure, prevent, or rehabilitate endures because it engenders politically useful ceremonies that are, using Meyer and Rowan's (1997) term, *isomorphic* with cultural values. Unfortunately, dominant cultural values rarely embrace true effectiveness for needy and otherwise marginal groups, with the result that social services often are more acceptable than profound, forever in the business of moralizing points of social preference and etiquette.

Effectiveness is measured against programmatic criteria—established goals, emergent obligations, and social need that is itself a partisan notion. Most social welfare programs in the United States are not effective against any programmatic criteria, even though the extant outcome literature typically boasts, at a minimum, the discovery of hopeful leads, small steps forward, helping hands, oases in the desert, intermittent successes, and glimmers of light. Yet, the body of research consistently reports levels of achievement and asserts conclusions about the causative ability of the interventions that cannot possibly be sustained by its own data and methodologies.

Randomized controlled trials rarely are employed; rare instances of their sophisticated use invariably turn out to be disheartening misadventures of reason, money, and motive. The strongest of the negative income tax experiments of the 1960s and 1970s, conducted in Seattle, Washington, and in Denver, Colorado, contained large randomized groups but inaccurately measured income and work participation while failing to estimate broader social impacts, created a distorting demonstration and not a true field test, and used biased samples, among other major methodological faults. Moreover, its reported outcomes were not readily accessible, and its methodological compromises reflected the preferences of the designers more than the needs of the nation for a valid assessment of the impact of a guaranteed income (Brasilevsky & Hum, 1984; Epstein, 1997b; Haveman, 1986). The experiment probably underreported the extent to which a guaranteed income would interrupt work behavior while ignoring both its influence in encouraging illegal work and the broader social effects of discarding the productive capacities of a large portion of American citizens.

The most credible evaluation of a family preservation program was conducted in Illinois. The experiment, reported in *Putting Families First* (Schuerman, Rzepnicki, & Littell, 1994) and in photocopied quasi-publications, is perhaps the most sophisticated study ever conducted within the social work orbit, comparing favorably with the negative income tax experiments. Yet, in spite of multiple measures, randomization, and extensive follow-up, the conclusion of the experiment—that family preservation fails—is undercut by numerous design flaws: Family preservation services might not have been delivered in their intended form (treatment integrity), the experimental samples probably did not contain the true target population, randomization was breached in 24% of the cases, both the measures and the measurement procedures were unreliable, and the experiment might have provided not a true field test of family preservation but rather only an instance of worker behavior under demonstration conditions (Epstein, 1997a).

Similarly, other randomized controlled trials in the social services, notably the Collaborative Research Program to treat depression (Elkin et al., 1989; Imber et al., 1990; Sotsky et al., 1991) and the Manpower Demonstration Research Corporation's extensive evaluations of manpower training programs (Epstein, 1993a, 1997b; Friedlander & Burtless, 1995), are debilitated by so many design flaws that the only tenable conclusions point to failure in spite of the authors' strained attempts to pick through the rubble of their numbers in search of hope. Indeed, some of their methodological problems are classic reasons to abandon research before incurring the enormous costs of data collection. Both studies experimented with participant populations that were *knowingly* unrepresentative of the underlying populations of concern while attrition, particularly in the Collaborative Research Program, reached derisive proportions.

These four experiments are among the very strongest in the social services. Weaker methodologies such as single-subject designs and other types of "practical" research are by far the more common fare and produce even less credible findings. The entire psychotherapeutic literature, constituting evidence for the effectiveness of the "nuclear" intervention of social work, should be interpreted skeptically given that it contains not one single credible study that testifies to the effectiveness of the field. Indeed, it is possible to reinterpret much of outcome literature as actual evidence of failure and perhaps harm. Even Smith, Glass, and Miller's (1980) massive tribute to the effectiveness of psychotherapy, among many other shortcomings, notably steps into the pitfall of interpreting standard errors as if they were standard deviations. As a result, the tightly clustered outcomes of psychotherapy that they report actually hint at a "Wild West" of the effects of the field.

The near universal disjuncture in the social services between reported outcomes and actual outcomes—the most fundamental and discrediting bias of any research with claims to science—indicts the communal life of the field's intellectuals. Numerous studies have pointed to the biases of the publication process in social work and the social sciences (Lindsey, 1978; Epstein, 1990; Pardeck & Meinert, 1999), the elusiveness of quality research (Manski & Garfinkel, 1992), and crabbed academic environments that recognize golden work with only bronze rewards (Ravetz, 1971). The attentiveness of social services research to funding instead of objective social conditions is complicit in the culture's tolerance for deceptive and ineffective social welfare interventions.

The skeptical tradition in the social services is tiny, and the number of those who base their criticism on the rational grounds of science is even tinier. This little band of loyal critics includes the early Fischer (1973), Segal (1972), Wood (1978), Wootton (1959), and very few others in social work; Martinson (1974; see also Lipton, Martinson, & Wilks, 1975) and his few descendants in criminology; Eysenck (1952), Prioleau, Murdock, and Brody (1983), Rachman (1971), and a few others in psychotherapy; only the rarest voice in child welfare (Epstein, 1999); and a scattering in other social services areas (Epstein, 1993a). Contentious commentary in the social services usually occurs between different schools of interventions arguing their cases on largely intuitive grounds and in protection of their own professional stakes. The interplay rarely is occasioned by any knowledge of actual outcomes or live attention to the needs of vulnerable groups. It is most frequently precipitated by changing social tastes, that is, fads in philanthropy and the public's mercurial will.

Not surprisingly, the summary reviews of the primary research, acting more like vacuum cleaners than discerning eyes, simply absorb, codify, and anthologize its biases (Andrews et al., 1990; Fischer, 1981; Gorey, 1996; Luborsky, Singer, & Luborsky, 1975; Reid & Hanrahan, 1982; Rubin, 1985; Smith et al., 1980). Like any pseudo-science, the discourse of the social services seems relieved from embarrassment by the absence of definitive outcome information, taking liberty from ignorance to press untested claims.

SOCIAL SCIENCE THEORY AND IDEOLOGY

The second branching point of critical analysis takes note of the methodologically porous, misreported research to question the role that social services play in society. Deprived of a production function, institutionalized social services play, by default, ceremonial political roles that engender cherished social values or at least the ideological preferences of the powerful. Very few social services researchers have been courageous enough to state the reality of program outcomes, and even fewer Isaiahs castigate the sins of established practice by deflating its scientific pomposities to ideological proportions.

Following Figure 23.1, the authority for an explanation of social events can be either empirical or nonempirical. Empirical explanations are rational theories whose credibility depends on their point of development, that is, as either immature or mature sciences. Nonempirical explanations cover the full range of the nonrational—intuition, superstition, religion, and politics. The authority for the nonrational, the test of its value, is subjective with some form of political satisfaction as its abiding criteria. Preempting objective outcomes with political satisfaction compounds the field's initial fallacy of misrepresenting the effectiveness of social services with the misuse of scientific social theory as ideology.

The explanations of human behavior that are central to social discourse (Panel A in Figure 24.1) do not bear the cachet of science. They radiate from the nonempirical (Panel B in Figure 24.1), although they wrap themselves in the finer cloaks of science. The science of genetics has little relationship to the politics of adjudicating inferiority and establishing priorities for social rewards. The issue of moral responsibility at the center of the dispute between subcultural and structural disputes cannot be settled on grounds of proof. Rather, social explanations are forms of political argument, per-

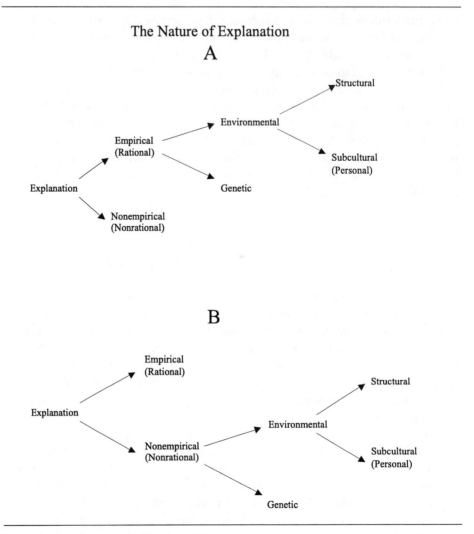

Figure 24.1. The Nature of Explanation

haps inspired by the metaphors of science but abstracted from its authority. What is known is very little, but what is believed is vast.

As rational forms, social theories are consciously limited to the conditions—the operations—of the individual tests of their predictive (explanatory) value. Yet, the empirical theories of social behavior have been given a greater life as ideology in the heat of factional disputes and political contests over limited resources. In turn, ideological truth is evaluated as satisfaction with their ability to promote partisan interests, not as empirical proof of their role in producing effective services. Thus, scientific authority is debased and transformed into social authority. In its more general application, this principle, philosophic nihilism—that culture perfuses all of its forms, even those (e.g., science) that claim acultural authority—is a pillar of modern consciousness. As a narcissistic exaggeration, it swells into the intellectual curiosity of postmodernism.

In spite of Enlightenment promises, science has not demonstrated a consistent ability to inform public discourse. By default, social decision making is necessarily nonempirical and political. That is, political systems seek power and consensus, not objective truth that might be an impossibility. In industrial societies, the drama of politics has adopted scientific and technological props, the totems of their beliefs. The dynamics of political theory contend over the degree to which empirical methods can influence social policy, with the more hopeful professing a faith in humans' rational impulses and the bleaker citing history.

Critical analyses of the ideological distortions of science can avoid the postmodern pitfall of equating the empirical with the nonempirical as political forms. The central observation that ideology is extended past the authority of defining social theory has been made with some power. Genetic theory is not the frequent barbarity of genetic ideologies, and a great divide exists between the works of the Minnesota Center for Twin and Adoption Research (Bouchard, Lykken, McGue, Segal, & Tellegen, 1990), on the one hand, and those of Herrnstein and Murray (1994) and Shockley (1992), on the other. Gould's (1981) attention to the fallacies of the genetic ideologues exemplifies critical analysis that stays clear of postmodernism. Even Kuhn (1970) maintains a loyalty to the rational while prominently accepting the sociology of knowledge. In direct rebuke to postmodernism, journals have been created as critical voices to guard scientific theory from ideological distortion (e.g., *Scientific Review of Alternative Medicine*).

The social sciences have produced many critical analyses of theory and social policy but very few of the social services themselves, a desert for the critical analysis of ideological subterfuge. It is as though their discerning eye has gone blind as the social sciences become realized in specific interventions. Nevertheless, trenchant commentaries on the political misuses of the social services occasionally appear. Cloward and Epstein (1967) and, more recently, Smith and Lipsky (1993) document the responsiveness of social services to elite interests. Kutchins and Kirk (1997) debunk the *Diagnostic and Statistical Manual of Mental Disorders (DSM-IV)* as science but without discarding the rational underpinnings of medicine. Wootton's (1959) magisterial work confronted psychological theory with its use as conservative dogma. A few others, and usually within the social sciences per se, concede the ideological determinants of social services practice and theory. Yet, the routine avoidance of critical analysis and the unwillingness to scrutinize social welfare programs are not unexpected in a field dominated by true believers. Those who have found secular salvation through commitments to social work and psychotherapy rarely are equipped emotionally or motivated professionally to question the broader meaning of their personal epiphanies.

Critical analyses of reigning social ideology, along with challenges to established empirical theory, create the intellectual disjunctures that facilitate change. They are occasions for celebrations proportionate to their theoretical depth, although original thinkers such as Freud and Marx rarely emerge in the social services. Still, Harris (1995) reminds the psychological community of the importance of peer groups in child development and socialization. If Harris is correct, then the fields of child therapy and child welfare, including services focused on family preservation, family reunion, and foster care, need to be redesigned. The observation of persistent differences between blacks and whites in test scores challenges the value of existing services and institutionalized practices as well as comfort with the degree of social and economic mobility (Jencks & Phillips, 1998). Cans (1992) aired out the "Wally and Beaver" myth of the American family that justifies much of the strategic direction of family services.

Still, the far more common offering applauds the field's progress (e.g., Bowen & Bok, 1998; Crane, 1998) and, therefore, its fundamental theoretical assumptions but does so, predictably, without substantial and credible empirical evidence. Social reality itself is the best test of theory and offers the toughest conundrums for social services. Scholarship's scientific contributions emerge from challenges to explain social reality. Its typical political role is performed in denial of need.

In the end, explanations of social outcomes (including programmatic outcomes) lack rational proof. Instead, they are ideologies that serve as flags for politically competitive factions. In this way, social science becomes a belletristic pursuit of the mot juste rather than an attempt to capture social reality. The need in the social services for self-reflection and honesty provides a vast opportunity to analyze social welfare interventions against their effectiveness and political utility and to question the social motives that prematurely graduate untested social welfare services into accepted practice.

SOCIAL MOTIVE

It is a an act of faith meriting canonization to maintain that cure, rehabilitation, and prevention motivate social services when hardly any credible evidence of effectiveness can be adduced; when the community of scholars responsible for measuring effectiveness routinely conducts biased research that is invoked to justify continued support for the failed services; and when social science theory is routinely aggrandized and distorted to justify questionable practice. Therefore, the problem for the third branching of critical analysis is to identify the live collective goals—the motives—that explain consistent social policy choices.

In addition to cure, prevention, and rehabilitation, there are numerous candidates for social motives in America—socialization, social harmony, social control (both legitimate and illegitimate), financial profit and other types of material gain, power, status, God's will, justice, progress, the realization of human potential, security, the social ethos, received values in general, the Protestant work ethic in particular, ideal benefaction, and many others, some of which might yet remain latent. Social motives may be specific to epoch, culture, and social structure, they may operate singly or in tandem, and they may be grounded in biology or sociology. Social motives are implemented through the acquiescence of constituent social institutions, in this case, the social services enterprise and, in particular, its intellectuals who profit by creating the nation's cultural ceremonies. These rituals—communions, school graduations, marriages, parades, funerals, and social services (including the rare ones with true production functions)—enact the myths of society.

The critical analysis of social motive entails a number of moderating considerations. The rational pursuit of social motives (as distinct from the pursuit of rational social motive) may be impossible both theoretically and practically; it also may lead to very little awareness, probably being only a marginal condition of change. Motive as cause may be arbitrary given that an infinite regression of causes always is possible. The simplifying assumptions of functional analysis—that the purpose of inquiry is to discover a sufficient *controllable* cause or causes and not the "prime mover"—may fail on the possibility that social motive is uncontrollable except as the behavioral specifics of actual programs; in this case, the search becomes trivial. Furthermore, and in tribute to Heisenberg, the discovery of motive also may change it and do so in unpredictable ways. Moreover, the methodological requirements of the search for social motive may be beyond any capacity to fund, reconstruct, or conduct. Finally, having identified social motive, there is no assurance that it will produce any particular political response.

In spite of numerous problems of meaning, the identification of social motive imposes a coherence on social discourse with inevitable theoretical implications. For example, the following observation is a fixture of American dialectics:

What is beyond debate is the enduring authority of Calivinist values. However often overlaid by transient moods, however often proclaimed dead and buried, they remain most vigorously strong just below the surface of American life, invisibly shaping both everyday choices and fundamental attitudes. (Luttwak, 1999, p. 17)

If indeed Calvinist belief is the core American motive, then any substantial change in American society must be coincidental with a changed ethos. Yet, mirroring the dispute between Weber and Tawney, the social ethos may be a logical consequence of economic and societal change, in this case the emergence of capitalism. American Calvinism may be less the root cause of American behavior than simply the very human tendency to rationalize social adaptation and political position.

Nonetheless, critical analyses of social services that challenge motives of civic virtue with less congratulatory possibilities give greater standing to disaffected groups. In this way, the socially efficient notion that American policy consistently chooses (is motivated by) inexpensive and socially compatible interventions despite their service failures ennobles an alternative to current policy. The nation might not be motivated by fairness and compassion and might simply be satisfying the blind justice of Solomon but without his wisdom and through a callous political process that slices the baby in half. The nation might indeed be doing the best that it can with resources that are limited by the federal deficit, inflation, the need for economic investment, and unexpected but critical emergencies (e.g., storms, medical bills of the elderly, youth crime, illegal immigration). Then again, the nation might be in disrepair, mindlessly satisfying shortsighted and selfish dictates to appease its most powerful actors.

A FEW FINAL WORDS

Then again, the intellectual life of the social services may be vital, truth-centered, erudite, accurate, courageous, independent, objective, coherent, and skillful. But to diminish the need for critical analyses of the social services, actual evidence must be enumerated that their intellectual community is performing well. In the first instance, studies should be identified that are scientifically credible and that point to effective services, that is, production functions of cure, prevention, and rehabilitation. Without proof of effectiveness, explorations of the social and political roles of the social services are called for to probe the suspicion that the intellectual community actually has become complicit in programmatic ineffectiveness. Finally, without proof of production functions and without the identification of ceremonial roles, the intellectual life of the field should be scrutinizing the social motives that perpetuate ineffective services. In the absence of this type of scholarship, the critical obligations of intellectuals, especially those who profess with the regularity and noise of ocean surf a commitment to the downtrodden, the marginal, and the poor, are unfulfilled.

The demise of Matthew Arnold, and with him the cloying insistence that scholarship be infused with sweetness and light, permits a tough-minded, resilient, unabashedly materialistic social reality. Against the group imperative of a profession biased toward superficial interventions and an insistence on effectiveness, the productive scholar best serves the social goals of the Enlightenment through an impersonal yet critical commitment to objectivity and coherence.

REFERENCES

Andrews, D. A., Zinger, I., Hoge, R., Bonta, J., Gendreau, P., & Cullen, F. (1990). Does correctional treatment work? A clinically relevant and psychologically informed meta-analysis. *Criminology, 28,* 419-429.

Bouchard, T. J., Lykken, D. T., McGue, M., Segal, N. L., & Tellegen, A. (1990). Sources of human psychological differences: The Minnesota Study of Twins Reared Apart. *Science, 250,* 223-228.

Bowen, W. G., & Bok, D. (1998). *The shape of the river.* Princeton, NJ: Princeton University Press.

Brasilevsky, A., & Hum, D. (1984). *Experimental social programs.* San Diego: Academic Press.

Cans, S. (1992). *The way we never were.* New York: Basic Books.

Cloward, R., & Epstein, I. (1967). Private social welfare's disengagement from the poor. In G. Brager & E. Purcell (Eds.), *Community action against poverty* (pp. 40-64). New Haven, CT: Yale University Press.

Crane, J. (1998). *Social programs that work.* New York: Russell Sage.

Elkin, I., Shea, I. T., Watkins, J. T., Imber, S. D., Sotsky, S. M., Collins, J. F., Glass, D. R., Pilkonis, P. A., Leber, W. R., Docherty, J., Fiester, S. J., & Parloff, S. (1989). National Institute of Mental Health Treatment of Depression Collaborative Research Program. *Archives of General Psychiatry, 46,* 971-983.

Epstein, W. M. (1990). Confirmational response bias among social work journals. *Science, Technology, & Human Values, 15,* 9-38.

Epstein, W. M. (1993a). *The dilemma of American social welfare.* New Brunswick, NJ: Transaction Publishers.

Epstein, W. M. (1993b). Randomized controlled trials in the human services. *Social Work Research and Abstracts, 29*(3), 3-10.

Epstein, W. M. (1997a). Social science, child welfare, and family preservation: A failure of rationality in public policy. *Children and Youth Services Review, 19,* 41-60.

Epstein, W. M. (1997b). *Welfare in America: How social science fails the poor.* Madison: University of Wisconsin Press.

Epstein, W. M. (1999). *Children who could have been: The legacy of welfare in wealthy America.* Madison: University of Wisconsin Press.

Eysenck, H. (1952). The effects of psychotherapy: An evaluation. *Journal of Consulting Psychology, 16,* 319.

Fischer, J. (1973). Is casework effective? A review. *Social Work, 18,* 5-20.

Fischer, J. (1981). The social work revolution. *Social Work, 26,* 199-209.

Friedlander, D., & Burtless, G. (1995). *Five years after.* New York: Manpower Demonstration Research Corporation.

Gorey, K. M. (1996). Effectiveness of social work intervention research: Internal versus external evaluations. *Social Work Research, 20,* 119-128.

Gould, S. J. (1981). *The mismeasure of man.* New York: Norton.

Harris, J. R. (1995). Where is the child's environment? A group socialization theory of development. *Psychological Review, 102,* 458-489.

Haveman, R. H. (1986). Social experimentation and social experimentation [review]. *Journal of Human Resources, 21,* 586-605.

Herrnstein, R. J., & Murray, C. (1994). *The bell curve.* New York: Free Press.

Imber, S. D., Pilkonis, P. A., Sotsky, S. M., Elkin, I., Watkins, J. T., Collins, J. F., Shea, M. T., Leber, W. R., & Glass, D. R. (1990). Mode-specific effects among three treatments for depression. *Journal of Consulting and Clinical Psychology, 58,* 352-359.

Jencks, C., & Phillips, M. (Eds.). (1998). *The black-white test score gap*. Washington, DC: Brookings Institution.

Kuhn, T. (1970). *The structure of scientific revolutions*. Chicago: University of Chicago Press.

Kutchins, H., & Kirk, S. (1997). *Making us crazy: DSM—The psychiatric bible and the creation of mental disorders*. New York: Free Press.

Lindsey, D. (1978). *The scientific publishing system in social science*. San Francisco: Jossey-Bass.

Lipton, D., Martinson, R., & Wilks, J. (1975). *The effectiveness of correctional treatment*. New York: Praeger.

Luborsky, L., Singer, B., & Luborsky, L. (1975). Comparative studies of psychotherapies: Is it true that "Everybody Has Won and All Must Have Prizes"? *Archives of General Psychiatry, 32,* 995-1008.

Luttwak, E. (1999). *Turbo capitalism*. New York: HarperCollins.

Manski, C. F., & Garfinkel, I. (Eds.). (1992). *Evaluating welfare and training programs*. Cambridge, MA: Harvard University Press.

Martinson, R. (1974, Spring). What works: Questions and answers about prison reform. *Public Interest,* pp. 22-54.

Meyer, J. W., & Rowan, B. (1997). Institutionalized organizations: Formal structure as myth and ceremony. *American Journal of Sociology, 83,* 340-363.

Pardeck, J. T., & Meinert, R. G. (1999). Scholarly achievements of the *Social Work* editorial board and consulting editors. *Research on Social Work Practice, 9,* 86-91.

Prioleau, L., Murdock, M., & Brody, N. (1983). An analysis of psychotherapy versus placebo studies. *Behavioral and Brain Sciences, 6,* 275-310.

Rachman, S. (1971). *The effects of psychological treatment*. Oxford, UK: Pergamon.

Ravetz, J. R. (1971). *Scientific knowledge and its social problems*. Oxford, UK: Clarendon.

Reid, W. J., & Hanrahan, P. (1982). Recent evaluations of social work: Grounds for optimism. *Social Work, 27,* 328-340.

Rubin, A. (1985). Practice effectiveness: More grounds for optimism. *Social Work, 30,* 469-476.

Schuerman, J. R., Rzepnicki, R. L., & Littell, J. L. (1994). *Putting families first*. Hawthorne, NY: Aldine.

Segal, S. (1972). Research on the outcome of social work therapeutic intervention: A review of the literature. *Journal of Health and Social Behavior, 13,* 3-17.

Shockley, W. (1992). *Shockley on eugenics and race*. Washington, DC: Scott-Townsend.

Smith, M. L., Glass, G. V., & Miller, T. I. (1980). *The benefits of psychotherapy*. Baltimore, MD: Johns Hopkins University Press.

Smith, S. R., & Lipsky, M. (1993). *Nonprofits for hire: The welfare state in the age of contracting*. Cambridge, MA: Harvard University Press.

Sotsky, S. M., Glass, D. R., Shea, T., Pilkonis, P. A., Collins, J. F., Elkin, I., Watkins, J. F., Imber, S. D., Leber, W., Moyer, W., & Oliveri, M. (1991). Patient predictors of response to psychotherapy and pharmacotherapy: Findings in the NIMH treatment of depression collaborative research program. *American Journal of Psychiatry, 148,* 997-1008.

Wood, K. M. (1978). Casework effectiveness: A new look at the research evidence. *Social Work, 23,* 437-458.

Wootton, B. (1959). *Social science and social pathology*. London: George Allen and Unwin.

PART IV

General Issues

The chapters comprised by this final part of the handbook could just as easily have been placed at the beginning of the volume rather than near the end given their centrality to all research endeavors.

Frederic Reamer (Chapter 25), one of social work's foremost ethicists and chair of the committee that drafted the National Association of Social Workers' (1996) current *Code of Ethics,* has prepared a chapter on ethical issues as they pertain to social work research. Informed consent, the role of institutional review boards, deception in research, confidentiality, and privacy are a few of the important issues presented by Reamer.

Antoinette Rodgers-Farmer and Miriam Potocky-Tripodi (Chapter 26) describe the relevance of gender, ethnicity, and race matters when designing and conducting research. These issues may be relevant at all stages of the research enterprise, from initial conceptualization to final report writing.

Elaine Jurkowski and Martin Tracy (Chapter 27) describe the design and conduct of comparative international research, a highly specialized form of study that cuts across countries, thus posing its own unique set of challenges. They discuss common impediments to undertaking cross-national investigations and the various perspectives or conceptual frameworks that can be used to formulate such studies. Comparative international research can be either qualitative or quantitative in orientation, and mixed-methods research is not uncommon.

Charles Cowger and Goutham Menon (Chapter 28) make the case for integrating qualitative and quantitative research methods, admittedly not a difficult argument but one that they present skillfully. They lead off by noting that the differences between the two positions are in their areas of emphasis, not content or approach, and that in the middle ground the distinctions can become muddled. It can be anticipated that increasing numbers of such integrated studies will be making their appearance within the social work literature. This is a good thing.

Scott Geron and Gail Steketee (Chapter 29) discuss applying for research grants, a skill increasingly necessary for the successful social work researcher but one rarely taught in any type of a formal manner. Most often, an apprenticeship model is used, wherein a doctoral student or junior faculty member collaborates with a more experienced grant writer. This model works well if one has access to such a rare being. If not, then the options are few. This chapter reviews the available federal funding sources most often tapped for social work research projects and the various funding mechanisms available within each source. The writing of grant applications and the use of pilot data also are covered.

The concluding chapter by Dianne Harrison and Aaron McNeece (Chapter 30) has been written, appropriately enough, by two very successful research authors. Like grant writing, writing for scholarly publication is a research skill more noted for its omission from the curriculum than for its inclusion. It can be said with some degree of truth that research that is not published might as well not even have been undertaken—or, perhaps from a social constructivist position, does not even exist. If a tree falls in the woods and no one hears it, does it make a sound? If a research study is completed and no one reads it or makes use of its findings, is knowledge advanced? Harrison and McNeece review the various methods that one can use to disseminate research knowledge. Professional journals, monographs, book chapters, books, the Internet, and conference presentations are the major venues, and the authors tell the reader how to gain his or her place at these tables.

This part of the handbook concludes our overview of major social work research methods. Space limitations precluded including all potentially important topics, omissions for which the editor apologizes while regretfully acknowledging the necessity. The reader's comments and suggestions to improve future editions are welcome and can be directed to the editor by postal mail or the Internet (bthyer@arches.uga.edu).

REFERENCE

National Association of Social Workers. (1996). *Code of Ethics of the National Association of Social Workers.* Washington, DC: Author.

CHAPTER TWENTY-FIVE

Ethical Issues

FREDERIC G. REAMER

The chapters in this handbook demonstrate clearly the remarkable maturation of social work research and evaluation. Especially since the 1970s, social workers have cultivated an impressive array of quantitative and qualitative methods to help them monitor and evaluate practice, conduct needs assessments, and develop practice guidelines (Grinnell, 1997; Reamer, 1998a, 1998b; Rubin & Babbie, 1997).

Paralleling these developments, social workers also have enhanced their understanding of ethical issues related to research and evaluation. Interestingly, social workers' enriched understanding of ethical issues also began in earnest during the 1970s. During recent years, for example, social workers have begun to appreciate that their mastery of technical issues pertaining to research design, sampling, validity and reliability, measurement, instrument development, and data analysis must be supplemented by a firm grasp of ethical issues. After all, even the most sophisticated and rigorous research and evaluation methodology would be suspect, and possibly destructive, if it did not conform to prevailing ethical standards. This chapter traces the development of social workers' understanding of ethical issues in research and evaluation, focusing especially on guidelines for research-based practice.

A BRIEF HISTORICAL OVERVIEW

During recent years, but especially since the 1970s, members of all professions—including professions as diverse as social work, psychology, psychiatry, nursing, medicine, accounting, business, law enforcement, and engineering—have paid closer attention to ethical issues in general. This has occurred for several reasons (Reamer, 1999). New technology, especially in the health care and computer fields, has brought with it a number of complex and compelling ethical issues. Examples include ethical issues concerning the termination of life support, genetic engineering, organ transplantation, and the privacy of computer-based records.

In addition, widespread media coverage of ethical misconduct and scandals has enhanced professionals' knowledge of and interest in ethical issues. For example, international, national, and local stories of ethical misbehavior involving politicians, lawyers, doctors, nurses, athletes, and social workers have helped to put the subject of ethics on the professions' front burners.

Also, our current preoccupation with ethical issues is a legacy of the intense focus during the 1960s on various social justice issues including patients' rights, consumers' rights, prisoners' rights, civil rights, and welfare rights. That decade's visible protests and advocacy made a lasting impression. One consequence is that the language of "rights" now is firmly entrenched in our culture, and we see evidence of this in the proliferation of mechanisms to protect the rights of research and evaluation participants.

Furthermore, there is no question that increases in litigation (lawsuits) and ethics complaints filed against professionals have generated increased interest in ethics. Formal allegations of ethical misconduct and professional negligence involving ethical issues have motivated many professionals to pay closer attention to ethical standards.

Along with these factors that explain the expansion of professionals' interest in ethics in general, we must consider a number of unique developments related to research and evaluation ethics. Perhaps the most significant historical event was the trial of the Nazi doctors at Nuremberg in 1945 (Levine, 1991). These legal proceedings broadcast the fact that profound harm can result from unethical research (Ashcroft, 1998). The hauntingly inhumane experiments conducted by the Nazi doctors for the benefit of the Third Reich military demonstrated the unspeakable pain and suffering that unprincipled research can cause. Fortunately, from this horror came the Nuremberg Code and other international codes of ethics designed to protect research participants. These pioneering documents have shaped contemporary guidelines requiring that individuals' participation in research be both voluntary and informed and that participants be protected from risk to the greatest extent possible (Levine, 1988).

Two other key historical events involving unethical research must be noted. First, the famous Tuskegee syphilis study involved a 40-year project begun in 1932 by the U.S. Public Health Service to investigate the natural history of untreated syphilis. The study's participants included poor black men from Alabama who were told that they had "bad blood" and that they would receive procedures such as spinal taps as free treatment. These men were not provided with what then was the standard and widely accepted treatment for syphilis, nor were they provided with penicillin when it became available later during the study. The men in the sample were not told about the research design or the risks they faced. Many of the men died, but the study's unethical design and procedures did not come to the public's attention until 1972.

In the second important study, known as the Willowbrook study, researchers investigated the natural history of another untreated disease, in this instance infectious hepatitis. A group of children diagnosed with mental retardation, and who lived at the Willowbrook State Hospital in Staten Island, New York, were deliberately infected with hepatitis. The researchers' goal was to study the history of the disease when left untreated and later to evaluate the effects of gamma globulin as a treatment option. Public debate about this project focused especially on the ethical issues involving the deliberate infection of the children with hepatitis and the attempts to convince their parents to enroll the children in the study in exchange for admission to the hospital (which had limited space).

The first prominent regulations designed to prevent these types of abuses were introduced in the United States in 1966 when Surgeon General William Stewart issued a U.S. Public Health Service directive on human experimentation. This directive announced that the Public Health Service would not fund research unless the institution receiving the federal funds documented the procedures in place to ensure research participants' informed consent, the use of appropriate and ethical research procedures, an adequate review of the risks and medical benefits of the research project, and the procedures designed to protect research participants' rights. Also during the 1960s, the World Medical Association promulgated the Declaration of Helsinki, which elaborated on the informed consent standards set forth in the Nuremberg Code in 1946 (Whitbeck, 1998).

The most prominent current guidelines to protect research participants appear in two key documents: the *Belmont Report* (National Commission for the Protection of Human Subjects of Biomedical and Behavioral Research, 1978) and the *International Guidelines for Biomedical Research Involving Human Subjects* (Council for International Organizations of Medical Sciences, 1993). The landmark *Belmont Report* sets forth guidelines to protect human participants in accord with three core ethical concepts: respect for persons, beneficence, and justice (Weijer, 1998). The *International Guidelines for Biomedical Research Involving Human Subjects* includes 15 specific standards for the conduct of research, addressing issues such as informed consent, the extent to which a research project is responsive to community needs, and scrutiny of a project's research methods by an ethical review committee.

A key historical development that is especially important to social workers concerns the ratification of the 1996 *Code of Ethics* of the National Association of Social

Workers (NASW, 1996). This code, only the third in the NASW's history, greatly expands the number of ethical standards pertaining to research and evaluation. The 1979 code, which preceded the 1996 code, contained 7 ethical guidelines governing research and evaluation. By contrast, the 1996 code contains 16 specific ethical standards that I explore later (Table 25.1).

ETHICAL ISSUES IN SOCIAL WORK RESEARCH AND EVALUATION

Ethical issues related to research and evaluation can arise at every stage of the evolution of a project or research activity. Some ethical issues emerge at the beginning stages when social workers formulate their research questions and basic methodology. Other issues arise while the research and evaluation actually are being conducted. Still others emerge at the conclusion of the research and evaluation, particularly in relation to data analysis and the reporting of results.

Ethical Issues During the Early Stages of Research and Evaluation

Social workers should be especially knowledgeable about several ethical issues when they begin research and evaluation projects. These include the initial formulation of research questions, sample selection, informed consent, and institutional review.

Initial Formulation of Research Questions

Before social workers dwell on ethical issues pertaining to the technical aspects of research design and methodology, they must explore overarching questions concerning the research project's broad goals. How compelling is the research question in the first place? In light of social work's mission and ethical norms, are the project's results likely to generate important information that will enhance social work's ethical duty to assist people in need? Research projects that are directly related to the profession's moral mission—"to enhance the basic human needs of all people, *with particular attention to the needs and empowerment of people who are vulnerable, oppressed, and living in poverty*" (NASW, 1996, p. 1, italics added)—are more compelling than projects that explore abstruse subjects that might be only remotely related to the core aims of social work.

Sample Selection

Social workers also should be mindful of the research participants (or samples) they include in their work. Given the profession's enduring commitment to issues of

TABLE 25.1 Ethical Standards for Evaluation and Research: Excerpts From the National Association of Social Workers' *Code of Ethics*

Section 5.02. Evaluation and Research

(a) Social workers should monitor and evaluate policies, the implementation of programs, and practice interventions.

(b) Social workers should promote and facilitate evaluation and research to contribute to the development of knowledge.

(c) Social workers should critically examine and keep current with emerging knowledge relevant to social work and fully use evaluation and research evidence in their professional practice.

(d) Social workers engaged in evaluation or research should carefully consider possible consequences and should follow guidelines developed for the protection of evaluation and research participants. Appropriate institutional review boards should be consulted.

(e) Social workers engaged in evaluation or research should obtain voluntary and written informed consent from participants, when appropriate, without any implied or actual deprivation or penalty for refusal to participate; without undue inducement to participate; and with due regard for participants' well-being, privacy, and dignity. Informed consent should include information about the nature, extent, and duration of the participation requested and disclosure of the risks and benefits of participation in the research.

(f) When evaluation or research participants are incapable of giving informed consent, social workers should provide an appropriate explanation to the participants, obtain the participants' assent to the extent they are able, and obtain written consent from an appropriate proxy.

(g) Social workers should never design or conduct evaluation or research that does not use consent procedures, such as certain forms of naturalistic observation and archival research, unless rigorous and responsible review of the research has found it to be justified because of its prospective scientific, educational, or applied value and unless equally effective alternative procedures that do not involve waiver of consent are not feasible.

(h) Social workers should inform participants of their right to withdraw from evaluation and research at any time without penalty.

(i) Social workers should take appropriate steps to ensure that participants in evaluation and research have access to appropriate supportive services.

(j) Social workers engaged in evaluation or research should protect participants from unwarranted physical or mental distress, harm, danger, or deprivation.

(k) Social workers engaged in the evaluation of services should discuss collected information only for professional purposes and only with people professionally concerned with this information.

(l) Social workers engaged in evaluation or research should ensure the anonymity or confidentiality of participants and of the data obtained from them. Social workers should inform participants of any limits of confidentiality, the measures that will be taken to ensure confidentiality, and when any records containing research data will be destroyed.

(m) Social workers who report evaluation and research results should protect participants' confidentiality by omitting identifying information unless proper consent has been obtained authorizing disclosure.

(n) Social workers should report evaluation and research findings accurately. They should not fabricate or falsify results and should take steps to correct any errors later found in published data using standard publication methods.

(o) Social workers engaged in evaluation or research should be alert to and avoid conflicts of interest and dual relationships with participants, should inform participants when a real or potential conflict of interest arises, and should take steps to resolve the issue in a manner that makes participants' interests primary.

(p) Social workers should educate themselves, their students, and their colleagues about responsible research practices.

SOURCE: National Association of Social Workers (1996).

cultural, ethnic, and social diversity, social workers must ensure that their samples sufficiently represent, when methodologically appropriate and sound, diverse groups and clientele. Studies based on narrowly drawn and culturally homogeneous samples are less likely to yield information consistent with social work's ethical obligations to address issues of diversity and social justice (see Standards 1.05[a,b,c] and 6.04[b,c,d] in the NASW's [1996] *Code of Ethics*).

Informed Consent

Perhaps the most important by-product of the unconscionable Nazi medical experiments and experiments such as the Tuskegee and Willowbrook studies has been the development of strict informed consent guidelines. Based on this concept, research participants must be *informed* about the purposes, methods, and risks associated with the research, and they must voluntarily *consent* to participate in the research.

The landmark legal ruling in the United States on informed consent was in the 1914 case of *Schloendorff v. Society of New York Hospital* (1914), in which Justice Benjamin Cardozo stated his widely cited opinion that "every human being of adult years and sound mind has a right to determine what shall be done with his own body" (President's Commission for the Study of Ethical Problems in Medicine and Biomedical and Behavioral Research, 1982, pp. 28-29). A second well-known court case pertaining to informed consent, one in which the term *informed consent* actually was introduced, was decided in 1957 (*Salgo v. Leland Stanford Jr. University Board of Trustees,* 1957). In this case, the plaintiff became a paraplegic following a diagnostic procedure for a circulatory problem and alleged that the doctor had failed to properly disclose ahead of time important information concerning the risks associated with the procedure (President's Commission for the Study of Ethical Problems in Medicine and Biomedical and Behavioral Research, 1982).

During recent years, various court decisions, regulations developed by government and private sector organizations (e.g., the NASW), and scholarly writings have generated a list of core elements that should be included in informed consent procedures pertaining to research and evaluation. These are reflected in the NASW's (1996) *Code of Ethics:*

> Social workers engaged in evaluation or research should obtain voluntary and written informed consent from participants, when appropriate, without any implied or actual deprivation or penalty for refusal to participate; without undue inducement to participate; and with due regard for participants' well-being, privacy, and dignity. Informed consent should include information about the nature, extent, and duration of the participation requested and disclosure of the risks and benefits of participation in the research. (Standard 5.01[e])

TABLE 25.2 Sample Informed Consent Form

You are invited to participate in a research/evaluation project being conducted by [insert name of agency]. This project involves [briefly describe the nature of the project]. I am a [social worker, student, etc.] at the [insert name of agency]. [If you are a student, explain how the project relates to your academic program.] The purpose of this project is to [describe the purpose and possible value of the project]. You are being invited to participate in this project because [state reason].

This project will involve [describe the specific procedures that will be followed; the reasons; the timetable or schedule for the various procedures; the possible risks, inconveniences, and benefits; alternative procedures or options that the participants might want to consider; and any standard treatment that would be withheld].

Any information obtained from you or about you in connection with this project will remain confidential and will be disclosed only with your permission, as permitted or required by law. [Describe plans, if any, to release information to third parties, the purpose for the disclosure, the nature of the information to be released, and the circumstances under which it would be released.]

You are not under any obligation to participate in this project, and your decision will not affect your future relationship with [insert name of agency]. Furthermore, if you decide to participate, you may stop at any time without penalty or prejudice. [For projects using mailed surveys or questionnaires, you might want to include the following or a similar statement: "Your completion and return of the enclosed survey/questionnaire will indicate your willingness to participate in this project and your consent to have the information used as described above."]

Please contact [insert names and telephone numbers of all appropriate contact persons] if you have any questions about this project or your participation in it.

Your signature below indicates that you have read the information provided on this form, it has been explained to you, you have been offered a copy of this form to keep, you have been given an opportunity to ask questions about this form, your questions have been answered, and you agree to participate in this project.

Signature_____Date_____

Signature of Parent or Legal Guardian (if necessary) _____Date_____

Signature of Child (when appropriate) _____Date_____

Signature of Witness_____Date_____

Signature of Project Director/Investigator _____Date_____

More specifically, social workers must be mindful of several key elements of informed consent (for a sample informed consent form, see Table 25.2):

1. *Not using coercion.* Social workers should not use coercion to convince people to participate in their research and evaluation activities. People should agree to participate willingly and voluntarily. This is especially important in circumstances where clients might believe that they are being pressured to participate in research so as to receive social services or other benefits.

2. *Ascertaining competence.* Consent is valid only when participants truly understand the nature of the research and evaluation activity, possible benefits, and associated risks. Social workers must ensure that participants' understanding of these issues is not compromised by their mental status, literacy, or language difficulties. Persons who are not competent or whose competence is questionable should not be asked for their consent. Either they should be excluded from the research or their consent should be obtained from their legal representatives.

Unfortunately, there is no clear and widely accepted definition of competence. Some believe that professionals should consider individuals' ability to make choices, comprehend factual issues, manipulate information rationally, and appreciate their current circumstances, whereas others believe that there ought to be a single standard for determining competency based simply on people's ability to retain information or "test reality." The President's Commission for the Study of Ethical Problems in Medicine and Biomedical and Behavioral Research (1982) concludes that competency should be determined by a person's possession of a set of values and goals, ability to communicate and understand information, and ability to reason and deliberate.

Although there is some disagreement about the conceptual criteria that should be used to assess and determine competence, there is general agreement that incompetence should not be presumed across the board for any particular client group (e.g., the elderly, children, people with mental illness) except for people who are unconscious. Instead, some groups of individuals, such as people with active psychotic symptoms and individuals under the influence of alcohol or other drugs, should be considered to have a greater *probability* of incompetence. Even in instances where clients or other potential research participants do not appear to be competent, social workers still should consider explaining the purposes and methods of the research project or activity and, if appropriate, should obtain the potential participants' *assent* to participate (along with formal consent from appropriate proxies as permitted or required by law). As the NASW's (1996) *Code of Ethics* states, "When evaluation or research participants are incapable of giving informed consent, social workers should provide an appropriate explanation to the participants, obtain the participants' assent to the extent they are able, and obtain written consent from an appropriate proxy" (Standard 5.02[f]).

3. *Waiving informed consent.* Some research and evaluation projects and activities do not require formal informed consent. Using clinical assessment tools during work with clients primarily for clinical rather than research purposes might warrant *implied consent,* where the social workers provide clear explanations of their approach and rationale. Implied consent also might be appropriate when social workers interview agency colleagues for their suggestions about topics such as potential in-service training curricula, needed resources, and personnel policies. According to the NASW's (1996) *Code of Ethics,*

Social workers should never design or conduct evaluation or research that does not use consent procedures, such as certain forms of naturalistic observation and archival research, unless rigorous and responsible review of the research has found it to be justified because of its prospective scientific, educational, or applied value and unless equally effective alternative procedures that do not involve waiver of consent are not feasible. (Standard 5.02[g])

4. *Obtaining participants' consent to specific procedures or actions.* When formal informed consent is warranted, social workers must explain clearly to potential participants the purpose of the research activity, possible benefits and costs, and alternatives or other options that the participants might want to consider. Broadly worded and vague explanations will not suffice. Furthermore, the language and terminology on consent forms must be clear and understandable, jargon and technical terms should be avoided, and potential participants must be given reasonable opportunity to ask for clarification.

5. *Having the right to refuse or withdraw consent.* Social workers should ensure that potential participants understand their right to refuse or withdraw consent. This is a standard element of the informed consent process. According to the NASW's (1996) *Code of Ethics,* "Social workers should inform participants of their right to withdraw from evaluation and research at any time without penalty" (Standard 5.02[h]).

Social workers should understand that merely having participants sign a consent form generally is not sufficient. Informed consent is a process that should include the systematic and deliberate disclosure of information and an opportunity for individuals to discuss and ask questions about the research (Reamer, 1987). In conjunction with this process, social workers should be aware of and sensitive to clients' cultural and ethnic differences regarding the meaning of concepts such as self-determination, autonomy, and consent. In some cultural groups, the concepts of individualism and consent are contrary to prominent values; in other cultural groups, there is a greater expectation that individuals will be asked for their permission before engaging in a research project (President's Commission for the Study of Ethical Problems in Medicine and Biomedical and Behavioral Research, 1982).

Institutional Review

One of the most important developments concerning research ethics was the creation of *institutional review boards* (IRBs). IRBs, often known as human subjects protection committees, became popular during the 1970s as a result of the national attention to ethical issues in research in general. Currently, all organizations and agencies that receive federal funds for research are required to have an IRB review the ethical aspects of proposals for research involving human participants. (There are some exceptions for research that constitutes a routine requirement of an educational or academic program, involves analysis of secondary or existing data in a way that preserves confidentiality, depends on interviews or surveys, or entails observation of public behavior.) An IRB may request additional information and details or may request certain changes in a study's research design before approving a proposal. As the NASW's (1996) *Code of Ethics* states, "Social workers engaged in evaluation or research should carefully consider possible consequences and should follow guidelines developed for the protection of evaluation and research participants. Appropriate institutional review boards should be consulted" (Standard 5.02[d]).

Ethical Issues in Research Design and Methodology

There are four main issues that social workers must be concerned about during the actual research project or activity: ethical aspects of research designs, the use of deception, confidentiality and privacy, and conflicts of interest.

Ethical aspects of research designs. Ethical issues often arise when social workers design projects that explore cause-effect relationships between variables. In an effort to control for extraneous factors in group designs (e.g., contemporaneous events, demographic factors, measurement effects), social workers may want to randomly assign participants to experimental and control groups or to contrast groups. Similarly, in single-subject or $N = 1$ designs, social workers may attempt to control for extraneous factors by withdrawing and reintroducing an intervention (e.g., ABAB and related designs).

Potential ethical problems in such instances are well known. On the one hand, social workers understand that it might be difficult, if not impossible, to control for extraneous factors without using control groups, random assignment, reversal designs, and so on. On the other hand, social workers sometimes find it difficult to withhold interventions from clients with demonstrated and serious needs or to withdraw interventions that might be efficacious from clients who are demonstrating progress.

Whether social workers are willing to use a control group, random assignment, or a reversal design always is a matter of judgment. Consultation with an IRB can provide useful insight into the ethical trade-offs involved in these decisions. In some instances, compromises are reached, for example, when an agency uses clients on a waiting list as a "natural" control group and as a way in which to avoid completely withholding services from a control group or when a practitioner uses a multiple-baseline design in an effort to avoid withdrawing services from clients in need.

The use of deception. As a group, social workers generally find anathema any form of deception in professional practice (see Standard 4.04 in NASW's [1996]

Code of Ethics). Fortunately, the vast majority of research and evaluation activities, whether needs assessments, program evaluations, or clinical evaluations, do not call for any significant deception.

There are instances, however, when social workers may feel that some degree of deception might be necessary so as to generate meaningful research information. An example includes withholding information from clients about concerns staff have that constitute the "real" reasons for the agency's client satisfaction survey; staff might feel that completely honest disclosure about their reasons for the research project would be inappropriate and might bias clients' responses. Another example involves giving clients only vague information about changes in clinical interventions that clinicians are evaluating using a single-subject design; completely candid disclosure might interfere with social workers' ability to evaluate the intervention.

Certainly, thoughtful and reasonable people can disagree about the extent to which any type of deception in research and evaluation is reasonable or acceptable. Diligent consultation and IRB reviews can help social workers to make sound decisions about these issues.

Confidentiality and privacy. Social workers have a keen understanding of the importance of confidentiality and privacy. Complex ethical issues concerning confidentiality and privacy arise in every professional capacity, whether related to direct practice, community organizing, administration, supervision, consultation, or research and evaluation.

Several confidentiality issues pertain directly to research and evaluation. Perhaps the most prominent concerns social workers' obligation to protect the confidentiality of data. Data collected by social workers often concern very sensitive issues such as clients' troubling feelings, illegal behaviors, and controversial attitudes or agency employees' concerns about personnel issues or administrative problems. Social workers need to be scrupulous in their efforts to protect such data. As the NASW's *Code of Ethics* asserts,

> Social workers engaged in evaluation or research should ensure the anonymity or confidentiality of participants and of the data obtained from them. Social workers should inform participants of any limits of confidentiality, the measures that will be taken to ensure confidentiality, and when any records containing research data will be destroyed. (Standard 5.02[l])

Furthermore,

> Social workers should protect the confidentiality of clients' written and electronic records and other sensitive information. Social workers should take reasonable steps to ensure that

clients' records are stored in a secure location and that clients' records are not available to others who are not authorized to have access. (Standard 1.07[l])

In addition to safeguarding the confidentiality of research data, social workers should be concerned about individuals' privacy. Social workers should recognize that clients and other data sources might be uncomfortable in disclosing information about very private and sensitive issues. Accordingly, social workers should take steps to prevent unnecessary intrusions into people's lives. However, once individuals disclose private information in the context of research or evaluation activities, social workers must take steps to ensure confidentiality. According to the NASW's (1996) *Code of Ethics,*

> Social workers should respect clients' right to privacy. Social workers should not solicit private information from clients unless it is essential to providing services or conducting social work evaluation or research. Once private information is shared, standards of confidentiality apply. (Standard 1.07[a])

Social workers also must be prepared to assist individuals who become upset during data collection or at any other point in their involvement in research activities. Because social workers often address sensitive and sometimes traumatic issues, they need to anticipate the possibility that research and evaluation participants might become upset during the process. According to the NASW's (1996) *Code of Ethics,* "Social workers should take appropriate steps to ensure that participants in evaluation and research have access to appropriate supportive services" (Standard 5.02[i]).

Conflicts of interest. Social workers involved in evaluation and research need to be careful to avoid conflicts of interest, especially when the research participants are current or former clients. Relating to clients as clinicians *and* for research purposes (e.g., collecting data from clients for social workers' master's degree projects or doctoral dissertations) has the potential to constitute a problematic "dual relationship" (see Standards 1.06[a,b,c] of the NASW's [1996] *Code of Ethics*). Social workers must avoid exploiting clients or placing them at risk for research purposes. Thus, social workers should not knowingly subject individuals to undue stress and discomfort so as to meet their own professional or personal aims. As the NASW's (1996) *Code of Ethics* states,

> Social workers engaged in evaluation or research should be alert to and avoid conflicts of interest and dual relationships with participants, should inform participants when a real or potential conflict of interest arises, and should take steps to resolve the issue in a manner that makes participants' interests primary. (Standard 5.02[o])

Evaluation and Research Results

Several ethical issues can arise once evaluation and research data have been collected. These concern reporting results, disclosing results to participants, and acknowledging colleagues' contributions.

Reporting results. Social workers must be careful to protect the confidentiality of final results and to report results accurately. Practitioners need to be sure that sensitive information does not fall into the wrong hands, for example, ensuring that clients' comments about past illegal activities are not shared with law enforcement officials. According to the NASW's (1996) *Code of Ethics,* "Social workers who report evaluation and research results should protect participants' confidentiality by omitting identifying information unless proper consent has been obtained authorizing disclosure" (Standard 5.02[m]).

Reporting results accurately also is essential. In some instances, social workers might be reluctant to disclose certain "negative" or unflattering results because of possible ramifications for their programs. For example, an agency director might be uncomfortable in reporting evaluation data showing that a major program has not had good results; this could affect future funding or the agency's reputation. In spite of these understandable concerns, however, social workers are obligated to be honest and accurate in their reporting of results. To do otherwise would undermine the integrity of evaluation and research in general and, ultimately, could damage social workers' and agencies' reputations and harm the people they serve. The NASW's (1996) *Code of Ethics* states, "Social workers should report evaluation and research findings accurately. They should not fabricate or falsify results and should take steps to correct any errors later found in published data using standard publication methods" (Standard 5.02[n]).

Disclosing results to participants. As a matter of principle, social workers ordinarily share evaluation and research results with their data sources, whether clients, colleagues, or the general public. In some instances, however, social workers might be inclined to withhold results in an effort to protect potential recipients from psychological harm or trauma. In clinical circumstances, for example, social workers might be tempted to withhold results obtained from rapid assessment instruments or other measures that suggest serious psychological or emotional symptoms or trauma. Ethically, of course, social workers must consider the extent to which clients have the "right to know" information about themselves, even when the information might be painful or emotionally threatening.

Unfortunately, there are no easy answers to these dilemmas. In general, social workers support clients' right to know information about themselves; at the same time, social workers have an understandable instinct to protect people from harmful information—what ethicists refer to as *professional paternalism* (Reamer, 1983). When social workers encounter these issues, they should take assertive steps to address them using available ethical decision-making frameworks, protocols, and standards (Loewenberg & Dolgoff, 1996; Reamer, 1999). When possible, social workers should obtain consultation from thoughtful and knowledgeable colleagues (e.g., supervisors, agency-based ethics committees, IRBs, ethics consultants).

Acknowledging credit. Many evaluation and research activities in social work entail some type of collegial collaboration. Common arrangements involve collaboration among agency-based colleagues and between principal investigators and research associates or assistants. Social workers responsible for the dissemination of results must be careful to acknowledge the contributions of those who provided meaningful assistance. According to the NASW's (1996) *Code of Ethics,* "Social workers should take responsibility and credit, including authorship credit, only for work they have actually performed and to which they have contributed" (Standard 4.08[a]). Furthermore, "Social workers should honestly acknowledge the work of and the contributions of others" (Standard 4.08[b]).

Although there is no precise formula to determine how credit should be given in every circumstance, there are widely accepted guidelines. These include ensuring that all individuals who made meaningful contributions receive acknowledgment as co-authors, usually in descending order of their respective contributions. Individuals who contributed equally may be listed alphabetically, although occasionally the parties decide to list names in random order. Individuals who made useful contributions but who were not central to the project's conceptualization, data collection, or data analysis may be acknowledged appropriately in a footnote (e.g., a graduate student or clerical employee who conducted a number of interviews over several weeks or who helped with data entry).

A related issue concerns social workers' honest acknowledgment of literature and data sources they rely on during the course of evaluation and research. Ideas reflected in a research report or a project's instruments that are based on, or directly draw from, other professionals' work, whether published or not, should be acknowledged accordingly.

CONCLUSION

Clearly, social workers must be cognizant of a wide range of ethical issues germane to evaluation and research. These include ethical issues involving the formulation of research questions in the first place, research designs, sampling, measurement, data collection, confidentiality and privacy, and the handling of results.

Our current preoccupation with these issues reflects the maturing grasp of ethical matters in social work and other professions. In part because of past unethical practices and in part because of professionals' increased understanding of the inherent importance of ethics, during recent years, social workers have developed increasingly substantial and rigorous ethical guidelines and standards related to research and evaluation. Certainly, this is reflected in the current *Code of Ethics* (NASW, 1996).

Underlying social workers' concern about the protection of research and evaluation participants and ethical methodology, however, is a fundamental question facing the profession: To what extent do social workers have an ethical duty or obligation to incorporate research and evaluation into their practice? The short answer is that contemporary social workers strongly believe that there is such an ethical obligation (Curtis, 1996; Myers & Thyer, 1997). In fact, the NASW's (1996) *Code of Ethics* asserts this definitively when it states, "Social workers should critically examine and keep current with emerging knowledge relevant to social work and fully use evaluation and research evidence in their professional practice" (Standard 5.02[c]).

We must ask ourselves, however, what social workers can do to meet this ethical obligation. The answer is twofold. First, social workers have an obligation to keep current with research-based knowledge and draw on it routinely and systematically during their careers. Social work's fund of research-based knowledge has grown dramatically, especially since the 1970s. The profession's journals and texts now regularly include the results of both quantitative and qualitative studies evaluating social work intervention. Social work's literature also contains many secondary reviews and meta-analyses of multiple studies on a subject. Social workers should consult this literature as a matter of course when they design and implement interventions (see Standards 4.01[b,c] and 5.02[c] of the NASW's [1996] *Code of Ethics*).

Second, social workers should use the ever-growing number of research and evaluation tools available to practitioners to conduct needs assessments and to monitor and evaluate their practice (see Standard 5.02[a] of the NASW's [1996] *Code of Ethics*). As various chapters in this handbook demonstrate, social workers in clinical and nonclinical settings now have access to an impressive assortment of research and evaluation tools that can strengthen the quality of their work.

Without question, social workers' understanding of the relevance and value of research and evaluation has progressed during recent years, especially with respect to the ways in which user-friendly tools and techniques can be used for very pragmatic purposes by social workers in all practice settings, supplementing contributions based on studies conducted by professional researchers. This phenomenon demonstrates noteworthy progress in the evolution of social work. Along with this developmental progress, social workers have enhanced their understanding of a diverse range of compelling ethical issues related to research and evaluation. This understanding, along with social workers' enduring commitment to upholding high ethical standards, will serve the profession and its clients well.

REFERENCES

Ashcroft, R. (1998). Human research subjects, selection of. In R. Chadwick (Ed.), *Encyclopedia of applied ethics* (Vol. 2, pp. 627-639). San Diego: Academic Press.

Council for International Organizations of Medical Sciences. (1993). *International ethical guidelines for biomedical research involving research subjects*. Geneva, Switzerland: Author.

Curtis, G. C. (1996). The scientific evaluation of new claims. *Research on Social Work Practice, 6,* 117-121.

Grinnell, R. M., Jr. (Ed.). (1997). *Social work research and evaluation* (5th ed.). Itasca, IL: Peacock.

Levine, C. (1991). AIDS and the ethics of human subjects research. In F. G. Reamer (Ed.), *AIDS and ethics* (pp. 77-104). New York: Columbia University Press.

Levine, R. J. (1988). *Ethics and regulation of clinical research* (2nd ed.). New Haven, CT: Yale University Press.

Loewenberg, F., & Dolgoff, R. (1996). *Ethical decisions for social work practice* (5th ed.). Itasca, IL: Peacock.

Myers, L. M., & Thyer, B. A. (1997). Should social work clients have the right to effective treatment? *Social Work, 42,* 288-298.

National Association of Social Workers. (1996). *Code of Ethics of the National Association of Social Workers*. Washington, DC: Author.

National Commission for the Protection of Human Subjects of Biomedical and Behavioral Research. (1978). *The Belmont Report: Ethical principles and guidelines for the protection of human subjects of research*. Washington, DC: Author.

President's Commission for the Study of Ethical Problems in Medicine and Biomedical and Behavioral Research. (1982). *Making health care decisions: The ethical and legal implications of informed consent in the patient-practitioner relationship* (Vol. 3). Washington, DC: Government Printing Office.

Reamer, F. G. (1983). The concept of paternalism in social work. *Social Service Review, 57,* 254-271.

Reamer, F. G. (1987). Informed consent in social work. *Social Work, 32,* 425-429.

Reamer, F. G. (1998a). *Ethical standards in social work: A critical review of the NASW Code of Ethics*. Washington, DC: NASW Press.

Reamer, F. G. (1998b). *Social work research and evaluation skills*. New York: Columbia University Press.

Reamer, F. G. (1999). *Social work values and ethics* (2nd ed.). New York: Columbia University Press.

Rubin, A., & Babbie, E. (1997). *Research methods for social work* (3rd ed.). Pacific Grove, CA: Brooks/Cole.

Salgo v. Leland Stanford Jr. University Board of Trustees, 317 P.2d 170 (Cal. Ct. App. 1957).

Schloendorff v. Society of New York Hospital, 211 N.Y. 125 (1914).

Weijer, C. (1998). Research methods and policies. In R. Chadwick (Ed.), *Encyclopedia of applied ethics* (Vol. 3, pp. 853-860). San Diego: Academic Press.

Whitbeck, C. (1998). Research ethics. In R. Chadwick (Ed.), *Encyclopedia of applied ethics* (Vol. 3, pp. 835-843). San Diego: Academic Press.

CHAPTER TWENTY-SIX

Gender, Ethnicity, and Race Matters

ANTOINETTE Y. RODGERS-FARMER

MIRIAM POTOCKY-TRIPODI

As we enter the 21st century, it is increasingly important that social workers become more competent in conducting research with culturally diverse populations, women, and gays and lesbians. The need to become more competent is dictated by the realization that traditional research paradigms, research methods, and data analytic strategies might not be appropriate for enhancing our understanding about the complex challenges that these populations face.

The aim of this chapter is to enhance the reader's awareness of the need to consider the issues of gender, ethnicity, and race in the planning and conduct of research. Using the stages of the research process as a conceptual framework, the chapter examines how issues related to gender, ethnicity, and race can be incorporated into each stage of the research process. Before discussing each of these stages, the research paradigms that have influenced the research methodologies that we use are explored.

RESEARCH PARADIGMS

Historically, social work research has been conducted from a positivist perspective. Positivism assumes the following:

There is a single tangible reality out there, independent of any observer and operating in a lawlike fashion. It is fragmentable into independent variables and processes, any of which can be studied independently of the others. From this position, the goal of social inquiry is to find the regularities and relationships, converging on reality until, finally, it can be predicted and controlled. This is possible because, in principle, it is always possible to discover the causes of social phenomena. (Chambers, Wedel, & Rodwell, 1992, p. 279)

Critics of this perspective argue that, having been developed by European men, it ignores the worldviews of women and persons from non-Western cultures. There is nothing in the positivist perspective that prohibits one from examining issues related to gender, ethnicity, and race. However, it has been suggested that this perspective allows us to examine these issues only in a limited matter. For example, Barton (1998) states that the positivist perspective merely allows us to examine the issues of gender, ethnicity, and race as "parameters to include in multivariate model specification" (p. 286).

Numerous alternatives to the positivist perspective have been suggested including the feminist, ecological, and empowerment perspectives. The feminist approach to research aims to "develop versions of reality that more accurately reflect the experience of women, versions that affirm women's strengths and value and can transform society itself" (Davis, 1994, p. 65). This approach is based on the assumption that the worldviews of women and other oppressed people are fundamentally different from those of the people in power. Feminist research emphasizes documenting the everyday lives of women so as to make their perspective visible (Swigonski, 1994).

The ecological perspective is embodied in constructivist research, which holds that reality can be understood accurately only in the context of the total person-in-environment situation. Like feminism, constructivism holds that there are multiple viewpoints among the people who live in a common environment. That is, there is not one single truth; rather, there are many truths. The aim of the constructivist approach is to articulate these differing viewpoints and, sometimes, to "co-construct" a mutually acceptable view of reality among the different participants in an environment (including research respondents, researchers, and other stakeholders) so as to address social problems (Rodwell, 1998).

Finally, the empowerment perspective is embodied in participatory action research, which aims to enlist research respondents as "co-researchers" who participate in defining the research questions, establishing methodology, and interpreting and applying the results. The purpose of participatory action research ultimately is social action on behalf of the population that is the focus of the research. By participating in all stages of the research process, the members of the population are able to influence the resultant social action and, thereby, are empowered (McNicoll, 1999).

The feminist, ecological, and empowerment research perspectives overlap in many ways. All aim to document the viewpoints of oppressed people with the ultimate goal of lessening their oppression. Researchers within each perspective often have advocated the use of qualitative methods as being more appropriate than quantitative methods to achieve the desired ends (Davis, 1994; Rodwell, 1998). Although some researchers argue that these perspectives are fundamentally incompatible with positivism, many others see the value in combining both positivist and nonpositivist approaches so as to achieve greater understanding of the problem under investigation and greater relevancy of the findings (Padgett, 1998; Tutty, Rothery, & Grinnell, 1996).

STAGES OF THE RESEARCH PROCESS

In this section, we highlight each of the major phases of the research process—problem formulation, population definition, research design, data collection, data analysis, data interpretation, and reporting the results—in which the researcher must be sensitive to issues related to gender, ethnicity, and race.

Problem Formulation

The formulation of a research problem is the initial stage in the research process. By the very name of this stage, it is implied that the researcher is operating from a "deficiency model." That is, the research questions or hypotheses may be stated in such a way as to focus on "problems" of minority groups (often in relation to the dominant group) rather than focusing on their strengths and resiliencies. For example, a research question addressing why there is a higher incidence of low-birthweight newborns in ethnic minority populations as compared to the white population (Kleinman & Kessel, 1987) focuses on a problem. By contrast, an investigation into the family or community factors that prevent low birthweights among the minority population would focus on strengths.

In formulating the research problem, the researcher may be using his or her own experiences, his or her own interests, and the findings of previous research (Hughes, Seidman, & Williams, 1993). Using these methods may lead to formulation of the "wrong problem" or errors in "conceptualization of the problem" (Seidman, 1978). One way in which to avoid these errors in conceptualization of the problem is to have the participants define the research question.

Another issue that may arise in the problem formulation stage is that of sexism in research concepts. This occurs when behaviors, attributes, and/or traits are conceptualized as applying to only one gender when, in fact, they may be present in members of both genders (Eichler, 1988). For example, throughout the 1980s, the official AIDS definition was based on the symptoms typically observed in men with the disease. Women with AIDS do not present many of the same symptoms. As a result, these women were not diagnosed with AIDS and, therefore, were largely excluded from much of the research on the disease (Rosser, 1991).

Population Definition

When defining the population under investigation, one must carefully consider whose definition one plans to use—the U.S. Bureau of the Census's categorical definition or the person's self-definition. The choice has implications for the generalization of the study's results. For example, research on black ethnic identity consistently has shown that "Blacks are not a monolithic group and that how individual Blacks see themselves, see other Blacks, and view non-Blacks reflects the extent to which they identify with their Blackness" (Thomas, Phillips, & Brown, 1998, p. 77).

Ignoring the fact that African Americans, Hispanics, and other ethnic groups are not monolithic has resulted in the continuation of culturally encapsulated research, which assumes that all persons within the group share the same norms and values and that they use and define concepts in the same manner (Pedersen, 1988). Such research results in overgeneralization of the findings obtained and ignores the diversity within the groups.

Research Design

During the past 18 years, the use of between-group designs to examine the differences between majority and minority groups has come under scrutiny (Phinney & Landin, 1998). Critics state that these designs focus on showing the differences between European Americans and African Americans, usually from a deficit perspective (Howard & Scott, 1981), and do not attempt to adequately explain why the differences found occurred (Hughes et al., 1993). On the other hand, supporters of the use of between-group designs (e.g., Azibo, 1992; Phinney & Landin, 1998) believe that these designs are helpful in demonstrating how cultural characteristics are related to different outcomes among various groups.

Within-group designs also have been criticized. These designs have been criticized for their lack of generalizability. Despite this criticism, Hughes et al. (1993) believe that these designs are appropriate when "(a) the design question is solely oriented toward a within-culture understanding, (b) conceptual equivalence across cultures is not possible, or (c) conceptual equivalence exists, but measurement equivalence is not possible to achieve" (p. 696).

Data Collection

During this phase of the research process, the researcher should be concerned with three issues: gaining access to the population of interest, who should collect the data, and how the data should be collected (e.g., surveys, direct observations).

Gaining Access to the Population of Interest

Gaining access to the population of interest might be the most challenging stage of the data collection phase because of the historical relationship between the research community and the population of interest. It frequently has been the case that the exchange between researchers and research "subjects" has been one-way, benefiting only the researchers and exploiting the participants. To address this injustice, a social action model of research recently has been promoted involving the research participants as co-investigators throughout the research process (Wagner, 1991). To start this active process, Becerra and Zambrana (1985) suggest several strategies for engaging members of minority communities. These include gaining the sponsorship of a well-known ethnic community service agency, explaining the purpose of the research to a variety of appropriate community groups, and training indigenous personnel to participate as interviewers or in some other staff capacity.

Who Should Collect the Data

Some experts in the field of multicultural research argue that the researcher must be of the same ethnic/racial background as those being studied. Marin and Marin (1991) state that ethnic matching of the interviewer and the interviewee enhances the validity of responses to sensitive questions. On the other hand, Becerra (1997) argues that ethnic matching of the interviewer and the interviewee may result in biased responses. Furthermore, the use of ethnic matching of the interviewer and the interviewee may ignore other important variables that have implications for data collection such as trustworthiness of the interviewer and the interviewer's awareness of biases about the group under study.

Gender matching of the interviewer and the interviewee also must be considered when deciding who should collect the data. In a recent study examining the effects of interviewer gender on mental health interviews, Pollner (1998) found that both male and female respondents interviewed by women reported more symptoms of depression, substance abuse, and conduct disorders than did respondents interviewed by men. He attributes his findings to women creating a more conducive atmosphere for disclosure.

Because gender, ethnicity, and race of the interviewer have implications for the quality of the data obtained, we suggest that one should have a standardized procedure for training all interviewers. Once these interviewers have been trained, periodic retraining on the administration of the survey instrument also should be done to ensure that the interviewers still are administering the survey properly. The effects of gender, ethnicity, and race on the dependent variable also can be examined statistically once the data have been collected. One way in which to do this is to conduct a t test or analysis of variance using gender, ethnicity, or race of the interviewer as the grouping variable. If it is detected that any of these variables had an effect on the outcome variable, then one should address this issue in the discussion section of the article with an emphasis on its implications for the findings obtained.

How the Data Should Be Collected

Data may be collected via standardized measures, interviews, direct observations, and so on. In conducting research with minority participants, however, it is critical that the researcher use measures that are culturally appropriate. The reason for this is that it is well documented that many assessment tools are biased against minority clients (Sue & Sue, 1990) because they have been normed on white middle-class respondents. Even though these measures are valid and reliable, they might not be valid and reliable for minority participants (Hughes et al., 1993). Similar concerns have been raised about using measures normed in Western cultural settings with persons who are not from a Western culture (Ortega & Richey, 1998).

When conducting research with persons whose language is not English, the researcher is faced with the dilemma of trying to establish various types of equivalence such as linguistic, semantic, and metric equivalence. Linguistic equivalence can be established by translating the instrument from English to the language of the respondents. Back-translation also is used to establish linguistic equivalence. For a detailed description of this procedure, see Brislin (1970). Semantic equivalence can be established after the measure has been translated or back-translated by determining whether the meaning of each item is congruent with the respondents' understanding of the phenomenon. Metric equivalence can be established by comparing the factor structure of the translated measure to the factor structure of the original measure. According to Burnett (1998), metric equivalence is used to determine whether the "observed indicators have the same relationships with the theoretical constructs across different cultures" (p. 77).

The need to establish metric equivalence also is important when conducting research with men and women. In examining the factor structure of the Beck Depression Inventory-II, Dozois, Dobson, and Ahnberg (1998) found that Factor 2 for women (Somatic-Vegetative) represented Factor 1 for men and that Factor 1 for women (Cognitive-Affective) represented Factor 2 for men. They also found differences in factor loadings. For example, they found that punishment feelings loaded on the Cognitive-Affective factor for women and on the Somatic-Vegetative factor for men.

Data Analysis

Because most measures have been normed on white middle-class respondents, it is recommended that these measures be assessed for their psychometric adequacy when using them with minority populations (van de Vijver & Leung, 1997). Assessing these measures for their psychometric adequacy would involve computing the reliability and the item statistics (e.g., item-total correlations, item means and variances) and determining their construct validity. The item statistic can be used to determine whether there is a ceiling or floor effect (van de Vijver & Leung, 1997), whereas confirmatory factor analysis can be used to assess construct validity. For example, confirmatory factor analysis has been widely used for assessing the construct validity of the Center for Epidemiologic Studies Depression Scale for use in cross-cultural research (Ortega & Richey, 1998).

After determining the reliability and validity of the measure, one is faced with the challenge of deciding how the construct of ethnicity or race should be used in the data analysis. In examining the literature on adolescent development, Steinberg and Fletcher (1998) found that ethnicity or race has been used in data analyses as a grouping variable, as a control variable, as a dynamic process, and as a moderator variable. Using ethnicity or race in any of the just-mentioned ways is not without its problems, both methodological and statistical. For example, using ethnicity or race as a grouping variable may result in overlooking important demographic variables that covary with ethnicity or race and that may account for the findings obtained. In other words, using ethnicity or race as a grouping variable may lead one to wrongly conclude that there are ethnic or racial differences when none exists. For a more detailed description about the methodological issues related to the use of ethnicity or race as a control variable, as a dynamic process, and as a moderator variable, see Steinberg and Fletcher (1998).

In addition to dealing with the issue of ethnicity or race in the data analysis, one also has to deal with the issue of gender. Eichler (1988) notes that when it comes to dealing with the issue of gender in the data analysis, one usually does not analyze the data separately for men and for women. Therefore, the results of these analyses cannot be generalized to either group alone. To make the results generalizable, it is important that separate analyses be done for both men and women.

Data Interpretation

One of the hazards at this stage is that of overgeneralization (Eichler, 1988). Data collected from one gender or one ethnic or racial group should not be generalized to apply to all persons. Another potential pitfall is in interpreting observed differences between diverse groups as indicative of "problems" or "deficiencies" in the minority members when, in fact, they are simply that—differences—and in many cases could be seen as strengths. For example, if ethnic minority or gay males were found to have elevated scores on the paranoia scale of the Minnesota Multiphasic Personality Inventory (MMPI), it would be erroneous to interpret this as indicative of psychopathology when, in fact, it is more likely indicative of a healthy survival skill in response to a hostile society (Sue & Sue, 1990).

Reporting the Results

In accordance with the social action model of research, study results and their implications should be shared with the research participants. Ideally, the results should be immediately usable by the community rather than having implications only for the future or for persons outside the community. Feedback from the research participants should be solicited to identify strengths and problems of the study and to suggest future directions. As a further component of the action research model, results should be used to influence policy and other activity at the macro level (Wagner, 1991).

CONCLUSION

In this chapter, we have highlighted some of the issues that researchers must consider when conducting research with diverse populations, women, and gays and lesbians. With increased attention to these issues, we will begin to develop a body of knowledge that will help us to better understand the complex challenges that these populations face.

Exemplary Studies

Hughes, M. (1998). Turning points in the lives of young inner-city men forgoing destructive criminal behaviors: A qualitative study. *Social Work Research, 22,* 143-151.

This study formulates the research problem in terms of strengths and resiliencies rather than deficiencies. It demonstrates the use of community leaders to access members of the population. The study uses qualitative data collection to obtain in-depth views of participants' perspectives.

Shin, H., & Abell, N. (1999). The Homesickness and Contentment Scale: Developing a culturally sensitive measure of adjustment for Asians. *Research on Social Work Practice, 9,* 45-60.

This study demonstrates the process of translating and establishing validity and reliability of a culturally specific instrument.

REFERENCES

Azibo, D. (1992). Understanding the proper and improper usage of the comparative research framework. In A. Burlew, W. Banks, H. McAdoo, & D. Azibo (Eds.), *African American psychology* (pp. 18-27). Newbury Park, CA: Sage.

Barton, W. H. (1998). Culturally competent research protocols. In R. R. Greene & M. Watkins (Eds.), *Serving diverse constituencies: Applying the ecological perspective* (pp. 285-303). Hawthorne, NY: Aldine.

Becerra, R. M. (1997). Can valid research on ethnic populations only be conducted by researchers from the same ethnic group? No. In D. de Anda (Ed.), *Controversial issues in multiculturalism* (pp. 114-117). Needham Heights, MA: Allyn & Bacon.

Becerra, R. M., & Zambrana, R. E. (1985). Methodological approaches to research on Hispanics. *Social Work Research and Abstracts, 21,* 42-49.

Brislin, R. W. (1970). Back-translation for cross-cultural research. *Journal of Cross-Cultural Psychology, 1,* 185-216.

Burnett, D. (1998). Conceptual and methodological considerations in research with non-white ethnic elders. In M. Potocky & A. Y. Rodgers-Farmer (Eds.), *Social work research with minority and oppressed populations: Methodological issues and innovations* (pp. 71-91). New York: Haworth.

Chambers, D. E., Wedel, K. R., & Rodwell, M. K. (1992). *Evaluating social programs.* Needham Heights, MA: Allyn & Bacon.

Davis, L. V. (1994). Is feminist research inherently qualitative, and is it a fundamentally different approach to research? Yes. In W. W. Hudson & P. S. Nurius (Eds.), *Controversial issues in social work research* (pp. 63-68). Needham Heights, MA: Allyn & Bacon.

Dozois, D. J. A., Dobson, K. S., & Ahnberg, J. L. (1998). A psychometric evaluation of the Beck Depression Inventory-II. *Psychological Assessment, 10,* 83-89.

Eichler, M. (1988). *Nonsexist research methods: A practical guide.* Boston: Unwin Hyman.

Howard, A., & Scott, R. (1981). The study of minority groups in complex societies. In R. H. Munroe, R. L. Munroe, & B. Whiting (Eds.), *Handbook of cross-cultural human development* (pp. 113-152). New York: Garland.

Hughes, D., Seidman, E., & Williams, N. (1993). Cultural phenomena and the research enterprise: Toward a culturally anchored methodology. *American Journal of Community Psychology, 21,* 687-703.

Hughes, M. (1998). Turning points in the lives of young inner-city men forgoing destructive criminal behaviors: A qualitative study. *Social Work Research, 22,* 143-151.

Kleinman, J. C., & Kessel, S. S. (1987). Racial differences in low birthweight: Trends and risk factors. *New England Journal of Medicine, 317,* 749-753.

Marin, G., & Marin, B. (1991). *Research with Hispanic populations.* Newbury Park, CA: Sage.

McNicoll, P. (1999). Issues in teaching participatory action research. *Journal of Social Work Education, 35,* 51-62.

Ortega, D. M., & Richey, C. A. (1998). Methodological issues in social work research with depressed women of color. In M. Potocky & A. Y. Rodgers-Farmer (Eds.), *Social work research with minority and oppressed populations: Methodological issues and innovations* (pp. 47-70). New York: Haworth.

Padgett, D. K. (1998). *Qualitative methods in social work research: Challenges and rewards.* Thousand Oaks, CA: Sage.

Pedersen, P. (1988). *A handbook for developing multicultural awareness.* Alexandria, VA: American Association for Counseling and Development.

Phinney, J. S., & Landin, J. (1998). Research paradigms for studying ethnic minority families within and across groups. In V. C. McLoyd & L. Steinberg (Eds.), *Studying minority adolescents: Conceptual, methodological, and theoretical issues* (pp. 89-109). Mahwah, NJ: Lawrence Erlbaum.

Pollner, M. (1998). The effects of interviewer gender in mental health interviews. *Journal of Nervous and Mental Disease, 18,* 369-373.

Rodwell, M. K. (1998). *Social work constructivist research.* New York: Garland.

Rosser, S. V. (1991). AIDS and women. *AIDS, 3,* 230-240.

Seidman, E. (1978). Justice, values, and social science: Unexamined premises. In R. J. Simon (Ed.), *Research in law and sociology* (pp. 175-200). Greenwich, CT: JAI.

Shin, H., & Abell, N. (1999). The Homesickness and Contentment Scale: Developing a culturally sensitive measure of adjustment for Asians. *Research on Social Work Practice, 9,* 45-60.

Steinberg, L., & Fletcher, A. C. (1998). Data analytic strategies in research on ethnic minority youth. In V. C. McLoyd & L. Steinberg (Eds.), *Studying minority adolescents: Conceptual, methodological, and theoretical issues* (pp. 279-294). Mahwah, NJ: Lawrence Erlbaum.

Sue, D. W., & Sue, D. (1990). *Counseling the culturally different: Theory and practice* (2nd ed.). New York: John Wiley.

Swigonski, M. E. (1994). The logic of feminist standpoint theory for social work research. *Social Work, 39,* 387-393.

Thomas, K. M., Phillips, L. D., & Brown, S. (1998). Redefining race in the workplace: Insights from ethnic identity theory. *Journal of Black Psychology, 24,* 76-92.

Tutty, L. M., Rothery, M. A., & Grinnell, R. M. (Eds.). (1996). *Qualitative research for social workers.* Needham Heights, MA: Allyn & Bacon.

van de Vijver, F., & Leung, K. (1997). *Methods and data analysis for cross-cultural research.* Thousand Oaks, CA: Sage.

Wagner, D. (1991). Reviving the action research model: Combing case and cause with dislocated workers. *Social Work, 36,* 477-482.

CHAPTER TWENTY-SEVEN

Comparative International Research

ELAINE T. JURKOWSKI
MARTIN B. TRACY

Research methods in comparative international social welfare policy research, especially studies of industrial nations, tend to cluster around frameworks that explore causal explanations relative to applied knowledge and theory building. This is reflected in a variety of comparative international social policy conceptual predictive models that have emerged over recent decades including convergence, class, political party, ideological, and diffusion theories (Midgley, 1997). Whereas comparative international social welfare policy analyses rely heavily on models based on macro policy determinants, studies of social work programs and practices in other countries have, for the most part, focused on descriptive case analyses.

Comparative international social work research has emphasized analysis of the pivotal characteristics of social work programs and practices. Indeed, a common critique of cross-national comparative social work studies is the scarcity of analytical conceptual frameworks that are attentive to the aggregate impact of social, economic, and political processes shaping social work services and practices (Ginsburg, 1992; Hoefer, 1996; Tracy, 1992).

There are several explanations of why comparative international research in social work has been so dependent on descriptive methods. One significant reason is that the preponderance of comparative theory in social policies reflects only a marginal interest in social work as a distinctive area of study. Cross-national studies on social welfare policy, as distinguished from social work programs and practices, are largely defined by macroanalytical frameworks and methods derived from comparative public policy analysis in political science and sociology (Dierkes, Weiler, & Antal, 1987; Heidenheimer, Heclo, & Adams, 1975).

In this chapter, we provide a brief summary of the major impediments to research and an overview of selected comparative international research methods and models used in studies on social welfare policy, with references to social work programs and practices where appropriate. We also discuss specific trends in comparative international social work methods as reflected in a review of research published in major social work journals.

IMPEDIMENTS TO RESEARCH

There are a number of impediments to conducting comparative international social work research. One barrier is the substantial logistical difficulty in obtaining reliable program- and practice-related data and information. Travel costs to obtain data can be prohibitive, language translation often imposes difficulties for researchers who are not fluent in the languages of the countries under study, the lack of comparability in terminology can be a problem, and access to documents by foreign researchers can be another major impediment to research. These and related factors discussed throughout this chapter make it difficult to obtain critical information on the social, economic, and political forces driving programs and practices in a given nation or set of nations.

Quality comparative international social welfare and social work research requires an adequate level of understanding of programs in terms of development, implementation, administration, and practice. This usually entails ready access to governmental and agency documents that often is dependent on personal connections in study countries so as to obtain empirical, or even secondary, data necessary to a research project. The acquisition of materials also may be dependent on travel to library and government holdings abroad and, when necessary, on translation of documents. This process can be a prohibitively expensive and time-consuming complex enterprise that discourages the use of analytical comparative frameworks conducive to theory building. Such research is compounded by problems of measurement and inconsistent operational definitions of variables across nations.

Secondary analysis of data on social work practice in a comparative research context also is a challenge, particularly at the practice level. The primary problem is the lack of access to social work practice information from public and private agencies. Most readily available data from agencies relate to basic social program components of income, in-kind, and health care systems rather than practice. Accessible data generally includes descriptive information on program features such as benefit amounts, qualifying conditions, demographic characteristics of recipients, level of expenditures, and sources of revenue. There is much less information on what social workers, and professionals in related disciplines, actually do or on the methods of intervention that are used at the client level. Again, language can be a barrier even for secondary data, particularly with regard to terminology used to define aspects of social work practice in different cultures.

Given the complications of conducting comparative international analysis that goes beyond descriptive studies, it is not surprising that very little international research in social work uses methods and frameworks that explain causal differences in policies and programs among nations. The predicament often has led social work analysts down the path of least resistance in comparative international research to identify differences using more easily obtained descriptive policy and programmatic information.

This is not to suggest that descriptive research on social work policies in other countries has been unproductive. In fact, many descriptive studies have produced valuable information on how different countries approach similar societal problems while increasing knowledge of the administrative and functional aspects of social work programs and practices. In particular, descriptive comparative international social work studies have contributed to a better understanding of funding streams, administrative structures, qualifying conditions, interpersonal interventions, therapeutic methods, evaluation, and related practices in a variety of countries.

A sizable literature base in comparative studies also has contributed to interest that resonates within social work education for comparative international research (Healy & Asamoah, 1997; Ramanathan & Link, 1999). Almost universally, social workers view themselves as agents of social change and institutional reform with the goal of empowering disadvantaged and vulnerable people, regardless of the country or locale. However, local resources, social and economic conditions, and political situations create dramatic differences in the roles and needs to which social workers minister. Consequently, international approaches to social work practice and policies, social and economic justice, and social work values may differ. Comparative international research can, and does, contribute to improving the level of understanding of why programs and policies vary.

There has been no systematic assessment of the impact of comparative studies on social work practice, but there are indications that such studies have advanced the expansion of innovative social work programs and practices. The transfer of the concept of hospice from the United Kingdom to other countries is one such example. The use of community programs for the learning disabled in Britain to Canada and the United States is another.

In addition, there are many examples of the successful transfer of program provisions from one country to another that have significantly affected social welfare systems, especially social insurance programs. Multiple-country adoptions of early retirement provisions, indexation of old-age benefits to wages and salaries, credit splitting of pensions among men and women, and child raising and caregiving credits are just a few of the provisions recently initiated in one country and adopted in others (Tracy & Tracy, 1998). The proliferation of similar programmatic provisions across nations reflects the ongoing interactions among policymakers and social welfare analysts in industrial countries, many of whom know each other personally and exchange ideas at professional international conferences or through publications. These forums provide a fertile environment for sharing knowledge based on research, particularly applied research and policy analysis.

OVERVIEW OF COMPARATIVE/INTERNATIONAL RESEARCH METHODS

Various analytical methods are used to examine social welfare and social work policy and programs within a cross-national context. Comparative international social welfare studies aimed at theory development and explanation frequently are found in academic research. Descriptive analyses of social welfare policies also are common in academic research but are even more likely to predominate in studies conducted by policy and program analysts in government and nongovernment agencies. As noted, comparative international studies related specifically to social work practice and programs tend to be descriptive and appear to be of more interest to academics than to practitioners.

The rationale for theoretical frameworks in comparative social welfare and social work policy analysis is to provide a tool, or a set of tools, that lends itself to a causal explanation of the differences in approaches in different nations. That is, theory-based research helps to answer the question of why Country A addresses a social welfare issue, common to many nations, differently from Country B or Country C. In other words, the research provides insight into what accounts for variance in programs and interventions for social problems and issues that have similar characteristics and root causes. Research within a theoretical comparative context typically entails analyses of the transcending impact of pervasive macro social, economic, and political factors that shape social welfare and social work. This includes dominant political philosophies, economic systems, and class structures in a given nation or group of nations.

In contrast to research that focuses on macro explanations, descriptive analytical methods stress research that is aimed more at an applied understanding of policies and programs in terms of *who gets what, where, when, and how*. Methods that emphasize descriptive research, however, do not often get at the question of *why* a given nation has a particular policy and program at a given point in time. Data on basic characteristics of policies and programs are necessary components of both theoretical and descriptive analytical methods, but answering the question of *why* there are differences relies on a level of analyses and methods that examine the reasons underlying the development of specific policy approaches. Several of the prevailing methodological models that vary in their emphases on theory and description are briefly discussed in the following sections. They include the welfare state framework, the industrialization perspective, welfare regimes, political economy, social cohesion and social exclusion, policy process analysis, case studies, and data-based studies.

The Welfare State Framework

One prevailing approach to comparing social welfare policies from a theoretical perspective is analysis of the development of the welfare state in industrial nations. There are numerous conceptual typologies used in comparative research based on the origins and sustainability of social welfare and social work policies and programs. As Midgley (1997) points out, these explanatory theories emphasize quite different influential factors. Among the theories are hypotheses related to social conscience (Prigmore & Atherton, 1979), citizenship (Marshall, 1950), functionalism (Mishra, 1977), interest groups (Rimlinger, 1971), and ideology (Gough, 1979). A leading conceptualization in comparative studies of social welfare policies in economically developing nations is diffusion theory (Midgley, 1984), suggesting that similarities in program characteristics do not adequately account for significant variations among the vast array of different approaches developed through social policies.

The Industrialization Perspective

Although all of these theories have influenced comparative research on social welfare, it is useful to focus on industrialization (which is an aspect of functionalist theory) as having had a distinctive impact on how social welfare and social work programs are viewed in a comparative context. Based on research from the 1960s and 1970s, it has been widely assumed that industrialization led to the development of a welfare state, as defined by similarities in social welfare programs and benefits (Rimlinger, 1971; Titmuss, 1968, 1974; Wilensky & Lebeaux, 1965). This perspective hypothesizes that economic structures common to all industrialized nations generate social welfare provisions that converge toward similar characteristics. This has, in turn, led to a "convergence hypothesis" emanating from analysis of parallel safety net benefit provisions, especially comparable program features such as old age, survivors', and disability benefit formulas; retirement-age trends; universal health care features; and related aspects of social insurance and social assistance systems.

Welfare Regimes

A contemporary derivative of assumptions about the impact of industrialization on the welfare state is Esping-Anderson's (1990) typology of welfare state "regimes." This framework has played a prominent role in recent analyses of comparative welfare state policies and programs, especially in research conducted by European policy analysts. In essence, the framework is based on the notion that industrial capital turns labor into a commodity that can be bought. However, to reduce the potential of labor abuses in a situation where industry has excessive control of wages, it is necessary to institute public social insurance and social assistance programs to provide alternative sources of income that are available even when an individual is not working for wages. The typology consists of three prevailing welfare state regimes in industrial nations (Esping-Anderson, 1990; see also Taylor-Gooby, 1991). These regimes are classified as being liberal, conservative, or social democratic, using the classic definitions of these terms, which are the opposite of modern political use.

Liberal regimes in the typology are viewed as those countries that develop social welfare programs targeted for specific categories of populations in need. For example, this is typical of the approach to government social welfare programs in Australia, Britain, and the United States.

A conservative regime in the typology is one where a country has developed universal programs that provide benefits for both employed and "nonactive" populations (e.g., children, working-age unemployed, elderly, disabled, sick). This approach is reflective of government welfare systems in France and Germany.

The third regime, the social democratic regime, is where the country has instituted programs that not only provide income and health care protection on a universal basis but also are designed to promote social solidarity and social cohesion. The Scandinavian countries are good examples of social democratic regimes.

There are, however, numerous other theory-based approaches to comparing social welfare and social work programs that are commonly used within the literature. Five such analytical frameworks are briefly noted next: political economy, social cohesion and social exclusion, policy process analysis, case studies, and data-based analysis.

Political Economy

One popular framework in comparing social welfare is the concept of political economy, especially as it applies to aging policies and programs (Estes, 1991). Political economy highlights awareness of structural pressures and constraints, particularly those that are related to class, gender, and ethnicity within the larger political and economic context.

Social Cohesion and Social Exclusion

A framework that is increasingly being used in comparing social policies focuses on the interrelated concepts of social exclusion and social cohesion (Gilbert, 1998; Silver, 1998). The terms have varying definitions, but social cohesion often is used to refer to the role of public and private sector organizations in promoting solidarity and social and economic stability (Leeuw, 1997; Miller, 1997; Organization for Economic Cooperation and Development [OECD], 1997). Social exclusion typically alludes to an individual's restricted access to adequate employment, cash transfers, and personal social services. It also refers to the exclusion of beneficiaries, consumers, and clients in participating in decisions about programs and policies that directly affect recipients of benefits and services (OECD, 1998; Silver, 1994).

Highlighted in the 1988 European Community (now the European Union) Social Charter and in the 1989 European Community Council of Ministers, social exclusion has been used to refer to the dynamic processes that form the basis of poverty (inadequate social programs, low wages, single parenthood, mental illness, drug and alcohol addictions and abuses, discrimination, inadequate education, and other factors that lead to marginalization). This dynamic process makes the concept more multidimensional than typical definitions of poverty and more attentive to the constantly evolving environmental factors that contribute to economic and social dependency (Berghman, 1996; Jordan, 1996).

Policy Process Analysis

Comparative policy process models are designed to help policymakers and analysts in international organizations to understand the conditions under which a given country, or group of countries, has adopted a specific program or provision (Tracy, 1992, cited in Ramanathan & Link, 1999). The information is intended to facilitate in planning the development, implementation, and evaluation of programs (Jones, 1985; Rose, 1973). The model provides a diagnostic tool to obtain practical information that a person or group in a decision-making or advisory position would want to know about a program in another country.

Information in policy process analysis is derived from answers to questions such as the following. What is the country's program intended to do (goals, objectives, or strategies)? What public issue or problem is being addressed? How is the issue defined (measured, understood, or perceived)? Why is government involved? What level of government is involved (local, regional, state/province, or federal)? What is expected of government in addressing the problem? What other organizations and official bodies are expected to play a role (private sector, business, or not-for-profit agencies)? What are the obstacles to implementing the program? How does the program reflect the nation's cultural, political, and economic environment? Does the program reflect principles of social insurance or social assistance, prevention or remediation, comprehension or categorization, integration or independence, public governance or privatization? The model also is based on information that describes how the program is funded and administered as well as who is covered and what benefits and services they are entitled to receive.

Information about the process in decision making is particularly useful for policymakers and professional analysts who seek to understand why one approach to a social issue, out of an infinite number of options, has been chosen. This is particularly important to analysts in governments. Understanding the process also is useful to social policy analysts in international advisory organizations including the World Bank, International Labor Organization, International Monetary Fund, World Health Organization, OECD, and International Social Security Association.

Case Studies

Each country shares common programmatic approaches to social welfare problems with other countries, yet each country also has marked differences. As noted earlier, case study models that identify the commonalities and differences frequently are used in comparative international social policy and social work research. This method is used to explain and describe basic program characteristics—assessment, development, administration, implementation, and delivery in a given nation or group of nations. Many case studies are similar to the analytical models mentioned previously in terms of describing *who gets what, when, where, and how.* Some case studies also attempt to explain *why* one or more countries have adopted a particular policy approach. However, in most case studies, there is less emphasis on a systematic analytical approach to making explanatory comparisons.

Case studies do often provide valuable information on identified needs for social welfare and social work programs among countries with common social conditions in comparative context. The most recent comparative research is on a wide variety of topics such as children (Bergmann, 1996; Kamerman, 1993), women (Koven &

Michel, 1993), retirement (Gruber & Wise, 1999), country studies (Mayadas, Watts, & Elliott, 1997), old age (Williamson & Pampel, 1993), and social security (Dixon, 1999; Midgley & Tracy, 1996).

There also is a body of case study literature that focuses on social work (Harris, 1990; Hokenstad, Khinduka, & Midgley, 1992; Schindler & Brawley, 1987). Whereas much of the research on all of these related topics concentrates on industrial societies, there also is a body of case study literature that focuses on social issues and programs in economically developing nations, as reflected in research published in *Social Development Issues* and related studies (MacPherson & Midgley, 1987).

The case study method does not necessarily indicate that the research will not involve a systematic theoretical approach to analysis. Many case studies are based on a variety of methodologies including socioeconomic and political theory. Examples include research on old-age policies (Williamson & Pampel, 1993), social welfare (Ismael, 1996; Jones, 1993; Midgley, 1997; Van Wormer, 1997), social services (Munday, 1989), and social work practice (Cannan, Berry, & Lyons, 1992).

Data-Based Studies

Another framework for comparative international studies uses social welfare program data and demographic indicators that have been standardized to varying degrees of comparability. This approach focuses on secondary data such as program and governmental expenditures, numbers of claimants, conditions of entitlement, coverage, benefit levels, and administration. Secondary data also are used to provide comparative differences in social indicators relative to quality of life, morbidity, and mortality. This format often is used to examine similarities and differences in social assistance (Eardley, Bradshaw, Ditch, Gough, & Whiteford, 1996), social insurance (U.S. Department of Health and Human Services, various years), and social indicators (Estes, 1984; International Labour Organization, 1999; World Health Organization, 1999), and social expenditures (OECD, 1997, 1998). The appendix provides a list of Web sites that can be useful resources for retrieving secondary data.

One of the most standardized comparative data banks on socioeconomic variables is the Luxembourg Income Study on income distribution and poverty (Popova, 1996; Rubin, 1996; Osbourg, 1991). Standardized data are of value to any analyst studying comparative international social welfare and social work. The data are essential to research among academics and policymakers, but businesses with employees in foreign nations also need to know the extent of their payroll tax, social service, and health care obligations to their workers.

PREVAILING METHODS

There are, then, several distinguishable analytical methods and areas of emphasis used in comparative international research methods on social work and social welfare policy in the literature. The methods reflect a wide range of analytical approaches to examining social and economic needs, programmatic approaches, and typologies of welfare states. To provide a snapshot view of the types of prevailing analytical methods used in comparative international research, a longitudinal review of articles published in selected refereed journals was conducted for this chapter. Four international social work and social welfare journals were reviewed over varying periods from 5 years to 40 years to determine comparative content areas and methods. The journals that were reviewed were the *British Journal of Social Work* (1975-1998), *International Social Work* (1958-1998), *International Social Security Review* (1990-1999), and *Social Work in Europe* (1995-1998). The review of *International Social Work* covered a much longer period of time because it generally is accepted as the leading international social work practice journal, representative of the aforementioned frameworks over its tenure. The *British Journal of Social Work* and *Social Work in Europe* have been in print since 1975 and 1995, respectively. All of the volumes in these journals were reviewed. The *International Social Security Review* has been published since 1948, but only the past decade was reviewed.

The methodology used to determine the prevalence of comparative international content and methods concentrated on three components in articles in these four journals: (a) the type of study design or analysis undertaken (qualitative or quantitative), (b) the domain within which the article was written (practice, policy, or research), and (c) the type of research analysis or outcome of the presentation (descriptive, theoretical, or analytical/empirical). In addition, the specific content areas (up to two) and geographic areas under study in the article were recorded. Each article published in the review periods for the four journals was reviewed.

A total of 2,000 articles were reviewed in all four journals. The findings support the contention that the preponderance of research in these journals has been descriptive and that there is a paucity of articles that incorporate theoretical or empirical analysis (Table 27.1). The highest incidence of empirical research in these journals was found in *International Social Security Review.* Theoretical frameworks appear only occasionally in research in the journals (Table 27.1).

The journals also were examined for differences in quantitative and qualitative content. Articles within the sample were categorized as either qualitative (e.g., theory driven, political process analysis, ethnographic, case studies) or quantitative (e.g., data analysis, empirically driven, secondary analysis). Table 27.2 shows the findings for each journal. *International Social Security Review* has the greatest balance between qualitative and quantitative frameworks. Conversely, *Social Work in Europe*

TABLE 27.1   Prevailing Analytical Methods in Articles With Comparative International Content in Selected Journals Over Varying Periods (N = 2,000)

Journal	Years	Percentage of Descriptive Articles	Percentage of Analytical (Empirical) Articles	Percentage of Theoretical Articles
International Social Work (*n* = 1,022)	1958-1998	81.7	16.3	2.0
British Journal of Social Work (*n* = 691)	1975-1998	67.5	28.5	4.0
Social Work in Europe (*n* = 181)	1995-1998	96.7	1.1	2.2
International Social Security Review (*n* = 106)	1990-1999	49.6	48.0	2.4

SOURCES: *International Social Work*, Vols. 1-40; *British Journal of Social Work*, Vols. 1-33; *Social Work in Europe*, Vols. 1-5; *International Social Security Review*, Vols. 43-52.

TABLE 27.2   Percentages of Qualitative and Quantitative Content in Selected International Journals Over Varying Periods, 1958-1999 (N = 2,000)

Journal Cited	Sample Size	Percentage of Qualitative Articles Published	Percentage of Quantitative Articles Published
International Social Work	1,022	84.0	16.0
British Journal of Social Work	691	71.5	28.5
Social Work in Europe	181	94.5	5.5
International Social Security Review	106	52.0	48.0

SOURCES: *International Social Work*, Vols. 1-40; *British Journal of Social Work*, Vols. 1-33; *Social Work in Europe*, Vols. 1-5; *International Social Security Review*, Vols. 43-52.
NOTE: Chi-square tests indicate that there is a statistical difference between groups, $p < .0000$.

was almost exclusively qualitative in content. Over the 40-year period under review for *International Social Work,* the content was predominantly qualitative.

The review suggests that there was an increase in empirically driven and quantitative articles in two of the journals: *International Social Work* and the *British Journal*

TABLE 27.3   Qualitative and Quantitative Research in Three Selected Journals Over Varying
Periods, 1958-1999 (N = 1,894)

Type of Article Published	1958-1969	1970-1979	1980-1989	1990-1999
Qualitative	100	85.7	84.0	53.4
Quantitative	0	14.3	16.0	46.6

SOURCES: *International Social Work*, Vols. 1- 40; *British Journal of Social Work*, Vols. 1-33; *Social Work in Europe*, Vols. 1-5. *International Social Security Review* was excluded from this table in an effort not to bias results due to the quantitative nature of the journal.
NOTE: Chi-square tests indicate that there is a statistical difference between groups, $p < .0000$.

TABLE 27.4   Proportions of Analytical Frameworks in Four Selected Journals Over Varying
Periods, 1958-1999 (N = 2,000)

Years	Percentage of Practice-Based Articles	Percentage of Policy Framework Articles	Percentage of Research/ Theoretical Articles
1958-1969	93.7	5.7	0.6
1970-1979	64.9	24.2	10.9
1980-1989	66.3	25.3	8.4
1990-1999	47.9	32.4	19.7

SOURCES: *International Social Work*, Vols. 1-40; *British Journal of Social Work*, Vols. 1-33; *Social Work in Europe*, Vols. 1-5; *International Social Security Review*, Vols. 43-52.
NOTE: Chi-square tests indicate that there is a statistical difference between groups, $p < .0000$.

of Social Work. This is illustrated in Table 27.3, which shows a higher proportion of quantitative research that primarily reflects data from these journals. The data in Table 26.3 exclude research in *International Social Security Review*, which included a high proportion of empirically based articles over the past 10 years.

An examination of the research in the four journals under review also provides insight on the type of content through the lens of practice-based articles, policy-oriented articles, and research/theoretically driven articles (Table 27.4). There has been a statistically significant increase in the proportion of policy-based and research/ analytical articles over the past decade. However, this appears to be a relatively recent practice.

In addition to the use of specific frameworks and analytical methods within the international realm, it is interesting to note what topics have been researched in which

TABLE 27.5   Primary Issue/Topic in International Social Work, 1950-1999 (N = 1,022)

1950-1959	1960-1969	1970-1979	1980-1989	1990-1999
1. Social work education	Social work education	Social work practice	Social work practice	Social work practice
2. Health	Health	Social work education	Social work eduction	Reform
3. Social work intervention	Social work practice	Policy issues	Social policy	Welfare
4. Consultation	Students	Training	Children	Women
5. Social welfare	Training	Communities	Health care	HIV
6. Collaboration	Communities			Child welfare
7.	Children			
8.	Families			

SOURCE: *International Social Work*, Vols. 1-51.

geographic areas. This also helps to identify areas that traditionally have not been examined or researched. The information in Table 27.5 provides an overview of the primary social policy issues and topics that were covered in *International Social Work* over the past five decades. Social work education was the most widely published topical area in this journal. Whereas health was a leading topic during the 1950s and 1960s, the concept of system reform took a major platform during the past decade. Community work was relevant and topical during the 1960s and 1970s, whereas HIV and child welfare became more prevalent during the 1990s.

A closer examination of the content reveals that there has been a movement away from direct practice and purely descriptive study to analysis of global issues within the context of several countries or between the developing world and the developed world. This might reflect growing interest in the impact of technology and movements toward globalization and integration of concepts on a global basis. The topical areas for which there have been significant numbers of publications in *International Social Work* also seem to dovetail with global and social issues.

The geographic areas that appeared as studies in *International Social Work,* as shown in Table 27.6, most often reveal differences in the major focus of international comparisons drawn from decade to decade. During the past two decades, global comparisons prevailed. Geographic areas that experienced significant political, social, and/or economic changes during specific decades appear to be studied most often during the same time period. Although not specifically reflected in the Table 27.6 data, content in *International Social Work* indicates that the influence of North

TABLE 27.6   Geographic Areas Included in Comparative International Research in
International Social Work, 1950-1999 (N = 1,022)

1950-1959	1960-1969	1970-1979	1980-1989	1990-1999
1. Generically referenced	Multi-comparisons	India	Global	Global
2.	Sweden	Africa	Hong Kong	Israel
3.	India	China	Africa	Hong Kong
4.	Africa	Israel	Japan	Multi-comparisons
5.	Britain	Sweden	Korea	South Africa
6.	Developing countries	Thailand	India	China
7.	United States	United States	United States	United States
8.				Sweden

SOURCE: *International Social Work*, Vols. 1-51.

American practice on other countries was the focus of research for international social work practice during the early decades under review. However, the geographic
research emphasis seemed to shift to multiple comparisons beginning as early as the
1960s.

The information in the tables in this chapter provides some understanding of the
prevalent methods used in comparative analysis by analysts engaged in comparative
international research. The data also provide some useful insights into areas for social work curriculum development and social work education. The information helps
to build a profile for social workers interested in international research and identifies
topics and areas in which there has been a dearth of research.

CONCLUSION

Comparative international research in social work has been primarily focused on descriptive case studies in industrialized nations that have significantly contributed to
knowledge of social work policies and practice relative to *who* receives *what* type of
benefits and services, *when, where,* and *how*. There has been much less emphasis on
why a particular practice or program is in place in a given nation, or group of nations,
at a given point in time. Most of the research that attempts to explain *why* a particular option has been chosen to address identified social problems is structured around

macroanalytical frameworks centered on public social welfare policy, as distinguished from social work practice.

One impediment to comparative international research in social work that is more analytical than descriptive is the logistical problem of collecting reliable comparative data. However, the primary difficulty in understanding why a nation, or group of nations, has adopted a particular approach is the underuse of analytical frameworks that systematically examine the reasons and processes underlying the development of policies, programs, and practices.

An examination of the trends in frameworks used in comparative international analysis provides some useful insights into areas for social work curriculum development and education. The information helps to build a profile for the social worker interested in international research and identifies topics and areas in which there is a dearth of research.

APPENDIX

Links to Resources and Sites for Demographic and Background Materials

The following Web sites are useful links that can provide background resource materials to the researcher when seeking useful comparative resource materials on specific countries. The sites that are listed provide both demographic components and background information on structural components of various social policies in a country.

Structural Factors

Luxembourg Income Study: http://lissy.ceps.lu/access.htm
International Labor Organization: http://www.ilo.org/
International Social Security Association: http://www.issa.int/
United Nations development programs: http://www.undp.org/
United Nations: http://www.undcp.org/unlinks.html#admin
NGONet (Central and Eastern Europe): http://www.ngonet.org/
World Bank: http://www.worldbank.org/html/extdr/data.htm
Social security programs throughout the world: http://www.ssa.gov/statistics/ssptw97.html
Social Security in other countries: http://www.ssa.gov/international/links.html
Organization for Economic Cooperation and Development: http://oecd.org

Cultural Factors

Action without borders: http://www.idealist.org/

Historical and social background information: http://www.worldbank.org/html/
extdr/regions.htm and http://www.etown.edu/home/selchewa/international_
studies/firstpag.htm

Demographic and Social Indicators

Census and demographic data: http://www.clark.net/pub/lschank/web/
census.html and http://www.unesco.org/general/eng/infoserv/index.html
International database: http://www.census.gov/ipc/www/idbnew.html

Children

Child Welfare League: http://www.cwla.org/
Children's Defense Fund: http://www.childrensdefense.org/
UNICEF: http://www.unicef.org/statis/
National Center for Children in Poverty: http://cpmcnet.columbia.edu/dept/
nccp/

Health

UNAIDS: http://www.aidsnyc.org/
Centers for Disease Control and Prevention: http://www.cdc.gov
World Health Organization: http://www.who.int

Social Development

http://www.worldbank.org/data/databytopic/databytopic.html
http://www.worldbank.org/html/extdr/regions.htm
http://www.worldbank.org/html/extdr/toc.html

REFERENCES

Berghman, J. (1996). Concepts in social protection: The lack of a common language. In *Social Challenges of the EU and the Intergovernmental Conference* (pp. 12-20). Helsinki, Finland: Ministry of Social Affairs and Health.

Bergmann, B. (1996). *Saving our children from poverty: What the United States can learn from France.* New York: Russell Sage.

Cannan, C., Berry, L., & Lyons, K. (1992). *Social work and Europe.* London: Macmillan.

Dierkes, M., Weiler, H. N., & Antal, A. B. (Eds.). (1987). *Comparative policy research: Learning from experience.* Brookfield, VT: Gower.

Dixon, J. (1999). Comparative social security: The challenge of evaluation. *Journal of Comparative Policy Analysis: Research and Practice, 1,* 61-95.

Eardley, T., Bradshaw, J., Ditch, J., Gough, I., & Whiteford, P. (1996). *Social assistance in OECD countries: Synthesis report* (Vol. 1, Department of Social Security Research Report No. 46). London: Her Majesty's Stationery Office.

Esping-Anderson, G. (1990). *Three worlds of welfare capitalism.* Cambridge, UK: Polity.

Estes, R. J. (1984). *The social progress of nations.* New York: Praeger.

Estes, R. J. (1991). Models, social modeling, and models of international social work education. In R. J. Estes, *Internationalizing social work education: A guide to resources for a new century* (pp. 20-37). Philadelphia: University of Pennsylvania, School of Social Work.

Gilbert, N. (1998, March). *Social security as an instrument for social cohesion: An overview of possibilities and limitations.* Paper presented at the Second Technical Conference of the International Social Security Association, Naples, Italy.

Ginsburg, N. (1992). *Divisions of welfare: A critical introduction to comparative social policy.* London: Sage.

Gough, I. (1979). *The political economy of the welfare state.* London: Macmillan.

Gruber, J., & Wise, D. A. (Eds.). (1999). *Social security and retirement around the world.* Chicago: University of Chicago Press.

Harris, R. (1990). Beyond rhetoric: A challenge for international social work. *International Social Work, 33,* 203-212.

Healy, L., & Asamoah, Y. (1997). *Global perspectives in social work education: A collection of course outlines on international aspects of social work.* Alexandria, VA: Council on Social Work Education.

Heidenheimer, A. J., Heclo, H., & Adams, C. (1975). *Comparative public policy: The politics of social choice in Europe and America.* New York: St. Martin's.

Hoefer, R. (1996). A conceptual model for studying social welfare policy comparatively. *Journal of Social Work Education, 32,* 101-103.

Hokenstad, M., Khinduka, S., & Midgley, J. (1992). The world of international social work. In M. Hokenstad, S. Khinduka, & J. Midgley (Eds.), *Profiles in international social work* (pp. 1-11). Washington, DC: National Institute of Social Workers.

International Labour Organization. (1999). Available: http://www.ilo.org/public/english

Ismael, J. S. (Ed.). (1996). *International social welfare in a changing world.* Calgary, Alberta: Detselig Enterprises.

Jones, C. (1985). *Patterns of public policy: An introduction to comparative analysis.* London: Tavistock.

Jones, C. (Ed.). (1993). *New perspectives on the welfare state in Europe.* New York: Routledge.

Jordan, B. (1996). *A theory of poverty and social exclusion.* Cambridge, UK: Polity.

Kamerman, S. B. (1993). International perspectives on child care policies and programs. *Pediatrics, 91,* 248-252.

Koven, S., & Michel, S. (Eds.). (1993). *Mothers of a new world: Maternalist politics and the origins of welfare states.* New York: Routledge.

Leeuw, F. L. (1997). Solidarity between public sector organizations: The problem of social cohesion in the asymmetric society. *Rationality and Society, 9,* 469-488.

MacPherson, S., & Midgley, J. (1987). *Comparative social policy and the Third World.* Hemel Hempstead, UK: Wheatsheaf.

Marshall, T. H. (1950). *Citizenship and social class and other essays.* Cambridge, UK: Cambridge University Press.

Mayadas, N. S., Watts, T. D., & Elliott, D. (Eds.). (1997). *International handbook on social work theory and practice.* Westport, CT: Greenwood.

Midgley, J. (1984). Diffusion and the development of social policy. *Journal of Social Policy, 13,* 167-184.

Midgley, J. (1997). *Social welfare in global context.* Thousand Oaks, CA: Sage.

Midgley, J., & Tracy, M. B. (Eds.). (1996). *Challenge to social security: An international exploration.* Westport, CT: Auburn House.

Miller, R. (1997). Economic flexibility and societal cohesion. *Organization for Economic Cooperation and Development Observer, 207,* 24-28.

Mishra, R. (1977). *Society and social policy: Theories and practice of welfare.* London: Macmillan.

Munday, B. (Ed.). (1989). *The crisis in welfare: An international perspective on social services and social work.* Hemel Hempstead, UK: Wheatsheaf.

Organization for Economic Cooperation and Development. (1997). *Beyond 2000: The new social policy agenda* (OECD Working Papers, Vol. 5, No. 43). Paris: Author.

Organization for Economic Cooperation and Development. (1998). *The battle against exclusion: Social assistance in Australia, Finland, Sweden, and the United Kingdom.* Paris: Author.

Osbourg, L. (1991). Cross-national comparisons of inequality and poverty position. In L. Osberg (Ed.), *Economic inequality and poverty: International perspectives.* Armonk, NY: M. E. Sharpe.

Popova, M. (1996). *Income inequality and poverty of economics in transition.* Working Paper No. 144, CEPS/INSTEAD, Luxembourg.

Prigmore, C. S., & Atherton, C. R. (1979). *Social welfare policy: Analysis and formulation.* Lexington, MA: D. C. Heath.

Ramanathan, C. S., & Link, R. J. (1999). *All our futures: Principles and resources for social work practice in a global era.* Belmont, CA: Wadsworth.

Rimlinger, G. (1971). *Welfare policy and industrialization in Europe, America, and Russia.* New York: John Wiley.

Rose, R. (1973). Comparing public policy: An overview. *European Journal of Political Research, 1,* 67-94.

Rubin, M. (1996). *Poverty, labor force status, and the social safety net in Eastern Europe.* Working Paper No. 141, CEPS/INSTEAD, Luxembourg.

Schindler, R., & Brawley, E. A. (1987). *Social care at the front line: A worldwide study of para-professionals.* London: Tavistock.

Silver, H. (1994). Social exclusion and social solidarity: Three paradigms. *International Labour Review, 133,* 531-578.

Silver, H. (1998). Policies to reinforce social cohesion in Europe. In J. B. Figueiredo & A. de Haan (Eds.), *Social exclusion: An ILO perspective* (pp. 38-73). Geneva, Switzerland: International Institute for Labour Studies.

Taylor-Gooby, P. (1991). *Social changes, social welfare, and social science.* Hemel Hempstead, UK: Wheatsheaf.

Titmuss, R. M. (1968). *Commitment to welfare.* London: George Allen and Unwin.

Titmuss, R. M. (1974). *Social policy: An introduction.* London: George Allen and Unwin.

Tracy, M. B. (1992). Cross-national social welfare policy analysis in the graduate curriculum: A comparative process model. *Journal of Social Work Education, 28,* 341-352.

Tracy, M. B., & Tracy, P. D. (1998). Negotiating the boundaries of the welfare state: Changing perspectives on social cohesion. In *Developments and trends in social security, 1996-1998* (pp. 1-19). Geneva, Switzerland: International Social Security Association.

U.S. Department of Health and Human Services. (various years). *Social security programs throughout the world.* Washington, DC: Government Printing Office.

Van Wormer, K. (1997). *Social welfare: A world view.* Chicago: Nelson-Hall.

Wilensky, H. L., & Lebeaux, C. (1965). *Industrial society and social welfare.* New York: Free Press.

Williamson, J. B., & Pampel, F. C. (1993). *Old-age security in comparative perspective.* Oxford, UK: Oxford University Press.

World Health Organization. (1999). Available: http://www.who.int/home/othersites/index.html

CHAPTER TWENTY-EIGHT

Integrating Qualitative and Quantitative Research Methods

CHARLES D. COWGER
GOUTHAM MENON

Both quantitative and qualitative research methods have distinctive and important contributions to make to the development of new social work knowledge. Used together, they provide unique advantages in the advancement of our knowledge base. This chapter promotes the integration of methods, demonstrates how the distinction between qualitative and quantitative methods is one of emphasis and not of discrete difference, presents the advantages of integration and the complementarity of the two approaches, and describes four ways in which to integrate these methods while giving examples of each. Integration makes reference to using both quantitative and qualitative methods in the same study and often is referred to in the literature as using *multimethods*.

Definitions of research and, in turn, definitions of qualitative and quantitative research methods were explicated separately in earlier chapters of this handbook. To provide a context for understanding their integration, their differential meanings again are presented. These definitions are limited to notions of alternative procedures (i.e., research methods) that social workers might use. The social work epistemological debates over qualitative versus quantitative paradigms during recent years, although interesting, are essentially ignored because they are not informative for our purposes and do not give coherent direction for the development of new social work knowledge. Campbell (1978) is essentially correct when he comments on the quantitative versus qualitative debate by stating, "Each pole is at its best in its criticism of the other, not in the invulnerability of its own claims" (p. 204).

Whatever else it is, research is a way in which to discover, generate, and/or test the truth of statements about events in the world of human experience. Research is empirical in that it relies on systematic procedures for making observations of events (i.e., methods of gathering and measuring observations), for organizing and analyzing observations (i.e., data analysis), and for making statements about them. Research also is dependent on reason in that its methods are based on logic that is attached to epistemological-cultural conventions that constitute the rules whereby some agreement is reached or has evolved about the "best practices" (i.e., best procedures/methods) to use in the achievement of knowing. These procedures used by researchers are important, as are their specificity in research reports, because they provide others with the opportunity to verify the results and replicate the research.

Quantitative research methods are those research procedures that involve counting and assigning values to units of attention/observations, and they rely primarily on mathematical analysis for generating findings. The careful design of research and the assignment of numerical values to observations of reality provide quantitative researchers with the opportunity to discover and test relationships between variables and to rule out alternative/extraneous explanations for those observed relationships. Surveys, needs assessments, outcome studies using group designs, randomized-controlled trials, single-system designs, program evaluations, and cost-benefit studies typically rely heavily on quantitative methods. National and community studies of employment; poverty; infant mortality rates; employment rates; commitments to mental hospitals; and violence against elders, minorities, women, and gays are examples of research that provides quantitative knowledge that is extremely important to social work practitioners and planners. Quantitative studies based on data that provide outcome measures demonstrating social program and/or practice effectiveness are particularly important because social services are increasingly under scrutiny as to their effectiveness.

Qualitative research methods are those research procedures used primarily to seek understandings of human behavior from the actors' own frames of reference. Researchers seek to obtain firsthand knowledge about the empirical social worlds in question and typically conduct research in the natural settings of everyday life. Narrative case studies, in-depth interviews, ethnographic studies, participant observation, and studies based on grounded theory rely primarily on qualitative methods. Qualitative studies that examine the ordinary events and everyday activities of communities, organizations, clients, social work practitioners, and social service delivery are particularly important in the development of social work knowledge. To discover and understand things such as the meanings that clients ascribe to their own behavior, how they view their own physical and mental health, and how they perceive and give meaning to the behaviors of professional helpers all are examples of qualitative findings important to social work practice.

COMMONALITIES AND DIFFERENCES BETWEEN QUANTITATIVE AND QUALITATIVE RESEARCH METHODS

A number of attributes have been ascribed to qualitative and quantitative approaches as a way in which to differentiate between them and/or argue for one versus the other (Bogan & Taylor, 1975; Cook & Reinhard, 1979). However, these attributes appear to be somewhat contrived and are more reflective of emphasis than of discrete categories. Indeed, Harrison (1994) argues that quantitative and qualitative research methods exist "only artificially," are "inseparable," and, hence, make the "integration of quantitative and qualitative methods inevitable" (p. 412).

Grinnell (1997) refers to the quantitative and qualitative distinction as being a "false dichotomy" (p. 148). As a way in which to demonstrate the proposition that the differences are mostly a matter of emphasis, a discussion of one of the characteristics that typically is used to show these differences follows.

The Objective and Subjective Distinction

Subjectivity is commonly ascribed to qualitative studies, and objectivity is commonly ascribed to quantitative studies. However, this is a confounding distinction. The word *objective* has been used in a variety of ways in the research literature. To some, it is associated with the notion of the law of large numbers. We say that it is *subjective* if only one or a few persons observe something but that it is *objective* if enough people observe it so that we can manipulate the number with mathematics. Because numbers are central to quantitative research, one might give undue weight to this distinction. However, numbers also are important in qualitative research. Identifying that something exists establishes that, at the least, it exists numerically in the number of one. Harrison (1994) states, "It is impossible to express qualitative perspectives, methods, perceptions, and conclusions without communications that are at least partially amenable to quantitative representation and, therefore, quantitative analysis" (p. 413). Identifying themes in qualitative data analysis requires some type of rule of evidence that establishes a minimum number of times something is mentioned before it is characterized as a theme. Analysis of qualitative data such as multiple comparisons of sentence structure, words used, and classifying questions and responses uses quantitative analysis. An important component of new qualitative research computer software is its ability to more efficiently locate and count the number of times a particular theme/finding, sentence structure, or word is in the text. Qualitative research reports that use this software typically make reference to those numbers. On the other hand, qualitative studies often are defined as having the distinguishing characteristic of subjectivity. They often are concerned primarily with a state of the mind and/or the feelings of the people being studied. However, researchers often use quantitative research methods to examine subjective attributes of people such as love, happiness, and loneliness. In addition, quantitative researchers use subjective criteria to identify their research questions, develop their instruments, and discuss the implications of their findings. Identifying factors in a factor analysis, identifying paths in a structural equation model, and identifying the order of variables to enter in a multiple regression model all are qualitative exercises.

We also use the word *objective* to refer to discrete categories such as an objective test. Such discrete categories assume that we have sufficient criteria to distinguish and clearly differentiate one phenomenon from another and, with large samples, that we can do so with calculable risk of mathematical error. However, the use of the notion of "objective" when referring to discrete categories also does not adequately differentiate between qualitative and quantitative research. Both quantitative and qualitative researchers use data that assume discrete categories and design their research to acquire them. By the fact that qualitative researchers use comparative analysis, they strive to develop discrete categories as they search for themes in their data, compare responses to questions, and examine differential responses to differential questions.

Finally, we often use the word *objective* to mean *without bias*. Bias is considered a threat to good quantitative research because it might be responsible for extraneous explanations for researchers' findings. In quantitative research, an attempt is made to rule out bias through research design and/or statistical manipulation. However, bias is ever present in the selection of research questions, the selection of participants, the selection of concepts in the development of an instrument, and the selection of theory that is used to construct the instrument and interpret the findings. In qualitative research, bias has come to be assumed, and concern about bias is not about whether it exists but rather about whether researchers are aware of their biases and are honest in their preparation of research reports in foreclosing those biases. Quantitative researchers also operate under an ethical canon of exposing any bias that is not self-evident in their studies. Bias is ever present and is a serious issue for both approaches.

In each of these uses of the word *objective,* we find that the application to qualitative and quantitative research is a matter of emphasis and that using the characteristics of objectivity versus subjectivity is questionable if used as a criterion to draw a sharp distinction between the two approaches. However, although notions about epistemological divisions between quantitative and qualitative methods are essentially abstract social constructions, the distinction may help us to understand the strengths and limitations of the approach that we are using.

WHY THE INTEGRATION OF QUALITATIVE AND QUANTITATIVE METHODS?

Research that integrates qualitative and quantitative methods has advantages in that it (a) proffers increased validity due to the triangulation of methods; (b) provides an opportunity to take advantage of the strengths of each approach; and (c) allows congruence with the principles of social work to study things holistically, in context, and from more than one frame of reference.

Triangulation

Although the basic meaning of the term *triangulation* is similar to how it is employed by land surveyors to describe locating oneself by using three fixed points in the landscape (Gunnysack, 1994), the meaning of the term has added complexity when referring to research. Triangulation is the process of incorporating multiple viewpoints of the same phenomenon so as to provide greater validity to the research endeavor. It provides additional evidence that we are observing what we really think we are observing. The combination of multiple methods, empirical materials, perspectives, and observers in a single study is best understood as a strategy that adds rigor, breadth, and depth to any investigation (Flick, 1992).

Denzin (1978) identifies four basic types of triangulation as *data, investigator, theory,* and *methodological* triangulation, the latter of which is the focus of this chapter. To explain the four types, let us consider the following hypothetical research project. In this project, which is intended to examine homeless mentally ill people, Professor Chronic included the following components in his design. First, he used in-depth interviews with the respondents in which he kept extensive field notes and logs. Second, he had two of his graduate research assistants live in the homeless shelters at night. They mingled with the respondents, talked to them about how the day had gone, and observed and kept notes about what they saw and heard. Third, he sent out a survey to all the shelter directors in the city asking them questions about the number of homeless mentally ill people who used their services during a year, the major issues that these people faced, the issues that service providers faced, and so on. Fourth, he used two different theoretical frameworks to examine, analyze, and give meaning to the data: a mental health deficit model (which considered client pathology) and a social work strengths perspective model (which considered personal and environmental strengths, skills, and resources that participants had available to them). Following these procedures, Professor Chronic used each of the four methods of triangulation in his study. He used interviews, field notes, and logs so as to triangulate data. By using other observers (his graduate research assistants), he managed to get multiple observers so that he achieved investigator triangulation. By sending out a survey and collecting quantitative data from directors of homeless shelters, he fulfilled the protocol for methodological triangulation. He then took the difficult step of analyzing his data using two different (often opposite) perspectives, namely the deficit model and the strengths perspective, to carry out theory triangulation. The use of multiple viewpoints, whether data, investigator, methodology, or theory, enhances any study in that it brings out trustworthiness in the data.

Strengths of Each Approach

Rennin and Toukmanian (1992) advocate a methodological pluralism and epistemological synthesis, whereby the strengths of each approach would be optimized. Tutty, Rothery, and Grinnell (1996) demonstrate how the two approaches differentially contribute to our knowledge base in six areas: the objectivity of the findings, the generalizability of the findings, the reductionistic properties, the differential use of theory, the number of words they use, and the flexibility of the research techniques. Padgett (1998) proposes a multimethod approach that "offsets many of the weaknesses" and "highlights the strengths" of the two approaches (p. 126).

Reid (1994) suggests that we need both methods because the strength of each tends to be the weakness of the other. He further states,

> Quantitative methodology can provide more exact statements of the degree of linkage between specific variables, better control over alternative explanations for these relations, more precise measures of phenomena that lend themselves to quantification, and larger databases for purposes of generalization. Qualitative methodology is better able to depict the workings of social systems in holistic ways, to take into account contextual factors, to detect elusive phenomena, and to generate more thorough descriptions as a base for generalization. (p. 477)

Congruence With the Principles of Social Work

From its beginning, social work has been grounded in the central premise of the "person in situation." The problem situation of the typical client presents the social worker with multiple stakeholders, multiple contexts, and multiple perspectives on the nature and meaning of the problem. In the same manner, useful knowledge that is relevant to the multiple contexts of social planning and administration is unlikely to be acquired by singular and narrow notions or research methods. Social work practice simply does not lend itself to a singular research method to understand what is going on, to evaluate a service, to examine one's own practice, and/or to develop new practice knowledge. Some argue that the choice of quantitative versus qualitative methods should be determined by the nature of the research question (e.g., Proctor, 1990). As indicated previously in this chapter, some questions are more amenable to a particular method than to another. However, the researcher should not let this principle confine his or her research approach to thinking about the use of only one method.

ALTERNATIVE WAYS IN WHICH TO INTEGRATE QUALITATIVE AND QUANTITATIVE METHODS

Padgett (1998) notes that, despite widespread endorsement of using multimethods, "few multimethod studies can be found in the literature" (p. 127). She suggests that some reasons for this are that (a) researchers usually are trained in one method but not the other, (b) there is confusion over which components of the methods can be integrated, and (c) multimethod studies require dual competencies and considerable outlays of time and resources, making it easier for researchers to follow separate paths (p. 127). Grinnell (1997) states that an additional reason is the desire to limit a study's scope (p. 141). Despite these obstacles, researchers do use multimethods. Following is a discussion on four ways in which to use multimethods, with examples presented for each.

Four ways in which to integrate quantitative and qualitative research methods are (a) qualitative research as a beginning step to quantitative research, (b) quantitative research as a beginning step to qualitative research, (c) simultaneous triangulation of methods, and (d) a dominant-less dominant model. The first two of these ways in which to use multimethods depend on temporal sequencing, whereas the last two use both methods at the same time. The conceptualization of this section evolved from earlier work by Grinnell (1997) and Padgett (1998), each of whom developed three models of integration.

Qualitative Research as a Beginning Step to Quantitative Research

Some argue that qualitative research is important, but important primarily as a phase or step that one must go through to get to more rigorous and scientific research. A textbook widely used in social work during the 1970s and 1980s (Fellin, Tripodi, & Meyer, 1969) held this position and classified qualitative research as "exploratory." Qualitative research was considered exploratory but important because it provided the foundation or first phase of a hierarchy of research methods that had the laboratory experimental study method at the top.

Padgett (1998) refers to this approach as the QUAL →QUANT model. Although Campbell (arguably the most influential experimental research theoretician in the social sciences of the past 50 years) also held this position early in his career (Campbell & Stanley, 1963), he later proposed a "unified perspective for both quantitative and qualitative knowing" (Campbell, 1978, p. 184). Campbell (1978) broadened his view to include qualitative research as an important endeavor in its own right. However, he did not rescind his earlier notion that qualitative research provides an important foundation for quantitative research in that "quantitative knowing depends on qualitative knowing" (p. 184). He pointed out that qualitative underpinnings of quantitative data lie in the verbal or written instructions of the test administrator, the verbal and written explanations given by the test administrator, and the participant's qualitative comprehension of the question (p. 194). Whether one assumes a research methods hierarchy or not, the basic proposition that quantitative knowing depends on qualitative knowing appears valid. As Campbell noted, "this dependence is poorly represented in much of quantitative social science" (p. 184).

This sequence of methods in which qualitative research precedes quantitative research is particularly useful for the development of quantitative instruments. Some recent studies that used qualitative methods to develop quantitative instruments include Kauffman, Silver, and Poulin's (1997) research on gender differences in attitudes toward alcohol, tobacco, and other drugs; Greenley, Greenberg, and Brown's (1997) measuring of quality of life; and Cook, Selig, Wedge, and Gohn-Baube's (1999) study of access barriers and the use of prenatal care by low-income inner-city women.

Quantitative Research as a Beginning Step for Qualitative Research

A researcher might well integrate quantitative and qualitative methods by beginning with a quantitative study. An example of such a study would be one in which the researcher might first wish to determine the characteristics and magnitude of a problem such as the use of methamphetamines and then gather qualitative data to learn more about their use in the everyday life of the user. The quantitative data would provide the important information needed to determine the magnitude of resources that would be required to deal with the problem, whereas the qualitative data would provide important planning knowledge for determining the type and structure of services to be implemented. In the same manner, assume that a school social worker wants to understand the psychosocial factors related to children being successful in his or her school. The social worker might first use a standardized instrument that would help to provide an assessment of his or her particular school and also provide normative data to compare the school to other schools. However, to get a complete picture and to understand the findings of the standardized instrument in context, the social worker then would gather qualitative data that relate to the unique characteristics of the school. In designing programs, findings from both sets of data would be important.

The Simultaneous Triangulation of Methods

To triangulate methods is to simultaneously combine both research approaches in the same study. This is similar to Grinnell's (1997, p. 151) "mixed model" and Padgett's (1998) QUANT ↔ QUAL model. An example might be to use both approaches to discover factors associated with teen pregnancy. One could examine comparative community demographic data to discover factors that are associated with high teen pregnancy rates and also do an extensive qualitative study of pregnant teens to learn about teen pregnancy and teen sexual behavior from the perspective of teens. The community demographic data could be focused on variables that would be susceptible to planning community intervention, and the qualitative data could be structured in a manner to discover factors that would be important in designing pregnancy prevention counseling.

An example of the simultaneous triangulation of methods is Kelly and Clifford's (1997) study of coping with chronic pain. They used qualitative research as their primary approach to answer their first two research questions, each of which focused on "understanding the phenomenon more than explaining it" (p. 268). For their third question, which was concerned with whether a narrative intervention approach was effective in improving coping skills, they used a quantitative quasi-experimental research design that included random assignment to treatment and control groups and the pre- and post-administration of five standardized questionnaires.

A research project that was able to simultaneously triangulate both method and researchers is reported in Mulroy's (1997) qualitative study of interorganizational collaboration to prevent child abuse and neglect. Mulroy's qualitative study of the community was done by one university unit, while a concurrent quantitative outcome study was done by another independent, university-based research center (p. 258).

Dominant-Less Dominant Model

Grinnell (1997) describes this "model" as a study that has a single dominant research approach "with another smaller component of the overall study drawn from the alternative approach" (p. 150). Typically, the researcher uses the less dominant method to gather limited information.

Studies that are predominantly quantitative sometimes include open-ended questions on questionnaires. An example of this is Ben-Ari's (1998) quasi-experimental, nonequivalent control group study of attitude change of social work students' homosexuality attitudes. An open-ended question was added to explore the students' associations with the term *homosexuality*.

Some qualitative studies that are predominantly qualitative have enough participants to include quantitative analysis of qualitative findings, and others analyze their qualitative data in the context of quantitative demographic data they have collected on their participants. Garcia and Van Soest's (1997) study of the effect of a required course on 43 M.S.W. students' changing perceptions of diversity and oppression first generated pretest qualitative data by using self-administered, audiotaped interviews. They also gathered demographic data on the students. Near the end of the course, the tape recordings were returned to students along with an assignment to write a paper reflecting how they felt hearing their views from the beginning of the course. Data included the papers at the end of the semester and demographic information on the students. The researchers did qualitative analysis to identify themes and patterns. However, they had enough participants that they also could do a quantitative analysis of these themes and patterns. Although their study is primarily qualitative, their findings are a mixture of quantitative descriptive statistics and a qualitative description of themes and patterns.

SUMMARY PROPOSITIONS ON THE USE OF QUALITATIVE AND QUANTITATIVE METHODS

Assumptions and principles affecting the use of both qualitative and quantitative methods in a singular research study include the following:

- The distinction between qualitative and quantitative methods is one of emphasis, not of discrete differences.
- Research questions can, in most cases, be examined using quantitative and qualitative methods, although one particular method might be more pragmatically viable and, therefore, receive the primary emphasis.
- Research studies are given further validation with the addition of multiple methods.
- Integrating qualitative and quantitative methods provides an opportunity to take advantage of the strengths of each approach.
- Integrating qualitative and quantitative methods is congruent with the principle of social work to study things holistically.

- The choice of methods is a pragmatic choice depending on things such as the congruence between the research question and the research method, time constraints, and the availability of data. However, none of these constraints matters if the research does not meet the test of being convincing to others. Using qualitative and quantitative methods provides collaborative evidence for making the case that one's findings are essentially valid.
- Researchers may use quantitative and qualitative methods sequentially or simultaneously. In some cases, a dominant-less dominant model is most practical and more viable.

Integrating quantitative and qualitative research methods can be particularly important for program advocacy. For example, at a state legislative hearing on housing subsidies for low-income people, one of the authors, who was well prepared, believed that the quantitative data he was presenting was thoroughly convincing. When he had completed his presentation, a state legislator asked, "Can you tell me about just one family who would benefit from this and how it would change that family for the better?" A good case study at that point would have made a considerable difference. Some want to know something about the people behind the numbers when reading or hearing about national and state housing data regarding families in poverty. When reading or hearing the story of a family in poverty and its housing needs, someone else might want to know how many others like that are "out there." To be effective in discovering, generating, and/or testing the truth of statements about events and experiences in the world of our clients, and to demonstrate the effectiveness of our practice and programs, social workers have the responsibility of using all the tools available.

REFERENCES

Ben-Ari, A. (1998). An experiential attitude change: Social work students and homosexuality. *Journal of Homosexuality, 36*, 59-72.

Bogan, R., & Taylor, S. J. (1975). *Introduction to qualitative research*. New York: John Wiley.

Campbell, D. T. (1978). Qualitative knowing in action research. In M. Brenner, P. Marsh, & M. Brenner (Eds.), *The social contexts of method* (pp. 184-209). London: Croom Helm.

Campbell, D. T., & Stanley, J. C. (1963). Experimental and quasi-experimental designs for research on teaching. In N. L. Gate (Ed.), *Handbook of research on teaching*. Chicago: Rand McNally.

Cook, C. A., Selig, K. L., Wedge, B. J., & Gohn-Baube, E. A. (1999). Access barriers and the use of prenatal care by low-income, inner-city women. *Social Work, 44*, 129-139.

Cook, T., & Reinhard, C. (1979). *Qualitative and quantitative methods in evaluative research*. Beverly Hills, CA: Sage.

Denzin, N. K. (1978). *The Research Act: A theoretical introduction to sociological methods* (2nd ed.). New York: McGraw-Hill.

Fellin, P., Tripodi, T., & Meyer, H. J. (1969). *Exemplars of social research*. Itasca, IL: Peacock.

Flick, U. (1992). Triangulation revisited: Strategy of validation or alternative? *Journal for the Theory of Social Behavior, 22*, 175-198.

Garcia, B., & Van Soest, D. (1997). Changing perceptions of diversity and oppression: M.S.W. students discuss the effects of a required course. *Journal of Social Work Education, 33*, 119-129.

Greenley, J. R., Greenberg, J. S., & Brown, R. (1997). Measuring quality of life: A new and practical survey instrument. *Social Work, 42*, 244-254.

Grinnell, R. M. (1997). *Social work research and evaluation*. Itasca, IL: Peacock.

Harrison, W. D. (1994). The inevitability of integrated methods. In E. Sherman & W. J. Reid (Eds.), *Qualitative research in social work* (pp. 410-422). London: Croom Helm.

Gunnysack, V. J. (1994). The dance of qualitative research design: Metaphor, methodology, and meaning. In N. K. Denzin & Y. S. Lincoln (Eds.), *Handbook of qualitative research* (pp. 209-219). Thousand Oaks, CA: Sage.

Kauffman, S. E., Silver, P., & Poulin, J. (1997). Gender differences in attitudes toward alcohol, tobacco, and other drugs. *Social Work, 42*, 231-234.

Kelly, P., & Clifford, P. (1997). Coping with chronic pain: Assessing narrative approaches. *Social Work, 42*, 266-277.

Mulroy, E. (1997). Building a neighborhood network: Interorganizational collaboration to prevent child abuse and neglect. *Social Work, 42*, 255-264.

Padgett, D. K. (1998). *Qualitative methods in social work research*. Thousand Oaks, CA: Sage.

Proctor, E. K. (1990). Evaluating clinical practice: Issues of purpose and design. *Social Work Research and Abstracts, 26*, 32-40.

Reid, W. J. (1994). Reframing the epistemological debate. In E. Sherman & W. J. Reid (Eds.), *Qualitative research in social work* (pp. 464-481). New York: Columbia University Press.

Rennin, D. L., & Toukmanian, S. G. (1992). Explanation in psychotherapy process research. In S. G. Toukmanian & D. L. Rennin (Eds.), *Psychotherapy process research: Paradigmatic and narrative approaches* (pp. 234-251). Newbury Park, CA: Sage.

Tutty, L. M., Rothery, M., & Grinnell, R. M. (1996). Introduction. In L. Tutty, M. Rothery, & R. M. Grinnell (Eds.), *Qualitative research for social workers: Phases, steps, and tasks* (pp. 1-17). Needham Heights, MA: Allyn & Bacon.

CHAPTER TWENTY-NINE

Applying for Research Grants

SCOTT M. GERON

GAIL S. STEKETEE

Sherlock Holmes, frustrated at the absence of clues in a case, once exclaimed, "Data. Data. Data. I can't make bricks without clay!" Social work researchers have the same complaint, but unlike the famous detective, they rarely have their own resources to conduct investigations. Today, more than ever, social workers who conduct research—and the agencies and universities that support them—will require grant funds to do so. Unfortunately, the search for grant funds often seems harder than solving an intractable mystery. This is true for a number of reasons. The past two decades have seen the federal government cede to the states increasing responsibility for the organization and management of social services, but with fewer federal dollars to meet identified needs as a result of the decline of important sources of federal funding. At the same time, the sophistication of methods and research expertise required to compete for federal funds has increased. Pressures on practitioners also have increased, limiting the time to conduct research and making the ideal of the practitioner/researcher more elusive than ever. Social work faculty face constant pressures to obtain research dollars, while they also must fulfill teaching, publishing, service, and administrative responsibilities, often making proposal writing a distant goal.

Despite the pressures and frustrations, there is good news to report. Social work doctoral students are receiving better training than ever in a competitive research environment (Task Force on Social Work Research, 1991). The growth of the Internet means that clues for obtaining funding are easily accessible. More important, opportunities for conducting social work research are better than ever before. Some 40,000 private foundations provide more than $15 billion in funding annually, and state and local sources of funding have stabilized or increased during the economic boom of the 1990s. Although funding for social services is down, the amount of federal dollars for research at the National Institutes of Health (NIH) has doubled during the past decade, and the likelihood of receiving an award for traditional research projects—slightly more than one in four—is much higher than many people believe. Social work also has made important inroads in the National Institute of Mental Health (NIMH) and the other institutes within the NIH. The recent NIMH initiative to support the development of social work research development centers and to provide information and training for prospective investigators through the Institute for the Advancement of Social Work Research is a sign of continued interest in social work mental health research.

In this chapter, we discuss the skills needed for writing successful research grants. We describe some likely funding sources, review some resources that guide the search for information on grants and proposal writing, and discuss how to write a research proposal. We direct our comments to social work researchers at beginning to middle levels of experience, particularly those interested in conducting experimental or quasi-experimental research, qualitative studies, impact assessments, intervention research, and/or clinical trials.

FUNDING SOURCES

Successful grant writing requires a substantive match between the grantor's interests, priorities, and aims and the investigator's capabilities and interests, an obvious point that is too important to gloss over. A well-written research proposal that addresses a problem that does not interest a grantor will not be funded. The first step in successful grant writing is to identify appropriate funding targets. The solicitation of research grants can be divided roughly into three categories: (a) federal funding, (b) private or public foundations, and (c) state and local sources of funding such as agency and university sources. Although we concentrate mainly on the first of these sources, the principles and strategies that we outline are applicable across most funders.

Federal Funding

The federal government is the most significant source of funds for research projects, providing approximately five times more money than foundation grants (Bauer,

1995). These grants are highly sought after because they enable researchers to undertake larger and more complicated projects. They also are highly prized in universities because of their larger indirect cost rates, some portion of which may directly or indirectly benefit the researchers. However, federal grant applications often are longer, more complex, and more time-consuming, requiring repeated revision for sometimes changeable review committees. Federal funds are, in fact, harder to get, but the rewards of successful efforts are substantial and increase the likelihood of obtaining future federal funding.

Among the most likely sources of federal funding for social work researchers are the Department of Health and Human Services (DHHS), the Department of Labor, the Department of Education, Housing and Urban Development, and the Department of Justice. Funds available vary considerably across these divisions, and many solicit research proposals in targeted priority areas that usually are quite broad. In addition, support is available through various fellowship mechanisms, and unsolicited proposals are accepted in some departments. Because the DHHS is the largest granting agency in the federal government, providing some 60,000 grants a year, we concentrate on describing this funding source.

The DHHS is primarily responsible for providing essential human services to client populations served by social workers. The department has more than 300 programs including some of the largest social welfare programs. Among the DHHS institutes likely to support social work research, the largest is the NIH. In fiscal year 1999, the NIH provided support to more than 35,000 research projects, approximately 80% of which funded extramural research projects in more than 1,700 organizations and research institutions throughout the United States and abroad. The NIH has 17 separate health institutes, the most notable for social workers being the following.

National Institute on Drug Abuse. The National Institute on Drug Abuse (NIDA) supports research on the health aspects of drug abuse and addiction in a broad range of disciplines including social work. The NIDA is committed to the rapid dissemination and use of training and research to significantly improve drug abuse and addiction prevention, treatment, and policy.

National Institute on Alcohol Abuse and Alcoholism. In 1970, the U.S. Congress identified alcohol abuse and alcoholism as major public health problems and created the National Institute on Alcohol Abuse and Alcoholism (NIAAA) to fight them. The NIAAA supports and conducts biomedical and behavioral research on the causes, consequences, treatment, and prevention of alcoholism and alcohol-related problems including dually diagnosed clients with both mental health and alcohol problems.

National Institute on Mental Health. The NIMH supports research and research training on mental health and mental illness in biological, behavioral, clinical, epidemiological, economic, and social science aspects of mental illnesses. Most funded NIMH studies are on diagnosable mental health conditions such as schizophrenia, depression, anxiety disorders, and eating disorders; on health problems such as Alzheimer's disease, trauma/stress, and HIV/AIDS; and on the delivery, financing, quality, and costs of mental health services.

National Institute on Aging. The National Institute on Aging (NIA) promotes healthy aging by conducting and supporting biomedical, social, and behavioral research and public education. The NIA sponsors extramural programs that fund research and training at universities, hospitals, medical centers, and other public and private organizations nationwide.

Other DHHS divisions pertinent to social work research include the Centers for Disease Control and Prevention, which support research on disease and injury prevention including violence and teenage pregnancy. The Health Resources and Services Administration supports research initiatives for medically underserved populations to reduce infant mortality and improve child health. The Substance Abuse and Mental Health Services Administration (SAMHSA) works to improve the quality and availability of substance abuse prevention and mental health services. In addition to state block grants, SAMHSA has supported training grants to schools of social work to improve substance abuse treatment. The Agency for Health Care Policy Research supports interdisciplinary research on quality, cost, and effectiveness of health care systems. Finally, the Office of the Assistant Secretary for Planning and Evaluation (ASPE) is the main policy development arm of the DHHS. ASPE funds research on policy issues for the legislative and executive branches and on the evaluation of DHHS programs and policies. Funding usually falls into one of four broad categories: income security and employment, health policy, social services policy, or long-term care policy.

Types of Federal Grant Support Mechanisms

Within the NIH, as in other federal agencies, a number of possible types or mechanisms of grant support are available, each with different program requirements, eligibility standards, funding constraints, and relevance to individual researchers with different levels of experience. It is important to identify the appropriate mechanism for support because some are designed for researchers just beginning their careers, others for mid-career and senior researchers, and still others for multidisciplinary teams of researchers that may involve multiple sites. Candidates typically must be

U.S. citizens, noncitizen nationals, or permanent residents. In what follows, we describe grant mechanisms pertinent to social work researchers including some designed for beginning or less experienced investigators.

R01: Traditional research projects. The R01 is a prestigious award conceived by individual researchers that is highly competitive. R01 proposals must meet the highest standards of research and undergo an independent review by a team of other scientists and researchers. Most candidates must have a doctoral degree, have already received independent research support, and have substantial preliminary data that support the proposed project. Recent changes might have improved the chances for newer investigators to receive R01s because the mechanism now allows for principal investigators to be clearly identified as new investigators.

K Series: Research career development grants. These types of grants provide mainly salary support to free time for research activities. The Mentored Research Scientist Development Award (K01) provides mentoring to enable beginning investigators with some postdoctoral research experience to become independent investigators. Experienced investigators also can use this award to acquire specialized mentoring to make substantial changes in their areas of study. The Independent Scientist Award (K02) provides salary support for experienced investigators who wish to devote large amounts of time to research activities. It does not provide funds to do research because principal investigators already are expected to have received funding, such as an R01, to cover these costs.

R Series: Support for young investigators. The NIH also supports training that enables young investigators to develop more advanced skills. Small Research Grants (R03) provide limited research support for preliminary short-term projects. Not all NIH institutes offer the R03 grant, and some institutes will accept R03 grant applications only in response to a specific program announcement or request for application. The small grant program provides research up to $50,000 per year for 2 years for new projects. This program provides support for less experienced investigators, for those at institutions with limited research resources, and for experienced investigators who are changing their research directions or are testing new methods or techniques.

One NIMH program, the Behavioral Science Track Award for Rapid Transition, uses the R03 mechanism to facilitate the entry of newly independent investigators into behavioral sciences research by providing 1-year support for small-scale pilot projects or for projects that entail novel research approaches. NIMH dissertation grants also are available for doctoral students pursuing mental health research careers as well as for dissertation research in child and adolescent developmental psychopathology, HIV/AIDS research, and mental health services research. Exploratory/Developmental Grants for Psychosocial Treatment Research (R21) are available from the NIMH for pilot research to develop the theoretical model, intervention/prevention protocol manual, fidelity procedures, training, and pilot testing. Up to $100,000 in direct costs for up to 3 years is provided.

F Series: National Research Service Awards. National Research Service Awards for Individual Predoctoral Fellowships (F31) and for Postdoctoral Fellowships (F32) are available to students pursuing research training. Prospective applicants for these fellowships choose sponsors with appropriate research skills who will participate in application writing and serve as mentors during the research projects.

Foundations

Foundations are nonprofit private organizations that maintain principal funds or endowments to provide assistance to charitable, educational, religious, or other nonprofit organizations. Although some foundations provide substantial awards, most give smaller grants than do governmental funding sources, but many of these are focused on improving services or client well-being. As a result, foundation proposals usually must include evaluation and research as one of several project objectives. Foundations typically are more flexible than government agencies and have easier application procedures with fewer reporting requirements. However, foundations typically do not fully reimburse indirect costs for expenses such as office space, supply maintenance, and administrative support.

Foundations typically have special interests or emphases that the researcher must target to be successful. Many thousands of applications each year are rejected because they do not clearly match the foundations' interests. Like the individuals or companies that established them, foundations can be quite focused in their giving interests, and success in obtaining foundation funding requires careful research. Many foundations publish specific guidelines and forms, publish lists of grants awarded, and maintain Web sites. Other sources of information include annual reports, Internal Revenue Service returns (Form 990-PF), published directories, and CD-ROM products. It will be important to examine funders' profiles and recent giving histories to especially target those that have supported projects similar to that of the researcher, especially those in the researcher's geographic area.

Finding the Right Funder

Local grants office. Often, the university's or agency's grants or development office can provide valuable assistance in searching for funding resources. At some research universities, the grants office relays grant information to social work schools and/or to individual faculty members. Staff in these offices often are very facilitative, providing help in preparing project budgets and obtaining the necessary signatures and budgetary approvals. They also might notify investigators of others within the universities who are responding to the same requests for applications.

Library resources. Most university library reference sections contain publications that list government and foundation sources of research support. Prominent among these is the *Catalogue of Federal Domestic Assistance* (Office of Economic Security, 1998), an authoritative listing of federal assistance programs published annually in June. The essential published resource for foundation grants is *The Foundation Directory* (Falkenstein, 1999). Arranged by state, the directory includes indexes by type of support, subject, foundation name, and geographic location.

Internet resources. The Internet has made searching for grant funds and applying for grants easier than ever before. There are literally hundreds of foundation and federal human service Internet sites including on-line grants and funding sources (Karger & Levine, 1999). Some useful Internet Web sites for grant sources for social work researchers are listed below.

The Mariner Gateway, from the University of Maine System Libraries (http://libraries.maine.edu/marreference/grants.htm), helps researchers to locate and access local and remote databases. Under Virtual Reference Library, Grants, the Web site contains the following useful links to grant funding resources:

- *Illinois Researcher Information Service,* or *IRIS,* contains information on federal and nonfederal funding opportunities in the social sciences.
- *Catalogue of Federal Domestic Assistance,* a government-wide compendium of federal programs, projects, services, and activities, is searchable by key word.
- *GrantsWeb* provides Web links to government agency and private foundation funding information from The Society of Research Administrators.
- *Fundsnet Directory* is a directory of foundations and organizations by area of interest and provides Web links to grant-writing advice.

The Institute for the Advancement of Social Work Research (IASWR) was founded by social work professional organizations to serve the research needs of the social work profession. The IASWR Web site (http://www.sc.edu/swan/iaswr/about.html) contains links to government funding sources and to assistance in proposal writing.

Community of Science Inc. (COS; http://www.cos.com) is a network of scientists and research organizations on the Web designed to help researchers find funding, collaborate with colleagues, and promote their research. Since 1994, COS has worked with 200,000 scientists, 215 universities, leading research and development corporations, and government agencies. The COS Funding Alert notifies subscribers of available grants weekly.

The Society for Social Work and Research (http://members.aol.com/ythand/sswr/home.htm) was founded in 1994 to improve support for research among social workers. This site contains links to the IASWR and New York University's World Wide Web Resources for Social Work, which also contain useful government Web links.

The Foundation Center, a New York City-based, nonprofit information clearinghouse, provides information and various services pertaining to foundation grants. The Foundation Center's Web site (http://www.fdncenter.org) contains detailed information about foundation grant sources, training seminars, and an orientation to grant seeking and funding research. Cooperating collections are located in libraries and nonprofit agencies in every state.

The Web sites of the DHHS (http://www.hhs.gov) and the NIH (http://www.nih.gov) help investigators to monitor federal research funding. The DHHS Web page includes an overview of different institutes within the NIH, phone numbers of staff, and summer internship opportunities. The Grants page provides a guide to NIH grants (http://www.nih.gov/grants/guide/index.html). The key word "social work" identified 52 program opportunities for research, training, and fellowship grants across the federal government, most of which were relevant for social workers.

The *Federal Register* Web site (http://www.access.gpo.gov/sudocs/aces/aces140.html) lists every new government funding initiative. The *Catalogue of Federal Domestic Assistance,* described earlier, also can be accessed on-line (http://www.gsa.gov/fdac/).

THE GRANT-WRITING PROCESS

In a review of this length, it is not possible to describe the process of writing research proposals in depth. Fortunately, other comprehensive reviews are available (see, e.g., Krathwohl, 1977; Coley & Scheinburg, 1990; Gitlin & Lyons, 1996; Miller, 1991; Reif-Lehrer, 1995; Ries, 1995). In particular, we recommend Gordon's (1996) excellent review of writing proposals for federal funding, available from the IASWR Web site or from the NIMH. Another excellent source is *The Foundation Center's Guide to Proposal Writing* (Geever & McNeill, 1997). These books, in addition to the other resources listed, provide a range of texts designed to help the reader seeking specific recommendations about writing research proposals. Internet booksellers' Web pages, such as amazon.com and barnesandnoble.com, also provide easy access to grant-writing resources. For example, on barnesandnoble.com, in the Searches category, the search of "proposal writing" in the key word section returned 107 recent titles in print.

Ideas for research proposals usually build on established interests, a thorough understanding of current theory and research literature, and discussions with colleagues and experienced researchers. Formulating research ideas into proposals usually is a gradual and time-consuming process. For relatively inexperienced investigators, the involvement of more experienced researchers in this process is critical to developing a state-of-the-art research design. One strategy for formulating a role for collaborators is to establish an informal advisory panel of experts. These should include experienced funded researchers familiar with the problem or population and those with special statistical and methodological expertise. Preparing a one- or two-page summary of the research project will help the investigator to answer important questions about the basic aims of the research, the importance of the study, study hypotheses, design, sampling, data collection, and analysis.

Prior to writing a full proposal, the investigator should contact likely funding sources to discuss research plans with the appropriate project officer or program staff. These calls provide important answers to specific questions on a grant project or grant mechanisms. In a phone contact with the program officer, the investigator should provide a very brief description of the project and be ready to provide more detail about study, rationale, importance, and methodology (in case he or she is asked). The questions to ask the program officer include the following: Does the proposal match the funder's current granting priorities? Is the research plan the type that the funder is interested in funding? Will the funder review a draft of the application? What level of funding can be expected? How will the proposal be reviewed? When are the proposal deadlines?

Once a funding source has been targeted, it is essential to understand the basic components of most requests for applications and to develop a systematic approach to writing. Components of a proposal that convince a reviewer that the investigator's study deserves funding typically include aims and scope, study questions or hypotheses, rationale based on a literature review, study design and time frame, sample, measures and procedures, data analyses, detailed budget, and capabilities of the research team. We review each of them in what follows, but the reader should bear in mind the following tips before beginning any research proposal:

- Be sure that the proposed study matches the funder's interests. Do not try to force a poor fit.

- Because each grantor has specific requirements for research proposals, carefully review specific program guidelines and maintain a checklist of all required components. Especially note requirements that will take longer or will involve others to complete (e.g., letters of reference, budgetary approval from the university).
- For inexperienced researchers, including one or more experts as co-principal investigators, investigators, or consultants in the proposal can significantly increase the chances of receiving funding.
- Contacting a funding source prior to submitting a proposal substantially increases the chances of getting a proposal funded—threefold for government grantors and fivefold for private grantors (Bauer, 1995).
- Incorporate the specific language and objectives of the grant organization.
- Give oneself enough time to write the proposal. Good proposals take time. Write clearly, simply, and precisely. Avoid technical language and jargon wherever possible.
- Check thoroughly for spelling, grammatical, and factual errors. Match text citations to the reference list.

Making One's Case Up Front

Critical to the success of the proposal is clearly conveying the overall significance of the proposed study in the abstract and in an introductory aims and scope section. First impressions are important, so the investigator should be sure that reviewers quickly get an overall impression of a study and its importance. The investigator will want to convey that he or she is providing a clear, if not definitive, answer to an important question. Occasionally, the abstract is the only part of the proposal seen by those reviewing a recommendation either to fund it or not to fund it (Miller, 1991). All funding organizations seek to support projects that address important questions and are likely to succeed. In the abstract, the investigator should move quickly to make a case for conducting the study. A common mistake is to spend too much time describing the problem and not enough on the proposed solution to address the problem.

Keep the Literature Review Focused

The typical proposal requires a problem statement, literature review, or statement of significance to provide a background for the study and to confirm its significance. This problem statement expands on the abstract and convinces the reader that the project is important. The investigator should clearly and concisely explain the nature of the problem, its severity and scope, and the generalizability and implications of the research. The investigator should indicate how the proposed study builds on previous theory and research literature, thereby demonstrating his or her grasp of the most recent literature on the topic. To keep this section focused, the investigator should include only studies that undergird the proposed study, noting any recently funded projects that use similar methods. The researcher should describe the results and implications of those studies so that a lay reviewer will understand their importance. He or she should demonstrate why the proposed study fills an important gap in knowledge. The following points are important to remember:

- Be sure that the literature review clearly supports the research questions or hypotheses.
- Demonstrate gaps in theory or knowledge.
- Show how the proposed study will contribute important information to the theoretical and research literature.
- Be concise; parsimony promotes attention, whereas a wandering literature review raises concern about one's discipline and clarity of aims.

Pilot Data

Pilot data are important because they demonstrate the applicant's expertise in a target area and serve as a basis from which the proposed research is built. Pilot data are essential for obtaining most federal funds and show the investigator's capacity to complete the study (Gordon, 1996). As with the literature review, the investigator should highlight results from pilot studies that illustrate the need to conduct the proposed research including the relevance of the findings to specific hypotheses, the proposed sample size and methodology, and the likelihood that the study hypotheses will be supported. The investigator seeking larger scale funding will need more substantial pilot data illustrating good effects in the predicted direction. Key points to consider in describing pilot studies include the following:

- Complete pilot studies before submitting federal grant proposals.
- Refer only to pilot studies or related research experience that clearly demonstrates technical skills and expertise in the proposed research area.
- Note how the pilot data are promising but insufficient and that, therefore, more data are needed.

Research Plan

Although the specific requirements of the research plan section vary widely, at least five components usually are required: (a) conceptual framework and design, (b) sampling plan, (c) measurement of key variables, (d) procedures for data collection, and (e) data analysis. These standard components for federal proposals serve as the basis for review (Gordon, 1996).

Conceptual framework and design. This section identifies key constructs, and specifies the interrelationship between and among them, following logically from the literature review, usually in the form of hypotheses or research questions. Hypotheses should flow from the literature review, encompass all of the major constructs in the model, and be specific enough to be testable. This section also should consider plausible intervening variables or alternative explanations to the proposed model. The investigator should bear in mind the following:

- The conceptual or theoretical framework must follow from the literature review.
- A limited number of hypotheses (one to five) are preferable to help focus reviewers' interest.
- Hypotheses should be interesting and testable.
- Anticipate reviewers' criticism and include justifications, especially for controversial procedures.

Sampling plan. In describing the sampling plan, the investigator should state clearly whether it is a probability or nonprobability sample. The researcher should describe the recruitment of participants, criteria for their participation, informed consent, and human subjects aspects and also should discuss whether sampling bias issues may affect the representativeness of the sample and the generalizability of the findings. Key points include the following:

- Provide a power analysis that justifies the proposed sample size (Cohen, 1988) pertinent to all main hypotheses.
- Avoid nonprobability samples for experimental or quasi-experimental research designs. If using nonprobability samples (e.g., for qualitative research or hard-to-research populations), indicate why this is necessary.
- Note any special strengths associated with the sampling plan.

Measurement of key variables. The investigator should clearly operationalize key variables. According to Gordon (1996), the two major problems in the measurement plans of federal research proposals are the absence of instruments or procedures that adequately measure key constructs and the use of measures, instruments, or procedures that are not fully described or are unrelated to the conceptual framework. If possible, the investigator should use existing standardized measures with known psychometric properties and should state these in the proposal. If the researcher proposes to adapt an existing instrument or to develop his or her own, then the researcher should present evidence to support the necessity of doing so. Finally, the investigator should describe any known or expected measurement biases (e.g., social desirability, acquiescence response set). Key points to address include the following:

- Use and cite the most recent versions of established measures. The reviewers might be familiar with them.
- Include copies of all measures.

- Provide succinct summaries of the psychometric properties of the instruments.

Procedures for data collection. The investigator should specify how data will be collected, who will do it, how long each phase will last, the order of administration of measures, recruitment and training of data collectors, and data management procedures. The investigator should be sure to address issues of respondent burden and the appropriateness of data collection strategies for settings and subjects. If data collectors must be "blind" to participant characteristics or study hypotheses, then the researcher should describe how this will be arranged. This section typically includes a project time line showing when each task will begin and end, usually at 1-month intervals. Some charts show when products (e.g., reports) will be produced. Most time lines prove useful for tracking progress after funds are received. Points to consider include the following:

- Anticipate criticism and justify all choices.
- Revise time lines as plans for data collection are refined. Detailed discussion of data collection often helps to anticipate problems.

Data analysis. Finally, the investigator should describe the statistical analysis procedures that pertain to each hypothesis. For multiple indicators used to measure a single construct, the researcher should include analyses for each indicator as well as methods to address the multicollinearity of similar measures. Some standard statistical procedures (e.g., multiple regression, analysis of variance, factor analysis) will not be challenged unless they are applied inappropriately. If a consultant helps to write this section of the proposal, then the investigator should be sure that the consultant clearly understands the purpose of the study so as to ensure that the statistical analysis section is well integrated with other proposal sections. Some points to consider include the following:

- Use state-of-the-art statistical procedures, but only if they are established.
- Time-honored methods may win reviewer approval over flashy new techniques that are not well understood or justified. Save experimentation until after obtaining the money.
- It always is prudent to obtain a statistical consultant for advice, even if the proposed analyses are simple. Including such a consultant in the proposal can bolster the funder's confidence in the analytic plan and help the investigator to respond to data problems when they arise.
- Map analyses precisely onto research hypotheses questions.

Budget

The investigator should be sure to consult with the grants office to draft the budget for the proposal. This must match the funder's expectations and appear realistic and well justified. For federal grants, some categories are disallowed or restricted, so the investigator should be aware of allowable costs. A common early mistake is to underestimate personnel time to complete tasks. The researcher should consult an experienced investigator in budgeting unfamiliar research components.

Capabilities of the Applicant

Few funders are interested in allocating funds if there is doubt about the investigator's ability to conduct the project research. Pilot research helps to dispel such concerns, and the background section should point to the principal investigator's role on projects that provided preliminary findings for the current study. Likewise, the principal investigator's biosketch accompanying the proposal should highlight previous funding or publications pertinent to the area of study. If the investigator's credentials could be questioned, then the researcher should include a senior investigator as principal investigator or a co-principal investigator, investigator, or consultant so as to bolster the apparent level of investigator expertise.

CONCLUSION

Even carefully crafted proposals will meet with rejection or receive priority scores outside the funding range. This almost always is true for first-time submissions for federal funds. Although it is disappointing and frustrating to receive a rejection, the reviewer's critique of the project is a key to revising the proposal successfully. For proposals that can be resubmitted, responding precisely and thoughtfully to each critique usually will substantially increase chances for approval in the next round. The investigator should consult with colleagues to determine how to improve the research or satisfy the previous reviewers' concerns. If changes would be inappropriate to test the hypotheses, then the investigator should justify the original plan carefully so as to address reviewers' concerns. Finally, the researcher never should let fear of rejection deter him or her from seeking research funding. Funds for social work research are available and obtainable, and the process of obtaining them can be relatively straightforward—even fun. Sherlock Holmes thought of sleuthing as a complicated puzzle to be solved. The social work researcher should view the quest for grant funds in the same way, with proposal writing the key to the puzzle. The researcher should approach proposal writing as vigorously as Holmes pursued his quarry.

REFERENCES

Bauer, D. G. (1995). *The complete grant sourcebook for higher education.* Phoenix, AZ: Oryx Press.

Cohen, J. (1988). *Statistical power analysis for the behavioral sciences*. Hillsdale, NJ: Lawrence Erlbaum.

Coley, S. M., & Scheinburg, C. A. (1990). *Proposal writing*. Newbury Park, CA: Sage.

Falkenstein, J. A. (1999). *The foundation directory*. New York: Foundation Center.

Geever, J. C., & McNeill, P. (1997). *The Foundation Center's guide to proposal writing*. New York: Foundation Center.

Gitlin, L. N., & Lyons, K. J. (1996). *Successful grant writing: Strategies for health and human service professionals*. New York: Springer.

Gordon, M. (1996). Writing a grant proposal. In E. B. Carlson (Ed.), *Trauma research methodology* (pp. 244-287). Lutherville, MD: Sidran Press.

Karger, H. J., & Levine, J. (1999). *The Internet and technology for human services*. New York: Longman.

Krathwohl, D. R. (1977). *How to prepare a research proposal: Suggestions for those seeking funds for behavioral science research* (2nd ed.). Syracuse, NY: Syracuse University Press.

Miller, R. C. (1991). *Handbook of research design and social measurement*. Newbury Park, CA: Sage.

Office of Economic Security. (1998). *Catalogue of federal domestic assistance*. Washington, DC: Government Printing Office.

Reif-Lehrer, L. (1995). *The grant application writer's handbook*. Boston: Jones & Bartlett.

Ries, J. B. (1995). *Applying for research funding: Getting started and getting funded*. Thousand Oaks, CA: Sage.

Task Force on Social Work Research. (1991). *Building social work knowledge for effective services and policies*. Austin, TX: Capitol Printing.

Disseminating Research Findings

DIANNE F. HARRISON

C. AARON McNEECE

If the major purposes of research are to build empirically based knowledge, corroborate or disconfirm theories, test the effectiveness of social work practice approaches, and ultimately benefit social work clients and client systems, then the dissemination of research findings is an integral component of the research process. Without dissemination, there is no knowledge building, theory confirmation, or benefit to clients. *Dissemination* refers to the diffusion or spread of ideas that stem from research studies out to those who need and can use them. In social work research, we need to be concerned with disseminating findings to other researchers, practitioners, policymakers, and sometimes the consumers of our services. In this chapter, we discuss the role of dissemination in research, what types of findings should be disseminated, and various dissemination methods and venues.

THE ROLE OF DISSEMINATION IN RESEARCH

Most well-designed research studies can take a minimum of 1 year from the time the studies are conceptualized to the completion of data collection and analyses. Depending on the nature of a study and the funding source (e.g., federal grant, state or private foundation funding), some large-scale and longitudinal research projects can span from 5 to 20 years. Vailant and his associates (1995) followed a cohort of high school and college men with alcohol problems for a record-setting 45 years. Given the amount of time and resources directed to the actual conduct of research efforts, the dissemination of findings to relevant audiences is an essential and mandatory part of the process. Without dissemination, research studies are of little value. An unpublished, nondisseminated study is an incomplete study, and so its findings, whether significant or not, add nothing to our knowledge base because they are unknown to others. It might be obvious, in instances where studies yield either statistically or clinically significant results, that the researchers have a professional obligation to share results with other researchers, practitioners, funding agencies, policymakers, and/or consumers. But, in fact, all findings, even nonsignificant ones, are important and add to knowledge development. Results indicating that a particular method or service did not make any difference to outcomes or that theoretical concepts were not supported by data also can inform our thinking and practice.

Whether findings are significant or not, they need to be shared in a timely manner. Some granting agencies require quarterly or annual reports that indicate statuses of research projects as well as any findings. Aside from these types of required reports, researchers need to incorporate into their research plans time for additional dissemination efforts. Findings, which literally sit on office shelves or in file drawers for months or years after completion, can quickly become out-of-date due to changes in policy or societal events. For example, a 2-year-old study of the effects of a food stamps program that subsequently was discontinued will not likely be of much interest to policymakers. Similarly, the drug use patterns of adolescents 5 years ago might not be relevant to current patterns of adolescent drug use when information is needed to design intervention strategies to deal with drugs being abused today. Therefore, the timeliness of dissemination can influence the use of research findings not only by other researchers but also by those external to the profession, namely, the public and consumers of services.

The professional dissemination of research also affects the willingness of some funding agencies to either continue or discontinue funding. Federal agencies, in particular, look for publication track records and publication products from grants that they fund. Such track records indicate to agencies that the investigators have the capacity to publish or present findings in peer-reviewed journals or professional conferences. The capacity to publish in peer-reviewed journals, in particular, is judged in scientific circles to be an important measure of scholarly merit (Thyer, 1994). Granting agencies not only value the dissemination of research for knowledge advancement purposes but also appreciate the added visibility to their agencies when their grantees' work is published in professional journals.

INFORMATION TO DISSEMINATE

Although the discussion in this chapter so far has emphasized the dissemination of overall results or findings (both positive and negative) of research studies, there are several other types of knowledge gained from research that should be shared with others. Often, a researcher's experience with a variety of methodological issues can prove to be invaluable to other researchers. For example, in a study that involved tracking homeless families, diffusing information about tracking strategies that were successful and those that were unsuccessful could save future researchers and practitioners much time and money. Similarly, methods that decreased participant attrition in a community agency-based intervention for teen parents might be very helpful to programs facing client dropout in their own settings. Basically, any time a researcher confronts a methodological dilemma and either solves it or finds that a particular strategy is not useful, that information should be disseminated. From the appropriateness of different measurement tools to a range of additional methodological issues involved in the actual implementation of research studies (e.g., maintaining intervention integrity, participant recruitment, securing agency cooperation, training interviewers), communicating these experiences to others who can use them is beneficial.

CONNECTIONS TO KNOWLEDGE DEVELOPMENT

Whether a researcher is attempting to disseminate overall results from a research study or information about methodological issues, it also is the researcher's responsibility to connect whatever is being reported to how (or whether) it advances our knowledge. These connections can be made in several ways. Most typically, the researcher needs to communicate, together with a review of relevant literature, how the current findings relate to previous findings; that is, the current findings either confirm, fail to confirm, or modify existing knowledge. Stated differently, how are the current findings the same as, better than, or different from previously reported findings? Connections also should be made with the theory or conceptual framework used to guide the research. In this instance, the researcher should address the extent to which the theory is supported or not supported without going beyond the scope of the study findings and within the context of the study's limitations. By establishing the links with existing research and theory, the researcher clearly articulates how the research study contributes to our knowledge development.

METHODS OF DISSEMINATION

In deciding where and how to disseminate research findings, researchers have a variety of different methods or avenues from which to select. Some of the methods to be discussed generally are thought to be more valuable than others. However, depending on the purpose of the dissemination and the intended audience, each method can be useful. In practice, multiple methods of dissemination often are used for findings from the same research study. The major exception to using multiple methods is that potential journal articles should be submitted to only one journal at a time, even though this practice undoubtedly increases the length of time in disseminating results. Multiple submissions of the same manuscript to different journals at the same time is not an acceptable practice in virtually all of the social and behavioral sciences including social work. It does present a dilemma to the researcher, however, in that he or she might have to wait as long as 2 years for a decision on a manuscript. By that time, the information already could be out-of-date.

SCHOLARLY JOURNALS

The dissemination of research findings in scholarly journals generally is agreed to be the most important and prestigious avenue for researchers to follow. The importance and prestige value placed on journal articles, as compared to other written formats (e.g., books, newsletters), derive primarily from the peer review system. *Peer reviewed* refers to the evaluation of a manuscript by a panel of experts (two or more) in the same field or topic area who have no connection with the author and who make recommendations to the journal editor as to whether a manuscript should be published or not. In a blind peer review system, which most journals in the social and behavioral sciences use, the reviewers ostensibly do not have knowledge of the authors' identifications or institutional affiliations. As a result, such reviews are the closest process to objectivity that exists in the scientific arena. Although the system is not perfect (Cicchetti, 1991), it still is regarded as the most desirable option for research dissemination.

For the novice author, and even for the more experienced researcher, the process of writing and getting an article published in a journal can be intimidating. The steps involved in publishing begin with actually writing a manuscript, making decisions about which journal is appropriate, submitting the manuscript, and dealing with the reviewers' and editor's comments including revisions, rejections, and (rarely) outright acceptances. Once a manuscript is accepted for publication, the author still has to edit galley proofs prior to final publication. It is not uncommon for many journals to have a backlog of manuscripts waiting to publish. Thus, it usually takes an author

1 year or longer (2 years is not uncommon) after initial submission of a manuscript before it actually appears in print.

Because manuscripts should be prepared according to specific journal guidelines, it is useful to have a journal (or possibly two) in mind when composing the manuscript. Selecting the right journal for the author's manuscript involves making several determinations. First, the quality of one's work will determine the ultimate quality or "tier" level of the journal to which a manuscript is submitted. In judging the quality of the research and manuscript, senior colleagues who have established publication track records can be called on to review the author's written work and give feedback. To target the right journal, the author should learn something about the tier level of the various journals and recent trends in what a particular journal is interested in publishing. *Tier level* refers to the prestige value of a journal (e.g., top tier, second tier, third tier). Tier ranking, both formal and informal, usually is based on factors such as acceptance and rejection rates (i.e., a higher rejection rate is viewed as more prestigious), number of subscribers (larger generally is better), and the citation impact factor (i.e., extent to which the articles in this journal are read and cited by others).

The potential author also needs to know whether or not a manuscript is appropriate for a particular journal based on the types of articles generally published by that journal. For example, some journals focus strictly on particular types of research studies; others focus on more practice-oriented pieces; and still others may publish a combination of conceptual, research-based, and practice-oriented articles. Perhaps the best single source for potential authors and researchers to use in selecting the right journal is the fourth edition of *An Author's Guide to Social Work Journals* (National Association of Social Workers, 1997). In this guide, the reader will find the editorial foci, special issues, circulation levels, submission and format instructions, review times, acceptance rates, and lag times to print for nearly 200 journals in social work and related fields. Senior colleagues also can advise about the appropriateness of various journals.

Once a decision is made as to which journal the manuscript will be sent and it is submitted, an author generally will wait from 3 to 12 months for a review decision. Such decisions take the form of either acceptance without revisions (very rare), acceptance with revisions, rejection with invitation to resubmit on revisions, and outright rejection. One of the most difficult lessons for novice authors to learn is that revision and resubmission of manuscripts usually is a necessary, albeit unwanted, part of the journal publication process. Rather than viewing this as a reason for quitting, authors should take the perspective that, in general, reviewers' recommendations for revisions will improve their manuscripts and, therefore, the value of their research dissemination efforts. For an excellent and informative guide to the journal publishing process, we recommend that potential authors consult *Successful Publishing in Scholarly Journals* (Thyer, 1994).

Monographs, Books, and Book Chapters

Researchers sometimes will choose to disseminate the findings from their research in the form of monographs or books. A monograph and a book usually share the characteristic of presenting, in one treatise, the description and results from an entire research project. For some researchers, the option of having a more complete collection of their work in one place is more attractive than publishing 6 to 10 articles in different journals (even though they still may publish some of the work in journals). Well-respected university or academic presses often publish monographs, either as part of a thematic series (e.g., HIV prevention research) or as a "stand-alone" topic (e.g., HIV prevention research with culturally diverse populations). Monographs typically are shorter in length than books and might not be marketed as aggressively.

In large part due to the lack of a blind peer review system, monographs, books, and book chapters represent second-choice outlets for the dissemination of research findings. There certainly are exceptions to the review process for these types of publications. Some monographs and books do undergo a system of peer review (even blind or anonymous ones), and some publishing houses (university and/or proprietary ones) are held in very high esteem. However, some book publishers and vanity press operations (i.e., works are published for substantial fees) exist on a for-profit basis and without regard for peer opinion. Thus, the likelihood is increased that the scientific merit of a research endeavor becomes less important in publication decisions than the potential market value of the work. As a result, these whole classes of publications (monographs, books, and book chapters) often are viewed as less prestigious than peer-reviewed articles in scholarly journals. At a minimum, we would advise potential authors to avoid vanity presses. If the only publication venue available is one in which researchers must pay for it, then the research probably is not worth disseminating.

Professional Presentations

Disseminating research results at professional conferences is an excellent and timely way in which to diffuse a study's findings. For most researchers, this venue represents the first opportunity for professional feedback on their research and stimulates the writing of manuscripts prior to publication. In contrast to the lag time for journal articles, monographs, and books from submission to print, annual national, state, and regional conferences occur frequently and offer the possibility for relatively instant feedback. Although not a substitute for published work, a presentation can be prepared in manuscript format such that, on any revision on the basis of audience feedback, it immediately can be submitted to a journal or other venue.

To present at professional meetings, an author generally submits an abstract (from 150 to 500 words) for blind peer review consideration as either a paper or poster session. A paper presentation carries more value than a poster presentation. The latter consists of preparing a visual depiction of the research project and findings (on a poster or backboard), with the author being available for a certain specified time to converse with interested parties. In a paper session, the author actually delivers a verbal presentation of the work, often as part of a panel of two or more papers on a related theme, in a specified time to an audience gathered for that purpose. Regardless of the audience size in a paper presentation, this venue is more prestigious than a poster session because the selection criteria are viewed as more stringent.

Getting abstracts accepted for presentation at professional conferences is similar (albeit easier), in some ways, to getting journal articles accepted. That is, the researcher must be familiar with the exact procedures for submission and the current conference theme or purpose and then must write the abstract to be congruent with the purpose and trends of the conference.

Some conferences, such as the Council on Social Work Education's (CSWE) annual program meeting, offer useful workshops and sessions on how to successfully write and prepare conference abstracts. Although the acceptance criteria for abstracts also are provided in the CSWE's call for proposals, it is interesting that a substantial proportion of authors ignore them, apparently thinking that the obvious merits of their research will outweigh the need to adhere to those criteria.

Some smaller conferences held at state or even regional levels are less stringent than national meetings in their selection criteria due to the paucity of abstract submissions. The larger the scope of the meeting (international vs. state, regional, or local), the more prestige and opportunity for wider dissemination of findings.

Bridging Research, Practice, and Policy

So far, we have discussed methods for research dissemination that involve professional audiences and primarily other researchers. Although these methods are critical for scientific and peer review purposes, we also recognize that there often is a huge gap between research and the needs of practitioners, policymakers, and consumers of social work practice. In this section, we discuss methods for disseminating findings from results that will have relevance for nonresearch and nonacademic audiences.

Basically, our premise is that we must narrow the gap that exists between research and practice, and by *practice* we refer to any primarily nonresearch entity (e.g., policymakers, consumers, clinicians). To accomplish this, dissemination of research findings needs to occur in venues other than scientific and professional journals or monographs/books (Sobell, 1996). Most practitioners do not read research journals or even research-based articles in journals focused on practice (Fensterheim, 1993;

Rose, 1992). To build our knowledge base and have it accessible to those who might benefit from it, researchers need to consider including in their plans for dissemination the use of methods that will facilitate the use of their research by those external to the research (generally academic) community.

One method for accomplishing this type of "user-friendly" dissemination is the use of professional newsletters that summarize research results in a manner without jargon. Such newsletters might be available on an agency-wide basis (local, state, or regional) or might originate from a statewide association. In such venues, researchers also can offer training or presentations to local groups on the research and findings. One of the most exciting initiatives designed to bridge the gap between research and practice is the publishing of treatment manuals (also called *manualized treatment*) that are produced from controlled research investigations and distributed (usually for a minimal price) to clinicians. Making such treatment manuals available to regular practicing clinicians either through mail or through continuing professional education is an excellent way of bridging the research-practice gap. In the past, such manuals that documented effective treatment approaches were too lengthy to be published in journals (or even books) and remained on the shelves of the researchers or funding agencies. This type of dissemination also aids other researchers who are attempting to devise new treatment procedures.

To inform policymakers and policy analysts, the use of the "bullet approach" is the best method. By *bullet,* we refer to short, jargon-free communications that make use of executive summaries and key points (or bullets) that outline or highlight only the main points of the research and findings. Lengthier, more technical reports or publications can be attached to such summaries, but researchers should assume that only the bullets will be read. Policymakers and even analysts often have little time or interest to do thorough reviews of technical academic materials.

Many federal agencies have developed in-house procedures for more rapid and efficient dissemination of research findings to selected audiences of scientists, analysts, policymakers, and consumers. Most now provide researchers with agency guidelines for publication at the time a grant is approved. For example, the National Institute of Justice (NIJ, 1991) issues a handbook for depositing data with the NIJ's Data Resources Program as well as a guide to writing reports for the NIJ (1996). Final research reports are to be written in a specific format and may be published in 1 of 11 different publications sponsored by the NIJ that are sent monthly or bimonthly to target audiences of 5,000 to 80,000 persons. The time lag between receipt of the final report by the NIJ and the dissemination of research findings through one of these publications may be as short as 4 to 8 weeks.

Even if the results of federally funded research projects are not published, final reports generally are archived in the form of microfiche and can be reproduced and disseminated to other interested parties very quickly and at minimal cost. For several decades, these reports were copied to microfiche and indexed in publication catalogs of various federal agencies. More recent reports are directly available on federal agency Web sites. Some agencies, such as the National Criminal Justice Reference Service, issue CD-ROMs each year containing abstracts of *all* final reports on grant-funded research projects during the past 5, 10, or 20 years. At least one private agency, the National Center for Juvenile Justice, produces a CD-ROM each year with national data on juvenile court statistics. The Substance Abuse and Mental Health Data Archive (SAMHDA) at the University of Michigan provides ready access to substance abuse and mental health research data that may either be (a) downloaded from the Internet or (b) obtained on CD-ROM. The SAMHDA Web site features an on-line data analysis system that allows the user to compute certain statistics (e.g., cross-tabs, correlations) and perform other operations (e.g., creating subsets of existing records). Available data sets include the Drug Abuse Treatment Outcome Study, Monitoring the Future, the National Comorbidity Survey, the National Household Survey on Drug Abuse, the National Youth Survey, and the Treatment Episode Data Set. Eight additional databases currently are scheduled to be archived.

The archiving of otherwise unpublished research reports from grant-funded projects on microfiche or CD-ROM greatly expands the volume of research that is available to scientists and other interested parties. Although a manuscript may be rejected by a professional journal for being poorly written, untimely, or inconsistent with the editor's current research interests, this rarely happens with final grant reports. Whatever the quality of the writing may be, they are archived and available for other researchers doing literature reviews.

With respect to disseminating research findings to consumers of services, several methods are available. Public forums, where consumers are specifically invited to attend, are an effective way of beginning to diffuse the research results. Visiting and making presentations at consumer group meetings (e.g., at the local National Alliance for the Mentally Ill to report on findings related to caregiving and the mentally ill) can be a useful venue, provided that the researcher is clear about the scope of the findings and the study's limitations. Similarly, producing press releases for local, state, and national media that are realistic from the standpoint of the implications of the study's findings and its limitations can assist in disseminating such results to those in need. If the researcher is located in an academic community, then the university media relations office can greatly assist and provide some guidance in this area. The biggest danger with press releases is that reporters often want to make a study's findings more exciting or "newsworthy" than they actually are. The risk is that reporters will go beyond the study's findings and make conclusions that cannot scientifically be made on the basis of the actual study.

The most common examples of this danger can be found when reporters begin making causal statements from correlational studies. For example, suppose that a researcher conducted a correlational study finding that African American youths who attended church regularly had lower levels of sexual activity than did Hispanic and non-Hispanic white youths. A reporter might attribute this finding to religion or race (more newsworthy) as opposed to acknowledging (as did the researcher) that the study did not test for causal effects. It might be the case that youths of any race or religion who attend church regularly are less inclined toward sexual activity prior to their church attendance, and so that is why they attend church (i.e., to be around peers who are similar). The point is that the study and findings did not answer this question because of the nature of the research design. Researchers attempting to disseminate findings through media channels should be cautious about the willingness of many reporters to make inferences and draw conclusions beyond the scope of the study findings.

Disseminating Research Through the Internet

The Internet already has radically transformed many aspects of American life and culture—how we shop, how we communicate, and how we seek and use information. This revolution in information and communication has affected the profession of social work as well as the dissemination of research, and it has the potential to have even more far-ranging consequences on each.

On April 7, 1999, if one had searched for the term *social work* using Netscape and the Excite search engine (as one of the authors of this chapter did), then there would have been exactly 4,564,445 "hits." Some of these hits included chat rooms, Web sites for individual social workers, and Web sites for practice journals and other publications. A substantial number of these hits were research-related Web sites.

Many government agencies now sponsor Web sites that include, among other things, recent research reports involving social work programs and social services. For example, the National Institute of Mental Health operates a Web site that includes a special section on technology transfer. It can be found at http://www. nimh.gov/research. Perhaps one of the most sophisticated Web sites is operated by the National Criminal Justice Reference Service (http://www.ncjrs.org). It has a self-contained search engine that allows the user to browse its research archives for everything from "adult corrections" to "zip guns," and it contains links to a number of other Web sites operated by other state, federal, and private agencies. The Office of Juvenile Justice and Delinquency Prevention, the National Institute on Alcoholism and Alcohol Abuse, and the National Institute on Drug Abuse all operate similar Web sites that provide access to recent research reports.

The Internet also contains Web sites for dozens, if not hundreds, of social work organizations, networks, bulletin boards, and chat rooms. One of the oldest and most comprehensive is the Social Work Access Network (SWAN; http://www.sc.edu/

swan), operated by the University of South Carolina. SWAN provides, among other things, access to a number of mainstream social work journals including research abstracts that can be downloaded by the user.

There is little doubt that the Internet has increased access to research; increased the rate of dissemination of research; and increased the volume of research available to scientists, policymakers, and consumers. There also is little doubt that it has the potential to continue these increases in an almost unlimited manner. However, there are several issues and problems brought about by this remarkable change in our technology:

How do we maintain quality control over research reports that appear on the Internet?

Many of these Web sites are maintained by individuals, with no attempt at peer review. Some of them are maintained by advocacy organizations that may promote "causes" by citing bogus research or by misinterpreting the findings of legitimate researchers.

How do we process the sheer volume of research now available through the Internet?

Imagine increasing the volume of literature to be covered in a literature review by a factor of 10 (or perhaps 100). Although there is a definite bias among social work and social science researchers to cite only the literature found in conventional sources (journals, books, and monographs), there undoubtedly will be increasing pressure to cite the most *recent* research, and that probably will be found on the Internet. The American Psychological Association publication manual already has conventions for Web site citations, and "www" is appearing more often in the reference sections of scientific articles.

Is it possible that "hard copy" of the printed word will become an outmoded format for efficient communication of research findings?

We already have CD-ROM books available. The exchange of business cards is a thing of the past for the fortunate few who own a personal digital assistant (e.g., Palm Pilot) or similar device. Information can be processed faster, stored more efficiently, and retrieved faster when it is in electronic form rather than printed on paper.

CONCLUSION

This chapter has described the critical role that the dissemination of research findings plays in the research process as well as the rapid changes that are occurring in the dissemination process. Depending on the purpose of the dissemination, whether for professional audiences or for policy-/consumer-driven purposes, many avenues exist for spreading the ideas and results that stem from research. Even negative findings about results and methodological issues are important in knowledge development. It is important that researchers consider dissemination methods that go beyond the usual professional scholarly ones so as to include policymakers and consumers. At a minimum, research that has not been disseminated in any avenue does little good to our advancement of knowledge. To paraphrase Hudson (1978), research that is not disseminated does not exist.

We also must do a better job of preparing future researchers in methods of dissemination. One of the authors of this chapter pulled 23 textbooks on social science/social work research off his shelves and looked for the word *dissemination* both in the tables of contents and in the indexes. It was found in only 2 books. One devoted a short paragraph to the need to disseminate research but gave no hints, advice, or instruction about how this should be done; the other contained only one short sentence about dissemination.

Dissemination is an integral component of the research process. Future social work researchers need to integrate the process of research dissemination into their research plans as routinely as they do the other steps in their plans. Dissemination is essential.

REFERENCES

Cicchetti, D. V. (1991). The reliability of peer review for manuscript and grant submissions: A cross disciplinary investigation. *Behavioral and Brain Sciences, 14,* 119-135.

Fensterheim, H. (1993). Comments on "Practice—It's Not What We Preached." *The Behavior Therapist, 16,* 149.

Hudson, W. W. (1978). The first axioms of treatment. *Social Work, 23,* 65-66.

National Association of Social Workers. (1997). *An author's guide to social work journals* (4th ed.). Washington, DC: NASW Press.

National Institute of Justice. (1991). *Depositing data with the data resources program of the National Institute of Justice: A handbook.* Washington, DC: Government Printing Office.

National Institute of Justice. (1996). *Guide to writing reports for NIJ.* Washington, DC: Government Printing Office.

Rose, S. (1992). Utilization of research in group work practice: An example. In A. Grasso & I. Epstein (Eds.), *Research utilization in the social services* (pp. 133-147). New York: Haworth.

Sobell, L. C. (1996). Bridging the gap between scientists and practitioners: The challenge before us. *Behavior Therapy, 27,* 297-320.

Thyer, B. A. (1994). *Successful publishing in scholarly journals.* Thousand Oaks, CA: Sage.

Vailant, G. E. (1995). *The natural history of alcoholism revisited.* Cambridge, MA: Harvard University Press.

Name Index

Subject Index

About the Editor

Bruce A. Thyer received his M.S.W. from the University of Georgia in 1978 and his Ph.D. in social work and psychology from the University of Michigan in 1982. Having previously taught at the University of Michigan and Florida State University, he joined the University of Georgia faculty in 1987 and currently is Research Professor of Social Work and Adjunct Professor of Psychology. He also is an associate clinical professor of psychiatry and health behavior at the Medical College of Georgia as well as a visiting professor of social work with the University of Huddersfield in England and with the Queens University of Belfast in Northern Ireland. He is the founding and current editor of the bimonthly peer-reviewed journal *Research on Social Work Practice,* published by Sage Publications and sponsored by the Society for Social Work and Research. He has produced more than 180 journal articles, 40 book chapters, and 18 books in the fields of social work, psychology, behavior analysis, and psychiatry. He and his wife, Laura Myers, are the proud parents of John (age 7 years), William (age 5), Joseph (age 3), and Cynthia (age 1).

About the Contributors

Alean Al-Krenawi, Ph.D., is Senior Lecturer in the Department of Social Work at Ben-Gurion University of the Negev in Israel. He is an international authority on cross-cultural social work and mental health practice. He is the author of *Ethno-Psychiatry Among the Bedouin-Arab of the Negev* and of numerous book chapters. His recent works have appeared in publications such as the *American Journal of Art Therapy; British Journal of Social Work; Contemporary Family Therapy; Health and Social Work; Family Process; Family Relations; Social Psychology; Social Psychiatry; Culture, Medicine, and Psychiatry;* and *Transcultural Psychiatry* as well as in other professional forums.

Michelle Ballan, Ph.D., is a doctoral candidate in the Ph.D. program at the School of Social Work at the University of Texas at Austin.

Jerrold R. Brandell, Ph.D., is Professor of Social Work at Wayne State University in Detroit, Michigan.

Ram A. Cnaan, Ph.D., is Associate Professor in the School of Social Work at the University of Pennsylvania. He is the director of the Program for the Study of Organized Religion and Social Work and is the associate director of the Center for Religion and Urban Civic Society. He serves on the editorial boards of seven academic journals and teaches research methods, statistics, and social policy. He received his Ph.D. in social work at the University of Pittsburgh and received his B.S.W. and M.S.W. from the

Hebrew University in Israel. He has published numerous articles in scientific journals on a variety of social work issues. He is the author of *The Newer Deal: Social Work and Religion in Partnership* (1999) and *The Invisible Caring Hand* (forthcoming).

Kevin Corcoran, Ph.D., is Professor of Social Work at Portland State University. He has M.A., M.S.W., Ph.D., and J.D. degrees and has written or edited eight books. His areas of interest are psychometrics/measurement and mediation. He maintains a practice in commercial and community mediation in Portland, Oregon.

Charles D. Cowger, Ph.D., is Professor and Director of the School of Social Work at the University of Missouri. He taught for 26 years at the University of Illinois, where he directed the Ph.D. program for 17 years and directed and/or served as chair for 24 doctoral dissertations. He is the president of the Inter-University Consortium for International Social Development, an organization with membership representing 51 countries. He recently became the first non-Russian to be inducted into the Russian Academy of Social Education. He has a bachelor's degree from Doane College, a master's of theology from the Chicago Theological Seminary, an M.S.W. from the University of Chicago, and a Ph.D. in social work from the University of Illinois–Urbana-Champaign. During recent years, his research interests have focused on the assessment of individual and community strengths, assessment/labeling of clients in personal social services and communities, labeling processes in community development programs, social development program evaluation, and social work cross-cultural technology transfer.

Peter J. Delany, Ph.D., is Acting Deputy Director of the Division of Epidemiology, Services, and Prevention Research at the National Institute on Drug Abuse (NIDA). Before assuming his current position, he was the deputy chief of services research responsible for the development of research programs focusing on treatment services with correctional populations, organization and management, and health services research with underserved populations. Prior to accepting a commission in the Public Health Service and joining NIDA, he taught at both the Catholic University of America (where he received his Ph.D. in social work) and the University of North Carolina at Chapel Hill. He is a licensed clinical social worker and a member of the Academy of Certified Social Workers, with 18 years of experience in the fields of addictions and mental health. His primary research interest has been in the development of organizations and service systems to meet the needs of underserved populations.

Dorothy Lockwood Dillard, Ph.D., is an independent consultant conducting program evaluations and training for drug treatment and social agencies, courts, corrections, and prevention programs. She serves as a consultant to federal, state, and county governments as well as to private and nonprofit organizations. Her research and evaluation has focused on treatment effectiveness in a number of modalities, cost-effectiveness, gender differences, treatment for offenders, program implementation and improvement, and case management. She is an expert in process evaluation. She has written numerous articles and book chapters and given presentations addressing drug abuse treatment, treatment effectiveness, treatment for offenders, juvenile and adult corrections, system development, and evaluation techniques.

Jeffrey Draine, Ph.D., is Assistant Professor affiliated with the Social Work Mental Health Research Center in the School of Social Work at the University of Pennsylvania. His research interests are focused on individuals with psychiatric disabilities and services with them. He is particularly interested in involuntary and coercive outpatient mental health treatment and the interaction of the mental health and criminal justice systems. He received his Ph.D. in social welfare from the University of Pennsylvania and his M.S.W. in social planning from Temple University.

Rodney A. Ellis, Ph.D., is Assistant Professor in the College of Social Work at the University of Tennessee, Knoxville.

Guy Enosh, Ph.D., is Assistant Professor at Haifa University School of Social Work. He received his Ph.D. from the School of Social Work, University of Pennsylvania, and was expecting to graduate by September 2000. His dissertation research focuses on "Attitudes of Israeli Youth Towards Social Activism: Between Violence and Altruism." His work has focused on various areas related to youth and family violence including evaluation of programs and policy. He has been teaching research-related courses in the School of Social Work at the University of Pennsylvania since the summer of 1998. His areas of interest include youth violence and family violence, youth social and political activism, and research methods in social work (both quantitative and qualitative).

William M. Epstein, D.S.W., is Professor of Social Work at the University of Nevada, Las Vegas. He has written extensively on social welfare. His latest books are *Welfare in America* and *Children Who Could Have Been.*

Cynthia Franklin, Ph.D., is Professor of Social Work at the University of Texas at Austin. She teaches courses on clinical practice, family therapy, and research methods. She is the author of several books including *Clinical Assessment for Social Workers: Quantitative and Qualitative Methods* and *Family Practice: Brief Systems Methods for Social Work.* She is the editor-in-chief of the National Association of Social Workers' journal, *Social Work in Education* (soon to be renamed *Children &*

Schools). She is a clinical member of the American Association of Marriage and Family Therapy and holds practice licenses in clinical social work and in marriage and family therapy. Her current areas of interest include school social work practice, effectiveness of practice methods (especially solution-focused therapy), brief cognitive and family therapies, development of clinical theory, prevention of teen pregnancy, and assessment and measurement.

Scott M. Geron, Ph.D., is Associate Professor in the School of Social Work at Boston University. He has extensive experience in conducing applied policy research with the elderly, chronically mentally ill, and other long-term care populations as well as in developing teaching and training materials for social workers, care managers, geriatricians, mental health professionals, and other health professionals who work with frail, chronically ill populations. He currently is working with the U.S. Administration on Aging to develop performance outcome measures for state and local programs for older adults. He completed his Ph.D. in the School of Social Service Administration at the University of Chicago.

Jane F. Gilgun, Ph.D., is Professor of Social Work at the University of Minnesota, Twin Cities. A child welfare social worker for more than eight years, she has published on topics such as how persons overcome adversity, the development of violent behaviors, the meanings of violence to perpetrators, and qualitative research methods. She currently is writing a book, *The Design and Analysis of Qualitative Research*. She has won awards for her research and for a violence prevention program that she developed. She has a Ph.D. in family studies from Syracuse University, a master's in social work from the University of Chicago, and a licentiate in family studies and sexuality from the University of Louvain in Belgium.

Harriet Goodman, Ph.D., is Associate Professor in the School of Social Work at Hunter College, where she has taught social work research for 10 years in the M.S.W. program and as a member of the social welfare doctoral program in the Graduate Center at the City University of New York. She also is the project director of the Human Services EdNet Program, a distance learning initiative that delivers graduate and postgradate social work courses over a broadband fiber-optic network; the project includes an extensive formative and summative evaluation using multiple data sources. She chairs the Protection and Social Justice Field of Practice and has a long-standing interest in work with people in the criminal justice system.

John R. Graham, Ph.D., is Associate Professor of Social Work at the University of Calgary, Canada. He sits on editorial boards of seven academic journals, has published extensively on social policy analysis, social welfare history, and international social work practice. He recently co-authored *Canadian Social Policy: An Introduction,* 2000. The author of numerous journal articles, recent publications appear in *British Journal of Social Work, Culture Medicine and Psychiatry, Health and Social Work, International Social Work, Social Development Issues, Social Science and Medicine, Social Service Review,* and *Transcultural Psychiatry.*

R. Kevin Grigsby, D.S.W., is Professor of Behavioral Science and Special Advisor to the Senior Vice-President for Health Affairs in the College of Medicine at the Pennsylvania State University. He has an extensive history of program planning, implementation, and evaluation in the area of innovative home- and community-based health and mental health services. His practice experience has been primarily in underserved rural and inner-city areas. He has published more than 50 articles, chapters, abstracts, and reports and has edited one book. He has been an editorial board member for *Research on Social Work Practice.* During recent years, his research interests have been in evaluating innovative service delivery through advanced telecommunications technology and in studying Georgia women who ingest kaolin, a naturally occuring clay. He holds a D.S.W. from the University of Pennsylvania and an M.S.W. from Florida State University. He also is an L.C.S.W. in the state of Georgia.

Dianne F. Harrison (Montgomery), Ph.D., is Dean and Professor of Social Work at Florida State University. She received her doctoral degree from the School of Social Work at Washington University and her M.S.W. and B.A. degrees from the University of Alabama. Her areas of teaching and research specialization include social work education, negotiation and conflict resolution, intervention research, and HIV prevention. She currently is principal investigator on a National Institute of Health-funded project related to HIV prevention with ethnically diverse couples at risk. She has published books and numerous articles for social work and related research journals. Recent books have focused on cultural diversity in social work practice and on academic job searches. She currently serves as a board member for the Council of Social Work Education; vice president of the National Association of Deans and Directors; and chairperson of the Southeastern Graduate Deans and Directors and the Florida Association of Deans and Directors. She currently chairs the Florida National Association of Social Workers Task Force on Licensure.

Richard A. Hoefer, Ph.D., is Associate Professor in the School of Social Work at the University of Texas at Arlington. He also is the co-director (with Catheleen Jordan) of the Work Life Project and is the editor of the *Social Policy Journal.* His work has appeared in publications such as the *Encyclopedia of Social Work, Social Work, Journal of Community Practice, Administration in Social Work, Journal of Sociology and Social Welfare,* and *Social Service Review.* He is the president of the Social

Policy and Policy Practice Group and is a former president of T-PACE, the political action group of the Texas chapter of the National Association of Social Workers (NASW). In 1999, he was named Social Worker of the Year by the Tarrant County NASW unit for his efforts in promoting advocacy among social workers.

Michael J. Holosko, Ph.D., is Professor of Social Work at the University of Windsor in Canada.

Catheleen Jordan, Ph.D., is Professor of Social Work at the University of Texas at Arlington, where she has taught in the master's and doctoral programs for 15 years. She is the director of the Ph.D. program and is the co-director (with Richard Hoefer) of the Work Life Project. She is the chair of the National Association of Social Workers' Tarrant County unit. Her areas of expertise are family assessment and treatment, clinical research, and family-work issues. She has published in journals and books and is co-author of *Clinical Assessment for Social Workers, Family Practice,* and *Introduction to Family Social Work.*

Elaine T. Jurkowski, Ph.D., is Assistant Professor in the School of Social Work at Southern Illinois University, Carbondale. She teaches courses primarily in research and social policy, with an emphasis on health, disability, and aging. Previously, she taught at the University of Windsor in Canada. She also has served as a program evaluation consultant in a range of public and private settings including India, Hong Kong, and Niger. Her research interests include public health, community planning for health and social services, citizen participation, and international models for disability and health. Her current research projects include comparative models of service delivery for health services (rural vs. urban), trends in aging/disability services, the use of technology to enhance teaching, and student learning/outcome competencies.

T. K. Logan, Ph.D., is Assistant Professor in the Department of Psychiatry, Center on Drug and Alcohol Research, University of Kentucky. She also serves as the principal investigator on several project evaluations working with the Kentucky Drug Court program. She has conducted more than 20 process evaluations of different Drug Court programs across the state of Kentucky and currently is conducting outcome evaluations for three Kentucky Drug Court sites. She is an evaluator for a family prevention program targeting children of Drug Court clients. She has been funded by the National Institute on Drug Abuse (NIDA) to examine the nature, extent, and co-occurrence of HIV risk behavior, victimization, and drug use among crack cocaine users. She also serves as a co-principal investigator on two NIDA-funded studies focusing on criminal justice populations and on the Kentucky Treatment Outcome

Study. Her primary interests are in the areas of violence, health and mental health issues, substance use, and HIV risk behavior.

Christine T. Lowery, Ph.D., is Associate Professor in the School of Social Welfare at the University of Wisconsin–Milwaukee (UWM). She received her Ph.D. from the University of Washington in 1994. She is a member of the Hopi and Laguna Tribes (Southwest). She is a scientist with the Center of Addictions and Behavior Health Research at UWM. Using her 13 years of direct practice with Native Americans, she contributes to teaching undergraduate foundation courses. At the graduate level, she teaches qualitative research methods. Her research work centers on spirituality in the recovery processes of Native Americans. During the summer of 1999, she began a 10-year study of sociocultural change and aging at Laguna Pueblo, New Mexico.

C. Aaron McNeece, Ph.D., is Professor of Social Work at Florida State University, where he also is Director of the doctoral program. He received his M.A. in political science from Texas Tech University and his M.S.W. and Ph.D. from the University of Michigan. A former probation officer, he has 30 years of experience in higher education. He is the author of more than 100 articles and books. His latest publications have focused on the connections among drugs, crime, and public policy. Since 1989, he has conducted evaluations of approximately 130 justice system programs.

Goutham Menon, Ph.D., is Assistant Professor in the College of Social Work at the University of South Carolina. He received his master's degree in social work from the Madras School of Social Work in India and his Ph.D. from the University of Illinois, Urbana-Champaign. His main area of work concerns the use of technology in social work practice and education.

Nancy Meyer-Adams, M.S.W., is a doctoral student in the College of Social Work at the University of Tennessee, Knoxville. She now has a C.M.H.S. work field education. Her academic interests include child welfare, foster care, mental health, field education, program evaluation, working with families, and evidence-based services. Her current research projects are in the areas of school readiness and kinship care.

Carol T. Mowbray, Ph.D., is Professor and Associate Dean for Research in the School of Social Work at the University of Michigan. Her major focus is on mental health services research. She has written extensively on gender differences in mental health and currently is conducting a National Institute of Mental Health-funded, longitudinal research study on women with serious mental illness coping with parenthood. Much of her work focuses on interventions for persons with serious mental illness using a psychiatric rehabilitation paradigm. She recently completed a research demonstration project to evaluate the effectiveness of supported education models for individuals with psychiatric disabilities who wish to pursue postsecondary education.

William R. Nugent, Ph.D., is Associate Professor in the College of Social Work at the University of Tennessee, Knoxville, where he also is Director of the Ph.D. program. He received his Ph.D. in social work from Florida State University in 1986. He has worked as a mental health counselor, as a residential counselor for the hearing impaired, and as the training director for the Florida Network of Youth and Family Services. He has done research in applied measurement and on ways of working with delinquent and antisocial youths. He is the author of more than 35 articles in peer-reviewed journals, has written numerous book chapters, and is the co-author of a forthcoming text on practice evaluation.

Miriam Potocky-Tripodi, Ph.D., is Associate Professor in the School of Social Work at Florida International University, where she teaches research methodology and data analysis. Her scholarly interests are in the areas of multicultural and international social work, with a specific focus on refugee issues. She is the founding co-editor of a new journal, the *Journal of Social Work Research and Evaluation: An International Publication.*

Frederic G. Reamer, Ph.D., is Professor of Social Work at Rhode Island College in Providence. He has served as a social worker in mental health, correctional, and housing agencies as well as in a governor's office. He was chair of the committee that wrote the current *Code of Ethics* of the National Association of Social Workers.

Antoinette Y. Rodgers-Farmer, Ph.D., is Associate Professor in the School of Social Work at Rutgers–The State University in New Brunswick, New Jersey.

Michael A. Rothery, Ph.D., is Associate Professor in the Faculty of Social Work at the University of Calgary in Canada. He received his M.S.W. from the University of British Columbia and his Ph.D. from the University of Toronto. His practice has been in the fields of child welfare and mental health, and his current research interests are in the family violence area.

David Royse, Ph.D., is Associate Dean and Director of Graduate Studies in the College of Social Work at the University of Kentucky. He is the author or co-author of five books: *Program Evaluation: An Introduction; Teaching Tips for College and University Instructors; Research Methods in Social Work; Field Instruction: A Guide;* and *How Do I Know It's Abuse?* In addition, a forthcoming text on data analysis for social workers is due to be released in 2001. His scholarly interests vary widely, as illustrated in recent articles and chapters addressing topics such as homelessness in out-of-treatment drug users, the ethics of gatekeeping practices in B.S.W. programs, and hospice volunteers' attitudes toward assisted suicide. He has served on the editorial board of *Research on Social Work Practice* and currently is serving as a consulting editor for *ARETE* and the *Journal of Baccalaureate Social Work.*

Phyllis Solomon, Ph.D., is a Professor in the School of Social Work, University of Pennsylvania who chairs the research sequence in the school. She has a secondary appointment in the Department of Psychiatry, School of Medicine, University of Pennsylvania. She has a M.A. in sociology and Ph.D. in social welfare, both from Case Western Reserve University. She has over 25 years of research, planning, and administrative experience. She has worked in the state psychiatric system and in a community research and planning agency, and she has served on numerous federal research and service review panels and reviews proposals for private foundations. She has published and presented extensively on issues concerning adults with serious mental illness and their families. She has co-edited two books on psychiatric rehabilitation, *Psychiatric Rehabilitation in Practice* and *New Developments in Psychiatric Rehabilitation,* and co-authored *Community Services to Discharged Psychiatric Patients.* She is Director of an NIMH Social Work Research Development Center, which focuses on service interventions for adults with severe mental illness and their families. In 1997, her article with others on the results of a family education intervention, which appeared in *Schizophrenia Bulletin,* received first place by the Society for Social Work and Research. She was the 1999 recipient of the Armin Loeb Award from International Association of Psychosocial Rehabilitation Services for her research in psychosocial rehabilitation.

Karen Sowers, Ph.D., is Dean and Professor of Social Work at the University of Tennessee, Knoxville. Previously, she served as the director of the School of Social Work and as the undergraduate program director of the School of Social Work at Florida International University. She received her B.A. degree in sociology from the University of Central Florida in 1974, her master's degree in social work from Florida State University in 1977, and her Ph.D. in social work from Florida State University in 1986. She is nationally known for her research and scholarship in the areas of case management with the frail elderly, child welfare, cultural diversity and culturally effective intervention strategies for social work practice, and social work education. Her current research and community interests include the development of initiatives to support responsible and involved fatherhood, the implementation and evaluation of community-oriented policing, and juvenile justice practice. She has authored or co-authored numerous scholarly articles, book chapters, and books. She has two forthcoming books, one (co-authored with Bruce Thyer) titled *A Survival Guide for*

Graduate Students in Social Work and one (co-authored with Rod Ellis) titled *Juvenile Justice Practice.* She also recently published (co-authored with D. F. Harrison) *Finding an Academic Job.*

Gail S. Steketee, Ph.D., is Professor and Chair of the Clinical Practice Department in the School of Social Work at Boston University. She received her Ph.D. from the Bryn Mawr Graduate School of Social Work and Social Research in 1987 and, prior to that, collaborated on research on behavioral treatments for obsessive compulsive disorder at the Temple University Medical School. She co-chairs an international group of obsessive compulsive disorder (OCD) researchers who are developing assessment measures for cognitions in OCD and is a member of the Scientific Advisory Board for the national Obsessive Compulsive Foundation. Her current research activities include cognitive treatment of OCD, group and family interventions for OCD, and cognitive and behavioral assessment and treatment for serious hoarding problems. She has published numerous articles and chapters on OCD and other anxiety disorders as well as three books: *When Once Is Not Enough* (for OCD sufferers and their families), *Treatment for Obsessive Compulsive Disorder* (a clinical guide for behavioral treatment of OCD), and *Overcoming Obsessive Compulsive Disorder* (a therapist and client protocol for cognitive and behavioral treatment).

J. Timothy Stocks, Ph.D., is Associate Professor in the School of Social Work at Michigan State University. He has worked as a protective services worker and a child abuse intake investigator for the Florida Department of Health and Rehabilitative Services. Prior to that, he was on staff at the Sex Offender Unit of the North Florida Evaluation and Treatment Center. He received his M.S.W. and Ph.D. from Florida State University. His areas of expertise include child maltreatment, application of technology in social work, ethical issues in research and practice, and research methodology. Over the past few years, he has been evaluating the delivery of advanced social work education through the Internet. Currently, he is working on the development of a virtual community to provide information, support, and other services to postadoptive families.

Barbara Thomlison, Ph.D., is Associate Professor in the School of Social Work at Florida International University, where she also is Acting Director of the Institute for Children and Families at Risk. She obtained her Ph.D. in social work from the University of Toronto and has a lengthy interdisciplinary practice history with children, families, and policy services research. Her teaching experiences involve both undergraduate and graduate programs at other universities. Her academic interests include child welfare, foster care, mental health, field education, program evaluation, working with families, and evidence-based services. Currently, she teaches courses on child welfare, child maltreatment, and practice interventions. Her current research projects are in the area of school readiness and kinship care. Her publications include articles in the areas of child welfare practice, family preservation, foster care, treatment foster care, family reunification, and social work field education. She is actively involved as a board and community member in local and national child welfare and family service organizations.

Martin B. Tracy, Ph.D., is Professor of Social Work at Southern Illinois University, Carbondale. He is a former research analyst with the U.S. Social Security Administration and with the International Social Security Association (ISSA) in Geneva, Switzerland. He is a consultant to the ISSA and the International Labour Organization. He also is a member of the National Academy of Social Insurance and a fellow in the Gerontological Society of America. His received his Ph.D. in social work and A.M. in political science from the University of Illinois, Urbana. His B.A. is from Murray State University.

Francis J. Turner, D.W.S., is Professor Emeritus of Social Work at Wilfrid Laurier University in Waterloo, Ontario, Canada.

Leslie M. Tutty, Ph.D., is Professor in the Faculty of Social Work at the University of Calgary in Canada, where she teaches courses in both clinical social work methods and research. A clinician since 1971, she primarily has worked in community mental health settings with both children and adults. Her research focus over the past 10 years has been on prevention and interventions with family violence in a variety of forms. Recently, she completed three projects for the Canadian government: a discussion paper on shelters in Canada for Health Canada, a discussion paper on husband abuse for the National Clearinghouse on Family Violence, and a research report for Justice Canada on firearms use in intimate partner relationships in which women are abused. She has expertise in both quantitative and qualitative research methods and has written or edited textbooks for social workers for both paradigms.

Theodore Varkas, M.S.W., is a doctoral student in the School of Social Work at Wayne State University in Detroit, Michigan.

Brian T. Yates, Ph.D., is Professor of Psychology at the American University in Washington, D.C., where he began as an assistant professor in 1976. He received his Ph.D. in psychology from Stanford University in 1976. He has published more than 55 articles, book chapters, and books. Most apply cost-effectiveness or cost-benefit analysis to the systematic evaluation and improvement of human services. His 1980 book, *Improving Effectiveness and Reducing Costs in Mental Health,* laid the groundwork for an integration of program evaluation, economics, and operations research in *Analyzing Costs, Procedures, Processes, and Outcomes in Human Services,* his fifth book. He has conducted cost →procedure →process →outcome analysis for service enterprises and research initiatives in prevention of alcohol, tobacco, and other substance abuse as well as suicide, treatment of opiate and cocaine addiction, residential programs for urban youths and mentally retarded adults, and consumer-operated services. He wrote the manual for helping substance abuse treatment programs to measure and improve their cost, cost-effectiveness, and cost-benefit that was published in 1999 by the National Institute on Drug Abuse.

Mieko Yoshihama, Ph.D., is Assistant Professor in the School of Social Work at the University of Michigan. She currently is coordinating a large-scale epidemiological study of women's health and domestic violence in Japan in collaboration with the World Health Organization. She is a founding member of the Tokyo-based Domestic Violence Action and Research Group, whose first nationwide survey of domestic violence provided an impetus for newly emerging battered women's movements in Japan. She has conducted a series of community-based studies of domestic violence including a study of women of Japanese descent in Los Angeles; focus groups with survivors of domestic violence in Japan; and a study in Detroit, Michigan, aimed at improving methods of data collection and analytical approaches to the study of domestic violence. Her research interests in the areas of violence against women of color reflect her advocacy work with Asian Pacific American battered women in Los Angeles and Japan over the past decade.